Rarely DIFFERENT

A SIBLING'S MEMOIR BY

Amanda Owen

**A SPECIAL NEEDS SIBLING MEMOIR &
REAL-LIFE ADVICE ON THE NEUROTYPICAL
CHILD'S UNIQUE PERSPECTIVE**

EDITOR, ASHLEY WEDDING

RARELY DIFFERENT

ISBN: 978-1-7367476-2-9

CONTENTS

ACKNOWLEDGEMENTS

I am profoundly grateful to many individuals who have supported and contributed to the creation of this book.

First and foremost, I want to thank my rockstar bestie, Ashley. With your degree in journalism, your role as an editor for a local parent magazine, and your impeccable design skills, you have been an irreplaceable partner in this journey. Your meticulous attention to detail and perfectionism have been pivotal in shaping this book. Without you, this story — my story — would not have reached those who need it most. Beyond your official role as editor, you've been a true collaborator, co-authoring a children's book series with me and offering unwavering support throughout this process. I am eternally grateful for your presence and partnership.

I am also deeply grateful to Greenwell Chisholm, my local printing partner, for your invaluable support in all of my print projects, especially this memoir. Your exceptional attention to detail and unwavering commitment to quality have been instrumental in bringing my vision to life. From the initial design to the final print, you have been a steadfast collaborator, ensuring that every aspect of my book reflects the care and dedication that went into its creation. Your expertise and personal touch have made a significant impact on this project, and I couldn't have asked for a better partner to help me share my story with the world.

Jamie Plain, thank you for the stunning photo on the cover. You captured quite possibly the best photo of Nick to date, and it perfectly encapsulates the essence of this memoir

Lastly, my heartfelt appreciation goes to my husband and our boys. Your patience and understanding as I dedicated every spare moment to writing meant the world to me. Your love and unwavering belief in me gave me the freedom and peace to dream, create, and truly discover who I am beyond the roles of mom and wife.

Thank you all for being an integral part of this journey.

Dear Mom and Dad,

As I write this, I'm overwhelmed by a deep sense of gratitude and admiration for everything you've done for Nick and me. It's only now, as an adult and a parent myself, that I truly understand the sacrifices you made and the endless love you gave us.

As I reflect on my childhood, I realize now just how much I didn't see – the quiet sacrifices, the endless juggling, the love that was always there, even when I couldn't fully understand it. You moved mountains every day to make sure Nick and I both felt loved, safe, and important. I couldn't have known back then the delicate balance you had to strike – making sure Nick got everything he needed while trying to give me the attention I deserved. I never saw the quiet moments when you wondered if you were enough for me because of all you had to be for Nick.

I wish I could have known then what I know now. I wish I could've told you that I saw you, even when I didn't have the words, that I felt your love, even when I didn't know how to express it. You deserved to hear, "I see you," and "You're doing more than enough." You deserved to know that every effort, every sleepless night, every worry you carried was not just noticed, but deeply appreciated in ways I couldn't articulate as a child.

I see it all now - your love, your sacrifices. It's all woven into every part of who I am today – as a sibling, a parent, and as a person. You showed me what it means to love unconditionally and to navigate life's challenges with grace. The strength, patience, and devotion you gave to our family shaped not only my childhood but the way I parent my own children. Your ability to give so fully, to love so deeply, and to face the complexities of our family with unwavering strength is something I will carry with me always.

I am who I am because of the both of you.

With all my love – Amanda

My Dearest Brother,

There's something I need to say that I'm not sure you fully understand, but it's so important to me that you hear it: I am who I am today because of you, and for that, I am forever grateful.

I love you exactly as you are, and I wouldn't change a single thing about you. Your rare chromosome disability is part of what makes you uniquely you, and I cherish every moment we've shared — every smile, every laugh, and even every challenge we've faced together. You are my brother, and my love for you is unconditional.

Because of you, I've been given a lens through which the world is brighter, more meaningful, and filled with purpose. You've always been more than just my brother — you're the heart that taught me how to love without conditions, the soul that showed me what true acceptance feels like, and the light that guides me to be a better person every day.

You've shaped my entire life, Nick. The compassion I carry, the patience I've learned, the deep empathy I feel for others — it all stems from growing up with you by my side. You've taught me that our differences don't divide us, they're the very things that make us beautiful, strong, and uniquely who we are.

This book, every word on these pages, comes from my love for you. It's not just about our journey together but a tribute to the moments — both beautiful and hard — that shaped who we've become.

God, in His infinite wisdom, made me your sister, and for that, I am endlessly grateful. You have been my greatest teacher, my inspiration, and my biggest cheerleader.

Thank you, Nick, for being the incredible brother that you are. Thank you for letting me share our love and our story with the world.

With all my love and gratitude — Your sister, Frog

FOREWORD

I can hardly believe it myself - but I've actually gone and written a book. And not just any book, but what I like to call a "book-book." See, ever since I started jotting down these thoughts back in September of 2023, I've referred to this project as my "book-book" because, despite having authored a series of children's books, I never quite considered those to be the real deal. Sure, they were books in their own right, but I had a burning desire to write something for adults, not kids.

(Oh, and speaking of which, consider this a shameless plug to check out Owen the Wonderer, my children's book series, aimed at teaching neurotypical children about acceptance and inclusion.)

Now, let me level with you right off the bat: I do not consider myself to be a writer. I know, I know, it sounds ridiculous - my name is on the cover of this book, which technically makes me an author. But the truth is, I've always struggled to embrace that title. Writing has never been a strength of mine. Without the help of my editor, this book would be tough to read.

Despite my imperfections as a wanna-be writer, I am fiercely passionate about speaking up and making a positive impact on this world. And when it comes to disability advocacy, I've got plenty to say. Specifically, my expertise lies in intellectual disabilities. I am the proud younger sister of Nick, my older brother by three years, who happens to have a rare chromosomal disability. From the moment I entered this world, I was handed two titles – "little sister" and "special needs sibling."

Little did I know then how profoundly that second title would shape the person I've become. In fact, my role as a special needs sibling set the trajectory of my life. I became a special education teacher to give students like my brother the education they deserve. Later, I left the classroom to start a nonprofit disability service provider, ensuring that individuals like my brother had a place to build social relationships and develop skills to live a life with purpose and independence.

Despite all of that, I didn't want to write this book.

Even with a life's worth of passion for individuals with disabilities and their families like my own, I never saw myself offering advice from my perspective as a sibling. You are only reading this now because of what I can best describe as divine intervention — a blessing I didn't realize I needed, but one that the world seemed to call for. It's as if this book was part of a larger plan, seamlessly intertwined with my journey as a special needs sibling.

Funny enough, I initially set out to write a different kind of book altogether, one titled "A Woman Who Wants It All But The Guilt Will Kill Her." (In case that sounds like a book for you, don't worry – it's already in the works.) I suppose I'm not your typical author, because who in their right mind attempts to juggle multiple books simultaneously? Hi, it's me, I'm the problem, it's me.

Yet here I am, driven by a newfound passion to share my most personal stories and deepest emotions, knowing that they will resonate with others who walk a similar path. This book has been a journey down memory lane, a chance to revisit and re-experience emotions that once lay dormant, memories that, in hindsight, held far more significance than I ever realized at the time.

My goal in writing this book is to show the beauty and strength that can come from having a sibling with a disability. I hope that by being open about my experiences, I can offer guidance and hope to special needs families. This book is meant to help siblings who find it hard to express their feelings and to give parents the insight they need to support all their children better. When we know better, we do better, and that's what I hope to achieve with these pages.

As I embark on this journey of putting pen to paper and reliving the chapters of my life as a special needs sibling, there's a weight on my shoulders that I can't shake off. It's the fear of laying bare my innermost thoughts and emotions, of exposing the raw, unfiltered truth of what it means to walk in the shoes of someone whose life has been touched by disability.

For that reason, I think it's important to say that in this book I have focused on sharing my own journey growing up with Nick, rather than delving into the full scope of his story or my parents' experiences. While I could recount his incredible achievements and the numerous obstacles my parents navigated, this book is intentionally written from a sibling's perspective. It's about my life as Nick's little sister, a narrative I've never fully explored or shared before.

And what I fear the most is the moment when my parents read these pages and see our family's story from my perspective. I worry they might discover feelings and struggles I couldn't express as a child — emotions that, while beyond their control or ability to change, only now make sense to me as an adult.

I want to give my parents the recognition they truly deserve and honor them for all they have done. They are the unsung heroes of my story, holding our family together through our disability journey. The stories and feelings I share on these pages were kept deep inside, not because of anything they did wrong, but because their unwavering support allowed me to focus on growing up. Their constant presence provided me with the strength and freedom to navigate my emotions and memories, helping me become the sibling my brother needed and the person I am today.

There's a certain vulnerability in baring one's soul to the world, which can be freeing, yet scary at the same time. I'm concerned that readers might misunderstand my story, thinking I want to change my life, my family. But that couldn't be further from the truth.

Despite the ups and downs that accompanied our special needs journey, I wouldn't trade a single moment of my life. Each trial, each triumph, has shaped me into the person I am today, giving me an understanding that I wouldn't have gained otherwise.

In many ways, this book represents a homecoming, a return to the essence of who I am and the core values that have guided me throughout my life.

It's a testament to the resilience of a humble family from Whitesville, Kentucky.

A celebration of a young couple given a devastating diagnosis for their child, but blazed a trail with little help or resources.

A boy with an extremely rare diagnosis, who defied all odds and expectations.

And a sister who is changing the world because her brother changed her.

Rarely Different is her story, intertwined with her brother's and her parents', uniquely told from the perspective of a sister – a special needs sibling – who lived it all firsthand, with the hope that her words will inspire, comfort, and heal.

CHAPTER 1

THE STORY OF MY BROTHER

A LOVE THAT CONQUERED FEAR

My parents' love story began in the mid-1970s on a softball field, at least that's how I always heard it.

My mom, Sharon, was recruited to play in a recreational league game by her close friend, Beth, who was covering left field while my mom played rover. Beth's boyfriend and future husband, Bob, brought his cousin, fresh out of the Navy, to watch the game. Beth was excited for my mom to meet Bob's cousin, Leon, and had been enthusiastically talking him up. After the game, Beth introduced them and from that moment on, as they both like to say, the rest was history.

Growing up, I heard this story countless times, but it's the eye rolls from my mom and belly laughs from my dad that make this story a family favorite. See, my dad had a friend on the bleachers with him that day. Rachel, a pal of his since childhood, was sitting in front of him, leaning back on my dad as she watched the game. My mom, even before even meeting my dad, was already mad at him as she believed he was flirting with this girl, when he was supposed to be there to meet her. We now joke that their first fight happened before they even met.

It's funny to think about how those small, seemingly insignificant choices led to my family – a happy marriage for my parents that eventually brought my brother and me into this world. A beautiful life. It's stories like these that make me believe in fate and the idea that what happens to us is simply meant to be.

My parents' love story is a testament to that.

It all started with a softball game and a bit of matchmaking by a friend. And from that point on, their lives were forever intertwined.

mom & Dad's wedding day
1977

Two years of dating later, my parents married on January 28, 1977. My dad was 22, and my mom was 19. They spent their early years together hanging out at ballfields, off-roading their Ford Bronco through the rural Kentucky woods, and relaxing at the lake. They were carefree, adventurous, and deeply in love.

After three years of marriage and building a life in their small Kentucky hometown, they decided it was time to start a family. But for a couple who had an easy start, this next chapter was anything but.

My parents tried for five long years but could not conceive. Despite facing the challenge of infertility, it was clear that Sharon and Leon Boarman were destined to become parents. Their patience, faith, and unconditional love made them perfectly suited for the role.

Determined to build a family, my parents turned to adoption. But just a few days before they signed papers to start the process, my mom found out she was pregnant. No matter how many times my parents tell this part of their story, their faces light up – their first pregnancy, the start of their family, their miracle baby.

Mom had a healthy, normal pregnancy, without even one episode of morning sickness. My big brother, Joseph Nicholas Boarman, was born on July 30, 1981. He was named after my dad, Joseph Leon, but they would call him Nick.

mom holding Nick the day he was born.

Dad feeding Nick for the first time.

They took their healthy baby home, the answer to a long-awaited prayer. At the time, my dad was a traveling boilermaker and although my mom had graduated from cosmetology school before Nick was born, she wanted to stay home and raise their precious baby for which she had prayed all those years.

Despite the exhaustion of being first-time parents, my mom and dad loved their life as a family of three. To them, life was perfect.

But everything changed at Nick's six-month check-up with his pediatrician.

My mom went to the appointment alone because my dad was at work. As the doctor began to examine Nick, he seemed concerned. He kept entering and leaving the room, a worried expression on his face, while my mom anxiously cradled Nick. He weighed Nick and measured parts of his body, examined his ears and feet, and then left the room again without saying a word.

After the third time, my mom demanded, "What are you doing? What is the problem?"

Dr. Neel, Nick's pediatrician, looked troubled as he said, "I don't want to upset you, but I think Nick has 4XY Syndrome."

He opened a medical journal to an article on Down syndrome and the next page described 4XY Syndrome, a rare chromosomal disability that meant Nick had four more X chromosomes than Y chromosomes. The doctor read from the book, telling my mom that Nick would be mentally retarded. The "R word" was written on those pages. The article detailed a bleak future for Nick, including dwarfism, the eventual inability to walk, talk or feed himself and a life expectancy of no more than 30 years.

Nick — 1981

My mom, who took her perfectly healthy baby to the doctor, was given what she felt was a death sentence.

In 1981, there was no internet to look up information about Nick's disability. My family is from a very small town in rural Kentucky where, at the time, individuals with intellectual disabilities were not seen, valued and oftentimes were kept hidden from the world. All my parents had was a small paragraph in a medical journal with a devastating prognosis.

The doctor told my mom that day that Nick was one of only eleven people in the United States with this rare syndrome. She asked if she could connect with the other ten families, but the doctor said they had all chosen institutionalization and he suggested that might be the best option for our family as well.

But my parents were trailblazers. Institutionalizing Nick was never an option. They had prayed for a child for so many years and they were going to raise their miracle baby – the son God gave them – to the best of their abilities.

To them, Nick was still Nick, perfect in whatever abilities he would have. Rarely different.

NICK'S LITTLE SISTER

It's hard for me to imagine the emotions my 24-year-old mother and 27-year-old father must have felt that day and the weeks after. To have your life flipped upside down after just one routine doctor's appointment?

They had no way of researching more information about their son's future and no way to connect with other parents facing a similar diagnosis. I can only assume they must have felt isolated and helpless.

They must have feared what Nick's life would look like and felt deep sadness, maybe even anger that their long road to parenthood led to a child with a rare chromosomal disability.

But I know they also felt a deep, unconditional love for Nick. They cherished every moment with him, celebrating his milestones and finding joy in his presence.

When I ask my mom about their life with Nick as a baby and toddler before I was born, she explains that it wasn't much different from any other family. Yes, they faced a diagnosis that had so many grim expectations for their son later in his life, but in his early years, Nick's differences weren't as noticeable. It wasn't until he got older that his deficits became more apparent, and the gap between his abilities and those of his peers started to widen.

As Nick grew older, my parents navigated increasingly complex and demanding circumstances that tested their resilience. They had to navigate a world that often failed to understand or embrace him. They found themselves advocating for rights and opportunities they never imagined they'd have to fight for on behalf of their child. Yet through it all, they remained steadfast in their love and commitment to him. When Nick was three years old my parents shared the news with him that he would be a big brother. Nick would kiss our mother's belly, eagerly anticipating a little brother to play alongside him with his favorite Hot Wheels. Nick loved cars and he was hopeful his little brother would love them as well.

My parents didn't know if their second child would be a boy or a girl, and honestly, they didn't care. Their primary concern was simply for a healthy baby. Before my conception, they underwent screenings to check for any genetic factors linked to 4XY Syndrome. Both screenings confirmed they weren't carriers of the syndrome, which only reinforced their belief that Nick was truly a miracle baby.

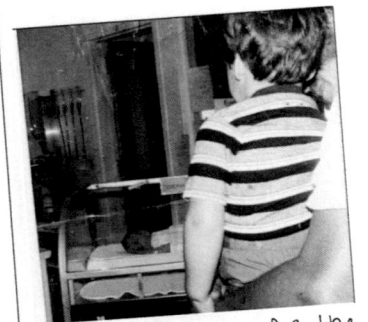

Nick meeting me foR the fiRst time iN the hospital.

I, Amanda Kate Boarman, was born on August 14, 1984. The only daughter to Sharon and Leon, and the best friend and protector to my big brother, Nick. My parents tell everyone that I came along at the perfect time. Three-year-old Nick was a "mother hen," according to my dad. He doted on me and kissed me often. That mother hen role would eventually reverse as my development would inevitably catch up to and surpass his, but it is special to hear that, in the beginning, Nick's priority was protecting me.

So, how did my parents balance raising a three-year-old with a rare disability and a newborn? The answer is: they just did.

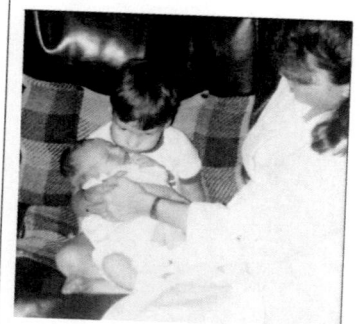

Nick loves his little sisteR.

Despite Nick's delays in walking, his ongoing therapies, and his open-heart surgery just weeks after I was born, they managed. They took each day as it came, putting one foot in front of the other.

Nick's diagnosis made them trailblazers, but it was these relentless, uncertain years that forged my parents into warriors.

They didn't just confront the unknown; they battled through it, carving out a path where none existed, guided by fierce love and commitment to their son.

I know my parents heard their fair share of, "I don't know how you do it," from family and friends. While these words were often intended as a compliment to their strength, they sometimes carried an undertone of pity—an implication that their lives were defined by struggle.

For my parents, there was never a choice — they had to figure things out, often relying solely on themselves. Every obstacle was met not with resignation, but with determination. They didn't just "do it;" they transformed every "can't" into "can," every closed door into a new opportunity. They redefined what it meant to be parents of a child with a disability, embodying the fierce, unyielding spirit of those who refuse to accept anything less than what their child deserves. They were not just surviving; they were setting a new standard for what it means to fight for your family, turning doubt into determination and pity into purpose. They were warriors in every sense of the word, and their legacy is a testament to the power of love, grit, and the relentless pursuit of what is right.

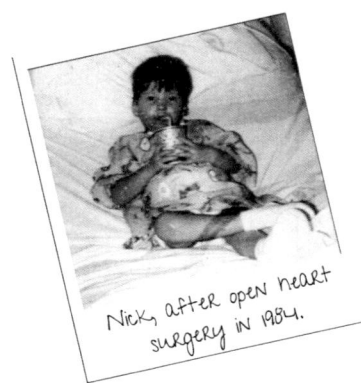

Nicky, after open heart surgery in 1984.

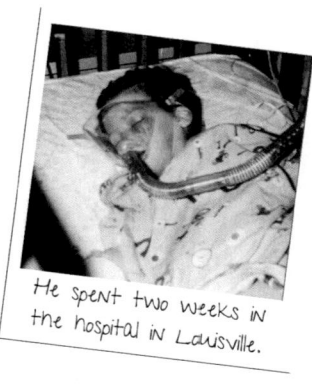

He spent two weeks in the hospital in Louisville.

" BEING A SPECIAL NEEDS
SIBLING MEANS GROWING UP
KNOWING THAT LOVE IS NOT
MEASURED BY

what's easy

BUT BY THE COMPASSION
AND STRENGTH IT TAKES TO
STAND BY SOMEONE
when it's hard "

CHAPTER 2
ALONG COMES ME

THE MOMENT I UNDERSTOOD HIS DIAGNOSIS

I have been asked countless times how my parents addressed my brother's disability with me. And really, the answer is: they didn't.

To be fair, maybe they did, and I simply don't recall the conversation.

What I do remember are small moments from our daily life. It was during these moments that I began to understand the full scope of Nick's disability and how it impacted him. His disability wasn't something we talked about or acknowledged — it was just who we were as a family, part of our everyday lives.

It was so much a part of our reality that it didn't need to be discussed; it just was.

A way of life rather than a topic for conversation.

And it was these moments that shaped our family's journey.

At the young age of 5, I was beginning to grasp the reality of my brother's disability. In fact, one of my earliest memories was the moment I realized Nick was different. On an ordinary day after school, I made a life-changing decision that would define my future: I would be a special education teacher.

In the heart of our humble single-wide trailer, I sat hunched over the coffee table in our living room, clutching a pencil that felt entirely too big for my kindergarten-sized hand. It was a weeknight, and my big brother, Nick, and I were in our homework routine, drowning in spelling and sight words. (Nick and I were three years apart, so in this season Nick was eight and I was five.) Our mom stood over us ensuring the work was getting done.

I was a fiery redhead, stubborn and strong-willed. So sitting down to do homework was not easy, especially when it came to my nemesis — spelling words. I couldn't help but resent them. For the third time that evening, I painstakingly rewrote letters onto the lined paper designed for the delicate handwriting of a kindergartner, my frustration building with each stroke of my pencil.

Amanda – 1990

Our trailer didn't have the luxury of a dedicated homework space, so the living room was our makeshift classroom. My mom, the epitome of patience and support, presided over the homework chaos, bouncing between Nick's struggle with his sight words and my frustration with my spelling words.

As I wrote the word cat for the umpteenth time, a cry from my brother pulled my attention. Nick's tears flowed freely now as he wrestled with his sight words, his frustration could be seen in the quiver of his lower lip.

I looked at Nick, crying, face red and something caught my eye. I could read the flashcard held tightly in my mom's hand. The bold handwritten letters had one single word: Mom.

Stubborn and strong-willed as I may have been, I was equally as passionate to be the best student possible, eager to impress my teachers, but more so my parents. My heart fluttered when I recognized the word.

"I know that word," I thought. Mom was the very first word on my kindergarten spelling test.

My confidence wavered as I leaned in close to my brother, my voice trembling with a strange mix of assurance and sadness. "Say 'Mom'," I whispered to my big brother.

My mom's gentle reprimand broke the stillness of that moment. "Amanda, do your spelling words," she said. "Nick needs to learn his words. It won't help him if you do it for him."

A heavy quiet fell over us and it carried with it an unfamiliar weight. Thoughts swirled in my young mind. It was the first time I felt an unsettling worry in the pit of my belly, and I couldn't quite figure out why. I felt sympathy for my brother that I couldn't understand. While I had helped Nick countless times before, it was the first time it felt as though I was an older sister. (Looking back, I realize this was the first time I recognized he needed me.)

And then, as I continued to labor over my spelling words, it dawned on me. Nick's sight words at age eight were the same as my spelling words at age five. In that instant, I realized that Nick was different from me, and a mysterious divide began to take root in our shared world. It was at that moment I became a different kind of sister. My innocence at five years old would slowly start to diminish because it took a mature little girl to accept and understand her role as this kind of sister.

This small moment was such a defining point of my life. From this point forward, I declared I would be a teacher. Five-year-old me simply wanted to help others like my brother. And because of Nick, I knew I could.

But as he and I grew older, that motivation evolved. Seeing Nick's continued struggles and his teachers failing to meet his needs, I dreamed of being the kind of teacher that my brother deserved.

But more on that a little later.

MY FIRST FEELINGS OF JEALOUSY

Despite our difference in age and ability, Nick and I were very close. I may have been younger, but Nick looked up to me, and to be honest, I sometimes took advantage of that. We spent countless hours playing pretend. Whether it was playing house, beauty salon, or with my baby dolls, Nick was always eager to join in and willing to let me take the lead. In our make-believe games, I was the mom or the salon owner, and Nick, my pretend son or obedient customer.

Nick and Amanda playing with baby dolls.

We lived in the country, and our big backyard had a playhouse my parents built for us. The light blue, A-frame house had a white front door and windows on either side. I don't know how many times we turned that playhouse into a McDonald's drive-thru, where Nick, my customer, would ride his bike up to the window to be served the make-believe Big Mac and fries I had just made.

When we played, everything was good until it wasn't. When Nick was done or had enough of my bossing, we would fight. But isn't that true of most siblings?

That's the thing – our parents allowed us to be siblings. We were Nick and Amanda, not a child with a disability and his neurotypical sibling.

While Nick received a certain unspoken protection from my parents, they did a great job of managing both of our feelings when we would fight.

The most common interest I shared with my brother was our love for swimming. At the bottom of the hill we lived on, we had a man-made swimming lake, equipped with a dock, slide, and, of course, a rope swing. Nick and I lived in that lake. It was a very natural common interest. I often coaxed Nick to swing into the water first, using him to scare away any fish before taking the plunge myself.

Despite occasionally taking advantage of his adoration, I recognized Nick's unwavering love for me. It was evident in every baby doll scenario I came up with, every pretend drive-thru transaction, and each time he scared away the fish in our backyard lake.

This dynamic continued into adulthood, with Nick still striving to meet my needs, albeit in more subtle ways. Today, he shows his affection by sending me thoughtful texts, with screenshots alerting me that White Claw is on sale or updates on the weather of my travel destinations.

Although most of the time Nick and I were rarely different. there are memories that stand out where I felt our differences profoundly.

Just as I recognized Nick was different that day in our living room doing our homework, I began to notice my parents' attention to Nick was different from their attention to me.

Yes, he got more of their time while we did our homework, but it was more than that.

I think even at that young of an age, I understood why Nick needed more.

MORE time.

MORE attention.

MORE grace.

MORE of everything.

So often this "more" stirs up emotions of frustration, jealousy, or loneliness within neurotypical siblings, which they mask with a smile or distraction because the last thing they want is to add any extra weight to their family's already heavy load. They don't want to be another person in need, another source of worry for their parents. So, they convince themselves they can handle it, that they are strong enough to bear it alone, determined not to burden their family with any "more" from them.

In my story, I can't pinpoint a time that this "more" affected me in this manner. Don't get me wrong, I was a young, emotional girl and my parents had to deal with all my BIG feelings, but those feelings were never about my brother. Those feelings I protected, shielding myself from the worry and guilt that admitting them out loud would cause me and safeguarding my parents, who were overwhelmed and tired.

My brother's complex needs were demanding enough, and truthfully, I was content with that, until one day, around age six, when my emotions began to spiral. I remember it was after a sleepover with my grandparents, that I returned home convinced I was adopted.

Nick was in the hospital a lot and he had weekly therapies. This meant I spent a lot of time with my grandparents. I had just returned home from another overnight stay with Ma & Pa where we had flipped through dozens of family albums reminiscing on my baby years.

I was the only freckled redhead in the family, but that wasn't what caught my attention. Those family albums were filled with pictures of my brother. Page after page, it seemed as though every milestone of Nick was captured and preserved. There seemed to be at least 100 photos of Nick's first steps. (I know now what a significant achievement this was for him at three years old.)

Of course there were pictures of me, but in comparison to Nick, it seemed as though there were none. The sadness this brought was a new feeling. I had never compared myself to Nick like this before.

Was I jealous?

Regardless of the feeling, I didn't like it and I didn't want to feel it, but I couldn't help it. Why did my parents take so many more pictures of Nick? They must be keeping a secret from me: I am adopted. It couldn't be because they love him more? No, I have to be adopted.

With sweaty palms and half-chewed nails – a bad habit I still can't kick – I finally had enough courage to ask, "Mom, was I adopted?"

My mom tilted her head to the side with a look of concern and said, "Lord, no, Amanda! What would ever make you think you were adopted?"

Although relief washed over me, tears still streamed down my face as I admitted to my mom I was sad there were more pictures of Nick than me.

My mom drew me close, hugging me tight and explained, "Oh, sweetheart, of course you're my baby girl. I'm so sorry there aren't more baby pictures of you, and I know that makes you sad. But let me explain why. When you were little, Nick was really sick, and it was a scary time for all of us. Some days still are. When you were just six weeks old, Nick needed open heart surgery. I had to leave you with Ma and Pa because the hospital wasn't the best place for a little baby like you."

After Mom and I talked, the following Sunday at our family dinner — an unshakable tradition at Ma and Pa's house with all my cousins, aunts, and uncles — Mom retold the story about how I thought I was adopted. As she shared it over the dining room table, everyone chimed in, recalling how life was certainly busy back then, but I was always in the center of it all. They shared stories about how, even amidst the chaos, I had been the heart of my parents' world. In that moment, any lingering doubts I had were replaced with a deep sense of belonging, surrounded by the love of my family.

Visiting Nick in the hospital

My mom later searched high and low to find all the baby photos she had of me and she spent time recounting each captured memory. I had noticed the obvious difference in the number of photos of my brother compared to me. But what I didn't see was that those photos documented Nick's triumphs, surpassing every expectation doctors told my parents all those years before. A little boy learning to walk, feed himself, ride a bike – living a life of purpose.

And I also couldn't see the blessing all of Nick's doctors appointments brought me: time with my grandparents. The silver lining was that I developed a deep bond with my grandparents, a relationship I might not have had otherwise.

Nick's needs would inevitably intersect with my own life, but my parents ensured my needs were also met, giving me love and care in the best way they could, which, in looking back I am grateful was enough. I never felt neglected or less valued by my parents, but I am sure they wrestled with their own guilt with having to give more attention, in whatever form, to Nick. And looking back, I recognize I was a bit more spoiled to compensate for Nick's disability.

I think all of those things are natural factors for special needs families. Navigating those situations will look different for each family. Did we do it perfectly? No. But I don't think there is a perfect way to approach parenting a child with a disability and a neurotypical child. I think you have to find what works for your family and allow yourself grace along the journey.

THE PRESSURE TO FULFILL THEIR DREAMS

At six years old, I couldn't identify that I was feeling jealous while looking at those family photo albums. However, looking back, I can definitely see that convincing myself I was adopted came from a feeling of jealousy. I was not inherently equipped with the emotional intelligence to recognize or manage the complex feelings that arise from having a sibling with a disability. At a young age, I lacked the maturity to mourn the loss of the typical sibling relationship I might have had. Nor was I yet capable of comprehending how my sibling's disability could instill in me the fundamental qualities of grace and empathy.

Jealousy just wasn't an emotion I remember feeling often. What I do remember was a sense of pressure, an immense weight resting heavily on my shoulders. It was the burden of an internal struggle that many siblings of those with disabilities know all too well — the relentless pressure to be the "good kid," to excel and achieve at levels that bring joy and pride to our parents. It's a constant need to compensate for what our sibling may not experience, to fill the gaps and alleviate the challenges they face.

The first time I recall feeling this weight, a pressure I imposed on myself, was after receiving my first report card in second grade.

I sat in the backseat of the van, clutching my report card reflecting all As and Bs. Not even giving in and letting Nick have the front seat could curb my enthusiasm. I couldn't wait to get the crisp $1 bills from Ma and Pa, a reward Nick and I always got for good grades.

We pulled up to our grandparents' house, and Nick and I excitedly burst through the door, yelling, "We have our report cards!"

Pa grabbed my report card, read the grades aloud and said, "Mandy, keep it up! Ma, get the money and pay this smart kid!"

It was Nick's turn. I don't recall what was on his report card, or what my grandparents said, but I remember the tone. Ma and Pa praised him, but the praise carried a different meaning.

That tone planted a seed that day.

Interactions like that set the stage for the role I felt compelled to play within my family. It wasn't asked of me or even suggested. I self-imposed this expectation that I needed to offer my family the hope, dreams, and achievements my brother might not provide.

Receiving our "A money" that day strengthened my drive to achieve at levels that would make my family proud. This one story marks the beginning of an internal narrative I crafted as a child, a narrative dictated not by desire but by the role I assigned myself as a special needs sibling. I imposed an unspoken pressure to be the good, smart, well-behaved, happy, overachieving, loving, and supportive kid.

Did my parents see the pressure I put on myself? I don't think they did. In all honesty, this pressure didn't feel like a burden to me. It didn't weigh me down. This role I gave myself changed me and the trajectory of my life, but it didn't hold me back. **It was simply an unspoken truth that I carried with me through my life.**

To be completely transparent and honest, I am vulnerably sharing the emotions I felt throughout my childhood knowing that my parents will eventually read these words. These emotions are not ones that I so openly shared with them at the time and for that reason, I feel the need to emphasize that the weight, pressure and worry I talk about was never a burden.

However, it's important to recognize that some special needs siblings may indeed view these feelings and their role as a sibling as burdensome. They might imagine a different life path for themselves — one that diverges from the spoken or unspoken expectations placed upon them. They may dream of leaving their hometown, pursuing a career in a bustling city, or choosing a life without marriage and parenthood. Simply put, the role of caretaker might not align with the dreams they hold for **their** future.

As a special needs parent, it's vital to understand the significant pressure that your neurotypical child(ren) might feel to assume your caregiver role, should anything happen to you. This pressure can be overwhelming and, at times, all-consuming.

The choices neurotypical children make as it relates to the future care of their sibling with a disability may be difficult for parents to accept, but it's crucial to move through any pain it may cause and prioritize the relationship above all else.
My advice? Communication. But we will get into that a little later.

I believe all special needs siblings grapple with some form of internal battle, shaping their understanding of what they must be for their family due to their sibling's disability. From the pressure to become a future caretaker to pursuing dreams that don't include their sibling, these battles are inevitable. Parents naturally want to prevent these struggles in their neurotypical children, aiming to lessen what they presume is a burden or pain. Just as they want to alleviate any pain their child with a disability feels, their ultimate goal is to protect all their children.

But I don't think there's anything a family could do to completely stop this narrative. It's a natural response for us siblings as we witness the daily demands and differences in our family dynamics.

Honestly, I don't see this as a bad thing. Don't bubble wrap your kids from their emotions, which are a catalyst to building character and helping them determine what they truly want for their future, especially in relation to their sibling with a disability.

The internal struggle I felt fueled my desire to make a difference for others and ultimately led me to become the woman I am today.

THE ROLES OF THE FAMILY

In families worldwide, each member typically assumes a distinct role that contributes to the overall dynamics.

Take my family for example.

My mom assumed the role of caregiver, ensuring both Nick and I received everything we needed. There were moments when her dedication bordered on over protectiveness, and I must confess, I sometimes took advantage of those instances. If she was getting Nick a snack, I, being the little sister, wouldn't pass up a hand-delivered sweet treat. But her unwavering support for my brother meant that she also extended the same level of care to me. In her hands, we never lacked anything.

(Have you seen the 2003 classic movie "Old School?" Let's just say that scene where Will Ferrell says "Ma... the meatloaf!" wasn't too far from a day in our home growing up.)

Our connection with our mom runs very deep and it is quite evident that Nick and I always came first in her priorities. The incredible progress Nick made in developing fundamental skills like walking, talking, and learning is a testament to my mom's dedication to her children. She beautifully balanced her role as his caregiver while

Our mom, the caregiver

encouraging him to strive for independence. Her ability to find the perfect balance between fostering his self-reliance and knowing when to step back was anchored in one fundamental principle: prioritizing his happiness above all else.

But, like many special needs moms, it pained my mom to see Nick struggle. The difficulty he faced made her want to make life easier for him. My sweet Momma often stepped in to do things for him, even if he could manage them himself. It was an act of love, a motherly impulse to lessen the challenges he faced.

This nurturing instinct seemed to come naturally to her, a trait that persists even now that Nick and I are in our 40s. I'm not entirely sure why this caregiving nature is so ingrained in her; perhaps it stems from all those years she yearned to have a baby or the initial realization that Nick would face challenges and wouldn't be able to do everything for himself. Regardless, in our family, she became the epitome of a caregiver, a role she embraced wholeheartedly.

My dad is the rock of our family, always ready to catch any of us when we stumble. My heart has always ached for him, recognizing the additional challenges men in special needs families often face in processing emotions and forging connections. But Nick was his son and he was a proud father. He took on the crucial role of being the voice of reason when emotions ran high. He supported my mom when she reached her limit and consistently served as our family's unwavering cheerleader.

I can't remember a time that my dad ever missed one of my softball games and he spent a lot of years on the field as my team's coach. He worked hard for his family, but he never allowed his job to become his priority. Reflecting now, I believe his career in the fire department and as an EMT provided our family with a profound sense of security. In the event of a medical emergency involving Nick, we took comfort in knowing that my dad would be there to assess the situation calmly and respond appropriately.

Our dad, the Rock

Throughout my life, my dad worked multiple jobs just to make ends meet. While Mom's career as a school bus driver allowed her the flexibility to support Nick's needs and schedule, Dad took on additional work to ensure that our family had everything we needed. His relentless efforts to balance these responsibilities were a testament to his dedication and love. He managed to create a stable and supportive environment for us all, even as he juggled the demands of several roles to keep our family secure and cared for.

His steady presence as a coach, provider, and protector made him the rock of our family, someone we could always rely on for guidance, support, and unwavering love. His dedication to both his career and our well-being shaped my understanding of what it means to be dependable and resilient in the face of challenges.

Nick, well he is the heartbeat of our family, while simultaneously taking on the role of entertainer. He never explicitly asserted himself as the center of our family or even anticipated it; it simply radiated from him effortlessly. But I think that may be the nature of his disability and our family's response to rallying around him. The expectations my parents were presented with upon Nick's diagnosis created this almost unearthly determination – and maybe a little stubbornness – that put Nick at the heart of who we were.

Nick, the Heartbeat

And then, there's me.

We have the devoted caregiver, the steadfast foundation, and the heartbeat, so where does that leave me?

I took on the role of the "light" within my family. By this, I mean being the one who offers the metaphorical oxygen mask when no one else can breathe, providing a refreshing breath of air in a stuffy room, or consistently embodying the persona of the dependable "good girl."

Amanda — the Light

Please know I wasn't an angel. I'm certain my parents still recall the time when, as a high school junior, I lied about my overnight plans in order to stay with my college boyfriend. (Mom, if you're reading this, I'm sorry!) I wasn't immune to the typical antics of a headstrong kid or a hormonal teenage girl who occasionally sassed her mother. But more often than not, I found myself being the light in a family impacted by disability.

Don't get me wrong, I cherished the fact that God blessed me with the ability to bring hope to my family. But to be honest, most often this role came with a pressure I placed upon myself.

As the neurotypical child, the hope that I provided was being "the one."

THE ONE who was granted a healthy life, for which I need to be appreciative and be grateful.

THE ONE who would graduate from high school with a diploma.

THE ONE who would get a driver's license.

THE ONE who would go to college.

THE ONE who would have a professional career.

THE ONE who would marry.

THE ONE who would move out and buy a house.

THE ONE who would provide the joy of grandkids.

THE ONE who would become Nick's caregiver if my parents could no longer care for him.

None of these roles within my family were imposed upon us. It was simply a natural process of assuming the roles we needed to fulfill. My parents never placed expectations on me to provide hope, nor did their actions reinforce such thinking.

However, at a young age, I learned that my gift – and my curse – would be the desire to be a source of joy in others' stories. I bore the responsibility of being the "good girl," driven by a desire to ease the challenges and uncertainties that accompanied Nick's disability by infusing positivity into our family dynamic. Looking back, I realize that this experience may have been where I naturally acquired a deep understanding of motivation and drive.

Do I harbor resentment for my role in our family?

The answer is no, but resentment is a powerful emotion.

It's an emotion that I couldn't escape, even from a young age. Although my resentment was never towards my parents for focusing more on Nick. Instead, it stemmed from the self-imposed role I felt I had to fulfill as "the light." I pressured myself to be everything for my parents and brother, to make our life as a special needs family easier. Reminders of Nick's disability and my perceived need to compensate for it were a daily part of my life.

Still, even with that pressure, I felt more pride than resentment in my role as his sibling. That pride didn't make the weight any lighter, but it was my way of embracing the responsibility that came with being Nick's

"THE MOST PROFOUND LESSONS OFTEN ARISE IN THE SPACES BETWEEN OUR PLANS AND *the reality of daily life*" sister. Now, as an adult, I understand that those experiences, with all their complexities, shaped me into the person I am today. The sense of duty, the strength, and the compassion I carry — it all comes from being Nick's sister.

And for that, I am eternally grateful.

ISOLATION, BULLYING & THE PUNCH

I can't speak for all families impacted by disability, but for us, the seasons of late elementary and middle school were particularly challenging. The gap between me, the neurotypical child, and Nick, my brother with an intellectual disability, began to widen, and our differences became more pronounced. This is also the first time I began to experience bullying. I learned that children, in their innocence, can be brutally honest, often highlighting the very insecurities that I struggled with during my adolescent years.

My school years were filled with countless moments that left a lasting mark on me as a sibling to someone with a disability. Although the landscape of today's society may differ from my experiences back then, there is still much work to be done to achieve true inclusion and acceptance for individuals with disabilities.

There was legislation mandating free appropriate public education for students with disabilities when Nick and I were in school. But he did not receive the accommodations or individualized education plan that students with disabilities receive today. In the 80s, public schools struggled to meet the educational and individualized needs of those with significant disabilities. At the time in my community, students with significant disabilities were bussed to one elementary school in the district, which had a self-contained classroom tucked away from the general student population. Nick, however, remained at the school closest to our home and was a part of the "special class," while I was in a typical classroom setting.

When he and his classmates would pass by in the hallways, my friends would stare and giggle. His class was the only door with a covered window, making it feel as though the school was hiding my brother away from me and the rest of the world. I can remember trying to process and understand why they wanted to hide my brother, because to me he was Nick. At home he was just my brother who needed a little more sometimes – more support, more love, more patience, more care, and more of his family.

Why did they want him hidden away and isolated? What was so scary about him?

Nick's disability was just a way of life for my family. It was very hard for me to grapple with the fact that he wasn't seen equally outside of our home.

Unbeknownst to my parents, Nick's teachers often used me to help console or support him. If he was upset because he missed our mom, wanted to go home or just didn't want to do his work, they summoned me from my own class to lend a hand. While being pulled from class initially felt like a cool sister privilege, I was unprepared for the questions that began to arise among my peers. They wanted to know why my brother needed my help, and I struggled to explain.

It was just one more way that made me – and our family – feel different from everyone else.

Nick was the only student in our school with significant needs and the staff's limitations eventually became evident. My parents advocated for Nick to receive a better education, even if that meant transferring him to the only school in our district that provided a classroom for students with significant needs. Despite being much further from our home, this school was better equipped to support him by offering a more accommodating setting for his needs.

As an adult, I understand this decision was made in the best interest of Nick. But as a second grader, it was hard not to wonder, "what about me?" I was no longer able to go to school with my big brother. Being Nick's sister was a huge part of who I was, especially when helping his teachers support his success became part of my everyday life. For my elementary aged brain, it was hard to comprehend how such a big decision was made without considering how it would affect me.

As the years went on, my parents' advocacy for Nick's education continued. In my middle school years, I started to hear my mom fight the world for my brother. Better schooling, more acceptance, needed therapy, and the list goes on. I heard these conversations, but I didn't really understand the significance of what was happening.

I have since come to understand that these seemingly insignificant moments – seeing Nick isolated in my own school and witnessing my mom stand up for what Nick needed – shaped my role as an advocate today.

My parents never pressured me to become an advocate, but I'll admit, my mom did tell me that if I ever got suspended from school for standing up for my brother, she'd take me shopping.

In hindsight, this might have motivated me to become an advocate far more than I ever realized.

I hated reading aloud.

It seemed like all of my teachers believed reading aloud was a way for an early learner to become more fluent in reading while also gaining confidence. But for me it did just the opposite: it highlighted my weakness, which destroyed my self-confidence.

In first grade, I was referred to speech therapy and where I often overheard adults discussing that my speech was impacted by my brother. I eventually graduated from speech before leaving elementary school, after mastering the word spaghetti.

But growing up alongside Nick undeniably shaped many aspects of my life — including my academic development. In my early years, as we both learned phonics, spelling, and speech, we were inseparable.

Naturally, we shared phrases, sounds, and ways of speaking, which became part of our bond. Looking back, I realize that while I wouldn't trade those moments for anything, they likely did impact my foundational learning. No one is to blame for this—it's simply a natural outcome of our dynamic as siblings. To this day, my phonics and spelling are a bit underdeveloped, and while I don't blame Nick, it's a reminder of how closely our lives were intertwined. Our connection was so deep that we even shaped each other in ways we never fully realized at the time.

Similarly, another natural outcome of being the neurotypical child was that my parents often stepped in to help me more than necessary, hoping to shield both of their children from any struggles. By over supporting me, they could have hindered a little of my early development. But there was no playbook for my parents as they navigated the challenges of supporting two children with completely different needs — one chasing milestones and the other building a foundation of skills. They naturally wanted both of their children to succeed and be fair in how they supported both of us.

Reading aloud in my class openly demonstrated my struggles to my peers, which is exactly when the bullying started. I heard the mumbles throughout the classroom.

"She is retarded like her brother."

"She can't read because her brother can't read."

I wanted to get up and punch the kids whispering about me. After all, my mom said I could.

I wasn't angry that they were making fun of me. No, that's not what hurt me. I was a strong willed, fiery redhead. I could take it. But I couldn't handle them talking about Nick like that.

They saw his weakness and what he couldn't do. They didn't see his value and all the things he could do. They didn't know my big brother.

I felt like a prisoner in that classroom of giggles.

The bullying continued. And the more I heard the laughter and the whispers of "retarded," the more I questioned – were they right? Did they know something I didn't know about my brother?

I never told my parents about what was going on. I knew it would hurt them too. I made the decision to sacrifice my feelings in order to spare them the same pain because I knew the weight they were carrying.

One specific day during my fifth-grade year, I found myself riding the bus back from a field trip alongside my fellow classmates. Our heads could barely be seen above those tall brown seats. The teacher was at the front of the bus with her back to us.

The bullying always started the same way. I was telling my classmates a story and I stumbled on the pronunciation of a word, and just like clockwork a boy named Danny called out, "You are so retarded."

That statement lit up my insides like fire. I never knew one word could make me want to cry and also burn with rage. Unfortunately for Danny, the right hook he took to his face was not just about him. That right hook was the fight that was building inside from all the people who bullied me. It was the fight I knew I would have for the rest of my life.

This was a pivotal moment in my journey as an advocate. Not because I was suspended and my mom took me shopping as promised, but because it taught me to stand up for what I believe in – although I have now learned to use words instead of my fists.

THE REFRIGERATOR BOX

I doubt many parents of special needs children sit their neurotypical children down and provide them with a playbook for navigating their advocacy journey. Siblings who have a brother or sister with a disability often find themselves naturally cast into the role of advocate, a responsibility that can be both a blessing and a burden. The weight of this expectation rests on their shoulders, demanding patience, understanding, and a profound knowledge of how to navigate a world lacking acceptance and inclusion.

Today, as a nonprofit service provider and someone with a small space in the social media world, I find that being an advocate is so often an unspoken expectation for siblings like me. In some families parents exert significant pressure on the neurotypical child to be the voice for their brother or sister with a disability. I consider myself so fortunate that my parents did not ask this of me.

Regardless of how you arrived at your role of advocate, the concept can be perplexing.

What does it even mean to be an advocate?

Is it a lifelong commitment, or can we eventually take off the advocate badge of honor?

There are days when we may not want to wage a continuous battle against a world that often fails to understand or accommodate those with disabilities. Does that make us bad siblings, or can we admit that we're not always ready to carry the weight of being an advocate?

These are questions that many siblings grapple with as they navigate the complex terrain of their family dynamics and societal expectations.

I told you about the moment I realized I wanted to be a special education teacher in order to help others like my brother. But do you remember when I told you I dreamed of being the kind of teacher that my brother deserved? I can recall just as vividly the moment I decided I would become the teacher my brother never had.

I was in elementary school when I overheard my mom, tears streaming down her face, passionately yelling over the phone. At the time, Nick was in middle school, and though I can't recall who was on the other end of that call, I can assure you they would have preferred hiding in a hole rather than facing my mom's wrath. As I listened at the door, my own tears welled up as my mom firmly said, "This is unacceptable, and I want it removed."

On that distressing day, I learned that my brother was placed in a refrigerator box for the remainder of the day as a punishment for his behavior. My mom vividly described this horrifying ordeal, creating a sickening image in my mind. The teacher had taken a refrigerator box, cut out one side, and placed it around Nick's desk against the wall, isolating him in this dark, solitary space.

You might wonder how my mom discovered what was happening in Nick's classroom. Mom simply asked Nick about his day. Nick was fortunately verbal, although he sometimes struggled to articulate details.

"I had to be in the box. That big box!" he said, oblivious to the inappropriateness of the situation.

Later, when Mom went to the school, she uncovered a mother's worst nightmare. As I heard my mom passionately retell this story with tears and anger, making phone call after phone call, I realized two undeniable truths in my life. I was determined to be the teacher my brother deserved, and in that moment, I knew I would become an advocate just like my mom.

If you're a parent of a child with a disability, I imagine that reading Nick's experience can evoke the same sickening reaction I experienced as a young child — an unsettling pit in the stomach. How does a human being, particularly a teacher, treat someone in a manner that devalues their very existence? I imagine that as a special needs parent, this is your worst fear. Trusting others with the care of our family members with disabilities is a difficult task.

Although this happened to Nick over 30 years ago, situations like this are not isolated incidents. Similar things continue to occur today, within our schools, workplaces, and communities. Headlines across the world provide examples of the continued abuse and neglect of individuals with disabilities – headlines of nanny cams capturing evidence of physical abuse or children with non-verbal autism being abused in the classroom.

These narratives, unfortunately, underscore the vital necessity for advocates to emerge. The need for individuals willing to champion the rights and dignity of those with disabilities is evident. Advocacy isn't just a reaction to isolated incidents; it's a continuous and vital duty rooted in a commitment to ensuring the well-being and fair treatment of individuals with disabilities in every aspect of life.

THE "R-WORD" MADE ME AN ADVOCATE

Whether it is a good thing to admit or not, the word "retarded" had just as much of an impact on my role as an advocate as any other experience in my life.

It's a term that packed a punch. It not only sent a shiver down my spine, but it simultaneously broke my heart. Growing up in the 90s, this term found its way into the everyday vocabulary of people of all ages, casually used to describe something as foolish or stupid. In high school, I heard it a lot.

But what my classmates didn't know was that "mentally retarded" was actually my brother's official medical diagnosis. It was written in his charts. After his diagnosis at six months old, this term was given to him as a label that would follow him for the rest of his life. Yes, even today his medical charts still label him as retarded.

When I heard others use the word "retarded" to describe something stupid, inferior, idiotic, or undesirable, it hit me hard and deeply affected me.

Friends tossed the word around so casually. But each time that word fell out of someone's mouth, everyone involved in the conversation would nervously cut their eyes toward me. It was as if their eyes were saying, "Uh oh," reminding everyone that I was a special needs sibling.

Hearing them use that word was bad enough, but it got even worse when they paused or hushed up to correct themselves. Something along the lines of: "Oh, her brother is retarded, I mean has special needs. Remember, she doesn't like that word."

To be honest, the ongoing fight against that word got pretty exhausting and was a constant reminder that those around me only cared that I was a special needs sibling when they chose to use a word that would inadvertently offend me. Sometimes I'd act like I didn't hear it, other times I'd ask them to use a different word, and every now and then, I'd go off on them, telling them how offensive it is and why they should never use it.

But one time, I will never forget, I had finally had enough.

Sitting in my freshman English class, two male peers were joking back and forth with each other. One said loudly, "You're retarded!"

He wasn't talking to me. It wasn't about my brother. But it struck a nerve.

"Hey, use another word," I yelled at him.

I don't know what had gotten into me. I had never disrupted class like that. Although I don't think there is ever an appropriate time to use that word, this peer was using it in a joking tone. But what he said next tipped me over the edge.

"Don't be so sensitive. It's just a word," he said back snidely.

In that moment, I was done. It was as if all of the R-words I have ever heard culminated in that moment, and I felt broken and defeated. I stood up from my desk, left all of my belongings and I bolted from that room in the middle of class.

I eventually returned to the class to retrieve my things and move on to my next period. I never received an apology from that student. My anger and hurt may not have impacted him, but his thoughtlessness and lack of remorse certainly impacted me. And it was this experience that made it clear to me that even adults like my teacher struggled to grasp the emotional weight of being a special needs sibling. This teacher never acknowledged my departure from class or even addressed the situation at all. Although she must have sensed my hurt, she didn't know how to approach or discuss it.

In truth, many people couldn't understand or empathize with my feelings.

It was that day that I first took a stand for what I believed in. In spite of embarrassment and the attention of the entire class, I made my first public statement for inclusion and acceptance for those like my brother.

But it wasn't – and never will be – my last.

Because, let's be real, even though society is better at telling people not to use it, folks still throw around the R-word to describe those with intellectual disabilities or as a way to call things stupid. I hear or read it almost daily.

Comments on my content across my social media platform are littered with this word. People hiding behind their keyboards comment about my brother or my friends with disabilities, calling them retarded, asking if they ride the short bus, or comparing them to stereotypical characters from pop culture that represent intellectual disabilities.

And with that day in high school in the back of my mind, I continue to take a stand for Nick, for the 400+ individuals I serve through my nonprofit and the disability families that I represent.

LEARNING FROM THE BEST, MY MOM

In those early years, securing a babysitter for Nick and I proved to be a daunting task, as he wasn't particularly fond of having babysitters. His ability to break in new sitters quickly turned them into "one and done" caregivers. Consequently, I often found myself tagging along to anything and everything, including Nick's Individualized Education Plan (IEP) meetings.

Times like these, and countless others, proved that my journey toward becoming an advocate wasn't planned by my parents; instead, it unfolded organically, almost as a byproduct of our family's unique circumstances.

Sitting at this IEP meeting, the only distraction available was a coloring book. As I sat there, attempting to divert my attention from the sometimes difficult discussions taking place, it struck me how these meetings solely focused on what Nick couldn't do. The list of things he hadn't yet mastered echoed through the room repeatedly. I now appreciate that my parents didn't shield me from these conversations, which inadvertently shaped and prepared me for my future as an advocate.

Within these experiences, one particular memory stands out — a moment that highlighted the remarkable strength and resilience of my mom and her fight for my brother. This memory became a pivotal point in my understanding of advocacy, showcasing not only the challenges but also the transformative power it holds in advocating for those with disabilities.

My mom took command of the room in a way I had never seen before. I had never witnessed her like this—her voice steady, her words powerful, and her energy filling every corner.

She was surrounded by a group of adults, all dressed in professional attire, seated around a table. Her advocacy, firm and resolute, cut through the air as she addressed the issue at hand.

"I would like to understand why my son is bringing home books he can't read. I understand this is a middle school and his reading level is not the same as his peers, but he should be given the opportunity to check out books he can read at his first-grade reading level."

The faces around the table displayed a collective sense of bewilderment; they were at a loss for words, grappling with the realization that what seemed like basic accommodations were not being met.

These individuals were so far removed from the realities of our daily lives, and their response reflected their lack of understanding. They offered a vague promise to "look into it," attempting to justify the oversight based on the fact that he was now in middle school.

My mother's response, however, was nothing short of epic. Unyielding in her advocacy, she declared, "That's not acceptable. It's what he needs. Do I need to call Frankfort?"

Frankfort, our state's capital housing the Department of Education, became the threat that underscored the gravity of the situation. In that small corner where I sat, absorbing the dynamics of that room, I witnessed a profound demonstration of what it truly meant to be an advocate — to become a voice for your child and articulate his needs.

In that very moment, my admiration for my mom deepened even further. It was a lesson etched in memory, a testament to the power of advocacy in navigating the complex terrain of a system that often falls short in understanding the individual needs of those with different abilities.

Becoming an advocate wasn't something my parents told me to do; it just kind of happened because of how I grew up. They never gave me a step-by-step guide or anything like that. Instead, they demonstrated through their own actions and allowed Nick and I to build a strong bond on our own.

When I talk with fellow families, I am often asked how to instill advocacy in their neurotypical children, particularly when it comes to advocating for their sibling. My response carries the weight of lived experience: instead of trying to teach advocacy by telling kids what to do or what you expect of them, demonstrate what advocacy looks like through your actions in your everyday family life.

" A FAMILY'S UNITY
ISN'T DETERMINED BY
HOW EASY LIFE IS,
BUT BY HOW
FIERCELY THEY HOLD
ONTO ONE ANOTHER
when it's not "

The things we learn through our shared experiences, challenges, and victories create a solid base for nurturing advocacy among siblings. **Make advocacy an essential element of your family story, something that is effortlessly woven into your shared journey.**

CHAPTER 3
BUILDING MY LIFE

FINDING CONNECTION BEYOND THE DISABILITY

I remember my mom once telling me about her life before having
kids. She compared it to my life today, which included girls' trips and
vacations with other families. She said that she and my dad were always
on the go with their friends – but then they had Nick. She explained that
having Nick changed everything.

Our safe place in the world became our family.

Working with so many individuals with disabilities today, I see the
reality of the isolation their families face. They lose friends and fall
distant from their loved ones, either because of variables associated
with their child's disability or simply because they feel more
comfortable, safe, and in control within their own homes.

I am lucky that this wasn't the case for us. We found connection through
my extended family – my parents' siblings and their children. Nick and I
grew up alongside a dozen or so cousins. We lived in a small, rural town,
with my mom's six brothers and sisters nearby. My mom's twin sister
was not only her best friend, but she was like a second mother to me.

In Whitesville, Kentucky, there wasn't much to do besides spending time
with family. We went to a small Baptist church on Sundays, which was

mostly made up of my family. After church, we had Sunday dinner at my grandparents. Honestly, we were always gathered for something – birthdays, holidays, and countless summer days swimming in the pond behind our house.

Our cousins filled such a void in not only my life, but in Nick's life too. For Nick, our cousins were the friends Nick didn't have outside of his self-contained special education classroom. They saw Nick for Nick, not just a kid with an intellectual disability.

Cousins playing
Summer 1985

Cousins
Christmas 1985

For me, my cousins became like brothers and sisters. And unlike my relationship with Nick, I could connect with them in a much different way. We matured at the same pace and shared an intellectual companionship that Nick's disability couldn't provide.

But as life progressed, we got older, learned to drive, made friends, and began exploring life beyond our family. This was typical. However, what none of them realized, but I knew to be true, was that we were leaving Nick behind.

During this uncertain transition, as our time with aunts, uncles and cousins began to diminish, the sport of softball saved us, giving my parents, Nick and I a new sense of community.

We weren't in dire need of saving, but softball became more than just an extracurricular activity for me; it became a significant part of my family's life. I started playing when I was five, and by the time I was seven, we were traveling and playing every weekend. The girls on that field and their families in the stands became our community, our friends who were more like family.

For us, softball was an outlet from being a special needs family, providing a sense of normalcy and a way to be part of something bigger.

Softball brought us together with other families, gave us shared goals, and helped us build relationships beyond our immediate family circle.

It wasn't just about the game; it was about the community, the camaraderie, and the connections we made along the way. It ensured we didn't experience the isolation that impacts so many families impacted by disabilities.

It allowed me to write my own narrative as a young girl trying to discover who she was.

HOW SOFTBALL SAVED US

One of the most valuable gifts my parents ever gave me was the opportunity to play softball. As with many families, there were moments when juggling the needs of two children, one with a disability, and one deeply involved in sports, posed unique challenges. From the moment my dad became my coach in tee-ball, my family could not have foreseen how softball would reshape our identity, moving us beyond the confines, even isolation, of being a family impacted by disability.

Softball became the bond that strengthened my relationship with my dad. It offered us the opportunity to direct our energies toward something we could control, providing a purpose beyond being Nick's dad and sister. I understood that my dad's role as my coach extended beyond nurturing my athletic talents; it also meant he was replacing his dreams of coaching his son. Although

Nick placed second at the Special Olympics in 1988.

my dad played a pivotal part in Nick's short-lived sporting debut in the Special Olympics, it was not quite the same as the traditional father-son sports dream.

From the early days of third grade until my senior year, my involvement in softball became a central focus of our lives, surrounding us with a community that would prove instrumental in providing acceptance and understanding for my family, Nick included. This softball family became the sanctuary we didn't know we needed, a place where the unique challenges of special needs families were met with open arms.

The discussions about upcoming games, pouring over my stats, and the regular commute to practices and games created a harmonious counterpoint. With more family dinners spent at the field than at our house, we found our rhythm and it worked.

Nick, in particular, thrived in this environment, relishing the long hours spent on the softball fields, provided he had the freedom to indulge in endless treats from the concession stand. Convincing others to contribute to his snack fund became Nick's special talent, and it's safe to say he single-handedly kept the concession stands of Kentucky ballparks booming with business.

Softball shaped my character, instilled in me the drive to aim high, and helped me carve out my own identity.

I vividly remember my journey of self-discovery during my formative years, feeling a sense of exclusion as family members and friends would consistently ask, "Where's Nick?" or "How's Nick?" In every retelling of significant memories, Nick was always the main character. He just was. We would recount his reactions, his experiences, and people naturally gravitated towards him.

Their genuine concern and affection for my brother were appreciated, and they truly missed him when he wasn't around. However, it was never about me – Amanda. Rarely did anyone ask, "How are you?" Nick's frequent health scares and his knack for cutting up understandably drew people's attention. But sometimes, their inquiries about him overshadowed my presence.

What was my story to tell? Simple – softball.

Being the youngest starting varsity pitcher in the high school's history.

Breaking both school and state records.

Becoming the best at my sport and the accolades I received became my identity.

How did our parents manage to balance Nick's needs and our passion for the game?

It was a beautiful give-and-take.

There were two things that brought endless joy to Nick during his childhood: food and swimming. Remarkably, his love for food remains unwavering even now. As I mentioned earlier, every softball field meant discovering what concessions were available, and Nick tried them all. He would memorize the offerings at each field complex. Weekend tournaments out of town meant hotel stays, bringing him his second joy – swimming. Booking a hotel without a pool was out of the question. My mom would spend countless hours by the pool while Nick swam, timing how long he could stay underwater. In those days, balance for us meant long hours on the field during the day, and hours in the pool by night.

Softball gifted Nick and me the chance to bond over what may seem like little things, but to me, they were monumental. To this day, Nick playfully calls me "Frog," a nickname I earned in the sixth grade when my frog necklace broke during high school softball tryouts. Hearing him call me Frog never fails to bring a smile to my face.

I will never forget being on the pitching mound and hearing my big brother yell from his camping chair at the fence, "Throw the spitball, Frog!"

I would always glance over at him and smile, letting him know I heard his cheer.

It became our thing.

And at some point during the game, Nick would bring Big League chewing gum and sunflower seeds to me in the dugout. While I knew it was just another ploy to get more money from our parents for yet another trip to the concession stand, I like to think it was his way of showing his love.

my family supporting me in my early softball years.

Our parents invested in my softball and his concession stand habit, and somehow, it just worked for us. We discovered a unique equilibrium that allowed both of us to be seen and valued.

It's what I like to call the glory days.

A GAME-CHANGING WAGER

Growing up alongside my brother Nick made me grow up faster. I felt a responsibility to support my family from a young age. At the same time, being the youngest pitcher on the softball team taught me how to handle pressure and excel. These experiences taught me resilience and the importance of balancing family responsibilities with personal goals.

This maturity, though ahead of my age, also brought concerns that were beyond my years.

One specific worry that weighed heavily on my mind was my parents' health. Ever since I was little, I had this persistent fear of them getting sick, or worse, dying.

But I never really talked about it. I think, deep down, it was because I wasn't ready to become my brother's caregiver. I loved Nick, but I wanted to live my life first.

Of course, every kid wishes their parents could live forever, but my wish was selfishly rooted.

Losing my parents would devastate me to my core. But for Nick, losing our parents would break him. He would lose his whole world.

How could I replace someone's whole world? How could I possibly guide him through his grief while also finding space to mourn myself? It seems crazy to think about my parents no longer being here, but because I've feared it so much, I think about life after them a lot. Yet I never talk about it. I have never shared these feelings with them – that is until now, as they read these words.

Growing up, my parents were smokers, and I despised it. The smell, the sight — everything about smoking just bothered me. I knew it served as a release for them, like many others. And living in Kentucky, surrounded by tobacco fields, smoking was just a normal part of life.

Even at a young age, I understood the risks of smoking and how it heightened their chances of lung cancer. I had asked them to quit, fearing that losing them early would thrust me into a caregiving role sooner than I could handle. But they didn't know the reason behind my plea.

While I know I'll never feel completely prepared, I've come to accept the inevitability of my future role as a caregiver. All I hoped for was to delay facing that reality for as long as I could. It was my sophomore year when I finally figured out the way to get them to quit.

In our district finals that year, we faced Owensboro Catholic High School, our biggest rival. We had equal records, so the game was really a tossup. As the pitcher, I felt the pressure that night to bring home the win for my alma mater, Daviess County High School. My dad and I discussed the gravity of this game every time he sat on a bucket, glove on his hand, catching what felt like thousands of pitches in preparation for this moment.

Walking into the game, with butterflies in my stomach, I gathered all my courage and asked my parents, "If we win and I pitch the game of my life, will you all stop smoking?"

Without hesitation, both of them agreed.

It might sound unconventional to wager on my pitching performance, but it turned out to be effective. Although we sidestepped a difficult conversation, we all knew the magnitude of this single game. I pitched the game of my life, with the most strikeouts I'd ever had against Owensboro Catholic. My mom smoked a whole pack of cigarettes to get through the nerves of that game, but it would finally be her last.

That win meant more to me than any other in my entire softball career for so many reasons beyond just beating our rivals.

MY HARDEST MOMENT, LEAVING NICK

For most people, leaving for college is a significant moment that symbolizes flying the nest, becoming an adult, and creating a life outside of parents and siblings. It's always expected for kids to grow up and leave their parents to build their own families and lives, but for our family, it looked different.

I was leaving, but Nick was staying.

During a season that should have been filled with excitement and adventure, all I felt was guilt. This was the starting line of building a life of my own, but I was more focused on what I was leaving behind.

Many people ask me about the hardest part of growing up as a special needs sibling, and without a doubt, leaving home was the hardest part.

I mentioned in a previous chapter that each member of my family played a role in our dynamic. These roles were not assigned or demanded of us, rather the roles were naturally assumed in order for our family to find balance. My mom was the caregiver, my dad was the rock, Nick was the heartbeat and I was the light.

Leaving for college, despite being only an hour away, meant that the light of our family was leaving as well. I think a part of me assumed this role in early childhood to not only provide hope for my family as a future caretaker, but also to be and accomplish all the things Nick would never be able to do. And while it was always assumed that I would be the first and only one in my family to attend college, when the day came for me to leave, it was devastating.

Mom and Dad were faced with the reality that their daughter was entering the next chapter of her life. I am sure my parents were abruptly met with the reality they would only become half empty nesters. I was moving out and building my life, while Nick would never leave.

This transition also meant leaving softball behind. My parents and Nick lost their social outlet, their connection to something that filled a significant space in our lives. Though the decision to attend college without pursuing collegiate softball was mine, the weight of this choice felt like I was making a life-altering decision for my family. The burden I carried was indescribable.

But my greatest source of guilt was leaving Nick, who was losing his best friend.

All our cousins had already grown up and moved on. Nick had graduated two years before me, so he had already lost any social connection he had outside of our family. He participated in Special Olympics, but it was only occasional and never provided him any long lasting friendships.

I felt guilty. I felt guilty for leaving my parents when our family unit worked so well. I felt guilty for going to college knowing that my brother never would. But as his best friend and protector, I mostly felt guilty for leaving Nick.

Guilt is a very important aspect of my story and I think all special needs sibling stories. So important that I will spend a lot of time on the emotional weight of guilt associated with my transition to college in a future chapter. But I thought it was worth sharing the significant impact of guilt here to underscore the fact that leaving for college marked the most challenging time in my life and essentially altered the landscape of my identity.

So, as the time approached for me to pack my bags and begin this journey of self-discovery, I grappled with all of these realities. Not to mention that the act of leaving meant that my identity as Nick's sister was flipped upside down. Although to my core I always was and always will be a special needs sibling, college marked the first time that I was Amanda before anything else.

I felt excited about the possibilities college had to offer – the chance to meet new people, and the prospect of establishing an independent identity beyond the label of "Nick's sister."

But I also felt a sense of fear and uncertainty. The security of my familial cocoon, where my role was clearly defined, was shattered and I was adventuring into uncharted territory.

Letting go of the familiar parts of my identity was a difficult task, but I was also worried that my departure would change our family's dynamics and shift everyone's roles and responsibilities.

What would it mean for my mom and dad, supporting Nick without his Frog?

What would it mean for Nick, who had grown accustomed to my presence as a consistent source of comfort?

The mix of guilt, excitement and fear created a complex emotional landscape. I was ready for newfound freedom, personal growth, and the opportunity to forge my own path. But, all of those things came at a heavy cost.

In those four years I was away at college pursuing my dream of becoming a special education teacher, Nick and my parents carried on without me. Although it was tough for them to adapt to my absence, it was equally hard for me to feel like an outsider to their new family dynamic. My parents shielded me from a lot of what was going on with Nick, not wanting me to worry. Nick was newly diagnosed with diabetes and my parents had to navigate a new life of insulin dependency for him and even more medical appointments. Additionally, his behaviors became more challenging, which meant adjustments in his medications. I am sure this was a very difficult time for my family, but I was never made fully aware of the details.

Guilt, sadness, loneliness – enough of that.

Sharing the toughest chapter of my life wouldn't be complete without injecting a bit of comic relief. That's how my family has weathered some of the most trying times with Nick — by finding humor even in the face of adversity.

You know the feeling, right? Laughing to keep from crying.

So, while I was away at college, Nick had an increase in behaviors, likely stemming from changes in his medication and the fact that his best friend wasn't a part of his everyday routine like I had been for 18 years. The confusion of me getting to leave while he stayed behind was something my family had to navigate. However, one phone call during my freshman year reminded me that my role as "the light" of the family would always remain, even though I was no longer living under the same roof. I believe you'll find as much enjoyment in this story as I do in telling it.

Walking into my dorm room after my less-than-favorite intro to mathematics class (a class that I barely passed, by the way), my cell phone unexpectedly began to ring. Glancing at the caller ID, I saw it was my mom. This was unusual; she seldom called during the day, respecting my college routine and my frequent naps between classes. But, as is my habit even now, I held my breath, fearing something might be wrong with my brother. When you've experienced the trauma of near medical crises involving a sibling, it's challenging not to anticipate the worst.

Answering the phone with a mix of concern and curiosity, I asked, "Mom, what's wrong?"

Her voice carried a strange blend of laughter, anger, and tears. Her next question caught me completely off guard.

"Is there any way you can sell 10 videos of Girls Gone Wild?"

(For those unfamiliar, Girls Gone Wild were explicit videos capturing snippets of college spring break escapades, featuring young women in swimsuits engaging in risqué behavior, often advertised on late-night MTV infomercials in the late '90s and early 2000s. It was no secret that my brother, Nick, was intrigued by these videos.)

I questioned my mother, "What do you mean sell videos of Girls Gone Wild?"

She explained, "A box of Girls Gone Wild videos was delivered today from the mailman. Come to find out, Nick ordered them. To top it off, he used your grandma Ruth's credit card to buy them. I called her to warn her of the charge, and she just told me to let him have whatever he bought."

At this point, I couldn't contain my laughter. My innate role as "the light" in the family instantly came into play.

I said, "Mom, let's look at the bright side here. These purchases are age-appropriate for him, which is something we always wanted — activities fitting his age. Besides, he employed some excellent independent skills he's honed throughout his life, like using the telephone to call people, following one to two-step tasks, and communicating his needs. He executed all these skills to get those videos. I think he should get to keep them, don't you?"

My mom, raised with strong morals and modesty, laughed with me and responded, "I don't think so, missy."

The fate of those Girls Gone Wild videos remains an unsolved family mystery. Whether my mom disposed of them, likely by fire, is still unknown.

I think the reason this story sticks out so much is because, looking back, memories of my brother from my college years are vague. He was learning to live without his Frog at home, and I was learning to live life on my own.

The college years were the best years of my life. Initially, it was hard to move away, but I quickly adapted to this newfound freedom and began discovering the woman I was meant to become.

I was given the gift of living, no strings attached, no pressure of how my decisions would one day impact my brother.

I was given the space to be me, Amanda.

I didn't know it at the time, but I know it now. The greatest thing my parents ever did for me was allowing me to go.

LOVING ME, LOVING NICK

My first "real love" happened in middle school.

Middle school love has a way of consuming adolescents completely. I was convinced I would marry this boy, and we were the typical love-struck middle schoolers who thought our love would last forever. This middle school romance made me confront my reality as a special needs sibling in a way I hadn't before.

While other kids dreamed about their future weddings, my romantic fantasies were different. I dreamed of a boy that would accept my brother, who without questions, would invite Nick to fit into our relationship.

Before my boyfriend ever met my brother, just as I did with all my friends, I prepped him. I told him what Nick was like, what he enjoyed doing, the kind of conversations he liked to have, how he might respond, and what to do if Nick got upset or did something I considered to be embarrassing.

I covered everything.

But what my middle school boyfriend didn't realize was that this conversation was different from the one I had with my friends. I was watching how he loved my brother back because it mattered. Any potential boyfriend could be a big part of Nick's future, and that was important to me.

Even as a middle schooler, I knew my future would someday include being a caretaker for my brother. This wasn't just an abstract idea; it was a responsibility I thought about often. Whenever a new boyfriend came into the picture, I wasn't just looking for my Mr. Right — I was also looking for Mr. Right for my brother. He had a high bar to reach.

In middle and high school, I was always the serious type. I only had two boyfriends, and I dated them for a long time. My high school sweetheart and I eventually broke up in college, but during our time together, we had many conversations about the future. These conversations weren't awkward or hard; they were just a natural part of who I was and my journey.

I never doubted my path.

I never wished for a different future.

I never imagined a different life for myself or my brother.

This was my reality, and I embraced it wholeheartedly. My brother's well-being was always a part of my decisions, and I knew that anyone who wanted to be with me had to understand and accept that. It was a unique situation, but it was my life, and I was committed to the responsibility of my role as his sister, knowing it came first.

You have to realize this is my story as a sibling, but it isn't every special needs sibling's story or desire, and that's OK. If I'm being honest, I've known this journey was what I wanted since I was a little girl. It was never a conversation my parents and I really had; it was something I always just knew to be true.

I would be my brother's future caretaker.

However, how I thought about that as a kid and how I think about it now as an adult feels different. Then, it seemed so far away, a future commitment that, at that time, didn't carry much weight. But as I've aged, reality is settling in, and my role as Nick's future caretaker sometimes scares me.

I wonder if I will be enough.

I had a nightmare once that woke me up crying. You know those dreams that feel so real you can't shake them when you wake up, and the tears paralyze you as you lie in bed? I dreamed that my parents had been gone for a year, Nick was living with me and my husband, though I didn't know who that was at the time. I was diagnosed with ovarian cancer. I was sick, and Nick needed me. That scenario from the nightmare plays over in my head sometimes.

It's hard not to worry. It's hard not to be anxious about the future. These are the times when I wish I had a second sibling to share the weight and worry with me. My mom always told me that she wanted a third child, but Dad didn't, thinking it might be too much. I often wonder what it would have been like to have someone else to help shoulder the responsibility and the fear.

But this is my reality, and I've accepted it. It doesn't mean the fear goes away, but I try to focus on the love and the bond I share with Nick. I remind myself that while the future is uncertain, the present is where I can make the most difference. And in those moments of doubt and fear, I lean on the strength that has carried me this far, knowing that I will do everything in my power to ensure Nick is cared for, loved, and most importantly happy.

As I navigated these fears and uncertainties, life had a way of surprising me in the most beautiful manner. It was during this time that I met the person who would become my partner, the one who would embrace not only me but also the responsibility and love I carried for Nick. The day he asked me to marry him marked the beginning of a new chapter, where my dreams and hopes for the future started to take shape in ways I had always wished for.

His name was Justin.

He understood. Just like my family had all those years, it was an unspoken understanding that didn't need much discussion. He often said he knew I came as a package deal. The topic of being future caretakers for Nick only really came up when we were buying a house, as we considered the number of bedrooms and how comfortable Nick would be living with us.

It all happened pretty quickly after I met Justin. We met on a weekend when I was home during my senior year of college. We dated for a short period before I graduated. When I moved home from college, I initially returned to my room at my parents' house. However, I gradually started spending more time at Justin's place, and eventually, I moved in with him. Reflecting back this was probably a blessing, so Nick wouldn't get used to me being back home and I wouldn't feel guilty about leaving him all over again.

I started my teaching career a few months later, and less than a year after that, we got engaged. Eight months after his proposal, we were married.

Our wedding day was magical, the kind of day every little girl dreams of.

Of course, every bride cherishes their wedding day, filled with love and the joy of marrying their prince charming, like living out a fairytale. However, I chose to do something non-traditional at my wedding, a choice that symbolized my life as a special needs sibling.

As I walked down the aisle to my future husband, my father walked on my right side, and my big brother, Nick, was on my left. Both men in my life equally "gave me away" to Justin.

Everyone there thought this gesture was about my brother.

But it wasn't. It was about me.

It may be traditional for a father to walk his daughter down the aisle. It symbolizes more of a "letting go" than a "giving away," a gesture of support in the daughter's next chapter.

But in my family, I knew it wasn't just my parents who were "letting me go" and extending their approval as I began my life with Justin.

Nick was letting me go too.

My wedding day felt different than when I moved out of the house for college. Then, I carried guilt because I was moving out and leaving my brother. But on my wedding day, I felt guilty that I was making a commitment to start another family.

Even on what was, at that time, the happiest day of my life, I couldn't help but feel the weight of Justin's "I do." His promise that day meant in sickness and in health for me and my brother. Nick and I were exactly what Justin had said when we were dating – a package deal.

Which is why it seemed so natural to ask my brother to "give me away" alongside my dad. Although I didn't want to overshadow this moment with my dad, I knew I wanted – and needed – Nick to be by my side too.

I chose to have my dad walk me down the aisle for the first half, and then Nick, who was sitting with my mom, came up the aisle to meet us. I walked toward my future husband with Dad and Nick both at my side.

The preacher asked, "Who gives this woman away?"

My dad's response symbolizes everything that only a special needs family could understand and grasp, "Her mother, Nick, and I do."

To those in attendance that day, my choice to let Nick walk me down the aisle must have looked like a sweet, thoughtful gesture.

My wedding day – 2007

Of course they did, because they couldn't begin to comprehend the symbolism or meaning behind why I wanted my brother to be part of my wedding.

Because if I am being honest with myself, part of that decision was for me to work through the guilt I felt for being able to get married and have a wedding, knowing my brother would never have that experience or create his own family.

But, selfishly, I also needed to know my brother accepted and invited my husband into his life. I needed to feel some sense of Nick's approval for what was about to happen.

My wedding wasn't just changing my life, it impacted Nick.

Who I chose to fall in love with and marry would greatly impact my brother's future.

The weight I carried of knowing this almost suffocated me. It had been a weight I carried through my entire relationship with Justin, a worry that began all those years ago with my first boyfriend in middle school.

What if I married a man that couldn't share the responsibility of caretaker with me?

What if Nick didn't bond with him or accept him?

In the moment when Nick was invited to give me away, I found the reassurance I yearned for, affirming that I was making the right decision. It was a declaration that Nick would be OK with me starting a new family.

Although he couldn't fully grasp that my wedding or choice of partner profoundly impacted his future, I needed this memory to symbolize Nick's approval, easing my guilt.

NICK'S NEW BEST FRIENDS

My husband and I had been married for a few years before we felt the desire to start a family. During this season of trying to build our family, I couldn't escape the feelings and fears that came with being a sister to a brother with a rare chromosome disability. I remember asking my doctor if I should get screened or undergo testing to see if I was a carrier for Nick's rare genetic condition or if my chances of having a child with a chromosome disability were increased. He reassured me it wasn't necessary.

That didn't stop Justin and I from having tough conversations about the "what if's." We both knew it wouldn't change anything. Just like my parents, we would love the child God gave us.

But at night before I fell asleep, or quiet moments throughout my day, I would secretly pray for a healthy baby.

These prayers continued for years as we struggled to conceive, especially after I was diagnosed with endometriosis. I couldn't help but think that maybe since I was praying for a healthy child, my infertility was God's way of answering those prayers.

I know it sounds crazy, but those deep-rooted emotions from being a special needs sibling made me question if God was sparing me the life of being a caretaker to two.

Eventually, in 2010, we were able to conceive our first child, Landon. Three years later, we became pregnant with our second boy, who we named after my brother, Nicholas, but called by his middle name, Layne.

As a child, Nick found companionship among our cousins, who were like siblings to him. As this first generation of cousins grew up and moved on, a new group of cousins entered the picture, giving him new friendships. Now Nick's new title of Uncle brought him his closest friendships yet. He wanted them to call him Uncle Nick-Knock, and they did.

Nick formed deep bonds with my two boys, his nephews, Landon and Layne. Witnessing their relationship develop and watching my sons grow up alongside my brother brought me immense joy. It was as if I was looking at my own childhood through a different lens, understanding it so much more as an adult.

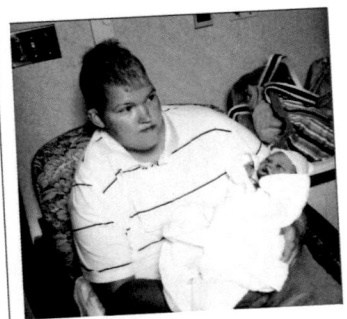

Nick holding Landon on the day he was born

Being a mom changed my life, but watching my boys grow up alongside Nick has been the highlight. And the happiness my boys have brought to my parents, now grandparents, has given their lives a new meaning.

It has been a beautiful, full-circle experience, seeing my parents find the joy of grandchildren, especially as they watched the special bond form between my boys and Nick. And I am grateful that my children brought me back into the lives of my parents and my brother.

Although not intentional, I had been somewhat distant since college. It was just the season of life I was in — from college to starting my career to marriage. The door was reopened for me to experience life with my brother all over again, this time with my husband and sons. This renewed connection not only enriched my children's lives but also reconnected me with the family I had unintentionally drifted from while I was building a life of my own.

Seeing my parents with my children, and watching the bond between my boys and Nick, has made me realize just how much love and support surround us. It has reinforced the idea that family is everything, and that includes all the ups and downs, the struggles and the joys. This dynamic has brought out the best in all of us and highlighted the incredible impact that Nick has had on our lives.

My sons' lives are forever impacted by their uncle. It's funny how small moments – seemingly insignificant conversations – prove just how much Uncle Nick-Knock influenced my boys, their character, who they are and what they stand for.

When my youngest, Layne, was about three years old, he shared Nick's love for food. One day, he was sitting at the table eating applesauce, shoveling it in as fast as he could. It was just the two of us in the kitchen, and I said, "Layne, you better slow down, buddy."

He grinned at me, pulled up his shirt to puff out his belly, and said, "When I grow up, I want to be big like Uncle Nick Knock."

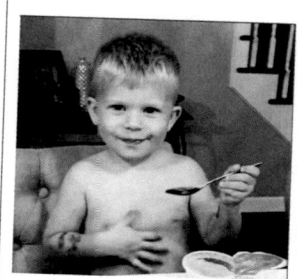

Layne – age 3

I couldn't help but laugh and asked him to do it again so I could capture it on video to send to my mom and brother. In that moment, Layne's innocence and pure love for Nick filled my heart in a way I can't describe.

I realized then that his life would be better because he already admired and loved his Uncle Nick in such a genuine way, just as I had growing up.

And as innocent as Layne was at three years old, he got it. He saw Nick for who he was, beyond his disability and limitations. My boys are older now and they are helping others get it too. Just as my advocacy naturally stemmed from the example set by my parents, it's now taking root in my boys as well.

From the moment my oldest son, Landon, could walk and talk, he formed an unbreakable bond with my Nick. Watching them together for the first time, I felt like I could finally breathe. It wasn't just me carrying the weight of trying to make Nick happy anymore. Landon naturally became his protector, his friend, always trying to bring him joy.

It was like we shared something deeply personal — a silent understanding, a connection that made us both stronger in this journey. Seeing Landon care for Nick the way I always had made me feel less alone, like we were in this together, determined to make Nick's life as full of happiness as possible.

There was a moment with Landon that will forever be etched in my memory, a moment that had me fighting back tears. It was one of those times that brought back the emotional weight and feelings I experienced as a special needs sibling, now seen through the eyes of an adult.

Heading into a summer weekend, Landon, who was 13 at the time, was bringing a school friend to our lake house. All three of us were piled into my SUV, with me driving and the boys in the back.

The lake house has been in our family since 1977. Before we had kids, my parents, my husband and I decided to build a shared cabin there. This cabin was meant to create lasting memories and connections, as every weekend from May to September was spent with my parents, my brother, and my children.

As we started to approach the lake house, I glanced in the rear view mirror and casually asked, "Hey, Landon, did you talk to Robert about Nick?"

His response sent me spiraling into a flood of childhood memories and emotions that I wasn't expecting, even though I was the one who had asked the question.

"Yes, Mom, I already covered everything," he said with such confidence.

In that moment, I knew exactly what he had covered. I knew what it felt like to have those conversations with your friends before they met Nick. It was a responsibility I had carried, and now my son carried, to prevent potential embarrassment for Nick and ensure our friends were comfortable. I had never felt more connected to my son for so many reasons than at that very moment.

My boys brought a new light into Nick's life, and in return, Nick brought a new perspective into theirs. They didn't just see him as their uncle with a disability; they saw him as their friend, someone to play with, laugh with, and learn from. Their innocence and acceptance mirrored my own childhood experience, but now, as a mother, I could truly appreciate the beauty and depth of these relationships.

Honestly, I am not sure you would be reading this book right now if it wasn't for seeing my boys build their relationship with Nick. It was as though I was looking at my life as a kid all over again, but this time through a more mature perspective.

Our Family — 2023

My childhood is woven together with memories of Nick. He was always there, experiencing life right beside me. Every cherished moment from my childhood, I not only remember how I felt, but I can vividly recall how Nick responded to those same moments — his laughter, his joy, his presence. We were just like any other siblings, navigating life hand in hand. **Rarely different.**

Now, watching my own children love their Uncle Nick, seeing him simply as he is, and creating their own cherished memories with him fills my heart in ways that words can't fully capture. It's a feeling that transcends explanation — a love that continues across generations. Our family is building a legacy of advocacy and acceptance that only special needs families can understand. **Rarely different.**

"IN A SPECIAL NEEDS FAMILY, ADVOCACY IS MORE THAN A RESPONSIBILITY—

it's the legacy we leave behind

IT'S THE PROMISE THAT OUR VOICES WILL CONTINUE TO SHAPE A MORE INCLUSIVE WORLD

for generations to come"

CHAPTER 4
FINDING MY PIECE, MY PURPOSE

FRUSTRATION TO ACTION: PUZZLE PIECES

Helping Nick with his vocabulary flashcards all those years ago is what initially lit the fire in me to pursue a career in education. Even in kindergarten, I knew that I wanted to be a teacher to help students like my brother. But seeing Nick's time in public education and watching my mom fiercely advocate for him inspired me to be the teacher he **deserved.**

I left for college to pursue a degree in special education, leaving behind my brother and family. I spent four years away from home, honing my knowledge and preparing to return to my hometown to see my dream come to fruition. I received a job right out of college at a local middle school and began the career I had been planning since I was five years old.

Dream come true, right? Wrong.

I was about five years into teaching when I began to realize the limits of my job. I couldn't address societal barriers or the complex needs of my students' families to prepare them for life beyond school. I was helping students for four years when they were at my school, but once they moved on to high school, I wasn't there to help them prepare for adulthood. (Students with intellectual disabilities often stay in school until they are 21 years old. Because of this, their time in each educational stage is extended. So, while most middle school students typically stay for three years, my middle school students were with me for four years.)

Countless parents were telling me that after graduation, their child had nowhere to go, no opportunities for socialization.

I realized that, like my brother, these students were left with limited opportunities for continued skill development, social interaction with peers, or making strides toward a more independent life. My desire for impact began to shift, and I discovered myself daydreaming about making change beyond my classroom walls. And so began a pivotal shift in my narrative — one that would connect the destinies of my students, my brother, and myself. My future would combine all that I learned as a teacher and the lessons I learned growing up with Nick, while also building a life that would support my future role as his caregiver.

If there was no place for my students to go post-graduation, I was determined to build it. I began to research starting a nonprofit, learned how to write a grant, and developed a business plan. In 2012, I left the classroom and opened Puzzle Pieces, a nonprofit service provider to adults and school-aged children with intellectual disabilities. We immediately served 32 clients with the support of less than 10 staff members, including myself. Puzzle Pieces quickly became a beacon of hope and resolved the fear of so many of my students' families. It wasn't until hearing their stories that I realized Puzzle Pieces is what was missing for my own family all those years ago.

Like the story of the mom with a 15-year-old son with severe autism who had never had a Saturday to herself. She walked into our weekend respite day with tears streaming down her face as she watched her son enter without hesitation. She looked at me and asked, "What do I do now?" I smiled and gently replied, "Do whatever makes you happy. This day is for you, because we've got him."

Or the story of the father of an 8-year-old boy with severe autism, who hugged me and said, "Puzzle Pieces didn't just help my son, you saved my family."

Then there's the story of a grateful mom who shared, "Puzzle Pieces gave our daughter the socialization and daily engagement she needed after high school. It allowed my husband and me to keep her at home with us longer. You gave her something we couldn't, and for that, I am forever grateful."

My dream for Puzzle Pieces was never just about creating opportunities for individuals with disabilities. Yes, I wanted them to have a safe place where they could build friendships and live with purpose, but my true motivation was about the families. Over the past 12 years, I've seen firsthand the difference our services are making in the lives of special needs families in western Kentucky. The same rural community that had nothing to offer my family 40 years ago is now supporting special needs families with whole-life services to ensure they are supported and thriving.

Today, Puzzle Pieces serves over 400 clients and employs more than 100 professionals dedicated to serving individuals with disabilities. While we began as a day center that provided respite and socialization, we have grown into so much more, now specializing in Applied Behavior Analysis, supported employment, and day training where we focus on targeted skill building for independent living and job skill development. We have the region's only targeted autism programming for summer and after school and we support multiple residential living homes.

While I could go on and on about Puzzle Pieces, I would rather use this space to talk about the defining moments that led me to my nonprofit. (Don't worry, I dedicated a bonus chapter in the back of this book to Puzzle Pieces and the full scope of our services and impact.) I think it's important to understand how my students and career as a teacher played a role in building something that has been so transformative to my community.

THE LESSON THAT SAVED MY CAREER

My time as a middle school special education teacher was spent in a self-contained multiple disabilities classroom. The class may have been small, but it was bursting with passion and intentional learning — the type of environment that I envisioned for my brother. My initiation into the world of teaching came at the age of 21, and it was during this first year that I discovered my love for working with students with autism. Naively, I believed that my college education would equip me with all the tools and experience I needed. Combine my education with my unique perspective as a special needs sibling, and I assumed I would be an exceptionally insightful teacher.

In my mind, every student would resemble my brother's needs, and their parents would mirror the love my own parents showered on us. Well, reality hit me like a ton of bricks. There's a saying, "When you know one person with a disability, you know one person with a disability," and I quickly realized the truth in those words.

I pursued additional education with a master's degree, which had a focus on autism. Surely this would arm me with strategies to best help my students? Little did I know, no amount of education could fully brace me for the whirlwind of experiences awaiting me in my early teaching years.

Navigating through the diverse needs of my students, overseeing paraprofessionals, drowning in paperwork, enduring emotionally charged IEP meetings, and managing the intense behaviors of my students were just some of the challenges I faced. The kind of teacher I became didn't involve grading papers on the couch while catching up on the latest season of The Bachelor. It didn't require memorizing standardized testing standards to prep my students for state exams and boost the school's overall scores. I wasn't the teacher standing in line at the copy machine to churn out multiple copies of next week's lesson plans.

No, my role as a teacher demanded so much more from me.

Unlike any other teaching position in the school, special education teachers have a unique relationship with their students' families. Whether through IEP meetings or collaborating on strategies to ensure their child's success, I was in constant contact with my students' families, working together to align our goals of what happiness and independence looked like for their child.

It was this responsibility that taught me the true meaning of trust.

Trust is a journey, and for families of children with disabilities, it can be a challenging and delicate process, especially when it comes to the education system. Parents of children with disabilities often struggle to trust schools because they are handing over the care of their vulnerable child — someone who may have difficulty communicating, advocating for themselves, or expressing their needs. These parents know, deep down, that no one can share the same intense love and protective instincts they have for their child. This deep-rooted fear can make it hard to trust professionals who, no matter how skilled or caring, don't have that personal connection or dedication to keep going when times are hard.

On the other hand, students with disabilities often take longer to build trust with their teachers. Many of these students have experienced frustration or misunderstanding in the past, which can lead to mistrust of anyone trying to push them to learn or engage in activities that may feel challenging or uncomfortable. This mistrust can make the learning process difficult, as students may resist or withdraw from the very people trying to help them grow. Teachers must understand that trust is not given easily, but it's an essential foundation for both learning and progress. It takes time, patience, and a genuine connection to build that trust, and only then can students truly thrive.

It was in these days that I started to understand why school was so hard for my brother, and why my mom was so fierce in her advocacy within the school.

It all came down to one word: trust.

This became the foundation of my classroom, a strategy not found in any textbook I studied.

With trust as my foundation, I began to build my lessons around the skills that I could teach my students to build their independence and support their wants alongside their families' dreams. Middle school is often when families truly begin to notice the widening gap between their child and their neurotypical peers. Behaviors once seen as cute or quirky in elementary school can become more pronounced barriers to development. It's during this time that many parents start to realize the future they envisioned for their child may no longer be attainable. I became part of their journey through this mourning process, helping them regroup, reassess, and create a new plan for their child's future.

In my first year as a teacher, I had a student, let's call him Brad, who would not just challenge me to be better for him, but would create for me a different level of love and understanding of autism.

Brad was nonverbal, had aggressive behaviors, and didn't trust a lot of people. His mother, like my own mom, was his warrior that would fight for him everyday.

To other teachers, this mom would have been considered the ultimate helicopter parent, a nightmare to deal with. But to me, she was the epitome of strength and I credit her with helping me succeed in my career as a teacher. (To this day, Brad's mom is not aware of the impact she had on my life and my love for autism.)

Brad's needs were complex and demanding for a first-year teacher. I remember specialists coming into my classroom to advise me on how to help him succeed. Their approach and what was being asked of me just didn't align with my philosophy of teaching. These specialists were recommending a reactive crisis approach, but I was determined to teach with a passionate, preventive approach.

I remember calling my college professor and mentor one night after a long week of aggression from Brad. My arms were bruised, my pride was

> **THERE'S NO MAGIC WAND THAT YOU CAN WAVE TO MAKE EVERYTHING BETTER, BUT THE GOOD NEWS IS THAT WE CAN CHOOSE TO FACE OUR CHALLENGES** *with courage and determination*

— MICHELLE OBAMA

shattered, and my hope was gone. Becoming the teacher I dreamed of being for Brad felt impossible. I was failing him and his mom.

When I called my professor in tears, overwhelmed by my sense of defeat, our conversation turned everything around for me.

"Amanda you need to teach him as though he was your brother," she said with a tender voice.

I replied, *"Brad is nothing like my brother. He has severe autism and is nonverbal."*

Her voice was soft spoken, but matter-of-fact. "His disability and communication may be different, yes, but his need to feel loved, accepted, and to trust others is just the same as anyone else's. You were born to do this. Stop letting other experts tell you what strategies, or what you need to do. Don't allow his mother to intimidate you; she needs you just as much as your mom needed someone. Stop trying to teach him, start trying to love him first, just like you wanted for your brother."

We got off the phone that night and it was like I had just spoken to a guardian angel.

I was restored.

I was ready to be the teacher for Brad and his mother that I so desperately wanted for my brother and mom.

Fast forward – Brad was a student in my classroom for four years and he changed me and I changed him. He taught me more than I could have ever taught him and it started with trust and love. It was truly incredible to experience breakthrough moments teaching him new skills.

Brad's mother, his fierce, unrelenting advocate, became my expert. I leaned into her knowledge of her son, and with an open mind I collaborated with her, just as I wanted my brother's teacher to do with my own mother.

Brad wasn't my brother, but when I started to love him like he was, everything changed.

HOW AN IEP MEETING SPARKED A DREAM

I taught Brad in my first year in the classroom. The struggle to help him succeed set the tone of my career, defining the type of teacher I wanted to be. Over the next few years, Brad would be one of ten students within my first three years of teaching. Each represented a variety of disabilities, varying in ability levels, and their needs stretched me far beyond what I thought I could personally handle.

Outside of their parents, I felt a pressure to be their everything.

My students – and their families – needed more than just a teacher. As a sibling, I knew what they were going through and I understood the isolating life of a disability family. Just like the self-imposed pressure I felt to be "the light" or "the one" in my family, I took on as many roles as I could to alleviate the stress of the families I served. Beyond a teacher, I would become:

A personal daytime caregiver, assuming the role of the parent while the student was at school.

A counselor, helping families navigate the emotions associated with their child's disability.

A PE teacher, ensuring my students were building the skills for a healthy lifestyle.

A hair stylist, helping my students look and feel their best.

An escort to the school dance, ensuring that my students felt included in school activities.

A friend, building trust with my students so that I could teach them lessons inside my classroom.

A future planner, collaborating with parents on their child's transition to high school and adulthood.

A dreamer and a realist, encouraging parents to maximize their child's potential, while also managing expectations for their future.

A provider of respite, giving parents a much needed – and deserved – break.

A supplier of hope, shining light on all the possibilities for their child.

College didn't prepare me for any of these titles, but when God made me a special needs sibling, He knew what He was preparing me for.

And it was in an IEP meeting that a parent asked me to take on a new role, something I never expected to be asked.

Individual Education Plan (IEP) meetings are annual gatherings convening a team of educators who collaborate with a student's family to establish a comprehensive plan outlining yearly goals, progress, and necessary support systems to facilitate the student's success. As a dedicated special education teacher, I found that IEP meetings serve as pivotal moments for the team to engage in deep reflection, evaluating the effectiveness of the school in meeting the unique needs of each student under our care.

These meetings prompt us to ask critical questions about our teaching strategies, interventions, and support systems, urging us to consider whether we are truly doing everything within our power to nurture the academic and personal growth of our students. Amidst the collaborative discussions around goal-setting and progress monitoring, there's often an undercurrent of anticipation and apprehension, as we grapple with the weight of responsibility placed upon us.

The process of identifying priorities for the upcoming year is important, but challenging, requiring us to strike a delicate balance between ambitious aspirations and realistic expectations. And yet, despite our collective expertise and dedication, there are moments when the sheer magnitude of the task at hand can evoke a sense of unease that is difficult to articulate.

This blend of anticipation, reflection, and occasional apprehension infuses each IEP meeting with a unique energy — an energy born from our unwavering commitment to the success and well-being of every student entrusted to our care.

As a special education teacher, I entered each IEP meeting feeling immense pressure. There was an expectation to know all the right answers, to promise improvements for the child, and to navigate the conversation with the school's guidelines in mind, all while respecting the parents sitting across from me.

But I felt an added weight, being a special needs sibling. I entered that room feeling an unspoken obligation to create a supportive space for these parents, to walk alongside them as they sought the best for their child. It was a reminder of my own family. The hopes and fears my parents expressed all those years ago echoed the families sitting across from me, highlighting the significant role I played in guiding them through this journey.

The pressure was often suffocating.

But the pressure I felt in this particular IEP meeting was different. I wasn't asked about what more I could do for the child in the classroom. Instead I was asked what I could do for life outside of school.

I remember sitting across the table from Robert's mother. (This student's actual name was changed in this story.) Her son was my third year student with level three autism. I was prepared for this IEP meeting to be more difficult than the ones in previous years, because it was time to discuss transition. Not just transition to high school, but developing goals and discussion about his future after high school.

What would his life look like?

As a middle school special education teacher, I had the responsibility of introducing the conversation to families about planning their future. Oftentimes describing what was possible, identifying the barriers, offering suggestions, but mostly navigating a conversation that no one was ready to have. These conversations offered hopeless resolutions, casted more fears, and ultimately ended in both myself and the parents crying.

This meeting with Robert's mom was no different. It wasn't that we couldn't identify Robert's needs or determine how to meet them, but rather that our small Kentucky town lacked opportunities for adults with disabilities.

I remember sharing the only story I knew of an individual with a disability working. He worked at Fazoli's handing out breadsticks. I only had one story. I didn't have the answers.

"Life after high school, for the most part, will fall on you," I told her. "My goal is to prepare Robert the best we can to help make that less difficult as you and he age."

It was hard to watch her reaction.

I felt as though I was the cause of her sadness, although I knew her tears were a reaction to the reality of how society was preparing individuals with disabilities to become adults.

I can still remember her cries that day.

She struggled to speak, breaths interrupted by sobs, and the tissues she used to wipe her tears couldn't keep pace with her streaming emotions.

When she was finally able to work up the courage to look me in the eyes she asked, "If something happens to me can you become Robert's legal guardian and make sure he is taken care of? His younger brother is too

young to understand right now, and with no options for the future, I just need to know someone will watch after him. I need to know he will be OK. Can you make sure he is OK if I am no longer here?"
That question changed the trajectory of my teaching career.

I got up from that conference table and walked around to Robert's mother. She stood up and we embraced each other in what seemed like forever.

While fighting every word through tears I said to her, "You know I can't become his legal guardian. That space is reserved for my brother. But I promise you one thing, I will figure something out and will somehow make sure he is taken care of. I promise."

This pivotal moment would be the spark that set my soul on fire.

I began to see a future for me past the walls of that self-contained classroom. From that moment on, I was constantly finding myself in these conversations with my students' parents about their unpromising future with limited support and lack of opportunity.

At the same time, I was seeing my brother living out his life after high school. Nick was 27 years old, just shy of ten years post graduation. Individuals with intellectual disabilities can attend school until they are 21 years old to help better prepare them for adulthood. However, my family chose to allow Nick to graduate with his class when he was 18. Their decision to do this was easy for them, just like most of the decisions they made as Nick aged.

My family always chose to prioritize Nick's happiness over chasing desired milestones. My parents were certain about two things when Nick graduated: he would be happy and he would be cared for with love. They didn't need an IEP meeting or transition plan to tell them those two things.

That's all they needed. That was their plan. But the truth is, Nick's life after high school was hard.

We saw little things creep in that my parents tried to fulfill the best they knew how. This season unfortunately came at the time I moved away for college, which meant Nick had twice the adjustment to make.

He lost touch with his friends. Without school to fill his daytime hours anymore, Nick was often bored. My parents tried a day program designed to meet the needs of senior citizens, but that was a short lived solution. Nick couldn't understand why he was around old people. My mom also discovered other participants were sneaking Nick cigarettes and tobacco. It was a hard time.

Eventually, Nick's health began to deteriorate. In part, this was due to his diagnosis, but I couldn't help but think his lack of movement and social engagement played a part.

How could I prepare my students for the future I envisioned for them, knowing that my brother was currently living their fate? A future of significant challenges, limited opportunities for engagement, lack of purpose, no meaningful routine, and zero social relationships outside of our home.

Don't get me wrong, Nick loves his life and has fully embraced being a homebody in every sense of the word. He's content where he is, and my parents did everything they could with what they had. For them, and for Nick, that was enough — they only had each other, and that was all they needed. But I couldn't help but wonder: What if there could be more? I wanted more. At the very least, I wanted families to have a choice, instead of feeling like they had to simply make things work with no other option.

MY OPRAH A-HA! MOMENT

Though I felt the weight of wanting more for my brother and my students, I couldn't shake the doubt — who was I to believe I could be the one to fix it?

I was just a teacher.

I never thought I could be the person to affect change, manifest a different outcome. But, in my fourth year of teaching, Karlie and her mom, Kathy, entered my life, providing me the "how to" behind executing a dream.

They helped me see that being "just" a teacher was actually the perfect role to make a profound difference.

I walked alongside Karlie as she used her hands to propel the wheels of her wheelchair on her daily visit with Jeff, the school's medical technician. Karlie, who has cerebral palsy and uses a communication device to communicate, visited Jeff each day for her necessary medication.

Karlie was my first student with cerebral palsy and my first student who used a wheelchair.

During our visit to Mr. Jeff in the health room that day, he asked me if I had watched an inspiring story on Oprah about a father and son who competed in running events worldwide.

Karlie listened attentively. Despite her inability to speak with words, some might assume she couldn't understand or communicate. This couldn't be further from the truth. I could tell she was absorbed in Mr. Jeff's story about Rick Hoyt, who was born with cerebral palsy, lacked the use of his limbs, and also didn't use words to communicate. His father built a custom stroller that allowed Rick to participate in 5Ks and marathons with him.

Mr. Jeff, a runner himself, found this story inspiring. As someone who is passionate about disability-related stories and a former athlete, I was eager to learn about Team Hoyt too.

Karlie and I hurried back to our classroom after leaving Mr. Jeff's health room, eager for the next class: peer mentoring. This program, which I initiated at our school, allowed students across all grades to become peer buddies in my class during their elective periods. I was passionate about this initiative because I had seen how much my brother cherished his relationships with peer mentors in high school. Understanding the power of such connections, I wanted to offer similar experiences to younger students, starting in middle school.

In this peer mentoring class, Karlie met Lauren, who quickly became her best friend. Their bond was indescribable, and I had the joy of witnessing it flourish during those 40-minute peer tutoring sessions.

Karlie and I returned to the classroom that day where Lauren was waiting eagerly. Karlie halted her wheelchair and lifted her arms high to embrace Lauren with a hug. As we settled into our seats, I asked Lauren, our middle school cross-country star, "Have you ever heard of Team Hoyt?" She replied that she hadn't, sparking a conversation that would unknowingly alter all three of our lives over the next ten minutes in that classroom.

I announced to the class that we were about to watch something special on TV. Sitting at my computer connected to the overhead projector, I opened YouTube and queued up the Oprah show featuring Team Hoyt. Dimming the lights, I hit play.

Karlie and Lauren sat with their backs to me as the story unfolded on the screen. When Rick Hoyt appeared on screen, pushed by his father in a custom stroller for marathons, Karlie's reaction etched itself into my memory forever. She pointed to the screen and then to herself, beaming with a smile. Glancing at Lauren, I saw her discreetly wipe tears away. Karlie repeated this gesture throughout the segment.

Before it ended, Lauren turned to me and asked, "Can I do this with Karlie?"

Holding back my own tears, I replied proudly, "Absolutely. I'll make it happen."

Lauren then turned to Karlie and said, "Karlie, do you want me to push you in a stroller like that so you can run with me?"

Karlie nodded eagerly and leaned in for a hug. As they embraced, I watched Karlie glance back at the screen, pointing once more.

After witnessing something magical between Karlie and Lauren that day, I knew I needed to figure out how to make this happen. Within three days I had raised enough money from fellow teachers at my school to purchase a $400 adult running stroller. Mr. Jeff embraced Karlie and Lauren's dream, offering to assist in training Lauren to prepare for the challenge of running while pushing Karlie.

Within a few months, Karlie's mother, Kathy, helped me create what would be our first of three nonprofits we would start together called, Team Karlie.

Team Karlie was born from my belief that this journey shouldn't end with Karlie — it was meant to be shared with others in our hometown who also had cerebral palsy. Kathy became my trusted confidant and partner in turning this vision into reality. The first 5K for Karlie and Lauren became an unforgettable event. The entire school turned out to cheer them on, and our community rallied around these girls, sparking something truly transformative within me.

Lauren & Karlie after their first race

Team Karlie ignited a belief in me that I was destined for more. Developing Team Karlie not only boosted my confidence but also sparked a mindset of "If I can do this, what else is possible?" It shattered the glass ceiling of my role as "just a teacher." I believe God placed Karlie and Kathy in my path for a reason. Kathy later became instrumental in starting Puzzle Pieces, leaving her job to join me in this venture. Karlie became one of our first clients, with Kathy stepping in as the Business Director.

It all began with Team Karlie.

(As a side note, I never dreamed that a casual conversation about a segment on Oprah and playing that video in my class would lead Lauren and Karlie to build a lasting relationship, bonding them forever. They remain best friends to this day. Karlie was in Lauren's wedding and takes her role as aunt to Lauren's children very seriously.

Karlie and Lauren's relationship was the inspiration for the second story in my children's book series, "Owen the Wonderer," which I wrote with the goal of educating youth about cerebral palsy, communication differences, acceptance, and inclusion.)

BORROWING CONFIDENCE

The creation of Puzzle Pieces didn't happen right away. It took me almost two years after launching Team Karlie to really understand I was destined for more. Through my journey, I've realized that gaining the confidence and courage to pursue your dreams often begins by borrowing belief and encouragement from others.

As I rounded the corner toward my classroom, I noticed the usual group of teachers and paraprofessionals by the side entrance, getting ready for bus duty. They were in the middle of an animated conversation, and as I got closer, I realized they were talking about me.

Shane, the paraprofessional from my class, was in the middle of it, and I caught him saying, "You guys are nuts. Amanda would totally quit if she could."

I felt a mix of curiosity and nerves. What were they saying?

Shane noticed me approaching and didn't hesitate to pull me in. "Settle a bet for us," he said, smiling. "I bet them that if you won the lottery, you'd quit teaching and spend your days relaxing at your lake house."

I was a bit caught off guard, standing there at the end of a long day, tired from a full day of teaching and sleepless nights with my 1-year-old. After a second, I replied, "I don't see my life without teaching." Another paraprofessional, who was also a parent of a child with disabilities, jumped in with a grin. "We tried to tell him," he said. "You're different. If you had that kind of money, you'd still do something for people with disabilities. No doubt."

His words hit me in a way I didn't expect, making me think about what they saw in me. I just shrugged, taking in the weight of their words, and headed back to my classroom, where my students were waiting to wrap up the day.

This small conversation I overheard by chance, happened around the end of my fourth year of teaching. The borrowed confidence I took away from that quick interaction, coupled with my experience with my student, Brad, Robert's mom, and the launch of Team Karlie were the impetus of leaving teaching two years later. I would spend the next two years crafting a vision, designing a business plan, and daydreaming about the possibilities of ... more.

THE SPEECH THAT CHANGED EVERYTHING

I left the classroom after six years, and opened Puzzle Pieces in September 2012.

I chose the name Puzzle Pieces for my nonprofit because, just like a puzzle, every aspect of a person's life is a vital piece of the bigger picture. When all these pieces — their supports, purpose, and opportunities — are thoughtfully placed together, they form a beautiful, complete image. Puzzle Pieces represents the idea that every individual deserves any and all support to create a vibrant, whole life.

I wanted my nonprofit to be a piece of our clients' stories. We are not meant to be their entire story. Alongside their families, caretakers, therapists, doctors, teachers, and friends, we become an essential part of their journey. We offer support, encouragement, and understanding, helping them discover meaning and purpose, contributing to their overall well-being and growth. Our nonprofit doesn't define their entire path but provides essential whole-life services, which contribute uniquely to their overall success.

During that first year after opening our doors, I remember crying in my pillow night after night. Running a nonprofit is like operating a business, and it was something very new to me. It didn't help that just a month after opening I found out I was expecting my second child, already having a 3-year-old at home. Maybe the crying had something to do with my hormones?

I remember thinking, "What have I done?"

I didn't know how to make this nonprofit work. I was 28 years old and had no business background. I didn't know how to fundraise and ask people for money. I didn't know how to lead people.

That "just a teacher" mentality inevitably crept back in.

Was I capable of hiring and firing? How would I figure out payroll?

Over 50 families were putting all their faith and trust in me to make this nonprofit a success for their loved one. They needed me.

The pressure I once felt as a teacher to find solutions for the future had now shifted to the ongoing challenge of sustaining the dreams I've helped shape for countless families.

Did I mention I was pregnant, figuring out how to balance being a mom and wife? And where did my brother fit into all of this, you may ask?

Nick briefly attended Puzzle Pieces, initially attracted by our cute, friendly staff. He soon lost interest though, and that was that. Puzzle Pieces just didn't align with the life to which Nick had become accustomed. After 12 years of him enjoying his apartment-style living in the basement at my parents' house — living his best life with no obligations, immersed in games and TV — Puzzle Pieces simply couldn't find a place in his schedule. And that's perfectly OK. In those initial years after graduation had been tough with additional behaviors, a more sedentary lifestyle and lack of friendships. But he eventually fell into a new routine and my parents gave him all that he needed, fulfilling roles as caretakers and best friends.

It was disheartening to see something I had envisioned for both my students and my brother not resonate with Nick. I felt I couldn't provide for my family what I was offering to others through Puzzle Pieces. I worried my family might resent the organization and my dreams for it, especially since it didn't meet Nick's needs. However, it was during the preparations for Puzzle Pieces' first anniversary banquet, an annual fundraiser, that I unexpectedly found solace in a conversation with my mom.

I was battling nerves, crafting a speech for the inaugural Puzzle Pieces Banquet, set to take place a year after we opened our doors. I wanted to express gratitude to those who believed in and trusted our mission, while also celebrating our journey and looking ahead. Finding the right words proved challenging as I struggled to convey the depth of Puzzle Pieces' impact.

Scheduled for a Friday night at a local church, the banquet was expected to draw about 150 attendees. On the Wednesday before the event, I called my mom to share my concerns about articulating our achievements and future goals effectively on stage. Little did I know, that conversation would not only provide the words for my speech but also offer me a profound sense of peace and reaffirm my purpose in life.

I could tell my mom started to cry. She paused and I asked her what was wrong.

She then fought through her crying to say something I will never forget: "Amanda, your dad and I are so proud of you. What you have done for this community by opening Puzzle Pieces is a reflection of your heart and love for your brother. When Nick was diagnosed, I would ask God, 'Why me? He knew I wanted a child so badly, why did He give me a child with special needs, with a disability?' It took me 30 years to finally get the answer, Amanda, and it's you. God gave me Nick so you could build Puzzle Pieces and provide this gift to so many."

With tears streaming down both our faces, her words resonated deep within me. They were a revelation and a validation of my journey thus far. Opening Puzzle Pieces wasn't just about fulfilling a need in the community; it was a profound purpose that came directly from our family's story.

As I stood at the podium that Friday night, surrounded by supporters and families whose lives we had touched, I shared my story. I spoke not only of challenges overcome and dreams realized but also of the unwavering love and support that propelled me forward.

In that moment, I understood. Puzzle Pieces wasn't just a nonprofit — it was a testament to resilience, hope, and the power of community. It was a piece of a much larger puzzle, connecting individuals with disabilities to a network of care, support, and opportunity. We were bringing visibility to disabilities and building a more inclusive community.

As I looked out at the faces in the crowd, I saw gratitude and pride reflected back at me. The journey had been fraught with uncertainty and doubt, but in that room, surrounded by love and belief, I found my answer. I was meant to be here, leading and inspiring, because of Nick and for countless others like him.

In the comfort of my mother's words and the encouragement of everyone there that night, I found the strength to keep moving forward, knowing that Puzzle Pieces was not just my dream — it was my destiny. And in sharing this journey, I hoped to inspire others to see the potential in every piece of the puzzle, to build a world where everyone, regardless of ability, could find their place and shine.

As the evening drew to a close, I felt a deep sense of gratitude and fulfillment. Puzzle Pieces had become more than I could have imagined — a source of hope, the result of a sibling's love for her brother, and my family's legacy. And with each passing day, Puzzle Pieces has continued to grow, adding new pieces to the services we provide and the change we want to see.

This is my story. This is our story. And as long as there are dreams to chase and lives to impact, Puzzle Pieces will continue to shine brightly, illuminating a path of possibility and purpose for all.

Vulnerability
IS NOT WEAKNESS.
AND THAT MYTH IS
PROFOUNDLY DANGEROUS.

- BRENE BROWN

CHAPTER 5
THE EMOTIONAL IMPACT OF BEING A NEUROTYPICAL SIBLING

THE BOOK I DIDN'T WANT TO WRITE

If I am being honest, I didn't want to write this book.

Writing this book required me to confront truths I had long avoided and unearthed emotions I had learned to suppress. The idea of my parents reading these pages added to my hesitation. Even at 40, I care deeply about their feelings and want to protect them. My parents are still navigating Nick's care, and I feared that sharing my perspective might make them question their parenting or, even worse, think I wanted our life to be different.

I didn't want my life to be different.

I am grateful for my parents. I am grateful for Nick. I am grateful for the gifts Nick's disability gave my family.

What writing this story has made me realize is that I owe it to other siblings like me to help explain our unique perspective. Overshadowed, misunderstood, weighed down with pressure, worried about their future – special needs siblings carry a lot of emotions. As a sibling, who pursued a career in special education, and then opened a nonprofit that serves those with disabilities, I have seen this both in my own childhood and in the lives of the families I serve.

So, when writing this memoir I felt it was important to tell my own sibling story. I dug deep in the vault to pull out stories – and emotions – to paint the picture of my life with Nick.

But from the beginning, I knew that I wanted this book to be more than a memoir. I wanted this book to have a deeper purpose, focused on the parents reading these pages.

Like my parents, you didn't intend on this journey.

Maybe you just got your child's diagnosis, and the journey is just beginning.

Maybe you have been on this journey for a while, but are at a point of transition and your path is becoming more unclear.

Or maybe you're a parent thinking about expanding your family after having a child with a disability, and you picked up this book because you're wondering what it might be like for a sibling to grow up in a family like yours, navigating the challenges and joys that come with having a brother or sister with a disability.

Here's what I know to be true about you:

You don't wish you were on a different journey. You love the life you have been given, but the unexpected twists and turns have been overwhelming.

Your journey is exhausting, as you advocate tirelessly for your children's well-being.

Your journey is a blend of immense joy and heart-wrenching moments.

You celebrate each milestone, but every step forward just means a new uncertainty.

But despite all of the uncertainty, your journey is one of love, resilience and strength.

I see you and I understand the journey you're on. I have lived this journey too, but from the unique perspective of the neurotypical sibling. God knew I could reach you, and this book I didn't want to write came from the gifts He gave me to impact families like yours and mine.

Honestly, I wanted to write a book for women struggling with mom guilt while chasing their dreams, a guide on how to find balance and empowerment. I wanted to inspire women to pursue their dreams despite their fears.

But God had different plans. He led me here – to this book and to you.

From this point forward, my goal is to create a space where you can recognize and embrace your strengths as a parent. You already possess all that is necessary to fulfill your role as mom or dad. You are enough.

LAYING THE GROUND RULES

This memoir is designed to be a companion on your journey, offering guidance and understanding as it relates to your neurotypical children. To ensure you get the most out of this book, I feel as though it is important to lay a few ground rules that will help guide you through the remaining pages.

To effectively address the emotions felt by special needs siblings, it's essential for parents to have the right mindset. This will allow you to support your neurotypical children as they learn to understand their role, while making them feel included and heard.

Understanding Through Reflection

Growing up as Nick's sister, I've learned so many lessons—about advocacy, conflict, and carving out my own identity. But perhaps the most valuable lesson has been the importance of reflection. It's through looking back that I've been able to truly understand how my role as a neurotypical sibling shaped me.

By reflecting on both the joys and the struggles, I gained clarity about my own perspective and feelings. This self-awareness has not only helped me process my childhood experiences but also given me the ability to offer genuine advice to other families navigating a similar path.

As you read this book, I encourage you to pause and reflect on your own journey, especially through the eyes of your neurotypical child. Approach these pages with an open mind, ready to see your life—and theirs—from a different perspective.

Communication Without Barriers

In families navigating the world of disability, communication becomes more than just important—it becomes essential. When you create space for open, honest conversations, you give every family member, including neurotypical siblings, the chance to share their emotions, fears, and hopes. This kind of communication isn't just about understanding each other better; it's about creating a home where everyone feels safe, supported, and valued.

Allowing every voice to be heard not only fosters empathy but also strengthens the family bond, helping each person feel understood and connected on this journey.

Honoring Each Journey

Every family's disability journey is deeply personal, and no two paths are exactly the same — even within the same household. As a parent, the key to building strong relationships with all of your children, both with and without disabilities, is learning to embrace this individuality. You might have expectations or visions for the future that don't align with your child(ren), and that's perfectly OK.

By being adaptable, patient, and open to your children's unique experiences, you not only honor their individual journeys but also create a stronger, more unified family bond that respects and supports everyone.

Avoid the Guilt & Doubt

As a parent, it's natural to want to create balance for all of your children, but when raising both a neurotypical child and a child with a disability, feelings of guilt and doubt can easily arise. You might find yourself second-guessing your decisions, wondering if you've done enough for your neurotypical child, or feeling regret over choices that now seem unfair. Confronting these emotions is essential. Taking an honest look at how your child's disability has affected the family dynamic is the first step toward growth, healing, and stronger relationships.

By addressing the emotional impact of having a sibling with a disability in this chapter, it is not my intention to make you feel as though you've been failing your children up to this point. No, far from it.

I hope to offer you a perspective from the other side, from the viewpoint of the neurotypical child who loves and cares deeply for her sibling with a disability.

You see, I firmly believe that understanding is the key to compassion, and compassion is the key to providing the best possible support for your entire family.

By sharing not only my personal experiences but also insights gained from conversations and coaching with other siblings who have walked a similar path, my goal is to help you understand our journey better. With practical steps and tangible advice, I will help you navigate this complex terrain with your children.

My goal isn't to change your family's circumstances, because I believe your family is uniquely beautiful as it is. Instead, my mission is to empower you to be the best parent you can be for your children.

Notice I said, "the best parent you can be?" Not perfect. There's no such thing as a perfect parent. You are human, which means you are wonderfully imperfect.

Forget being the perfect parent. What defines great parenting is your ability to embrace those imperfections, learn from your mistakes, and grow with your family.

It's about making progress, not chasing perfection, and simply being present for each moment. We're on this journey together, one imperfect step at a time.

EMOTIONAL INTELLIGENCE & BEING SPECIAL

When your child was diagnosed with a disability, you faced the complex emotions that accompanied such life-altering news as an adult. Your maturity and life experience provided you with the tools to comprehend and process these feelings.

However, your neurotypical child, who lacks the same level of emotional development and understanding, does not have this advantage. They may struggle to grasp the full impact of the diagnosis and experience a full range of emotions as a result.

As a parent, it's crucial to recognize this disparity and support your neurotypical child in navigating their own emotions as it relates to your family's disability journey.

Think about this: There are numerous support groups and online communities for parents raising children with disabilities to find connections and help them feel understood. But it's rare to find groups like this for siblings.

What I have learned is that sibling experiences and feelings often mirror those of their parents.

Feelings of guilt, embarrassment, jealousy — we must work through these emotions too. But we often keep these feelings to ourselves, not wanting to add to the emotional burden we see you carry daily.

I remember growing up hearing how "special" I was, just for being Nick's sister. If I had a dollar for every time I heard that word, I'd be retired and sipping cocktails on a beach by now. I may call myself a special needs sibling now, but hearing others call me "special" then was different.

I think every sibling of someone with a disability has heard these labels — 'special,' 'patient,' 'God's chosen one' — and the list goes on. As an adult, I've grown immune to these well-intentioned but misplaced compliments. But as a kid, hearing strangers call me a "guardian angel" simply for being a sister to my brother, left me confused.

With my outgoing personality, I'd usually respond with a hair flip and a nonchalant, 'I know, right?' But deep down, I was flooded with so many emotions that didn't feel very special.

I FELT GUILTY. Why did I get to be the version of "special" others were always applauding and my brother got to be the version of "special" they always felt sorry for?

I FELT EMBARRASSED. When coming of age, a child wants to blend in, not stand out. This word put a big label on me – "different."

I FELT HATE. I never asked to be considered "special." I never asked for this life, or for my family to experience such emotional weight.

I FELT JEALOUS. Other kids had "normal" lives. Why did I have to be "special?"

I FELT PROUD. Nick's disability made him visibly different to the world, and somehow, it made me different in a superhuman way. He needed me and I liked that he needed me.

I couldn't grasp these feelings; I didn't want to be different, and I didn't want my brother to be either. I simply wished people would stop seeing me as something 'special,' because, to me, I was just being a sister.

Emotions like guilt, embarrassment, hate, jealousy, and pride that are experienced by a neurotypical sibling in childhood can significantly influence – both positively and negatively – development and outlook later in life.

All families and all siblings are different though. We have different emotions, different experiences, and in return, this impacts each of us differently. I think some parents get lost in worry and fear that the family's disability journey will have a detrimental impact on their neurotypical children.

I am here to tell you that although there are emotions to work through, I fully believe the disability impact can be positive. I know that is the case for my story with Nick.

GUILT can evolve into a heightened sense of empathy and compassion.

EMBARRASSMENT can build a sense of humility and the ability to laugh at oneself.

HATE can teach valuable lessons in resilience and the importance of forgiveness as we grow older.

JEALOUSY could foster a drive for individual achievement or provoke a sense of injustice that fuels advocacy.

PRIDE in their sibling's accomplishments can instill a lasting sense of solidarity, influencing their career choices or personal values as they navigate adulthood.

The emotions neurotypical children experience can vary dramatically. The five emotions I will explore are the ones that I believe siblings most often feel and can be the hardest to understand. The stories illustrating these emotions are not solely based on my personal experiences. Instead, they encompass narratives generously shared with me by other siblings over the years.

It's also important to know that these emotions are not necessarily feelings your child is currently experiencing or has in the past. They may never experience any of these emotions or they may experience all of them at different seasons of their life. My goal in this chapter is to be unapologetically open and honest, offering you a candid look into my own experiences and those of other siblings I've interviewed.

These emotions are ones that you, as parents, have experienced on some level. But for your neurotypical children, these emotions manifest differently and often intertwine with the complexities of growing up.

GUILT

As a kid, I navigated through feelings I couldn't quite put a name to, let alone understand. It's only in the rear view mirror of adulthood that I find myself unpacking the emotional baggage of growing up with Nick, finally putting a name to the big feelings I had.

One of those feelings, probably one that I most often felt, was guilt.

Guilt was sneaky. It's the kind of emotion that slips in unexpectedly, an uninvited guest to our biggest moments in life. In my story, guilt is inextricably intertwined with some of my happiest moments and biggest achievements.

I FELT GUILTY for every childhood first — my first sleepover, my first boyfriend, my first straight A report card, and my high school prom.

I FELT GUILTY that I got my driver's license.

I FELT GUILTY when I made a best friend.

I FELT GUILTY when I left for college.

I FELT GUILTY when I got married.

But guilt is more pervasive than just life's biggest moments. Like a weed overtaking a garden, guilt weaseled its way into the everyday moments too. Every positive thought I had about myself, every compliment I received, and every trait I took pride in was entangled with guilt.

I FELT GUILTY doing things with my friends, while Nick stayed home.

I FELT GUILTY I was smarter than him.

I FELT GUILTY that things came easily to me.

I FELT GUILTY that I had better health than him.

I FELT GUILTY that I was me and Nick was Nick.

I can't even begin to count how many times I asked the question, "Why don't I have the disability?"

Without an answer to that question, I downplayed my successes to preserve Nick's feelings. When it came to celebrating myself or leaning into my natural talents or those first-time experiences, I learned to make myself small, ensuring I never overshadowed Nick's possibilities.

No one asked me to do this, it's almost like it was a natural, subconscious way of living for me.

My parents celebrated Nick and I equally, even if his wins looked different, like participating in Special Olympics, driving his go-cart around our property safely, or independently making his own lunch. My way of navigating my guilt was allowing Nick to do life alongside me, when he wanted. I made sure he could be included. I made sure he was seen. I tried to share my life with him so he never felt inferior.

But like any child, coming into their own, there were times I didn't want my brother around. I wanted space to breathe, to be me. But that only led to more guilt.

I FELT GUILTY when I would beg my mom to get Nick out of my room when I had a friend over.

I FELT GUILTY when I cried to my mom, asking her to stop Nick from texting my friends.

I FELT GUILTY when I would get mad at him, because he too needed that friend to hang with.

Guilt is so deeply rooted, it can arise when a sibling is being the epitome of support and understanding. Am I doing enough? Am I patient enough? Are my actions unintentionally contributing to the barriers my sibling faces?

No matter how I spun it, the guilt would be there lurking deep within me.

I would be remiss not to address the complex emotions of guilt and grief that are intricately woven into the fabric of special needs families. Grief, in this context, can arise from many layers of the disability experience. On one hand, there's the medical side of the disability — a constant stream of doctor's appointments, therapies, surgeries, and hospital stays. These challenges weigh heavily on the entire family, often leaving them grieving a sense of normalcy.

But grief goes deeper than that. It also stems from the unspoken loss of certain expectations. Special needs siblings may quietly mourn the shared experiences they imagined, like playing together on the playground, whispering secrets late at night, or hitting life's milestones in sync. They see their peers bonding with siblings in ways that might feel out of reach, and there's a sense of longing that's hard to put into words.

Families, too, experience a unique form of grief as they realize their dynamics don't align with what society defines as "typical." The realization that everything – holidays, family outings, vacations – will always be different can create a deep sense of loss. Yet, this grief isn't always obvious or openly discussed, as it often exists alongside immense love and pride for their sibling with a disability. It's a silent, heavy burden that shapes how we navigate our family's world and the world around us.

This grief is not about regret, but rather an acknowledgment of what is, what could have been, and the lifelong adjustments that come with loving someone with a disability. It is a part of our journey, and understanding it helps us embrace all the pieces — both the joy and the pain — that come with being part of a special needs family.

I can say with certainty that I have experienced each of these forms of grief, which were each accompanied by the co-dependent emotion of guilt. Nick's rare diagnosis came with a lot of additional medical issues, which he still battles today. I can still remember the time we almost lost him and the guilt I felt at the time thinking it was all my fault.

In late spring 2001, I was a junior in high school, and my family's weekends were consumed by the relentless demands of the softball season. Each Saturday found us at the ball field, where the sweltering Kentucky sun blazed down on our four-game marathon. At this particular game, my dad was stationed right behind home plate, meticulously listening to the murmur of college scouts' comments as he watched me pitch with pride. My mom, always the unwavering supporter, cheered enthusiastically from the sidelines, her voice carrying over the clamor of the crowd. Nick, who was 19 at the time, was sprawled out on a quilt in the grass beside her. The hot sun and extended games had drained him, and he drifted in and out of sleep.

Our trusty cooler, a staple for these long days, was packed with an assortment of drinks and snacks to keep us fueled. On this particular day, Nick seemed unusually thirsty, downing nearly a dozen of our childhood favorite Squeeze It drinks, which seemed like a lot even with the Kentucky heat.

As the games wore on, I was entirely immersed in the rhythm of competition, my focus sharpened by the whispers of college scouts and the pressure of living up to expectations. My parents' attention was on me, and not on Nick's excessive thirst or sleepiness. It wasn't until we returned home that the gravity of the situation became apparent. Nick struggled to stay awake and his eyes rolled back in his head. My dad, a former EMT, sprang into action, and we sped through the rural roads to the nearest hospital, a good 30 minutes away.

Upon arrival at the ER, we were hit with the seriousness of Nick's condition. His blood sugar levels were shockingly high — 1600, far beyond the normal range of 95 to 105. The doctors were astounded he could even walk into the hospital. Nick was swiftly admitted to the ICU, where he was placed in a medically induced coma to relieve the strain on his heart while insulin and IV fluids were administered. The sight of him, so vulnerable and still, is something I will never forget.

As the reality of Nick's condition settled in, the thought gnawed at me: If Nick hadn't been at the ball field, if my parents' attention hadn't been so focused on my games, could they have noticed the early signs of diabetes? Could they have seen something that would have prevented this crisis?

In the midst of this crisis, I had a scheduled college visit to Western Kentucky University, an hour and 15 minutes away from our hometown. This was an opportunity I had eagerly anticipated, but now it seemed overshadowed by this family crisis. My parents, determined that I would not miss this chance, arranged for a shortened visit. My mom took me, while my dad remained at the hospital with Nick. I felt a deep sense of guilt for experiencing a semblance of normalcy and relief at escaping the hospital's grim atmosphere while my brother was in such a dire state. But the excitement of the college visit, which should have been a shared family experience, felt tainted.

I felt guilty for having any excitement about my future while my brother's life hung in the balance. I mourned the fact that the visit, an event that was supposed to be a milestone, was overshadowed by the circumstances of Nick's condition. The emotional strain of navigating my aspirations while coping with the reality of Nick's health crisis became a poignant lesson in balancing personal dreams with family responsibilities, a lesson that would shape my journey in profound ways.

The guilt I had as a child was different from the guilt I felt that day on a college visit, which is different from the guilt I feel as an adult. Guilt has this funny way of growing with us it seems. It never really disappears, it just reshapes and morphs through life experiences, which only remind me of what I can do and what Nick can't.

I met a colleague through my career, who has a similar story to me. He is a sibling and found success in franchising a disability service provider business. I remember he once said to me, "I feel guilty that I made a successful career out of being a special needs sibling. What would my life look like had my brother not had autism?"

After hearing this statement, I couldn't un-feel it – a new level of guilt unlocked.

This is exactly what I have done with my platform. I have social media accounts, a website, and this book all centered around my identity as a special needs sibling.

But I can't ignore how much sharing my story in these spaces, especially writing this book, has helped heal my guilt.

Putting my feelings into words and sharing those with you makes all of my emotions – and my life – mean something. Honoring my big brother and giving my sibling experience purpose in a way that can impact others has been extremely therapeutic.

Honestly, the greatest support I received in overcoming the guilt I internalized came from my parents. They established clear boundaries between my life and Nick's, allowing us both to be involved in each other's lives while also creating space for our individual experiences. This balance allowed me to pursue my own path. My parents never pressured me to feel grateful or compare my situation to Nick's, which helped me navigate my own journey without added burdens.

After hearing other siblings share their personal stories, I've come to deeply appreciate the role my parents played in my journey. Many siblings I have spoken with have detailed how certain comments or actions from their parents shaped feelings of resentment, which only added to the guilt they naturally felt. This is your reminder as a parent that your neurotypical child's journey is uniquely theirs, filled with its own challenges and triumphs.

I don't want to leave you worrying about whether you're setting your child up for resentment, so I'm going to share some practical steps you can take to foster a healthy family dynamic.

Celebrate Individual Achievements
Allow them to embrace their path without the burden of comparison or competition with their sibling who has a disability. For example, if your neurotypical child excels in sports, celebrate their achievements with the same enthusiasm and pride as you would for any milestone your child with a disability reaches. Establish an environment of unconditional love and support, where each child is celebrated for their individual strengths and accomplishments

Allow Free Expression
Have regular one-on-one conversations with each child, providing them with a space to express their feelings and experiences freely. Start by gently asking them if they've been feeling upset, overwhelmed or carrying any heavy emotions, and reassure them that it's normal to feel a range of emotions when navigating life with a sibling who has a disability.

Let them know that guilt, while uncomfortable, is a common feeling, especially if they think they aren't doing enough for their sibling or when they feel resentment. Encourage them to share their thoughts without fear of punishment or shame, and emphasize that they are not responsible for their sibling's challenges. Explain that it's OK to have moments where they need space or time for themselves, and feeling conflicted doesn't make them a bad person. Your goal here is not to try to take the guilt away, but help to talk about it to help them create a healthy emotional balance.

Set Aside Dedicated Time

Plan special outings or activities that cater to each child's personal interests. This ensures that every child feels valued and understood, and it strengthens individual connections.

Avoid Comparisons

Focus on celebrating what makes each child special and unique, rather than drawing comparisons between them. If your child with a disability makes progress in therapy, highlight and celebrate their achievements, while also acknowledging your neurotypical child's milestones with equal enthusiasm. Remember, comparison is the thief of joy.

Embrace Differences and Celebrate Successes

Embrace each child's differences and celebrate their successes, nurturing their unique potential. This approach bolsters their self-esteem and fosters a family dynamic where every member feels equally cherished and supported.

Teach the Value of Compassion

Amid the guilt, help your child discover the enduring power of family. Teach them that guilt is not a reflection of their shortcomings but rather a testament to their love and compassion. It's a reminder that, despite the challenges we face, our journey is full of meaning and purpose.

EMBARRASSMENT

Embarrassment is a complex emotion that many siblings of those with disabilities experience, though it often remains unspoken. It's a feeling that can arise unexpectedly, even in the most loving and supportive families. For a child, the desire to fit in and be accepted by peers can clash with the realities of having a sibling who might behave differently or require extra attention. This internal conflict can create a sense of discomfort or even shame, which can be difficult to navigate.

Understanding and acknowledging this emotion is crucial, not only for the sibling's personal growth, but also for fostering a compassionate and supportive family environment.

Growing up with Nick, I had my fair share of these moments. It's not always easy to talk about, but it's a real part of the journey.

I can remember being out in public when an innocent comment suddenly felt uncomfortable, or noticing how Nick's unique behavior drew curious stares. It's like when a classmate at school asked why my brother didn't talk like other kids, or when a family member asked a question that unintentionally highlighted Nick's differences. These moments made me feel confused, self-conscious and a mix of emotions, including embarrassment.

I can remember thinking that if I could just have a sign proclaiming, "My brother has a disability — handle with care" things would surely be easier. People would surely understand and stop their judging stares.

Siblings like me often carry this constant, uneasy feeling of "what if," and it doesn't just surface in public places or around strangers.

WHAT IF my brother has a meltdown during a family gathering, and everyone starts giving me unsolicited advice?

WHAT IF someone makes an awkward comment about my brother's behavior, and I don't know how to respond?

WHAT IF my brother says or does something inappropriate in public, and I have to explain it to strangers who don't get it?

WHAT IF my brother doesn't understand personal space and makes someone uncomfortable, and I have to apologize for it?

What's surprising is how much stronger those feelings can be with family and friends. Their judgment hits harder, and their advice or comments can leave you feeling defeated or inadequate. I've felt more pity from those closest to me than I ever have from complete strangers. Strangers don't know your story, so their judgment doesn't sting as much. But with family and friends, you expect understanding, support, and love. When that falls short, it hurts more because their opinions matter so much. Strangers are easier to dismiss as part of a distant, flawed society, but with those close to you, the impact is far more personal.

As a young girl, I often felt embarrassed, not so much as an adult. Back then, I was just trying to fit in and navigate social circles, which made me want to hide my family's less-than-perfect dynamics. I was also afraid that my brother might draw unwanted attention, adding a whole other layer of anxiety to hanging out with my friends.

Many special needs siblings have shared their personal stories with me, revealing moments where they felt embarrassed or awkward in social situations because of their sibling's behaviors or needs. These experiences, though deeply personal, are a common thread in the fabric of sibling relationships and highlight the unique challenges we face.

We might feel embarrassed by our sibling during public outings, especially in settings like restaurants, due to our sibling's eating habits not being considered appropriate by societal standards. These eating habits could include behaviors such as messy eating, making loud or disruptive noises while eating, or exhibiting difficulty with utensils or table manners.

We may feel embarrassed by our sibling in social settings, particularly when our sibling exhibits behaviors that draw attention or cause disruptions. These behaviors could include tantrums, outbursts, or other forms of emotional distress that are common manifestations of their sibling's disability.

If the sibling struggles to communicate effectively or exhibits different speech patterns, we may feel embarrassed when he/she is attempting to engage in conversations with others. They may worry about others' reactions to their sibling's speech or their own ability to effectively communicate on their sibling's behalf.

If our sibling requires assistance with personal care tasks, such as toileting or dressing, we may feel uncomfortable or embarrassed when helping them in public. We worry about others noticing or commenting on their sibling's needs, leading to feelings of self-consciousness and embarrassment.

If our sibling struggles with social cues and has difficulty reading the room or recognizing when a conversation has ended, we may feel a strong urge to manage these interactions carefully. We might find ourselves feeling pressured to navigate social situations in a way that minimizes discomfort for others, often at the expense of allowing our sibling to fully engage in their own way. This pressure can lead us to try and "fix" the situation or redirect conversations, hoping to make everyone feel more at ease.

We may inadvertently suppress their unique ways of connecting with others, driven by our desire to smooth over potential awkwardness and make others comfortable. We may want to protect our sibling from discomfort or judgment, but this may be at the expense of honoring their individuality and allowing them to navigate social interactions at their own pace.

My parents may not appreciate my decision to include some of my own personal examples of embarrassment in this book, but hopefully you know enough about me at this point to know that I believe you deserve honesty. I'm committed to keeping it real, even when it means delving into the less flattering truths.

As I've shared before, our family has a unique way of using humor to navigate challenging moments. Yet, as a young girl still discovering my identity, my brother's recurring behaviors often left me feeling an intense, sometimes overwhelming, sense of embarrassment. I vividly remember moments when I wanted nothing more than to hide and cry.

One particularly memorable instance was with a new babysitter. Nick was clearly upset about our parents being away and made his displeasure known by refusing to cooperate with the babysitter's bedtime efforts. How did he express this? By pulling his pants down for either a good ol' school mooning or a full frontal display.

Yep, you heard that right—Nick had a way of channeling his frustration into behaviors that were definitely not considered appropriate. Whether it was an unexpected mooning, a full-on frontal display, or the classic middle finger salute, my brother had a remarkable talent for expressing his mood.

While I can laugh about these antics now, back in my elementary and middle school days, I was a young girl desperately trying to blend into the background.

Sure, anyone might cringe at the type of displays Nick chose when acting out, but the embarrassment I felt wasn't always about extreme gestures. Words he said and decisions he made would embarrass me too, I just learned to move through it and pick my battles of asking mom or dad to make Nick stop. I remember wanting to hide when Nick would stretch his whole body across the church pew for an impromptu nap during service, or feeling judged when he told his tall-tales that never made sense.

In those moments, I felt a strong compulsion to become an apologetic mediator, trailing behind him as I rushed to offer hasty explanations to anyone who witnessed his behavior.

"Excuse us, this is my brother; he has a disability," became my mantra.

Looking back, I realize how misguided that instinct was. It wasn't my role to hide him or apologize for his presence; rather, I should have felt comfortable to embrace and normalize our experiences, even if they didn't align with societal expectations. As an adult, I've learned that Nick's right to take up space in this world is non-negotiable, and the discomfort of others is not my burden to bear.

But, that doesn't mean it's easy.

From as far back as I can remember, Nick had a simple but profound desire: to be a part of the conversation, to join in the usual banter that seemed so effortless for everyone else. He delighted in chatting about things like having a girlfriend, living on a houseboat on the Mississippi River, or what he would do if he won the lottery — anything with a some-day dream. These were the conversations Nick lived for, thriving in the back-and-forth, yet never expressing a deeper desire to turn these dreams into reality.

Nick's desire to connect with others knew no boundaries. Pre-cell phone days, Nick had an uncanny ability to memorize phone numbers — a talent he used with surprising precision. My friends, and sometimes my boyfriend, would get unexpected calls from Nick, who would enthusiastically dial their numbers, to share tall tales or just shoot the breeze. My friends and boyfriend would play it cool, but Nick called multiple times and eventually they had to hang up. I was mortified.

I would frantically call my mom, confessing yet another awkward situation, feeling a mix of frustration and embarrassment. It wasn't just that Nick had the habit of calling; it was the reality that his actions were due to his disability. In those moments, it felt like his disability was the glaring spotlight that magnified every awkward interaction. My parents often stepped in to smooth things over, but looking back, I see that my feelings of embarrassment were intensified by the awareness that our situation was different — not just annoying sibling behavior, but a reflection of a deeper struggle.

Navigating the emotional landscape of having a sibling with a disability can be incredibly complex, especially for a young child still discovering their identity. The fear of judgment and embarrassment can create significant anxiety, particularly when their sibling's behavior diverges from societal norms. This embarrassment often stems not from the disability itself but from the behaviors that attract unwanted attention and the societal expectations that accompany them.

A neurotypical sibling may find themselves torn between their deep love and loyalty towards their sibling and their own desire to fit in and avoid negative attention. They might worry about how their sibling's actions reflect on their family and feel the pressure to maintain a certain image in public.

Parents and caregivers play a crucial role in helping neurotypical children navigate these challenging emotions. Here are some tangible ways to provide support:

Open Communication
To foster open conversations about embarrassment, create a safe space where your child can express their feelings without fear of judgment. Start by acknowledging that it's normal to feel embarrassed at times, especially in public when others may stare or ask questions about their sibling.

Encourage them to share specific situations that make them uncomfortable, and validate their emotions by letting them know it's OK to feel that way — it doesn't mean they love their sibling any less. Ask about peer reactions and offer to role-play responses to help them feel more confident in handling awkward situations. Check in with them after social outings to understand how they're feeling, and brainstorm solutions together for handling moments of discomfort. The key to remember here is not thinking you have to offer them a solution, but just be able to listen and empathize with them through the journey.

Validate Their Feelings
Acknowledge that feelings of embarrassment and discomfort are normal and valid. Let them know it's OK to have these feelings and that they don't make them a bad sibling.

Promote Understanding
Help the neurotypical child understand their sibling's behavior in the context of their disability. Education can foster empathy and reduce feelings of embarrassment.

Set Boundaries and Provide Support
Establish clear boundaries regarding behavior in public and provide guidance on how to handle awkward situations. Offer practical strategies to manage challenging moments like:

If your sibling becomes overwhelmed in a busy place, prepare a calm phrase like, "We're just having a hard moment," and focus on the sibling rather than on others' reactions.

If they feel overwhelmed, have a plan in place to allow them to signal when they need a break or want to leave a public situation.

Have a family discussion where everyone shares their worries or fears about being in public, and agree that these feelings will be handled with compassion rather than frustration.

Encourage Independence
Allow the neurotypical sibling to develop their own coping mechanisms and support systems. Give them space to grow and mature while providing reassurance and guidance.

Model Positive Behavior
Demonstrate how to handle embarrassing situations with grace and confidence. Your actions can serve as a model for how to manage similar situations.

Reflecting on my own experiences, I appreciated how my parents never dismissed my feelings of awkwardness or pressured me to simply accept everything without question. Instead, they provided me with the space and support to grow, helping me shift my focus and mature. **More often than not, a sibling's embarrassment is not about the disability itself but about navigating societal expectations against behaviors that are not considered typical.** By offering understanding and empathy, parents can help all children build resilience and create a supportive family dynamic.

HATE
When I was in fourth grade, I started to worry a lot about what other kids thought of me.

I even remember cutting the tags off my Walmart clothes because they weren't cool brands like Tommy Hilfiger and Gap. Let me

Amanda – 3rd grade

tell you, Walmart clothes in the '90s were nothing like the trendy stuff you find there today. And if my jeans weren't tight-rolled just right or my bangs didn't have that perfect teased "wave," I'd cry and beg to stay home.

As a young girl growing up in a single-wide trailer with no money for name-brand clothes, and a family dynamic different from my peers, I worried a lot about what others thought of me.

I bet most girls have been there. Fear of not fitting in and being on the receiving end of bullying is simply a given when it comes to growing up.

Honestly, I'm glad I didn't have to deal with Instagram or Snapchat back then. These platforms are a constant battle of comparing and competing, and I'm not sure I would've handled it well at that age. I just wanted to fit in with the "in-crowd," to feel like I belonged.

I'm sharing all this because the next part of my story really shook me. It messed with everything I thought I knew about who I was and where I belonged. Being a young girl is tough. You're trying to find your identity, figure out your circle of friends, and understand where you fit in. What happened to me at that age felt like the universe saying, "Good luck with that, Amanda."

I will never forget that day in elementary school, as we sat in our small classroom, the air thick with the smell of crayons and chalk. We were reading aloud from "Tales of a Fourth Grade Nothing" by Judy Blume, a book I should have enjoyed. But for me, the joy of reading was overshadowed by dread. The game of "popcorn," where students took turns reading paragraphs and calling on others to continue, filled me with paralyzing anxiety. My palms would grow clammy, and my right leg would jitter uncontrollably, causing my desk to shake with each rapid bounce. The sight of the book in front of me, the words blurred together, made my heart race with a fear I couldn't shake.

The moment I had been dreading arrived when Matt, the boy I had a hopeless crush on, called my name. My throat tightened as I began to read, and I stumbled over the words almost immediately. The frustration of not being able to pronounce a word correctly, with the whole class and teacher watching, was a crushing blow to my self-esteem. The paragraph felt endless, stretching on like a cruel test of my patience and endurance, even though I genuinely enjoyed Judy Blume's stories.

As I neared the end of the paragraph, the sting of humiliation hit its peak. I remember the exact moment when a whisper, piercing and cold, floated through the air.

"She is retarded like her brother."

I would never forget the boy who uttered those words, his face etched in my memory. It felt like his words were amplified, echoing in my ears despite the hushed tones. Though only a few classmates might have giggled, it felt like the entire room was laughing at me. I sank deeper into my chair, struggling to keep my composure. I fought back tears, my anger simmering as I envisioned punching him in the face, but I was too paralyzed by shame to act on it.

In that moment, my heart ached with a new kind of pain. I hated that my brother had a disability, not just for the struggles he faced, but because it cast a shadow over me, too. I felt branded by association, my identity overshadowed by the stigma attached to my brother. To my classmates, I wasn't Amanda — I was simply the sister of a boy with a disability. This unwelcome label was a heavy burden to carry, a cruel reminder of how society often projects its biases onto those closest to the ones it deems "different."

As a young girl, desperately trying to fit in and concerned about how others perceived me, this added layer of worry was unbearable. It wasn't just that people saw me through the lens of my brother's disability; it was the feeling of being unfairly judged and labeled by others who didn't understand. This painful experience of being unfairly categorized stuck with me through my elementary years, a lesson in how even the youngest children can be influenced by societal prejudices.

That is my first memory of hatred.

We've all heard the familiar parental wisdom when a young child exclaims their strong dislike for something: "Hate is a strong word. You might not like it, but saying you hate it is too extreme."

And it's true — "hate" is a powerful emotion, often marked by a deep and passionate dislike. But sometimes, that word feels too real, cutting deep into our emotions. In this section of the book, I explore the complex emotions involved in grappling with the difficulties of my brother's disability, all while deeply loving him. It's about understanding how the word "hate" can impact us, recognizing the intensity of those feelings, and learning how to navigate hate within the framework of the special needs family.

Although we'll dive deeper into this advice more in upcoming chapters, I want to make a sincere plea to parents reading this book: take a moment to understand your neurotypical child's perspective, allowing them the space to feel their emotions. My parents never made me feel ashamed of my feelings, but articulating them was a challenge, overshadowed by guilt and shame.

I loved my brother for who he was, yet there were times when I hated his disability. I never gave myself permission to say it out loud, but it simmered deep within me. Hate was too powerful of a statement, but sometimes it was the only word I could find to describe this deep emotion because his disability didn't align to what society said was typical. Yet in the same breath I can also say he was rarely different from me.

How is that possible?

How could he be different, yet just like me? How can hate and love coexist in the same space?

Nick's disability was a part of him, so if I claimed I hated it, was I saying I hated my brother?

NAVIGATING THE JOURNEY OF SPECIAL NEEDS PARENTING REQUIRES NOT JUST PROBLEM-SOLVING SKILLS, BUT *a heart open to learning and adapting*

That's why I kept any hate I felt buried. As an adult, I can grasp the hate that I felt, and sometimes still feel. But today I have the words.

I HATED how society couldn't see Nick as I did, and I feared when his disability caused impulsive behaviors.

I HATED the pressure I felt to be Nick's protector.

I HATED negotiating his defiance in public, especially the full-frontal expressions of frustration. I hated it for him, but selfishly, I hated it for me.

I HATED the worry I carried for my parents' health, which would have a direct impact on their role as Nick's caregivers.

I HATED that Nick struggled with reading social cues, which often led him to overstep boundaries around my friends. This left me in the uncomfortable position of having to explain his disability while trying to protect his dignity and privacy. I can remember so many times hollering, "Mom, come get Nick! "Mom, tell Nick to stop!"

My parents were great at not pushing me to become a peacemaker or simply tolerate the situation. Instead, they gave me the space to navigate and understand it in my own time.

In reflection, it's probably the thing my parents did that I appreciate the most. I think deep down they knew my time would come to be Nick's caregiver when they couldn't, so they allowed me the time I needed to be a kid and young adult.

They allowed me to navigate these hard feelings in my own way. They never forced me to push down my "hate" for Nick's disability. To be fair, I don't think I ever expressed to my parents the hate that I often felt. But they never expected me to feel or act any certain way when it came to my brother. I was given grace to explore my role as Nick's sister, and simply given their positive example of loving someone with a disability.

As an adult, I can see that my parents were constantly navigating a complex balancing act that I found so challenging. They were tirelessly managing the needs of both my brother and me, but that was their way of showing their love. It was simply our life unfolding.

Now, as a professional in the field, I understand these things I hated were parts of Nick's disability. When talking with other siblings, I've found they, too, struggle with this emotion when they are brave enough to share how they truly feel. Just as I feared as a child, they, too, worry that talking about hate out loud sounds as though they hate their sibling. Parents, I encourage you to be a safe place for your neurotypical children so they can express emotions as strong as hate and not worry they will be reprimanded or taken out of context. We siblings already carry enough guilt and inner turmoil; we don't need an extra layer of judgment on top of that.

Even though I haven't personally experienced all of these feelings, I want to share what other siblings have identified as sources of their hate when it comes to their sibling's disability.

"I hate that my sister can't walk."

"I hate that my brother can't talk."

"I hate that my brother pinches me all the time, and he never gets in trouble."

"I hate that my sister causes me to miss out on going to places I really want to go."

"I hate that my brother flaps his hands and jumps up and down when we are out in public, because it draws attention to us. I hate the attention."

"I hate that my brother doesn't understand how to play with me."

"I hate that I will never be an aunt." (This one is from me.)

"I hate that my brother ruins all of our family time and steals the attention."

"I hate that my sister's disability means my family does not go on vacations."

"I hate that my brother gets more attention and is more known than me."

"I hate that my family can't do normal activities like other families because my sister is in a wheelchair."

When parents hear these phrases from their child, it's a natural reaction to minimize the extreme emotion of hate and tell them something that defends their sibling, like:

"You know he/she can't help that."

"You should be grateful that you can do the things they can't."

"You really don't mean that; one day, you will understand."

"You should not feel that way, that is your sibling and they need you."

Maybe you have said something similar. These statements are not necessarily wrong. However, from my own personal experience and from working with siblings throughout my career, I know we just need to feel validated and heard.

While growing up, kids' emotions are big.

Just because parents have navigated these emotions doesn't mean their children have. Parents, with their adult perspective and experience, often handle these feelings more gracefully. It can be really valuable to share with your children how you've worked through these emotions, including any feelings of resentment, or hate because they may be experiencing similar feelings themselves.

I also like to have siblings identify what about the disability they love, while allowing them the freedom to say what they hate in the same breath. Creating a space where they can express these feelings honestly — without guilt or shame — can be incredibly freeing. This exercise allows them to openly share their mixed emotions and provides a safe outlet for their true feelings.

I never recalled asking my parents if they wish Nick didn't have his disability. I was mature enough to know that was never an option, so I never allowed myself to go there. I guess I didn't want my brother to be different. Although I have shared how I hated his disability, please know it coexisted with so much love for him.

HE WAS THE OLDER BROTHER that always wanted to play and be around me.

HE WAS THE OLDER BROTHER who could make me laugh at the littlest things.

HE WAS THE OLDER BROTHER who trusted me.

HE WAS THE OLDER BROTHER who loved me unconditionally.

HE WAS THE OLDER BROTHER who needed me, and I was the sister who wanted to be needed.

To change him was never a thought inside me.

The only time I can remember my mom ever wondering "what if Nick didn't have a disability" was in reference to his height. Despite doctors predicting Nick would have dwarfism due to his syndrome, he grew to be 6 foot 4 inches. It was a casual comment from my mom, one that didn't seem significant at the time, yet it's funny how I still remember it vividly.

Mom said, "Can you imagine if Nick didn't have his disability? With his height, he'd make an incredible basketball player."

My response was simply, "Yeah, he probably would."

And that was the end of that.

I recall a social media post from my friend, Tiffany, who's raising two boys, one of whom has autism. Her words deeply resonated with me and left a lasting impression. It was clear she was reflecting on her own experiences, but also those of siblings like me. Her neurotypical 8-year-old son had made her think deeply about their family dynamics, and her response was spot-on. It's fascinating how kids process their feelings and how those reflections can prompt meaningful conversations.

Tiffany's Facebook post read:
My 8-year-old recently asked me, "Mom, are you happy that he has autism?"

It took my breath away and for a minute I struggled to answer it.

I know he is a person not just a diagnosis, but when your child has a profound disability, it's so enmeshed in who they are that it's difficult to separate the two.

If I say no, does that mean I don't love him as he is? If I say yes, does that mean I love the difficulties and struggles he faces everyday?

Every single day, parenting a child with a disability is filled with mixed emotions and questioning EVERYTHING.

So my answer was simple and as honest as I could be.

"I wish he didn't have to struggle so much, but this is his journey and his story, so we will love him as he is and support him the best we can."

Her response was spot on. I am no therapist (and actually Tiffany is), but she couldn't have navigated her response any better for her son. Special needs families often find themselves in a precarious position of justifying their emotions, especially when expressing the difficulties and challenges of their journey. There's an inherent societal pressure to balance any mention of hardship or frustration with an overwhelming display of love for their child with disabilities.

Unlike parents of neurotypical children who might freely express frustration without needing to justify their love, we feel compelled to immediately back up any negative emotion with a testament of our deep affection and commitment. This societal expectation forces us to suppress raw and authentic feelings, creating a perception that hate cannot coexist with love and joy in our lives. It's a constant battle against judgment and misunderstanding, where every statement of struggle must be carefully accompanied by reassurances of unwavering love.

Hate is a difficult emotion to unpack, but a necessary one to identify and express. Here is a summary of the advice I recommend on helping your neurotypical children grapple with any hate they may feel toward your family's disability journey.

Encourage Open Expression

To encourage open expression about difficult emotions like hate, it's important to normalize these feelings and reassure your child that experiencing them doesn't make them a bad person or mean they truly "hate" their sibling. You could start by saying something like, "I know sometimes it might feel really hard, and you might even feel like you hate your sibling in those moments. That's OK to feel, and I want you to know it doesn't mean you actually hate them."

Ask gentle, non-judgmental questions, such as, "Can you tell me about what made you feel that way?" or "What's the hardest part for you right now?" This allows your child to explore their emotions and feel heard without guilt or shame. You can also model understanding by acknowledging the challenges they face: "I can understand why you feel that way — it's frustrating when things are tough or when it feels like everything is focused on your sibling."

Reassure them that these deep emotions are temporary and don't define their relationship with their sibling. Help them find ways to process those feelings, saying something like, "It's OK to feel anger or frustration, but let's work on ways to handle those feelings when they come up, so they don't overwhelm you."

Teach them how to cope and move through these feelings by offering strategies like talking through their emotions, taking breaks when they're feeling upset, or finding ways to focus on their own interests. Reinforce the idea that it's healthy to express difficult emotions, but that those emotions don't define who they are or the love they have for their sibling. By helping them navigate these intense emotions, you're showing them that even feelings like hate are part of being human — and that they can move through them with support and understanding.

Share Your Own Experiences
Share with your children how you've navigated similar emotions. By showing them that you've experienced and managed these feelings, you help them feel less isolated in their own internal, emotional struggles.

Help Them Identify Positive Aspects
Encourage them to also identify and express what they appreciate about their sibling or the situation. Balancing negative feelings with positive reflections can provide a more comprehensive view and reduce guilt.

Provide Emotional Support
Offer emotional support and guidance. Help them work through their emotions by discussing coping strategies and reassuring them that their feelings are normal and manageable.

JEALOUSY
Of all the emotions I cover in this book, jealousy is the one that least affected me. I don't remember feeling jealous while growing up with Nick, except for when I thought I was adopted because there were more photos of him in the family albums. To be honest, I think I was overwhelmed with guilt so much that there was no room to feel jealous. I also think my personality kept jealousy at bay. I was a strong,

independent girl with fierce determination to write my own story. It was the way my parents raised me, but honestly it was a gift God granted me. My parents never allowed me to doubt my potential. I remember, as a kid, Mom and Dad telling me more times than I can count that I can do anything I set my mind to.

Maybe that was formed as a direct result of my brother having a disability? Nick's life was filled with limitations, which meant that my parents saw only possibilities for me.

For the sake of research and accuracy, I texted my mom and asked if she remembered a time that I was jealous of Nick? To my surprise, she had a clear memory that she immediately texted back. If you knew my mom, you would understand why this is a surprise. I love her, but Sharon Boarman can't really remember most things.

Her text: We always took your brother to the races. (In my hometown we had a local stock car racetrack and my brother loved going there to watch the races on Sunday.) At one of the races we won a Dr. Pepper themed go-kart. When we brought it home and you saw it, you wanted to be the first to ride it, but we said your brother was going to ride it first. You said, "Nick always gets to go first."

But to me, this memory depicts a typical sibling jealousy. It seems to be no different than any other siblings fighting for the front seat, fighting over who went first, or sharing a favorite toy – all of which Nick and I did.

It wasn't until working through this chapter that I realized the times I felt I went unnoticed, were times I felt jealous. When people were making small talk with me or with my family, everyone would ask about my brother and want to hear the latest funny Nick story. While I genuinely enjoyed sharing these stories and talking about Nick, it was like that was all we ever talked about.

People saw me as the go-between, the one who could relay the news about Nick or give them the inside scoop on his latest antics. He became everyone's friend, even within my own circle of friends. On one hand, I loved that they cared about him and that he could bring so much joy to people. But on the other hand, there were moments when I wished they'd ask about me or take an interest in my life. It sometimes felt like I was just the messenger, the one who made the connections happen, but I wasn't the focus of anyone's attention.

I was grateful for the bond they shared with him, yet there were times when I wished they shared the same with me. The jealousy was never about not wanting Nick to have friends, but more about wanting to be seen too.

Expressing these feelings of jealousy makes me feel guilty and selfish. Just talking about it out loud feels wrong, like I shouldn't think this way. It feels awkward and uncomfortable, the kind of thing that makes you cringe and wonder if you've crossed a line. I don't want anyone to think that I didn't love my brother or that I wasn't happy for him. It's just that the focus on him sometimes left me in the background, and admitting that hurts.

But that's why so many siblings stay silent; it's easier to keep those feelings to yourself than risk being misunderstood. Or, we come to understand that things can't always change, and while our family and friends are doing their best, we learn how to process, cope, and move forward.

And yet, not talking about it can make you feel isolated, as if you're the only one who struggles with these thoughts. It's a tough place to be, feeling like you can't win whether you speak up and risk being misunderstood or stay quiet and risk isolation.

A sibling once shared something with me that I believe every parent needs to hear: "My parents fight so hard for inclusion for my sister — it's always their top priority. But sometimes, it feels like that means I'm left facing my own kind of exclusion." That insight carries so much weight, revealing the unseen struggles siblings sometimes face. It's a reminder that while advocating for one child, it's crucial not to unintentionally overlook the emotional needs of another.

Create a safe space for your children to talk. Let them feel jealous, even if you can't fix it. It doesn't mean they're wrong for feeling that way. Siblings often get jealous of each other, whether there's a disability in the mix or not.

But when it comes to a sibling with a disability, we often act like jealousy is something to be ashamed of, like it's something that should be hidden away. This isn't true, and it's unfair to the sibling who feels this way. It's OK for them to feel whatever they're feeling, even if it's complicated. Acknowledge it, talk about it, and give them the support they need to process it without judgment. By doing this, you help them work through their emotions and let them know that it's OK to be honest about how they feel.

Although jealousy wasn't a profound emotion for me, I believe it needs a place in this book. In fact, it is one of the most common ones that I hear from the families that I am connected with in the disability community. And like I stated while laying the ground rules, special needs siblings may feel some, all or even none of the emotions I describe. Each of our journeys is unique to our own story.

I can't even count the number of times I've spoken with special needs families where jealousy runs deep. In many cases, parents feel a frustration toward their child's jealousy that they may not openly admit. They are frustrated because they believe they are doing their best, yet still feel the need to justify and defend themselves. This complex emotion in their children can stir up feelings of inadequacy for parents, making it even more challenging to navigate and address.

I can understand their frustration, however jealousy is a real emotion that needs to be handled delicately, not shut down. The most common conversation I have with parents about jealousy is when it is related to attention. Regardless of the family dynamics, when there are multiple children, parents constantly navigate the challenge of giving balanced attention to each one.

Parents strive to make sure all their children feel equally loved and supported. But in a special needs family, the challenge of balancing attention can feel overwhelming, especially when one child's needs are more demanding. It can leave you feeling exhausted as you work tirelessly to ensure everyone gets what they need.

Let me give you examples of when a child whose sibling has a disability might feel jealous in various situations:

Attention
Children may feel envious when their sibling receives more attention from parents or caregivers due to their disability, especially if it means their needs or achievements are overlooked.

Special Treatment
If the sibling with a disability receives special privileges or accommodations, such as extra time with parents or allowances for certain behaviors, or public recognition, their other sibling(s) may feel resentful or left out.

Resources
A neurotypical child might feel jealous when resources like time, money, or energy are primarily focused on their sibling's needs, leaving less available for them. For example, while a parent sees a new wheelchair, learning toy, or communication iPad as essential tools for their sibling with a disability, the neurotypical child might simply see it as their sibling getting something new that they didn't receive. This difference in perspective can create feelings of imbalance or unfairness.

Achievements
If the sibling with a disability achieves milestones — like learning to walk with assistance or communicating a new word — these accomplishments often come with an outpouring of praise and celebration from family members and friends. The neurotypical child might feel overshadowed, especially if their own achievements, like excelling at school, scoring a goal at soccer, or learning a new skill, don't receive the same level of excitement or attention.

For example, the neurotypical child may ace a test, but if the family's focus is on the sibling's progress in therapy, their success might feel less acknowledged or even overlooked. This can create feelings of being unnoticed or unimportant, even though both milestones are valuable in different ways.

Relationships

A child may feel jealous if their sibling's disability influences social interactions or relationships in ways that set them apart. This can happen when the sibling receives more attention from friends or family, or when others intentionally focus on the sibling in social situations to include them or make them the center of attention.

I often hear parents grappling with feelings of guilt and confusion as they try to navigate the delicate balance of attention within their family dynamic. They express concerns about their child's potential resentment and desperately seek solutions to justify the attention given to their sibling with a disability.

But here's the thing — parenting isn't about justification. It's about love, understanding, and empathy. Here are some tips to help your neurotypical children grapple with jealousy.

Acknowledge and Validate Emotions

While it's natural to feel defensive when faced with accusations of favoritism, it's essential to acknowledge and validate the emotions of all children involved. Dismissing or discrediting a child's feelings of jealousy only serves to invalidate their experiences and deepen any existing rifts.

Encourage Open Conversations

To address jealousy with your neurotypical child, start by acknowledging that it's a natural feeling, especially in a family where attention and resources may often be focused on a sibling with a disability. Begin the conversation by saying something like, "I know it might be hard sometimes when your sibling needs extra attention or gets things that you don't. It's OK if that makes you feel upset or jealous

— it doesn't mean you love them any less or that you're a bad person for feeling this way."

Ask them open-ended questions to encourage sharing, such as, "Can you tell me about a time when you felt jealous?" or "How do you feel when your sibling gets something new or when we have to spend extra time helping them?" This helps create a space where they can freely express their feelings without fear of judgment.

After listening, explain that while their sibling's needs might sometimes require more focus, it doesn't diminish their own importance. Let them know, "Your feelings are important, too, and I want to make sure you feel seen and heard." Reinforce that jealousy is a normal part of any sibling relationship, but what matters is how you handle it as a family. Assure them that they will have moments where the focus is on them and that both their needs and desires are equally valued.

By openly discussing jealousy, you help your child understand their feelings and realize that it's OK to feel conflicted at times, all while reassuring them of their unique and valued place in the family.

By creating an environment of understanding and mutual respect, you can navigate these complex emotions together as a family, without the need for justification or defense.

Plan Individual Time
If you're worried about not giving your children enough attention, try asking them what they'd like from you this month. Plan a date or a one on one activity with them — whatever you can do to show you care. This dedicated time can be used for activities they enjoy, allowing them to express themselves and receive undivided attention. It doesn't have to be anything grand; sometimes it's just about being intentional.

Be Intentional in Your Love
People often think that love should just happen naturally, that if you care enough, everything will fall into place. Stop feeding yourself that line. It's a comforting thought, but it's not always true. Sometimes you

have to work at it, even plan it. Just like marriage, love takes effort. If you need to put a reminder on your phone or mark it on the calendar, do it. Don't worry about what others might think. It doesn't mean you love your family any less; in fact, it shows that you care enough to make them a priority. So don't let shame or guilt hold you back from doing what you need to do to be there for your spouse, children, family, friends – all of the people who need you.

Celebrate Their Achievements

Balanced attention plus encouragement is key. Celebrating their achievements and milestones, no matter how small, ensures they feel valued and recognized. Praising their efforts and accomplishments helps build their self-esteem and reminds them of their unique contributions.

Involve Them in Sibling Care

Involving neurotypical children in the care and support of their sibling with a disability can also be beneficial. When done appropriately, this involvement provides a sense of teamwork and shared responsibility, reducing feelings of competition. However, it's important that these responsibilities do not become burdensome or overwhelming.

Maintain Open Communication About Family Dynamics

Maintain an open dialogue about the family dynamics, explaining why certain accommodations or attention might be necessary for their sibling. This helps the neurotypical child understand the reasons behind the special treatment, reducing feelings of resentment.

Encourage Regular Dialogue

Encourage your neurotypical child to regularly voice their feelings and concerns. This practice ensures they feel included, important, and connected to the family's journey.

PRIDE

As a special needs sibling, I've encountered countless others who, like me, feel a deep sense of pride in the role they play in their sibling's life. This pride is often rooted in love, compassion, and a desire to be there for someone who may need extra support. It's a beautiful emotion, one that parents cherish as they see their neurotypical children step up with such responsibility and care. However, this pride, while powerful and positive, can sometimes evolve into an unhealthy sense of possession. It can manifest as a belief that their sibling or family cannot succeed or be cared for without their involvement. This shift, while well-intentioned, can lead to challenges that we will explore as we discuss how to empower both the journey of the neurotypical child and their sibling with a disability.

As Nick's sister, I've always felt a deep sense of pride and responsibility towards my big brother. This feeling isn't uncommon among other siblings in similar situations. It goes beyond just being a brother or sister; it's about being an advocate, a cheerleader, and sometimes a protector. I remember feeling as if Nick was not just my brother, but also a part of me. After all, so much of my own identity was rooted in being his sister. This pride influenced how I interacted with others, especially when discussing Nick's achievements or challenges — I took great joy in highlighting his strengths and bringing him into the spotlight.

One of the most rewarding parts of having a sibling with a disability is celebrating their victories, no matter how small. Whether it was mastering a new skill, overcoming a fear, or navigating a challenging situation, each accomplishment felt like a triumph for our entire family. These moments taught me resilience, perseverance, and the value of never taking life for granted.

Despite the challenges, I wouldn't trade my experience for anything. The bond Nick and I share is unique and special, built through a lifetime of shared experiences, laughter, tears, and everything in between. As his sister, I've had the privilege of being his confidant, ally, and friend — roles that define who I am, even today.

But it's not uncommon for that pride to progress into possessiveness. Parents, it's important to recognize when siblings to those with disabilities might overdevelop that sense of possessiveness. Your child may feel that no one else can be the kind of friend or caregiver their sibling needs, driven by the belief that only they truly understand what their sibling is going through. This can lead to an overprotective nature, fueled by the fear of how society might treat their brother or sister.

This protective instinct is a sign of deep love, but also extreme internal pressure. While it reflects their commitment, it can also become a heavy burden, making it difficult for them to find their own space and pursue their own goals. When they see themselves primarily as a protector, it can limit their personal growth and development.

In the next two stories, shared with me by friends, we'll explore how some siblings navigate this complex blend of emotions, showing how pride in caring for their sibling can also carry a heavy weight and the desire to always be present.

Emma, a bright and caring 10-year-old, has a younger brother, Liam, who has cerebral palsy. They share a special bond that is unlike any other. Each night, Emma reads Liam his favorite bedtime story, tucking him in with a gentle kiss on the forehead. This nightly ritual was their time — a moment of peace and connection that Liam cherished deeply.

One Friday night, Emma was spending the night at her best friend's house. It was supposed to be a night of fun, laughter, and sleepover games. But as the evening went on, Emma couldn't shake the feeling that something was missing. She knew Liam would miss their story time and that he would need his medicine before bed.

Around 8 p.m., Emma asked her friend's parents if she could call home. Worried about her brother, she asked her mom if Liam had taken his medicine and if he had asked for her. Her mother assured her that everything was fine, but in the background, Emma could hear Liam's soft cries. Her heart sank. She knew he was missing her and their nightly routine.

Without hesitation, Emma told her mom, "Come pick me up. I need to be there for Liam. He needs me." Her mom tried to comfort her, saying that Liam would be OK for one night, but Emma insisted. She knew the role she played in Liam's life, and she took immense pride in that. She couldn't bear the thought of him being sad and needing her.

Soon after, Emma's mom arrived to take her home. As soon as she walked in the door, Emma rushed to Liam's side, wiped away his tears, and picked up the storybook they always read together. Liam's face lit up as Emma began to read, her voice soothing him as only she could.

This story beautifully illustrates the depth of Emma's heart, compassion, and pride in her role as Liam's sister. Her decision to leave a fun sleepover to be there for her brother demonstrates a maturity and love beyond her years. Emma's sense of pride in caring for Liam is evident — she knows the importance of her presence in his life and the comfort she provides.

Yet, mixed with this pride is a weight of responsibility and worry. Emma's concern for Liam's well-being shows that while she embraces her role with love, it also comes with the heavy feeling and responsibility of ensuring his happiness and safety. It's a reminder of the emotional sacrifice some siblings may feel they need to make. This story is a powerful example of how pride in being a special needs sibling can be both a source of strength and a heavy load to carry.

I remember a similar situation occurring with one of my friends. This couple has two daughters: a neurotypical 8-year-old and a 3-year-old with intense medical needs. The younger daughter requires life-saving machines and full-time nursing staff at home. Because of my own personal experiences as a sibling, the girls' father asked for advice about how to understand the behavior he and his wife were seeing in their neurotypical daughter.

The father shared his worries with me, his voice trembling with emotion.

"I think my 8-year-old daughter is struggling with something I can't quite put my finger on, and I'd really value your perspective as a sibling," he said.

He described how his older daughter doesn't sleep well at night and seems uninterested in playing when she comes home from school. Instead, she's always by her sister's side — feeding her, giving her baths, stroking her hair. He admitted it gets frustrating because she's constantly there, and they can't convince her to step away. Sometimes, in their efforts to care for the younger daughter, they lose patience with her because she's always in the way.

I asked him if they had ever talked with her about why she likes helping so much or what she hopes to achieve by doing so. He told me she simply insists she wants to help her sister.

I explained that at 8 years old, she might not yet have the emotional maturity to fully understand or express what she's really feeling. It's possible that she's helping out of fear — fear that her sister might die. Or perhaps she's trying to connect with her sister in the only way she knows how, by mimicking how her parents care for her.

She might even see how overwhelmed her parents are, juggling care for her sister, work, and daily chores, and she wants to help ease their burden so they can spend more time with her. I reassured him that none of these reasons are bad; they're natural emotions that need to be talked about and worked through.

This 8-year-old feels a unique bond and responsibility towards her sister that goes beyond typical sibling relationships. This pride in being a crucial part of her sister's life can be a powerful and positive force, shaping her identity and fostering a strong sense of empathy and compassion. While it's essential to guide and support her through her fears and anxieties, it's equally important to recognize and celebrate the pride she feels in her role. This pride can be a source of strength for her, helping her navigate the challenges and joys of being a sibling to someone with a disability.

Here are some tangible ways to help your neurotypical children understand the pride they feel for their sibling with a disability and cope with any possessiveness or fears that may come with that sense of

> **EMOTIONS ARE OUR GREATEST TEACHERS. WHEN WE LEARN TO UNDERSTAND AND EMBRACE THEM, WE GAIN THE STRENGTH TO** *grow and heal*

pride.

Encourage Open Communication

Regularly checking in with your child about their feelings and experiences as a sibling is crucial for their emotional well-being. Create a safe space where they can openly express how they feel about their role in the family. Encourage them to talk about the pride they may feel in helping their sibling with a disability — whether it's assisting with daily tasks or being a source of comfort.

While this pride can be a positive and empowering emotion, it can sometimes lead to an overwhelming sense of responsibility or over protectiveness. Your child might feel that it's their job to shield their sibling from challenges or negative reactions from others, which can be a heavy emotional burden.

By discussing these feelings, you help your child recognize that while it's wonderful to care deeply for their sibling, they don't have to carry the weight of protecting them from everything. It's important to help them find balance, allowing them to feel pride in their supportive role without feeling like they have to be a constant caretaker.

Open dialogue also reinforces that it's normal to have mixed emotions — feeling proud but also sometimes frustrated or overwhelmed — and that these emotions are valid. Acknowledging both the positive and challenging aspects of their sibling relationship will give your child a more rounded understanding of their role and ensure they don't feel isolated in their feelings.

Balance Praise and Independence

While it's important to acknowledge and praise your child for their role in their sibling's life, also encourage them to pursue their own interests and activities. Remind them that their value is not solely tied to their sibling role and that it's OK to have separate goals and hobbies.

Guide Healthy Boundaries

Help your child understand the importance of setting boundaries.

Teach them that while their pride in supporting their sibling is admirable, they don't have to be involved in every aspect of their sibling's care. Encourage them to take breaks and have time for themselves without feeling guilty.

Model Self-Care and Compassion

Demonstrating self-care sets an important example for your child, showing that caring for themselves is just as vital as caring for others. By making self-care a family value, you help your child understand that their own needs matter too, which encourages a more balanced approach to pride and responsibility.

When a child feels proud of supporting their sibling, it can sometimes lead to overextending themselves. Teaching them the importance of setting boundaries and caring for their own well-being helps them manage that pride without feeling overwhelmed or guilty for stepping back when necessary. This balance fosters healthier relationships and ensures that their sense of responsibility remains a source of positive connection rather than pressure.

Acknowledge Their Unique Perspective

Validate not only the pride they feel but also the weight that comes with it. Acknowledge that their role in the family is significant, and the pride they take in helping their sibling is a positive and valuable trait. However, emphasize that it's normal to have mixed feelings — such as pride mixed with worry, anxiety, frustration or fatigue — and that both are valid.

By recognizing and celebrating the child's contributions, you reinforce their confidence and sense of self-worth. At the same time, it's essential to remind them that their worth is not solely tied to their role as a helper, ensuring they don't feel overly defined by it. This balance of validation helps them maintain a healthy relationship with the pride they feel, without letting it become overwhelming.

Provide Reassurance and Flexibility

Reassure your child that they are not solely responsible for their sibling's well-being. Emphasize that it's OK to step back sometimes and that their sibling will still be well cared for. This flexibility allows them to take pride in their role without feeling overwhelmed by it.

EMOTIONS HAVE TO BE PART OF THE STORY

I know I've talked a lot about the tougher emotions that special needs siblings often face, and I get that for some, it might feel like a heavy load. But it's important to remember that these emotions, while difficult, aren't necessarily bad. A lot of them are just a natural part of growing up, for all siblings, regardless if they have a brother or sister with a disability.

It's almost as if parents believe that their child's emotional struggles are a direct reflection of their parenting or that they've somehow failed by not shielding their kids from these feelings. But the truth is, emotions are complex and unpredictable, and it's natural for all children to experience a wide range of them.

My advice?

Don't get discouraged by your child's emotions. Instead of seeing these emotions as something to be fixed or avoided, they should be viewed as opportunities for growth and connection. By embracing the reality that these feelings are part of life, especially in families with disabilities, parents can better support their children in working through them, helping them to develop resilience and empathy.

My best friend, a therapist, once shared a profound insight with me: "It's OK to acknowledge your feelings and take time to sit with them. But remember, you can't stay there forever. Eventually, you need to move through them."

Encourage your neurotypical children to sit with and feel their feelings, but not to dwell on them. These emotions can actually turn into important life lessons, offering deep insights into what it means to be human.

Amidst the challenges, there are also beautiful emotions that can flourish in special needs siblings — gratitude, intentionality, meaningful love, and a strong sense of purpose. These are the kinds of feelings that even adults struggle to grasp, yet they come naturally to us siblings.

It might take some time to fully understand these emotions, but growth is a journey, not a race. Let it happen naturally, without rushing. Just like the seasons change, so do our emotions, sometimes appearing out of nowhere.

Looking back on my own childhood, I couldn't fully grasp or explain these feelings, even to myself. It wasn't until I became an adult that I could really process and appreciate them. To be honest, writing this book at 40 years old has helped me process feelings and events in my life that I didn't fully understand until typing them here.

So, if you ever find yourself lying awake at night, worried that your neurotypical kids might feel resentful or burdened by their sibling with a disability, I'm here to tell you that's likely not the case.

Kids will be kids. Let them feel, learn, and grow through their emotions. Don't always assume their big feelings are just because they're special needs siblings. Emotions are a part of being human, and as we walk this path together, we find that embracing and understanding them is a big part of our growth.

By investing your time into understanding your neurotypical child's perspective and the emotional impact of being a special needs sibling, you're showing just how much you care. It's a testament to your dedication as a parent, recognizing the unique challenges each of your children faces. You're putting in the work to help them navigate these emotions, ensuring they feel seen, valued, and supported as they grow.

As someone who has walked this path both personally and professionally, I've seen firsthand how these challenges can shape a family. In my career and life as a special needs sibling, I've learned that there are strategies that can truly make a difference. I want to leave you with tangible advice that I've found to be effective, drawn from my experiences working with families like yours and from my own journey.

Explaining the Disability
When parents explain the nature of the sibling's disability, it's crucial to gauge how much the neurotypical child understands and to address any confusion, fear, or misconceptions they might have.

Behavioral Differences
When the sibling with a disability exhibits challenging behaviors, parents should recognize the neurotypical child's feelings of embarrassment, frustration, or confusion and help them process these emotions.

Social Situations
In social settings where the sibling with a disability might be treated differently, parents need to be attuned to the neurotypical child's potential feelings of jealousy, exclusion, or protectiveness.

Time and Attention
When the sibling with a disability requires more parental attention, it's important to validate the neurotypical child's feelings of neglect or resentment and find ways to ensure they also feel loved, seen and valued.

Celebrating Milestones
When celebrating the achievements of the sibling with a disability, parents should be aware of the neurotypical child's feelings and ensure their accomplishments are equally recognized and celebrated.

School and Extracurricular Activities
Balancing the needs of both children can be challenging. Parents should consider the emotional impact on the neurotypical child if they have to miss out on activities or opportunities due to their sibling's needs.

"AS SPECIAL NEEDS PARENTS, YOU NAVIGATE A JOURNEY *without a manual* YET YOUR DEDICATION AND LOVE BECOME THE *guiding compass* FOR YOUR ENTIRE FAMILY."

Peer Reactions

When peers react to the sibling's disability, parents need to help the neurotypical child navigate their emotions, whether it's feeling defensive, embarrassed, or protective.

Family Dynamics

During family discussions about future plans, such as guardianship or care for the sibling with a disability, parents should be sensitive to the neurotypical child's concerns, fears, and sense of responsibility.

CHAPTER 6

SEEDS: YOUR GUIDEBOOK TO SUPPORTING NEUROTYPICAL CHILDREN

As we reach the final part of this book, I'm excited to step into a role that has always felt natural to me — guiding parents through the often chaotic and unpredictable journey we special needs families navigate.

You see, problem-solving has always been at the core of who I am. When I saw that my brother wasn't getting the education he deserved, I became a special education teacher. Later, when I realized my students had nowhere to go after graduation, I left the classroom to start a nonprofit, even though I had no experience running an organization. That nonprofit, Puzzle Pieces, now serves my community. providing essential services for those with disabilities.

With that same passion, I want to equip you with practical action steps to help you better understand and support your neurotypical children — providing solutions that can serve as a foundation for your journey. As special needs parents, you're doing everything you can for your child with a disability, even though there's no manual for this journey. You connect with other parents, go to conferences, and work closely with educators and therapists to find the best path forward.

But sometimes, in all of that, it's easy to overlook how your neurotypical children are processing everything.

How do you strike a balance?

How do you ensure ALL of your children are supported equally when the needs of one are so great?

And how do you avoid the guilt that creeps in, worrying that your kids might grow up resenting you if you fail to find that balance?

I get it. While I haven't been in your shoes, I've seen and heard the worry in my parents and with the hundreds of families I support through my nonprofit.

That's why I wanted to make things easier for you. I have put together a guide, a framework of five strategies that I call SEEDS, to help you connect with your neurotypical children, understand their perspective, and ease some of the pressure you might feel. This guide is about finding that balance, making sure every child feels seen and heard, and helping your family navigate your unique special needs journey together.

One thing about me: I love a good acronym. Not only does SEEDS stand for five individual strategies that I believe could be instrumental in helping you support your neurotypical children, but it is also a beautiful analogy of planting and cultivating practices to help you become a proactive, better prepared parent.

To me, SEEDS symbolizes the importance of nurturing knowledge, understanding, and empathy within a special needs family, especially when it comes to sibling relationships. Just as a seed needs care to grow, parents need to support and guide these relationships with patience and love. Over time, this care helps each member of the family thrive. How did I come up with SEEDS? It's an interesting story, one that I think is worth telling. Although the five strategies are drawn from what my parents did to help me become the sibling – and woman – I am today, the way this framework came together is pretty special.

When my friend, Kate, asked me to speak at her annual caregiver's retreat, I was honored. Kate is an autism mom who founded Finding Cooper's Voice, a blog that has garnered millions of followers for Kate's vulnerable approach to sharing her story. She and I met through our social media platforms and instantly connected.

My presentation, "Finding Joy in the Hard," was scheduled for the second night of the retreat. But when I arrived, I was asked to also lead a breakout session about growing up as a sibling to someone with a disability.

Without hesitation, I agreed. Although I didn't have a formal presentation ready, I felt like I could wing it. After all, if there was one thing I knew about, it was being Nick's little sister. My main concern was whether my perspective as a sibling would offer real value to the moms attending the retreat.

As I prepared for the 30-minute session, I reflected on my own experiences and realized how central my parents were to my story. They had never attended a retreat, never connected with other special needs parents, and never took time for respite. My brother, the heart of our family, was always with them, and I wasn't sure they even needed or wanted a break.

I remembered a specific moment from when I was in my 20s, living just 20 minutes from my parents and brother. On January 19th, I called to wish them a happy wedding anniversary. I was always in awe of how they managed to stay together and cherish their anniversary amidst the challenges of raising a child with a disability. During that call, I suggested that they let my brother stay with me for the weekend while they took some time for themselves.

My mom's response was exactly what I expected: "This wedding anniversary is no different than the years before, and we always have Nick there. He's just part of us. We wouldn't know what to do without him, and he probably wouldn't want to stay anyway."

That memory has stayed with me, highlighting how deeply ingrained Nick was in their lives. It made me realize how my parents never truly navigated life without him.

My goal for this retreat had been to inspire and uplift these women, reminding them of their incredible worth before they returned to their demanding roles. But that focus shifted in preparing for the breakout session, where I found myself reflecting on the challenges my parents faced without a road map or support system. This reflection helped me find the words to honor their dedication and share my perspective as a special needs sibling.

I walked into that breakout session with an index card that read:

S – Stop Thinking You Wear Two Different Hats
E – Emotional Intelligence Must Be Considered
E – Empower Their Journey
D – Don't Avoid The Hard Talks
S – Share Emotions Respectfully

As you read through the remainder of this book learning about SEEDS, I hope that each of these five strategies resonates with you, alleviating that feeling of being overwhelmed and burdened by guilt. I know you are stretched thin, struggling to balance your love for all your children while meeting the intense needs of one. Remember, you're not alone — many others are also seeking clarity in understanding their neurotypical children.

But most of all, I hope SEEDS becomes a voice for siblings who may not yet have the words to express their needs. Like me, I know they often carry their emotions quietly, not wanting to add to their parents' stress, worry and fears. SEEDS aims to provide the insight needed for parents to connect with and support these siblings, helping to prevent the family from feeling fractured.

Siblings, may you find validation and connection in these pages. Your feelings and experiences matter deeply. This chapter is meant to strengthen family bonds and remind you of your essential role in your family's journey. Your voice and your place in this world are significant and valued.

STOP THINKING YOU WEAR TWO HATS

Given my experience as a special needs sibling and through my role as a disability service provider, I've had numerous candid conversations with special needs parents who often describe an overwhelming sense of grief, grappling with the challenge of balancing two distinct roles – the feeling of wearing two different hats.

Does this sound familiar?

With one hat, you are a typical mom or dad who loves and supports your neurotypical child. You dream alongside them, celebrate their milestones, and invest in their future, trying to ensure they have every opportunity to thrive. You want to be there for their everyday moments, from school projects to baseball games, and to share in their hopes, fears, and aspirations.

With the other hat, you are an advocate, caregiver, and fierce protector for your child with a disability, often feeling the weight of the world on your shoulders. You worry about their future, their well-being, and whether they're getting the support and resources they need to reach their full potential.

This second hat comes with constant concerns — about navigating the complexities of medical care, therapies, and education, about finding the right balance of independence and protection, and about how to ensure your child's happiness and security in a world that isn't always accommodating.

You spend most of your time wearing this second hat because it's where you're needed most. So often, you feel that the "typical mom/dad hat" doesn't need to be worn as frequently because your neurotypical children are thriving in comparison to your child with a disability. It's a natural instinct for you to focus where you feel most needed and wanted, which often means that your "special needs hat" gets worn more often.

You write your own story in this role as a special needs parent, growing more comfortable with it over time. Yet, when you go out, you wonder: Is this hat all others see? Is this hat what I want them to see? The thought lingers, making you question how you're perceived and whether you're seen for all the complexities you manage daily.

The challenge lies in balancing these hats – these two roles – trying to be fully present for each child, yet feeling the strain of spreading yourself too thin, worried that one role may overshadow the other.

Let's examine Lydia's story.

Lydia was a mother who always seemed to be in two places at once. She had two children — Josh, her neurotypical son who was twelve, and Sophie, her eight-year-old daughter with cerebral palsy. From the outside, people saw a mom who balanced it all. She was at every school event, cheered at every sports game, and was deeply involved in the disability community. But what people didn't see was the constant battle Lydia fought within herself.

It was a regular Wednesday evening, and Lydia was in the kitchen, preparing dinner while keeping an eye on Josh and Sophie in the living room. Josh was doing his homework, and Sophie was playing with her adapted toys. Lydia was trying to split her attention between them, making sure Josh's math questions were answered while also ensuring Sophie was entertained and safe. It was a delicate balancing act, and she often felt like she was failing one child while focusing on the other.

The internal struggle was always there. When she spent time with Sophie, she felt guilty for not being more present for Josh. When she dedicated time to Josh, she worried that Sophie wasn't getting the support she needed. Lydia felt like she had to be two different moms — one who could cheer and keep up with Josh at his soccer games, and another who could shift gears to manage Sophie's therapy sessions and medical appointments.

One evening, as she was tucking Josh into bed, he asked, "Mom, why don't we ever go out to eat at a restaurant?"

It hit her that they hadn't had a simple family dinner outside of the house in months. The logistics of taking Sophie out with her wheelchair and medical equipment seemed overwhelming, and she realized how much she had been sacrificing to meet Sophie's needs. At that moment, Lydia felt the full weight of her internal battle. She was torn between giving Josh a normal childhood and providing the necessary care for Sophie.

That night, after the kids were asleep, Lydia broke down in tears. She felt she wasn't doing enough for either of her children.

While this story is fictional for the purpose of this book, it is very similar to the conversations I have had with the parents I serve. Special needs parents, especially moms, feel as though they have two distinct parental roles – raising their neurotypical children and raising their child with a disability.

I have heard countless stories like Lydia's and each time a parent shared this two-hat scenario with me, I was left at a loss for words.

During my childhood, I never felt my mom was trying to wear two hats, trying to be two different moms. To me, she was just Mom. The mom who tirelessly tended to both Nick and I, supporting our needs to the best of her ability. I never perceived any difference because, in my eyes, all my mom showed was love.

And I can tell you that, more than likely, your kids see the same – a mom or dad who does it all, providing them the love they need to grow and thrive.

But I will be honest. That isn't always the case. I have spoken with siblings who see and feel their parents assume a different parental role when it comes to their sibling with a disability.

One day during a mentoring session, a young girl asked me a question that struck a deep chord. She wanted to know why her mom always referred to herself as a "special needs mom."

"She talks about it with everyone," the girl said, "and even with other special needs moms. She says she has to put on this special needs hat now. But if she's a special needs mom, then what kind of mom is she to me? Do I get a different mom? I don't understand. What if I want her to be a special needs mom to me because she seems to enjoy that more?"

Her words were filled with confusion and a hint of hurt.

I took a deep breath and gently explained to her, "Your mom doesn't mean that she is literally a different type of mom to your sister than she is to you. It's not about comparing or competing. It's her way of describing the mindset she switches into to meet the different needs of each of her children. She loves you both deeply and equally, and being a 'special needs mom' is just one way she expresses the care and attention your sister requires."

The girl seemed to ponder this for a moment, and I could see the wheels turning in her mind. "So, she's the same mom to both of us, just in different ways?" she asked, seeking clarity.

"Exactly," I replied. "Your mom is a loving mom to both of you. She doesn't enjoy being a special needs mom more than being your mom. She loves you both and wants to be there for you in the best way she can. Sometimes, that means wearing different 'hats' for different situations, but it doesn't change her love for you."

As the call ended, I hoped my words had brought some comfort and understanding to her young heart. It's important for all siblings to know that their parents' love isn't divided but shared in unique and beautiful ways.

Reading the story above, it's crucial to recognize the profound impact your words and actions have on your children. As a parent, understanding that your children perceive the distinctions you make, even unintentionally, can help you shift your mindset and approach. Be mindful of the language you use and strive to communicate, both directly and indirectly, with equal love and dedication to all your children.

But also stop chasing unattainable perfection and simply be "Mom" or "Dad." Because that is more than enough.

What would happen if you let go of the belief that you're giving less to one child than the other?

What if you quit comparing yourself to your own evolving roles as a mom or dad to multiple kids with diverse needs?

You're raising unique children, and it's not about choosing one over the other. It's about making each child feel valued and loved. Find the path that works for you, and walk it confidently, knowing it's right for your family. There's no need to split yourself in half; instead, discover the harmony within the chaos and ensure each child knows they are deeply loved.

At the end of the day, you hold just one title in their eyes. Release yourself from the pressure of chasing a perfect balance or trying to measure up to an imaginary checklist. Perfect balance doesn't exist, and it's a burden you don't need to carry. **It's not about making every moment equal but about making your love count.** Focus on the quality of your connections, the meaningful moments you create, and the genuine care you show. Your children don't need a perfectly balanced scale; they need to feel valued, understood, and deeply loved in the unique ways they each require.

If you carry the weight of guilt, fearing you're not enough or worrying your child might resent you, they'll sense it. They'll see the guilt you carry and feel sad, thinking they're causing you pain just by needing your love. Break down those walls, relieve yourself of that burden, and show up without guilt. Embrace your role fully, and let your love shine

"
**TRUE STRENGTH IN A
FAMILY IS KNOWING THAT**
*vulnerability and resilience
can coexist side by side*
"

free from the shadows of self-doubt.

I once heard a profound idea that reshaped my perspective and mindset: there are essentially only two narratives that shape our lives in profound ways.

The first narrative is the story we tell ourselves. It's the internal dialogue that shapes our beliefs, attitudes, and sense of self.

"Am I doing enough to help my child thrive?"

"I feel like I'm failing them, no matter how hard I try."

"Why can't I be as patient and strong as other moms?"

"I'm exhausted, but I should be able to handle this better."

"Maybe if I did things differently, my child wouldn't struggle as much."

"Other moms seem to have it all together — why don't I?"

"I shouldn't need help, but I can't do this alone."

"If I were a better mom, my child would be making more progress."

"I worry that I'm neglecting my other children because of how much time my child with a disability requires."

"I'm constantly questioning my decisions — what if I'm making things worse?

"I love my child, but sometimes I don't know if I'm strong enough to keep going."

"Am I missing out on life because I'm so focused on managing my child's needs?"

"I wish I could take away their struggles — it's my job, but I feel powerless."

The story I know many special needs parents are silently telling themselves is that they aren't enough for all their children. They feel stretched thin, believing that one child's greater needs mean they're falling short with their other children. They fear their neurotypical child will one day resent them for the extra time and attention their sibling requires.

The story we tell ourselves can quickly consume us, shaping how we see the world and ourselves. When we repeatedly think we aren't good enough, those thoughts turn into emotions — feelings of inadequacy, guilt, and self-doubt. Over time, those emotions start to drive our actions, influencing how we engage with others, make decisions, and even take care of ourselves. It becomes a cycle where negative thoughts fuel negative emotions, which then impact our ability to show up as the best version of ourselves. Breaking that cycle starts by rewriting the narrative we choose to believe.

The second narrative, perhaps even more impactful, is the story others tell about us when we're no longer here. It's the legacy we leave behind, the imprint we make on the lives of those around us.

I imagine that the story your kids would tell about you would go something like this:

"Mom always made sure we both felt special, even when things were tough. She knew just when I needed a hug or some one-on-one time. She never let me feel less important, even when my sibling needed a lot of attention."

"She was the glue that held everything together. No matter how busy or overwhelmed she was, she made sure everyone felt loved and supported. She balanced her time and energy in a way that made each child feel seen and valued."

"Dad always knew when I needed to get away from everything. We'd go for walks around the neighborhood, just talking about anything. I didn't realize it then, but those walks were his way of making sure I felt understood."

"Mom always made sure we had Saturday mornings together, just us. She'd take me for donuts, and we'd sit in the car talking about whatever was on my mind. Those moments made me feel like I was her whole world, even when life was chaotic."

And the story your colleagues, friends and family members would tell about you would probably go something like this:

"I've always admired his strength and patience. He never complained, even when juggling so much. He taught his kids about kindness and acceptance through his own actions. He never shied away from the hard conversations or the challenges of raising his kids, no matter how different their needs were."

"She brought empathy and understanding into everything she did. Her perspective as a parent helped her connect with others on a deeper level. She always found a way to be present, whether at work or at home, and she never let anyone feel like they didn't matter."

Take a moment to let that sink in.

How you show up today — the love you give, the sacrifices you make, and the memories you create — becomes the legacy your children carry with them long after you're gone. Through the tired nights, the exhaustion, and the overwhelming uncertainties, it's being fully present in the moments that matters most.

Forget this idea of two hats. Embrace the fact that you are a unique and wonderful parent, capable of blending your roles into one powerful presence. You don't need to divide into different versions of yourself — each role is simply a part of who you are. By embracing all aspects of yourself, you're showing your children a powerful example of how to balance love and support in a unified way. Your ability to be present and supportive in every aspect of their lives makes you an incredible parent, and that's what truly matters.

EMOTIONAL INTELLIGENCE MUST BE CONSIDERED

Emotional intelligence is the ability to recognize, understand, and manage your own emotions while responding empathetically to others. It includes skills that help build strong relationships, communicate clearly, empathize, and make thoughtful decisions based on emotional awareness.

There is much debate on when one reaches emotional maturity. Researchers believe that women mature as early as a decade before men. Some experts say emotional maturity is reached in the 20s, others say as late as the 30s and 40s. Although there isn't a specific age or moment when someone fully matures in emotional intelligence, one thing is for sure: children are not emotionally mature.

Children's brains are in the early stages of development, making it difficult for them to fully grasp complex feelings or the emotions of others. They often react impulsively and may struggle to express themselves in healthy ways, needing guidance from adults to navigate their feelings and develop emotional intelligence over time.

Why does emotional intelligence factor into how you parent your neurotypical child in your special needs journey?

For siblings of individuals with disabilities, emotional intelligence plays a crucial role in navigating the unique dynamics of their family environment. Parents must recognize that each child may experience and express their emotions differently, emotionally maturing in their own time, and it's essential to provide a supportive and understanding space for them to do so.

You just read about a little girl who felt confused because her mom often talked about being a special needs mom, leaving her to wonder if she was getting a different kind of mom. Her thoughts and emotions reflect the reality of underdeveloped emotional intelligence.

I'd like to pose a question: Do you recall the day you first learned about your child's diagnosis?

I can imagine the intense wave of emotions you felt — shock, fear, heartbreak — as if the world you knew had suddenly shifted, leaving you uncertain of what the future holds. In that moment, you may have envisioned your child's life unfolding in ways you hadn't anticipated, with their milestones, education, marriage, and career looking different than you once imagined. For some, though not all, there's a period of grieving — not for the disability itself, but for the realization that the life you envisioned is now on a different path. Yet with this shift comes growth, acceptance, and the discovery of new, unexpected joys.

In the days, weeks, and even months after that diagnosis, you wrestled with this shift, possibly navigating the stages of grief as you grappled with the daunting uncertainties of your new reality.

I know that's how my mom recalls feeling when the doctor told her about Nick's rare diagnosis.

But as parents, you were processing these formidable emotions and coming to terms with your child's diagnosis as an adult, armed with an adult brain and perspective. You possess the capacity to process, reflect, draw from past experiences, foresee the future, and glean insights about what it means to embrace this journey with a child with a disability. **Yet, even armed with all the maturity and emotional intelligence that adulthood bestows upon us, it was and is still so damn hard.**

Now, let's shift our focus to your neurotypical child. Regardless of whether your neurotypical children are younger or older than their sibling with a disability, they are still children. It's essential to recognize that they can't navigate acceptance, understanding, and their emotions about their sibling's disability in the same manner as you did as an adult.

Why? Because they don't possess the same level of emotional intelligence. They lack the capacity to describe or fully comprehend the emotions they may be experiencing, especially when it comes to how those emotions relate to their life alongside their sibling.

It's crucial to appreciate this difference in emotional maturity and provide them with the guidance and support they need as they grow and learn to navigate the complexities of their unique family dynamics. Never assume they will understand one day and leave the conversation off the table. Talk about it. Find the words to help build their emotional experiences and form rational and empathetic emotions in their life experiences.

Here are examples I have witnessed in special needs families that illustrate how a parent may not fully consider their child's emotional intelligence on this journey:

They might hurriedly dismiss or avoid discussing their child's feelings because, as adults, they've already worked through those emotions and find it challenging to revisit them.

They could downplay their child's emotions in the moment or tell them not to dwell on it, thinking that because they've experienced and moved past those feelings, their child should too.

Parents might find it difficult to understand their child's emotions, assuming they appear out of nowhere because, from an adult's perspective, nothing major has changed in the family dynamic.

However, children and young adults often don't know how to grieve for the future or anticipate loss until they are directly confronted with real-life experiences that trigger these emotions.

Now, let's explore some communication insights for effectively meeting your child where they are at and considering their developmental stage: *Offer reassurance by saying, "It's completely normal to feel the way you do right now. It's normal to worry. I remember when I felt the same way."*

By sharing your personal experience, you can help your neurotypical children feel understood and less alone, creating a connection that eases their fears and provides comfort during a challenging time.

"It's natural to feel anxious about the unknown. We can't predict the future, but we can focus on what we can do now to help your sibling and support each other. Let's talk about your fears and find ways to manage them together. Remember, you're not alone in this, and we'll face whatever comes as a family."

Reinforce the idea that you are a family unit and will work through emotions together. Even if you are a single parent, you are still a family unit and that strong connection will bring your child comfort.

"It's completely normal to have mixed emotions. Supporting a sibling with a disability can bring up a lot of different feelings, including frustration and anger, alongside the love and support you have for them. It's OK to feel all these things. Let's discuss what's been making you feel frustrated and find ways to handle these emotions in a healthy way. You don't have to hide or suppress how you feel — talking about it can help."

Your child may not be able to identify a specific feeling or may feel many emotions at once. Help them find the cause of the feeling and put a name to it.

Next let's talk about language. While you want conversation with your neurotypical children to feel comfortable and relatable, you also need to realize that words matter. Your child's level of emotional intelligence will dictate how they interpret or misinterpret what you say in regards to your special needs family.

A friend of mine that teaches in a local middle school reached out to me about one of her students who she felt was struggling with her special needs family dynamic. This friend thought my sibling perspective could help her student process her emotions.

On an early morning Zoom call, I listened intently as this 11-year-old girl shared her experiences with her brother with severe autism. She spoke about his behavior and how it seemed to dictate "everything."

Curious to understand more, I asked her to elaborate on what she meant by "everything." She recounted instances where her desires, such as going to Disney World or having a slumber party with her friends, were hindered because of concerns her parents had about her brother's behavior.

Her father expressed doubts about a Disney trip, fearing her brother's ability to handle it, while her mother hesitated to host a slumber party, fearing her brother's potential behaviors.

Did you pick up on anything from this story?

When I have conversations with siblings like the example above, they often circle back to one realization: parents frequently attribute the inability to participate in certain family activities solely to the sibling's disability, without addressing the underlying fears and concerns. This lack of deeper explanation leaves young minds, still learning to understand their emotions, to interpret the situation from a limited perspective.

Instead of understanding the complexities of fear, embarrassment, or overwhelm, they simply hear that their sibling's disability is the cause of the restriction. When saying "no" to something because of a sibling's disability or struggles, it's crucial to go beyond the surface and provide context that fosters empathy and understanding. This involves not only explaining the reason for the decision but also offering alternative options that accommodate everyone involved.

By delivering the message in a thoughtful and compassionate manner, you can teach your children to navigate challenging situations with resilience and grace, rather than resentment or frustration. It's about empowering them to see beyond limitations and approach life's obstacles with empathy and understanding.

Throughout my entire life, I can't recall a single moment when my parents attributed a change in our family activities or dynamics solely to my brother's disability. Even when his disabilities may have presented challenges, my parents always found alternative explanations that were never tied directly to his disability. My parents' dedication to meeting our family's needs while valuing inclusivity has deeply influenced me, shaping how I approach both personal and professional challenges to this day.

As you navigate the ever-changing seasons of life with a family member who has a disability, remember that understanding and considering your child's emotional intelligence is crucial and recognize that each child is unique in their ability to process and express their emotions. There's no perfect formula for addressing these complex feelings, and you can't do it wrong if you approach each situation with a willingness to meet your child where they are. Don't assume maturity or readiness; instead, engage in honest conversations and offer support that aligns with their current emotional capacity. By doing so, you create a nurturing environment where all your children feel heard and valued, fostering their emotional growth and strengthening your family bond.

EMPOWER THEIR JOURNEY

Many women grapple with the challenge of their personal identity being overshadowed by their various roles — such as being a mother, wife, daughter, or sister. These roles often dominate their sense of self as they strive to meet the expectations and responsibilities attached to them.

Children typically don't face this struggle about being overshadowed by another role, with one notable exception: special needs siblings. From a young age, these children assume a significant position within their family, carrying unique pressures and responsibilities.

When I talk about the pressures and responsibilities of being a special needs sibling, many might assume it's solely about the future caretaker role — knowing that, in some capacity, we'll be responsible for ensuring their well-being, whether that means they live with us or we oversee their care through others. And while that is certainly part of our journey, I want to dive deeper and give you a glimpse into the often-overlooked burdens we siblings carry with us daily.

More than just future obligations, siblings take on unspoken responsibilities in the here and now, which shape our lives in ways that go beyond what most see. These responsibilities include helping our siblings make friends, ensuring they are safe and accepted at school, acting as a guard in public to shield them from stares or a society that still struggles with inclusion. We also take on the responsibility of helping our sibling understand social cues when others don't, stepping in to explain things when adults aren't sure how to respond, and constantly advocating for their needs, even when we're not sure how to navigate our own. We manage our own emotions when family plans change because of their needs, and try to balance our own desires for independence with the inherent responsibility we feel toward their well-being.

The impact of this role can vary greatly depending on the family's dynamics, shaping their life experience and character in profound ways.

In order to empower their journey, you must allow your neurotypical children the space to discover who they are, what brings them joy, and embrace their childhood fully, so that being a special needs sibling doesn't overshadow their sense of self.

It's about finding a balance within your family that allows each child to be free from the pressures of being a special needs sibling and simply enjoy being a kid. Every family dynamic is unique, but in my own experience, my parents managed to give me that freedom and space to just be myself. Looking back, I deeply appreciate and admire my parents for allowing me to just be a sibling, free from expectations or pressures. They gave me the space to fully experience my childhood, which, in turn, made my bond with Nick more genuine and natural, rooted in love rather than obligation.

I want to share a story about a sibling who had a different experience from mine and how it affected her, based on what she shared with me. My intention in sharing this is not to induce guilt or judgment, but to provide a safe space for learning and growth. I hope you can approach this story with a perspective of understanding and openness, rather than through feelings of sadness or self-criticism.

During a sibling mentor session via Zoom, I was speaking with a 12-year-old girl whose brother has autism. I found myself stumbling over my words more than usual on this particular call. The weight of this girl's raw, honest emotions was palpable. This was the first sibling session I had with her, and while I spent time getting to know her, she was eager to dive straight into the conversation — my kind of girl.

"Can I tell you something and you won't tell Mom or Dad?"

I assured her that while I was a safe space, I would have to inform her parents if what she was about to share involved harm to herself or others.

"I'm not going to hurt anyone, but I need to tell someone this. I hate autism," she said. "I hate that my younger brother has autism. I hate that I'm always forced to play with him. I hate that before I do anything I want to do, I have to watch him. I hate that my parents put pressure on me to include him with my friends, because it's hard for him to make friends. I hate that I always have to help others understand him. Every day after school, I have to play and watch him for Mom because Dad is at work. I want to help, but it sometimes makes me sad."

Her words felt like she was finally letting out a deep frustration that had been building up for too long.

"Have you told your mom how you feel?"

Her response was something I understood: "I don't want to hurt my mom's feelings. My brother needs her, and he needs me too. I don't want to be mean, and I really do want to help. It just seems like I'm always expected to sacrifice my own wants and needs for my brother."

I encouraged her to take a deep breath and explained that many special needs siblings share her feelings. "Sometimes we carry a weight out of love that was never asked of us."

What she said next is the heart of the "Empower Their Journey" strategy within SEEDS: "I do love my brother and I like to play with him sometimes. I just want to do what I want to do and have fun, but he doesn't want to do those things. It's hard for him. I'm afraid if I tell Mom, she'll be upset. She reminds me how much it's my responsibility to protect and love my brother because things are hard for him. I want to be a good sister and make him happy, but sometimes I just want to be me."

I used the rest of the call to validate her feelings and guide her in finding a way to talk with her mom about creating a plan that would work for both of them. I reminded her that all siblings, regardless of disability, struggle with finding a balance while growing up. Although the responsibilities she has now will serve her well in the future, it's important to communicate the pressure and sadness she feels from being expected to constantly care for her brother.

This story is a powerful reminder of the emotional struggles siblings may struggle with internally. As you read, I encourage you to pause and consider the pressure or expectations you might inadvertently place on your neurotypical children. I'm not suggesting you abandon those expectations altogether. Instead, I urge you to engage in open conversations with your neurotypical children to establish a balanced and supportive dynamic.

It's normal to ask children to help with their siblings, regardless of whether they have disabilities. But just as the mother in the last story didn't intend to pressure or overwhelm her daughter, I know you wouldn't want to either. That's why it's crucial to recognize that expecting a child to take on caregiving responsibilities too soon or too often can take away their childhood and force them to grow up faster than they should, which may have lasting effects.

The most powerful statement that stood out to me from the sibling's story was, "It just seems like I'm always expected to sacrifice my own wants and needs for my brother." What overwhelmed her wasn't just the responsibility, but the unspoken pressure that her feelings always had to come second. Now, let me be clear — I'm not suggesting you remove all expectations or responsibilities for supporting their sibling. Instead, focus on finding balance. Have honest conversations with your child about their feelings, and make sure they know they don't always have to put their own needs aside.

Parents often ask me, "How did you develop such a deep love for your brother? How did you become such a passionate advocate? I want my neurotypical children to have that same understanding – to accept, advocate, and fully embrace this life." Their questions are humbling, but it's as if they are seeking a well-kept secret behind how I became who I am today.

The simple answer is that I wasn't forced or expected to become a caregiver, advocate, friend maker, or babysitter at the expense of my own desires. While there was an expectation to be a good sister, I never felt pressured to sacrifice my own dreams and aspirations for my brother. I believe this is because my parents made countless sacrifices themselves and wanted to shield me from those responsibilities until I was older and could choose for myself. They treated and supported us as typical siblings, a brother and sister who were rarely different.

At the start of this book, I recounted my softball journey and how it became a lifeline for my family and an integral part of my empowerment journey. Through softball, I found a space where my happiness mattered, where I didn't have to search for activities that were solely adaptable for my family's needs (although my brother thoroughly enjoyed attending my games).

For some families, their loved one with a disability may face challenges in fully participating in such activities. A neurotypical sibling may love to run, but it's difficult for his brother who uses a wheelchair to attend his cross country meets or a neurotypical sister may play in her school's band, but the instruments are too much for her sister with sensory issues. A neurotypical brother might play baseball, but the long games can be challenging for their sibling to sit through.

I realize this makes life hard. I don't know the answer for your situation, but I do know that how a family navigates these circumstances will have an emotional impact on the neurotypical children.

Supporting your neurotypical children's journey involves more than just encouraging their extracurricular activities and hobbies. It also means embracing their aspirations for their future roles, even if that means they are not ready to take on the responsibility of caring for their sibling. Parents might worry they've failed if their children's dreams don't align with becoming future caregivers. However, it's important to recognize that each child's path is unique, and their personal goals and desires should be valued and respected, even if they differ from the role of a future caretaker. Avoid letting your concerns about the future and fears shape how you support and dream with your child.

Here's some advice I frequently share with parents on how to empower their neurotypical children:

- Create space to talk about it.

- Be mindful not to impose your expectations on them without first understanding their own needs and desires.

- Never assume or expect what they want or how they feel.

- Aim to support their journey without overshadowing it with the needs of their sibling with a disability, avoiding a "what about them?" mindset.

- Encourage individual interests and passions by creating a supportive space where your child feels free to explore their interests without guilt or the need to justify their choices. Even if you can't be the one to take them to their activities, provide the opportunity for them to pursue what they love, and encourage exploration without strings attached. This allows them to embrace their passions openly, without feeling like they're seeking an "escape" or betraying family responsibilities.

- Encourage your child to develop independence and take on responsibilities that focus on their own interests and personal growth, rather than those related to their sibling with a disability.

In short, don't let their identity revolve solely around accepting or advocating for their sibling. Give them the space to be themselves and support them when they're ready to engage.

I understand that family dynamics can sometimes make it challenging, but whenever possible, strive to let your child be a sibling first, not a caregiver. They shouldn't have to bear the weight of balancing roles like best friend, nurturer, protector, advocate, and caregiver all at once. You might be thinking as you read this, "My child is sweet and amazing — they naturally step in without me ever placing extra pressure on them to do so." I completely hear you and understand. I was the same way; it came naturally to me, and my parents never made me feel like it was expected. However, it's important to pay attention and recognize that your child may be placing internal pressure or expectations on themselves. Just take the time to acknowledge that. Regularly check in with them through intentional conversations about their journey and their interests/wants.

Reflecting on my own experience, the greatest lesson from my parents was their commitment to empowering my journey. They allowed me to be myself and simply expected me to be an ordinary sibling, not weighed down by extra responsibilities. This approach made all the difference, and it's a powerful principle to embrace in nurturing your own children.

DON'T AVOID THE HARD TALKS

Parents often avoid hard conversations with their children, especially when it comes to navigating the complexities of a special needs family. There are countless reasons for this — maybe the topic feels too overwhelming to discuss, or perhaps they believe their child is too young to understand. Sometimes, it's the fear of not having the right answers, or the worry of instilling unnecessary fear in their child.

But avoiding these conversations doesn't make them any easier in the long run.

The reality is, the emotions tied to these discussions are incredibly raw and intense. Even now, when my mom and I try to talk about Nick's future, we often can't get through it without breaking down in tears. My mom can't picture Nick navigating life without her, even though he has me. And I can't imagine how I'll ever fill the void my brother will feel when our parents are no longer here.

It's hard. It's overwhelming. It's a lot. So, we avoid talking about it.

The uncertainty of the future and the challenges it brings are probably the most difficult topics for special needs families to confront, but they are also some of the most important conversations we need to have. Things like navigating social situations, where their sibling will live in the future, and the meaning of guardianship are not easy talks to have.

Avoiding these difficult conversations sets an unspoken boundary that can have lasting effects on your neurotypical child. When parents shy away from addressing the tough realities, it sends a silent message that certain topics are off-limits, creating a barrier that the sibling may internalize. In turn, they learn to hold their own feelings and thoughts inside, believing they must carry the weight of their emotions alone. This silence can lead to feelings of isolation and confusion, as they struggle with the belief that their worries and fears are not valid or welcome. Over time, this unspoken boundary can prevent them from sharing their true feelings, deepening the emotional divide within the family.

Here's a personal story about a conversation I avoided within my family:

I still remember gripping my Grandma Ruth's hand tightly as we walked through those stark, white nursing home hallways. The harsh smells were almost unbearable, and I even asked her if I could hold my nose. We navigated down two long corridors before arriving at Kip's room. Inside, his bed was positioned against the right wall. He lay there, gazing blankly at the ceiling and twirling a sock.

When Grandma Ruth's voice broke the silence with, "Hey Kip, it's Sissy. I'm here," he instantly stopped twirling the sock and turned his head towards her. Grandma Ruth released my hand — though I wasn't quite ready for her to— and moved to Kip's bedside, gently stroking his head and kissing his forehead. Even at around seven years old, the vividness of that moment remains etched in my memory.

I only knew Kip from our family's holiday gatherings at Grandma Ruth's house. He was always dressed in bib overalls, clutched a knotted sock, crawled instead of walked, and never spoke. I hadn't asked many questions about him; he was simply Kip. However, during one of my overnight stays with Grandma Ruth, I finally mustered the courage to ask, "Grandma Ruth, where does Kip live? Can I go with you one day to see him?" Grandma Ruth mentioned that I had actually visited Kip with my mom and Nick before, though I didn't remember it. Despite this, I felt a strong urge to visit him again.

That day with Grandma Ruth opened a door to realizations I wasn't prepared to fully understand. The questions I had about Kip — where he lived, why we only saw him on holidays, and whether he and Nick shared similarities — remained unasked and unanswered. These were conversations I longed to have but avoided because they seemed too painful and complex. As a seven-year-old, I struggled with thoughts and emotions I couldn't articulate, but they

Uncle Kip

matured me in ways I didn't fully grasp at the time.

Watching Grandma Ruth interact with Kip, sharing stories and memories, deepened my connection with her. While people assumed my fondness for her was due to her spoiling me, there was something deeper — a shared bond that went beyond words. We both had brothers with disabilities, an unspoken connection that drew us closer in ways I hadn't fully realized.

That day in Kip's room, I saw Grandma Ruth not just as my biggest supporter but as someone who truly understood the unique role of being a sibling to someone with a disability. This bond, though never discussed, was a revelation to me. Grandma Ruth was the first person I encountered who truly understood my experience as a sibling.

As I walked through those dreadful-smelling hallways, I felt a deep-rooted fear that Nick's future may involve a place like Kip's care facility. Grandma Ruth explained that Kip had to move there after her parents passed away, as his needs were too great to be managed elsewhere.

I fought back tears, overwhelmed by the thought of Nick's future and whether he might one day need such care. Despite Kip's needs being more severe than Nick's, I couldn't shake the fear of what might happen if Nick's condition worsened. I resolved in my young mind that when the time came, Nick would live with me. This decision, made quietly and with determination, was one I kept to myself, a secret promise I made at seven years old.

Just as much as parents avoid tough talks, siblings do too. As siblings, we often shy away from difficult conversations to spare our parents from additional worry. We hesitate to share our own struggles and feelings, knowing they already carry so much on their shoulders. However, as difficult as they may be, we cannot afford to shy away from them.

Avoidance only prolongs the inevitable and prevents children from understanding and processing their feelings in a healthy way. Instead, you must embrace these conversations with courage and honesty, acknowledging the complexities of our circumstances while offering reassurance, love and support. By being open and transparent, you empower your children to understand their sibling's disability, helping them navigate challenges with resilience, empathy, and compassion.

So, which conversations do families most frequently sidestep?

Undoubtedly, discussions about future care, guardianship, living arrangements, and financial plans top the list. However, many other challenging topics can also be easy to avoid. Here are some age-appropriate conversations that can confront the challenges head-on and help you emerge stronger as a family.

YOUNG CHILDREN (AGES 4-7)
Understanding Differences
"Your sibling has different needs than you. Sometimes, they might need more help, and that's OK. What are some ways we can show them we care?"

Handling Frustration
"I know it can be hard when your sibling needs gets more attention than you. How can we make sure we connect and spend time together to meet your needs and wants?"

Explaining Behavior
"Sometimes, your sibling might act differently or do things that seem strange or even scary at times. They're not trying to be difficult; they just need to do things in their own way. They process the world we live and communicate what they need or want in ways that don't always come out in words. How does that make you feel?"

MIDDLE CHILDHOOD (AGES 8-12)
Balancing Time and Attention
"We need to make sure everyone in the family gets what they need. How do you feel about the time and attention you're getting compared to your sibling?"

Discussing Responsibilities

"You might have to help more with your sibling sometimes. How does that make you feel? Are there ways we can make sure you have time for your own interests?"

Navigating Social Situations

"When you're with friends, your sibling's disability might come up. How do you want to talk about it with them? What do you need from us to feel supported or figure out what to say?"

Future Living Arrangements

"We're thinking about where your sibling might live when they're older. Would you like to help us research options, or do you have any thoughts on this?"

Safety Plan and Crisis Management

"We're developing a safety plan for situations where your sibling might act out or have a crisis. How do you feel about this plan, and do you have any concerns or fears that we should address?"

TEENAGERS (AGES 13-18)

Future Planning and Career Choices

"As you think about your future, how do you feel about potentially taking on more responsibilities for your sibling? How does this fit with your own goals and dreams?"

Emotional Impact and Mental Health

"It's essential to talk about how your sibling's disability affects your mental health. I want to make sure you feel supported in managing any feelings of stress, anxiety, or sadness that may arise. Are there specific challenges or emotions you're experiencing that we can address together? Your well-being is important, and I'm here to help you navigate this."

Family Dynamics and Independence

"Balancing family needs with your own independence can be tough. How do you feel about the expectations placed on you? What changes could help you feel more balanced and supported?"

Guardianship and Legal Responsibilities

"We need to talk about what guardianship means and how it might impact you in the future. There will come a time when we won't be here to care for your sibling, and we want to make sure you feel prepared for that reality. Do you have any questions or concerns about what that might look like? We're here to discuss any feelings or thoughts you have as we plan for their future together."

Financial Arrangements

"We're making important plans to ensure your sibling's future is secure, including arrangements for their long-term care and support. This involves setting up resources and ensuring they'll have what they need, even when we're no longer here. How do you feel about these preparations, and do you have any questions about how these decisions might impact our family or your own role in the future?"

Determining the best time to have these tough conversations is less about a specific age and more about gauging your child's emotional maturity and readiness. Children develop at different rates, so the key is to observe how they process and express their feelings about everyday situations. If they're asking questions, showing concern, or expressing curiosity about their sibling's needs, it's a sign that they're ready for more information.

The right time to start these conversations is when you notice your child is capable of understanding and handling complex emotions. If they can express empathy, ask thoughtful questions, or reflect on their own experiences, they may be mature enough to begin discussing more challenging topics. Start with simple, honest conversations that match their level of understanding, and gradually introduce more complex ideas as they grow.

It's also important to create a safe environment where they feel comfortable asking questions and expressing their feelings. Be patient and listen to them carefully; their reactions will guide you in knowing how much to share and when to pause. Trust your instincts as a parent, and remember that it's OK to have these conversations in stages, revisiting the topic as your child's understanding deepens over time.

Once you start the conversation, give them space to express their thoughts and feelings. Aim for a balanced exchange where both of you share openly. You might also ask if there's anything you can do to help them feel more prepared for the future, regardless of the circumstances.

Next, I encourage you to take a deep breath and try not to let this feel overwhelming. I know that you, as special needs parents, think about the future more deeply than many others do, and constant discussions about it can be exhausting. What I'm suggesting requires time and intention. It's easy to say, "I know I need to do this," and then put it off. As a sibling who may eventually take on the role of caretaker, I urge you to prioritize this and take the next step I'm about to share.

Buy a notebook and keep it by your bedside. Start an ongoing letter to the "future caregiver" of your child with a disability, even if you're unsure who that will be. Focus less on who it will be and more on how you can make their future role easier and more meaningful.

Use this journal to express all your hopes and dreams for the care of your child. Think of it not as a secret diary, but as a thorough and heartfelt guide that you want others to read in order to understand your vision for caregiving. Include detailed instructions that go beyond the basics.

For instance, instead of simply listing a bedtime routine step-by-step, write about what makes it special, what your child loves about it, and why it's important. Imagine different scenarios, like if the routine needs to be adjusted while traveling, and explain how to handle it with care and thoughtfulness. Paint a vivid picture by describing everyday moments like getting ready in the morning, favorite hobbies you share, holiday traditions that bring your family together, milestones you celebrate, and even the dreams and goals you envision for the future.

Not a writer? That's OK. Pick up your phone and record yourself with your camera. Take these video talks and store them in an online file storage or cloud platform that can later be accessed and viewed by your child's future caretaker.

Here are some great prompts to get you started in journaling for your child's future caregiver:

> What is the toughest part of my day as a caregiver, and what challenges do I face? What strategies or insights have helped me navigate these challenges?

> What is my most cherished memory with my child, and what makes this moment significant? How can I ensure it remains a treasured part of their life?

> If my child becomes ill, what steps would I take to care for them and provide comfort during their sickness?

> What actions do I take to ensure my child's happiness and create joy and fulfillment in their life?

> When my child is feeling sad, what words or actions do I use to comfort them and provide support and understanding?

> What simple things do I do each day that might go unnoticed but are important to my child, and why are these actions meaningful to them?

> What key elements of life do I want my child to remember and cherish after I'm gone, and why are these aspects important for their ongoing well-being and happiness?

While it's crucial to manage practical details — updating your will, organizing medical contacts, tracking medications, and documenting service provider information — don't stop there. Let this be a reminder to look beyond the logistical details and express what truly matters:

your genuine hopes, fears, and values. These deeper reflections will serve as guideposts for those you leave behind, providing them with a connection to you and a framework to navigate life without you.

As you navigate the complex journey of parenting, especially within a special needs family, remember that avoiding tough conversations only delays the inevitable and may even deepen misunderstandings. Embrace these moments as opportunities to connect and grow together. Be open, honest, and compassionate in your discussions.

Your children, both neurotypical and those with disabilities, deserve to feel heard and understood. By addressing difficult topics head-on, you are teaching your children invaluable lessons about facing challenges with courage and love. Don't shy away from these conversations; they are the foundation of a stronger, more unified family. There is no such thing as the right age, the right time, the right way – just lean into what feels right and start there.

SHARE EMOTIONS RESPECTFULLY

Sarah, a 10-year-old fourth-grader, sat in the school's guidance counselor's office, tears streaming down her face. I, not a licensed therapist or an expert, but a sibling to a brother with a disability, had been asked to come talk to her. As I looked at her, all I could see was a freckled-faced, red-headed little girl. It was like I was looking into a mirror of the past, speaking to my former self. I was there to offer her words of love and validation that we siblings often don't realize we need.

Sarah attended the same school as her younger brother, who had been diagnosed with autism. Her brother's struggles with school life, intense aggression, and disruptive behaviors were known throughout the school, which meant Sarah was equally known.

The school counselor had reached out to me because Sarah, once a great student who loved school and maintained excellent grades, had started to change. She no longer wanted to come to school and complained of bellyaches. Her grades were slipping, and her once-outgoing personality had given way to shyness and insecurity. Concerned parents and teachers couldn't pinpoint the cause. Was she being bullied? Did she have an underlying health issue?

It was Sarah's guidance counselor, with a background in special education, who connected the dots. Sarah's desire to stay home from school coincided with her brother's struggles at school, which included an incident where his teacher was injured. As the school and family focused on providing support for her brother, Sarah was the one left on the outside looking in. She was worried whether the other kids in the school knew about what her brother did and if they would ask her questions about it. She was worried that teachers would not just judge her brother, but now feel differently about her as well.

Sitting across from her on that blue couch, tears welling up in both our eyes, I introduced myself, saying, "Hi, I'm Amanda. We have a lot in common. I'm here because I know you've been having a tough time. You don't have to talk about it with me. But I'd like to share something special about me and you."

Sarah looked up from her tightly clasped hands, and her response said it all, "The counselor told me you have a brother with a disability."

And that's all she had to say. We bonded instantly without sharing our stories because we just knew. We saw each other. Even as an adult, I felt seen by her, and it felt comforting.I didn't waste any time, as I knew what she needed to hear.

"Are you embarrassed to be at school because your brother hurt a teacher, or do you want to stay home to be with your mom one-on-one without your brother?"

She started to cry, and I cried with her, but the tears weren't from sadness; they were tears of relief. With a quivering voice, she replied,

"Both. I don't want the teacher to hate me or be mad at me. I'm sorry my brother did that; he can't help it. I'm worried about my mom. She's sad all the time because autism is hard. I want to make her better. I want her to rest. She needs to get rest and I want to make sure she is resting when he is at school."

And I told her what every little kid needs to hear when they are a special needs sibling.

"I totally get it. It's really tough on you, and it's OK to feel embarrassed — I would feel the same way. It's also normal to be sad when the people we love are going through a hard time. But remember, you don't have to carry the whole burden or always be the strong one. The teacher will be fine; she's trained and knows how to handle these situations. She's not upset with your brother or with you.

As you grow up, you'll get better at navigating life with your brother's autism, one experience at a time. You don't need to be strong for your mom all the time; she will handle things in her own way, both the easy and the tough moments. Her sadness is part of her learning process, and that's OK. It won't last forever, I promise. You don't have to fix everything — but your worries are completely normal."

Then, I asked her to tell me about a fun thing she likes to do with her brother, something special just for them, and something she loves to do with her family. She shared how she likes playing trains with her brother because he likes them so much, and helping her mom cook spaghetti for dinner.

I reminded her that during the toughest times, it can really help to hold onto the things she loves. I assured her that her place in the family is special just as she is — she doesn't need to be the one who fixes everything, but instead, she can just be the fun-loving and determined little girl she naturally is. I encouraged her to embrace her feelings and give herself the space to experience and work through them, while focusing on what she can control.

I have talked with thousands of families and siblings over the years, all with varying stories. Too often I have witnessed parents trying to discredit their children's feelings. Telling them things like:

"You shouldn't feel that way."

"I haven't done anything to make you feel that way. I give you the attention you need."

"Your brother can't help his disability, but you can control how you react to it."

"Your sibling needs you."

"This is our life, I can't change it. You will just have to accept it."

"It makes me sad you feel that way, because I can't change the fact that your sibling has a disability."

"You should feel grateful you can do the things you are able to do, because your sibling can't. You should appreciate what you have."

Sharing emotions respectfully involves creating a safe space where both you and your children can openly express and release feelings. Statements that dismiss or invalidate these emotions prevent this safe space from forming. When children feel ashamed of their feelings, they may internalize that shame, isolate themselves, or struggle privately with intense emotions they believe they shouldn't have. For siblings already grappling with guilt, making them feel ungrateful or pressuring them to behave differently can deepen their resentment and exacerbate their struggles. **It's crucial to foster an environment where emotions are welcomed and understood, rather than suppressed or judged.**

Let me be clear: I'm not a therapist, nor do I claim to be. However, drawing from my personal experience growing up with my brother and from countless conversations with siblings navigating their own journeys, I've gained a deep understanding. I'm here to share that insight in a way that I hope resonates with you and helps you learn from those who have already lived this journey.

Creating a space for children to share emotions respectfully is crucial for their emotional development. Here are some ways parents can create such a space to allow all children to thrive.

Establish Regular Check-Ins
Set aside regular times, like during family dinners or before bed, to ask your children about their day and feelings. Consistent check-ins show that their emotions are valued and important.

Model Emotional Expression
Demonstrate healthy emotional expression by sharing your feelings openly and calmly. When parents express their emotions respectfully, children learn to do the same.

Create a Safe and Non-Judgmental Environment
Ensure that your child feels safe to express any emotion without fear of punishment, ridicule, or dismissal. Validate their feelings, even if you don't fully understand them.

Active Listening
Practice active listening by giving your full attention, making eye contact, and nodding to show understanding. Repeat back what you heard to ensure clarity and show empathy.

Use Open-Ended Questions
Encourage deeper conversation by asking open-ended questions like, "How did that make you feel?" or "Can you tell me more about what happened?"

Create Emotion-Friendly Zones
Designate specific areas in the home where children can retreat to express their feelings, such as a cozy corner with comforting items like

pillows and books.

Validate Their Feelings
Even if you don't understand or agree with their emotions, acknowledge that their feelings are real. Say things like, "I can see that you're really upset," or "It sounds like this is really hard for you."

Stay Calm
Maintain your composure, even if your child's emotions are intense. Your calmness will help them feel more secure and less overwhelmed.

Ask Clarifying Questions
Gently ask questions to better understand their perspective. "Can you help me understand why you feel this way?" can provide insights into their emotional state.

Offer Reassurance
Let them know that it's OK to feel whatever they are feeling. Reassure them that all emotions are valid and part of being human.

Problem-Solve Together
Collaborate on finding solutions or coping strategies. Ask, "What do you think might help you feel better?" This empowers them and shows respect for their ability to manage their feelings.

Encourage Healthy Expression
Suggest constructive ways to express emotions, such as drawing, writing, physical activity, or talking it out.

Reflect and Empathize
Share similar experiences you might have had to show empathy and solidarity. This can help them feel less alone in their emotions.

Set Boundaries
While validating emotions, it's also important to set boundaries on behavior. Explain that while all emotions are OK, not all actions are. "It's OK to feel angry, but it's not OK to show disrespect with harsh words or

yelling."

By creating a respectful space for sharing emotions and responding thoughtfully, parents can help their children develop strong emotional intelligence and foster a supportive, understanding family environment.

As we wrap up the SEEDS chapter, remember this is not a scorecard for judging yourself or measuring your worth as a parent. It's all too easy to feel overwhelmed by the constant pressure to evaluate if you're doing enough, but this chapter isn't meant to make you feel inadequate or defeated. Instead, it's designed to help you understand and embrace the journey of raising a child with disabilities while balancing the needs of your neurotypical children.

If you ever find yourself questioning whether you're getting it right, keep in mind that this is a learning process, not a test you need to ace. Think of SEEDS as a tool for growth, resilience, and confidence. Approach this journey with an open heart, knowing that you have the strength to adapt and thrive. Your willingness to read, reflect, and engage shows you're already on the right path.

Perfection isn't the goal and every family faces its own set of challenges. What truly matters is your commitment to making the best choices and putting in the effort. Let this chapter be a source of enlightenment and encouragement rather than stress or self-doubt. You are doing everything you can for all your children, and that's something to be proud of. Keep moving forward with the assurance that you're not alone and that you have what it takes to be the parent your children need.

CHAPTER 7

UNTIL NEXT TIME

Well, I guess this is it — we are drawing to the end. I've spent a lot of time staring at the screen, trying to find the right words to close this journey with you. It's not easy. Part of me doesn't want it to end, because as I write these final lines, I feel like I'm letting go of something important. We've walked this path together, and it feels like I've been holding your hand and wiping away your tears as we explored these stories and memories. It's hard to say goodbye when it feels like I've shared so much of my heart with you. How do I just leave you now?

So instead of saying goodbye, I'll just say, "Until next time."

If you are a parent who picked up this book seeking reassurance that you're not inadvertently causing resentment in your children, I hope you've discovered that you are enough. It's important to recognize that your presence here signifies your commitment to being the best parent you can be. While some passages may have been difficult to read, don't be hard on yourself. Instead, view this book as an opportunity for growth and reflection. Use it as a guide to move forward with a renewed sense of direction and confidence in your parenting journey.

If you're a parent who has read this book and feels that life — and your children — are currently in a good place, I hope you tuck away these words in case you need them in the future. Life's circumstances can shift unexpectedly, and while things may be smooth now, challenges can always arise. Your neurotypical children might have complex emotions simmering beneath the surface, and the insights from this book will equip you to support them effectively. Don't assume they aren't experiencing their own set of emotions or internal struggles just because they seem to love their sibling and embrace their role. These lessons will prepare you to guide your children through their feelings, ensuring they have the tools they need to navigate whatever comes their way.

To the incredible special needs sibling who picked up this book, I want you to know that I see you. I see the unique and sometimes heavy load you bear as the sibling of someone with a disability. While our individual journeys are far from identical, I see that we all share the expectation to find inner strength and understand our own stories.

I hope this book has made you feel truly seen and understood, and that you've found words that resonate with emotions you may have kept hidden for years. As siblings, our struggles are often overlooked or underestimated, with the assumption that we're unaffected. My deepest wish is that my words have helped you step out of the shadows and recognize your true value and purpose, which goes far beyond simply being "the special needs sibling."

Special needs siblings are far more than just "special" or "chosen." We are pillars of support within our own families who possess a unique ability to connect with and uplift other siblings who share similar experiences. No one truly understands what it means to be a sibling in this context better than another sibling who has walked the same path.

Your role is invaluable. You offer insights and empathy that others might not fully grasp. By sharing your journey, you not only help your own family navigate the complexities of the disability but also provide understanding for others who face similar journeys. Your experiences and resilience become a powerful bridge, connecting you with other siblings and creating a network of support and solidarity.

Embrace this role with pride. Your story and strength are not just contributions to your own family but are also gifts that can inspire and guide others. In a world where only those who have lived it truly understand, your voice is essential. You have the power to connect, support, and make a difference, both in your family and in the wider community of siblings who share your journey.

To the one who read this book who isn't part of a special needs family, thank you for joining me on this deeply personal journey through my life as a special needs sibling. Whether you picked up this memoir out of curiosity or a desire to gain insight, my hope is that you find a piece of my story that resonates with your own experiences or opens your heart to a new perspective. I want you to see the world through my eyes, understanding the quiet strength and profound love that comes from living in a family where disabilities are a part of daily life. My wish is that as you close these pages, you carry forward a sense of empathy and awareness, and perhaps feel inspired to foster more inclusive and compassionate connections in your own life. Remember, every story shared can bridge gaps, transform perceptions, and ignite change.

Lastly, as I look at my own reflection, I am filled with immense pride. I took on the challenge of writing a book that once seemed daunting, and in doing so, I've come to see that my sibling story is not just worth telling but essential. Sharing my relationship with Nick and the journey of my trailblazing parents has revealed how truly unique and impactful our story is – **rarely different.**

Some passages have been tough to write, bringing raw emotions to the surface and leaving me staring at a blank screen, tempted to abandon this project out of fear. I worried that my parents might question their roles or second-guess what they could have done differently. Yet, through this process, I've learned that our story, despite its ups and downs, is a testament to the strength and resilience that define us, and it's meant to be shared with other families who are on their own journey of learning and growth.

Writing this book has given me the chance to share special memories of

Nick with my own boys. Nick holds a special place in their hearts, and if they ever read this book, I hope they understand why it means so much and why I was so passionate to get these words on paper to share with families like ours.

As I reflect on my journey, I've come to understand that my identity is deeply rooted in being Nick's sister. Despite the challenges we faced, I wouldn't trade a moment; each trial and triumph has shaped me into who I am today. This book is a homecoming — a return to my foundation and the core values that have guided me throughout my life.

"Rarely Different" stands as a testament to my parents, who confronted a devastating diagnosis with unwavering determination. It celebrates a boy with an extremely rare condition who defied all odds, and a sister inspired to change the world because her brother changed her.

The title itself reflects two profound truths: Nick's unique diagnosis and the bond we shared, which, at its core, mirrors any other sibling connection. Our love, memories, and the challenges we faced together are universal, reminding us that while our journeys may differ, the essence of love and connection unites us all.

ABOUT THE AUTHOR

It feels strange to call this section "About the Author" when you've just finished a book filled with my thoughts, stories, and heart. You've walked through my journey, so you know me pretty well. But you've mostly seen the little girl who grew up and looked back, and that's just one part of my story. I'd like to take this moment to introduce you to who I am today.

This book was a journey, and now I want to invite you to continue it with me. I'd like to give you a glimpse into my current life, not just as an author, but as a person who is constantly evolving. I want to show you how the experiences I've shared have shaped the dreams I'm pursuing and the values for which I stand. It's not just about tying up loose ends; it's about opening a new chapter, one where I'm striving to make a difference for others who might be walking a similar path. I hope you'll stick around with me a little longer.

This book was launched to the world on my 40th birthday. I was dreading this birthday for a long time, and as it got closer, I started to feel like my body was falling apart. I'm not kidding; I actually had to take a heating pad to work and position it just right in my office chair because my back was giving me trouble. That's never happened to me before.

But turning 40 wasn't just about aches and pains — it was also about setting goals and reaching them. Writing this book was one of those "I did it" moments I wanted to achieve by my 40th birthday, even though I knew that finishing it wouldn't magically transform anything in my life. It was more about proving something to myself. I am a woman of impact, demonstrating to my young sons that women are bold, resilient, smart, and capable of achieving their dreams while being mothers.

My boys played a significant role in the creation of this book, though they had no idea they were doing it. Watching them interact with my brother brings me immense joy, reminding me of my own childhood memories with Nick. As I observed them laughing and playing together, it felt like stepping back in time, reliving moments I'd nearly forgotten. It was as if my boys were opening a window to the past, allowing me to reflect on memories I hadn't visited in years.

Although I did not develop the SEEDS strategy for raising my boys, I admit that I have had to use these reminders for myself. It provides me with practical tools to help them navigate life alongside their uncle's disability. Being Nick's nephews, they have their own experiences with disability, and it shapes their perspective. We've had difficult conversations about what the future might look like, but we've also used humor to lighten the mood and keep things from becoming too heavy. These moments have shown me that humor can be a powerful way to connect, even in the most challenging discussions.

It's hard to believe that I've spent over 20 years teaching and supporting individuals with disabilities. In some ways, it feels like a lifetime, but in others, it feels like I've only just begun. This journey has shaped me in ways I never expected, and along the way, I've learned some invaluable life lessons that have become a part of who I am.

The Impact on Families
There's no clear way to measure how deeply a disability impacts a family. Each family carries their own unique circumstances, and I've come to understand that what feels manageable one day can feel overwhelming the next. Every family's story is different, but each one is powerful in its own way.

Supporting Parents

No matter how many years I've done this work, it never gets easier to listen to parents share their feelings when they are in a season of hopelessness. Their tears, their fears — it's these moments that keep me awake at night. I carry their worries with me, and I often find myself searching for the right words to let them know that they're not alone, that they're doing enough.

Teaching and Advocacy

I've learned that my role isn't just to teach or advocate for change — it's to plant seeds of awareness in those who might not even know they need it. My mission is to keep teaching and advocating, not advocating to change the extremist mindset, but to reach people who don't even realize they need to know more. I believe in showing them how much more they can do once they know better.

A Lasting Legacy

I won't lie—I've thought about the kind of impact I want to leave behind. One day, when I'm gone, I dream that the people who cross my mind now will fill the room, standing shoulder to shoulder, sharing stories of how I made a difference. Not for recognition, but because my work, my heart, touched them. That's the legacy I hope to leave.

Struggling to Celebrate Wins

It's always been hard for me to celebrate my own victories. Growing up, I didn't want to make a fuss about things, worried that it might take attention away from my brother or make him feel left out. It became a habit — downplaying achievements, brushing off compliments. Now, I'm slowly learning that it's OK to acknowledge the good things. There is room for my wins to be celebrated along with the wins of others. It doesn't have to be either or, it can be both.

Making Space for Others

I've spent a lifetime navigating how much space to take up in a room, always cautious not to overshadow my brother or anyone else. I've learned to put others first, but I've also realized that it's just as important to make space for myself. My journey matters, too, and I've worked hard to embrace that.

Advocating with Purpose

Above all, I've learned that my advocacy can't come from frustration or scarcity. It has to be grounded in love, in the belief that there's enough room for everyone. I advocate not because the world is broken, but because I see the beauty in what it could become if we keep working, keep believing, and keep building.

Despite all I've learned over the past 20 years, I still have so much more I want to accomplish in the next two decades. It feels like I've only just begun, like I've built the groundwork for something far greater. Now, I'm eager to share that with the world. The journey isn't over — in fact, it's just starting to take shape. I have a vision of where I want to go and a drive to make a lasting impact. As I move forward, I want to invite you to join me in exploring the possibilities that lie ahead. Together, we can build on this foundation and create something extraordinary.

PUZZLE PIECES

When I first founded Puzzle Pieces over 12 years ago, I had a vision of creating a place where individuals with disabilities could feel safe, supported, and empowered to live their best lives. What started as a dream to fill a gap in our community has blossomed into something far greater than I could have ever imagined. That small idea has grown into a thriving organization that now touches hundreds of lives, providing services I never even knew were possible when we opened our doors.

Puzzle Pieces was built with the belief that everyone deserves a place to belong, where their unique strengths and abilities are celebrated, not just tolerated. From day one, our mission has been to provide opportunities for individuals with intellectual disabilities to learn, grow, and thrive — whether through job training, social programs, or person-centered support services.

As I reflect on the growth of Puzzle Pieces, it's impossible not to think of the incredible team that has carried this vision forward. I once believed that only family could truly understand the depth of love, patience, and acceptance required to work with individuals with disabilities. But over the years, I've learned that love and passion transcend bloodlines. Our team has shown me, time and time again, that you don't have to be related to someone to love them unconditionally or to be fully invested in their success. They've embraced each client with open hearts, proving that empathy, dedication, and compassion are at the core of everything we do.

Puzzle Pieces has evolved into a true whole-life service provider. We offer programs that support people at every stage of life — early childhood development, transition services for young adults, employment training and long-term living supports to help adults build independent, meaningful lives in the community. We focus on their strengths, we work on their dreams, and we are by their side as they achieve milestones that once seemed impossible.

Looking at what Puzzle Pieces has become, I am filled with gratitude for the individuals who've trusted us with their care, the families who have walked this journey with us, and the community that has supported our mission. We've grown beyond the walls of a center — we've become a movement. A movement of acceptance, opportunity, and hope for individuals with disabilities. It's a reminder that, together, we can build a world where everyone belongs, and no piece of the puzzle is left behind.

All nonprofits must create a mission and vision, so I wanted to share ours here with you:

OUR MISSION
To equip those with a disability with individualized skills that enable them to become productive citizens. We believe in providing individuals with disabilities access to the community and a community center to socially engage with peers while meeting their individualized goals.

OUR VISION
At Puzzle Pieces, we are dedicated to bringing visibility to disabilities through education and awareness to our community.

We are on a mission to build a more inclusive community, where individuals with disabilities feel empowered and have an equal chance at employment.

We provide clients with a person-centered approach to programming and care, meeting their individualized goals and building the skills they need to become productive citizens.

We strive to provide the highest quality of services with a client choice approach, reinforcing the individual's value and self worth.

The direct services we provide include:

Day Training: Provides structured daily activities and skills development to support personal growth and independence for individuals with disabilities.

Community Living Supports: Offers assistance with daily living tasks and community engagement to help individuals with disabilities thrive in their homes and neighborhoods.

Residential Homes for Long-Term Living: Delivers comprehensive care and support for individuals with disabilities in a stable, long-term residential setting.

Supported Employment: Assists individuals with disabilities in finding and maintaining meaningful employment through job coaching and support.

Autism Services - After school/Summer Programming: Provides specialized programs and activities during after school hours and summer breaks to support the social and developmental needs of individuals with autism.

Applied Behavior Analysis (ABA): Uses evidence-based techniques to improve behavioral and developmental outcomes for individuals with autism through personalized interventions.

Autism College Support Programming: Offers tailored support and resources to help students with autism succeed in higher education settings and transition to adult life.

As I look to the future of Puzzle Pieces, my heart is filled with hope and determination. I envision a world where our organization continues to break barriers and open doors for individuals with disabilities, creating opportunities for them to shine in ways that reflect their true potential. My deepest aspiration is for Puzzle Pieces to be a catalyst for change, helping our community not only to embrace but to actively seek out and celebrate the diverse talents and contributions of those with disabilities.

I dream of a future where every individual is given the chance to do more and be more. I dream that our collective understanding and acceptance of those with disabilities grows stronger each day. Together, we can build a community that recognizes and values the unique strengths of every person, and where the impact of our efforts reaches far beyond our immediate circles, inspiring others to join in the journey towards greater inclusion and empowerment.

BRIDGING THE GAP

I founded Bridging the Gap to close the divide in understanding and inclusion for individuals with disabilities across various fields. The name embodies this mission. I'm passionate about the idea that greater knowledge leads to better practices, and I'm committed to teaching others how to enhance their support for people with disabilities.

Bridging the Gap is a consulting company focused on areas of impact that I deeply care about, starting with healthcare. I've created a comprehensive training program for healthcare professionals, introducing them to the ACCESS pyramid — a framework designed to improve care for patients with disabilities. This training comes with a workbook and guide to raise awareness and provide a clear path towards better health equity.

But my vision extends beyond healthcare. I plan to expand Bridging the Gap into training for starting nonprofits, developing effective business models for disability services, and creating empathetic classroom environments that understand the complexities of special needs families. Through this work, I aim to make a significant impact by equipping others with the knowledge and tools necessary to foster true inclusion and understanding.

OWEN THE WONDERER

As an advocate for as long as I can remember, I've always been the person who eagerly shared insights about disabilities and my brother's unique journey. I never shied away from questions, no matter how curious or probing they might be, because I believed that genuine curiosity and open dialogue are key to fostering understanding and empathy.

It troubled me to see how parents often discourage kids from asking questions or expressing curiosity about disabilities, fearing awkwardness or not having the right answers. This approach can unintentionally teach children that there's something to be uncomfortable about or avoidant toward.

That's why co-authoring the Owen the Wonderer series became such a significant part of my story. I wanted to create a space where those curious questions could be answered thoughtfully and respectfully. Through Owen's adventures, I aimed to provide a narrative that encourages children to ask questions, learn about differences, and understand that everyone has unique qualities that make them who they are. Owen's journey is designed to be a tool for teachers and parents alike, offering a gentle yet impactful way to spark meaningful conversations about acceptance and inclusion.

Through captivating narratives infused with educational themes, my goal is to inspire children to approach the world with empathy and curiosity. I want them to recognize that it's not only acceptable but vital to ask questions and learn about others. These stories serve not just as entertainment, but as a stepping stone toward nurturing a more inclusive mindset in young readers.

THE GRATITUDE JOURNAL

The Gratitude Journal holds a special place in my heart, born from a personal journey of growth and a deep-seated desire to support others like myself. As I immersed myself in personal development workshops and embraced the practice of gratitude, I discovered a profound sense of peace and empowerment. At each of these workshops I found myself surrounded by inspiring women and I couldn't help but think about how special needs moms — who often face overwhelming challenges alone — could benefit immensely from gratitude and building a village of support.

I saw firsthand how empowering and transformative these experiences could be, but I also recognized the unique struggles that special needs moms face in carving out time for themselves. The idea of stepping away from their families to focus on personal growth seemed like a distant dream for many. It was from this understanding that the concept of The Gratitude Journal was born.

I envisioned a tool that would not only help these incredible women practice daily gratitude but also connect them with a community of others who truly understand their journey. To make this vision a reality, I collaborated with 30 remarkable special needs moms, each of whom contributed their thoughts and experiences to the journal. Their voices and insights are woven throughout the pages, creating a supportive and relatable guide.

The journal is designed as a 30-day self-reflection guide, crafted to encourage daily practices of thankfulness and positive reflection. Each page invites users to recognize and appreciate both the small and significant blessings in their lives, nurturing a deeper sense of joy and fulfillment. With carefully crafted prompts and inspirational quotes, it aims to shift focus toward gratitude and build resilience, especially through the challenging times that come with raising a child with a disability.

This Gratitude Journal is more than just a book — it's a testament to the power of community and the strength found in shared experiences.

It's my hope that it brings comfort, encouragement, and a sense of connection to every special needs mom who embarks on this journey of reflection and gratitude.

FUEL YOUR PURPOSE PODCAST

Starting my podcast was a journey of self-discovery and a response to a deep, personal revelation. I had always felt a stirring within me — a sense that I had a voice and valuable insights to share, but I didn't fully grasp its significance until a pivotal moment.

I vividly remember sitting in church one day, listening to a sermon about using the gifts God gives us. The message was clear: if we don't use our talents and voice, we're not honoring the gifts we've been given. Those words hit me hard. I realized that while I had been impacting those close to me, there was a whole world of people who could benefit from the messages and lessons I had gathered throughout my life. I had a purpose that extended beyond my immediate circle, beyond my community.

That moment of clarity led me to launch my podcast, Fuel Your Purpose. I wanted to create a platform that went beyond my personal sphere and reached out to inspire and empower others. The podcast became a way to share the myriad experiences and lessons I've learned along my journey — lessons about pursuing passions, overcoming obstacles, and achieving goals.

Each episode is crafted to ignite listeners' motivation and offer practical advice. Through conversations with thought leaders, entrepreneurs, change-makers, and individuals impacted by disabilities, I aim to provide valuable insights and actionable steps. My hope is that every episode helps listeners fuel their purpose, make meaningful changes in their lives, and connect with a broader community.

The podcast is more than just a series of episodes; it's a space where stories and strategies come together to inspire others to chase their dreams and embrace their potential.

BE COLLECTION

At 28, I was a teacher with dreams that seemed too big for my reality. I wanted to make a real difference and chase my dreams, but I often felt constrained by doubt and the opinions of others. People laughed or told me my dreams weren't needed or feasible. I was met with skepticism instead of encouragement, and I felt alone in my journey.

Many women, like myself, get caught in a cycle of self-doubt and fear. Too often we are silenced by our own insecurities, feeling as if we aren't enough or don't have what it takes to become the woman we dream of being. We stand still, paralyzed by the weight of our own limitations, and often remain trapped in the shadows of our own fears.

It was this realization that gave birth to the Be Collection. I wanted to create something that would serve as a constant reminder of our inherent potential. The Be Collection isn't just about a phrase or a mantra — it's about empowerment. It's about reminding ourselves that we can "be" whatever we need to be in the present moment to evolve into the woman we aspire to become.

Whether it's being present amidst chaos, being humble in our achievements, being intentional in our actions, or simply being courageous enough to face each day, the Be Collection serves as a symbol of encouragement. It's for those times when you're feeling depleted and questioning your ability to show up as the person you want to be — whether that is a mother, a leader, or simply as yourself.

This collection is a tribute to the strength and resilience within every woman. It's a reminder that no matter where you are on your journey, you have the power to "Be" anything you need to be. Through the Be Collection, I hope to inspire others to embrace their own path, overcome their fears, and believe in their limitless potential.

Before we close, I want to share a bit more about the lighter side of who I am — something I haven't touched on as much. While I've shared deeply about my dreams, my work, and my journey, there's a fun, everyday Amanda that you should also get to know. I've been married for almost

17 years to my wonderful husband, and together we have two amazing sons who bring joy and laughter into our lives every single day. They've inherited their dad's humor and my love for life, which makes every day a little brighter.

I'm a self-proclaimed lake girl, a tradition that started with Nick and me growing up on the water, and now we continue that cherished pastime with our family every summer. Reading is a passion of mine, though I stick to personal development books — leisure reading just doesn't fit into my busy schedule. My friends are like family to me and play an integral role in my family's life.

Though my weekdays are all business, I truly come alive on the weekends, enjoying lively gatherings with friends and savoring an occasional White Claw or vodka drink in hand. (Yes, Mom, only in moderation.) Despite a busy schedule, I've found a steady balance in the chaos, creating a sense of calm and joy through cherished moments with my family. As an introverted extrovert, social events can make me a bit anxious, but I genuinely treasure those opportunities to connect deeply with others and share in meaningful conversations.

I hope you see not just the professional side of me but also the person who finds joy in the everyday moments, the family traditions, and the simple pleasures of life.

As I reflect on the journey that has shaped me, I'm deeply grateful for the chance to share my story and experiences with you. Each chapter of my life, from leading Puzzle Pieces to creating impactful projects, has been a significant part of who I am. Being a special needs sibling has profoundly influenced my perspective and fueled my passion for advocacy and support.

My dreams extend beyond these pages; I envision connecting with others who share similar journeys, fostering supportive communities, and continuing to inspire and empower through every endeavor.

I invite you to continue this journey with me, knowing that our connection doesn't end here. My hope is that within these pages, you find a piece of me that resonates with your own experiences, making you feel seen and empowered. Let this book be a starting point for our shared experiences and dreams. Together, let's build a community where every story is valued and every voice is heard. Thank you for joining me, and I look forward to the future we can shape together.

Horses, Hotels, and Hospitality:

Harry W. Child's Epic Vision for Yellowstone

by Ruth Quinn and Nan Sigrist

Cover artwork by Jim Reed, Casper, Wyoming.
Front cover text by Donna Reed, Casper, Wyoming.
Book design and layout, and back cover and spine by Becky Sheehan, Jackrabbit Graphics, Bozeman, Montana.
Printing by McNaughton & Gunn, Saline, Michigan.

Library of Congress Control Number: 2020917318

ISBN: 978-0-9760945-2-4 (hardback)
978-0-9760945-3-1 (paperback)

1 3 5 7 9 10 8 6 4 2
First Edition

Our Purpose

Our purpose in writing this book is to share the life stories of three young men of vision and courage who were drawn to an adventurous life in Montana Territory. It is our hope that you will come to know the principals of our story as the real people that they were – Harry W. Child, Silas S. Huntley, E.W. Bach, and their loyal, supportive wives, children, and friends. Their adventures led them to Yellowstone National Park, where together they maintained a family legacy that lasted seven decades – spanning the creation of the National Park Service, the coming of the automobile, World Wars, and personal challenges.

Yellowstone National Park, America's crown jewel and "The First Greatest Tourist Attraction in the World," as seen today, is a fine example of government and private enterprise working together. Congress preserved the place, but private enterprise – including financial investment of the railroads, along with Harry's vision, built the grand hotels. The public transportation system is the product of Silas Huntley's ingenuity and organizational skills. The less visible contributions of the third partner, loyal numbers man E.W. Bach, acted as a steady anchor to Helena home base.

Their successes made them stars of the local society columns of their day, but their contributions are not celebrated in history as remembered in the state or the national park today. As two long-term employees of park concessionaires, we feel OUR history is often forgotten.

Many hours and months – and even years, have gone into the research, documentation, and writing. We have relied heavily on other historians and authors who have written fragments of this saga. Their work is detailed in the endnotes. In our daunting attempt to condense over seventy years into a readable tale, we have left out dates while organizing the narrative in roughly chronological order. The appendix contains a detailed time line for readers with that interest.

We came too late to have personally known the people presented here, but their stories live on in Yellowstone folklore. Every summer over four thousand eager employees call Yellowstone home, while providing guest services in historic hostelries lovingly built and maintained. We love both the natural unspoiled park with its many attractions and the concessioner services enjoyed by its numerous visitors.

We wish to express a heartfelt THANK YOU to the newspaper writers of the day. We have quoted them often because they so aptly presented each character's own particular manner of speech, as well as colorfully describing their personalities and actions.

Nan Sigrist & Ruth Quinn

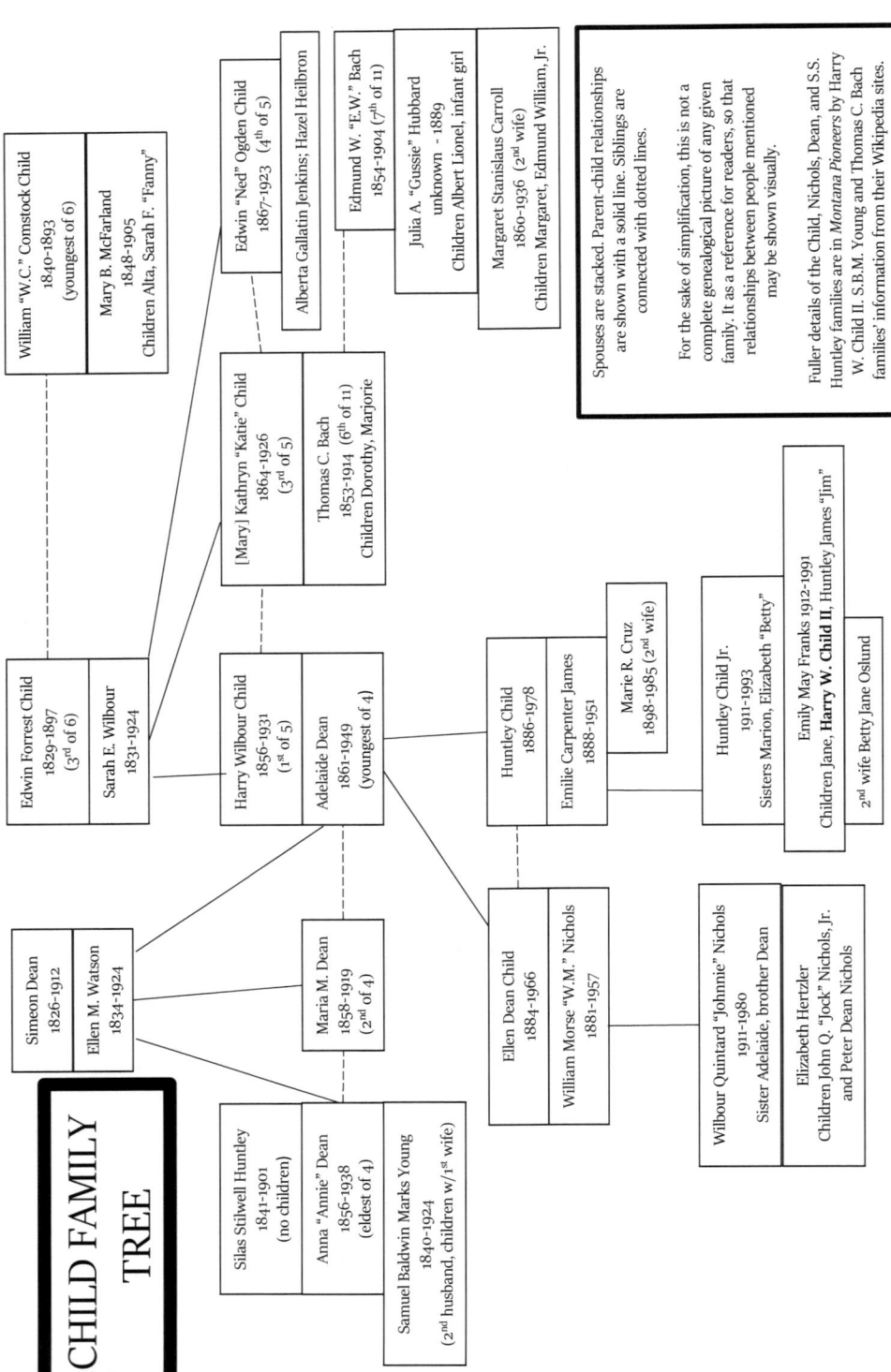

CHILD FAMILY TREE

William "W.C." Comstock Child
1840-1893
(youngest of 6)

Mary B. McFarland
1848-1905
Children Alta, Sarah F. "Fanny"

Edwin Forrest Child
1829-1897
(3rd of 6)

Sarah E. Wilbour
1831-1924

Edwin "Ned" Ogden Child
1867-1923 (4th of 5)

Alberta Gallatin Jenkins; Hazel Heilbron

Edmund W. "E.W." Bach
1854-1904 (7th of 11)

Julia A. "Gussie" Hubbard
unknown - 1889
Children Albert Lionel, infant girl

Margaret Stanislaus Carroll
1860-1936 (2nd wife)
Children Margaret, Edmund William, Jr.

Spouses are stacked. Parent-child relationships
are shown with a solid line. Siblings are
connected with dotted lines.

For the sake of simplification, this is not a
complete genealogical picture of any given
family. It as a reference for readers, so that
relationships between people mentioned
may be shown visually.

Fuller details of the Child, Nichols, Dean, and S.S.
Huntley families are in *Montana Pioneers* by Harry
W. Child II. S.B.M. Young and Thomas C. Bach
families' information from their Wikipedia sites.

[Mary] Kathryn "Katie" Child
1864-1926 (3rd of 5)

Thomas C. Bach
1853-1914 (6th of 11)
Children Dorothy, Marjorie

Harry Wilbour Child
1856-1931
(1st of 5)

Adelaide Dean
1861-1949
(youngest of 4)

Huntley Child
1886-1978

Emilie Carpenter James
1888-1951

Marie R. Cruz
1898-1985 (2nd wife)

Huntley Child Jr.
1911-1993
Sisters Marion, Elizabeth "Betty"

Emily May Franks 1912-1991, **Harry W. Child II**, Huntley James "Jim"
Children Jane, Nichols, Dean
2nd wife Betty Jane Oslund

Simeon Dean
1826-1912

Ellen M. Watson
1834-1924

Maria M. Dean
1858-1919
(2nd of 4)

Ellen Dean Child
1884-1966

William Morse "W.M." Nichols
1881-1957

Wilbour Quintard "Johnnie" Nichols
1911-1980
Sister Adelaide, brother Dean

Elizabeth Hertzler
Children John Q. "Jock" Nichols, Jr.
and Peter Dean Nichols

Silas Stilwell Huntley
1841-1901
(no children)

Anna "Annie" Dean
1856-1938
(eldest of 4)

Samuel Baldwin Marks Young
1840-1924
(2nd husband, children w/1st wife)

Table of Contents

Prologue

The fire watch tower has survived renovations and even an earthquake. It is Helena's most famous landmark, "The Guardian of the Gulch."

When Harry Child stepped from the stagecoach in Helena, Montana Territory, he was 23 years old. In his early years, he experienced life in the city of San Francisco, then two years in Boston, Massachusetts. Next, he went back to his home in San Francisco where he joined his father at the San Francisco Stock Exchange. To make that exciting trip, he booked passage on a deep-water sailing ship from Boston to Panama, and then rode the new train through the jungle to the west coast.

Now, the year was 1878. In Helena, after a long dusty stagecoach ride from California, he stood briefly reconnoitering, and instinctively he walked toward the old wooden fire watch tower standing on a knoll overlooking the town. From all directions he saw mountains, wide open spaces, and streams feeding into the mighty Missouri River.

Helena was a collection of handsomely built houses on well laid-out streets and stately business structures lining the main street, Last Chance Gulch. Missing from this scene were electric street cars or any other means of public conveyance. Single men rode astride high-stepping horses; the ladies rode in horse-drawn buggies. Harry was gazing upon a very different way of life in a new, rich, and isolated area.

W.C. Child, Harry's uncle, had come to Montana Territory in 1866 as an agent of Wells, Fargo & Company. Being a farmer at heart, he purchased a piece of land near the spot that would become the

1

town of Helena. Here he began planning his dream of establishing the western equivalent of a farm, namely a large stock ranch. He had a jovial personality and excelled at social networking. He volunteered for the Library Association, the poor fund, and the Helena Board of Trade – becoming well-acquainted with the town's most prominent businessmen. He participated in and promoted a very active social life. He married a local girl (Mary McFarland), built a house, and put down strong, solid roots in his new home. He soon became interested in mining as well as farming. When a young mining engineer named Lionel R. Nettre came to town, they became partners in buying up abandoned mine claims.

Montana Territory was a vast land bursting with opportunity, not yet an official territory of the U.S. Government – much less a state. Many young men, having just come through the struggle of the Civil War, followed the cry of Horace Greeley, "Go West, Young Man." One such man was Silas Huntley, who had studied land surveying and road building in his native New York. He traveled on a steamboat up the Missouri River to the port town of Fort Benton. Silas' cousin, Charles C. Huntley, came from California bringing along two Concord stagecoaches.

As partners, they first built a stagecoach road connecting Fort Benton to Helena, and then a road following the Musselshell River to Fort Peck. His cousin soon moved on with plans to build a road all the way to the west coast. Silas stayed on and went to work on his plan, which was to connect the small communities in Montana with good roads and stage service carrying passengers, freight, and the U.S. mail. It was in large part the government contracts to carry mail that would make his venture lucrative.

Contemporaries and social acquaintances of W.C. Child were Nathaniel Pitt Langford [32] and Samuel T. Hauser [31]. Langford, youthful, energetic, and ambitious, came to the region in 1862 with a wagon train as second assistant and commissary for Captain Fisk's Overland Expedition from Minnesota. He saw promise of a future here beyond gold and fertile land. Considering the number of emigrants pouring in, he decided to go back to Washington, D.C. to lobby for territorial status for Montana. At the electoral convention that nominated Abraham Lincoln for re-election, Langford represented the territory (then less than two weeks old) as a delegate. He was named Collector of Revenues for the new territory, and he later became the U.S. Bank examiner for the states of the west coast and the western territories.

Samuel T. Hauser came by steamboat, up the Missouri River from St. Louis to Fort Benton, in 1862. He first prospected around the Bannack area, but he was more successful along the Yellowstone River. Within a few years he owned six silver mines, some coal mines, and several smelters. He joined with Langford to open a bank in Virginia City, and on his own, he opened banks in other Montana towns as they developed. He founded and was president of the First National Bank of Helena. Besides banking and mining he had interests in ranching, and he owned a considerable amount of land.

To the south, a remote area of Wyoming Territory was beginning to attract the attention of Helena residents. In September of 1870 an expedition of more than twenty men left Helena to explore the Yellowstone area – a high altitude plateau, completely surrounded by mountain ranges. This became known as the Washburn Expedition.

Samuel Hauser and Nathaniel Langford were both expedition members. Afterward, both men supported and promoted the idea of Yellowstone becoming a national park, but it was Langford who became the voice of the expedition. He lectured in the east gathering support for the idea, as well as influential people with means to financially back such a plan.

By an act of Congress in 1872, Yellowstone became America's first national park, but with no operational funds appropriated and no set of governing rules established. Langford was appointed the first superintendent.

At the heart of this narrative are Silas Huntley and Harry Child as they became concessionaires in Yellowstone National Park. We follow them through their lives as they gain diverse business interests in mining, ranching, merchandising, and real estate. Their enthusiasm, combined with the status of their neighbors and partners, prepared them to take the reins of tourist services in the nation's first national park.

Route of the 1870 Washburn Expedition through Yellowstone (current borders shown). Prominent Helena businessmen accompanied the groundbreaking trip. Map design by Becky Sheehan.

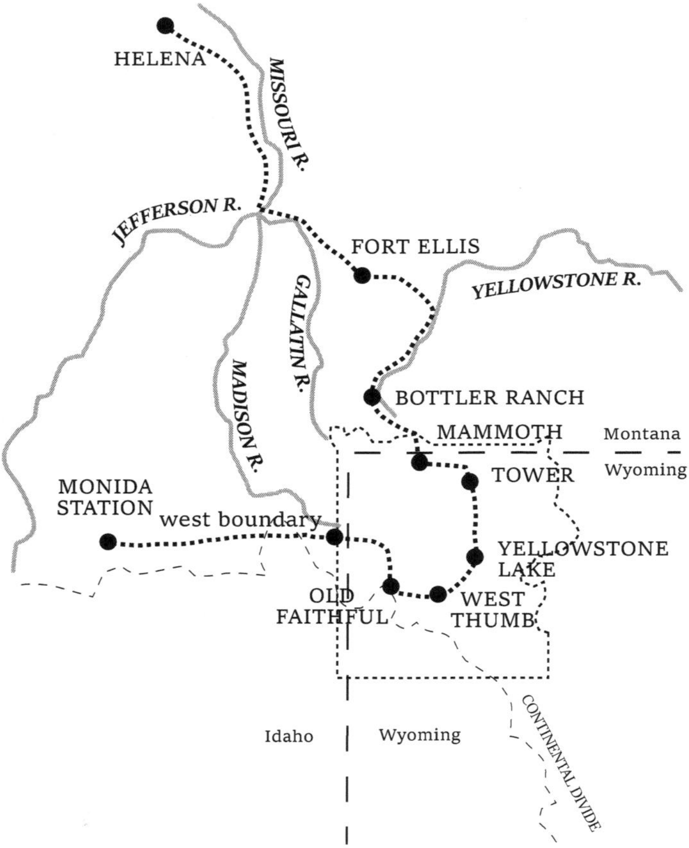

Chapter 1: Setting the Scene
1864-1877

*Introducing important pioneer builders and events
in one section of Montana Territory*

Helena began with gold discoveries in 1864. Discouraged by previous strikes that did not pan out, the miners named their camp *Last Chance*. This strike, however, proved to be the big one. As the town grew with the construction of fine homes and businesses, its citizens began to take issue with the name of their community. After a number of town meetings, and many suggestions, the name was changed to *Helena*, with the main street keeping the name *Last Chance Gulch*.

Many prospectors who discovered gold worked their claim for a year or so, taking the gold they could obtain through surface mining without needing a lot of equipment. Then they moved on, selling or abandoning the claim. Very often those who acquired the old mines were the ones able to take a fortune from them by means of newer and better equipment. W.C. Child and Lionel Nettre capitalized on the opportunity to purchase claims for these unclaimed or abandoned mines at low rates.

W.C. (William Comstock) Child [1] first became involved in smelting operations, joining with partners to form the Helena Reduction Works. Much of his early personal wealth came from strikes in the Lexington Mine, three miles northwest of Helena.

5

The Gregory Mine [16], twenty-five miles southwest of Helena, was perhaps the first major mine discovered in *that* area – also in 1864. Ore from the Gregory was being processed by a smelter a few years later, but the best methods for extracting the silver had not yet been developed, so "the majority of the wealth went into the tailings." W.C. and Lionel patented four mines in 1876; the Gregory, the Compromise, the Banner, and the Matchless – forming the Gregory Mining Company.

W.C. and Lionel also bought the Gloster Mine [17] which produced mostly gold – calling this enterprise the Boston & Montana Mining Company. "The new owners erected a ten-stamp mill and developed the mine to the 200 foot depth, with gold assaying at an average of $15 per ton being mined." In one fifteen-day ore run, processing 160 tons, the Gloster Mine produced "a beautiful bar of bullion" valued at $3,308.54.

Ore was plentiful, but transporting ore to the smelters was a problem. Although the two mines proved profitable for the two partners, in the end, they did not possess the capital to develop either to its full potential. After W.C. Child and Lionel Nettre had sold their interest in the Gregory Mine, they both invested in sheep ranching.

———

Even in his youth, Harry Child was not one to idle away time. Born in California in 1856, he was the eldest of five children. In his early teens, he traveled from San Francisco to Boston – his father having New England roots. He enrolled in the West Newton Preparatory School to prepare for Harvard. He also worked as a clerk in a fashionable men's clothing store. He found nothing that appealed to him as a lifelong career, so he abandoned his college plans. He did acquire an appreciation for well-fitting and well-tailored suits. He became known as a "snappy dresser." He never lost sight of a vow he had made to himself "that he would rather become an asset than a family liability."

"to get up in the world, a man must get up in the morning. Then, when you get up, get busy!" HWC

When the Panama Railroad extended its tracks so that deep-water ships could meet the train at the wharf of Panama, Harry booked passage on a steamer. From the Panama wharf he took the train through the jungle – considerably shortening his travel time to the west coast.

At home, Harry worked with his father Edwin F. Child (brother of W.C.) at the San Francisco Stock Exchange. This venture did well, and held Harry's interest for some time before he began to feel a restlessness. He did not like being in a stuffy office all day. He preferred being outside in the fresh air and sunshine, exerting some physical energy.

While Harry languished at the Stock Exchange, there was excitement in Montana Territory. With the advent of new smelting methods, mining operations were growing. Harry invested in his uncle's Gregory Mining Company, purchasing the Matchless Mine.

The Huntleys' plans for stagecoach service and road building throughout Montana hit a snag following the success of their first summer. All was well until Wells, Fargo & Company announced that it had been granted a four-year contract, starting October 1st of 1867.

The Huntleys were taken by surprise, however, they were not easily beaten or even discouraged. They made a new plan. Helena would remain their base of operation, but they would build a road eastward below the Musselshell River to its mouth – intercepting the Missouri River ships some hundred miles before they reached Fort Benton. They sold their Benton-Helena line to Wells Fargo.

They hoped to receive the mail contract for their new route, but confusion amongst government agencies got in their way. The Post Master General in St. Louis let a contract to a Pony Express outfit for carrying U.S. mail from Fort Abercrombie, near the eastern border of [North] Dakota Territory, all the way to Helena, Montana. The U.S. Army was building forts along and just below the Missouri River to protect the proposed route. After 1862 and before 1866, a delegation of peace commissioners had won permission from the Assiniboine Indians for a mail route within their territory – along the Yellowstone River, but not above the Missouri. The tribe was promised that no white man would travel above Fort Union.

But the Pony Express Route loosely followed Captain Fisk's trail of 1862. From Fort Peck the trail followed westward along the Milk River – well above the Missouri. The natives became hostile upon discovering that white men were carrying U.S. mail through their territory. With the trust broken, the Indians decided to raid and harass whites anywhere and anytime they found them. Although the Huntleys' new road to Fort Peck would not be finished until the spring of 1868, they agreed that it would be far enough along to accommodate the Pony Express riders, so Captain Charles Huntley (who kept his military rank from the war) entered an agreement.

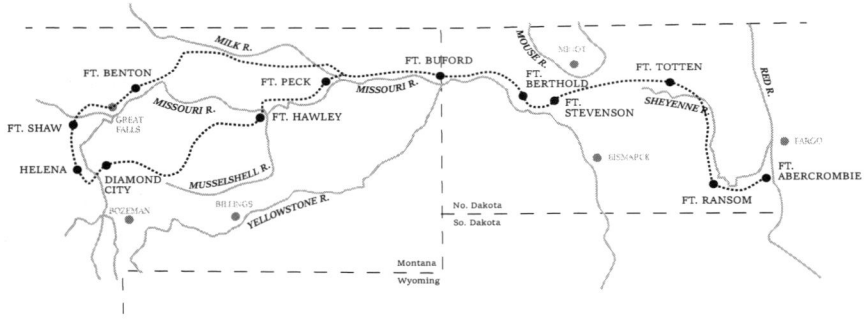

The Huntleys planned the Musselshell Road to intercept Missouri River traffic at Fort Hawley, miles before reaching the established Fort Benton landing. Map design by Becky Sheehan.

Silas (Silas Stillwell, often S.S.) Huntley [2] and his crew now worked through the winter – south and east of Helena following the Musselshell River below the Missouri. They fought not only some cruel weather conditions, but also many Indian attacks. Most of the Indian raids were small groups out to steal horses or rummage through the mail bags. There were however occasional casualties and severe mistreatment of the express riders. Single riders had little chance of getting through unharmed so they began to go in pairs, and then three together. Mail was piling up at the forts and the express riders were refusing to go out. At times Silas could find no workers willing to go out in the open country exposing themselves to a sudden attack. Even though the worst hostilities were against the express riders, horses, equipment, and supplies were also stolen from the road crews.

As the bitter winter of 1867-68 dragged on, the problems grew more and more serious. The commanding officers in the field were constantly lobbying Washington for more recruits to man the forts. Silas began getting letters from the officers and his agents at the forts about the express riders saying, "They had done everything contrary to my instructions and I can say very little in their favor. ... mostly they are a set of lazy, worthless dogs. ..." The men were stealing guns, selling horses, charging goods against the company, and hanging around the forts causing trouble. A decision regarding the fate of the Musselshell route had to be made. Silas took care of the problem in short order. In March of 1868, he issued this statement, "The mail service between Fort Abercrombie and Helena has been discontinued." He made "no excuses, no comment, no elaboration." His men at the forts were told to "wind up affairs on the line and return to Helena."

When the Musselshell route was finished, it connected with the Northern Overland Trail at Fort Peck making it the last link in the Great Overland trail from St. Paul, Minnesota to Helena, and on to Walla Walla, Washington. Silas now turned his attention to building shorter roads connecting the settlements throughout Montana Territory. As each road was finished, he went to Washington, D.C. to secure the proper contracts and permits. He maintained the roads and subcontracted with local drivers to cover each route. Isolated ranchers and miners were happy to see a local man roll into their towns bringing news and supplies.

Captain Charles' health steadily declined. As a Union soldier, he had been captured and held prisoner for some time in the deep South which had affected his health. He became partially paralyzed so he decided to dissolve his affairs in the west and go back to Ohio to be in his father's care. In doing so, he ordered one audit done for both of the stage lines – not only the line in Montana Territory, but another stage line across the lower tier of the westerns states and into Idaho, Washington, and Oregon.

Yellowstone National Park's first years saw minimal visitation. No roads accessed the area, so only travelers on horseback reached the interior. The lack of services meant stopping outside the park to provision one's party for a multiple-day visit. The sole accommodation in 1871 was declared "the last outpost of civilization."

The Golden Spike completing the first transcontinental railroad was driven at Promontory Point in 1869, but completion of the northern routes came more than a decade later. The Northern Pacific's major financier, the banking house of Jay Cooke and Company, had already put its financial backing toward the advancement of the railroad. With the collapse of that company and the ensuing economic depression in 1873, the building of tracks stalled at Bismarck, [North] Dakota Territory.

Mr. Jay Cooke had become interested in Yellowstone after hosting one of Mr. Nathaniel Langford lectures in his home. That interest continued after the NPR emerged from bankruptcy and joined its two ends in eastern Montana Territory.

Langford's superintendency extended five years. But with no working funds, and no power to establish or enforce rules, and a full time job far away, his appointment was rather ineffective.

Silas was a well-known and liked figure in Montana. As long as the stagecoach business continued, he needed to keep negotiating and renewing contracts with the government. Therefore he established permanent living and office space in Washington, D.C. Being a handsome, reputable, and available young bachelor, he was soon highly favored in society circles.

In the spring of 1876 a very lovely young lady named Annie Dean [9] appeared on the Washington social scene. Annie was the eldest of three sisters. By the time they were teenagers, their father was no longer involved in their lives, so their mother, Ellen Dean, worked as a dormitory matron at the University of Wisconsin. One of Annie's school friends invited her to assist as hostess in their Washington home. While her two sisters attended classes in Madison, Wisconsin, Annie was being introduced into society.

It was inevitable, maybe even destiny, that Silas and Annie would meet. Both were gifted conversationalists, and they soon discovered strong mutual interests, especially their love of horses. By the end of the next season their engagement was announced glowingly in the Helena newspapers. Silas Huntley's bride-to-be was described as "intellectual and accomplished in addition to her conspicuous beauty." Silas and Annie Dean were married on February 11, 1879 in Wisconsin, Annie's home state.

Silas was now 37 years old. With the promise of marriage on the horizon, he set about establishing a new livelihood and building a home for his elegant bride. After ten years in the stagecoach business, Silas dissolved the partnership with Captain Charles, selling routes and equipment to others. In the summer of 1878 he filed on a nice piece of land a few miles south of Helena, near Toston, along the Missouri River, and devoted himself to developing his ranch and a large horse racing track [12].

P.B. (Philo B.) Clark, one of the Huntleys' contract stagecoach drivers, owned a neighboring ranch at Radersburg. Each man had a considerable amount of land along each side the Missouri River in the Crow Creek Valley, providing ample water for stock. That summer P.B. accompanied Silas on business trips to purchase 17,000 sheep in Utah and Canada. They made purchasing trips to the east and shipped stock via the steamboats coming up the Missouri River. Sheep along with herders and their dogs and blooded horses were among the arrivals at Fort Benton.

Montana ranchers had learned that sheep fared very well in the climate and could be left alone to graze in the high mountains. Huntley & Clark soon had 20,000 sheep on their Horseshoe Bend range, east of Fort Benton under the Belt Mountains. As a favor to a San Francisco buyer of wool clips, Silas decided to go and take a look at the different flocks in the Smith River area where he had worked building roads in 1867, "when there was but one human habitation and not a settler in the valley." Ten years hence ranchers and sheep were thriving.

———◦◦◦———

Helena, up to this time, was still very isolated. The most established means of getting into Montana Territory were the steamboats that traveled from St. Louis up the Missouri River over three thousand miles to Fort Benton – leaving well over one hundred miles of overland travel on horseback or horse and wagon on to Helena. One stagecoach road operated from the transcontinental railroad line in Utah, which was about four hundred miles south of Helena. The NPR was working its way west across the northern plains, but it would be twenty years until its tracks were laid all the way to Helena. Emigrant homesteaders mostly followed Captain Fisk's Northern Overland Trail from Minnesota, across North Dakota to Fort Benton.

A large population had grown up around the fabulous gold strikes of 1864 in Last Chance Gulch. Other assets in the area along with the gold were readily recognized. The wide open fertile lands, the mighty rivers, and the towering mountains attracted people who had a mind to build a thriving city with substantial homes and successful businesses.

The community of Helena prospered as new streets filled with large beautiful houses of various architectural styles. But twice, horrific wildfires swept through town burning many homes and businesses. These disasters did not cause a mass exodus; the people stayed and built even bigger and better houses. A wooden fire watch tower was constructed overlooking the main business district with a platform and a bell to be sounded as soon as a fire was spotted by the watchman.

W.C. Child and his wife Mary had built their home [21] in the original townsite near Last Chance Gulch. But the new arrivals developed an area of grand homes on Madison Avenue, on a rise north of the town center.

Silas and Annie planned to reside in Montana and raise standard bred horses. Silas built a house at 812 Madison [22] in this new prominent neighborhood. Annie soon endeared herself to the other ladies of the neighborhood. She loved to entertain and socialize. The housewives of Helena were social and civic-minded. Aided by the newspapers' society column writers, the ladies' causes, activities, and even their latest eastern fashions were kept in the news.

Such was the scene around Helena when Harry W. Child stepped off the stagecoach early in 1878.

Madison Avenue homes of (L-R) Sam Word, Samuel
Hauser, A.J. Seligman, and H.W. Child

Chapter 2: New Faces in Helena
1878-1887

Harry arrives in Helena, building begins in
Yellowstone, trouble at the Gregory

Harry Wilbour Child [5] was an adventuresome man with a competitive spirit. He arrived in Helena, responding to an invitation from his uncle, W.C. Child, coaxing him to visit and experience Montana Territory. Harry, now twenty-three years old, and his good friend E.W. (Edmund William) Bach [3], both caught the attention of newspapermen soon after they arrived in 1878. These communities and towns were still young, and they welcomed ambitious and energetic young men of business.

Harry decided he would not patent or work his Matchless Mine just yet. Instead, he first got a job selling cigars and stationery, and worked for a time as an agent for a stage company – probably the Shasta Stage from Salt Lake City, Utah. In his first years in Helena, he shared a

15

boarding-house room with Lionel Nettre.

Harry's friend, E.W. Bach came with him from San Francisco. E.W. was born in New York City. After spending a few years in Connecticut, he too entered the stock brokerage business in San Francisco. Upon arriving in Montana, E.W. immediately took a position with a dry goods store in Deer Lodge. The lure of mining took him, the next year, to join the North-Western Company in Philipsburg as a clerk in its quartz mill and reduction works.

E.W. was described as affable and accomplished. Among other talents, he was a champion foot racer -- a popular sport at that time. Harry too joined the races, but friends said that "while being a good breaker, lacked the length of legs necessary in a good runner." Harry was only five feet-five inches tall. However, what he lacked in height was made up for in business shrewdness, trustworthiness, loyalty, and personality.

E.W. was a numbers man – very quickly being hired as a clerk. Once he learned how these pioneer developments worked, he saw his future in supplying goods and food to the mining camps and the growing community of Helena.

By 1886, E.W. joined with Canadian emigrant, David C. Cory, becoming partners in Bach, Cory & Company. They first established a mercantile store at the mining community of Wickes, and a few years later opened another branch at the Gregory Mine. In downtown Helena they leased from businessman Colonel Broadwater his "fine brick building ... one of the best in the city" at the corner of Sixth Avenue and Main Street [24].

E.W. soon ran on the Democratic ticket for Lewis and Clark county assessor. He seemed to enjoy politics, serving with Samuel Hauser as a county delegate at the Territorial convention in 1884. He was trusted to examine the financial records of the Territorial offices, and when Samuel Hauser was appointed the Territorial Governor by President Cleveland in 1885, he appointed E.W. as ordinance officer.

A.J. (Albert Joseph) Seligman [4], a dapper young man of twenty-two and a mining engineer, arrived in Helena in 1881. With his New York City roots, and his wealthy upbringing, he quickly became part of Helena's elite. He built a magnificent home at 802 Madison Avenue, between those of Samuel Hauser and Harry Child/Silas Huntley, and designed by a nationally renowned architect. His father was one of seven brothers who emigrated from Bavaria. Financial success in the clothing business allowed the Seligman brothers to enter banking, establishing branches in multiple cities. A.J.'s Uncle Joseph, head of the New York branch, decided to work with the people in Montana Territory to assay, purchase, and ship gold directly to his New York office. He, in turn, planned to sell the gold to the U.S. Treasury. He invested $25,000 in a Helena firm that operated both an assay office and a street-front bank.

In the first year business was brisk – both for the bank and the assay office. They turned out a gold bar valued at $24,722.58 that was shipped by them to Joseph's New York office on the Wells, Fargo & Company stagecoach. Gold dust and gold melted together into bars had a combined coin value of $259,478.70. Joseph Seligman doubled his initial investment in what he liked to call "Our Montana House." But after the death of one of the principal owners of the Helena bank, Joseph began to question the integrity of the successors. After sending two confidants to investigate he learned that, through convoluted dealings loaning to mines and smelters, they had apparently done the Seligman firm out of a quarter of a million dollars. He instructed the men to liquidate everything as soon as possible, preserving as many assets as possible. Joseph said, "I don't care what happens to those Montanans, they can go to jail or to H - - -."

When Joseph Seligman died in 1880, his brother Jesse Seligman took charge of the dynasty. In the beginning, Joseph had only been interested in profits produced by the mines. Now, Jesse sent A.J. to oversee their mining interests in Montana. Through correspondence with Lionel Nettre, in 1881 A.J. purchased a partnership in the Gregory

Consolidated Mines and Works for J. & W. Seligman & Company.

By 1882 Harry Child was manager of two producing mines, the Gloster and the Gregory. Rather than working his own mine, he chose to learn the business from the bottom up. He seemed to have a natural instinct for communicating with and getting along with everyone whether it be the local workmen, eastern financiers or even presidents of the United States. Harry also lived by a motto, "What's worth doing is worth doing well."

Harry enjoyed great success and publicity as manager of the Gregory Mine. Under his direction the mine had reached a depth of 350 feet and had horizontal levels and side drifts extending 4,000 feet. It had rich veins of galena, coal, and silver, as well as gold. Concentrators, smelters, furnaces, and crushers had been added making the Gregory the most complete works in Montana Territory.

After Eastern financiers began developing the Gloster Mine it employed over 300 men. With the combination of these two enterprises, Harry assumed great responsibilities at a very young age.

———————

Annie and Silas' first years together were marred with controversy in his business life by way of court battles. The first was an investigation by the post-office committee of the U.S. House of Representatives about the awarding of mail contracts. Silas was found to be innocent of any wrongdoing.

A few years later Captain Charles, based on the audit of his stage lines, filed suit against both Silas and Bradley Barlow, his partner on routes farther west. He alleged that during their partnerships the two men failed to give him an equal share of the business.

Silas was recognized as a good organizer and manager but perhaps not so meticulous with numbers in his record keeping. He testified that to get anything done in Washington, he had to go through many levels. His attitude was to be friendly, starting with the clerks and messengers, by presenting them with what he called "trifles," such as a cigar or opera ticket. Silas had topnotch horses and carriages, and he often made them available to department heads or members of Congress. He also said that after clerks and messengers, department heads and congressmen, came members of the press, to whom he often gave dinners in the amount of $10.00 to $50.00 a head. Being reported and repeated daily put the whole thing in the spotlight. Having these practices exposed piqued the ire of the reporters.

Silas did not detail each time a trifle was presented. He knew how much money he went to Washington with, and how much he had left when business was done. That difference told him the figure he put on the books as cost of doing business. The Washington reporters chose to describe that money as used "to grease the wheels" of his business. The local Montana newspapers reported that "S.S. Huntley, the spruce young man who made liberal payments in Washington, D.C. had been investigated [before] and cleared of any wrong doing."

The Huntley vs. Huntley case dragged on for several years, making it to the Supreme Court of the District of Columbia. It ended in 1882 – part of the case was decided in favor of Charles. Silas had to sell his carriages and some Washington, D.C. real estate to satisfy the execution of the court decision. Silas and Annie were at last free of the cloud that had hung over the first three years of their marriage. Charles died before the rest of the trial was settled. His father was appointed executor of Charles' estate.

Silas may have lost one battle to his cousin, but by 1882 he was financially secure enough to join L.H. Hershfield's bank. When it became the Merchants National Bank of Helena with an associated bank in Fort Benton, Silas Huntley was appointed to the Board of Directors. He served on the Board for more than ten years.

Even while the court battle was dragging on, Silas got contracts for two new stagecoach lines – one to carry mail between Helena and White Sulfur Springs, the other to carry mail between Helena and

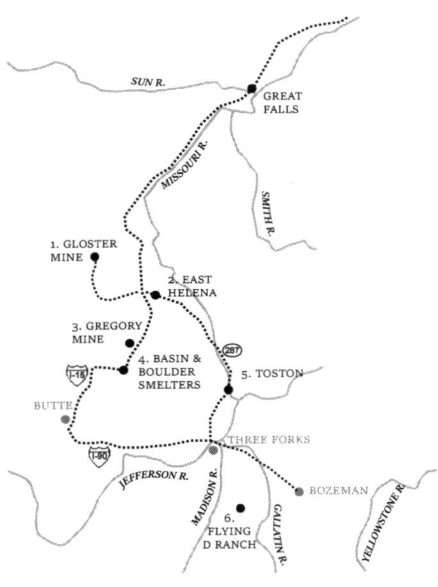

1) Gloster Mine
2) East Helena, H.W. Child Ranch
3) Gregory Mine
4) Basin and Boulder smelter locations
5) Tosten, Huntley & Clark's Riverside Stock Farm
6) Flying D Ranch

Diamond City. It was reported that for each of the new lines, "four brand new coaches have been ordered. S.S. Huntley and his new partner, Mr. Philo B. Clark propose to put on good stock and plenty of it and fit up the finest stage lines in the Rocky Mountains." The partners joined in a business venture which they called the Huntley & Clark Riverside Stock Farm.

Silas and P.B. continued to extend their Riverside Stock Farm by launching an aggressive breeding program. They advertised regularly in local newspapers and a catalogue was printed yearly. An early catalogue featured names and pedigrees of twenty stallions and colts, and thirty-five mares and fillies. Their specialty was trotting and racing horses. An impressive pedigree went with each animal sold. In the beginning, they harbored some doubts about the success of their breeding business yet were convinced that their customers "would soon become educated up to discarding the treacherous cayuse for a reliable and valuable animal."

While in Kentucky to purchase horses with certain blood lines they wanted to introduce into their breeding practices, Silas said in an interview, "The demand for road horses in Montana Territory is good and growing. The striking feature of American civilization is the love of the trotting horse. As soon as a man builds himself a home and lays up a little for a rainy day, no matter how far from New York or San Francisco, he hankers for a light wagon and a stepper who will not take the dust of his neighbor."

Silas purchased a three-year-old colt named Bishop. It was predicted that "the blood of Bishop could not do otherwise than improve the equine stock and ultimately add much to the wealth of the Territory." So began the Huntley & Clark creation of the Montana blooded horse.

As horse racing grew in popularity, Silas finished the race track on his side of the ranch. The track "drew enthusiasts from throughout the region and even as far as the east coast. Horses from his ranch became distinguished on the eastern trotting tracks."

Ben Lomond, son of Bishop, was their first prize racing horse. He became one of the best known and most valuable stallions in Montana and the Northwest. Ben Lomond, Jr. won recognition at the Montana Territorial Fair as "the fastest trotting horse in Montana" – "trotting a full mile without a skip or a break and came under the wire in 2:28," – earning him the reputation as "King of the Montana Turf." One year later, he won a heat in 2:27, beating his previous time.

"Throughout the late 1880s, Helena's track was intrinsic to the state's racing circuit, where breeders, horses and jockeys influenced the national racing scene." Huntley & Clark erected training stables at the Helena Fair grounds and began training their trotting horses for competition. They traveled to the fair grounds of the Montana Agricultural, Mineral & Mechanical Association in Butte, and the Deer Lodge Fair & Racing Association Grounds. Their finest horses, Ben Lomond, Maxim, and Kentucky Volunteer dominated the reports.

Activities at Silas's track and regional races were important social occasions – providing entertainment for the locals and the social class. Local businessmen like Silas and Harry also used the events to make contact with eastern railroad men and investors.

The Riverside Stock Farm continued to grow and Silas began to move into the realm of politics governing the growth of agriculture in Montana. He first became active in the Montana Stock Growers Association and was appointed their representative at the first National Convention. He served on the Executive Committee representing Jefferson County and eventually was elected Vice-President of the Association.

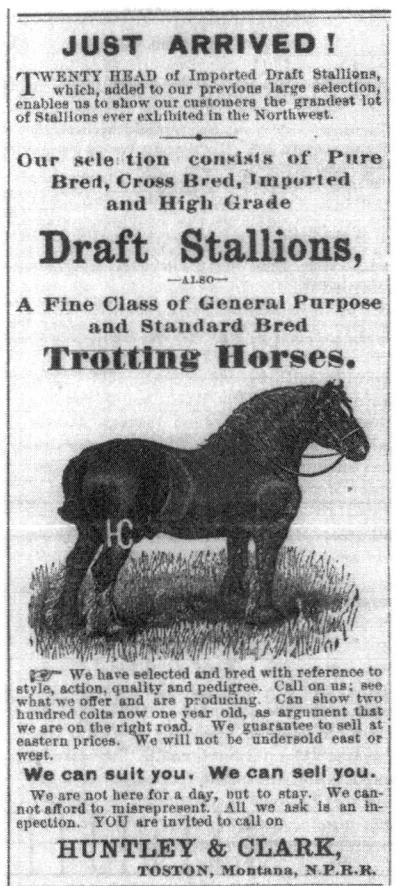
The horse in this ad bears the Huntley & Clark brand.

The mid-1880s was a prosperous time for Huntley & Clark's Riverside Stock Farm as they promoted their breeding program and began entering horses in trotting races at fair grounds around Montana Territory. "Some of the animals described [in their catalog]" observed one newspaper, "have pedigrees as long as the moral law." Their sales of thoroughbred working type stallions, Norman and Clydesdales, appeared in the livestock sections regularly. Demand for their stud services spread from Jefferson county to Lewis and Clark, Gallatin, Meagher, and Choteau counties. "These gentlemen are good judges of horses," declared one reporter. Phrases such as "handsome model of a horse" and "beautiful specimens" filled the columns.

Their struggles were noted as well - such as the loss of a prize-winning horse along with seven or eight others to an epidemic inflammation of the lungs. There was an accident where a mule team with two wagons backed off the ferry and was a total loss. Horses bearing their HC brand were also identified among stolen stock recovered in Crow Indian Territory.

Back in 1881, W.C. had incorporated the Montana Sheep Company with Harry, Lionel Nettre, D.L. McFarland (his wife's brother), and W.W. DeLacy. They had nearly 3000 acres in the timbered foothills of the Snowy Mountains, along Flatwillow Creek. Their flock numbered 10,000. D.L. McFarland died tragically in 1884, and W.C. and his partners disposed of that ranch the following year.

In 1886 W.C. purchased 4,000 acres along Prickly Pear Creek to the east of Helena where he established the *White Face Farm* [14], stocking the first purebred Herefords in Montana Territory. The first winter was one of the worst in Montana history. This tragedy was the inspiration for Charles Russell's famous drawing "Waiting for a Chinook," showing an emaciated cow on a frozen plain.

Because W.C. suffered great losses of cattle in the severe winter of 1886-1887, he began building a massive stone barn to protect livestock indoors. "This monumental three-story barn with full-length side wings made of local fieldstone measures one hundred feet by one hundred feet on the first two levels and one hundred by sixty five feet on the third hayloft level. It was designed to hold five hundred cattle; 350 tons of hay could be stored in the loft." He imported thirty stonemasons from Italy for his projects.

It was reported that gold was discovered while excavating for the barn, but "Mr. Child does not intend, however, to sluice away his model stock farm to get to the gold dust and nuggets it contains." He proceeded with the construction. He claimed the first water rights in the Helena valley and irrigated 2,000 acres of hay.

In 1888 he started construction on a massive octagonal home. "The ranch house... was intended for recreation purposes, rather than as a permanent residence, because Mr. Child lived in Helena. The entire second floor of the house is an open ballroom." A spur of the Jefferson County and Elkhorn Railroad ran to the ranch, making it an easy destination for the young people of Helena – specifically the Childs' two daughters, Alta and Fanny, as they reached their teens.

―――⋙●⋘―――

Dr. Maria Dean [11] settled in Helena to be near sister Annie – Mrs. Silas Huntley. Dr. Dean completed her studies at the University of Wisconsin, graduated from Boston University School of Medicine, and spent a year training abroad. She set up a homeopathic practice, specializing in the diseases of women and children.

Diphtheria had reached epidemic proportions in the area and quarantine flags had been placed in front of the homes affected by the disease. Some folks resented being quarantined and removed the flags – prompting the *Helena Herald* to question the Board of Health. Dr. Dean, though new to Helena, was the chairperson of the Board.

Dr. Dean stood her ground insinuating that some citizens had removed the flags unlawfully. She promised prosecution and a fine for defying the Board's actions. She requested that all members of the households affected by the disease and any visitors should "abstain from intermingling with others." In case of either death or recovery, "the premises should be thoroughly disinfected, and no bedding exposed to the public by being hung out on the fences near the sidewalks."

Her stern remarks were resented by some, but she became a loved and very special citizen.

———◦———

Within a year the third Dean sister, Adelaide [6], came to Helena for a visit. Adelaide also attended the University of Wisconsin and then on to Boston. While there she was instrumental in organizing a Kappa Kappa Gamma chapter.

At that time, the NPR tracks lacked a few miles of being finished all the way to Helena; however a taxi service was provided to convey travelers the remaining distance into the city. Adelaide said, "I found no dearth of young men in Montana Territory. The carriages were lined up at the depot so the bachelors of Helena could view the young ladies descending from the train cars."

Throughout the summer and fall of 1882 Miss Adelaide was the star of the society columns of the *Helena Herald* and other local papers. She was properly escorted and introduced to the folks of Helena in the company of Mr. and Mrs. S.S. Huntley and Mr. and Mrs. W.C. Child.

One afternoon they "left for the Gregory mine behind Mr. McFarland's spanking four-in-hand" as guests of Mr. Harry Child, manager. The outing provided opportunity for Harry to shine, introducing his friends "to the process through which the ore product passes for treatment, under as favorable circumstances as modern inventions render practical." Gregory, at the time, was "working a full force of men. ... The smelter is in full blast, and the concentrator and other appliances of the reduction works are also at work ... They will find a rambling through its glittering levels not merely interesting as novel, but as giving a better idea of what real mining is." Through the ensuing months, on the guests list of many social events, were the names of Mr. Harry W. Child and Miss Adelaide Dean. While courting, one of their favorite outings was strolling Last Chance Gulch to the old fire watchtower.

At the end of a very romantic and publicized summer, Adelaide traveled to Cincinnati, Ohio to spend the winter with her mother's family. Her presence must have been missed. One columnist wrote, "In a recent visit to Helena, Miss Dean not only made a host of friends, but she captured our 'Handsome Harry'."

Harry, before much time was lost, made an extended trip to Cincinnati. They were married on October 23,1883 at the residence of Mr. W.H. Wyman. "They pledged their vows beneath a floral marriage bell, with surrounds made beautiful by plants and flowers." "The services... were impressive." "The bride, lovely in white silk with diamond ornaments, was given away by her mother, Mrs. Ellen Dean." Harry's parents and sister attended: Mr. and Mrs. Edwin F. Child and Miss Kate Child. Mr. Jesse W. Lithenhal of New York, Harry's best man, was a partner in mining concerns. Silas and Annie also made the trip to Ohio.

After an elegant wedding breakfast, the happy couple departed on the evening train for their home in Montana. Congratulations to the newly wedded couple and Best Wishes for their happiness were extended through all the local publications.

Harry and Adelaide moved to the house on Madison Street, next door to A.J. Seligman. This was a prominent neighborhood, near Samuel Hauser's house which became the Governor's Mansion. All three Dean sisters, Silas and Annie Huntley, the Childs, and Dr. Maria Dean, now lived in the same neighborhood. The city of Helena was thriving.

In 1884, Harry and Adelaide welcomed their first born, a daughter. They named her Ellen Dean Child in honor of her maternal grandmother, Mrs. Ellen Dean. Two years later their second baby was born. They named their son Huntley Child after brother-in-law and good friend Silas S. Huntley. Although Harry's work sometimes took him away from home, Adelaide was not alone. She had her two sisters and her mother close by. And the women of Helena opened their homes for receptions and parties.

———————

The Northern Pacific Railroad (NPR) tracks were growing farther and farther across Montana, and a spur line was built from Livingston down to Gardiner, the north entrance to Yellowstone Park. With such a large investment, there was concern about adequate facilities for accommodating the tourists the NPR planned to carry throughout the summer season. Already there were business ventures of many types operating within the Park boundaries – rustic hotels and camps, lunch stations, souvenir stands, and various types of transportation.

The Park superintendent who followed Nathaniel Langford, Philetus W. Norris, was successful in getting some appropriations from Congress. He laid out a road system and posted signs to guide visitor use. The location of roads in Yellowstone was laid out to highlight the major attractions such as the Mammoth Hot Springs, Norris Geyser Basin, Lower and Upper Geyser Basins (Old Faithful area), Yellowstone Lake, and the Grand Canyon of the Yellowstone River. * *[see map p. 39]* The Army Corps of Engineers, beginning in 1883, surveyed and built roads and bridges to connect these spots.

The NPR was granted exclusive rights to provide accommodations for transportation inside the park. Railroad officials determined that the necessary business of handling tourists should be placed in independent hands, thus the creation of the Yellowstone Park Improvement Company (YPIC). They started construction on the National Hotel at Mammoth and built tent camps at Norris Geyser Basin, the Upper Geyser Basin, and the Lower Falls. Interest in the Park remained high among Helena citizens, and happenings were followed almost daily in the local newspapers.

But by the mid-1880s things were getting out of hand to the point that the U.S. Army was sent in to take over the administration of Yellowstone [33]. The Army's purpose was to roust out poachers of wild game, to protect the natural features, and to keep the peace. Commanding officers were called "Acting Superintendents" during their temporary tours of duty at Fort Yellowstone.

The National Park System (not Service) was created (in the Department of Interior) which opened the way to create other national parks and provided for the creation of the National Park Rangers. Eventually, after the establishment of the National Park Service, park superintendents would be appointed from those who had come up through the ranks of the National Park Rangers.

Harry diversified his investments by purchasing land in Crow Creek Valley in 1885. Calling it *Willows Stock Farm* [15], it was six miles south of Toston, near Huntley & Clark's Riverside Stock Farm. He continued to add to it for the next fifteen years until he held a total of 640 acres. He stocked "the largest herd of pure bred Galloway" cattle in Montana and "twenty-five head of full blood and grade Clydesdale mares" for breeding. The business was a profit making venture "besides offering an occasional recreation from business cares."

In 1887 Harry purchased 800 acres of land on the north side of Helena for $250,000 in cash. This was said to be "the largest cash deal in real estate, that is not connected with mining interests, that had ever taken place in Montana. ... Incorporators include Harry W. Child, Silas S.

Huntley, E.W. Bach and others from St. Paul and Bismarck with HWC as president of the corporation." After four years of being related through their wives, for the first time Harry and Silas entered a business deal together.

A short time later Harry and Adelaide conveyed by deed to St. Paul Land and Improvement Company all the property known as the Fant, Benedict and Kessler ranches. This corporation included several officers of the Northern Pacific Railroad along with the Helena men.

Another real estate venture of Harry's that same year was the construction of Oro Fino Terrace [23], an elegant family residence, at the corner of Benton and Stuart streets in Helena. This was a personal investment for the Child family. A glance at city directories over the years shows that Harry did become an asset to his family, including extended family members. From time to time Oro Fino Terrace welcomed Harry's brother George B. Child, and their sister, Miss Katie Child and later she and her husband Thomas C. Bach (brother of E.W. Bach). The E.W. Bach family lived there for a time too, as did Harry's parents, the Edwin F. Childs, Silas and Annie Huntley, and Dr. Maria Dean. The mother of the Dean sisters, Mrs. Ellen Dean, eventually moved there. Harry and Adelaide twice made Oro Fino Terrace their home (1892-1895 and 1899-1909).

⟶➤◆◄⟵

As the bitter winter of 1886-87 set in, troubles mounted at the Gregory mine. The weather and Indian raids were hampering the shipments of gold sent by wagon or coach to the railhead of the Northern Pacific Railroad which was still some distance from Helena. Therefore bouillon was being stored in Helena until it could be safely shipped by rail. For two months, Harry managed to keep the miners working while no payroll money was sent from the New York office. By the end of January, the miners were getting nervous and decided to take matters into their own hands.

As Harry arrived at the mine that January morning in the

company of E.W. Bach, accountant, Mr. Thomas West, the mine foreman, and A.J. Seligman, as representative of Eastern investors, a group of miners surrounded the four men and informed them that they were being held hostage until the back wages were paid. Harry and A.J. were put in a hoist and lowered into the mine. E.W. and West were allowed to move freely about the mine works but were kept under close guard.

Harry, quickly assessing the situation, asked to speak with the ringleaders of the kidnaping scheme and was able to persuade them that nothing could be done as long as he was held hostage. He promised not to involve the law and would pull no kind of shenanigan if he would be allowed to go to Helena and make arrangements to get the money. Having had no previous reason to doubt Harry's word, the miners agreed to let him leave on horseback under cover of darkness to make the twenty-five mile trip to Helena. E.W. and West were not allowed to leave the mine, and A.J. Seligman was held prisoner inside the mine until the matter could be resolved.

Harry went first to the Territorial Governor, Samuel T. Hauser, founder and president of the First National Bank of Helena. They decided to get Western Union to hook up Helena with New York and hold the line open until Mr. Jesse Seligman, A.J.'s father, head of the banking firm and major stock holder of the Gregory mine could be contacted. Harry then went to the Chief Justice and explained that the miners had threatened A.J. Seligman's life if there was any interference from the law. Harry meant to follow the miners instructions alone.

Within twenty-four hours the money was telegraphed to Harry Child, with Samuel T. Hauser as intermediary and E.W. Bach as distributor. The money was gathered from the local banks and stowed in a sleigh for transporting to the mine. The miners had stipulated that they preferred gold but would accept some paper money, no checks.

Being alone with the sleigh full of money, Harry became suspicious that there might be bandits or groups of miners who would waylay him and steal the money. He remembered an old stagecoach road that had not been used for several years and now lay under twelve inches of snow. He would have to break trail, but thanks to Silas S. Huntley, his good friend, brother-in-law and future business partner, he had at his command a high-stepping and strong Montana horse that could do the job. He broke away from the well-trod trail in favor of the unused stage road. The miles slipped away as the sleigh runners slid over the snow making soft sighing, singing sounds.

Harry arrived at the mine without incident delivering the payroll money to E.W. Bach, who would distribute to each miner his allotted amount as determined by Mr. West, the foreman and timekeeper. That done, A.J. Seligman was released, and he graciously thanked his captors for the kind treatment they had given him while being held prisoner. He had suffered no mistreatment and was well fed.

With the immediate crisis over, Harry's success in handling this difficult situation earned him wide fame and a reputation of acting squarely – being a man of his word and being able to take care of himself without feeling the need to carry a gun. This event brought him to the attention of railroad men and financiers, catapulting him into the world of big business and high finance. Harry made a short foray into politics, but declined a nomination when he accepted a job in Great Falls with the Montana Smelting Company.

The NPR had just put on a "Fast Train" that traveled at thirty-two miles an hour making the trip between Helena and Great Falls in only three hours. Harry was on the inaugural trip and because of this convenience, for the next several years, he and Adelaide were able to stay involved with many interests in both cities.

MONTANA SILVER SMELTER, GREAT FALLS, MONT.

Chapter 3: Winds of Change
1888-1891

*Building a smelter, campaigning
for statehood, Silas
awarded Yellowstone contract*

As General Manager of the Montana Smelting Company's project in Great Falls, Harry was charged with the monumental challenge of overseeing all the construction. The buildings, machinery, and equipment were massive. The facility was being built to process 1000 tons of ore per day.

The spot chosen to build the plant was below Giant Springs on the southern slope of the Missouri River – a beautiful setting [19]. The people of Great Falls were especially fond of the huge smoke stack that stood 155 feet high for more than forty years. It became a beacon for airplane pilots and at ground level could be seen for miles around. It was built under the direct supervision of Harry Child at a cost of $75,000. He believed that it would serve for seventy-five years.

The general office building was 50 by 60 feet. Another building, 150 by 408 feet, housed the twenty roasting furnaces. The engine and boiler rooms were in an 85 by 200 foot structure, and, connected with this, were five ore bins. There was also an assay office, laboratory, and smaller residences for assistants and employees [18]. When all of that was completed, the manager's residence would be built.

He had a crew of three hundred men to oversee and to keep the project moving in an organized fashion. Harry proved himself equal to the task. The whole project was brought in on time and under budget. Harry was paid one million dollars for the job. When all was ready for the smelter to start working, Harry employed "the dainty hand of Mrs. Child to pull the lever, setting the mighty machinery in motion as if by a magic touch."

Harry occasionally acted as the smelter's public relations representative. He hosted the Press Association to visit the works and "take a 'lunch.' It was one of the finest repasts ever spread in the Territory, and eaten with gratitude beaming out of every eye of his hungering and grateful guests," touted the *Great Falls Tribune*. He entertained the eastern financiers at the meeting of smelter directors, "H.W. Child of Helena, arrived here today in a special car, accompanied by W.S. Gurnee, A.C. Gurnee and C.W. Cromwell, all of New York. The party will leave in the morning for a trip to the National park, and on their return will visit Tacoma and Portland, stopping a day in Helena on their way west."

Again the Childs were the darlings of the social columnists. Their every move was reported in the evening papers: "Mrs. Child is again visiting this scenic region and stopping with her husband at the reduction works." On this occasion, Adelaide was probably considering the location and plans for their new home. "Before many months she will reside in the elegant $10,000 residence to be built by Mr. Child on the beautiful plateau that overlooks the Giant Spring."

The house was a three-story structure, sixty-feet square, of

French architectural design [20]. It had many rooms – each with its own tiled fireplace. A winding staircase of solid oak and a carriage entrance were also features. Christmas of 1889 was a splendid occasion at the manager's residence. Mrs. Adelaide Child hosted a Christmas Eve party for the children of all the company employees.

The spacious home also provided the opportunity for the three sisters to celebrate the holiday together, "Si Huntley and wife, Annie, and Dr. Dean spent a Merry Christmas with Mr. and Mrs. Harry Child at the smelter."

In Helena, the Dean sisters, Annie, Dr. Maria, and Adelaide, along with friends, Mrs. Hauser, Mrs. Seligman and Mrs. Julia A. Bach, affectionately known as "Gussie," were actively participating in social and community events. Fortunately, all families enjoyed prosperity, because it "took a long purse" to keep pace with Helena society.

As a city Helena was in its infancy despite the wealth of the area. After twenty-five years, the residents were only a small part of Montana Territory. Now they were looking toward the coming statehood. When the dispute between cities battling for the honor of becoming state capitol began boiling up, the prominent ladies of Helena took the matter in hand and formed "The Helena for Capitol Club." The *Helena Independent* backed their efforts with the headline: "Women, God Bless 'Em. Women in Montana Generally and Women in Particular Who Work for a Living. The Wealthiest Women in the State - Helena's Professional Females."

Helena needed a new hospital to compete as a capitol city. Dr. Dean had helped in founding the first hospital in a wood frame building. Through the years, the effort continued as the facility suffered set-back after set-back, namely overcrowding and in one case even fire damage.

The ladies of the fine houses in Helena were not idle. They went on hunting trips and donated the meat. They went on fishing trips and brought back a large catch, also to be donated. And they entertained.

Whether it was a progressive euchre party or an elegant evening of music, dancing and beautiful hospitality, the gracious hostesses opened their homes and donated the proceeds.

———⋙●⋘———

With the advent of the new smelter, the city of Great Falls enjoyed a growing spurt. The Bach, Cory & Company established a branch in Great Falls. The firm constructed on Central Avenue a three-story structure of local sandstone. The local press touted their efforts: "The firm are widely known for their energy, public spirit and business capacity. They will receive a cordial welcome from the mercantile community here..." E.W. Bach and his wife "Gussie" Hubbard Bach, moved their residence to Great Falls.

As the Territory of Montana moved closer to statehood, there was a convention to frame the constitution of the State of Montana. Three delegates were to be elected from each of twenty-five districts, for a total of seventy-five members. In each district the Democrats had two nominees and the Republicans the same. After several votes, the Republicans declared Harry Child their choice to the attend convention. The party was hopeful that his participation would bring along the votes of the miners.

The politics soon turned nasty and personal, as two local newspapers, each backed by a different political party, dueled over Harry's nomination. The *Great Falls Daily Leader* "had not a good word to say for Mr. Child." After Harry declined the nomination, the *Great Falls Tribune* defended his decision, declaring him "a great deal shrewder politician than may have been supposed."

E.W. Bach took his politics seriously, once becoming involved in a public brawl that produced local headlines, "There was a knife and a good deal of talk but nobody was badly hurt." Harry Child, a Republican, and Bach, a Democrat, continued a close personal friendship and joined in business enterprises, such as real estate or co-ownership of competitive racing and trotting horses.

34

After living in Great Falls a short time, tragedy struck the E.W. Bachs. Their first child, Albert Lionel Bach, named to honor two dear friends (A.J. Seligman and Lionel Nettre), died at age eight months in 1883. In 1889 Gussie died giving birth to a second baby. The child, a girl, also died and was buried in Helena with her mother. After Gussie's death, E.W. stayed with Harry and Adelaide, while his brother Judge Thomas Bach and his wife Kate, Harry's sister, stayed at the Bach home in Helena, taking care of the necessary arrangements.

After the burial, the Childs, the Thomas Bachs, Silas and Annie Huntley, and E.W. engaged in one of Harry's prescriptions for "a saner, healthier, more rational, more friendly life" – a week-long camping and fishing trip to the Belt Mountains. In his words, "you can do more work and you can get more fun out of doing it in the sunlight ... riding, fishing, game hunting, ... all in the open, all healthy, leading to no 'morning after.'"

Eventually E.W. Bach went back to Helena and established his reputation as a trusted businessman and community promoter. He was a member of the Helena Board of Trade, county election judge, a member of the Chamber of Commerce, the Athletic Association, and the Commercial Club. He became a director of Samuel Hauser's First National Bank. He disassociated himself with Bach, Cory & Company around 1893, but still appeared in the Helena City Directories, now listed as a mining broker.

———⟫●⟪———

The Riverside Stock Farm prospered in the late 1880s. Huntley & Clark "have 11,000 acres of land under fence," recorded the *Great Falls Tribune*. "Their stock at Toston includes 1,500 head of horses ... 500 head of ... cattle. They own 15,000 sheep." Sale of a horse brought $1,500 to $2,000 to the partners. (today's equivalent of $40,000 - $53,000) In April 1888 they sold Ben Lomond and Maxim for $9,000 (equivalent to $239,000 today!) – Silas "hesitated the sale but felt constrained to do so on account of the necessity of unloading somewhat of their marketable stallions." Their 1889 catalogue featured one hundred and twenty-two head of trotting stock, each with an impressive pedigree.

Huntley & Clark's horses scored big at the Helena fair in August 1889:

Prize	Category	Winner	owners
First Premium $10	stallion 2 yrs and under 3 yrs	"Scandle"	owned by Huntley & Clark
Second Premium $5	mare 2 yrs and under 3yrs	"Sweet Brier"	owned by Bach and Child
Sweepstakes $50	Stallion with 5 of his colts, regardless of ownership, under 2yrs of age	"Maxim"	owned by Huntley & Clark

The ladies planned a celebration dance at the new Broadwater Hotel, which opened to the public just days before. For the past year Helena citizens watched in anticipation as the grand hotel took shape, "transforming the area from an arid waste and tangled wilderness into a paradise." Among those present at the *Fair Hop* were Mr. and Mrs. A.J. Seligman, Mr. Hauser, Mr. and Mrs. Harry Child, Mr. and Mrs. S.S. Huntley, Judge Thomas and Mrs. Bach. The various committees fulfilled their duties well. Mr. W.C. Child made a most efficient floor master. Mrs. S.S. Huntley wore white silk, lace overskirt with bead trimming. Mrs. Harry Child wore pink silk with pink Tule overskirt. Mrs. Thomas Bach wore black lace.

Silas Huntley was active in the organizations and associations that supported and promoted the farm and ranching industries. He was on the executive committee representing Jefferson County when the two Montana associations -eastern and western -joined into one. Although Harry, "a large cattle and stock man," was not himself involved in the association, Silas was working side-by-side with two men who later became part of Harry's inner circle – Charles Anceney of Gallatin County, and Theodore Roosevelt, then representing Dakota Territory.

Silas' travels began to extend beyond Montana to livestock shows in Chicago and New York. Diamond City's *Rocky Mountain Husbandman* was a widely read publication that carried much news, plus many interesting articles. Huntley & Clark, recognized as some of the area's horse kings, "know the value of printer's ink." Silas regularly visited the offices of the *Husbandman*, the *Chicago Horseman*, the leading horse paper in the U.S. – *Spirit of the Turf*, and the *New York Sportsman* to promote the Montana breeding programs.

While in Chicago Silas had a chat with a representative of the *Horseman*, which wrote: "Mr. Huntley says that he tried blanketing and keeping growing stock in the stable during the winter, but found that they did not thrive any better than other animals that were turned out and in a measure shifted for themselves on dry grasses to be found in the shaded nooks and fertile spots. He thinks that such rearing in the pure air of Montana makes its horses more rugged and enduring on track and road than those bred and pampered in milder latitudes and more settled regions."

Silas continued to be quoted about the horse-drawn days. He wrote this letter to the *Husbandman* in response to an article written by another reader:

> Your experience of riding the cayuse fifty and one hundred miles a day in early times, brings vividly to mind many old timers, stagers and prospectors feats accomplished by the Montana horse that now seem incredible. I remember as only yesterday, when we had no thoroughbreds and high breeds in Montana, we used to make with six-horse stage from Helena to Deer Lodge, via Blackfoot, a distance of sixty miles, and the route over the main backbone of the Rocky Mountains, in five hours - a quicker time than one now makes the same distance by cars. And without injury to horses we have driven a six-horse from Bozeman to Helena, a distance of one hundred miles in less than twenty hours, never urging them, and they would be as fresh as ever the next day. This early – not hearsay – experience, with the endurance and bottom of Montana horses, led me to pin my faith to them, where it still sticks...

———————

Late in the year 1889 Montana residents were consumed with the excitement of becoming the 41st state. Montana's first Governor, Joseph Toole, appointed Silas Huntley to the State Board of Stock Commissioners. Helena got a new hospital – St. Peter's, and was named the state capitol.

Dr. Dean was granted a full medical license – she was the 27th doctor to receive a state license and the only woman doctor. *The Helena*

Herald's description of her was admirable: "She is one of the most popular and prominent residents in Helena. Although full of pluck, she is not a bit masculine. She is an excellent shot and can hit eleven or twelve birds out of thirteen on the wing. ... [She] does not want to marry and probably never will." Of medium height, "Dr. Dean is a blonde, remarkable for her strength, and can handle a high-spirited horse with the dexterity of a veteran turfman and is an expert in the saddle." She drove her own horse and buggy when making her numerous house calls.

Annie and Silas were spending summers at the Riverside Stock Farm and winters at Oro Fino Terrace in Helena. This allowed them to join the social scene with their friends in the fall and winter months. "Last Thursday evening a delightful tally-ho party was given by Mr. E.W. Bach to Mr. and Mrs. S.S. Huntley." announced the society column, "Mr. Huntley skillfully piloted the horses and Prof. Peterman was bugler. After visiting the race track and watching the flyers, an extended drive over the magnificent roadways followed, and then a delightful dinner at Hotel Broadwater. The ladies wore elegant corsage bouquets and the gentlemen boutonnieres. This is the first tally-ho party ever given in Helena."

Helena's society was changing. Not only were some of the newspaper readers growing weary of reading about the lives of the elite few, but the elite themselves were ready for something new. However, their toned-down methods of entertaining still made the newspapers, as in this entry titled, *Society in the Solstice*:

> Realizing the dissatisfaction and actual discomfort consequent upon crowded gatherings when there is room for the sparkle of neither wit nor jewels, some of the ladies of Helena are adopting the plan so long in vogue in the east and elsewhere, where the number of one's friends outgrows the rooms in one's house, namely that of giving a number of small entertainments in place of a single large one from which everyone retires more or less crushed, both physically and spiritually. One of the most delightful of these small entertainments was that given at the elegant house of ex-Governor Hauser, on Wednesday evening last, when some of the numerous friends of the hostess were invited to meet Gov. and Mrs. Toole, and Mrs. Spofford of New York city ... Those invited ... were ... Judge and Mrs. Bach, Mr. and Mrs. Harry Child, Dr. Dean, Mr. Huntley, Mr. D.A. Cory.

~ ~ ~

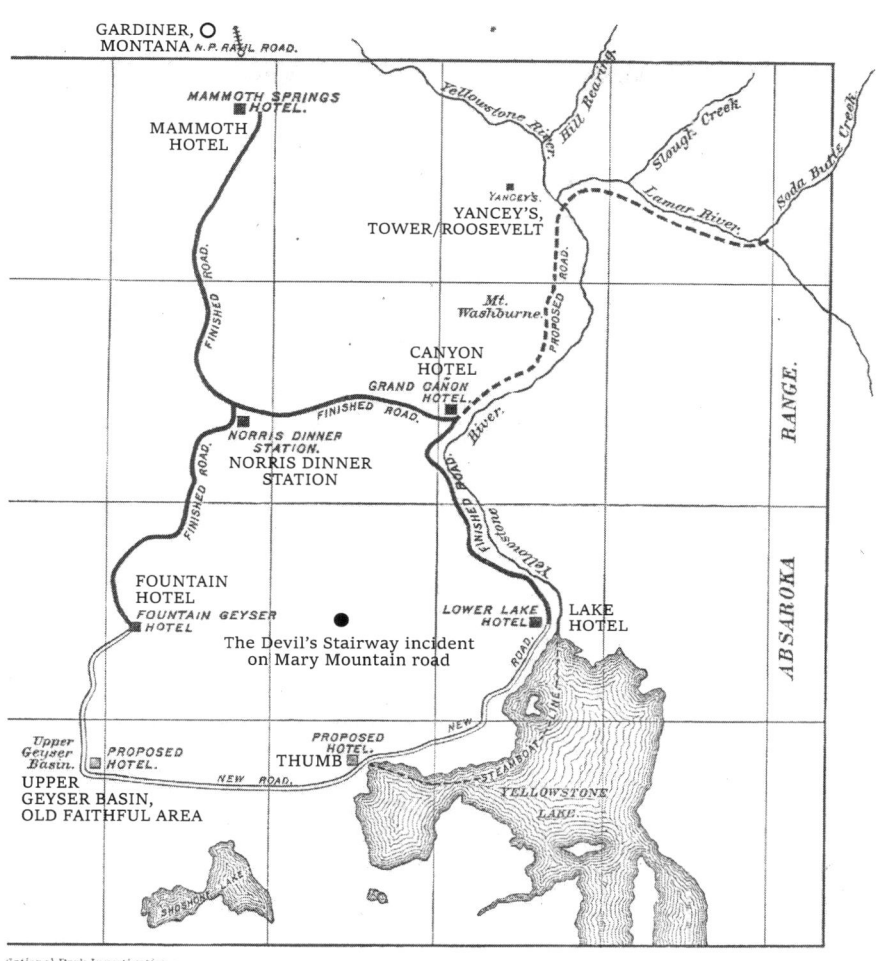

Yellowstone National Park road system about 1892. The Devil's
Stairway incident took place on Mary Mountain road (now a hiking
trail) between Fountain Hotel and Lake Hotel. Map courtesy of NPS.

Congress had approved a very large appropriation of funds for
road improvements in Yellowstone. Other services were provided by
private enterprise companies that contracted with the government. The
railroads were financial backers for many of these private companies.

Since the days of YPIC when the NPR officials first became
concerned about adequate tourist facilities, [George] Wakefield &

[Charles] Hoffman had provided transportation by stagecoach from the train terminus to the hotels operated by the YPIC (owned by the NPR but managed by a group of independent businessmen). When the YPIC failed, the railroad brought in a new group of businessmen who formed the Yellowstone Park Association (YPA) [60]. Wakefield & Hoffman continued to act as agents of the YPA. As early as 1882 the NPR had had exclusive rights to carry railroad passengers to the hotels, but there were to be no railroad tracks in the park. This created a loop-hole that Wakefield & Hoffman slipped into.

In those days, the stagecoach road that went from the Lower Geyser Basin over Mary Mountain was a long steep haul and very difficult for the horses to pull a loaded coach. That piece of road had been dubbed the "Devil's Stairway." It was normal procedure for the drivers to ask the passengers who were able and willing to stretch their legs a bit to spell the horses. In midsummer of 1890, a sixty-four-year-old man who had a heart condition started walking with the other passengers behind the coach. It was a slow walk, but the day was hot – and sadly, he collapsed and died.

The recent national election had put a Republican, President Benjamin Harrison, in the White House. He appointed a fellow Republican, James Noble, to be his Secretary of Interior. After the Devil's Stairway incident, Secretary Noble began to look more deeply into the numerous other complaints reaching his office about the stage service in Yellowstone. He discovered that more than a few of the 'other' complaint letters concerned the idea that liquor was being carried on the same coach as Uncle Sam's U.S. mail, and that perhaps some of the drivers had imbibed. Also, he discovered that Wakefield & Hoffman had no legal government contract, but operated only as an agent of the YPA – while using all their own equipment and their own company name. Noble saw them as "an independent association" operating with "no responsible party" to be held accountable. He split the Yellowstone business, leaving the hotels to the YPA with transportation to be operated separately. Now Noble was looking for a new transportation concessionaire.

It was rumored that Russell Harrison, the President's son, had done some lobbying for Silas Huntley – a fellow Republican. Be that as it may, whether he lobbied or not, on March 30, 1891 Silas Huntley received a contract from the Department of the Interior to operate a stage and transportation line in Yellowstone Park. Of course, George Wakefield was not happy with this decision, and he took his complaint to his Democratic Representative who was able to gather enough support to demand a congressional investigation. Feeling sure that the investigation would go his way, Wakefield continued to prepare for the coming summer's business. However, the investigation dragged on and on. In the end, the investigative committees ruled that Wakefield was not responsible for the Devil's Stairway incident. His only infraction was operating without a contract – and the YPA, as well as the NPR, was remiss in allowing that to continue. Silas' contract stood firm, but George Wakefield was able to conduct his business as usual for one more summer (1891).

Silas was well-known and remembered from his earlier days of negotiating for road building and permits and contracts for his stagecoaches to carry passengers, freight, and the U.S. mail, as well as being popular in the social circles. Secretary Noble could not have found another man more suitable for the job in Yellowstone.

Both Silas Huntley and George Wakefield benefitted from the transitional season of 1891. Silas was making preparations for his Yellowstone franchise which was to begin operations the following November. He went into the Park early in the summer, checked in with the Superintendent, and spent some time "looking over the field," and making his own plans.

But most of the summer he spent in Montana tending to his business of raising and selling blooded horses. They excelled in competitions in Denver and Dallas and cities to the east and west, establishing the Montana horse as equal at least, if not superior, to other horses. The Huntley & Clark partners had begun to sell colts outside of Montana. The stock columns in the Montana newspapers show that

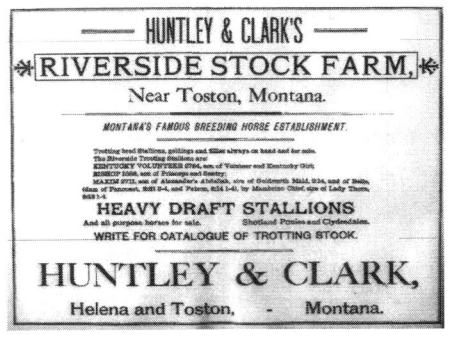

Around 1890 Marcus Daley, a Butte Copper King, began to devote his considerable wealth to horse breeding – overshadowing the contributions of Huntley & Clark.

Silas was slowly disposing of his blooded show horses. Huntley & Clark held their first public auction in Denver in October, and planned to have them annually.

Mr. P.B. Clark was moving heavily into mining, providing work horses, mules, and Shetland ponies that had also been bred at the Riverside Stock Farm, but without as much fanfare as the racers and trotters. The partners incorporated the Dunleith Mining Company in Jefferson County, and the Golden Chariot Mining Company at Pony, Montana, in Madison County. Mr. Clark put mule teams to work at their iron mine near Radersburg hauling ore to Monarch for shipment by rail.

George Wakefield still had a livelihood to pursue. As a private citizen with no ties to the railroad money, he could transport people to any or all of the camps using coaches, wagons, or buggies. NPR's exclusive contract covered their northern terminus to the hotels only. The government was leery of the railroads creating a monopoly in the park, which was the reason for adhering so strictly to the contracts.

George Wakefield received a license to provide transportation from the Union Pacific railroad on the west side of the park. Several Bozeman and Livingston men also received licenses to transport passengers through the Park. At the same time, Wakefield became co-manager of the new Bozeman Hotel in Montana.

Silas' contract was the usual form describing the obligations expected from "the party of the second part," including a $10,000 bond conditioned for the faithful performance of the agreement. It also listed park resources available for building his business, such as harvesting dead trees for lumber, water, grazing areas, and a certain amount of land. This attached addendum really laid down the law:

> Article 15: "It is further agreed upon and expressly understood by and between the parties hereto and to become a part of said lease, that said party of the second part [Silas Huntley] shall only retain in his employ and have in his services or engaged in and about the moving of passengers and tourists upon his line and upon his coaches careful, sober, experienced and courteous superintend, conductors and drivers and all employees of every kind and nature shall be faithful, careful and obliging. In no instance shall any but the most efficient drivers be employed, those who look to the safety of the passengers, and no intoxicants shall be used on any trip by anyone in the employ of the party of the second part, and no employee given to swearing, rude or boisterous conduct toward the passengers shall be retained in the service..."

Passenger complaints about questionable behavior on the part of Wakefield's drivers may have called for the inclusion of this passage. Historian Paul Schullery observes, "Swearing was regarded as part of the art of being a good teamster, since strong language seemed to inspire sluggish teams." Drivers were suspected of carrying secret flasks and hiding liquor bottles near park roadways. These practices brought obvious disapproval from park managers – and might have been the basis for Yellowstone's drivers earning the nickname *savage*!

By now Silas Huntley and P.B. Clark were "well-known old timers." Their frontier experience made them valuable to give testimony for Montana horses, "if we cannot breed Montana horses with better feet, better bones, larger lungs, to go faster, and to go longer than any other horse, it will be because our climate and air has changed, our soil and water not the same, our rolling hills have become level marshes, and our bunch-grass has lost its strength and become degenerated." One fellow Helena businessman raced a trotting horse called *S.S.*, probably a tribute to Silas S. Huntley.

The "winds of change" blew in with the 1890s spreading an aura of nostalgia amongst the old timers. While they were looking back to the glory days, the younger people looked to the future with different ideas. One columnist reminisced:

> Staging in Montana is rapidly closing out. Of the many lines that formerly centered in Helena, but two small affairs are left. The only lines now entering

here are Jay Gould and Diamond stages. Many of the old stage drivers and managers have gone into the stock business, which they are now successfully conducting. P.B. Clark, one of the best drivers that ever sat a coach entrusted with the custody of Uncle Sam's mails, has been in the stock business for a number of years with S.S. Huntley, a successful mail contract and stage manager. James H. McFarland has also done a great deal of staging and is reckoned one of the best drivers in the state. His love of good horses is undiminished, and he keeps a good string of roadsters in his stable on Clore Street for the accommodation of the public. Chris Vassube is probably the oldest stage-driver in the country. He drove on the Overland for many years, and is still a hale and rugged old man. But the days of the stagecoach are numbered, except in isolated districts, where of course, they will probably always be useful. The old timer still has a vivid recollection and kind remembrance of the Overland coach, and it is believed, if the truth were known, many of them would be glad to see the Overland drive up Main Street loaded with passengers, mail sacks and what not. But these wild desires are repressed out of consideration for the railroads and newcomers, and if indulged in at all it is only at times when a few congenial spirits congregate in a social way to relate stories of the early days.

Silas was now fifty years old. His entire adult career had been involved in the transportation business – building roads, hauling freight, passengers, and mail. Horses were his love and his business, but automobiles were becoming popular and change was coming. Instead, for Silas, this new opportunity in Yellowstone arose that allowed him to continue the horse-drawn lifestyle for another ten years.

Early Entrepreneurs in Helena, Montana Territory

[1] W.C. Child (1840-1893) was a brother of Harry Child's father Edwin F. Child. (MHS 941-710)

[2] Silas Stilwell Huntley (1841-1901). An attempt was made to change the name of Dome Mountain in the Gallatin Range to Mount Huntley. The change was not lasting. (YELL 133674)

[3] Harry's financial partner in several ventures was numbers man Edmund W. Bach (1854-1904). F.G. Kernan engraving. (MHS 940-665)

[4] Before arriving in Helena, Albert J. Seligman (1858-1935) trained as a mining engineer at Rensselaer Polytechnic Institute. He served in the Montana Territorial Legislature in 1884 and 1885. L. Alman photo. (MHS 944-909)

H.W. Child and Adelaide Dean

[6] Miss Adelaide Dean (1861-1949), born in Wisconsin, captured "our handsome Harry." Viroque Baker photo. (MHS PAc96-13.1)

[5] Harry Child (1856-1931) had "piercing eyes and a drooping mustache." 1904 photograph. (YNP photo)

[7] Harry was known as a snappy dresser. Shown here in later years with a YPTC vehicle. (YELL 133669)

[8] Adelaide, Grandmother Child, had "beautiful eyes and a lovely expression always on her face." (YELL 13357)

[9] Annie Dean Huntley (1856-1938) shared a love of horses with her husband Silas. She was the first of the sisters to venture to Montana Territory. (MHS H-3618)

The Dean sisters

[10] Annie is 4th from the left in this photo titled Woman Suffrage, captured in 1914 in Washington, D.C. Harris & Ewing Collection. (LC-H261-4951)

[11] After graduating medical school, Dr. Maria Dean (1858-1919) spent a year training in Germany before joining her family in Helena. (MHS PAc2014-23.3)

Riverside Stock Farm, Toston, Montana

HUNTLEY & CLARK'S RIVERSIDE STOCK FARM, NEAR TOSTON, MONTANA.

[12] Huntley & Clark's Riverside Stock Farm about 1887. They advertised stallions, trotting horses, and draft horses. The race track is pictured at middle right. (Board of Trade Report, p. 59)

[13] Rutledge Hargrove is pictured here (about 1908) with a perfectly matched team owned by Annie Huntley. He worked with Silas' horses at Toston, and later became a tenant farmer at the Flying D Ranch. (GHM P7889N)

White Face Farm, East Helena

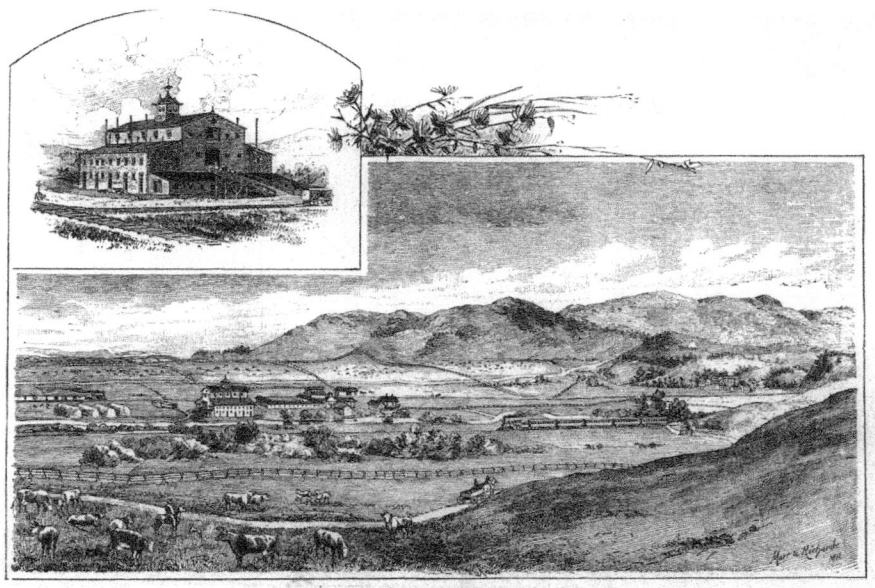

W. C. CHILD'S STOCK RANCH AND STOCK FARM, NEAR HELENA.

[14] W.C. "Billy" Child left his stamp on Helena through the enduring beauty of the buildings on his ranch, a beloved landmark in East Helena. Known today as the Child Ranch. (Board of Trade Report, p. 57)

Willows Stock Farm

WILLOWS STOCK FARM, NEAR COSTON, MONTANA, THE PROPERTY OF H. W. CHILD.

[15] Harry called his first livestock venture Willows Stock Farm. (Board of Trade Report, p. 63)

Helena area mines

[16] *Gregory mine in December 1886 – just one month before Harry and others were held captive. Events convinced miners that Harry was a capable manager who would protect their interests. F. Jay Haynes photo. (MHS H-1740)*

GLOSTER MINE.—HOIST AND MILL.

[17] *Harry also managed the Gloster Mine located near Marysville, Montana – northwest of Helena. (Board of Trade Report, p. 55)*

Great Falls, Montana

[18] Montana Smelting Company's operation was located on the south bank of the Missouri River, downstream from Great Falls. The smelter's history is interpreted along a hiking trail in Giant Springs State Park. J.C. Cowles photo. (HM, GF 2005.105.1-7)

[19] A family story concerns a guest who planted water cress near Giant Springs, upsetting Adelaide –who knew the plant did not belong there and thought it would mar the natural beauty. (HM, GF 1982.098.0003)

[20] Harry and Adelaide lived in the Manager's Residence at the Great Falls Smelter between 1889-1891. J.C. Cowles photo. (HM, GF 2005.105.1-16)

At Home in Helena

RESIDENCE OF W. C. CHILD.

[21] Mary and W.C. Child's house at 305 N. Ewing still stands, north of Last Chance Gulch. (Board of Trade Report, p. 35)

[22] Tree-lined lawns of Madison Ave include the elegant home Silas built for Annie. The Huntleys and the Childs lived here until around 1890. (RQ photo)

MESSRS. H. W. CHILD AND E. D. EDGERTON'S "ORO FINO TERRACE" ON BENTON AVENUE.

[23] Oro Fino Terrace, designed by St. Paul architect Ralph Edgerton, was planned to be six separate three-story houses under one roof. (Board of Trade Report, p. 35)

BROADWAY BLOCK, COR. OF SIXTH AVENUE AND MAIN STREET.

[24] Bach, Cory & Co. used this building for 5 years before constructing their own. (Board of Trade Report, p. 54)

[25] In 1889, Dr. Dean built this home at 508 Monroe Ave. Rather than living there, she leased it to St. Peter's Episcopal Church. (RQ photo)

[26] W.M. and Ellen Nichols purchased this home at 706 Harrison Ave. Known as the Edward C. Babcock Mansion in the Helena Downtown Historic District. (RQ photo)

[27] Sarah Child, Harry's mother, was the first to live at 801 Stuart Street. Harry and Adelaide called it home from 1910-1931. (YELL 133603)

[28] Annie and S.B.M. Young's home when they returned to Helena. It was student housing for Carroll College (1956-1968), named Dean Hall. Known as the Tatum-Young House in Helena Downtown Historic District. (RQ photo)

[29] Dr. Dean owned this home at 626 N. Benton Ave from 1908-1919. Part of the Women's Walking Tour of Helena, it recognizes her influence on the Helena community. (RQ photo)

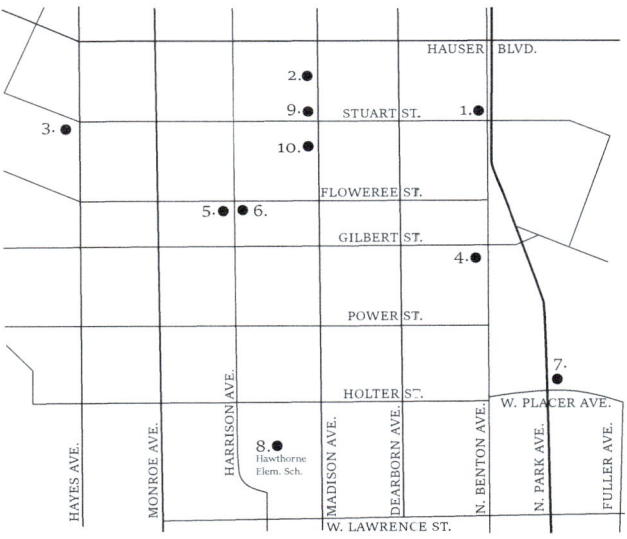

[30] Helena's West Side was just being developed when Harry and Adelaide, Silas and Annie, built near A.J. Seligman and Samuel Hauser. Several sites have family connections. (Map designed by Becky Sheehan)

¹ 802-806 N Benton Ave –owned 1887-1930 (burned 1985)

² 812 Madison Ave –Huntleys and Childs, 1886-1890

³ 801 Stuart St –Mrs. Sarah Child, Harry & Adelaide, 1905-1931

⁴ 626 N Benton Ave –Dr. Maria Dean, Ellen Dean, 1908-1919

⁵ 706 Harrison Ave –Ellen and W.M. Nichols, 1914-1956

⁶ 529 Floweree St (705 Harrison Ave) –Youngs, 1924-1938

⁷ YWCA building –assisted by Maria & Adelaide, 1919

⁸ Hawthorne School –Dean Memorial Clock, 430 Madison Ave

⁹ 802 Madison Ave –A.J. Seligman 1886-1899

¹⁰ 720 Madison Ave –Samuel T. Hauser –1885-1913

Yellowstone Explorers

[32] Nathaniel Langford (1832-1909) promoted the idea of preserving Yellowstone for future generations and the interests of the railroads. (YELL 02938)

[31] Samuel Hauser's (1833-1914) business interests paralleled Harry's in banking, mining, smelters, and land. (YELL 02940)

Early Yellowstone Protectors

[33] Prior to the creation of the National Park Service, Silas and Harry dealt with military commanders who had the title of "Acting Superintendent." (YELL 09192)

[34] General S.B.M. Young married Annie Dean Huntley in 1908. They met during his first tour of duty in the park. Harris & Ewing Collection. (LC-H25-14708-E)

Yellowstone Builders

[35] Hiram M. Chittenden (1858-1917) served the Army Corps of Engineers in Yellowstone between 1891-1893 and 1899-1906. (YELL 02970)

[36] Among Chittenden's triumphs was the bridge over the Yellowstone River above the Upper Falls. The feat required 150 men, a full moon, and a 72-hour continuous hand-mixing of concrete. It was replaced in 1962. (Quinn postcard collection)

[38] Harry's connection with the NPR helped Robert Reamer receive the commission to design their depot in Gardiner, Montana, at the park's north entrance. (YELL 11588)

[37] Robert C. Reamer (1873-1938), with head carpenter, H.L. George. Reamer was life-long friends with the Child family. (YELL 18182d)

[39] *Silas was the first member of the family to move to Yellowstone, and the first of the family to create unique stationery for park businesses. (MHSRC SC 888)*

[41] *Loading platforms were constructed at remote attractions so passengers could easily board. (YELL 13790)*

[43] *Silas kept meticulous care of this tack, equipment, and horses –as this coach shed interior shows. (YGM 2006.044.0628)*

[40] *One of Silas' stagecoaches loads passengers in front of the National Hotel. (YELL 02836)*

[42] *Silas purchased large coaches from the Abbot-Downing Company of Concord, New Hampshire. They carried thirty-six passengers, requiring a six-horse team, and fostered an elite cadre of drivers. (Quinn postcard collection)*

Chapter 4: Tally Ho
1892-1894

Silas and Harry arrive in Yellowstone,
W.C.'s ranch sees good days and tragedy

Silas Huntley's ten-year contract in Yellowstone went into effect in 1892. Just before the Park season opened, Harry Child and Silas purchased Wakefield's outfit for $70,000. The Yellowstone National Park Transportation Company (YPTC) incorporated in June 1892, with a capital stock of $250,000, by H.W. Child (President), E.W. Bach (Secretary/Treasurer), and Silas S. Huntley (General Manager) [39]. With the congressional hearings concluded, the new owners could settle in to the business of transporting park visitors to hotels and points of interest.

With minor changes over the decades, most of the roads as we know them today were completed by the Army Corps of Engineers between 1883 and 1905. The final section of the Lower Loop, between Old Faithful and the Thumb of Yellowstone Lake (now known as Craig Pass) was completed in 1891 (replacing the Mary Mountain Road). * *[see map p. 39]*

By that year the Yellowstone Park Association (YPA) operated four hotels for travelers. Their locations were determined by two things: the proximity to one of the attractions, and the comfortable distance for a day's travel by stagecoach. The National Hotel at Mammoth Hot Springs [64], eight miles from the Northern Pacific Depot in Cinnabar, Montana, served as a first night's stay. Between 1889 and 1891, the YPA completed the Fountain Hotel at the Lower Geyser Basin [68], the Lake Hotel on the north shore of Yellowstone Lake [80], and the Canyon Hotel near the Grand Canyon of the Yellowstone.

In the spring of 1892, Silas and Yellowstone's Acting Superintendent Captain George Anderson made a preliminary round of the park roads prior to the opening of the tourist season, and "they simply had an awful time. Every bridge in Spring Creek Canyon was washed out..." (On a section of the new road from Old Faithful to West Thumb.) "In one place the coach sank down on its side and water rushed over and came pretty near drowning the inmates." The new road over Craig Pass was obviously in no condition to be used; a call for help went over the wires to St. Paul, and Lieutenant Chittenden, of the Army Corps of Engineers [35], was sent to the park to see what he could do.

After a quick look, Chittenden decided that if Captain Anderson could spare him $500 and a few enlisted men, with supplies and a wagon, and if Silas' transportation company and park photographer F. Jay Haynes could each add as much, he could get together a work party that would make the roads passable in fifteen days.

While Silas was learning the lay of the land in his new home, Yellowstone National Park, he kept Harry up-to-date by telegram announcing that "the first National park tourists of the 1892 season have started into the park. The hotels will open on May 28th. There is a great deal of snow in the Park, but the weather is warm, and it is going off fast. By June 1st the Transportation Company will be in shape to accommodate all who may call upon it." A new career was beginning for both men.

Silas and Annie moved into the Wakefield house at Mammoth Hot Springs in Yellowstone [53]. Though more rustic in nature, it did have a certain prestige. A guest characterized it in her diary entry as, "the daintiest little cottage" she had ever seen.

After fulfilling the first year of their contract, Capt. Anderson reported: "The plant is in every way adequate and excellent."

———

The Great Falls smelter was handling ore in large amounts, and because of its good equipment, stoppages for repairs seldom happened. It was producing lead, silver, and gold faster than it could acquire raw ore, so Harry moved into the second phase of his obligation – negotiating the purchase of ore to be processed. The financial backers and mining experts were actively studying ways to get ore to the smelter faster.

Harry traveled far and wide, covering the territory between Chicago and Coeur d'Alene, Idaho as well as all of Montana. He was negotiating with the NPR to get spur tracks built from the Belt Mountains, northeast of Helena, so that mines and individual miners could easily transport their ore to Great Falls at a reasonable price.

James J. Hill completed his Minneapolis and Manitoba Rail Company (later to become the Great Northern) from Minot, Dakota Territory, to Great Falls in November of 1887. Col. Charles Broadwater, president of the Montana Central Railroad, had plans to connect Butte, Helena and Great Falls, joining mining regions. Harry, along with Samuel Hauser, invested in another railroad spur line: The Helena, Boulder & Madison Company.

Interest from the railroads was high. Harry dined with a representative of the Northern Pacific which was contemplating extending their line from Billings to Great Falls. Harry's reputation as a genial host began to show, "Mr. Child has made it so pleasant for me," the railroad man said, "that I positively couldn't get away, and I am loath to depart now."

The Great Falls Smelter combined with the Helena Smelter and the Chicago Refining Works to form the Union Smelting & Refining Company. "The consolidation of these interests means not only a union of the capital of the old companies, but the accession of new capitalists to the business, thus forming the strongest corporation engaged in the smelting industry in the United States," announced the *Fergus County Argus*. Stockholders included Samuel Hauser and A.J. Seligman. Harry stayed on as manager of the Great Falls plant.

When the price of silver dropped below $1 per ounce, the Union Company closed the Great Falls smelter. It had survived for twelve years. By 1900, one by one the smaller buildings had been moved away and the machinery was shipped to Helena and Butte.

The citizens of Great Falls were very proud of their smelter and became fond of Harry and Adelaide. The Childs had enjoyed their time in Great Falls but knew they would be leaving the elegant home when Harry's job was finished. They had built the Oro Fino Apartments in Helena as a temporary home for themselves with extra apartments to accommodate visiting family and friends. In the fall of 1890 Harry and Adelaide began a tradition that became a permanent part of their family life – they took an extended vacation to California.

———◆———

Late in 1891 the Great Falls paper reported that Harry "has been east interesting eastern capitalists in establishing a large smelter at Boulder City, Montana." He succeeded in incorporating two companies, The Boulder Smelting Company and the Basin Mining Concentrating Company. Incorporators included H.W. Child and E.W. Bach with Harry listed as general manager. Ground was broken for the Boulder Smelter in October 1891.

There was high anticipation that this organization would have a great deal to do with the future development and prosperity of Jefferson County and the state of Montana. The NPR had already made surveys for five miles of side track connecting with the smelter, and the Great Northern Railroad had plans to do the same. The Boulder operation was intended to be the largest of its kind in the state, with the best railroad facilities of any smelter in the state.

Despite the low price of silver, mines around the town of Basin were active. The Hope, the Minneapolis, and several others were "running full blast and likely to do so for some time." The ore bins at the smelter were rapidly filling with the ores from Basin, Wickes, Elkhorn, and Comet. Most of the mines in Jefferson County produced largely pyritic ores, carrying a small percentage of lead, together with gold and silver. The Boulder smelter processed low-grade ores that existing smelters had no interest in. Those willing to process it were some distance away, making the cost of shipping prohibitive for the local mines and miners.

The Boulder smelter was well-designed, not only for easy access but also for efficient operation, as the *Helena Independent* reported:

> In the boiler house are two enormous boilers, which furnish the necessary power. In one end of the boiler house stands the blast furnace and this furnace is the main factor in the reduction of pyritic ores. It is divided into three compartments, and consists of a series of nine heavy pipes or stoves incased in brick, in each compartment. A rotary pressure blower forces the air through these pipes, which are heated from the fireplaces below, and when the air leaves this furnace, to say the least, it is warmer than Satan's dominions. Formerly in the treatment of pyritic ore, it was customary to slowly roast out the sulphur; but in this process the sulphur is used as a fuel instead of being wasted, and thus enables them to treat the ores with less fuel than by any other known process. In the furnace room is a ninety ton Fraser & Chalmers water jacket furnace, with removable bottom plates, which enables the repair of the furnace with but little expense.

The Boulder Smelter went into operation in the summer of 1892. After an idle winter, it resumed operation the following summer. Harry had put in a lot of work and travel between 1890 and April 1893 and he now had the satisfaction of another great project finished.

Along with his work, Harry liked to have some fun. "A novel and interesting foot race took place at Meaderville yesterday, in which Harry Child and Dave Jones covered

> "There's more to life than money. There's more to life than business, and mighty little to life when a man lets business take complete possession of him." HWC

100 yards in their bare feet and through a foot of snow. The wager was a keg of beer, and Jones came in winner by half a yard. ... The time was not noted, but the beer hardly lasted as long as the contest."

Harry was adept at combining his business contacts with his social and recreational life. Mr. Val Laubenheimer, an accountant at the Great Falls Smelter, went with Harry to a ranch on Belt Creek and then to the mountains to fish and hunt. Their names appear together at social events as well.

In 1892, Harry Child and Mr. Laubenheimer were notified of Ben Lomond's death. They were partners in ownership of the horse, one of the best known and most valuable stallions in Montana and the Northwest. Although Silas had sold Ben Lomond and Maxim in April 1888, Harry and Val purchased them in May 1889 and returned them to Montana. Ben Lomond had been standing in stud at Huntley & Clark's Riverside Stock Farm for several years.

Harry and his friend, E.W. Bach owned Ben Cole, son of Ben Lomond. Two other prize-winning horses they co-owned were Ida D. and Sweetbrier. Harry became a "familiar figure at state fairs where harness racing was popular."

The fertile grasses of Riverside Stock Farm became a winter home for the YPTC herd of horses. At the end of the tourist season, "The total number of employees leaving at the same time is nearly 350, and it takes in the neighborhood of 35 coaches to transport them, after which the transportation company covers the stages with duck covering [canvas], and then comes the task of re-branding 500 head of horses after which the animals are driven to the ranch of Huntley & Clark at Toston, for the winter."

Silas was the man on the ground at Mammoth Hot Springs, while Harry Child served as president of the new company. The first record of Harry being in the park in some capacity is a memo, hand-written on YPA stationary, dated June 6, 1893, requesting action from the acting superintendent about the lack of restroom facilities (then called "earth closets") at Norris Geyser Basin:

"My Dear Capt.

We arrive here with Mrs. Nelson under the weather, and absolutely no place for the ladies to retire, except the woods. Larry has wired Dean

four times and written twice to have the closet put in running order,
but does not get an answer. He of course is a little hot. I would wire
Pearse but my telegram would go through Dean. He would be hot for the
balance of the season. There are twenty ladies here hunting the woods.
Can you not get a club and swing it a few times.

Sincerely, HWC"[1]

Here is a first glimpse of Harry's method of approaching problems by taking them straight to the top, while giving reasons why approaching others in charge would be ineffective.

The early Helena neighborhood was changing; the old timers moving on; and newcomers moving in. Harry and Adelaide now made their home temporarily at the Oro Fino Terrace Apartments, also some blocks away. It was a few years before they would build their residence in Yellowstone.

———➤●◄———

The World's Columbian Exposition in Chicago, Illinois, was the event of 1893. Always the promoter, Silas Huntley shipped a couple of Yellowstone stagecoaches to "be run between the fair grounds and hotels to show visitors at the fair the kind of accommodations in use in the park. They will also exhibit an old bullet-riddled coach of early days." Joining the State of Montana exhibit at the fair, "coaches will be run from the heart of the city to the grounds, making as many trips as it is possible for six teams to travel in a day."

The Northern Pacific Railroad promoted travel to Yellowstone in the annual *Wonderland* publications, which were available through ticket agents around the country. The railroad's photographer, F. Jay Haynes, became the Yellowstone Park Improvement Company's official photographer in 1882. Two years later he received a lease to build a studio at Mammoth Hot Springs. He produced his own guidebook to

[1] The people mentioned in this memo were: Capt. George Anderson – Supt. of YNP, 1891- 1897, known as the "Czar of Yellowstone;" Larry Mathews – manager of Norris lunch station; J.H. Dean – manager of the hotels for the YPA; W.G. Pearce – Vice President and General Manager of YPA and General Purchasing Agent of the NPR; Nelson – an unidentified park visitor. The authors have found no relationship between J.H. Dean and the Dean sisters of Wisconsin.

the Park, and in the off-season traveled the rails in his palace car, selling park views and promoting travel.

The park tour was sold as a package, including transportation and one night at each hostelry. To divide the longest days of travel, which measured forty miles, the YPA also ran tent lunch stations at Norris Geyser Basin and Thumb Geyser Basin (on the west shore of Yellowstone Lake). At Thumb, travelers could purchase a more leisurely trip across Yellowstone Lake on the *SS Zillah* [63]. The steamboat, operated by E.C. Waters, deposited passengers at the docks in front of the Lake Hotel.

Silas Huntley, as manager of the YPTC, operated separately from the hotels. He received permission from the park superintendent to build his own bunkhouses and mess houses at Norris, Fountain, Upper Basin, Thumb, Lake, and Canyon. Henceforth, the Transportation Company bunk houses, mess halls, and kitchens were in close proximity to the hotels. The wranglers and drivers, as far as eating and housing was concerned, were kept separate from the other employees.

Yellowstone Park Transportation Company

Coach Schedule

Leave Mammoth Hot Springs,		8:00 a.m.
Arrive Norris	- -	12:00 noon
Leave Norris -	- -	1:30 p.m.
Arrive Fountain -	-	5:30 p.m.
Leave Fountain	- -	8:30 a.m.
Arrive Upper Geyser Basin,		10:30 a.m.
Leave Upper Geyser Basin,		7:30 a.m.
Arrive Thumb of Lake	-	11:30 a.m.
*Leave Thumb of Lake	-	1:00 p.m.
Arrive Yellowstone Lake	-	4:00 p.m.
Leave Yellowstone Lake	-	8:30 a.m.
Arrive Grand Canyon	-	11:30 a.m.
Leave Grand Canyon	-	8:15 a.m.
Arrive Norris	- -	10:15 a.m.
Leave Norris -	- -	11:45 a.m.
Arrive Mammoth Hot Springs,		3:15 p.m.
Leave Mammoth Hot Springs,		6:30 p.m.
Arrive Gardiner	- -	7:15 p.m.

* Boat leaves Thumb 1:15 p.m., arrives Lake 3:15 p.m.

The management reserves the right to change the above schedule without notice.

The "Grand Tour" included nights in five grand hotels, with leisurely afternoon hours for sightseeing at the Upper Geyser Basin and Grand Canyon of the Yellowstone. YNPA

"Besides the drivers, the other employees in the park were not in the distinguished-category bracket, but, nevertheless, had titles of many descriptions. The barn men were called 'barn dogs,' the waitresses were 'heavers,' dishwashers were called 'pearl divers,' the chamber maids, 'admirals.' It was said that they had one arm longer than the other, caused from reaching under the beds for the vessels. The driver's mess was a 'mulligan dump.' The term 'necking' or 'smooching' as now used so universally was then called 'rotten logging.'"

The term *savage*, probably first attributed to the stagecoach drivers, was later expanded to include all who worked for the hotels, lodges and camps. Savage mess halls were located inside the hotel and lodge structures. They were separate from the guests' dining rooms, but both were served from the same kitchen. Some areas had cafeterias for park guests and a separate room, served from the same kitchen, for the cabin savages.

Several private camping companies were also licensed to provide accommodations and transportation through Yellowstone. One was granted to Bozeman schoolteacher William W. Wylie, who established the *Wylie Way*. His company erected a series of candy-striped tents throughout the park and equipped them with camping gear. Those who could not afford the hotels or preferred a less formal type of accommodation found the tent-tops comfortable and enjoyable [62].

Wylie provided horse-drawn buggies to transport his guests around the park. He used more than three thousand horses for his trips, and therefore he needed lots of good grass lands to winter them. In the Gallatin Valley, south of Bozeman and northwest of the park, he bought eight sections of Spanish Creek land, as well as eleven sections in the Cherry and Elk Creek basins.

———⟩●⟨———

Dr. Dean, home in Helena, was finding acceptance and challenge in her chosen profession. She began to specialize in the health concerns of women and children, having studied at the Women's Clinic in Berlin. She delivered the first Chinese child born in Helena, spent a summer taking a special course in surgery at Johns Hopkins University in Baltimore, and agreed to be the in-house medical provider at the Great Falls smelter. She began lecturing around the community to teacher's groups and women's clubs about hygiene, morality, and parenting. She accepted an elected post as a school trustee, served on the supervisory board of the Associated Charities of Helena, and was a director of the county branch of the Society for the Prevention of Cruelty to Animals. She was an active member of St. Peter's Episcopal Church and joined her close friends in incorporating the Helena School of Art. She was a study in contrasts – appearing on the lists of elegant balls and parties while the newspapers reported her numerous hunting and camping expeditions.

Perhaps Dr. Dean's most passionate interest was the position of women "with reference to the general advancement of society." She argued in 1891 for a woman's right to be self-supporting. Four years later at the first annual convention of the Montana Equal Suffrage association, Dr. Dean joined the cause.

———

Social lives in Helena had taken a turn – no more large receptions and dinners. Dancing in the grand ballrooms of the mansions or the Hotel Broadwater, where the ladies and gentlemen dressed in New York fashions, had become passé. Harry's uncle, Mr. W.C. and Mrs. Child were still holding forth. Ice cream from the White Face Farm's creamery made it a popular summer destination.

"A merry crowd left the city by way of the Union Pacific railway on Wednesday afternoon for the Child ranch," noted the *Helena Independent* in June 1891, "With baskets of lunch stored in all available corners of the coaches and the picnicers seated three or four to a seat, the train pulled up at the platform and the precious cargo began unloading. A short walk brought them to the house of Mr. Child, which was thrown open to their pleasure." On another occasion, the young people "... repaired to the large ball room at the top of the building and danced until the early hours of the next morning. They returned to their homes about 2:30 am on Thursday."

It seemed a lovely way to entertain the young people, but W.C.

opened it for other community events. "A handsome reception was also given on Tuesday evening by the Board of Trade to the members of the general assembly. Universal pleasure reigned when it was understood that the hospitable ranch of Mr. W.C. Child had been offered for the occasion. Mr. Child's ranch in the valley is one of the favorite resorts of Helena, so that an invitation to that fine place is always hailed with pleasure. ... Quite a jolly throng of pleasure seekers, about one hundred and fifty, filled the three cars chartered by the Board of Trade."

W.C. seemed to enjoy the limelight. When the city of Helena opened a new auditorium, he led the opening dance number and "announced in his own inimitable manner, the set times for the leaving of the electric cars, stating that the last would 'leave the auditorium at three a.m. All participators remaining in the hall after that time will be expected to stay to breakfast and walk home.'..."

Before the end of the next year, the jolly times would come to an end. W.C. mortgaged the ranch to invest heavily in the Boulder smelter. According to Child family lore, at some point W.C. and Harry had a falling out, whenever they were together at a social event, they never spoke – often occupying opposite corners of the room.

After the Silver Panic of 1893, Charles Broadwater's Montana National Bank and Samuel Hauser's First National Bank closed. W.C. found himself $30,000 in debt, much of it to First National Bank. He and his wife filed "separate deeds of assignment for the benefit of their creditors ..." But business cares weighed heavily on his mind, and the usually light-hearted, cheerful and generous man became moody and disheartened.

On October 14, 1893 he was found dead at the ranch. Although there were fears that he may have taken his own life by poison, none was found in evidence, and his physician determined he "died of exhaustion and nervous prostration" brought about by worrying over business troubles. A note was found in his pocket which read, "I arrived at the ranch very much worn out and need rest. Something tells me I shall never leave this place alive."

Perhaps the best way to remember William and Mary Child, members of The Society of Montana Pioneers, is this October 1892 announcement as the social season ended: "A great many ladies and gentleman will appear (at the Columbian Ball) in colonial costumes, but it is not absolutely essential, and there will be as many in ordinary dresses as there will be in costume. The old timers will be out in full force. Ex-Govenor and Mrs. Hauser, W.C. Child and Mrs. Child, and Major and Mrs. Davenport will lead the Virginia reel."

———◆———

The Silver Panic of 1893 also affected both E.W. Bach and Harry Child. E.W. joined Samuel Hauser's First National Bank as a Director in 1893. Later that year, when its closure and subsequent restructuring took place, his name never appeared in banking again. Harry seems to have lost his Directorship when the Second National Bank failed in September of 1893. But when the dust settled he regained a seat on the First National Bank board.

Merchants National Bank, where Silas continued as a Director, seems to have faired the best. It was recognized as "one of the strongest and best managed institutions in the country...The fact that the officers are 'the right men in the right places' is conclusively demonstrated by the success of the bank under their management."

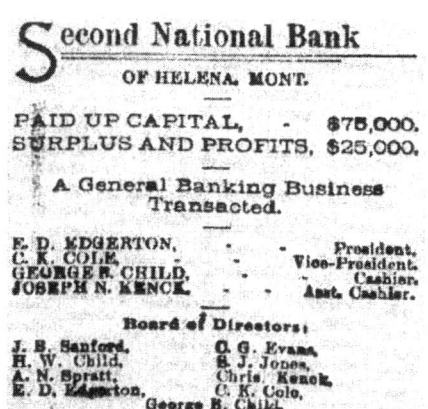

In 1889 Harry Child joined the Second National Bank's Board of Directors. This 1892 advertisement showed he still held that position.

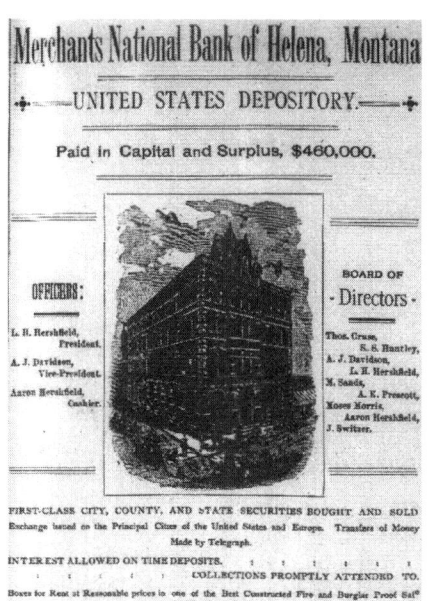
L.H. Hershfield and Aaron Hershfield put up the bond that allowed Harry and Silas to gain the transportation contract in Yellowstone. Silas was a long-time member of Merchants National Bank's board.

Following the Silver Panic of 1893, Second National was forced to merge with the Helena National Bank. They were absorbed into Samuel Hauser's First National Bank in 1894. Harry was listed as a Director in this 1896 ad.

Captain Anderson seemed satisfied with Silas Huntley's operation. "The Transportation Company has improved all of its sites, and kept them in thorough order," he wrote in his 1894 report. "... Their plant is the finest I have ever seen. Applications from outside parties for licenses to carry on transportation business in all forms continue to pour into this office. When I consider the obligations the regular company has assumed and the bonds that it has given for their faithful performance, I have not felt justified in recommending approval in more than one or two cases, and these were to parties who would furnish good accommodations for the cheaper class of travel."

Chapter 5: In the National Park
1895-1901

*Annie and Silas pass on their
love of horses, a little competition,
entering the hotel business*

Yellowstone was a small isolated community. The children of the families who operated businesses and served the government were playmates. Huntley Child, son of Harry and Adelaide, came to the park in 1895 to spend the summer with his uncle and aunt, Silas and Annie Huntley. He was nine years old. He was back in the park the next summer, learning a lot about such things as which type of coach, buggy, or wagon was used for each of the various chores, and if it required a four- or six-horse hitch. Later, in an interview with a park historian, he shared fond memories of the very large harness room [43]:

"The harnesses were all cleaned and oiled everyday. The coaches were painted at least every other year so they were always bright and shiny and the horses were the very best Montana horses. Silas had a man that went around to the ranches to pick them out. The horses, at first, wintered on ranches south of Livingston toward Billings. ... After a good winter, they came back fat and were held in the Park for three weeks before being put in service. They had to be shod and get in shape. They were driven some but not too much: they had to be in shape for going forty miles. After a couple of trips around, they were not too frisky."

The big tally-ho stagecoaches [42] required the six-horse hitch and were used only between Gardiner and Mammoth. Huntley remembered only one run-away with the six-horse hitch. The surreys needed only two horses. The wagons carrying freight to the hotels or hay to barns needed eight horses. Young Huntley Child was enthralled with the horses and their operation.

Like his father, Huntley found time for enjoying the great outdoors. He became the Champion Fisherman for the summer of 1896, "he caught 76 fish in a little over two hours. His fish basket was so full that he could not carry it, and had to return to camp and unload and return again. S. Turner, superintendent of Wells, Fargo & Company, in the City of Mexico, who was one of the party, and an old fisherman at that, says that the work of Huntley was simply wonderful. They fished in the same place together [at Willow Creek] and while he could not land any, little Huntley was pulling them in right along." Huntley also recalled weeks spent at Yellowstone Lake, where boat concessioner E.C. Waters had a son about his age. His pattern for the next several years was school terms in Helena or California and summers in Yellowstone.

———⟫●⟪———

Beginning from the days when Wakefield & Hoffman had an agreement to transport hotel guests around the park, local carriers felt their rights were not being considered. One serious issue brought to light during the congressional investigations was that the railroad depot was still several miles from the park border. The acting superintendent had no control over operators who picked up passengers there. Many of the complaints the Department received were about these out-of-park operators. During his tenure, Captain Anderson tried not to expand the number of licensed companies. In 1895 he wrote, "The only change to be noted ... is the refusal of the Department to grant licenses to any but the Park Transportation Company to take tourists to the hotels. Many licenses are issued but they are all ... restricted to camping parties. So long as the regular company maintains its very high standard of excellence, it is right and proper that it should be protected in this manner. It has, and is required to have, an extensive plant, always ready to accommodate the greatest volume of travel. Its whole equipment of horses, harness, and drivers is of the best." [40, 41]

In his last official report as acting superintendent, 1896, Captain Anderson continued to praise Silas Huntley's operation. "In every respect the transportation is conducted the same as last year. Horses, harness, and vehicles are the best procurable in the country. They are kept clean and in through repair and running order. There is no overcrowding; there are no avoidable discomforts. An occasional complaint is made of the lack of stop-over privileges. ... I believe that the business is conducted at a profit, and is the only enterprise in the Park that has so far reaped any material reward. It is only natural that the company should object to granting excessive stop-overs, as it materially increases expenses. In every other respect I have nothing but praise of the company and its management."

The town of Huntley, Montana (15 miles east of Billings) "was first established in 1877 as a Gilmer and Salisbury Company stage station, store, ferry, and post office .... Since both Gilmer and Salisbury had previously worked for Silas S. Huntley's stage line, it was logical to name the station for him."

Most Yellowstone visitors purchased a five-day tour of the park, spending one night at each hotel. For their convenience, they could arrange a stop-over – staying multiple nights at one individual hotel. This was long a difficulty to the transportation operators, as it meant sending coaches around the loop half-empty or keeping a seat open for someone to occupy late in the tour. The transportation company absorbed the financial loss of not having full coaches around the loop.

On June 23, 1897, Captain Anderson completed his tour of duty at Fort Yellowstone. On that day he was replaced by Lieutenant Colonel S.B.M. Young [34]. Young performed the superintendent duties until November 15, and he wrote the report for that year. It shows the extensiveness of Silas' operation:

A thorough inspection of the coaches, surreys, stables, harness rooms and paint shops, was made at the beginning of the season and everything was found to be in excellent condition, employees well organized, work systematized, and in all appearances a thorough discipline maintained. At the date of the first inspection, I found present, ready for business, 1 superintendent of stages, 1 foreman of stables, 1 railroad trainman, 1 agent for each hotel in the Park, 1 wagon maker (for repairing), 3 blacksmiths, 1 painter, 1 washer, 8 stable men, 2 day herders, 1 night herder, 2 six-horse Concord coaches, 4 two-horse surreys, 37 drivers, and 144 well-groomed horses. During the month of July another inspection was made, and I found in service 83 regular drivers, 155 temporarily employed drivers, two six-horse coaches, 83 four-horse coaches and spring wagons, 53 two-horse surreys, 24 four-horse, and 78 two-horse vehicles in temporary employ, 282 regular team horses, and 412 employed team horses. This does not include extra teams at park stations, no teams for baggage, for driving to formations, freighting, etc. I have always found Mr. S,S. Huntley and his assistants efficient, polite, and obliging. Mr. Huntley is the best manager and handler of coach transportation it has ever been my pleasure to observe.

———————

By late 1897, F. Jay Haynes and W.W. Humphrey (a former employee of both George Wakefield and Silas Huntley) applied for permission to transport passengers by stage coach from Yellowstone's west gate to the hotels. Their Monida & Yellowstone Stage Company [61] started at Monida, Montana, where the Union Pacific rails passed, seventy miles west of the park entrance. They were called the *Red Line* and painted all their coaches bright red. The hotels blocked a certain number of rooms each day for Haynes' *Red Line* patrons.

Huntley Child told of the precise procedure that was carried out to assure good service and the very same care of the guests whether traveling on the *Red Line* or Silas Huntley's *Yellow Line*. "Guests had their luggage packed and outside their door by a certain required time. Luggage tags were numbered to match the number of their coach. In this manner the porters could group the luggage and have it ready to load as each coach pulled up to the loading dock. They were held to a strict departure time taking turns. Yellow, Red, Yellow, Red. One day a Yellow coach went first and the next day a Red coach went first."

By season's end in 1898, the *Red Line* operated 18 vehicles, owned 80 horses, and employed 27 persons. Haynes was granted six more sites for the transportation business in addition to his photo shops at Mammoth and Old Faithful (built 1897). The park superintendent praised their operation: "This stage company is of the first order in every respect; has given first-class service to its patrons, has opened up a new route to the park through a beautiful country, and I have found its entire personnel, by courtesy and politeness, desirous of making its route popular with the traveling public, which it will undoubtedly be. ... Messrs. Humphrey & Haynes, who control the line, are both practical business men, with experience in this business, and are always courteous and obliging."

The two stagecoach businesses were now serving the park's hotels from two railroads – the Northern Pacific from the north entrance and the Union Pacific from the west entrance.

Between 1894 and 1900 E.W. Bach and Harry Child identified themselves as mining men. Harry continued as general manager of the Boulder Smelting Company, but also secured control of a mine to the south. "I went to New Mexico against the advice of San Francisco mine owners," he said in a newspaper interview, "but I found a piece of property that will cut a figure in the coming output."

Although Bach, Cory & Company continued in business, A.J. Seligman now partnered with David Cory. A.J. left Helena in the fall of 1899 and opened a brokerage house in New York.

For a few years, E.W. Bach remained active in business in Helena and continued his mining interests. In 1898 as America entered war with Spain, E.W. was appointed as chief of commissaries with the volunteer army - one of a few officers serving as a civilian. He maintained the rank of major given to him as ordinance officer for the Territory of Montana. Returning to Helena after the war, E.W. assumed an active role in the Yellowstone Park Transportation Company, acting as secretary and later joint manager.

During the last half of the 1890s many VIPs visited Yellowstone. A tour through the national park provided respite from the cares of business, politics, or war. The U.S. Army Acting Superintendent was on hand to greet the dignitaries, but either Harry Child, E.W. Bach, or Silas Huntley were called upon to act as escort.

Harry himself was handling the buggy reins in July of 1896, with noted Boston lecturer John L. Stoddard as his passenger. When the coach encountered the swollen waters of Alum Creek in Hayden Valley; "... the horses were compelled to swim and the vehicle was set afloat...," reported the *Livingston Enterprise*. "Both Messrs. Stoddard and Child were excellent swimmers, however, and succeeded in reaching the opposite shore with no worse experience than an enforced bath in the almost ice-cold water..."

Other visitors included ex-President Benjamin Harrison, Chicago street car magnate Charles T. Yorkes, William Jennings Bryan, the Pugh family of Pennsylvania, philanthropist Helen Gould, Speaker of the U.S. House of Representatives David B. Henderson, Wyoming Governor Richards, and Acting Secretary of the Interior Thomas Ryan.

The Pugh family were probably acquaintances of Silas when he spent time in Washington securing government contracts. In the summer of 1900, the family toured in Yellowstone and received special attention from the Huntleys – as recorded in daughter Annie Jane's diary. Silas personally escorted them from the Fountain Hotel to view the nearby geyser basin, and Annie Huntley invited the two young girls over to see their home at Mammoth. "After supper at Mammoth Hotel," Miss Pugh recorded, "Mr. Huntley sent his niece, Dean, (Harry and Adeladie's daughter Ellen Dean Child – now aged 16) over with her pony-cart to take us out driving."

Ellen, like her younger brother Huntley, adopted a love of horses from her family. Jack Haynes, son of photographer F. Jay Haynes, was a playmate of Ellen's. "... in those days she was an agreeable 'buggy horse' in their imaginative play. Properly reined with string, Ellen was 'driven' down to the livery stable – until the day Jack tried to make his 'horse' drink out of the watering trough."

—⇒●⇐—

Silas Huntley was nine years into his ten-year contract for operating the YPTC when the hotel company (YPA) developed unsurmountable problems. The NPR wanted to divest themselves of all interests inside the Park and to find new management. The NPR had brought in a new group called the Northwest Improvement Company.

In late September 1899 E.W. Bach was in Yellowstone. James H. Dean, then President, General Manager and Superintendent of the YPA spoke with him briefly on behalf of the Northern Pacific to consider "purchasing the plants, or enter into an agreement with the Railway Company to operate them on a fair basis." These discussions continued for another year. NPR president, Charles S. Mellen, wrote to his vice-president, Daniel S. Lamont, regarding Bach and Child in December 1900, "I believe we will receive as much benefit from the Park with the hotels in the hands of these people, as we do when we run them ourselves, ... My best judgment is, it is for our interest to sell to these people."

Harry's success at mining and smelter building had earned him the reputation of having natural management abilities and business acumen. The NPR was now willing to throw their backing behind these men. Harry put up some of his own money and the NPR, through their Northwest Improvement Company, loaned like amounts to both Silas Huntley and E.W. Bach so they would have equal ownership. By April 4, 1901 the transfer of the YPA stock from the Northwest Improvement Company to Child, Huntley, and Bach was complete.

Silas had the reputation of being a good organizer and Harry was known for his efficiency. Historian Robert Shankland wrote: "Child was a homemade efficiency expert, a student of drive, punch, and wham. He kept a stop-watch on all his operations and could say offhand how much time was required to load an *x*-type stagecoach with *y* passengers at point *z*. People liked him, however."

⟶•◦•⟵

When Silas, Harry, and E.W. assumed the hotel company in 1901, little had been done to improve the hotels in the past ten years. The National Hotel at Mammoth Hot Springs was largely untouched since its completion in 1886. The facility at Norris remained a lunch station, with only a handful of rooms to offer parties traveling independently. At the Lower Geyser Basin, the fashionable and grand Fountain Hotel, then ten years old, offered a respite from the dust and discomfort of stagecoach travel. But the YPA still carried a large debt from its construction – a debt assumed by the new owners.

The YPA had inherited the Upper Geyser Basin Hotel, but that structure burned in 1894 – to be replaced by a log registration building and tent accommodations. Large tents were divided into sleeping partitions with canvas curtains. Rather than sharing with strangers sleeping in adjacent beds, guests preferred to return to the comforts of the Fountain Hotel. Upgrading this situation was a priority.

Every year since 1894 the superintendents' desires were the same: "A hotel here has long been one of the greatest needs of the Park;" "there is an urgent need of a hotel to accommodate tourists at the Upper Geyser Basin;" and "frequent demands have been made for a hotel at this most wonderful spot." One park visitor took the cause to a popular magazine, publishing these words: "But what is there in reality? A small wooden shanty in which a poor lunch is served, while as for rooms, not one is to be had for love of money. But where do the tourists stay while they remain to admire the geysers? Stay? Foolish question! They do not stay at all. The stage gives them four or five hours, during which a hurried guide takes them hurriedly across the Basin, and if some of the geysers happen to play while they are being 'done,' the tourists are lucky. ... Something must be done soon. Congress ought to compel the company to build that hotel."

The YPA still offered lunch in a tent facility at Thumb, where E.C. Waters could be found soliciting steamboat passengers for the trip across Yellowstone Lake in the *SS Zillah*. The Lake Hotel, considered the finest in the park since its opening in 1891, boasted only 51 rooms.

The pre-fab Canyon Hotel was replaced with a permanent structure. Foundation problems were addressed in 1896, but little in the way of improvements could be documented.

The loop tour was complete – but accommodations were far from satisfactory. W.G. Johnson, in charge of park operations for the Northern Pacific Railway summarized, "… in the past this class of work has been done without the services of a competent architect and by day labor, with the result that, at great cost, the Association has one very ungainly structure, two fairly good looking structures and all three with defective features, especially as to roof designs."

——————————

For the 1901 summer season Harry assumed lead in the hotel part of the business, while Silas and E.W. focused on the transportation. Harry still had a number of concerns outside the park - mines, ranches, smelters and numerous partners that he financially backed – just as the railroads would do for him inside the park. His name began to appear as an officer of the YPA, and the next decade or so was a whirlwind of building hotels and other accommodations around the park, much as we see them today. Changes in the YPA hierarchy continued until Harry, little-by-little, gained control and formed his own Yellowstone Park Hotel Company.

Harriett Meloy, of the Lewis & Clark County Historical Society, wrote: "'Not every man is born with a silver spoon in his mouth.' Harry W. Child, was one of those not born to wealth, but one whose achievements accorded him fortune beyond that realized by many of his contemporaries who came to Montana nurtured by wealthy relatives." From mining to smelters, to banking and transportation, Harry gained more and more experience and success through his own drive and personality.

Yellowstone Park Transportation Company
Yellowstone Park, July 23, 1908.

Chapter 6: Passing the Reins
1901-1905

*Saying farewell, welcoming the President,
building a log hotel*

On September 11th, 1901, grief and disruption came to the new owners of the YPA company and their families. Young Huntley Child was living at Mammoth with his uncle and aunt, Mr. and Mrs. Silas S. Huntley. In his own words, this is what happened:

On the evening of September 11th, 1901, the Superintendent, Captain and Mrs. Pitcher invited Silas and Annie for dinner. Very soon after they had finished eating Silas started feeling badly so the Huntleys excused themselves and went home early. By eleven o'clock, Silas was feeling worse and called Dr. Dean in Helena as there was no doctor in the Park. Silas suspected food poisoning because the dessert that evening had been some mixture of pineapple and ice cream. Dr. Dean suggested that they start for Livingston; she would take the train and meet them there. When she arrived the Huntleys were not there. She waited for some time, becoming very, very nervous because the station was about to close and she feared being left there alone in the dark. At last, the station agent informed her that he had just received a phone call and it was too late. Silas had died. Silas had gotten too ill for further travel so they had stopped at a ranch for help. When Dr. Dean was able to examine the body, she determined that there was no food poisoning. Silas had died from a stroke. He was only 57 years old.

A number of newspapers and publications printed obituaries and tributes to his honor. From *The Progressive Men of Montana*:

Silas S. Huntley was born in Ellicottville, Catarangus, county New York... [He] was a student at Springville Academy when the dark cloud of civil war rose from the national horizon. Ever responsive to the call of duty, the young man abandoned his studies to participate in the greatest internecine strife in history, enlisting in the Thirty-seventh New York Volunteer Infantry. He was rapidly promoted, served on the staffs of Gens. Berry and Kearney, and was with each of these officers when he was killed. He was in service of first and second battles of Bull Run, the conflict at Williamsburg, the sanguinary Seven Days' fight and other early battles ... He was also warmly interested in his soldier comrades, being a zealous member of the Wadsworth Post No. 2, G.A.R at Helena and also of the Loyal Legion. ... his name is indissolubly connected with Montana history from early pioneer days until death placed its seal upon his brow.

The *Montana Daily Record* wrote:

In the death of Mr. Huntley one of the picturesque types of the Montana pioneer has been removed. His genius for the promotion and successful management of great western enterprises was recognized throughout the broad west years before the iron horse entered as a factor in the vast transportation business of the Pacific coast.

His contributions and character were well recognized:

When we state Mr. Huntley and his associates established and controlled every original stage line in Montana, some idea may be formed of the extent and importance of his business operations; but, above all this was the personality of the man, who stood four square to every wind that blows, and won the abiding friendship and regard of all with whom he came in contact, by the integrity and loyalty of his character, by his sympathetic and genial nature, and by his inflexible honesty. He was a distinct man, a true man, and none is more worthy of a tribute of honor. Such lives as his offer both lesson and incentive.

In his *1901 Report*, Superintendent John Pitcher wrote:

This Company [the Yellowstone Line] is by far the finest and best equipped transportation company operating in the Park, and there are few, if any, better to be found anywhere in the country. Their Concord coaches, seating seven to ten people are the finest and most comfortable wagons made. They also have a number of small surreys seating three people besides the driver, which are intended to carry small parties who prefer to travel by themselves. That their teams are excellent and drivers skillful and careful is shown by their remarkable freedom from accidents during the past season. This company has operated in perfect harmony during the season with the Yellowstone Park Association ... and has done away with many things which have heretofore caused friction between the two companies and inconvenience to the tourists. The company has recently suffered a serious loss in the death of its manager, Mr. Silas Huntley, by his genial and courteous treatment of all who come in contact with him, had made a host of friends not only for himself and his company, but for the Park as well. In his business transactions Mr. Huntley never lost sight of the true interest of the Yellowstone National Park, and was at all times exceedingly careful not to ask for anything or do anything that would in the least mar the beauty of the Park or conflict with its best interest in any way. By his death the Park has lost a true and valuable friend.

His friend and colleague Hiram Chittenden wrote:

The transportation system of the Park, which has now developed into the best equipped organization of its kind in the world, was, in its essential features, the creation of Silas S. Huntley, who gave it his undivided attention from 1892 until 1901, the date of his death. By virtue of his wide acquaintance throughout the country, his intimate knowledge of the Park, and his genuine interest in its welfare, he practically controlled its administration for many years, and died lamented as one of the best friends it ever had.

Annie again had to leave her home, the little cottage at Mammoth Hot Springs. She went back to Helena taking charge of selling the ranch which took close to two years. For that time it was one of the largest real estate deals ever made in Montana. She sold to the Riverside Land & Livestock Company, a corporation newly formed by mostly Helena stock holders. "The ranch includes 11,000 acres of land located on both sides of the Missouri River, together with about 6,000 acres of leased land. These lands control an immense range. Included in the deal are about four hundred head of cattle and in the neighborhood of twenty thousand head of sheep. The ranch is well equipped with buildings, fences and other improvements. Being on the railroad, and controlling, as it does, a vast range the ranch is said to be very favorably located."

After disposing of the ranch, Annie traveled for a few years, eventually going back to Washington, D.C. among her old friends.

<hr>

Silas' death was a double dose of disaster for Harry Child. The emotional loss of a long time friend and partner as well as a loved brother-in law was an undescribable blow. And then shortly after, his other long time friend and partner, E.W. Bach, being beset with family and political problems found it necessary to disassociate himself from the Yellowstone enterprises. The financial part eventually turned out to be not so devastating a disaster. The loan procured from NPR to buy the YPA was made to all three men equally. Now two-thirds of the shares reverted back to the railroad's Northwest Improvement Company, which continued to support Harry.

From 1893, he had been juggling his time and efforts between finishing the smelter and getting involved with the hotel division of the YPA. By 1903 he was writing long letters to the Department of the Interior and the Park Superintendents on YPA stationery and signed H.W. Child, President.

Some of the letters concerned complaints that needed to be explained and solutions addressed. Most were about over crowding of the hotels. Harry blocked a certain number of rooms each day for each of the railroads, but the Union Pacific consistently over booked their allotted space. The Union Pacific delivered its passengers to their Monida, Montana terminus, and F. Jay Haynes' Monida & Yellowstone Company accommodated as many as they could pile on the stagecoaches for the rest of the trip into the Park. But as they were delivered around to the hotels, some found "no room at the inn." Complaints went to Washington and were thrown back to the YPA. The demand for more hotel accommodations was urgent.

From 1883-1902 the NPR spur line from Livingston, known as the Yellowstone Park Line, ended at Cinnabar, three miles north of the park's northern border. A land dispute kept them from being able to finish their tracks all the way into Gardiner. After holding out for sixteen years, the miner relinquished his claim, and the way was clear for the line to be completed.

With this thought in mind, in 1902 Harry purchased most of twelve blocks of land in Gardiner (around 350 lots total) – including several blocks close to the location where the depot was planned. He sold most of this land in 1904. Pieces were sold to other businessmen, and Harry and Adelaide donated land to build the Gardiner Community Church [90]. They saved a portion for their own use.

Adelaide kept her interest in Helena through involvement with the Unitarian Church. After the wife of the minister died in 1905,

Adelaide commissioned from the Tiffany Company of New York a unique window in her memory. The design was "a 100" x 40" mountain sunset landscape, suggestive of the Helena valley. ... When no back lighting fell upon the window it appeared a marbled blue." When back lighted, "it had all the glory of a western sunset." The window was installed in 1907.

Harry and Adelaide were now spending more time in Yellowstone. Just as they had done in Helena and Great Falls, they became involved in lives of Mammoth and Gardiner residents. One old-timer was E.C. Culver, who rode the trains between Livingston and Gardiner, soliciting business for the park hotel and transportation companies.

Culver was hired by the YPA as winterkeeper of the Firehole Hotel for the winter of 1888-89. "Mr. Culver brought his wife, then suffering with tuberculosis, and [their] baby girl, to live in Firehole Basin, hoping the change in climate might benefit her [Culver's wife Mattie]. Her death occurred after a short sojourn there. At the time the snow was on an average of five feet deep and the nearest doctor nineteen miles away, at the Government Post ..." Her body was packed in snow to be kept frozen until a proper grave could be dug. Men from the Nez Percé Soldier Station helped by fencing the grave site. When Adelaide Child heard this sad story, she had a proper headstone made and placed inside a sturdy iron fence [91].

This long-held story in Yellowstone folklore has captivated employees and visitors for decades. From the late 1930s Mattie Culver was known as the "woman who died in childbirth." Several historians have thoroughly researched Mattie's life – raising questions about the truth of the details – while expanding her story. Her tragic tale continues to attract strangers to her lonely resting place – including mysterious unseen visitors who annually pull weeds from around the stone and place a bouquet of flowers. By helping to preserve Mattie's resting place, Adelaide's efforts help today's visitors honor Mattie Culver's short life.

⸻

The demand for a hotel at Upper Geyser Basin was strengthening.

A 1900 traveler described the "few log houses which constitute Upper Geyser Basin," but the superintendent was kinder, "... a frame building where meals are served, and a number of very comfortably arranged tents,... neatly floored, and comfortably warmed with stoves."

Time and energy had been devoted to plans, none of which ever came to fruition. St. Paul architect A.W. Spaulding, engaged by the YPA, prepared blueprints and detailed specifications. He advertised for bids on the job, and the Secretary of the Interior approved the plans, but the NPR postponed construction.

F. Jay Haynes suggested the erection of five cottages. He submitted plans for a hotel, drawn by St. Paul architect, E.J. Donohue, but his request for lease was never granted.

In the fall of 1902 the NPR agreed to furnish the money necessary to erect the hotel at Upper Geyser Basin (UGB). Harry wasted no time – first running with Haynes' cottage idea. That winter Harry left one hundred head of horses in the Park to be used for hauling wood to the Upper Geyser Basin. He knew the spring thaw would cause muddy roads and prevent hauling until mid-June or so. Hauling over the snow during the winter would allow construction to commence as early as possible in the spring. When Harry and Adelaide left Montana for San Diego, Harry was satisfied his plan was moving ahead.

While vacationing at the Hotel del Coronado, Harry instead made an acquaintance that would forever shape his business choices and change the hotel landscape of the Park. After seeing some recent renovations to the hotel and a few other nearby buildings, Harry inquired of his friend and hotelier Elisha Babcock, President of the Coronado Beach Company. Babcock went out of his way to recommend his architect, Robert C. Reamer [37] to Child. Babcock advised Reamer, "I have known Mr. Child for years. He is intimately connected with the president of the Northern Pacific Railway. If you went with him for a year, I am satisfied your ability would be recognized and it would probably connect you in a very prominent and permanent way with the Northern Pacific. If you would be inclined to accept from him $3,000 per year,

I believe you could secure the place, and I think it would lead to your being his main architect, and a very prominent place on the Northern Pacific in addition. They want to build hotels, as much as possible, in the rustic and your taste in that line would redound to your credit."

Reamer did accept Child's offer and drafted plans which both incorporated and enhanced the log cottage idea. His plans exploded simple ideas such as log construction, stone fireplaces, second floor balconies into a magnificent six-story high log cabin.

In the spring of 1903, while the new hotel for the Upper Geyser Basin was still a pile of logs and a simmering vision, U.S. President Theodore Roosevelt (TR) vacationed to Yellowstone [94, 95]. The park was still under a blanket of snow and closed for the winter, so TR's party had the interior of the park to themselves. At Mammoth the President stayed with Park Superintendent Pitcher, but Harry's transportation company was called upon to transport him into the park interior. In a meeting with Child and Reamer, Roosevelt put his stamp of approval on their plans. Harry noted that during his visit, the President "spent considerable time looking over and examining the plans of the buildings that we are contemplating building in the Park in the next two or three years, notably the Upper Geyser Basin structure and this Lake Hotel structure, and went into detail with our architect, and was very profuse in his compliments upon our efforts to improve the architecture of the Park buildings."

Many acquainted with the Great Camps of the Adirondacks and their unique, whimsical architecture, draw parallels in Reamer's completed Old Faithful Inn. Perhaps during this conversation ideas were transmitted. The presidential party may have passed through some of Yellowstone's diseased forests leading to the idea of using these "odd freaks of tree growth" as architectural accents.

Park officials and the YPA worked out a lot of details such as wood collection areas, contracts let to teamsters and businessmen to assist the wood cutters. Engineer Hiram Chittenden attempted to enforce wider wheels on freight wagons to preserve road surfaces during spring mud season. But Harry's negotiation skills allowed him to keep running with his existing equipment. Harry traveled to Washington with Reamer's plans. Approved by the Secretary of the Interior, construction commenced the next month [73].

Reamer lived on site at UGB during construction. During the winter of 1903-1904, Reamer and his wife lived in Haynes' Log Cabin Studio next to the construction site. In the spring of 1904, Harry and Adelaide made the arduous trip to Upper Geyser Basin to check on progress, but they found themselves stranded by an unexpected snowstorm.

Soon after this adventure, Adelaide became more involved in the plans for the new hotel. With her two children grown, her time was free for other interests. She and Robert Reamer began working together on decisions to decorate and furnish the new hotel. Their sharing of this creative task would continue for more than thirty years as Yellowstone's hotel expansion continued.

⸺⊷⊶⸺

One shadow was cast in the midst of the excitement around the completion of Old Faithful Inn – the death of Edmund W. Bach. He became ill while traveling in October of 1903 and had to be hospitalized in Chicago. He was staying at the Hotel Washington in Seattle when he died of Bright's disease (kidney failure) on April 20, 1904. He left behind his second wife, a nine year old daughter and a five year old son. "Major Bach was a man who made friends and he was known from coast to coast," wrote the Anaconda *Standard*. "While his best friends were undoubtedly those who were most closely associated with him, there will be men and women from New York to San Francisco who will regret to hear of his death."

⸺⊷⊶⸺

Old Faithful Inn opened June 1, 1904 [72, 74]. Touted as a "castle of logs," it boasted 140 rooms with steam heat, community bathrooms with indoor plumbing, and electric lighting designed to look like candles. "Finished in the rough, one might imagine material comforts lacking," declared an early advertising booklet, "but everything will be found here to suit the most fastidious."

Harry Child sought perfection in his hotel, not only in the unique structure but in the services rendered. He planned for every meal served in his dining room to be an unforgettable culinary experience. The tables were set with white linen tablecloths and adorned with sterling silver and Blue Willow china.

The featured menu item was roast beef. He kept a small herd of prime beef "on the hoof" in the Indian Creek area. Fresh watercress and vegetables were brought daily from the Chinamen's Garden, just inside the park's north entrance. The little stream of hot geyser water that ran behind the Inn had a section covered over to create a greenhouse environment for growing mushrooms – Harry's favorite accompaniment to roast beef. A company fisherman provided a never-ending supply of trout from park streams.

To promote travel to this new man-made wonder, a photograph of it was shipped to St. Louis to be displayed at the World's Fair that summer. After the summer season ended, the transportation company also "...sent one of the largest coaches and six horses with John Reynolds as driver to the World's Fair at St. Louis where they will be on exhibition during the remainder of the fair season. E.C. Culver, the company's old war horse, accompanied the outfit to St. Louis and will do the shouting, tell the weird western stories, etc."

For Adelaide the Inn was an opportunity to share her husband's passion for building. At the smelter in Great Falls, and in their home in Helena she began to establish herself as a gracious hostess. But soon she and Harry would begin spending the season off from Yellowstone visiting furniture shows.

Similarly, the construction of the Inn, and Harry's role as hotel and transportation chief of the Park, began to place him in contact with some major political players. William Loeb Jr. [94], private secretary to President Roosevelt, accompanied Harry on several fall camping/hunting trips and hosted him in Washington. Another ally was Thomas H. Carter, who between 1889 and 1911 served one term in the U.S. House, spent four years as Chairman of the Republican National Committee, and was elected to two (non-consecutive) terms as Senator representing the state of Montana.

Harry's contact with TR did not end after the president's visit to Yellowstone. The two continued correspondence that would endure. In 1911 when Roosevelt visited Helena, Harry was again on hand to act as his chauffeur [97]. In the personal family collections is a gift to Harry and Adelaide from one TR subsequent hunting trips. "He was close friends with four presidents and did not hesitate to use the friendships." Harry Child developed a knack for making connections with those in powerful positions – a skill that would serve him well for the rest of his working career.

Reamer stayed in Yellowstone for one year. For the Yellowstone Park Association he designed the Old Faithful Inn, major additions to Lake Hotel [81, 82], and a lunch station at West Thumb. For the Yellowstone Park Transportation Company he designed a massive barn and coach shed at Mammoth Hot Springs. For the Northern Pacific Railroad he designed the Gardiner, Montana depot [38]. Reamer collaborated with Army Corps engineer, Hiram Chittenden, on the landscaping design surrounding the depot, which included Chittenden's massive stone arch, known today as the Roosevelt Arch [122]. And for local business man, W.A. Hall, he designed a general store. Reamer's chance meeting with Harry Child set him off on his successful career path.

—————»●◄—————

The Monida & Yellowstone Stage Company, operated by F. Jay Haynes, was well on its way to an established position in the park. This company had twenty-five employees, 12 eleven-passenger Concord coaches, 4 three-passenger Concord surreys, 80 horses, and two Concord buggies. The company constructed barns at Upper Geyser Basin, Norris,

Mammoth Hot Springs, and they used the barns of the YPA at Fountain, Lake, and Canyon until they could construct their own.

Proprietors of the Monida & Yellowstone Stage Company were the first to explore introducing automobiles to Yellowstone's roads. In the spring of 1903 Mr. Haynes and his superintendent Mr. Humphrey toured the factories of several auto manufacturers. W.W. Humphrey, with more than a decade of experience in and knowledge of park transportation "... learned that the largest motors made are capable of carrying no more than six persons and even with this small number they must be packed so close as to be uncomfortable, while no room is left for baggage, without which the five days' trip cannot be made. In consequence of Mr. Humphrey's investigation his company will adhere to the old way of carrying its passengers." The time was not yet right for the automobile and Yellowstone to meet.

———◆———

In 1905 W.W. Wylie sold his *Wylie Way* to A.W. Miles, a prominent businessman in Livingston, Montana. Miles owned a profitable dry goods and grocery store and had carried Wylie's purchases on time for a number of years. At the age of fifty-seven "Wylie wanted to retire because of age, the nervous strain brought on by fighting for his lease every year, the difficulties of enduring the weather and high altitude as an older man..." Miles agreed to forgive Wylie's debts in exchange for one-third of the company shares, and Harry W. Child bought the other two-thirds as a silent partner. The name was changed slightly to Wylie Permanent Camping Company. Wylie stayed on for that summer only as a paid employee of the company. His name continued to provide credibility and assure guests a quality of service, though the man himself was gone after that summer.

With his sister, Wylie concentrated on building a guest ranch on his Spanish Creek properties. That venture lasted only one year. Wylie next tried raising sheep and cattle. Despairing of ever getting rich on Montana land, he sold his holdings to Harry and departed with a number of sheep, which he shipped to the Imperial Valley in California. The Montana-bred sheep died from the California heat shortly thereafter. Wylie did find the California climate to his liking, so he settled in Pasadena.

———————

At age 16 Huntley Child took a job with the U.S. Army Corps of Engineers, working with Hiram Chittenden building roads in the park. [*Italics are Huntley's words as spoken in an interview with Aubrey Haines*; **'bold' are Chittenden's words as remembered by Huntley**] Huntley admired Chittenden, described him as *"the fastest and most accurate engineer I ever saw, but he could be cantankerous."* Huntley drove stakes and worked the ball and chain. As they rode out to meet the work crew, Chittenden would give Huntley the orders, and Huntley would relay them to the crew. *"When we were working in Mammoth laying out water and sewer lines, we rode out on our saddle horses. When working out in the Park, I rode along with him in his buggy. Chittenden would drop me off someplace and say,* **'you fix that up and I'll pick you up tonight.'** *So we would stake that out and chain it off. Or he would say,* **'Huntley, I want to make a change,'** *so we would stake that out and go."*

They spent one summer working between Thumb and Lake. Huntley said, *"The original road went from Thumb around the shore-line of Yellowstone Lake. The road was soft along the lake making it difficult for the horses so we took a short cut up over the hill. I was out there for weeks working on that. The crews were working one from each end. At that time seventy-five percent of the people were taking the boat across the lake."*

"Eventually that road proved unpopular with the tourists because the only scenery was trees on both sides of the road ..."

Huntley worked with Chittenden again building the road from Canyon over Dunraven Pass, down to Tower Fall and to the summit of Mount Washburn. Today the former road is a popular hike up to the fire watch tower at the summit. Huntley worked three summers with Chittenden – 1902, 1903, and 1904.

In January of 1905 Harry wrote to the Secretary of the Interior: "The road from the Canyon Hotel to Dunraven Pass is in fair condition, but the road from said Pass to the top of Mount Washburn and return is exceedingly dangerous, and to convey tourists there over would necessitate the furnishing of specially heavy draft horses, specially constructed harness, and coaches so constructed as that they will not be blown over by the wind. The rigs in use by the Yellowstone National Park Transportation Company at this time, or other persons, firms and corporations, transporting passengers under contract, or under license in the park, are not such as can with safety to passengers make this trip to the top of Mount Washburn. ... it is the purpose of the company, in view of the dangers attendant upon taking this trip to the top of Mount Washburn, to issue a circular in relation to this side trip describing it and the dangers attendant thereon, and require all persons taking such trip the signing of a paper relinquishing any claim against the Transportation Company for damages in case of accident to them due to causes other than negligence on the part of the company and its employees."

Harry was granted: "This permit, which is of a special character and to meet a special condition of affairs existing in the Park at this time, is to continue during the pleasure of the secretary." It was strictly a side trip, not a part of any package, taken at a cost of $5.00 per person. During the era of stagecoaches, the transportation company's regular runs returned to Mammoth via Norris. Mount Washburn, Tower Junction, and the northern tier road to Mammoth were not a part of the official tours until after automobiles arrived.

Throughout the formative years of Yellowstone concessionaires, many good people came and went. For whatever reason, some stayed to make the park their lifelong venture. In1905, a young man from St. Paul, Minnesota, eager and energetic, took a summer job as assistant to the purchasing agent. He was Charles Ashworth Hamilton[109], friendly, fun-loving, unassuming, and a hard worker. He returned to the Park for several summer seasons working at one time as Harry Child's secretary. Yellowstone Park has a certain undefinable charm which to some cannot be denied. During those carefree summers in his youth, Ham, as he was fondly called, made special friends and such great memories which, in his later years he loved to share. One particular friend was Huntley Child, Harry's son.

F. Jay Haynes had been in and around Yellowstone since its earliest days. By this time he had two photo shops, one at Old Faithful area and one at Mammoth where he maintained a home for the summers seasons. He was also granted permission to sell his post cards and photos from a shop just off the Old Faithful Inn lobby.

During summers at the Park, Haynes' second son, Jack [111], became good friends with Huntley and Ham. These three brash young men enjoyed palling around and were especially fond of pranks and practical jokes. One Fourth of July they swiped a case of dynamite, and they mistakenly ignited the gathered explosive. The subsequent blast broke all the windows in the Mammoth Hotel. "Since Huntley was the son of Harry, [Ham] took the rap and was booted out of the Park, not to return until 1915." Beyond the usual exuberance of their youth, the three each found a start in business – with Yellowstone as the backdrop.

———————

A few years after the deaths of Silas Huntley and E.W. Bach, Harry's business acumen and his acquaintance with the NPR people came to his rescue. He was able to work out a 50-50 ownership deal with the YPA, and the NPR with confidence in Harry's ability, threw in their financial backing. In just a few years Harry was able to pay off the debt. In 1905, the NPR's Northwest Improvement Company sold shares of stock to Harry Child, such that he then owned half of the Yellowstone Park Association [70, 71] and the Yellowstone Park Transportation Company.

YELLOWSTONE PARK ASSOCIATION

HOTELS AT

MAMMOTH HOT SPRINGS   NORRIS GEYSER BASIN
FOUNTAIN GEYSER BASIN   UPPER GEYSER BASIN
THUMB OF LAKE   YELLOWSTONE LAKE
            GRAND CANON

H.W. CHILD,
PRESIDENT.

YELLOWSTONE PARK   August 30, 1908. B

Chapter 7: Love in the Rough
1906 - 1910

*Marriages and grandchildren add
to the family, a ranching partnership is formed*

Harry and Adelaide arranged for their children Ellen and
Huntley to be educated at prominent schools in the eastern U.S. Ellen
attended the Baldwin School, now part of Bryn Mawr College, west of
Philadelphia, Pennsylvania. As a young woman, she often accompanied
her mother or Aunt Annie to the park.

Huntley Child, a member of the 1908 class at MIT in Cambridge,
Massachusetts, played on the football team and joined the Delta Psi
fraternity. "Hunt is the man with the stretch – the greatest punt and
drop kicker ever seen in the Hub," declared the yearbook.

As Harry and Adelaide's children came of age, work and play
was not the only thing on their minds – romance was in the air. For
Ellen Dean Child [115], known in the family from childhood as "Dean,"
it was a dashing soldier who won her heart.

William M. Nichols (known to the family as Billie) [116], a
Connecticut native, received an appointment to the U.S. Military
Academy at West Point in 1899. He was a member of the fencing and
football teams, and graduated in 1903. Ellen was present at the Army-
Navy game on November 28, 1903 – compliments of family friend
General S.B.M. Young. Billie graduated as a second lieutenant, and he
joined the Cavalry, and was assigned to Fort Yellowstone, coming to the
park early in 1904.

According to a family story Ellen and Billie fell in love and wanted to marry. "Harry would have nothing to do with this as he did not want his daughter ... to leave the Park and travel to different Army posts with Billie. So Harry contacted someone in Washington, D.C., and had Billie transferred out of the Park." Ellen "was crushed and could not live without Billie so Harry contacted Washington again and had Billie transferred back to Yellowstone."

William Loeb, Jr., President Roosevelt's personal secretary, responded to Harry's request to transfer the "young Lochinvar[1] to some distant point." Loeb's son later explained, "Unfortunately my father was sympathetic to the young lovers' situation, so he arranged the transfer of Captain Nichols to be an instructor at West Point, but with an appropriate delay in the transfer. The following summer when he arrived at Yellowstone ... [my father] was met by Harry Child at the station, with fire in his eye. The first thing Child said, without waiting to greet him, was, 'What about this Nichols affair?' My father innocently remarked, 'Oh, I've arranged his transfer, to be an instructor at the military academy at West Point.' Child said, 'Yes, I know that, but you arranged it too late!'"

Perhaps realizing the true force of his beloved's father, Billie resigned his commission in 1905 and took a position in the Engineering Division of the Northern Pacific Railway.

General S.B.M. Young was enough acquainted with the Harry Child and Silas Huntley families, from his term as Yellowstone's Acting Superintendent ten years before, that he wrote President Roosevelt's secretary, "I start for Helena today to be present at the Child-Nichols wedding." Ellen and Billie (hereafter W.M.) married in November 1907, and W.M. became Harry's private secretary.

---

[1] "Lochinvar" refers to a fictional character in a Sir Walter Scott poem, 1808, "a brave knight who arrives unannounced at the bridal feast of Ellen, his beloved, who is about to be married [to another] ... Lochinvar claims one dance with the bride and dances her out the door, swooping her up onto his horse, and they ride off together into the unknown." https://www.britannica.com/topic/Lochinvar 1Apr2020.

As a Colonel, S.B.M. Young did a tour of duty in Yosemite before serving a five-month tour of duty at Fort Yellowstone in 1897. He was a highly decorated veteran of the Civil War. He did a tour of duty fighting Indians in the Southwest, and he was a fearless fighter in the Spanish-American War serving in Cuba alongside then-Colonel Theodore Roosevelt (TR). He was the eighth lieutenant general in our Army's history – George Washington being the first. He was the Army's first chief-of-staff.

By 1907 he was back as full Superintendent and higher in the military ranks. During his second tour of duty in Yellowstone, the Park was plagued by an escapee from the Fort Yellowstone jail, followed by a series of stagecoach hold-ups and robberies, as well as the poaching of trophy animals.

Despite these troubles, he was able to renew old friendships. In December 1907 he wrote to his old friend TR, "... on my return from a little visit and a Christmas dinner with the admirable woman whom I hope to have the pleasure of presenting to you and dear Mrs. Roosevelt as my wife sometime during 1908." The reply came, " we look forward to having you and her dine with us at the White House. Give her our warm regards." Three months later Young wrote from Chicago, "Dear Mr. President. The Ceremony will be in Grace Church at high noon on Tuesday March 3, and we shall leave at 4 pm on the Rock Island for Phoenix Arizona as our first objective point. Will be in Washington sometime in May." He received a letter from Theodore and Edith Roosevelt, "Heartiest Congratulations, We look forward to seeing you both in May."

The "admirable woman" was Silas Huntley's widow, Annie Dean Huntley. After their honeymoon, Annie and General Young settled in Army housing at Fort Yellowstone. Harry wrote to Washington suggesting improved housing due to the entertainment duties inherent in the park superintendent's job, but this would not come about until after the Youngs had left Yellowstone.

Cupid's arrow would also hit son Huntley Child [119] who at age 19 entered his father's business and maintained a residence in the Park. Huntley and Charles Hamilton "would look at all women coming into the Park and would make a bet who could get a dance and a kiss with any one of them. In 1907 a beautiful Southern Belle arrived in Yellowstone from Memphis, Tennessee, by the name of Emilie James. Both men tried to dance with her, and neither got anywhere. The next night the same thing – their advances were not accepted. Huntley told his mother, Adelaide, about this beautiful girl who would have nothing to do with him, and asked if she could help.

When Emilie and her mother returned to Mammoth from their trip around the Park, Adelaide invited them to tea at her home, and Huntley was finally able to meet her. Huntley danced with Emilie that night, but had to dance with her mother first. After the ladies returned to Memphis, Huntley and Emilie corresponded. Huntley was madly in love, and was invited to Memphis for Christmas." They were married in Memphis on October 12, 1908.

Today, Yellowstone visitors pass through the Mammoth Hot Springs village and notice the presence of private homes, but rarely give thought to their residents. Several of these homes were occupied by the Huntley, Child, and Nichols families during the seven decades that they operated businesses inside the park.

As the first of the family to reside in the park, Silas and Annie lived in the house George Wakefield had built at the base of the Mammoth Terraces [53]. When Harry assumed operations of the transportation and hotel companies fully after Silas's death, he and Adelaide moved into the Wakefield house. This was not large enough to accommodate the family of four comfortably, so Harry built a colonial-style house [54] a couple years later. This house (built circa 1903) sits north of the terraces, near Liberty Cap, between the stone house and the public restroom building.

After Billie Nichols and Ellen Child married, they moved into the Wakefield house. Their three children, Adelaide "Jackie" (1909), John Q. "Johnnie" (1911), and Dean (1914) grew up there. This house was certainly too small for the growing Nichols family, so additions were put onto the rear of the home [55].

Son Huntley Child and his new bride Emilie moved into the Colonial house. While living there, their first child, a daughter named Marion was delivered at home with Dr. Dean in attendance. The family story goes, "Dr. Maria Dean was once summoned to Mammoth Hot Springs to attend to her sister, Adelaide, who was ill. She was met at Gardiner depot by her nephew, Huntley Child, and was taken immediately to his home. His wife Emilie was in labor and after several hours gave birth to Marion Child (1909). All was well with the mother and baby when Dr. Dean suddenly exclaimed, "Oh, my poor, dear Addie! How is she? I must go to her." Two years later (1911) their second child, a son named Huntley Jr. was born in Tennessee. Elizabeth, called Betty, was also born in the house at Mammoth (1914) [120].

To provide a new home for Adelaide and Harry while their children were moving into the neighborhood, architect Robert Reamer designed a prairie-school style house [57] next to the old Wakefield house. The kitchen, dining room, and living spaces were spaciously laid out to accommodate entertaining, both for visiting dignitaries and for company social functions. Because the house was located adjacent to what was then a main roadway, the family bedrooms were well hidden behind a hallway that extends across the entire front half of the building.

A unique feature of the front room is a beautiful spiral staircase [58] – perhaps this is one feature Adelaide missed from her grand home in Great Falls. Well-designed for both its location and its purpose, the Child House still provides a comfortable home and a venue for hosting necessary social functions. It was and still is the grandest and most prestigious of the privately-occupied concessioner homes.

After the completion of Old Faithful Inn architect Reamer's career took him away from Yellowstone. He did not stay away for long, as his friendship with the Child family brought him back within a few years. Previously Reamer had constructed a large coach shed, stable, and drivers' living quarters adjacent to the Mammoth Hotel. In 1906 he designed a similar set of structures in Gardiner, just inside the park border. These lovely stone and wood buildings echoed the rustic features of the Gardiner Depot and Old Faithful Inn. One of these buildings survives – the mess house and bunkhouse. The two buildings were joined into a duplex and are currently occupied by two concession employee families.

Harry also had plans for a grand hotel to replace the aging National Hotel at Mammoth Hot Springs. Twice, in 1906 and in 1909, Robert Reamer created water color renditions of immense new structures. Twice, money concerns and failure to receive government approval for the site selected, delayed the construction. A new hotel for Mammoth would have to wait.

During this period, automobiles were becoming more common in cities. Harry, always on the forefront of innovation, owned a Franklin. He was not permitted, however, to bring the vehicle the five miles from Gardiner into Mammoth. He kept his auto in Gardiner where Robert Reamer constructed a handsome garage that could handle five vehicles [56]. Harry's garage was located on a piece of his Gardiner land, adjacent to the Roosevelt Arch. For a trip to Helena, Harry and family would leave Mammoth in a horse-drawn wagon, switching to the auto in Gardiner.

———◆———

General S.B.M. Young's 1907-1908 run as superintendent of Yellowstone was unique. He had retired from the Army, so another man served as commander of the troops at Fort Yellowstone. He was not an "acting superintendent," as all other officers had been. Young was a full superintendent. Several pieces of correspondence suggest he may have been on a special mission from his commander and chief, President

Roosevelt. "So far as I am concerned," Young wrote, "my services as Superintendent will be cheerfully and conscientiously given, without any remuneration whatever, so long as I am able to perform the duties and my services are acceptable to the authorities."

Young sent a multi-page letter to TR outlining his suggestions for replacing the Army's presence in Yellowstone with what he called a "National Park Guard." "It is my firm belief," he wrote, "that this park can be governed and protected in a manner creditable to our government with a civil guard ..." He recommended one to three guards at each of ten stations for the seven months of winter, and two to four guards at each of thirteen stations for June through October. TR's response was final, "I found it was simply not possible to do anything with it this year." Instead, the military presence in Yellowstone continued for another decade.

Another pressing matter concerned a park concessioner, E.C. Waters. Since launching his steamboat *Zillah* on Yellowstone Lake in 1891, Waters had served the park well. He was a consummate businessman – the numbers show he often transported fully half of the number of visitors accommodated by the hotels and camping companies. But he was often an annoyance to the lunch station staff at West Thumb and the hotel staff at Lake Hotel. Harry personally ejected him from the Lake Hotel after he failed to respond to polite requests to discontinue drumming up boat business while hotel guests enjoyed dinner.

Waters made an arrangement with W.W. Wylie to add the steamboat option to their regular camping tour. He unsuccessfully attempted to make the same deal with Harry. Despite building a larger vessel, the *SS E C Waters*, his forceful personality had rubbed too many people the wrong way. In 1907 S.B.M. Young assembled a set of documents recommending that "the existing permit of the Yellowstone Lake Boat Company ... be not extended or renewed ..." This landed on the desk of TR, who made the decision to cancel Waters' contract after the 1907 season.

In 1909 Roosevelt appointed General Young Governor of the Soldiers' Home in Washington, D.C. where he and Annie enjoyed a very active social life. The Department of the Interior required many conferences with concessioners in Washington which enabled the Childs and Youngs to maintain close contact.

———⊷∘⊶———

Late in 1907 the Union Pacific Railroad (UPR) completed its tracks to the west border of Yellowstone. Although the UPR attempted to contact Robert Reamer while they were planning depot construction in the growing town of Boundary (now known as West Yellowstone), they ultimately turned to an in-house architect whose name is unknown to history. Today the Union Pacific Depot houses the Museum of the Yellowstone. Gilbert Stanley Underwood designed their beautiful stone dining hall, now used for community gatherings and educational programs.

The Monida & Yellowstone Stage Company moved their operations to a location just inside the Park border – and changed their name to the Yellowstone-Western Company. Their new location, an area known as Riverside, was later used as a bus dispatch and drivers' dormitory location until 1975. Two miles inside the west entrance, there is currently a fishermen's access road to an open meadow along the Madison River – the former location of Riverside.

Monida, once a busy train destination, is now a cluster of about thirty buildings, located at exit 0, along I-15 between Idaho Falls, Idaho and Dillon, Montana. Travelers today may enjoy some of the former stage route between Monida and West Yellowstone as it travels through Red Rock Lakes National Wildlife Refuge. Interpretive signs along the way whisper the story of the now distant whinny of the horses and rumble of the stagecoaches.

F. Jay Haynes, largely backed by Edward Harriman, president of the Union Pacific Railroad, began circulating complaints in Washington suggesting Yellowstone's guest services were a railroad monopoly. The NPR decided to dispose of all their hotel stock to Harry by 1907. He was now full owner of both the YPA and the YPTC. NPR president Howard

Elliot wrote an internal memo showing the true story, "The relations between the Park Companies and our Company will continue as now, in so far as close working together is concerned. We will help Mr. Child where we can, and may make advances of money to him from time to time rather than to force him to borrow outside. He, in turn, will do all he can to manage the Park so that it will be satisfactory to the Northern Pacific Company."

Two years later Harry dissolved the YPA and formed the Yellowstone Park Hotel Company, with his son Huntley Child as treasurer, and son-in-law W.M. Nichols as secretary.

Since acquiring the Wylie Permanent Camping Company in 1905, A.W. Miles continued to act as its head and began to grow the business. It continued to operate Wylie's four camps at Willow Park, Upper Basin, Lake, and Grand Canyon. The peak year for W.W. Wylie was 1902 when he hosted one-thousand-eight-hundred-and-seventy tourists. 1905 was the first year the company turned a profit – hosting over thirty-five-hundred guests – but Wylie no longer had a financial interest.

Within the next four years, the company added three more camps. Miles replaced the Willow Park location with a larger facility at Swan Lake Flats in 1906. According to long-time employee Edward Moorman, "He constructed a much better camp than the one at Willow Park, bought a much better type of tents, wainscoted the tents from about four feet from the board floors and bought many new tents and much camp equipment; also had better kitchen and dining-room equipment. He installed flush toilets in this camp. He also bought some new Concord Coaches, harness and stage coach horses. Miles also constructed a large addition to the old Wylie Hotel in Gardiner [built in 1903] and bought all new equipment and furnishings."

Camp Roosevelt was established at a site near Tower Junction in 1906. Howard Hays [112], who had been promoting the Wylie Way as a railroad agent in Salt Lake City, became Miles' assistant. He delighted in showing the large Douglas fir tree under which the president had camped during his visit three years earlier – no matter that the actual camp was next to the Tower soldier station two miles east.

They established a lunch stop called "Sleepy Hollow" on the Gibbon River, and a camp at Riverside, five miles inside the West entrance. In 1910 the company built a bathhouse at the Old Faithful Camp, near Grotto Geyser. Although other entrepreneurs received leases as guides to private camping parties, the only ones that posed any major competition were the Holm Company on the east side of the park, and the Shaw & Powell Camping Company, established in 1898.

As Harry began looking to replace the National Hotel at Mammoth and to greatly expand the hotel at Canyon, he divested himself of a portion of his ownership in the camps. In 1909 he sold half of his share of the company to F. Jay Haynes.

———•———

Harry Child was by now full owner of the horse operations in Yellowstone. Each fall he had to take the horses out of the park and find a place to winter them. Silas Huntley had known many of the ranchers in Montana. His method of wintering the horses was making individual deals with the ranches – mostly in the area north of Livingston toward Billings. So it was a good day for Harry when Charlie Anceney [100] approached him about wintering the horses on the Anceney "Home Ranch" in the Gallatin Valley just west of the Park. He said he would winter all of the horses without resorting to hay or other grains, just good grass. Harry was interested, but he had heard rumors of loco weed (a plant harmful to horses) growing in that area. He decided to go out and pay a visit to the Anceney ranch. After visiting and taking the evening meal, it was decided that Harry should stay overnight, and early next morning he and Charlie would ride out and look over the land.

They rode out "to a point where, to the south, the Spanish Peaks sparkled in the sun, to the west the Madison River flowed north with the

Tobacco Root [Mountains] as a backdrop, and to the east the Gallatin River ran from its canyon and north to join the Madison [River] at the three forks of the Missouri River." [98]

The story goes that, at this point, "loco weed was forgotten," and as Charlie sat on his horse looking at the grandeur he lamented to Harry that someday he would like to own all of the land as far as the eye could see. "Mr. Child agreed to become interested in the ranch provided Anceney became his partner and undertook the practical management. Anceney readily agreed. 'Now, go out and buy all the land within sight,' Mr. Child instructed his partner. 'I'll finance your share of the cost.'" Thus began a partnership that would last over two decades.

And so it was, that while Child was busy building hotels in Yellowstone, Anceney was busy acquiring land that would one day become the "One Big Spread" in Montana's Gallatin and Madison counties. Anceney first bought land in small sections paying about $5.00 per acre. This was in the Cherry Creek area where many people homesteaded following the Civil War. The bachelors who came with one horse and a pack mule were inclined to choose the more mountainous areas with an eye for prospecting in the hills. The men who came with families were more inclined to choose the flatter areas with water available and good soil for crops. After twenty-five years or so, they had proved up on their land, lived there the required time, and had paid the twelve dollar fee to get a legal deed. They were ready to move on perhaps to a town or settlement. In the beginning of the Child and Anceney partnership (1907), the land purchases were strictly for the winter grazing of horses on the natural grass.

———◆———

Just as the west entrance to Yellowstone was growing in importance, so the east entrance from Cody, Wyoming was beginning to find its place on the map. The town's namesake, William F. "Buffalo Bill" Cody courted the Chicago, Burlington and Quincy Railroad to complete their rails to the site by 1901. One historian noted, "Tapping the Big

Horn Basin's agricultural productivity was the railroad's prime objective in building to Cody. Carrying tourists to the park would generate some additional source of revenue for the railroad, but this certainly was an insufficient justification for building an expensive branch to Cody."

In fact, two more years passed before the Army Corps of Engineers under Hiram Chittenden completed the road connecting Yellowstone grand loop road to the park's east border. The following year, Aron "Tex" Holm received a license to transport camping parties from the east – providing another competition to the Wylie Camping Company.

***

At the end of the first decade of the 20th century, Harry Child had been involved in Yellowstone for nearly twenty years. His and Adelaide's children were grown and producing children of their own. The couple were in their 40s. They maintained homes at Mammoth Hot Springs and Helena, Montana entertaining circles of friends at both places during the summer months. In the winter they continued to return to southern California, purchasing a home in La Jolla. The Huntley Child family and the William Nichols family, children and grandchildren, accompanied them to their winter haven. They could be proud of what they had built in Yellowstone, not only the magnificent Old Faithful Inn, but a solid, well-respected family business. The next decade would bring a multitude of unpredicted challenges – changes in the park's political climate, Harry's health concerns, updates to the transportation system, ups and downs of war time visitation, and expansion of the park hotels.

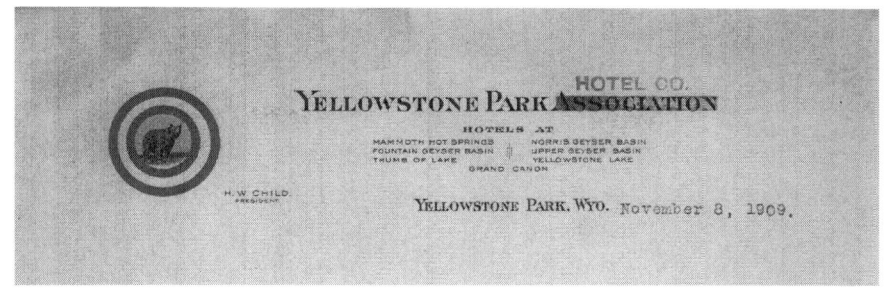

YELLOWSTONE PARK ASSOCIATION
HOTEL CO.

HOTELS AT
MAMMOTH HOT SPRINGS   NORRIS GEYSER BASIN
FOUNTAIN GEYSER BASIN   UPPER GEYSER BASIN
THUMB OF LAKE   YELLOWSTONE LAKE
            GRAND CAÑON

H. W. CHILD.
PRESIDENT

YELLOWSTONE PARK, WYO. November 8, 1909.

Chapter 8: A Miracle in Hotel Building
1910-1912

*On the Grand Tour, a monumental
building feat, cattle on the Flying D Ranch,
the fall camping trip*

Harry dissolved the YPA and created the Yellowstone Park Hotel Company. He was also full owner of the Yellowstone Park Transportation Company. All the parts were now in place for Harry to initiate his "Grand Tour." He continued Silas Huntley's precise system of handling luggage, loading passengers, and scheduling the stagecoaches. Now the tourists were delivered to newly remodeled, or in some cases, brand new luxury hotels.

Tourists arrived by the Northern Pacific train at the Gardiner terminus. They stepped off the train and into the very beautiful Robert Reamer designed depot, walked through the depot to the waiting "tally-ho" stagecoaches of the Yellow Line. Transportation Company porters loaded passengers and luggage on the coaches, that then proceeded through the Roosevelt Arch, beginning the five-mile trip up to the porte cochere of the Mammoth Hotel. The porters then unloaded the passengers and the luggage and turned the care of the tourists over to the hotel staff.

Rooms were assigned and lunch was served, leaving the afternoon free for the guests to explore the Mammoth Hot Springs area. Formal dress was not required for the evening but was appreciated as orchestra music and dancing followed the dinner. Attentive staff members were always present to meet the needs of the guests.

Day one required an early start. Luggage was packed and tagged with a number and waiting on the loading dock. After breakfast, each passenger was assigned a number matching their luggage number and assigned a seat on a stagecoach. That would be their seat assignment for the duration of the tour. Now they traveled in smaller coaches seating up to eight passengers. Some buggies seating only four people besides the driver were available for families or small groups to travel alone.

Lunch was served at the Norris Lunch station, then they proceeded to the Lower Geyser Basin and a night at the Fountain Hotel.

The Fountain Hotel was opened in 1891 by the YPA with financial help from the NPR's Northwest Improvement Company. It was modern in every way - electric lights, steam heat, and baths featuring natural hot spring water. Three hundred and fifty guests were accommodated comfortably.

It offered a social life as well as entertainment beyond the usual sightseeing. Ball gowns for the ladies and formal dress for the men was required at the formation dances which were often made more colorful by the attendance of soldiers stationed at the Fountain Soldier Station near Nez Percé Creek. The Fountain staff started the practice of feeding bears the left-overs from the dining room at dusk each evening [69, 71]. That became a tradition around the Park and was a favorite of the guests.

Day two was a shorter travel time to the Upper Geyser Basin and the exciting new Old Faithful Inn. The Inn was beautifully appointed and a pleasure to relax and enjoy. Meals were served on white linens and set with full sterling silver service. Men were required to wear coat and tie in the dining room. If they were not prepared, the staff would furnish suitable attire.

On this day the tourists had time to stroll among the geysers and hot pools in the Upper Geyser Basin. Witnessing eruptions of Old Faithful, Beehive, or any geyser offered great excitement. And Henry

Klamer's Curio Shop located next to the Inn provided shopping for souvenirs and sundries. Just below the Inn was F. Jay Haynes' Log Cabin Studio where travelers could purchase framed park views or boxed postcard sets. Both men received leases for their buildings in 1897.

On the third day, the same procedure was utilized for getting underway after breakfast. Now they drove on the new road over the continental divide and down to the West Thumb lunch station. The trip to the Lake Hotel could be made either by riding the stagecoach or by taking the boat across the Yellowstone Lake to the Lake Hotel dock. Beginning in 1908, Park guide Thomas Elwood "Uncle Billy" Hofer, was awarded the boat contract. He purchased the gasoline-powered *Jean D* in 1911.

Lake Hotel had an ambiance all its own – quiet and restful. Dinner was served in the lovely dining room with a view of the lake and the mountains. When dinner was finished, the guests moved to the spacious lobby to enjoy piano music and more of the fantastic view.

The fourth day entailed a short stagecoach ride to the Grand Canyon of the Yellowstone and Canyon Hotel, a look at the Upper and Lower Falls, and a visit to Artist's Point. As a side day trip, one could take a buggy ride to the top of Mount Washburn.

The fifth day consisted of a trip across the center of the Park by way of the Norris cutoff road. Lunch was taken at Norris, and the guests reached Gardiner in time to catch the afternoon train.

For those who did not want to take the first-class tour, there were other means of seeing the Park. The Northern Pacific "couponers" had a package deal which included travel by coach and overnight accommodations in cabins. Each cabin had cold running water, beds with bedding provided, wood stoves for heat, and outdoor "biffies." Meals were served in central lodges.

"Tent campers" were usually traveling with a guide who provided transportation. They stayed in cabins with four walls and a floor with a canvas top. There were cots and mattresses but no bedding. There was a stove for heat and wood could be purchased from the woodshed. Guests provided their own food, or in some locations there were cafeterias.

"Sagebrushers" brought their own camping gear and food, traveled in their own wagons, and camped wherever they wanted.

Part of the success of the hotel company was Harry's ability to partner with western railroads. Passenger agents in the east sold not only cross-country tickets, but beautifully illustrated guidebooks to the West and details about Park travel – much in the same way a contemporary travel agent might promote international destinations. Major touring companies such as Cook's Travel Company and Raymond & Whitcomb of Boston brought groups of travelers beginning in the 1880s. Occupational conventions, religious gatherings, and fraternal groups also attracted hundreds of pilgrims on adventure that included a glimpse at the Wonders of the Yellowstone.

Harry handled such "party business" himself, instituting a booking fee and cancellation penalty, and juggling requests from the competing railroads. While admitting that party business required more responsibility for his staff, he recognized its value. At the same time he maintained open rooms for individual travelers, the bulk of the hotel business. He and his railroad counterparts were not alone in promoting Western travel.

In 1906 the initial "See America First" conference was held in Salt Lake City, Utah. One-hundred-twenty-five delegates representing boosters, businessmen, and politicians from across the West gathered to forge a campaign to divert some of the $150 million that Americans had spent traveling in Europe the previous year. The idea was to educate citizens about their own country, including the "wonders and possibilities of the west." Taking his message across the nation, including an audience with President Theodore Roosevelt, the founder was successful in publishing a booster magazine for only about twelve months.

"Marshaling its resources to develop and disseminate this extensive advertising campaign," writes historian Marguerite S. Shaffer, "the Great Northern Railway appropriated what had been a motto for local and regional interests and publicized it on a national scale." In 1910 they financed two hundred fifteen-by-twenty foot billboards to promote Glacier National Park with the "See America First" logo as the center of the campaign. The first issue of another short-lived magazine *See America First*, published in March 1912, featured "articles on President Taft's automobile tour of Mount Rainier, the proposed San Diego Fair of 1915, Seattle's scenic boulevards, and Point Defiance Park in Tacoma. The issue also included brief notes on the See America First movement, National Parks, Pacific Coast carnivals, festivals, and conventions, and various hotels and resorts."

Now four railroads, the Northern Pacific Railroad (north entrance), the Union Pacific Railroad (west entrance), the Burlington Line (east entrance), and the Chicago Milwaukee & St. Paul (operating the Sacajawea Inn at Three Forks, Montana), were all promoting travel to Yellowstone. As visitation grew steadily Harry began to focus on expanding and upgrading existing hotels.

He had maintained a periodic business relationship with architect Robert Reamer and now invited him to Europe to "see something of the architecture in Germany, Switzerland, England and Scotland." "One inference to be drawn from this," observed one architectural historian, "is of a desire on the part of Child to leaven Reamer's affinity for the rustic with a sense of gentility." Harry and Adelaide, and their friend "Rob," set sail October 6, 1909 from New York – bound for Liverpool aboard the *SS Mauritania*, one of the palace steamers of the Cunard Line.

Returning December 17, 1909, Reamer immediately set to work on plans for expanding the 1890 Canyon Hotel, which a *Livingston Enterprise* reporter declared to be the "ugliest building in the world." The writer continued, "It is as ugly as the big icehouses that deface the banks of the Hudson river, but at the same time it is an illustration of the well-established principle that one cannot judge accurately by appearance. The attractions are all inside, and it is one of the most admirably kept and one of the most comfortable hospices a tired traveler ever entered. If all the hotels in the universe were as well kept as that at the Yellowstone Canyon there would be more happiness and contentment among mankind."

Early the next year Reamer took up residence at Mammoth, occasionally traveling to Helena to consult with Harry and Adelaide about the plans. The YPHC also employed a draftsman during this period to assist their architect. Blueprints for the structure, which incorporated the old building as one guest-room wing, were extensive.

Construction of the new Canyon Hotel was a monumental feat [85]. Its construction is also, fortunately, well-documented with photographic records and publications. J.H. Raftery, editor of the *Treasure State Press* in Anaconda, Montana, journeyed to the construction site in January 1911: "I saw the first 'order' prepared on the range of one of the largest and most perfect hotel kitchens in the world. The 'order' was for nails, hot nails, nails by the quart and by the gallon, piping hot, big and little, brads and spikes, ten-pennies and shingle nails, while from the walls inside and out, from the sub-cellar below and from the acres of gaping roof came the tattoo of the hammers of a hundred carpenters clamoring for nails, hot nails and plenty of 'em."

"Two hundred and fifty men, hardy, alert, emulous and undaunted, had been fighting with the frost and blizzard, bucking the snow drifts and freezing their fingers and toes in this far place all winter long," Raftery recorded, "to the end that one of the most remarkable, extensive, beautiful and complete summer hotels in the world would be ready and running for the approaching season. ... For the hauling of a carload of freight each day in the rapid building of the Canyon Hotel in the National Park, about fifty drivers and two hundred horses were required. When the snowstorms set in with their full winter fury, sleds

After the enhanced Canyon Hotel opened, YPHC published J.H. Raftery's construction tribute in pamphlet form. Quinn collection

with a capacity of three or four tons apiece could carry only 2,500 pounds or less. Horses downed in the drifts, loads overturned, sleds broken, harness torn apart, snow slides and sudden blizzards increased the hardships, the hindrances and the perils of the gigantic task."

Harry and Adelaide arrived at Mammoth in January hoping to journey to view the new construction. After receiving word from Norris station that temperatures reached -50° F, they altered plans and continued on their travels to Chicago, New York, and Washington. Howard Elliott, now president of the Northern Pacific Railroad, suspended freight charges and cancelled uncollected fees to move the construction along.

The hotel opened in June [84, 86]. A grand ball formally opened the new Grand Canyon Hotel in August 1911. The reception line included President and Mrs. Harry Child, Robert C. Reamer, Samuel Blythe, editor of the *Saturday Evening Post*, officers of the hotel association, and the commanding officers from Fort Yellowstone.

———◦———

Another opportunity in Yellowstone came to Harry during this time – the acquisition of the Yellowstone Lake Boat Company. "Uncle Billy" Hofer found himself underwater financially. When E.C. Waters' contract was cancelled, his boats remained in the Park, but they also

101

remained in his ownership. When Uncle Billy received the new contract, he was required to acquire his own vessels which he did with a loan from a wealthy easterner. When he was unable to make enough profit to make payments on the loans, Harry stepped in. Uncle Billy soon realized he was not a businessman, and he let the business go to Harry.

E.C. Waters continued to make a nuisance of himself, such that he was eventually banned from reentering the park. He was at least allowed to return in order to settle his affairs. Harry Child asked to have him brought to his office immediately. When Waters entered, Harry offered him a sum of money to buy out his entire outfit. Waters had no choice but to comply. *Zillah* and *E C Waters* would never steam across Yellowstone Lake again.

⎯⎯⎯⎯⎯⎯

By 1911 the Child-Anceney partners had acquired 27,898 acres of land, and had invested $262,000. This was mostly located in the Cherry Creek and Elk Creek drainages. Child and Anceney made plans for a townsite. A group of Gallatin businessmen had acquired land and built a fifteen mile branch line from the NPR mainline at Manhattan, Montana to Anceney's stockyards on the Norris road, site of an earlier stage stop. The line was called Camp Creek Railway and its terminus was called Anceney Station [99]. "The train was in full operation by 1912 and was successful enough that the NPR bought it two years later at Harry Child's behest." Child and Anceney hired an architect to draw up a plan for a town site at Anceney Station. It was an ambitious plan, but it did not come to fruition.

With the rapid development of auto, touring cars, and buses at this time, the Child-Anceney partners knew that horse travel to and within Yellowstone would diminish with the exception of pack trips, and they began to plan for a change in operations. They reduced the number of horses grazing on their land and made cattle grazing central to their business.

Since Harry Child had special knowledge of the meat

requirements for diners in the park, he was able to secure contracts for beef. It was estimated that two hundred and sixty beeves (beef cows) were needed for each season.

In their blacksmith shop, Charlie Anceney created a variation of an old brand known as the "Flying U." By rotating it 90 degrees it became the "Flying D." The "D" in the name was for Adelaide Child's maiden name, Dean. The curved left side of the brand, representing "flying," was a stylized "C" for Child. This brand was registered in 1929 when the Flying D Ranges were incorporated [101]. Previously, they used the "CA" brand on the left hip of their cattle.

Child and Anceney also started a breeding program. The breed was called "Chilancy," a combination of their sir-names. They started with 100 blooded shorthorns that Charlie had been able to save from the Anceney family ranch near Bozeman (Meadow Brook). They soon were taking prizes at the Chicago Stock Shows.

Harry Child moved the Rutledge Hargrove family onto the Flying D in 1911. Hargrove [13] had worked for Silas Huntley since the 1880s, and after Silas' death "Rut" stayed on with P.B. Clark at the former Riverside Stock Farm. He signed a contract with Charlie Anceney and became the first tenant farmer on the ranch land under Child and Anceney. He stayed for almost forty years. A number of the original homesteaders followed suit and became tenant farmers. Where there had been more than one hundred and ten homesteads on the land, now twenty-five or so tenant farmers operated. The unusual arrangement included tenant use of company equipment – mowers, rakes, overstack stackers – and half of each year's hay to Child and Anceney. The other half of each season's hay crop was sold by the tenant at eight dollars per ton, usually to the Flying D. At one time there were forty-four hay pastures, eleven of them irrigated. The arrangement was a special one, agreeable to both tenant and owner. There were no inspections and little supervision.

Nearby, the settlement known as Salesville had been platted back in the early 1880s. Zachariah Sales, one of the earliest settlers, cut trees along the Spanish Creek and Gallatin River and floated them down to a spot where he built a giant water wheel to power a sawmill. He constructed a large building around the sawmill. It became a social gathering place. Couple whirled across the floor to the tune of one violinist and one floor manager who called out the dance patterns. "Around the edge of the floor, sleeping children covered with patchwork quilts nested with piles of coats."

Salesville was lively by 1912. A blacksmith had opened his doors, a steam laundry had begun operations, in addition to a clothing store, a butcher shop, and a lunch counter. A number of the homesteaders had given up making a living on their land and sold their acreage to those developing the Flying D Ranch. They moved to Salesville for a fresh start in the business community. More new businesses appeared – two general stores, a brick Salesville State Bank, a drugstore, barber shop, lumber yard, hotel, meat market, doctor's office, three saloons, and several dance halls.

Later Mr. Sales partnered with Bozeman cattleman and businessman Nelson Story to construct a water-powered flour mill just north of the townsite. Mr. Sales left the area before long. Salesville was fondly called "Slabtown" until 1927, when the name was changed to Gallatin Gateway.

—————

1910 probably was not Harry's first "Fall Camping Party," but this is the year that was publicized by B.C. Forbes in his book, *Men Who Are Making The West*.

"Every year this man, out in Helena, Harry W. Child, the president of the Yellowstone Park Transportation Company, has the same yearning to go camping that a letter carrier has to take a walk. He is a little more elaborate in his methods, however. He never starts until the hotels in the Park system are about to close - somewhere about the last of September. His first step is to get three of the largest trucks on the system and go from hotel to hotel on a closing-up expedition. He generally starts at Mammoth Hot Springs, where he takes on four or five tons of food. Then he goes up to Norris, where he grabs a couple of cooks; at Old Faithful he sweeps up half-a-dozen waiters; at the Geyser he grabs not less than tons of ice; at Lake he cleans out all the vegetables and fruit and delicacies that have not been devoured by the tourists from the East. In his triumphant march, he grabs all the good horses and tents and portable ranges that are fit for service. Von Hindenberg going through Belgium was nothing compared to Harry Child raiding his hotel system for camping paraphernalia" ... "We pitched our tents in Red Canyon. Harry, known along the frontier as 'Harry Hardup' for the reason he owns only a young empire of land and 30,000 head of stock, ordered up a pitcher of lemonade and superintended the laying out of the camp site. As soon as night falls, Harry eats three trout, a couple of elk steaks, drinks another quart of lemonade, smokes another box of cigars and climbs into the hay. If the fishing is good and there is a wind behind him, he trots down to the river, makes a dozen casts (the higher the wind the better), picks up a few fish [96] and comes back to his canvas chair" ... "As soon as we got comfortable in Red Canyon, Harry rolled out a large map of the state of Montana and suggested thirty or forty other places that he thought were better. His whole idea of camp life is to get away from the spot where he happens to be. When Harry Hardup is finally tucked away into the mold and a large marble slab is erected over him, a voice will roll forth exclaiming: "I know a better place; let's move." But he was the noblest host in the world".

With some variation, the Yellowstone Park Hotel management carried on a scaled-down version of this well into the 1960s.

<hr />

In the fall of 1910 William Loeb, Jr. returned to the Yellowstone region. Loeb, as President Roosevelt's personal secretary, had accompanied the President's April 1903 visit, but he was left behind at the railhead in Cinnabar and was able to view little of the Park. He returned in the fall seasons of 1904, 1905, and 1907, when accompanied by Harry Child, they hunted and fished in the areas around Slough Creek and Cooke City. Loeb expressed his satisfaction to a Livingston reporter, "I come out here every year a physical wreck and return a new man." The 1910 trip he brought Samuel Blythe with him. This adventure centered in the Gallatin Valley and the Madison Valley – exactly the spot where Child and Anceney were slowly acquiring land. Campfire talk must have been full of future plans.

"There's more fun in doing things for others than in doing others."
HWC

Child and Anceney made another use of the Flying D Ranch Lands outside of the business of raising and marketing cattle. They "produced a handsome promotional pamphlet in 1912 entitled 'Western Life for Eastern Boys' with a Charles Russell sketch for its cover and, inside, ... photographs of the area." The experience would "surely enhance each boy's understanding of the world." A few weeks on the Flying D Ranch would be like "the old West of [Theodore] Roosevelt, of [Owen] Wister, of [Brett] Harte..." The hard work of roping and riding would be offset by more leisurely days of enjoying the beauty of "the great fields ... when the millions on millions of wild flowers are in bloom."

The boys were to be "housed in large ... double-roofed tents, of newest design, with matched wooden floors. There will be a large assembly tent, ...a dining tent, and a large plunge bath, with sparkling mountain stream water ... The food 'will not be a rough camp table' but would feature 'fresh, pure, perfect milk, cream, butter and eggs,' and 'camp grown vegetables such as peas, tomatoes, lettuce, corn, radishes, and potatoes. The managers of the camp will kill their own beef, mutton, veal, and pork,' as well as serving 'fresh-caught Montana mountain trout.'"

Even with the support of the head masters of prep schools, several railroad presidents, and Sam Blythe, editor/writer for the *Saturday Evening Post*, the project failed after only three summers.

Adelaide and her sister Maria were devoting much of their energy to a project in Helena. Dr. Dean noted a need in Helena for an agency to provide help to women seeking employment or attending school in the community. She became "the driving force behind the early membership in Helena YWCA." By March 1911 dues from the three hundred members allowed them to rent an office, and Dr. Dean hired the first staff person. The following year they incorporated, but "members chose to be an independent organization," rather than an affiliate of the national organization. Over the next few years, the Helena YWCA continued to grow with the need, moving into successively larger houses.

Adelaide could see how much energy her husband was investing outside the park in the Boy's Ranch project and his Flying D pursuits. Concerned for his health, she wrote personally to Howard Elliott, President of the Northern Pacific Railway: "May I make so bold as to write you ... We have brought him to the point of selling this Yellowstone property so I am going to ask you to give him an added shove. ... I am so afraid he will sell only on a basis of what he knows the investment can produce. It is taking too much out of him physically to carry that alone and keep it abreast of the time. His heart is in the Gallatin project and that work might hurt him. I feel that he must get out of the Yellowstone no matter who gets it..."

It was an eventful few years for Harry, having assumed full ownership of the hotels and transportation and completed the unprecedented construction of the Canyon Hotel.

[45] Buses of the Cody-Sylvan Pass Motor Company, touring on the East Entrance Road, 1916. (YELL 11519)

[46] Harry pioneered the Geysers to Glaciers Road, linking Yellowstone and Glacier National Parks through Helena, MT. (MHSRC Ephemera collection: Broadwater Hotel and Natatorium)

[49] Although private autos were admitted in 1915, Harry's transportation company stagecoaches shared park roads with them in 1915 and 1916. (YNPA)

[44] Two automobiles, on the test trip around the park (June 1915), arrive at Wylie's Upper Basin camp. This road, between Morning Glory pool and Grotto Geyser, was closed to motorized travel in 1972. (YELL 50774)

[47] Gerard Pesman (1906-2000) drove in the park before and after his career with NASA. (Quinn collection)

[48] Harry Child (left) with Walter White, of the White Motor Company, Cleveland, OH. (courtesy Harry W. Child II)

NOTICE.

ALL DRIVERS:

Private Automobiles are to be allowed to enter the Park August 1st

They are to run on a schedule which has been figured out by the Government Officials in the Park in connection with the Transportation Officials and we have protected the terms of the four transportation lines so that there should be no occasion for any of the transportation outfits seeing an automobile during the Park trip.

If, however, should an accident occur to an automobile and it should be stalled on the road or side of the road, do not run any chances with your teams and your tourists but in every case, upload your tourists before attempting to pass a machine either stalled or along side the road or in motion.

APPROVED
H. W CHILD, PRESIDENT

JOE PHILLIPS,
SUPERINTENDENT

[50] Bus fleet behind the Mammoth Garage, looking south toward Bunsen Peak. When the building burned in March 1925, YPTC lost ninety vehicles, including some that were less than one year old. J.E. Haynes photo. (MHS H-20005)

[51] Company letterhead, 1942, showing White model 15-45, purchased by YPTC between 1920 and 1925. (MHSRC MC292 GC b13 f5)

[52] Bus fleet, Gardiner Garage –now home to Xanterra's Vehicle Service Center, Human Resources, Transportation Offices, and the YPSS offices. (YELL 133539)

At Home in Yellowstone

[54] Emilie and Huntley Child's oldest and youngest children were born in the Colonial House at Mammoth Hot Springs. (YELL 133605)

[56] The Child's garage was located on a piece of Harry's Gardiner land near the Roosevelt Arch. J.E. Haynes photo. (MHS H-21160)

[53] Annie and Silas moved into George Wakefield's house, the "dainty, little cottage," at the base of the Mammoth Hot Springs terraces. (MHS H-1952)

[55] Ellen and W.M. Nichols expanded it after their children were born. A rear apartment was added for Bessie Ferguson. After Harry died, Adelaide called it home. (RQ photo)

[57] The Child House at the base of the Mammoth terraces was designed by Robert Reamer for Adelaide and Harry. It is alternately known as the Executive House. (YELL 02818)

[58] A spiral staircase adds distinction and elegance to the main room of the Child House. (YELL 11269)

[59] When Huntley Child Jr.'s family returned to the park in 1938, they lived in the mail carrier's cabin, built in 1897. The term "Love in the Rough" was coined there. (YELL 18203d)

All the buildings on this and previous page are still standing.

Early Yellowstone Concessionaires

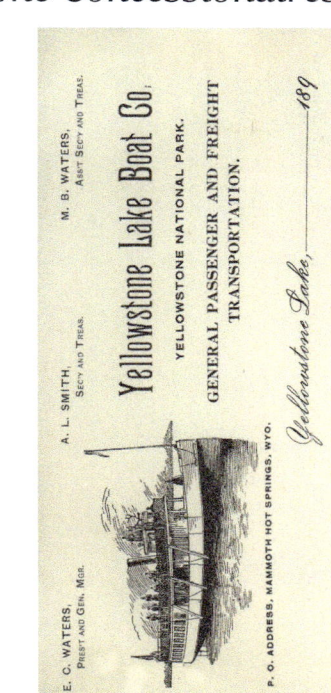

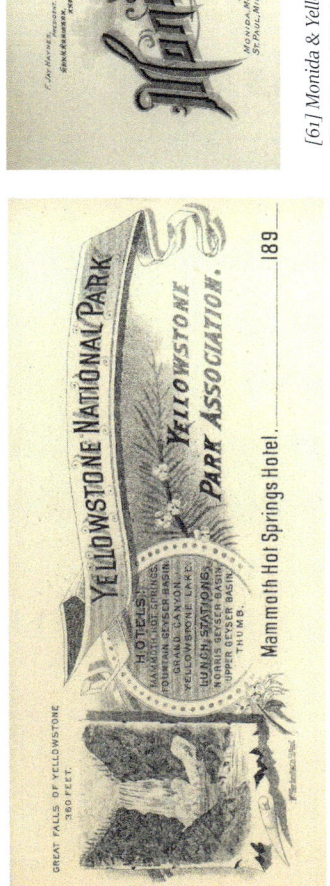

[61] Monida & Yellowstone Stage Co. (the Red Line) provided service from the "Mon"tana/ "Ida"ho border (exit 0 on I-15) through what is now Red Rock Lakes National Wildlife Refuge. After 1908, when Union Pacific tracks reached west gate they renamed themselves Yellowstone-Western. (YNPA RG00 s1 b013 doc2071)

[63] A trip across Yellowstone Lake, from Thumb to Lake Hotel, gave relief from dusty roads. E.C. (Ela Collins) Waters brought the SS Zillah (1891-1907) from Lake Minnetonka, MN. (YNPA RG00 s1 b017 doc551)

[60] The YPA (1886) completed a system of hotels in the park. Huntley, Bach, and Child acquired their assets in 1901. (YNPA RG00 s1 b017 doc415)

[62] Licensed camping companies provided an inexpensive option for seeing the park. W.W. Wylie hired teachers as guides and college students as camp help. (Quinn postcard collection)

At Mammoth

[64] The National Hotel at Mammoth Hot Springs, constructed by YPIC between 1883 and 1885, was dismantled in the 1930s. (YELL 02819)

[65] The current Mammoth Hot Springs Hotel, shown in an artist's rendering during the 1935-1936 planning stages. (MHSRC MC 86 f25 i12)

[66] This photo of the Map Room in the 1936-38 Mammoth Hotel shows the map on the west wall – preventing it from being seen from the registration desk. Bert L. Brown photo. (MHS H-53132)

[67] The Map was restored in 2016 and redisplayed on the north wall of the room that bears its name. Johnnie Nichols and his sister Jackie point at the map. (YELL 133554)

Lower Geyser Basin, Fountain Paint Pot area

[68] *Fountain Hotel (1890-1917) shows how early hotel architects applied popular eastern styles to the wilderness setting. (Quinn postcard collection)*

[69] *Western novelist Owen Wister observed in 1887: "In these days, the Park bear has almost completed his education. His children for generations have known the way to the garbage pile. And all have learned the hour when the train of stages passes along the road through the various woods." (Quinn postcard collection)*

[70, 71] *Around 1905 Harry began using a new logo on company stationary. (Quinn collection; YNPA RG00 s1 b20 d6520) A black bear photographed at Fountain Hotel dump was the model. E.J. Westlake photo. (YELL 11537)*

Upper Geyser Basin, Old Faithful area

[72] Old Faithful Inn opened June 1, 1904. "It is a craftsman's dream realized," wrote a visitor in 1905. (YELL 02781)

[73] Construction of Old Faithful Inn, October 1903. (Jane Reamer White collection, courtesy Richard A. Bartlett)

[74] Robert Reamer used native stone and wood to create a rustic charm that revolutionized architecture in parks. Adelaide Child worked with the architect to select furniture and furnishings. (YELL 02776)

The Beguiling Bear Pit Lounge, Old Faithful Inn

[75] A fashionably dressed couple out for an evening stroll encounter a begging bear – perhaps mirroring a nation emerging from the Great Depression. (YNPA MSC019 sIX fB)

[76] The dancing moose and squirrels harken a park tradition that was still popular in the 1930s and 1940s. (YNPA MSC019 sIX, fB)

[77] Roast beef sandwiches made with Flying D beef, for many years a Yellowstone favorite, are shown on the table. When this panel was recreated in glass for the Inn in 1988, they were replaced with fish. (YNPA MSC019 sIX, fB)

[78] The Inn's 1926 Bear Pit lounge was a collaboration of W.M. Nichols, Robert Reamer, and artist Walter Oehrle. (YELL 133436)

[79] A full-size replica of Old Faithful Inn was built at the Panama-Pacific Exposition in San Francisco in 1915. Stephen Mather entertained in its massive dining hall. (YELL 09188)

[81] The Colonial styling that Harry and his architect chose for the Lake Hotel expansion (1903-1904) make it unique in national parks today. It received National Landmark status in 2015. (YELL 09187)

At Yellowstone Lake

[83] Lake Hotel's dining room continues to offer elegant fine dining, overlooking beautiful Yellowstone Lake. 1920s photograph (YELL 133572)

[80] Lake Hotel (1891) provided respite and relaxation despite its plain exterior. (YELL 128122)

LAKE HOTEL~YELLOWSTONE PARK

[82] Interior furniture and furnishings (shown here about 1905) reflect Adelaide's superior taste. (Quinn postcard collection)

In the Canyon area

[84] Boasting over three-hundred rooms, the craftsman-style Canyon Hotel was ¾ mile around. It occupied the hillside about 1 mile south of today's Canyon junction. (YELL 02769)

[85] Construction of Grand Canyon Hotel (1910-1911) was a monumental feat at nearly 8000' in elevation. (Jane Reamer White collection, courtesy Richard A. Bartlett)

[86] On August 8, 1960 fire destroyed the remains of the Canyon Hotel. It was "the greatest architectural loss in Yellowstone history." (YELL 14292)

yellowstone park division
TWA SERVICES, INC.

yellowstone national park, wyoming 82190-0165 — phone (307) 344-7901

[87] YPC's contract was cancelled in 1979. TWA Services, Inc., a subsidiary of the airline, was brought in to replace them. The NPS purchased the Yellowstone Park hotels and lodges. (Quinn collection)

[88] When TW Recreational Services (a successor of TWA Services) was sold in 1994 it was purchased by Amfac Parks & Resorts, which started in Hawaii as American Factors. (Quinn collection)

[89] A corporate-branding contest in 2000 resulted in the name Xanterra – combining Samuel Taylor Colderidge's poem "Xanadu," with "terra," meaning "beautiful places on earth." (Quinn collection)

[90] Adelaide and Harry donated land for the Gardiner Community Church in 1905. (YELL 133624)

[91] Adelaide helped protect and maintain the grave of Martha "Mattie" Culver, Nez Percé Picnic area in Yellowstone. (RQ photo)

[92] Orchestra leader Henry Nuernberger dedicated "Yellowstone Park March and Two Step" to H.W. Child in 1904. (Courtesy Randy Ingersoll)

[93] In 1937 pianist and orchestra leader Gene Quaw dedicated his composition "Yellowstone" to Mr. and Mrs. W.M. Nichols. (Quinn collection)

JOHN LEGGERINI
MANAGER

H. W. CHILD

GREEN MEADOW FARM

THE HOME OF

BREEDERS OF REGISTERED
SHORT HORN CATTLE
PERCHERON HORSES
POLAND CHINA HOGS

RINGMASTER

GROWERS OF
POTATOES   BARLEY
CABBAGE   OATS
ONIONS   HAY

HELENA, MONTANA   September 30, 1920.

Chapter 9: The Next Generation
1913-1914

children assume positions of power,
Green Meadow Farm, Cherry Creek Land Association,
autos honking at the gates

Harry was becoming more and more involved in the Gallatin/ Madison Valley operations. He felt that the next generation was capable of taking on more responsibility in managing the YP companies. He promoted W.M. Nichols from private secretary to Assistant to the President. Huntley was made General Manager of the YPTC and Treasurer of both the YPHC and the YPTC.

Both growing second-generation families had two children, with thirds on the way. With all the young children around, and both fathers committed to helping run the operations, around 1913 Harry engaged a young woman, Bessie Ferguson [125], to act as care giver for the grandchildren.

Bessie was originally from Scotland, but she left there broken-hearted after her fiancé was killed in the Boer War in South Africa. She worked in Yellowstone beginning in the early 1900s, serving the company at Larry's Lunch Station at Norris, the Fountain Hotel in the Lower Geyser Basin, and Old Faithful Inn. She worked as a baker for the construction crew during the building of the Canyon Hotel in the winter of 1910-1911. There is an interesting account of her cross-country skiing to deliver freshly-baked apple pies to the workman. It was during that time that Bessie came to the attention of Harry.

Bessie soon became an integral part of the families' households, traveling with them as they spent winters in California and made

109

frequent visits to Helena. After several years maintaining one of the apartments at Oro Fino Terrace in Helena, Harry and Adelaide purchased a larger home at 801 Stuart Street [27], near their old Madison Avenue neighborhood. In 1910 Huntley and Ellen, along with their spouses and one child each, were all living together in this home.

The Nichols family purchased a home at 706 Harrison Avenue [26] in the fall of 1914; and the Huntley Child family lived at 706 Monroe Avenue beginning in 1915. Bessie taught the grandchildren to be polite and respectful. They always addressed Harry and Adelaide as Grand Father Child and Grand Mother Child. Bessie stayed with the Child family until both Harry and Adelaide died.

———

After the Canyon Hotel was completed, Robert Reamer took a position back east with the New York, New Haven, and Hartford Railroad. He returned to Yellowstone in the fall of 1913-1914 to superintend the east wing addition to Old Faithful Inn and the renovation of National Hotel. The World's Fair was to take place in California in 1915, and the railroad companies were aware that this would be an opportunity to attract international visitors to see the wonders of Yellowstone.

During construction of these expansions, W.M. Nichols received a letter from the acting superintendent requesting to see construction specifications. Nichols replied, "We are doing all the work at the Old Faithful and at Mammoth Hotel by day labor with the architect on the ground and at this writing have no specifications and it is impossible for us to draw them up until the buildings are completed. ...You know from the work that Mr. Reamer has done that he does much better to build as he goes along rather than to draw up a set of specifications and be tied down to them." The company's confidence in Reamer allowed them to stand up to growing pressure from the government.

In January 1914 Harry and Adelaide traveled to a Grand Rapids, Michigan furniture show to purchase furniture for these additions. They continued to their winter home in the west. "I am leaving for

California to-morrow with Mrs. Child to complete our purchases of furniture, linens, carpet, etc. etc., for the various hotels, as I have the men of whom I purchase, in California now, together with the house-keeper, Superintendent of Hotels, Chief Engineer, etc., etc; this was much cheaper for me than having these people congregate at Helena at my expense, and avoids putting them on the pay-roll now as against the 1st of June. Fortunately the employees are located in California through the winter, so that I can do my figuring with them on their own time."

With these hotel additions completed, Harry kept his architect busy with improvements to land north of Helena that he had purchased and sold in 1887. He re-acquired this land from the St. Paul and Helena Land and Improvement Company to create Green Meadow Farm [106]. In July 1914 the *Helena Independent* suggested it would "become one of interesting points of interest to all sight-seers who visit this city and valley in the future." Harry's plans were to transform the property into "a farm de luxe."

Harry employed a manager on the property who had been serving for the past thirty years. Like the Flying D Ranch, Green Meadow Farm raised blooded stock – Percheron horses, shorthorn cattle, and Poland China swine. "All varieties of grains" were also grown on the 1,900 acres in the Helena valley.

The buildings Robert Reamer designed for Harry, completed between 1914 and 1915, included a private residence, a bunkhouse, a granary, a blacksmith's shop, outbuildings, and a unique barn. The house was lost to fire in 1924 and the barn in 1956. Only the bunkhouse, granary, and blacksmith shop remain today [108].

Much has been written about the buildings at Green Meadow Farm, especially the huge barn: "The main barn," wrote historian David Leavengood, "was designed as four separate smaller structures but was covered with a large, single, wood-shingle roof. The entire barn was 450 feet in length and varied in width from 40 feet to 50 feet. It rose

40 feet high in the ridge [107]. There were three passageways which cut transversely through the barn allowing for a team and wagon to be driven [through]. ... The dormer windows on the south elevation of this structure had a carved likeness of a bull's eye and eyelid set into it. ... No two windows were the same; every window in the barn had a hand-carved animal in it."

The granary and blacksmith shop carried the same heavy timber frame construction with steep-gabled roofs. But the house and the bunkhouse had more of a Scandinavian feel. In total, Harry expended $100,000 on these improvements.

Perhaps these words, offered after the barn burned, best pay tribute to Harry's vision: "Strong and sturdy, so many years she stood, seemingly as eternal as the surrounding hills, but in spite of all our care, an accident last Thursday struck the fatal blow and sent her to her flaming death. For this was not just another barn and not just OUR barn. From her sloping roof of old time shakes, her length and breadth of hand-hewn timbers, and down to the native rocks of her foundations, she was the realization of one man's dream of beauty, a landmark and beloved possession in the minds and hearts of Helena and its valley."

—————

In 1913 Harry hired the vice-president of the State Bank of Montana, based in Helena, to act as purchasing agent to acquire more land in the Gallatin/Madison Valley. Now they were paying about $40.00 an acre for land in the Spanish Creek area. The Child-Anceney partners began moving their cattle onto this newly acquired land.

As far back as 1911, Harry knew of plans by the Northern Pacific and the Union Pacific railroads to build their tracks into the Park and take over as many of the facilities as possible – meaning the hotels that railroad money had built – just as had been done in Grand Canyon National Park. The government was able to squash the idea by declaring it a monopoly.

The railroad officials, as well as Harry, were concerned about the coming of the motor cars and the effect that would have on the tourist trade. Harry assured these people that he intended to motorize in the park as soon as possible, and he began selling land within the Flying D boundaries. He was able to interest railroad presidents and directors in this plan. A corporation was formed in Massachusetts called the Cherry Creek Land Association. Howard Elliott, president of the NPR, joined the group. The Cherry Creek Land Association bought large blocks of land amounting to twenty-three percent of the acres within the boundaries of the Flying D and took an active interest in association management.

—⇒•◦⇐—

In 1908, Dr. Maria Dean was fifty years old. She purchased her own home at 626 North Benton Avenue [29], moving a few doors down from her previous residence at the family's Oro Fino Terrace. She shared the new home with her mother Ellen Dean, Mary Wheeler, her co-founder of the Helena School of Art, and Georgia Young, administrator at St. Peter's Hospital.

Dr. Dean had remained active in the cause of women's suffrage in Montana from her time helping found the Helena Business Women's Suffrage Club in 1896, to assuming presidency of the Montana Suffrage Association in 1900. But after the Montana legislature failed to pass amendments in 1903 and 1905, the women's efforts would founder. Dr. Dean continued to travel the state speaking on issues of concern to women and their rights.

Success for women in Washington State brought Montana native Jeanette Rankin home to address the Montana legislature in February 1911. Dr. Maria Dean was one of the "old guard of women's rights activists" who appeared on the platform with Miss Rankin – twenty years her junior. After failures in 1895, 1897, and 1911 legislatures, the women continued the fight. In 1913 a woman suffrage amendment passed in both houses of Montana legislature. The women then focused on the public vote to follow.

Maria and other members approached the Helena city council for clearance to form a rally for Women's Day at the State Fair in Helena in September 1914. Supporters turned out in force that day – marchers from every county and even surrounding states. They formed a mile-long parade through the streets of the capital city, with Jeannette Rankin and Maria Dean carrying the yellow suffrage banner at the front of the pageant. Dr. Dean and her sister Mrs. Annie Young served as hostesses in the suffrage booth. "What has become of the old-time politicians who used to stump the state and kiss the babies?" posed the Helena-based *Suffrage Daily News*, "Answer: Kissing is declared unsanitary by Dr. Dean. The candidate takes care of the baby now on election day so mother can vote."

"Optimism prevailed on election day, November 3, 1914, because the press was genuinely favorable, friends were enthusiastic, enemies, except for a few antis, were quiet, the powerful Amalgamated Copper Company did not openly oppose. As it turned out, however, the vote – 41,302 to 37,588 – was closer than most suffragists had expected." Regardless, Montana became one of a handful of states to pass a suffrage bill [11]. Two years later, the state sent Jeannette Rankin to Congress, the first female in the nation to be elected to that office.

———>●●<———

The Child family owned automobiles – one for Harry, one for Adelaide, one for Huntley, and one for Ellen and Billie Nichols. They were great enthusiasts for this new mode of travel outside of Yellowstone. Automobiles had become a way of life outside the park, but they would be a menace to the great system of stagecoach travel that was so much a part of Yellowstone. Since 1902 visitors had been clamoring for the right to bring autos into the park.

A Union Pacific passenger agent from Salt Lake City requested permission to take a moonlight drive through the park when no horse teams were present – even offering to include Harry Child as a passenger. The Army superintendent denied his request.

Other western parks had allowed cars since 1908 and pressure was building against the practice of banning them in Yellowstone. Harry had a big investment in stagecoaches, horses, etc., and his transportation company was popular and profitable. Quite naturally he lobbied to keep things as they were.

Incidents of auto drivers sneaking into the park were happening more regularly, and it was bothersome for the superintendents. In one incident a long distance traveler tried to enter the park at the south gate but was turned away. He rented a wagon and horses and wanted to pull the auto behind the wagon. "They got in communication with General Young who denied them the request ..., but finally did authorize them to take it through, but only on condition that it be taken apart [drained of gasoline] and loaded on to the wagon."

A party of local people drove their machine up to Mammoth for a dance one evening. The superintendent allowed them to drive it home – but only under cover of darkness and a promise to never do it again.

Huntley Child took his White touring car on a freight wagon from Gardiner to Mammoth to have it repaired at the Transportation Company's carriage shop. This was 1914 and Huntley had just been appointed by his father to be General Manager of the Transportation company. By this time automobilists were exerting such pressure to get their machines admitted to the Park that no exception could be granted for any purpose. Huntley was ordered to haul the White touring car back to Gardiner immediately.

———>●●<———

A new road was under construction, south from Bozeman, Montana along the Gallatin River to West Yellowstone, Montana. Some portions of the road crossed the Yellowstone boundary, but none of the park's major features could be visited along its route (which remains true to this day). From the time this road opened in October 1911, it had no restrictions against automobile travel. Commercial clubs in Cody and Livingston were pressuring park managers to open the entire park to automobiles.

Businessmen in Wisconsin and Minnesota began efforts to improve auto roads in their local areas. As more communities did this, roads could be connected from one section to the next, forming *The Yellowstone Trail*. Travelers could follow the route using brochures and booklets. Advertised as "A Good Road from Plymouth Rock to Puget Sound," much of it was completed between 1913 and 1914. A yellow circle or oval, containing a black arrow, was used in some areas to guide the motorists. America's first national park was providing inspiration for its first coast-to-coast highway.

———

Huntley Child was taking a more active role in running his father's business. Beginning in 1910 the Department of the Interior began imposing a franchise or "usage tax" on all concessionaires "for enlargement of the maintenance fund of the Park." It was assigned to the local superintendents to collect the tax of twenty-five cents for each person accommodated at the hotels and carried by the stagecoaches during the season. The superintendent would then forward the funds to the Interior Department. The initial tax would be retroactive to the 1909 season. The first payment was due in July 1910.

For several years, the Secretary of the Interior, the park superintendents, and Yellowstone's hotel and transportation companies negotiated how and when these taxes would be paid. Two problems arose. One was the discrepancy between actual passenger counts and the taxable numbers reported by the company. The company subtracted their "dead-heads," a term of Yellowstone in-house lingo that had to be translated for the government. These were "conductors of parties, traveling government officials, lecturers on the park and photographers who were in position to do the park some good." These persons, like dignitaries, were allowed to travel fare-free. A second, larger part of the adjustment was reconciling the payment due date to accommodate Yellowstone's May-September operating season with the federal fiscal year. Although both Harry Child and W.M. Nichols began these talks, it was Huntley Child, as treasurer of both companies, who ironed out the final arrangement with the department.

Chapter 10:
Storm on the Horizon:
the beginning of the
National Park Service
1911-1915

Mather and Albright inspect facilities
autos for Yellowstone
Park-to-Park Highway discussed

Harry W. Child, as astute and energetic as ever in his mid-50s [7], was about to be faced with great changes in his personal and professional life.

Probably the most challenging was the diagnosis of diabetes. This came from a higher power, and at that time was pretty much a death sentence. Harry approached it by finding and staying in close contact with the best doctors, especially those searching for the best treatment and hopefully, someday, a cure. He learned to keep the progression of the disease in check through diet and exercise.

Harry was not caught unaware of other changes about to affect his business life. Throughout the years he had kept his thumb on the pulse of Washington, D.C., and he kept up with political and business trends across the country.

By 1916, Yellowstone National Park had been in existence for forty-four years. For twenty-three of those years, Harry Child had held government contracts to operate the concessions. He had built the Old Faithful Inn, remodeled the Lake Hotel, built the great new Canyon Hotel, and remodeled the Mammoth Hotel. His Yellowstone Park Transportation Company, along with the beautiful hotels, was being hailed as "The Greatest Tourist Attraction in the World." Harry favored the creation of the National Park Service for the sake of continuity, with one set of rules for all the National Parks.

As years passed, other worthy areas were accepted and joined to the national park system. Since Yellowstone became a park, ten more parks and twenty-one monuments had been added to the system and administered by the Department of the Interior. The rule was, if the new addition was grass or timbered, it was put under the agriculture department; if it was military, it was placed under the direction of the army. Therefore, in Washington, the parks and monuments were known as "orphans," – no one department wanted to claim them. In Yellowstone's case, because of Fort Yellowstone, the acting superintendents answered to the Secretary of the Interior, plus the Secretary of War.

In the fall of 1911, a group of park superintendents and concessionaires gathered in Yellowstone at the spot of the Washburn pow-wow, now called Madison Junction. At the end of their sessions, the sixty attendees recommended the creation of a new National Park Bureau, with one director who would report directly to the Secretary of the Interior. This bureau would include all the parks and monuments – establishing one set of governing rules and making them eligible for government appropriations. This would take another act of Congress. The idea of continuity was not only popular with the superintendents, but it was well received in Washington.

These participants at the pow-pow had no need to sit around camp fires or sleep in tents, as the Washburn Expedition had done in 1870. Harry Child hosted them in his newly opened Grand Canyon Hotel. Featured speakers were Louis W. Hill, Glacier Park hotel developer and president of the Great Northern Railroad, and Horace McFarland, a big promoter for a national park in Colorado and president of the American Civic Association. Secretary of the Interior, Walter L. Fisher, called it "the first historic activist mobilization of park officials, See America-Firsters, and park boosters."

1912 was an election year. With the change in administrations came a Democratic regime. President-elect Woodrow Wilson chose a graduate of U.C. Berkeley, Franklin K. Lane, as his Secretary of Interior. Lane had a particular interest in the parks, and he too turned to Berkeley alumni to fill his roster of appointments. By late 1914, Stephen

T. Mather [114] came on board as Assistant to the Secretary, and Horace M. Albright [113] as Mather's personal secretary. Before Mather's arrival in Washington, an attempt was made to get the National Park Service bill through Congress. It failed because too many lawmakers felt the wording was so loose that it could, through different interpretations, lead to another large bureaucracy.

Stephen Mather was a man of energy and personality extraordinaire. Immediately he began to spread his charm around Washington. Horace Albright described him as "an experienced public relations man, [who] created instant rapport with strangers, had a personality that radiated poise, friendliness and charm, could talk easily with anyone he met, confidently instilling strangers with his enthusiasm." Other writers took up the cry and wrote glorious words like a hymn of praise for Mather: his good looks, his pleasing personality, as well as his mission. Male writers were more inclined to describe him as "an eight-cylinder, 60 m.p. (man power) sort of personality."

Mather wasted no time. His first chore was to lobby congressmen and get votes lined up to pass the National Park Service bill. He was not one to sit through meetings in dull offices. Instead he preferred to entertain lavishly at long lunches, capturing an audience of financial supporters as well as congressmen. By March of 1915, he felt assured of enough votes to pass the bill. His next step was to get the population interested and excited so that they would put pressure on Congress. He intended to flood the country with a massive dose of favorable propaganda. He contacted his friend, Robert Sterling Yard, a colleague from their days as young reporters at the *Chicago Sun*. Using his own money, Mather paid Yard a yearly salary.

Mather wanted to visit the parks and get to know his personnel. He planned his first Superintendent's Conference to be held in California, followed by a week-long camping trip in the Sierra Nevada mountains. Yard went along for publicity, writing exciting articles – enticingly illustrated with just the right pictures furnished to him by his photographer friends. All the excitement of California in 1915 was delivered to homes across the country on the pages of *The Saturday Evening Post* or *The National Geographic*.

The expositions in San Diego and San Francisco offered an excellent opportunity to publicize the national parks and help to push the park bureau through Congress. The See-America-First campaign also received a boost at the Panama- Pacific International Exposition [San Francisco]: "On four and a half acres and at a cost of 'half a million dollars,' the Union Pacific created a 'best of Yellowstone' exhibit, including a replica of Old Faithful [geyser]. The Santa Fe Railroad countered with their creation of the Grand Canyon on six acres. The Great Northern Railway focused on Glacier National Park, the Southern Pacific on Yosemite and its marvelous sequoia [trees]." The UP's exhibit included a full-size replica of Old Faithful Inn [79] where one publicity luncheon occurred. Mather's guests romped up and down the California coast drawing national attention to their cause.

The next month back in Washington, the concentration was on producing more publicity and getting it through the government printing and mailing process. Thousands of copies of *The National Parks Portfolio* were mailed to names and addresses on lists collected from all departments and volunteer sources. Stephen Mather did not break the law, but he took liberties to the limit – like "franking" unauthorized publications through the U.S. mail and paying Yard's salary from his own pocket.

———>●<———

Mather attached himself to a group of Reclamation Service people who were traveling the mountain west. They made a swing through Yellowstone, touring mostly the west side of the park. Mather's priority was to prepare for the entry of automobiles to YNP. Sharing the roads with stagecoaches would mean traveling on a tight schedule, and Mather wanted to see how that arrangement would work. Three days later, the first regulations, schedules, and general instructions were published.

Mather and his crew were in California again in July. The highlight of this trip was Mather's famous "Mountain Party." This time he was entertaining, again with his own money, a group of wealthy acquaintances he hoped to convert to heavy donors to the cause. Then the trip was extended to include a visit to the proposed new Rocky Mountain National Park. While in the Denver area, Mather met with leaders of the Park-to-Park Highway project and threw his full support behind that. He made arrangements to make a trip through Yellowstone with that group later in the season. Also it was about this time that Mather let it be known that Secretary Lane would allow automobiles to travel the roads in Yellowstone in the month of August on a trial basis [49].

Knowing that cars would be admitted in August, Harry Child proposed that a test trip be made concerning the matter of working out a schedule by actually running an automobile over the park roads. Mr. Mather agreed and suggested to Yellowstone Acting Superintendent Colonel Lloyd Brett that "Mr. Child become a member of your party. It would be well for him to join you in order that you may be able to avail yourself to his suggestions." Mr. Mather also offered to send someone to "help you whip the schedule into shape."

A telegraph dated May 12, 1915 from Mr. Mather to Colonel Brett stated, "Child's proposition automobile trip through the park in next few days with you and Major Fries. Would road conditions on account of snow, etc., make trip advisable at this time? Could it not be made better about June first?" The telegraph wires hummed as messages flew between Colonel Brett and Mr. Mather.

The test auto trip was planned for June 4th, but "heavy storms in the park made it impossible to make the test ride. Now snowing very hard. Impossible to set a date for this test." A few days later Huntley Child drove lead car, a 1915 White. His passengers were his father, Colonel Brett, and Major Fries, the government's road engineer. Gardiner resident L.H. VanDyck accompanied in his 1912 Franklin. They followed the same route the stagecoaches traveled, spending one night at Old

Faithful Inn. The final communication on June 8 read, "Automobile test trip accomplished. [44] No accidents. Much valuable data gathered for schedules and regulations."

As August 1st neared in Yellowstone, Colonel Brett feared that there might be "a run" at the park gates, overwhelming gate staff. He noted on July 29th that thirty-five vehicles were lined up at the north entrance awaiting admittance. He was allowed to permit vehicles to enter on July 31st – seven vehicles did so.

One of those vehicles was "an official White car [that] led the procession to the hotel..." On board were Brett and Fries, H.W. Child, and Robert S. Yard, as representative of the Department of Interior. "Promptly at 7:00 o'clock the next morning, the official White left Mammoth Hotel for a complete circuit of the Park." They arrived at Old Faithful Inn at noon, spending two-and-a-half hours for lunch and sightseeing. Proceeding across the Continental Divide, "where good brakes and a substantial steering gear come in handy," the travelers found "it seemed impossible to overheat the engine, no matter how long or severe the grades were." After dinner at Lake Hotel, they spent the night at Grand Canyon Hotel, crossing Dunraven Pass on their return to Mammoth Hot Springs. This trip "formally signifying an official welcome to motordom."

Fifty automobiles entered on August 1st, carrying 171 tourists. Through August and until the park closed in mid-September, 3,513 tourists enthusiastically drove their 958 autos around the loop road.

The trip Mr. Mather had planned earlier with the Park-to-Park Highway Association materialized in early September. Since cars were now traveling in the park, Mather wanted "to see how the mix of car and stagecoach was working out." He decided that he and Albright would travel by stagecoach from Cody. Albright recalled that "we were traveling right along, bumpy and uncomfortable but moving at a pretty good clip." They came upon a string of automobiles having "a terrible time, trying to get up a steep grade; the road was just one big muddy mass of ruts." Mather didn't expect to catch up with the Park-to-Parkers until inside the park, but here they were. "He fretted and stewed over it, taking it all personally," because he had so highly promoted car travel to his friends. "... the roads were absolutely impassable – or impossible. When we got into the park itself, we found conditions vastly better. ..."

Albright and Mather began to lay the ground work for future changes: "We stayed in Yellowstone for only a few days, but it was long enough to make a thorough inspection. We covered the so-called Grand Loop, now traveling by automobile, as one day on a stagecoach had been quite enough. Mather was in and out of the car at every hotel, geyser, camp, cascade, garbage dump, and ranger station. I was right beside him with my ever-present notebook and pen, taking dictation."

A history-making change happened the same year in the operation of park souvenir shops. When Huntley Child heard that the Klamer Curio Shop in the Upper Geyser Basin was for sale, he thought of his friend, Charles Hamilton, from their youthful days in Yellowstone. Klamer's, in proximity to the new Old Faithful Inn, was basically a souvenir shop, but it also had a soda fountain, and sold groceries and other necessities.

Huntley made a phone call to "Ham," and told him the situation. Ham was back home in Minnesota, and at age thirty, he was looking for something permanent in the business field. Klamer's store was exactly the kind of business he was wanting. He liked the challenge and excitement of merchandising – buying and selling for a profit. There was just one big problem – he did not have the money to buy the business. Huntley decided he would finance the buy-out, and Ham "would be the front man," actually running the business.

Ham took the first train from St. Paul to Livingston, Montana. The two men, Huntley Child and Charles Hamilton, went to Harry Child to tell him of their plan. Having recently made Huntley treasurer of both the hotel and transportation companies, Harry told his son, "No, you're staying out of it. You have enough to do here." But he agreed to loan

Ham $5,000 to purchase the business.

From Mammoth, Ham rushed over the next fifty miles to get to Old Faithful and make a deal with Mrs. Mary Klamer. After sharing a leisurely cup of tea, Ham wrote two bad checks – one for the down-payment and one for the inventory. Trotting his horse slowly out of sight, he galloped off for a quick stop in Mammoth to cement a deal with Harry Child, and drink a quick toast to his future. By driving all night, he was at the Livingston bank early to make the checks good before Mary could get there to cash them.

This is a well-known, often repeated tale around Yellowstone. It illustrates one of Harry's strongly held beliefs – and one he felt represented the success of the West: "Easterners seem to have a code of ethics which is entirely different from our code out West ... We try to win our wealth from the soil, from mines and from oil wells. You Easterners, in the cities at least, try to win your money from one another. We don't want another man's money. We would rather help a fellow to make money than scheme to get away from him any money he may have made."

"Our national parks are just as much the possession of the workmen as of the millionaire ..."
HWC

That was the beginning of over seventy-five years of success for the Hamilton Stores in Yellowstone, and a lifelong friendship between the Child and Hamilton families. Ham's business flourished to the point that eventually a major Hamilton Store could be found at each Park location, plus outside businesses in West Yellowstone, Montana. Ham's favorite was always his original store at Old Faithful. He kept an apartment above the store and delighted in visiting with customers and young seasonal workers in the Park. He liked to encourage young people by inviting them up to his office to show off his walls covered with canceled checks – including the two "bad" ones that worked out so well for him. He also pointed out the check he received that represented the first million dollars he had made. Charles Hamilton died at his desk in the Million Dollar Room in 1957 [110].

His son-in-law, Trevor Povah and daughter Eleanor, known as Miss Ellie, ran the business for many years. The family continued to operate the general stores until 2003. After the National Park Service radically changed the way concession contracts were awarded, their contract was not renewed.

———❦———

Once the first auto "test trip" was made successfully, the die was cast. Harry's "Greatest Tourist Attraction in the World" was doomed. Of course, he had become a master hotel builder, and the wonders of Yellowstone would always be an attraction. But one great symbol of the American West, the horses and stagecoaches, would soon be gone.

Child was a hands-on type of manager and stayed on top of all aspects of his business. His employees liked him and were loyal because he made a point of getting personally acquainted with as many as possible, from the top down to the most humble positions.

Mather's way of operating was not unlike Harry's. Both men loved time outdoors and valued the benefits of assembling business associates in the casual camp setting, away from the structure of office meetings. Though Mather and Child clashed over issues now and then, they genuinely liked one another and worked well together. As their associations strengthened over the years, they had fun making and collecting on frivolous bets. They wagered on such things as park visitation numbers and whether certain improvements would come about. Their stakes were high – the winner receiving the cost of a "well-tailored suit."

CODY-SYLVAN PASS MOTOR COMPANY
YELLOWSTONE NATIONAL PARK

OFFICERS
F. J. HAYNES, Pres.
A. W. MILES, Vice-Pres.
LEO C. SHAW, Sec.
HUNTLEY CHILD, Treas.
CHAIRMAN OF OPERATING COMMITTEE
A. W. MILES

(Post Office)
Yellowstone Park, Wyo.

DIRECTORS REPRESENTING
YELLOWSTONE-WESTERN STAGE CO. { F. J. HAYNES
                                                              JAMES R. HICKEY
YELLOWSTONE PARK TRANSPORTATION CO. { WILLIAM M. NICHOLS
                                                                       HUNTLEY CHILD
WYLIE PERMANENT CAMPING CO.—A. W. MILES
SHAW & POWELL CAMPING CO. { LEO C. SHAW
                                                      JOHN D. POWELL

Chapter 11: "Those Infernal Machines" 1916

official visits from Washington, autos and stages
share the road, enter the rangers, extended monopoly

The National Park Service bill that failed in 1913 was not dead. Congress was passing it from one committee to another and doing numerous rewrites. Mather and Albright kept up the lobbying pressure. "In the midst of all the Washington work on the national park service bill ... [Mather] had again become vitally concerned with the Park-to-Park Highway and planned another trip to Yellowstone to go over the route ..."

This time Mr. Mather's party included his wife and a number of personal and official friends. They arrived in July 1916 on the Chicago, Burlington and Quincy Railroad. Seven-passenger, chauffeur-driven, White touring cars were waiting, and off they went. Their overnight in Cody was less than favorable, and the roads from Cody to the east entrance showed no improvement from the previous year's condition. Inside the park the roads provided a pleasant ride. While Mather and his party were sightseeing, Albright and Major Amos Fries, the army engineer in charge of road-building in the park, traveled their own route in another car. As the Major "poured over a flood of valuable information," Albright "made copious notes and recommendations, such as signs that should be erected to locate and explain attractions to tourists, parapets that should be built at dangerous curves or precipices, hiking trails that must be constructed to scenic spots."

Albright wrote this account of their second night:

I always thought the Canyon Hotel one of the most beautiful in the world. Built during the fearful winter of 1910 - 11, it hugged the contour of the hill above and beyond the grand canyon of the Yellowstone River, though too far away to see the canyon itself. [The hotel] was huge, a mile around, and yet it blended as one into the landscape. The architect, Robert Reamer, who also designed the Lake and Old Faithful hotels, commented on this, his masterpiece: 'I built it in keeping with the place where it stands. To be in discord with the landscape would be almost a crime.' Inside it was equally breathtaking, especially the lounge, projecting forward from the main hotel two hundred by one hundred feet [86], with a grand staircase descending to lounge areas and, at night, a ballroom with soft, discreet lights and a dance orchestra. What a relief it was that night to be in this beautiful, luxurious hotel, to eat in the lovely dining room with windows framing the vista toward the canyon, to luxuriate in clean bathrooms with large tubs of hot water, to sleep in comfortable beds with fresh sheets and Hudson Bay blankets, and with not a crawling thing in sight.

The Park-to-Park Highway Association was established to connect all of the national parks of the Rocky Mountain region and the Pacific coast. The group convened at Harry Child's new and grandest hotel; Stephen Mather was the featured speaker. Harry and Adelaide supported the Park-to-Park Highway with both their time and money. For Horace Albright, his most memorable day was spent in the Teton Valley south of Yellowstone – an area he had only glimpsed from a distance the year before.

Later that year Mr. Mather hosted a "Glacier Mountain Party," in Glacier National Park, Montana, gathering more support.

———>●<———

Mather wanted cars permitted in Yellowstone, but the stagecoach transportation was so accomplished and popular. How to get the two modes of travel to operate on the same narrow roads, safely, was a formidable problem. The summer of 1916 brought controlled chaos to park roadways. Experiences from the year before were showing that the backfiring and noise of the early autos was frightening the horses. So the government published a booklet entitled *A Motorists Guide* that included elaborate time schedules – cars were required to leave road junctions by certain times. This got them off the roads before the horses

AUTOMOBILE SCHEDULES, YELLOWSTONE NATIONAL PARK.

EFFECTIVE JUNE 15, 1916.

Automobiles may leave the park by any one of the authorized routes of entrance. Automobile drivers should compare their watches with the clocks at checking stations.

Automobiles stopping over at points other than the hotels and permanent camps will be allowed to resume travel only at such time as permits them to fall in with a subsequent regular automobile schedule past the point of stop-over. Such automobiles while stopping over must park out of sight of, or at least 100 yards from, the main road.

Automobiles stopping over at permanent camps must leave the same at the proper time to conform with the published schedules from the nearest hotels. Detailed times of departure to comply with this provision will be posted at the particular camps concerned.

When, due to breakdowns or accidents of any other nature, automobiles are unable to keep going, or to reach the next stopping place on time, they must be immediately parked off the road, or, where this is impossible, on the outer edge of the road, and wait until the next schedule for automobiles past that point, or until given special permission to proceed by park guards.

Automobiles will not be permitted for use on local trips around hot springs formations or other points of interest off the main roads, except in the case specially noted at Artist Point, in the morning schedule from the Lake Hotel to Canyon.

SPEEDS.—Speeds must be limited to 12 miles per hour ascending, and 10 miles per hour descending steep grades, and to 8 miles per hour when approaching sharp curves. On good roads with straight stretches, and when no team is nearer than 200 yards, the speed may be increased to 20 miles per hour.

HORNS.—The horn will be sounded on approaching curves, or stretches of road concealed for any considerable distance by slopes, overhanging trees, or other obstacles; and before meeting or passing other machines, or riding or driving animals.

TEAMS.—When teams, saddle horses, or pack trains approach, automobiles will take the outer edge of the roadway, regardless of the direction in which they may be going, taking care that sufficient room is left on the inside for the passage of vehicles and animals. Teams have the right of way, and automobiles will be backed or otherwise handled as may be necessary so as to enable teams to pass with safety. In no case will automobiles pass animals on the road at a greater speed than 8 miles per hour.

In addition to the schedules herein given, automobiles must keep clear of any horse-drawn passenger vehicles running upon regular schedules which may be following them; and upon overtaking any horse-drawn passenger vehicles running upon regular schedules, automobiles must not attempt to pass or approach closer than within 150 yards of the same.

REDUCED ENGINE POWER—GASOLINE, ETC.—Due to the high altitude of the park roads, averaging nearly 7,650 feet for the belt line and east, north, and west entrances, the power of all automobiles is much reduced, so that about 50 per cent more gasoline will be required than for the same distance at lower altitudes. Likewise one lower gear will generally have to be used on grades than would have to be used in other places. A further effect that must be watched is the heating of the engine on long roads, which may become serious unless care is used. Gasoline can be purchased at regular supply stations as per posted notices.

	Miles	SCHEDULE A.		SCHEDULE B.	
		Not earlier than—	Not later than—	Not earlier than—	Not later than—
GARDINER TO NORRIS.					
Leave Gardiner Entrance	0	6.00 a. m.	6.30 a. m.	2.30 p. m.	3.00 p. m.
Arrive Mammoth Hot Springs	5	6.20 a. m.	7.00 a. m.	2.50 p. m.	3.30 p. m.
Leave Mammoth Hot Springs	0	6.45 a. m.	7.15 a. m.	5.45 p. m.	6.15 p. m.
Leave 8-Mile Post	8		8.00 a. m.	(See Note 3.)	
Arrive Norris	20	8.30 a. m.	9.00 a. m.		
NORRIS TO WEST ENTRANCE.					
Leave Norris	0			4.00 p. m.	4.30 p. m.
Arrive West Entrance	27			6.00 p. m.	6.30 p. m.
NORRIS TO CANYON.					
Leave Norris	0			2.15 p. m.	2.30 p. m.
Arrive Canyon	11			3.00 p. m.	3.30 p. m.
(FOR GALLATIN STATION ENTRANCE SEE NOTE L.)					
NORRIS TO FOUNTAIN HOTEL.					
Leave Norris	0	8.30 a. m.	9.15 a. m.	4.00 p. m.	4.30 p. m.
			(Via Mesa Road.)	(Via Mesa Road or Madison Junction.)	
Leave Firehole Cascades	14.7		10.30 a. m.		
Arrive Fountain Hotel	20	10.30 a. m.	11.00 a. m.	5.45 p. m.	6.15 p. m.
(FOR GALLATIN STATION ENTRANCE SEE NOTE L.)					
WEST ENTRANCE TO FOUNTAIN HOTEL.					
Leave West Entrance	0	6.45 a. m.	7.15 a. m.	7.30 p. m.	8.00 p. m.
Arrive Fountain Hotel	21	8.30 a. m.	9.00 a. m.	(See Note 3.)	
FOUNTAIN HOTEL TO THUMB.					
Leave Fountain Hotel	0	10.30 a. m.	11.00 a. m.	5.45 p. m.	6.15 p. m.
Arrive Upper Basin (Old Faithful Inn)	9	12.00 m.	12.30 p. m.	6.45 p. m.	7.00 p. m.
Leave Upper Basin (Old Faithful Inn)	0	2.30 p. m.	3.00 p. m.	7.00 a. m.	7.30 a. m.
Arrive Thumb Station	19	4.30 p. m.	5.00 p. m.	8.30 a. m.	9.30 a. m.
(FOR SOUTH ENTRANCE SEE NOTE L.)					
THUMB TO LAKE HOTEL.					
Leave Thumb Station	0	4.30 p. m.	5.00 p. m.	8.30 a. m.	9.30 a. m.
Arrive Lake Hotel	15	5.45 p. m.	6.15 p. m.	10.00 a. m.	11.30 a. m.
LAKE HOTEL TO EAST BOUNDARY.					
Leave Lake Hotel (See Note 1)	0				
Arrive East Boundary	28				
EAST BOUNDARY TO LAKE HOTEL.					
Leave East Boundary (See Note 1)	0				
Arrive Lake Hotel	28				
LAKE HOTEL TO CANYON.					
Leave Lake Hotel	0	7.00 a. m.	7.30 a. m.	2.00 p. m.	2.30 p. m.
			(See Note 2.)		
Leave Canyon Soldier Station	16		10.00 a. m.		
Arrive Canyon Hotel	17	9.10 a. m.	10.10 a. m.	3.15 p. m.	3.45 p. m.
CANYON TO NORRIS.					
Leave Canyon Hotel	0	2.15 p. m.	2.30 p. m.		
Arrive Norris Hotel	12	3.00 p. m.	3.30 p. m.		
(FOR SCHEDULE FROM NORRIS TO FOUNTAIN, UPPER BASIN, AND WEST ENTRANCE, SEE ABOVE.)					
CANYON TO TOWER FALLS.					
Leave Canyon Hotel	0	1.30 p. m.	2.00 p. m.	7.00 a. m.	7.30 a. m.
Arrive Tower Falls					
Via Dunraven Pass	16	3.00 p. m.	3.45 p. m.	8.30 a. m.	9.15 a. m.
Via Mount Washburn	19	4.15 p. m.	4.45 p. m.	9.45 a. m.	10.15 a. m.
(FOR COOKE CITY ENTRANCE SEE NOTE L.)					
TOWER FALLS TO GARDINER.					
Leave Tower Falls	0	3.15 p. m.	4.45 p. m.	8.30 a. m.	10.15 a. m.
Arrive Mammoth Hot Springs	20	5.30 p. m.	6.45 p. m.	10.00 a. m.	12.15 p. m.

During his 1915 visit to Yellowstone, Secretary of the Interior Stephen Mather began drawing a schedule for stagecoaches and automobiles to share the roads. This 1916 publication shows the highly regimented result.

left those points. Drivers could be fined if they were not off the roads by the designated times. Certain rules held if stages and autos met on the road – always giving the horse-drawn vehicles the right-of-way. Admitting cars to Yellowstone National Park was already promising to have far-reaching effects.

A pilot project using multi-passenger touring vehicles was run that year. "... a concession was granted the Cody-Sylvan Pass Motor Company, authorizing it for the term of one year from January 1, 1916 to establish and maintain an automobile transportation line ... This company operated from Cody, Wyo. to the eastern entrance, thence inside of the park to the Yellowstone Lake, where they turned their patrons over to the transportation companies operating horse drawn vehicles." The Cody-Sylvan Pass Motor Company purchased "seven 10-passenger auto busses and five 7-passenger touring cars [45] ... a seating capacity of practically 100 daily or 50 each way between Cody and the Lake Hotel."

The directors of this new company included F. Jay Haynes, Huntley Child, W.M. Nichols, A.W. Miles of the Wylie Company, and the two principals of the Shaw and Powell Camping Company. The east entrance had never been all that profitable with horse-drawn vehicles because of the steep grades required to climb into the Absaroka Mountain range. A corkscrew bridge had been constructed allowing horses to make the climb to Sylvan Pass at more than 8500 feet. The Cody-Sylvan Pass Motor Company's trial season proved an improvement and a success.

———⟫●⟪———

The importance of the railroads to Yellowstone tourism was not forgotten. Mather worked a deal with the railroads whereby a traveler could purchase one ticket, arrive on one railroad at the east, west or north gate and depart, on the same ticket, on another rail line leaving the gate of the traveler's choice.

Harry cooperated with this plan by blocking a certain number of rooms for each railroad, that number being made clear to each.

However, the railroads sold tickets according to the number of seats available in a train car. The stage companies loaded as many people as they could carry and delivered them to Harry's hotels. On their arrival, some people found "no room at the Inn." Throughout the summer of 1916, privately-owned cars were allowed to travel in the park, and those people also expected to find a room at night. The Park was inundated with tourists and just not enough rooms to go around. Some nights, Harry felt compelled to give up his rooms to accommodate travelers. He wrote long pleading letters to Mather and the railroads but to no avail.

F. Jay Haynes complained to Stephen Mather that the Union Pacific was delivering more people than his Red Line coaches could handle. Mather's answer to that was, "cannot Child aid Haynes," to borrow some of his yellow coaches. Harry did not have stagecoaches sitting around empty. Clearly, Mather had no idea of what was happening on the ground in the park.

———————

There was chatter in the newspapers about a possible railroad strike in 1916. Harry was on a short trip to his ranch in the Gallatin Valley when he happened to call the chief dispatcher of the NPR in Livingston. Harry wanted to ask a question about his ranch operations, but the dispatcher said, "By the way, Mr. Child, do you know that we have notified all shippers that from this date we will receive no more perishable goods... on account of the strike. I hope you are provised with plenty of butter and eggs and fresh fish, etc., for your tourists." Harry asked if he was dead sure that the strike was coming off, and the agent answered, "Yes, at seven o'clock Monday morning, September 4th."

Harry asked the dispatcher if he would please locate the President of the NPR and the vice- president in charge of traffic and arrange for him to talk with them over the railroad wires. Harry left his ranch immediately and drove in his automobile to Livingston. After conversations with the two NPR officials, Harry received this telegram: "No question about wisdom about your plan if there is to be a strike, and nobody can say today that there is any other prospect."

Harry talked with the NPR superintendents in Livingston and found that they were spending thousands of dollars hiring men to protect the bridges and culverts along the entire system, and erecting barricades around all of their property. Harry drove on to Mammoth thinking about all this information – as well as another strike that had happened in 1894 when people were marooned inside the hotels. At that time, without trains running to the entrances, people had to be transported by stagecoach to distant cities. Harry made his decision, but was not yet ready to instruct his people to close the hotels. He wanted a conference with the traffic manager of the Union Pacific. They met late that night at Old Faithful Inn and made a plan. At seven o'clock the next morning they began executing the plan.

Telephone and telegraph operators were kept at their instruments all night notifying hotel managers around the park to alert their guests of the plan. Harry was in touch with his son Huntley, and W.M. Nichols in Mammoth. Col. Brett had had no communication with Mr. Mather, but he cooperated by arranging to delay the automobile schedule so that the stagecoaches would not run into them. Soldiers from all stations were called to duty, and the exodus went off with absolutely no difficulty. All refunds were made to the tourists before they left their hotels and the help was paid off. This was accomplished by Huntley sending money out into the park with clerks to take care of the pay-outs. Harry wrote, "Colonel Brett is entitled to most of the credit for this movement, together with my son Huntley, and my son-in-law Mr. Nichols."

The railroads reported the next day that the situation was exactly the same as it was the previous day, and that they were figuring on the strike being pulled off as planned. It never happened.

Mr. Mather had now reached Portland, Oregon and heard the news. He wired Col. Brett to inquire as to what action Mr. Child had taken to take care of independent motor travel in the park. Col. Brett responded, "Mr. Child made no provision to care for motor travel but permanent camps are open." With only a few days left in the season, it was not feasible to re-open the hotels.

The bill Lane and Mather wanted finally was passed through Congress – making the National Park Service the ninth Division of the Department of the Interior. President Wilson signed the bill August 25, 1916, the date still celebrated by the NPS as its official anniversary. Stephen Mather was sworn in as the first Director of the National Park Service.

Yellowstone, almost from the beginning, had been under the protection of the Army. Mather had plans of developing the National Park Rangers. The first Rangers were recruited from the army personnel at Fort Yellowstone. The War Department agreed to discharge a select number of volunteer cavalry on September 30 so they could go to work for the National Park Rangers. The final withdraw of troops was on October 25, 1916. But Congress failed to appropriate funds for the Park Service for 1917, and the Ranger force was disbanded.

Political pressure from the Montana Congressional delegation over the loss of economic revenue from the military's presence resulted in the recall of the Army, and 450 soldiers were sent back to Fort Yellowstone. Mather and Albright had a special dislike for Montana Senator Thomas J. Walsh, and they blamed him alone for the lack of funds. Huntley Child had acquired some small businesses in Gardiner that the soldiers frequented. These developments upset Mather greatly, and although it was out of his control, it seemed to sink him into a bout of depression.

Albright was sent to assist Col. Brett in the transition from military to civilian control. Administrative control remained with the Interior Department under acting superintendent Chester Lindsley, a long time civilian in the Park.

1916 had been a year of turmoil in Yellowstone. And then Mather called for a conference of the Yellowstone concessioners in Washington on December 10. During his three recent trips to Yellowstone, he had been making plans for just the right way to organize the concessioners in all the parks, a "controlled" monopoly or an "extended" monopoly. He chose the latter.

His power as Director of the NPS extended to all aspects of parks' services, from the location of buildings to the price of rooms, tours and sandwiches as well as the fate of the concessioners. He believed that concessioners should be afforded a large measure of protection, and that competition should be discouraged. He considered Yellowstone and its multitude of operators the perfect opportunity to demonstrate.

At the meeting of Yellowstone concessionaires: "There was not much give and take with the issue. Mather simply dictated that Harry Child got all the hotels in the park under the Yellowstone Park Hotel Company. His Yellowstone Park Transportation Company consolidated all the transportation lines. This was because the hotels were a losing business and the transportation was a money-maker and also because Child was heavily backed by the powerful Northern Pacific Railroad. As part of the deal, Child was ordered to get rid of all horses, stagecoaches, and other equipment and have his operation completely motorized by 1917."

The camping companies were also forced to combine into one business. The chosen winners were A.W. Miles, of the Wylie Permanent Camping Company, and J.D. Powell of the Shaw and Powell Camping Company. Harry Child and F. Jay Haynes were required to sell their shares to the new Yellowstone Park Camping Company. Mather's instructions were specific – dictating which camp locations would be permitted to continue in use. In some areas of the park, the location of the former Wylie camp was used – and in other, the Shaw and Powell camp could stay.

Mr. Mather's selection of the YPTC had put both the Yellowstone-Western Stage Company and the Cody-Sylvan Pass Motor Company out of business – therefore ousting the Haynes family from the transportation business. A deal was struck in which Harry's transportation company acquired the assets of the Cody-Sylvan Pass Motor Company, "at no financial loss to Haynes." What had been Yellowstone's "Red Line" was gone. F. Jay Haynes retired from the photography business, leaving his son Jack Ellis Haynes to run the family company.

From the perspective of those running businesses in the park, this move happened suddenly, without fair warning. In fact, the idea had been brewing in Mather's mind since his first visit to Yellowstone in 1914. After the conference, most of the concessionaires felt that Mather "had achieved his goal in a fair and honest manner."

Despite his success in getting the National Park Service bill passed and establishing the extended monopoly principle for the parks, Mather continued to be depressed. He complained that he had done nothing right, that perhaps he was not helping the Park Service movement at all. His friends rallied and tried to encourage him, but his mood swings continued.

Sometime back, Mr. Mather had become impressed with Robert B. Marshall of the U.S. Geological Survey, and was grooming him to be the director when the NPS was finally ratified. An interim title had been given to Marshall so he had some authority. Along the way, he and Mather came to cross purposes. Marshall was "a diligent worker, a versatile engineer, and much more," but to Mather "he began to look like a clumsy administrator." When Mather decided to take the job of director himself, Marshall did not take it quietly. It was another drain on Mather's nerves. And then, there was the problem of Rangers versus U.S. Soldiers in Yellowstone. Mather wanted NPS Rangers, but how could he get the Army out?

Woodrow Wilson's re-election was another major strain on Mather. Mather was a staunch Republican but was now supporting the Democratic candidate, Woodrow Wilson, knowing that he would be more favorable to plans for the NPS. Mather's friends rallied and planned an election night party. All the wives went off for a night at the theater while the men listened to the election results. Late in the evening, it appeared that Wilson had lost.

However California's electoral votes had not yet been counted. By morning the election did go to Wilson by one vote. This perked Mather up somewhat, and he began to plan the Fourth National Parks Conference for early January.

La Jolla, California,

Chapter 12: From Wranglers to Gear Jammers

1917-1918

*motorizing the fleet, closures during the war,
Huntley loses role, Army departs, Dr. Dean's death*

In the winter of 1916-17 Harry Child, still president of the Yellowstone Park Transportation Company, sold his stagecoaches, horses, harnesses, and all equipment. Following Stephen Mather's directive to motorize park transportation, he made a deal with the White Motor Company of Cleveland, Ohio to purchase 117 vehicles. Most of them had four bench-seats [51]. The cost was tremendous, but with the backing of the railroads, Harry managed.

Huntley Child was now general manager and treasurer of the hotel and transportation company. Huntley's background was mostly transportation. As a teenager he had worked with and was trained by his uncle, Silas Huntley. Now at age 31, partially due to his father's illness, he was given charge of a company that no longer dealt with horses and stagecoaches, but was suddenly totally motorized. Because Silas' system was so organized, it made for an easier transition to autos. W.M. Nichols for a number of years had been Harry's secretary. Now his title was Assistant to the President.

137

One young employee, Gerard Pesman [47], spent twenty-three summers working in the Transportation Department. He started while attending college, and returned after retirement. "Each spring," he recalled, "there was a campaign to recruit what they called 'chauffeurs' to drive buses ... they wanted local people who were used to driving these roads which were narrow, crooked, sometimes ungraveled, and in Yellowstone Park, of course, a lot of mountain work. So each spring they had a campaign in the local towns like Missoula, Helena, Bozeman, Billings, and Livingston, and there would be an ad in the paper saying, 'Try-outs for chauffeurs would be held on such and such days.'"

Pesman answered the ad, took the driving test in one of the yellow touring cars, and later received a postcard informing him that he was chosen. He described his first day of bus driving: "Well, when I walked in and saw that monster, it looked like it was twice as long as an ordinary car, and they were parked two in a stall, pretty close together. My first query in mind was, number one, I wonder if I can get this thing started? And number two, how am I going to get it out of that narrow space? Well, I finally got it started and by being real careful, twisted it out of the space. But those old buses, of course, used a fair amount of oil, and the inside of that storage shed was just blue with smoke. I got it out, got gas, signed for it, and parked the bus out along the road."

Each driver was issued robes – one for each seat in the bus – a jack, tools, fire extinguisher, instruction book, and copy of the rules and regulations. They signed out caps and uniforms, agreeing to be responsible for all items, and to turn them in in the fall. "The uniforms were something. Brown corduroy pants ... military-type pants and tight from [the knees] down. And I had puttees, stiff as a piece of stove pipe ... The jacket was what would probably be known as an English hunting-coat style. ... The cap was one of these flat affairs with a bill and you fastened your badge on top of it there. Well, you felt like an over-dressed turkey. That was all right – everybody looked the same."

A senior driver loaded up the "frolickers" (first year drivers) for a two-day tour of the roads. They received indoctrination as to the expectations and some special rules – like not being allowed to enter the hotels – except on business. They were permitted to socialize in the lodges where there were "savage programs," (variety shows staged by the employees), community singing, and dancing. The drivers were among the elite employees who had their own mess halls – a hold-over from the stagecoach era. "At our mess halls we got better meals than just about anybody else in the park. We got just as good of meals as the passengers. The attitude of the cooks was rather interesting. The cook at Old Faithful got a call from the chef over at the hotel and he said, 'Look, I've got a little bit of meat here. I really don't want to put on the table for the tourists. Would you want it?' The story is that she snapped back at him, 'Well, if it's not good enough for the tourists, it sure as hell ain't good enough for my men.'"

The buses were described as being either a *string* or a *parade*. "That also," continued Pesman, "is a holdover from horse days. If you have a bunch of pack animals, they are in a string. ... Oh, the buses, known as a *string*, but while they were in movement, it was called a *parade*. ... Spacing [between buses in a parade] was based primarily on two things. Number one was the dust. You stayed far enough back so that you were not riding in the dust cloud all the time, and this meant at least 100 yards, maybe 200 yards. The second thing was that you could not ride too close, you had to leave space enough so that the people with their own cars could get around you."

———

Mr. Mather had made plans for his fourth Superintendent's Conference. The first session was to be held in the new National Museum in Washington, D.C. The invited speakers on the guest list read like a "who's-who" in the fields of wealth, power, the arts, politics, etc. The plans were grandiose as usual, and he had high hopes of making new friends for the promotion of the NPS and making new contacts to solicit more financial help. Each of the invited guests would be speaking to the superintendents at the various sessions.

Mather had been displaying irrational behavior since late 1916. Besides the pressure of the conference plans, several situations in particular were making him more and more nervous and excitable. There was the lingering problem of what to do about Robert Marshall. The uncertainty of President Wilson winning re-election had affected him greatly. Another situation was the business of NPS Rangers versus U.S. soldiers in Yellowstone.

The Superintendent's Conference opened on January 2, 1917. The conference progressed according to plans, and Mather floundered through all of it. He did not even show up for a couple of days, so Robert Yard covered for him. The total melt-down came at the end of the conference. His friends found him in a confused state and contacted his wife. Under Mrs. Mather's instructions, Horace Albright, Mather's personal secretary/assistant, took him to his doctor who ran a sanitarium in Philadelphia. There he was put under his doctor's care, was assigned a male nurse who would care for him and be a constant companion for the next six months or so. Mrs. Mather confirmed that the symptoms he displayed were the same as he had suffered in 1903.

Only Robert Yard knew of Mather's illness because he was a long-time friend, had been Mather's best man, and had seen Mather through his last illness. Horace Albright and Secretary Lane chose to keep Mather's confinement a secret – nothing could stand in the way of their goal.

Through the summer of 1917, Mather was in the sanitarium still being protected from any kind of stress or worry. He was given a typewriter, however, and allowed to write some letters to his wife and to Albright. Most of those kind of letters were answered with just some uplifting and distracting conversation.

It was during this time that Albright received a message from Mather saying "that he had reconsidered on the Fountain Hotel, found it 'useless,' and wanted it destroyed." He desired to rid the parks of old buildings, and he saw the Fountain Hotel as an eyesore. It was twenty-six years old, and unlike the face-lifting renovations that Harry had done at Lake and Canyon Hotels, little work had improved Fountain Hotel over the years.

Albright resisted because it was considered modern, in that it had hot water, locally-generated DC electricity, and steam heat. "Furthermore, it was nicely located and had the dubious honor of being known as 'the bear hotel.'" Albright did not follow Mather's order right away. He hoped to talk Mather out of the idea of destroying a famous and popular landmark.

———⟫●⟪———

World War I had been raging in Europe for three years. By late 1916 when it looked as though America might enter the war, Mather put out an announcement that the Parks would remain open because people need rest and recreation in war time as in peace. On April 6, 1917 President Wilson asked the Congress for a declaration of war against Germany, and America joined the Allied forces. The Selective Service Act was signed the next month.

On June 1st, 1917 the hotels in Yellowstone were due to start opening. Harry, W.M., and Huntley had put together some figures which predicted a very grim season ahead. Because of the war, the trains had changed their schedules to accommodate the "troop trains," and they had raised their prices for the travelers. There was unrest in the country, and many people were working for the war effort. Therefore the companies were unable to hire adequate staff to operate the hotels properly.

The Childs were no longer allowed to run the business to suit themselves – they now answered to the new National Park Service. Because of his illness, Mather was unavailable, so Horace Albright did his best to keep things running. But he was mostly in remote areas and could not be reached. He was traveling in the west doing park inspections, and scouting areas that might meet their standards to become a park or monument.

The area just south of Yellowstone was certainly on Albright's list. The Grand Teton Range lies just south of Yellowstone's southern boundary, but within the state of Wyoming. Suggestions to protect this area surfaced repeatedly through the years – including Acting Superintendent S.B.M. Young (now Harry's brother-in-law) who suggested in 1897 that Yellowstone's authority be extended into Jackson Hole, thus giving protection to the migratory paths of the elk that summered in Yellowstone.

Despite slower business, the Yellowstone Park Hotel Company made some expansion plans. In the summer of 1917, Huntley Child, Howard Hays, and Jack E. Haynes made an expedition to the glacier on Mount Moran [117]. Their purpose was to scout possible locations for hotel expansion. As typical of young men of any generation, this group (now ages 31, 33, and 33 respectively), looked to establish their own paths in park concessions.

Mather's particular friend Emerson Hough accompanied the group, as did YPHC architect Robert Reamer. Hough published a stirring article in *The Saturday Evening Post* advocating for adding this area to Yellowstone. A bill was introduced in the spring of 1918, but the Idaho senator managed to block its passage. It would be another decade before formal protections were achieved for this mountain range and valley.

————⟫●⟪————

The Flying D was by now basically a cattle ranch [103]. Marketing their animals was a large part of the business. Charlie Anceney went to Mexico each year and brought back a train-load of yearlings. He turned them onto the Flying D grass to graze and fatten for another year. Then they were rounded up and sorted for market. Charlie rode on the train with his herd from Salesville to Chicago – making sure that they were cared for properly. He was very proud that his cattle brought the best price and were purchased by the most discerning buyers.

Harry had nearly completed what he set out to do in Yellowstone. Both the Hotel Company and Transportation Company were well organized and running smoothly, led by long-time loyal employees under the leadership of his son Huntley, and son-in-law, W.M. Nichols.

Harry, ever a builder, was finding new horizons in Gallatin Valley.

Harry and Charlie acquired the Sales-Tomlinson mill site that came with 2,500 inches of water-rights – a rancher's precious resource. They purchased several residences and businesses, including a hotel and the Salesville Mercantile. When a new Salesville State Bank opened, Harry and Charlie bought a majority of the shares offered for sale. The Child-Anceney partnership in the Gallatin Valley now included a successful breeding program, real estate holdings, and local business interests.

———⟶●◀———

Harry had been battling diabetes and related chronic illnesses for some time, and lately his health had worsened. He had moved Huntley and W.M. Nichols into positions of control of his companies.

Visitor counts for the 1917 and 1918 summers were dismal, and the only revenue for Harry's companies came from the transportation side. Huntley Child was 31 years old, and married, with three children to support. At home in Yellowstone, Bessie Ferguson had become one of the family, so Huntley knew that his family would be cared for.

In November 1917 Huntley took a government post at the appointment of Herbert Hoover, secretary of the Food Administration. With his Aunt Annie and General S.B.M. Young also in Washington, D.C., he obtained lodging there at the Soldier's Home.

Huntley had struggled to find his place in Yellowstone – out from under his father's formidable shadow. He passed up the general store opportunity to his buddy Charles Hamilton. In the fall of 1916 when Stephen Mather merged the camps companies and the transportation companies, Mather desired to include the hotels with the camps. But Harry's friendship with Senator Walsh and the Hotel company's twenty-year contract (from 1913) kept him from pushing his luck.

Recalling the situation in later years, Horace Albright wrote:

Director Mather of the National Park Service, had tried unsuccessfully in 1916 to merge the Camps Co and the Hotel Company. Evidently Huntley Child had in mind talking with [Howard] Hays in another effort to effect a merger which they both knew would please Mather, but Huntley Child disagreed with Mather on some fundamental issues, including removal of troops from protection of the park, while Hays fully agreed with Mather.

Stephen Mather was back in his Washington D.C. office by September [1918], and now was riding a high tide of his manic-depressive condition. In his mind, anything was possible. It was during this time that Huntley paid a visit to Director Mather's office. That did not go well, and ended with Huntley being tossed out.

Huntley was called for active duty [119], enlisting on October 14, 1918. In his words:

Before I left for the army, I went into the Interior Department and told Mr. Mather that I was going into the army. Mather said, "You can't do that. You have to run the Park." Huntley's reply, "I don't want to open the hotels and run the transportation service if the war continues." Mather said, "If you won't open the businesses, I will find someone else to run the Park." Huntley's reply, "I don't think it would be very practical as all efforts should be on the war." Quite an argument ensured. Finally Huntley said, "It doesn't matter what you say, I am going in the army, and we won't open." Mather responded with, "Well, I can't let you in the Park again."

Mather had little respect for Harry's son, calling him a "whipper-snapper," among other things. Perhaps Huntley had learned of the plans going on between Mather and a Mr. John A. Hill at the Chicago Stockyard Inn.

Letters written between Mather and Hill surfaced later, proving that considerable thought was being given to the details of their scheme to take over the Child concessions in Yellowstone. Starting on October 14, 1918, their plans were being finalized by telegraph. Mather did seize the company, and turned it into a public corporation with himself as the head and John Hill as president.

Secretary Lane sent an urgent message to Albright, calling him to Washington pronto. "I've got a wild man on my hands." Lane wanted Mather out of town and calmed down, lest his illness be discovered and embarrass the entire department. Albright got to Washington on October 31st.

Mather was put back under the care of his doctor, and was sent to a series of rest and spa-type places. By December he was at Hot Springs,

Arkansas. Albright suggested that Child and Mather should talk. Harry went to Hot Springs and enjoyed some rest and relaxation for a few days before he initiated a conversation by thanking Mather for taking those businesses off his hands. "I don't care. Those companies always were a trouble to me. I just hope you do better with them than I did."

This gave Mather the escape he needed, because by now he had realized how much this was going to cost him. He would give the business back to Harry, but he thought Huntley was "unfitted to engage in national park operations." Under threat of losing the hotel contract, Harry agreed to ban his son from the companies in late 1918. Harry got the combined hotel and transportation businesses safely back in his hands, but Huntley Child's altercation with Stephen Mather cost him his leadership role in the park. Relations between father and son were never mended.

After 1918 Huntley would never re-establish a residence in Helena or Yellowstone – a place he'd called home since age 9. His life changed irrevocably over a decision made by two men under impairment – one physically, one psychologically. It was heartening and touching to hear this incident told in Huntley's words, as recorded in an interview later in life. He spoke clearly, thoughtfully, and respectfully of everyone. Huntley said:

> The war was soon over, and of course, the Park did open. Mather told my father and mother that he relented on his decision, and as the war was over, I could go back into the Park. My father had been sick for several years, and was not active in the Park, but he hinted that he was going to write me a letter and say that I could NOT come back into the Park. Since he owned the stock in the companies, I didn't come back.

During his service, Huntley Child was commissioned a captain and served in the ambulance/transportation corps. When the war ended in November 1918, he returned to the Food Administration, and he was discharged April 3, 1919. He later moved to New York City, where Bessie Ferguson and the three children joined him. Emilie and Huntley were never reunited.

W.M. Nichols rejoined the U.S. Army in November 1917, commanding the ordnance depot in Rock Island, Illinois until October

1918. He was then stationed at Camp Sheridan, Montgomery, Alabama, and was discharged December 17, 1918.

Stephen Mather, finding Horace Albright indispensable to his work, requested and was granted a draft deferment for his young secretary.

S.B.M. Young, though retired from active service, did not remain inactive. During the war he promoted what he called "Universal Military Training," and shared the stand with the president – drawing names of young men drafted to serve.

———⟫●⟪———

With the hotels shuttered, and the young men serving their country, the women focused on their causes in Helena. In 1916 Dr. Maria Dean had been asked to represent the state of Montana in Congress. She declined, preferring to focus on her medical practice, her local community, and women's suffrage.

After many years of renting large houses where women were boarded and fed, ground was broken in May 1918 for a new YWCA building. A Helena investor donated land and funds – provided that an equal amount be raised in thirty days. Adelaide Child "was chairman of the Finance Committee during all the early fund-raising years." The donor also required that there be no debt remaining when the building was completed, and "Adelaide Child was the financial rescuer during this challenge ... Her personal contributions offset the deficits many times over, and they amount to the largest made to the YWCA independent."

Adelaide and Maria saw the building completed in February 1919. "The first board members rolled up their sleeves and scrubbed floors and painted woodwork to make a comfortable homey place for the first residents."

Dr. Maria also helped found the Mountain View School for Girls in 1918; she "tirelessly lobbied the Montana legislature to establish a girls' reform school." A dormitory bearing the name *Maria Dean Cottage* was part of the new campus.

In October 1918, Dr. Maria was in Washington, D.C. visiting her sister, Mrs. Annie D. Young, when she became ill. President Wilson offered the use of his private rail car to allow her immediate travel west. Her sister, Adelaide Child met her in Chicago and accompanied her the rest of the way to Montana. Maria died of cancer a few months later in May 1919, at age 61. She was in her beloved Helena in the home of Adelaide and Harry Child. Her older sister Annie Young was also at her side.

In memoriam to her life the *Woman Citizen* quoted about Dr. Dean, "to be a friend of the weak, the poor and the unfortunate; ... to be one whose soul is permanently engaged in the magnificent struggle

> Dean Memorial Clock, on Hawthorne School, 430 Madison Ave, Helena was donated in 1923 by Annie Young in memory of Dr. Maria Dean. It was damaged and removed after an earthquake in 1935.

for the uplift of humanity – ... this is to reach a character high above anything upon the merely material plain." In a time when few women were gaining acceptance in fields dominated by men, Dr. Maria Dean's advice was well-sought, and she served as a respected member of her profession and her community.

⟶►◄⟵

America's attention remained focused on its participation in war during the summers of 1917 and 1918. The hotels remained closed in 1918. Harry Child had to take extensions on his loan payments, but with his financial background and loyal support from the railroads, he was able to weather the storm. With the younger generation at the helm, a successful transition was made from stagecoaches to automobiles, from wranglers to gear jammers.

The camps and lodges were open for business, but they did not fare well. Having been so recently re-organized by Mather, they had not yet built sufficient capital to hang on by more than a thread. Also, that summer the NPS opened its FREE campgrounds, pulling away a sizable amount of otherwise potential business.

After August of 1916, Stephen Mather, as Director of the National Park Service, convinced Congress and the War Department that civilian control of national parks under the National Park Service was the right solution. But with enlisted soldiers needed overseas to help the war effort, the new civilian National Park Service struggled because of lack of funds. The two years of transition brought disagreements over proposed construction, ownership of buildings, and use of personnel. On October 31,1918 the Army left Yellowstone for the last time – Mather's Rangers were finally a reality.

The biggest loser of the era was one of Yellowstone's grande dames – the Fountain Hotel. The speedier automobiles and the strong attractions of the Upper Geyser Basin made the Old Faithful Inn a more desirable destination. As a result of the combination of the automobile's arrival, Stephen Mather's incapacitation, and the intrusion of war, the hotel never opened again.

Today with over four million annual visitors, the idea of more hotel rooms seems appealing. But at the time, the era of the elegant balls and white linen tablecloths was fading, and visitors favored a less formal accommodation. Yellowstone concessioners followed the tide of the times.

Chapter 13:
What's Horace Up to Now?
1919-1920

*Camping Company sold, Albright and Child lock horns,
growing grain on the Flying D, connecting the parks by road*

Under Stephen Mather's "extended monopoly" idea, the multiple small camping companies were all combined into one business, called The Yellowstone Park Camping Company. To act as partners to lead the company, he chose A.W. Miles (from the Wylie Company) and J.D. Powell (from the Shaw and Powell Company.) Both Harry Child and F. Jay Haynes were forced to sell their shares. Conflicts between the old competitors made a rough transition.

Now Horace Albright and Stephen Mather were supporting Howard Hays to buy the Yellowstone Park Hotel Company. Hays was a younger man with experience mostly as a travel agent and some big ideas. However, he had no money to back-up his plans. He was aware that Harry Child was ill, and he, along with a lot of other people, was wondering what would happen to the business in Yellowstone if Harry died. In his desire to buy the YPHC he recruited a couple of friends, and they decided their goal would be to take over, not only Yellowstone – but also the transportation in Glacier and Rocky Mountain parks. The key was to get a foot in Yellowstone first.

For financial backing, Hays went to the very people who had bankrolled Child for all the years of Harry's business career. All but one of these contacts stayed loyal to Harry. After the plans to purchase the hotel company fell through, Walter White [48], of the White Motor Company, did put up some money to purchase the Yellowstone Park Camping Company. So Hays, with White's money, bought the camping company in April 1919, retaining Edward Moorman as his manager. It became the Yellowstone Park Camps Company.

Shortly after Hays' purchase Harry's brother sent him a clipping from the *American Hotels & Purveyors* magazine:

HAYS TO MANAGE YELLOWSTONE

Howard H. Hays, who has been in charge of the Bureau of Parks, United States Railroad Administration, since the railroads were taken over by the Government, has taken charge of all concessions, hotels and lodges in the Yellowstone National Park, according to an announcement made by Stephen T. Mather, Director of Parks, a few days ago at the Clift Hotel.

PATHÉ EXCHANGE, Inc.
BRANCH OFFICE
985 MARKET STREET
SAN FRANCISCO, CALIFORNIA

June 25th, 1919.

Mr. Harry W. Child,
Mammoth Hot Springs.,
Helena, Montana.

My Dear Harry:

The enclosed marked copy is being run in all the hotel papers through-out the country and I would suggest for your own sake that you send out a general letter to each, correcting the impression which it is bound to convey to all hotel men that read it, namely that you are no longer connected with the Park, for remember that your name has been identified with it for so many years and you are so closely known by so many hotel people that they might lose a great amount of interest in boosting for you.

I am merely sending you one paper but it is appearing in all of them.

Sincerely yours,

Eo Child

EOC:L

150

Harry fired off a letter to Stephen Mather:

Yellowstone Park Transportation Company
Yellowstone Park Hotel Company
Office of the President

Yellowstone Park, July 1, 1919.

Personal

My dear Mr. Mather:-

Enclosed is a letter from my brother Ned in San Francisco, which seems to indicate that he is quite worked up over the fact that his oldest brother may lose a few white chips.

I am perfectly willing that Howard should have all the glory there is coming and I am getting too old to care much about the "hot air" part of the game. I used to eat it up twenty-five years ago but found there was no real money in it.

I was a little disturbed, however, along last April, when I had some prominent officials of the Montana State Government with me at Mammoth Hot Springs, and was confronted with the statements made by Yellowstone Park Government employes that I had been fired out of the Park and the hotels and transportation company confiscated by the Interior Department.

I am wondering whether there is any way you can correct the impression contained in the article in this hotel paper. Ordinarily these notices do not last more than fifteen minutes but in hotel papers which are taken by all hotel men throughout the country the Park hotels might suffer a little in not knowing just whom to take up Yellowstone Park Hotel business with.

Yours very truly,

H. W. Child

To
Stephen T. Mather
Department of the Interior
Washington, D. C.

By gaining the Yellowstone Park Camps Company, Howard Hays had firmly placed his foot in the door in Yellowstone, but Harry kept control of the park's hotels and transportation.

———

The year 1919 brought another big change to Yellowstone, Stephen Mather had decided to keep his job as Director of the NPS, and

151

Horace Albright was ready to change from his job as Assistant to Mather. However, Mather still wanted to lean on Albright in some matters. The two men worked out an arrangement whereby Albright would come to Yellowstone as the first NPS superintendent. In the winter months, when Yellowstone was closed, Albright could spend some time in Washington working with Mather. And at the same time Albright would serve as assistant to the director overseeing all the field operations.

Albright assumed the superintendency on July 1st. Along with his appointment came a house and an official car. The Albright family moved into the Commanding Officer's quarters at Fort Yellowstone. Mather gave Albright a personal gift of one thousand dollars so that Mrs. Grace Albright could throw out the army cots and other military furnishings and decorate the house to suit herself and her family.

Albright had absolute power to develop the NPS holdings to his liking under the general policy, the NPS creed, written by himself and Mather. Following the policy that everyone should be able to visit the parks regardless of their personal financial situation, Albright proceeded to redesign park facilities to meet the needs of the new era of the automobile. He established the public auto camps with bathhouses, and built museums where educational programs would be presented.

While Harry kept up a jovial bantering correspondence with Stephen Mather, at the local level, his relationship with the new NPS administration in Yellowstone was a contentious one. Where young Huntley Child had locked horns with NPS director Mather, his father Harry would lock horns with young Horace Albright. Before arriving to assume Yellowstone's superintendency in 1919, Albright already had a good base of knowledge about the park and its services from his 1915 and 1916 visits. At that time he was very complimentary of how Harry ran his Yellowstone concessions and spoke with admiration of his efficiency.

Harry may have experienced his own generational gap with young Albright. Horace, having just worked closely with Mather in establishing the Park Service, bringing new parks and monuments into the agency, establishing a ranger force, and writing both the

Park Service and Ranger codes to live by, may have been just a little bit full of himself. And it could be that Harry was a bit resentful after building and operating his businesses for twenty-four years (working long-distance with the Interior Department in Washington and military superintendents locally), that he now had a young uniformed Park Service Superintendent watching over his every move.

Shortly after Albright's arrival, W.M. Nichols began to find cryptic little notes scribbled on scraps of paper, written in Harry's handwriting. One scrap read, "What is Horace trying to dig up now. I'm not going to answer any of this." signed HWC. Another read, "What is this. How many more things is Horace going to dig up? Wish they would let you run the outfit during the summer as that is job enough. HWC."

—————

At the end of that summer, Albright wrote a scathing "poison pen" letter about Harry Child. He obviously felt his new authority under threat. "He [Harry] wants to operate in Yellowstone Park unhampered and unrestricted," Albright wrote, "He wants a superintendent of the park who will let him do as he pleases ... Child realizes that if some change is not immediately made in the personnel of the Park Service and of Yellowstone Park, he will be brought to a point where he will give service exactly in accordance with the policy of the Park Service. Such service he has not yet given, because we have not been able to make him do it ..." One copy was sent to Mather who advised Albright not to send the letter immediately, but to sit on it. He said you "may want to keep it in your confidential files for the time being ...," but somehow a copy found its way to YPHC files.

—————

Huntley Child, having lost favor with his father and the NPS director, returned to the government position he held before the war. Harry gave a statement to a local newspaper saying his son is now serving his country for one dollar a year as head of the bakers' division of the food administration under Herbert Hoover. Harry was in communication with Huntley, figuring out ways that he and Anceney could help the food shortage situation by turning some Flying D land into grain crop production that was so badly needed both at home and abroad. Huntley, recognizing the partners as leaders in food production in Montana, urged them to "use their success to serve their country."

Harry returned early from his winter in California to confer with Anceney. At first Charlie was hesitant. He had taken such pride in the fact that Flying D beef was fed only on the natural Montana grasses. He did agree to back Huntley and Harry all the way, and they converted a part of their grass land into wheat for human consumption. Harry estimated that with the cooperation of their twenty-five tenant farmers, they would be able to devote between 8,000 and 12,000 acres to growing wheat.

During his service at the Food Administration, Huntley wrote passionate letters to both Harry and Anceney. He spoke of the dire situation facing America and their allies, "France can raise and harvest a wheat crop only twenty-eight percent of normal. Do you know that on the farms in France, there is not a male between the ages of fifteen and fifty-five? Certainly we don't want that condition to come to us."

When asked how he would find workers to produce the large amounts of wheat that could be grown on the 12,000 acres, Harry replied that the Flying D partners "are using automobile trucks for this purpose. ... this will allow us to follow up our Caterpillars with a large number of horses that are used by us and our tenants in hauling for ourselves and them."

Harry met with other ranchers in the Gallatin Valley and convinced them to do their part in the effort, and promised that the Flying D would help them in every way they could.

As 1919 came to a close, Harry visited his son in New York. Two weeks later Huntley Child made one more attempt to return to Yellowstone. In a personal letter to Howard Hays on December 11, 1919, Horace Albright wrote "Huntley Child turned up in my office today, and surprised me by stating that within the next month he could raise enough money in New York to buy out his father's interest in Yellowstone Park, and put both the old man and Nichols out of the park. He stated he was also able to raise an extra half million for improvements. He said he had not seen you [Howard Hays] but wanted to take you in with him. He went up and saw Secretary Lane before he saw me, and he says the Secy. approved his proposal subject to Mr. Mather's attitude. After talking awhile with Huntley, I went in and put it up to Mr. Mather, but he could not see it."

Both Huntley Child, in a later-in-life interview, and Horace Albright, at the time of the second meeting, described the subsequent conversation between Huntley and Stephen Mather. Huntley said, "About a year later, I went to see him and told him I was sorry about what had happened. I didn't ask to go back to the park and didn't say I wanted to." Albright, writing to Howard Hays wrote, "Later, he [Mather] told Huntley that he would not have him back in the park, and refused to do any business with him. Huntley left as sore as a boil."

———

In the spring and summer of 1919, Harry turned his personal attention and his professional clout to the Park-to-Park Highway idea. He felt comfortable putting his companies in his son-in-law's hands for management. W.M. Nichols no longer had Huntley to deal with the financial end of the businesses; however Galusha, Higgins & Galusha Financial Firm of Helena had worked closely with Harry for years. The second generation was just taking hold there, so W.M. had good support.

Harry started his busy summer by driving around a loop of Yellowstone approach roads – Helena to Bozeman, to Livingston, to White Sulphur Springs, and finally to Mammoth Hot Springs. The mission of his "Yellow Car Party" was two-fold – one, to check out the road conditions and two, to contact commercial clubs, chambers of commerce and people to promote the National Park-to-Park Highway plan within the Rocky Mountain area, as well as throughout the western states.

Just slightly over twenty years before Harry had taken the inaugural trip on the NPR's first fast train between Great Falls and Helena. It traveled at thirty-two miles an hour making the trip in only three hours. Reporters now bragged that automobiles were making the same time, "Overland road records between Helena and Bozeman, a distance of 107 miles were smashed today by Harry W. Child's yellow car party on its preliminary park-to-park pathfinding tour when it made the distance in three hours and seven minutes, or better than a mile every two minutes for the entire distance."

Harry and other Helena businessmen invited representatives from the states of Idaho, Utah, California, Washington, Oregon, Wyoming, and Colorado to join them. The National Park-to-Park Highway plan had "the support and help of Secretary of the Interior Franklin K. Lane and the benefit of the publicity plans of the national parks service bureau and the United States railroad administration."

During the summer of 1919 the spectacular **"Geysers to Glaciers Trail"** [46], along the main range of the Rockies, was in full operation. "The Yellowstone, Glacier and Rocky Mountain transportation companies operated passenger cars on scheduled time from Yellowstone to Glacier," for a distance of 384 miles. The trip was easily made by the 12-passenger motor coaches in two days. For a stopping place on the Geyser-to-Glaciers Road, Harry talked the city of Helena into purchasing the Broadwater Hotel. "It seemed almost an impossibility," he wrote to Stephen Mather, "to raise the $100,000 necessary to open the hotel, but it was done in three days, and will be under operation during the Park season this year. [1920]"

In August, a big meeting was held in Glacier Park to promote plans for completing a good road from Glacier to the Canadian border. Horace Albright, Roe Emery of Glacier, and Harry Child along with many others like the president of the Calgary Board of Trade, Secretary Lane, Montana Senator Walsh, and Superintendent of Banff Park, were delegates. All the big guns were out promoting, but it was Harry's big yellow cars that drew attention from the public.

Later in August plans were made for a motor tour from Montana to California in the interest of the Park-to-Park Good Roads movement. On October 9th, "aboard their big yellow automobiles, the party of national park officials" arrived in Hood River Valley, Oregon. "Two Yellowstone Park cars reached Seattle by noon on Sunday, arrived in Klamath Falls last night and left this morning for Mt. Lassen, Sequoia, Yosemite and Grand Canyon." The newspaper reporters were busy all of October and November, following the various car clubs and park-to-park promoters.

Harry was a featured speaker at a number of the meetings along the way. He said, in a speech at Klamath Falls, that he would be interested in establishing an automobile stage line from Yellowstone, via Helena, Missoula, Spokane, Seattle and Tacoma to Mt. Rainer and Crater Lake. "This will not be possible however, until the roads across Idaho and from Davenport to Ellensburg in Washington are improved." Harry went on to say, "Transportation of tourists over most of the way would be practical as the entire trip from Klamath Falls to Helena is a scenic wonderland. The trip over the Columbia River highway is a most beautiful one and one which every automobile owner in the United States should some day take." Harry's friends made another major promotional stop in Grand Canyon National Park, promoting the Park-to-Park efforts.

This great enthusiasm continued into 1920. Harry and his big yellow cars drove many of the scenic by-ways, and he gave colorful speeches: "When your road is marked, it will take the tourists through the greatest scenery in the world," Harry said, "from Grand Canyon to Zion, Yellowstone, Lewis and Clark National Monument, the Butte Mines, the Gate of the Mountains, the Great Falls of the Missouri, Glacier Park, Banff, and Lake Louise." Forty thousand tourists cars traveled the National Parks Highway during the 1919 season.

Chapter 14:
Harry Spreads His Wings
1920-1930

yellow car parties, a home at
Spanish Creek, a devastating fire,
Harry controls it all, deaths in the family

Harry had fun driving his "big yellow cars" around the western states advertising and promoting the Park-to-Park Highway plan. Indicators were that the year 1920 would be even better for business. During the winter spent in California, Harry got even more exciting news. Insulin had been discovered and was proving to be a blessing for diabetics. Although it was not a cure, it did make personal control of the disease possible.

With W.M. Nichols at the helm in Yellowstone, Harry decided to expend his new-found energy in the Gallatin Valley. The Flying D partners had kept working with purchasing agents acquiring land – twenty, forty, one hundred acres at a time as discouraged homesteaders and ranchers decided to sell. By 1920, they owned 84,000 acres and controlled a total of 120,000 acres. The Flying D Ranch had become known as a "cattle empire," and was one of the largest, if not the largest ranch in Montana.

Harry built a new house for himself and his family, located to the west of the old buildings at the Spanish Creek ranch [102]. A long, low, ranch-style house, it contained four bedrooms and a three-car garage. It was considered an "elegant residence for a cattle ranch," but many of the family's eastern visitors thought it "delightfully rustic." On the grounds, Harry included a nine-hole golf course and even raised some polo ponies. The Spanish Creek Ranch house for the summer months and their La Jolla, California home for the winters became Harry and Adelaide's favorite residences through the 1920s.

⸻⸺⸻

Harry's big yellow cars and buses, along with all the private automobiles, brought excitement and a new look to Yellowstone, but also brought the need for new concession services. All those vehicles required a ready supply of gas, oil, and other auto needs. The NPS decided to utilize their tried-and-true concessioners, the YPTC, Hamilton Stores, and George Whittaker (whose stores at Canyon and Mammoth were eventually acquired by Charles Hamilton).

The three joined forces and shared in the efforts to build gas stations in all locations near the camps and lodges. This arrangement became a separate business known simply as *Yellowstone Park Service Stations* (YPSS). YPSS hired their own employees and made separate arrangements for feeding and housing them, and they contracted with their own suppliers. They built attractive gas stations that blended well with other "park-itecture."

Harry turned to Walter White repeatedly with automobile orders to meet the increasing volume of visitors [50]. White Motor Company countered by engineering Yellowstone-specific changes, such as vehicles with longer wheelbases to accommodate more passengers and the elimination of left-side doors which discharged sightseers into traffic. In 1920, Harry purchased twenty-four new vehicles, adding to the original one-hundred acquired in 1917. He purchased twenty vehicles each in the next two years and another sixty in 1924. By the end of that year he added forty-nine 7-passenger touring cars and several Lincolns for VIPs. Until the purchases were complete, the company relied on the problematic solution of hiring cars from outside sources.

Child and White took every opportunity to publicize the big cars and their business association. For Yellowstone's Golden Anniversary (1922), three cars were driven cross-county to announce the new purchases for that year. After Harry and Horace Albright personally toured the Harding Presidential party around Yellowstone, White made sure to publicize it in his in-house magazine. When Harry made the major purchase in 1924, the White Company hosted 600 teachers to a trip around the Cleveland, Ohio area before the cars were shipped to the Park.

The YPTC had been slowly remodeling and enlarging the 1903 garage at Mammoth, originally built for stagecoaches. The decision was made to move the operation to the Gardiner area. The company began construction of two concrete buildings.

Before the move could be made, a disastrous blow hit the YPTC. On March 30, 1925, the garage building at Mammoth caught fire and destroyed the main garage housing the machine shop, blacksmith shop, top shop, carpenter shop, a nearby oil house, storage shed, and general manager's house. Along with all these buildings, the company lost ninety-three vehicles – including some of the one-year-old fleet. Seventy-five vehicles were saved by alert employees. The fire was determined to be accidental.

The season opening day was just weeks away, and the cars and buses were needed. The White Motor Company responded. They put on an extra shift and built ninety cars in fifty-nine days. The last vehicle was delivered to Yellowstone on June 9th. As a final touch to the new Gardiner complex, the otherwise plain cement buildings [52] were decorated only with a prominently positioned YPTC logo – a black bear encircled by stripes of red, white, and blue.

For the transportation managers, Robert Reamer designed three new homes to be built in the immediate area of the new garage buildings. In a land trade with the NPS, he designed an additional house for the district ranger and family.

Gerard Pesman, an early *gear jammer*, described the chalk board used by the dispatchers at each location around the Park to keep the drivers and the buses on their rigid schedules. When it was nearing departure time, "we would be called, and it was the same signal the park over – three blasts on the whistle. No matter where you were, brother, you high-tailed it and showed up. You might be in the bunkhouse, you might be someplace watching Old Faithful from near enough so you could hear. The dispatcher would write the dispatch on a board. The board was divided up – Old Faithful to West Yellowstone, Old Faithful to Lake, Old Faithful to Jackson Hole, all those schedules. ... at the proper time, he would say, 'okay, go.' ... he would check you off his list as you departed.. You went out according to routine. If you came in after such-and-such a bus, you went out after that [same] bus ... So you stayed in that routine. That way they could dispatch the buses at the proper time, and so on." The cars and buses traveled in a parade just as the stagecoaches had done earlier with just enough space between for a private car to pull in.

Albright praised the system saying, "Carefully prepared schedules made it possible to tell the whereabouts of any car or bus with reasonable accuracy at any time."

A driver enjoyed the same preferential treatment that the wranglers of the stagecoach era had received. In 1923, Gary Cooper, a rangy young man from Butte, Montana came to Yellowstone to be a *gear jammer*. After his second summer of entertaining dudes with his natural western drawl and dry humor, he decided to try his luck in Hollywood. His first movie was made in 1925. Titled *The Thundering Herd*, it was partially filmed in Yellowstone. Experiences gained from working a few summers in Yellowstone have boosted many youth into successful careers – not all their names are celebrated as much as Gary Cooper's.

———➤●◄———

Another employee of note was Miss Beulah Brown, a multi-talented young lady who was not the usual summer "savage," fresh out of high school or first-year of college. Beulah had graduated with a Bachelor of Philosophy. She had inherited from her minister father, a clear, well-modulated voice of ringing quality. She came west for her health, and found employment teaching high school students dramatic speaking and elocution.

In the summer months, she came to Yellowstone starting in 1915, and spent a total of eleven seasons in the Park. Beyond her regular job as a guide for the Yellowstone Park Camps Company, she wrote, choreographed, and presented evening entertainment for the guests. She recruited fellow "savages" with various talents such as singing, dancing, playing a musical instrument, or story-telling. For Yellowstone's golden anniversary, Beulah wrote and directed a series of skits presented in drama, song, and creative dance on stage at the new lodges. A different episode of Yellowstone history was presented at each location.

Beulah also revived the group singing of campfire songs, but with lyrics written especially for Yellowstone, and sung to familiar tunes such as *My Darling Clementine* or very often popular college fight songs. The following song is not necessarily one of Beulah's, but still a favorite:

> *Rotten-logging, rotten-logging,*
> *That's what we do each night;*
> *Strolling along under Yellowstone skies*
> *Whispering secrets and making up lies.*
> *They may all say, to hug and kiss is a crime,*
> *But as soon as it's dark in Yellowstone Park*
> *It's rotten-logging time.*

"Singing out the dudes" became a tradition at the lodges in which employees assembled on the front porches at departure time to share some of these clever selections. Beulah published several versions of a small booklet titled *Songs of the Yellowstone Camps*.

To satisfy her adventurous spirit, Beulah stayed through the winter of 1923. A "winter keeper" was employed in the off-season to look after Old Faithful Inn and keep the snow shoveled off the roof. That winter a family of five were doing the winter keeper chores. Beulah agreed to stay with the family and tutor the three children. In turn, they taught her to travel on skis and snow shoes. She also learned about growing fresh vegetables in the greenhouse built over a stream of hot geyser water. This same water was piped into their house, providing the comfort of steam heat. Beulah wrote a booklet about her experiences, *My Winter in Geyserland*, and sold it the next summer in Hamilton Stores. With those proceeds, she was able to travel through Europe.

Beulah proved her self capable and reliable and soon became a manager for the company, serving at Canyon, Mammoth, and Old Faithful Camps. After her summer in Europe, she began managing the new Furnace Creek Inn at Death Valley. Many of her Yellowstone staff followed her in the winters, returning to Yellowstone in the summers.

Beulah went on to become an officer in the National Park Concession, Inc., a group put together by government officials to run concessions in smaller areas, and in some cases, new national parks and monuments including the Blue Ridge Mountains, Mammoth Cave, Isle Royale, Olympic and Big Bend. She and her husband held positions in this company until they retired.

⎯⎯►◄⎯⎯

The Yellowstone fleet began serving two new railroad destinations. In Moran, Wyoming [current GTNP north entrance station] the buses met the Lander-Yellowstone Transportation Company, bringing tourists from the trains of the Chicago Northwestern Railroad in Lander, Wyoming. Passengers were transported by the YPTC to Lake Hotel where they could join the in-park tours.

Harry, with his Gallatin Valley connections, convinced the Chicago, Milwaukee, St. Paul & Pacific to build the elegant Gallatin Gateway Inn in the hamlet of Salesville. The Spanish-style hotel served as a YPTC pick-up point beginning in August 1926. Salesville then changed its name to Gallatin Gateway, and the post office changed its postmark.

In Cody, the pick-up point of the Chicago, Burlington, and Quincy Railroad was also improved with the construction of the Burlington Inn in 1924. The Yellowstone buses now served five railheads as well as its in-park tours leaving from the hotels and lodges.

With the expansion of railroad service and the motorized fleet, the hotels were also increased in size. W.M. Nichols was now dealing directly with Robert Reamer and a Montana firm, Link & Haire, on these additions. But a new voice had to be heard – the landscape architecture division of the NPS.

At Lake Hotel, Reamer added one hundred rooms by extending the building to the east. Link & Haire took on the smaller job of expanding the dining room and creating a Presidential Suite above it. Not built to attract national leaders, the "president" was Harry and Adelaide who occupied the rooms on their visits around the park. Their granddaughters recalled that, as children, their families were assigned rooms on the *opposite end* of the three-hundred-foot-long structure.

One U.S. president, Calvin Coolidge with wife and son, did occupy the suite during their visit in 1927. Their escort Horace Albright recounted the story that one evening, Coolidge informed him that he had made a decision. Albright hoped it might concern the protection of the Teton area, but Coolidge instead exclaimed that he decided to stay another day and go fishing.

At Canyon Hotel "The melody of an old-time waltz proved too alluring for Mrs. Coolidge Friday night and she accepted an invitation from her son John to dance. While the orchestra in the lounge room ... was playing the barcarole from 'Tales of Hoffman,' she and John stepped on to the dance floor almost unnoticed by the other dancers. They danced encores to the strains of 'My Hero' and 'My Gypsy Sweetheart.' As the orchestra played another waltz they left the floor, but Mrs. Coolidge then accepted the invitation of her host, W.M. Nichols, general manger of the hotel, to complete the dance; John also danced with Adelaide, daughter of Mrs. Nichols."

Four railroads made a joint loan to the YPHC to add 150 more rooms to the Old Faithful Inn. But the NPS landscape architects did not like Reamer's roof design. Because the new west wing was prominently visible from the main road, which then went through the geyser basin past Morning Glory Pool and Old Faithful Geyser, they demanded he continue the A-frame lines of the original building's roof. In a telegram to Harry Child, Reamer argued, "As I designed the old building and wasn't shot for it, I, according to the code of ethics, feel I should be trusted to finish the designing." Reamer won the argument in the end, and the west wing was built with a flat roof matching the east wing, which had been added in 1913.

Canyon Hotel also received ninety-six new rooms in 1930. The only hotel that saw no attention during these prosperous years was the Fountain Hotel. Fountain had never re-opened after Mather closed it in 1917. Five years later, expensive elements like windows, doors, and stair rails were salvaged to serve a new dorm at Old Faithful Inn. "When NPS director Mather visited Yellowstone in 1925, shortly after a well-publicized excursion to Glacier National Park, where he dynamited a troublesome sawmill, Child, never one for sentiment, suggested that 'if he has any sticks of dynamite left, he may slip them under the Fountain Hotel.'" The shell of the Fountain Hotel was razed in 1927.

———>•<———

The Yellowstone Park Camps Company grew by leaps and bounds, under the ownership of Howard Hays, and the efficient management of Edward Moorman. They built "recreation halls" at the established locations – Lake, Roosevelt, Old Faithful, Mammoth, and Fishing Bridge. In some cases, earlier buildings were enclosed into the new – creating larger, more attractive buildings that were called "lodges." New tourist areas were developed as Sylvan Pass Lodge rose at East Entrance, and the Thumb Lodge at Yellowstone Lake's west shore. Where the camping company went, they were followed by a General Store, a YPSS gas station, and a Haynes Photo Shop – now operated by F. Jay Haynes' son Jack.

To serve the new NPS public auto camp patrons, Hays and Moorman opened delicatessen tents at Old Faithful and Fishing Bridge. These were "very popular and greatly appreciated." With the rail passengers patronizing hotels and lodges, the auto travelers had the choice of lodges, free NPS auto camps, or "housekeeping cabins," also called tourist cabins. The cabins, though located near the Lodges, had a separate registration building.

After about five years, the YPCC was offered for sale. Howard Hays was ready to move on to greener pastures. Harry, W.M., and a new partner, Vernon Goodwin, bought the company, and changed the name to Yellowstone Park Lodges and Camps Company. Goodwin brought along plenty of prestige and expertise, being a past president of the California Hotel Association, and managing director of the Alexandria Hotel Company in Los Angeles. He was made Manager of the new company, and W.M. Nichols was President. Harry's Helena banker acted as secretary and treasurer of the company. Though Harry was not actively managing the daily affairs, he now had "more pies than fingers." From this point forward, he controlled the Yellowstone Park Hotel Company, Yellowstone Park Transportation Company, Yellowstone Park Boat Company, and Yellowstone Park Lodges and Camps Company.

———>•<———

The Child and Anceney partnership agreement had worked well. Charlie, forever a rancher, continued to build on their land holdings in the Spanish Creek area and was building a true western cow camp. "A cow camp is a place for the branding of steers, gentling of horses accustomed to winter freedom [on the open range], rounding up and sorting of cattle, and accomplishing all those chores central to the smooth running of a large cattle ranch."

The Flying D Cow Camp consisted of the bunkhouse, the lodge, the cookhouse, the blacksmith shop, and the ice house with the creek running under it. Five to eight cowboys and the foreman lived at the Cow Camp. The cook occupied her quarters attached to the cookhouse. She was revered by the cowboys, not only for the good food she presented at meal time, but for her congeniality. " ... when she wasn't milking the cow, churning butter, setting out dough to rise or seeing to her chickens, [Cow Camp Mary] crocheted." Her way to the cowboys' hearts was through her pies and cakes, and especially her doughnuts. In the fall at haying time, Mary fed as many as thirty-five men. She was part of the Flying D Ranch for twenty-one years. By some of the younger cowboys, the Flying D was referred to as "the company."

Long ago, Harry Child and Charlie Anceney had sealed their partnership with a handshake. After nineteen years, they decided to officially become incorporated. Their venture became the Flying D Ranges, Inc., in 1929. The Cherry Creek Land Association turned their land holdings back to the Flying D Ranges, but held stock in the amount of 188.90 shares. Child held 811.10 shares. Anceney through the years had opted to work on salary. Child was named president of the Flying D Ranges, Inc. Anceney and Charles Perkins, of the Cherry Creek people, were named vice-presidents. W.M. Nichols became secretary and treasurer. Anceney was named manager, and Frank Stone, manager of the Salesville Bank, now became Anceney's bookkeeper and assistant manager of the ranch.

When journalist B.C. Forbes was seeking subjects for his essay collection, *Men Who Are Making the West*, both Harry Child and Charlie Anceney caught his attention. Admiring their "... agriculture empire of more than a half-a-million acres," he found Charlie to be a "real ranchman." Forbes wrote, "Yet he is as modest, as industrious, as constantly on the job in working togs as in the days [of old] ..." The Flying D now officially registered their brand – a slightly modified version of one that had been in use since 1911.

———»•«———

In the twenties Adelaide turned her attentions to family and community. When General Young's tour of duty at the Soldier's Home in Washington D.C. was completed, he and his wife Annie, heeded the call of the West and retired to Helena. They purchased a home at 706 Harrison Avenue [28]. Annie made their home a showplace and again became active in women's organizations and Episcopal Church functions. Her reputation as a hostess was well-known.

General Young died at their home in Helena on September 1, 1924. Annie continued to live there for fourteen more years until her death, spending most winters in La Jolla, California. Ellen and W.M. Nichols lived in the home across the street. Harry and Adelaide purchased a home on Stuart Street just a few blocks away. The family held on to Oro Fino Terrace until 1930.

Mother, Ellen Watson Dean, returned to Helena and lived out the rest of her days near her two surviving daughters. She was active in the Unitarian Church, serving as president of the Women's Alliance for many years. Ellen died in February 1924 and the following tribute was published, "For the last 20 years she was one of Helena's most beloved and respected citizens interested in every progressive work and for all that was noble and good in the community life."

A plaque on the Grandstreet Theatre, Helena reads "The First Unitarian Society of Helena gave this building to the city for a public library in memory of ELLEN M DEAN and the early members to whose efforts the structure is due MCMXXXIII"

Adelaide had the honor of hosting one U.S. president in her Mammoth Hot Springs home. After touring the Black Hills in South Dakota, President and Mrs. Calvin Coolidge and their son John, extended their holiday to include a five-night visit to Yellowstone National Park. The day of their arrival, August 22, 1927, was the planned execution date of convicted robber/murders Nicola Sacco and Bartolomeo Vanzetti. The verdict drew much controversy because the evidence against them was largely circumstantial, and they maintained their innocence. They were acknowledged anarchists and Italian immigrants, so national attention was focused on the case.

Fearing the possible interference by protestors, the Secret Service imposed extra security precautions, and monitored gate arrivals for several days prior to the President's visit. After the Coolidges arrived at Mammoth, they were whisked off to the seclusion of the Roosevelt area for the day, while the family's traveling gear was transferred into the Child House.

The President and First Lady slept undisturbed in Harry and Adelaide's home that night while Secret Service staff patrolled the grounds. The execution in Boston proceeded without incident, as did the First Family's Yellowstone visit.

Following the visit Adelaide received a handwritten note:

My dear Mrs. Child: We have spent a quiet, happy evening beneath your wide-spreading, friendly roof. - We have warmed ourselves at your fire-side, tended by your faithful Bessie, we have played your records and made ourselves generally at home. We are grateful to you and want you to know that we deeply appreciate your generous hospitality – Many times during the year ahead I shall recall this peaceful scene. – With our thanks and friendly good wishes. Sincerely, Grace Coolidge.

———➤◆◄———

Stephen Mather continued as director of the National Park Service until 1928. Late that year, he suffered a stroke. After fourteen years of successful but exhausting campaigning to establish the NPS, he named Horace Albright to succeed him as Director.

After six months in the hospital, Mather continued to see improvement in the use of his affected leg, arm, and fingers. It appeared he was returning to his normal self, but on January 22, 1930 he died unexpectedly.

Mather's right-hand man, Horace Albright, served as Yellowstone's first superintendent under the NPS from 1919 to 1929. His leadership saw greater focus on providing education at museums and outdoor amphitheaters and on increasing visitation.

[95] Taking the President to Old Faithful, April 1903. (L. to R) Freighter Joe DeBarr, TR, John Burroughs, and Harry Child. (courtesy Harry W. Child II)

[94] Major Pitcher, John Burroughs, President Roosevelt, his secretary William Loeb Jr., and Harry Child at Mammoth Hot Springs, 1903. (L to R) (LC-USZ62-35722)

[96] "Harry can handle a Rainbow better than any man I ever saw," wrote B.C. Forbes, "in the stream or on a plate." (L. to R) Harry, Capt. Geo. Anderson, unknown. (courtesy Harry W. Child II)

"Teddy" Roosevelt's visit at Helena, April 12, 1911

[97] In 1911 when Roosevelt (seated in car closest to camera) visited Helena, Harry (wearing the white hat to TR's right) was again on hand to act as chauffeur. C.E. Hedges photo. (MHS 944-646)

Flying D Ranch,
Gallatin & Madison Counties, Montana

[98] It's easy to see why Harry was attracted to the beauty of the land of the Flying D ranch. View of the Spanish Peaks from the Flying D Ranch. F. Bertil Linfield photo. (MOR 84.73.100)

[99] Anceney Station at the Flying D Ranch Lands in Gallatin Valley, Montana. Note the stock corrals in the center and the grain silo – both were commodities sold by the Child-Anceney partnership. (GHM P1149N)

[101] The partners used three brands on the Flying D lands. Images recreated by Becky Sheehan from Livestock Brand Registrations for Montana. (digital collection, pp. 2442, 5788)

[100] Charlie Anceney (left) and Harry Child with their first prize bull, Ringmaster, the only three-time Grand Champion at the Chicago International, winning high honors in 1910, 1911, and 1913. (GHM P1700N)

[102] A favorite family retreat – the Ranch House at Spanish Creek, Artist's rendering. J.E. Haynes photo. (MHS H-21248)

[103] Cattle sale at the Flying D. Current ranch owner Ted Turner runs bison on the land. In celebration of the ranch's history, one can order "Karen's Flying D chili" off the menu at Ted's Montana Grill, in nearby Bozeman, MT. (MHS PAc 2003-12.6)

[104, 105] Lee Martin, a real cowboy, shown during the spring horse roundup, 1967. (Nan Sigrist photos)

Green Meadow Farm, Helena, Montana

[106] Artist's rendering, Green Meadow Farm, Robert Reamer, architect – developed beginning in 1914. (MHS Farms and Farming Collection)

[107] The Green Meadow barn, a famous landmark at the farm north of Helena, was lost to fire in 1956. (MHS PAc 89-70)

[108] A few buildings remain at the Green Meadow Farm, this bunkhouse, the granary, and the blacksmith shop. (RQ photo)

[109] Charles A. Hamilton (1884-1957) started his general store empire by purchasing one store at Old Faithful with a loan from Harry Child. (YELL 31187)

[110] Ham in the Million Dollar Room at Old Faithful lower store. J.E. Haynes photo. (MHS H-58515)

[111] As young men, photographer Jack E. Haynes (1884-1962) and Ham joked around with Huntley Child. (BSC-MSU 116, coll 1507)

[112] Howard Hays (1883-1969) worked for W.W. Wylie, and later owned the camping company before ultimately selling to Harry Child. J.E. Haynes photo. (MHS H-21269)

Business Associates

[114] Stephen T. Mather (1867-1930), father of the National Park Service. (YELL 03036)

[113] Horace Albright (1890-1987), first Yellowstone superintendent under the new NPS, 1919-1929. (YELL 13699)

The second generation

[115] Daughter Ellen Dean Child Nichols (1884-1966) with NPS Director Conrad Wirth (L) and YPC Exec. VP and Gen. Mgr. Geoge Beall (R). (YELL 114050)

[116] Son-in-law William Morse Nichols (1881-1957). (courtesy Harry W. Child II)

[117] (L to R) Robert C. Reamer, Huntley Child, E.M. Newman, Emerson Hough, Howard Hays, I.L. Peil, Charles d'Emery, and J.E. Haynes scouting opportunities in the Teton area, 1917. (MHS H-17213)

[118] Son Huntley Child (1886-1978) holding his firstborn, daughter Marion (born 1914). (YELL 22953)

[119] Huntley Child joined the efforts during World War I. (courtesy Harry W. Child II)

The third generation

[120] Harry with his six grandchildren. Ellen & W.M. Nichols and Emilie & Huntley Child had three children each. (YELL 133567)

[121] Bessie on horseback with Huntley Jr. (YELL 133671)

[122] Huntley Jr., Adelaide "Jackie" Dean Nichols (1909-1998), and Wilbour "Johnnie" Quintard Nichols (1911-1980) at Roosevelt Arch. (YELL133602)

[123] Speedboat Adelaide on Yellowstone Lake, 1922. W.M. later named two vessels, Adelaide II and Marion, after granddaughters. (YELL 1335577)

ROCKY MOUNTAIN HOTEL ASSOCIATION

Affiliated with
THE AMERICAN HOTEL ASSOCIATION

[124] Rocky Mountain Hotel Association stationary. (Adeline Moulton collection, courtesy Addie Wickham)

[125] Bessie Ferguson and Huntley Child Jr. (1911-1993). Bessie began working for the family when the grandchildren were small and cared for Harry and Adelaide in their later years. (courtesy Harry W. Child II)

[126] Huntley Child Jr. (3rd from the left) brought company executives to Old Faithful to personally award a cash prize to Chef Walley Hendrickson who won the baseball pool in 1955. Bruce Sigrist is standing upper right. (Nan Sigrist photo.)

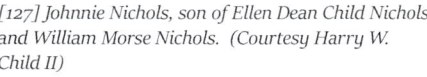

[127] Johnnie Nichols, son of Ellen Dean Child Nichols and William Morse Nichols. (Courtesy Harry W. Child II)

W. M. NICHOLS, President

VERNON GOODWIN, Vice-President

Yellowstone Park Company

HOTELS   LODGES   CABINS   CAFETERIAS
TRANSPORTATION   BOATS

Helena, Montana

4 3

Chapter 15: Riding into the Sunset
1931 – 1938

friends applaud Harry's life,
death of Anceney and cattle sale at the Flying D,
combining of all Yellowstone businesses

"Harry Child entered the Park via the west gate on August 18, and left for his ranch near Bozeman on August 21st," noted the Superintendent's Report for 1930. This may have been Harry's last visit to the Park. In his later years his favorite place to live was the Ranch House at Spanish Creek.

On February 4, 1931 Harry died at his home in La Jolla, California. He was seventy-four years old. For fifty of those years he had dedicated himself to building tourists' accommodations in Yellowstone Park that would serve and be loved by generations to come. He saw rough times – wars, train strikes, and other national and personal calamities. Harry kept a level head and found a way to survive. The coming of the Park Service was a contentious time, but he adapted because he believed in the NPS purpose, especially a strong set of rules for the sake of the continuity – for all the parks then in existence and the ones to come in the future.

Harry did not just work – he took time for recreation with friends and family. During his early years in Helena and Great Falls he was keenly interested in horse racing. He invested in fast racing horses, liked owning champions, and enjoyed receiving accolades of his competitors in the social celebrations around the track. He shared his love of the outdoors by entertaining business associates and friends on camping and fishing trips. "He had a passion for running water; a nose for trout and grayling; a sort of sixth sense that enabled him to drop a fly in the right place."

He turned his hobbies into businesses at the Green Meadow Farm and the Flying D Ranch. He in turn used their by-products to supply his hotels and camps in Yellowstone. Historic structures he envisioned and saw completed grace these ranch properties today.

Despite their clashes when the NPS was new, former Superintendent Horace Albright remembered Harry as "an efficient and successful business man, a great sportsman, a wonderful story teller, a royal entertainer and a steadfast friend, he was in a class by himself."

Upon his death, many accolades honoring Harry appeared in print locally and around the country.

Acknowledging his role as a supporter of civic causes, "Harry Child had as much to do with promoting an intimate knowledge of the Northwest as did any other citizen. He worked quietly and without asking for any credit for many wonderful programs accomplished through his effort to bring the Northwest to the attention of the East." Through his partnership with western railroads, the tourist tide was turned away from Europe "toward Montana's two national parks and other scenic features of the west."

Others wrote of his pleasure in giving, without having his name on it – not just in large civic things, but even more individual causes. He was "unaustentatious in his benefactions and his public-spirited undertakings, only those who happened to be present at such times as he freely gave of his wealth would have any way of knowing that he bestowed upon those public works in which he was deeply interested, his moral as well as his financial support. Many, many times he has been host to groups of young people on visits within the park. At the time the high school band from Helena was making a tour to Denver and return, that wonderful aggregation of musicians were his personal guests in the park, and in addition to this generous hospitality he added several hundreds of dollars to their fund to make possible their trip going and coming from Denver."

Writer and sportsman Robert Davis called Harry "the noblest host in the world." "It is doubtful if any living man has entertained so many presidents and distinguished captains of industry. The list of those that have written their names in his guest book would, without a doubt, fill volumes. Among this number are Presidents Roosevelt, Taft, Harding and Coolidge, the Crown Prince and Crown Princess of Sweden, A. Barton Hepburn, president of the Chase National Bank, New York, Sam Blythe, Robert H. Davis, William Loeb, Jr., Carmi Thompson, Nicholas Longworth, Uncle Joe Canon, Irving Cobb, Howard Elliott, Charles Perkins, and literally scores of others."

Harry played host to Sweden's Crown Prince Gustaf Adolf and Crown Princess Louise as they toured Yellowstone in July of 1926. They bestowed upon him the *Cross of the Royal Order of Vasa.*

And finally, summarizing his business successes: "The name of H.W. Child has been closely associated with pioneer history in this section of Montana. Not only was he one of the principal factors in the making of Yellowstone National Park a playground where the comforts of the best hostelries of the nation could be obtained, but in stock raising pursuits and the development of the Treasure state. In every way he was a leader and a devoted booster."

A more humorous characterization came from his friend, Jack Haynes, who quipped, "If Harry Child died and appeared at the Pearly Gates, and St. Peter suggested they flip a coin to see if he would enter Heaven or Hell, Harry would have agreed. Then he would have caught the coin in mid-air and run away with it."

This beautiful tribute was written by a recent historian:

Early in 1931, before the Summer Savages arrived to open the park for another year, before Yellowstone awakened yet again to greet the hordes of raucous vacationers, Harry Child died at his home in La Jolla, California. For seventy-four years he had lived at a breakneck pace. His legacy would endure for decades, both in the businesses he built and in the legend that grew up around his memory. A dedicated Republican in a Republican age, he had been a friend to Presidents Roosevelt, Harding, Coolidge, and Hoover, entertaining each at one time or another on visits to Yellowstone. In fact, some say that Harry Child first interested Roosevelt in big-game hunting. He always accommodated important visitors ... His business associates, who numbered in the dozens across the West, and his competitors as well – men such as Howard Hays and Jack Haynes – considered him a close personal friend, a man they respected for his character as much as for his success. His companies would endure, less prosperous at times, without his dynamic leadership, but unchanged to most tourists. In fact, few were probably ever aware that their host in Yellowstone – "the noblest host in the world," according to one friend – one of the truly visionary park architects, was gone.

———>●◄———

On February 23, 1936 Charles Anceney died of internal injuries received in a car accident caused by icy roads. He was seventy-four years old. Frank Stone, Charlie's bookkeeper and banker, took over as manager of the Flying D ranch. W.M. Nichols had assumed control of the Child family affairs, but he was "not a cattle man," so he did not interfere with the management of the ranch.

Child and Anceney had had lots of fun with their Shorthorn breeding program and enjoyed winning at the stock shows. Harry had used proceeds from the YPTC to finance their hobby. Frank Stone had realized that the Flying D could not financially support the expensive Pure Bred Shorthorn herd. He along with Adelaide, W.M. Nichols, and Charles Perkins, (representative of the Cherry Creek Land people), decided the shorthorns, and eventually the ranch, would have to be sold.

Some of the animals were moved around the state and put on display to advertise the sale, along with a very handsomely printed catalog containing pictures of the animals with very long pedigrees. The slogan was, "Child and Anceney's – The Best is None Too Good."

On September 28, 1936 the sale of the shorthorns was most successful. Many agents representing wealthy people approached the owners about purchasing the ranch itself, but no firm offer was forthcoming.

———>●◄———

After Harry's death, W.M. changed the way business was conducted in Yellowstone. Some of the management staff loyal to Harry for many years drifted away.

The Yellowstone concessioners weathered some rough times during the Great Depression. A new Secretary of Interior appointed in 1933 opposed private development within parks – further threatening the company's presence. In what seems a defensive move, W.M. Nichols consolidated the company holdings. The Yellowstone Park Company (YPC), formed in 1936, merged the Yellowstone Park Hotel Company (YPHC), the Yellowstone Park Transportation Company (YPTC), the Yellowstone Park Lodges & Camps Company (YPLCC), and the Yellowstone Park Boat Company. W.M. Nichols served as President, Vernon Goodwin, as Vice President. W.M. and Ellen's son John Q. Nichols [127], age 25, was named Secretary. The Galusha Firm continued to monitor the financial details.

Within the YPC, W.M. Nichols appointed officers for each aspect of the operations – Hotels, Lodges, and Transportation. Other functions fell to Division heads – such as general operations manager, reservations manager, personnel manager, food & beverage manager, and engineering & construction superintendent. That year, the National Park Service granted the Yellowstone Park Company a 20-year contract.

Huntley Child Jr. [125], son of Huntley and Emilie Child, graduated from MIT in 1934 – studying mechanical and electrical engineering. He began working for the Murray Corporation in Detroit, Michigan. He started designing machinery for the auto manufacturer, and soon he became a plant layout and production engineer.

Late in 1937 he wrote to W.M. and Adelaide asking if he could go to work in family business in the park. After spending a summer with his mother in Joplin, MO, his young family arrived in Helena in the fall of 1938 to work in the company offices there.

Huntley Jr. moved to the Murray Hotel in Livingston early in 1939 to become Ed Moorman's assistant in the Lodges and Camps Division. He stayed in Livingston during the week, but returned to his family in

Helena on weekends. When the operations moved to the park in the summer, there was no house available at Mammoth. He, his wife, three-year-old daughter Jane, and two-month-old son, Harry II, moved into the former mail carrier's cabin [59]. They had electricity, but cooked on a wood stove, and heated water on the stove. When Huntley Jr.'s sister visited that summer, she coined the phrase "love in the rough."

By the next summer, they moved into a three bedroom house near the Mammoth Lodge. The family spent two summers there, returning to Helena during the winters where Huntley Jr. worked in the company accounting offices.

In the 1930s, more new vehicles were purchased for the Park. Bus enthusiasts Bruce Austin, Robert Goss, and Gerard Pesman give a wonderful description of a joint effort between several parks:

"In December, 1935, transportation managers and representatives from Yellowstone, Glacier, Grand Canyon and Yosemite National Parks met to evaluate chassis for a proposed standard National Park Tour bus, and to draft specifications for a standard body which could be modified to meet the needs of all four Parks. The tests were made at Yosemite ... [White Motors, General Motors, Reo, Ford Motor Company all participated] ... They all did their stuff, and after completion of the test, the verdict was that while none of the vehicles met all the requirements of the prospective users, the White 706 with a longer wheelbase would come the closest. ... As a result of the Yosemite trials, Yellowstone ordered 27 White model 706 buses to be delivered for the 1936 season. There were 98 by 1939, the largest number of these 'Park Buses' operated anywhere."

Visitors today see the White Model 706 Tour Bus driven by "Jammers" in Glacier National Park and Yellowstone. The bus's designer, Count Alexis Wladimirovich de Sakhnoffsky, was smuggled from Russia just before the Communist Revolution. Emigrating to the United States in 1928, he found success in designing stream-lined motorcars, trains, trucks, furniture, etc. When one of these unique vehicles is parked in front of Old Faithful Inn, crowds gather with cameras to pose with these national park icons. According to one current Yellowstone driver, "Any day I drive one, I'm a rock star."

Joe Mitchell, a driver between 1947 and 1995, remembered Mrs. Nichols as a very particular woman. The bus drivers, now with 1936, 1937 and 1938 buses, ended their day at the Gardiner garage. The main road went in front of the Prairie-style house where the Nichols now lived. If a driver happened by, missing their hat or having rolled up their sleeves against the heat of the summer day, by the time they reached Gardiner, Ellen had already reported the infraction to the dispatcher.

———————

Harry entered Yellowstone as one-third owner of the transportation company. Through time he assumed full ownership of the transportation company and the hotel company. Eventually he acquired the lodges and camps and the boat companies as well. Before his death, the second and third generations were in charge. But Harry's was the driving force that inspired hard work and company loyalty.

When B.C. Forbes asked about his secret, Harry replied, "'Wizardry? Shucks! Whatever I know has come from trying to keep my eyes wide open and all my faculties tuned up to concert pitch. I have always acted on the motto that, to get up in the world, a man must get up in the morning. Then, when you get up, get busy. Observe as well as work. By constantly keeping your eyes wide open, in time you learn to see things that the other fellow doesn't.'

'From what I am told, you keep something else besides your eyes open – your heart and your pocket,' Forbes remarked.

Harry shot back, 'The man who doesn't ... is a fool.'"

Four generations of the Child/Nichols family. Adelaide is seated, front row holding a toddler.

Chapter 16: Grandmother Child, Anchor of the Family
1937 – 1949

*finishing touches for Old Faithful Inn and Mammoth Hotel,
Adelaide's final visit to Yellowstone, sale of Green Meadow Farm,
her death and gifts to the community*

After Harry died, Adelaide [8] moved her Yellowstone residence from the larger Prairie-style house into the smaller cottage next door. She started using a guest book, a leather-bound volume with an image of the cottage (the former Wakefield home) tooled on the cover. On the reverse are her initials ACD. Inside she inscribed "My Summer Guests 1932."

Robert Reamer, thirty years a friend of the family and recently widowed himself, brought his 21-year-old daughter to visit in 1934. Jane's entry in the guest book shows her affection for Adelaide, "'Grandma' Child has found a new brat." Two-and-a-half years later Jane entered, "My first visit to La Jolla and what a delightful one! If it weren't for a round trip ticket, 'Grandma' Child would have a permanent 'brat' in her house."

The fall after his 1934 visit, Reamer sent his first sketches to W.M. Nichols for what would be his final project for Yellowstone – a rebuild of the aging Mammoth Hotel. They replaced the remains of the National Hotel (1883-1885), too deteriorated to be saved, with three smaller service buildings. Hotel rooms were replaced with cottages, and Reamer's 1913-1914 wing of guest rooms would remain standing – incorporated into the new vision [65]. Although W.M. was making the business decisions and supervising the company checkbook, Adelaide was again called to "work her magic" on the interiors.

The new Mammoth hostelry would have a central registration desk for both hotel guests and cottage guests. Although the era of grand balls and elegant teas had largely passed, a spacious lounge was included in the plans. At Adelaide's suggestion, the building was designed "to prevent the cabin people from going into the lounge room" [66] – a few class distinctions remained.

Grandmother Child (Adelaide) and Robert Reamer worked together on a project for the Mammoth Hotel lounge – a large map of the United States. The finished full-size map (ten-feet tall and seventeen-feet wide) was completed in Seattle, and sent by rail to Yellowstone in six panels, divided along longitudinal lines. It highlighted early coast-to-coast highways like the Lincoln Highway and the Yellowstone Trail, and the major railroads, including the five that serviced Yellowstone. Inlaid wood of fifteen varieties from nine nations created state and national boundaries [67].

During the planning stage, craftsmen in Reamer's Seattle office created a small scale sample of ideas they had discussed. Sending it to Mrs. Child with his ideas of what they liked and did not like, Reamer joked, "When you are through with the map possibly Bessie can start a fire with it or your chauffeur would like to carry it on his seat so he could find La Jolla without inquiring."

Unrecognized by visitors who enjoy this delightful piece of artwork today, are locations related to the family that W.M. requested be included – Gallatin Gateway and Anceney, besides Helena and Butte, ... "Of course, La Jolla and San Mateo and Burlingame." Although W.M. also suggested Reamer add his own family locales, he did not.

Before the Mammoth Hotel and Cottages renovations were completed, Reamer died in his Seattle home (January 1938), leaving partners in his office to complete the Yellowstone work.

———————

At the same time Adelaide and Reamer were planning on the map for Mammoth, Old Faithful Inn was receiving the architect's final addition. Prohibition had ended, and evening cocktails along with entertainment were in great demand. Robert Reamer worked with a popular artist to create the decor of the new lounge – called *The Bear Pit* [78].

Yellowstone by this time had become famous for its native grizzly and black bears. The Fountain Hotel was gone, but there were garbage dumps at Old Faithful, Lake, Otter Creek (near Canyon), and West Yellowstone. They decided to bring life to those popular bears – inside the hotel.

W.M. contacted Chicago advertising artist Walter Oehrle, who created cover art for the Union Pacific Railroad. Oehrle drew the designs – imaging a human engaged in activity – and imposing a bear's features on top. As to his creative process, Oehrle wrote that he did not "humanize animals, I animalize humans."

I THINK OF THIS – THEN DRAW THIS – AND THIS

For the Inn's *Bear Pit*, bears strolled, danced, laughed, sang, ate, and watched geysers – everything the humans did [75, 76, 77].

Reamer, along with his crew, made the wall-size panels. They were first cut into stencils of thin plywood. Various stains and sand blasting techniques were used on each layer. They were then glued together to make the finished product. The procedure was actually much more complicated than described here. The final panels were, and are today, each a charming piece of art.

———

Over its years of gracing the Mammoth area landscape, the Child House has hosted uncounted receptions and VIP visits. One notable event in the summer of 1937 was the visit of President Franklin Delano Roosevelt and First Lady Eleanor Roosevelt – August 25 and 26. The Nichols family extended the hospitality of their home to accommodate the President's wishes for privacy because of his physical disability. According to one source, F.D.R. "was so impressed by the plan [of the house] that he expressed a desire to have it duplicated at Hyde Park."

In October 1938, Adelaide lost her sister Annie Dean Huntley Young. Described as a "kindly woman, always quick to aid those in need. She was known for her participation in charitable endeavors during the past 50 years." Annie was 82 years of age.

Adelaide and Bessie returned to the Wakefield-Huntley house throughout the 1940s. Adelaide's artistic taste continued to have an impact on Yellowstone hotels. Summers in Yellowstone allowed her precious family time. She did not return to Helena or the park after November 1948.

———

"Adelaide was the vice-president of the Yellowstone Park Company until her death ... Her advice was sought by other officers, by bankers and businessmen. ... [Her] knowledge and understanding of the money market equaled that of any banker ..." One family member said, "Those who had the privilege to know Adelaide Dean Child found that she added a new dimension to their life – that of loving and giving, and learning from her great store of knowledge."

In Harry Child's last will and testament, Adelaide received the Green Meadow Farm with all livestock, poultry, and equipment. "This [was] the one entity the Nichols family was not involved in. Adelaide, not a farm operator, listed the property for sale ..." After unsuccessful attempts in 1933, 1941, and 1944, the farm sold in 1947. It included 2741 acres and a second ranch that Adelaide had acquired after Harry's death.

In the 1940s Adelaide gave generously to the communities that had fostered her and Harry's life together. She donated a portion of the Green Meadow Farm land to the Green Meadow Country Club in Helena. At St. Peter's Hospital "the Maria M. Dean Foundation and the H.W. Child fund were both established by Adelaide to underwrite free beds for the hospitalization of women, children, and men who could not afford the costs." She gave gifts for wading pools at the Beattie tennis courts at the Civic Center, the Deaconess school, and the East Helena Public Park.

In 1939 she "made a gift of 17 acres along the Little Blackfoot River, near Elliston, Montana, 25 miles from Helena, for a camp for the youth of Helena," through the YMCA. Her funds help construct a lodge there between 1940 and 1941 which was dedicated Camp Child on May 26, 1941. She provided tents, equipment, furnishings, and extra funds to complete the lodge and adjacent cabins. The Child descendants continue to support the camp to this day.

From the land Harry had purchased in Gardiner, Montana back in 1902, Adelaide donated land for a new school. The 1952 school annual was dedicated to her. The final lots in Gardiner were sold by the H.W. Child Trust in 1961.

At the age of 88, Adelaide died at the family home in La Jolla, California, in October 1949. Bessie Ferguson [125] stayed with her for all the last years. Bessie inherited Adelaide's guest book, with the treasured letter from First Lady Grace Coolidge tucked in the pages. The last entries were addressed to Bessie who continued to use the book well after Adelaide's death. The family bought Bessie a house in La Jolla, and she lived there until her death in 1960.

Adelaide was described as being "the anchor of the family." From working crossword puzzles with her grandchildren to presiding over Sunday fried chicken dinners, she was "a friend to everyone."

⟶∞∞⟵

Between the time Robert Reamer met Harry and Adelaide Child in Coronado in 1903 and his death in 1938, he drafted over forty projects for the park. From barns and garages, to grand hotels, and to residences and dormitories, his work also spilled out into Helena through the Childs's greater social connections and land ownership.

When introducing Robert Reamer to Harry Child, his then-employer Elisha Babcock predicted correctly that his "ability would be recognized." The partnership and friendship between the Childs and the Reamers bestowed to Yellowstone its most cherished and beloved man-made spaces.

Chapter 17: The Last Roundup
1940 - 1966

the family's final years, Mission 66 and
the loss of Canyon Hotel, Huntley's life apart

On September 30th, 1944, the Flying D Ranch was sold to James Irvine, a California rancher. The YPC continued to winter horses in the Gallatin Range, on Flying D land – now leased from the Irvine Family Trust. In the stagecoach days, Harry had wintered many hundreds of horses at open range on the Flying D lands.

From that sale the Nichols family retained fifteen sections of Spanish Creek land which included Harry's elegant ranch house to be used as a vacation retreat. Sixteen of Harry's original tenant farmers stayed on and continued to work their hay fields. The family continued to receive some income from the previous crop-sharing agreements. The water rights obtained before 1883 added value to the land. W.M. Nichols hired Archie Martin II, a long-time YPC employee, to manage the Spanish Creek operation.

Archie Martin Sr., his father, had worked in the Park with Silas Huntley. A younger son, Lee Martin, grew up on the family homestead between Pony and Harrison, Montana. He rode his horse to school, and at about twelve years old, he began to forget about school. Instead he followed his Dad and older brother to the Park. Before long he had worked his way into a regular job.

By the early 1960s the number of horses had dwindled somewhat, and Lee Martin [104, 105] was now head wrangler for YPC. The horse roundup on the Flying D Ranch was a big event every spring. For Yellowstone employees, the arrival of the wranglers and strings of horses they brought to each location meant that the entire quota of summer workers was in place and ready to perform the duties of another summer in Yellowstone.

A description of the last roundup in 1964 shows the awesomeness of the land and the skill of the horsemen: Lee arranged the roundup with his Yellowstone wranglers sorting out the YPC horses, and the wranglers of other ranchers in Gallatin Valley sorted out their stock. Lee was total cowboy, but he was getting up in age, so he stayed at the corrals to keep things organized there.

Roundup was a day of hard work for the wranglers, and spectators were generally not welcome. The younger wranglers had been riding the high country since early morning, gathering the horses into groups. The show at the corrals would start about 10:00 am and be all over by noon.

The scenery was spectacular – high peaks all around, with draws leading down to the closed, bowl-shaped valley. There were two very large corrals with several smaller connected corrals. When the first horses appeared, Lee mounted up.

The show for the next hour or so was nothing short of awesome. The horses were in beautiful condition. Each looked as if it had been groomed for the occasion. The thick winter coats had been shed; they were sleek and shiny.

One after another, the groups of horses came down the draws from all directions, funneled into the large corrals and the gates were closed. The wranglers, working their lariats, were inside the corrals with the horses, and all were moving in a circular order. Now the horses were being sorted according to their brands. As a horse was roped, it was led to one of the smaller corrals, and handed over to another wrangler who led it into its respective horse trailer.

Before noon the corrals were empty, and the pickups with their trailers full of horses were all gone.

Silas Huntley's love of horses brought him to Yellowstone. Harry Child's and Charlie Anceney's western grit developed the empire that was the Flying D Ranch. Ellen Nichols, Harry and Adelaide's daughter, was the last family member to remain on the land. She ultimately sold the Spanish Creek Ranch in 1961.

Yellowstone's annual visitation reached an all-time high in 1940 – topping 500,000. But diminished visitation during WWII hit the companies hard. Two years during the war, visitation dropped below 100,000. Lake Hotel did not open between 1942 and 1946. Old Faithful Inn stayed closed for three years: 1943, 1944, and 1945. Mammoth Hotel was shuttered, as was Canyon Hotel. Without revenue, there was little spare money to upgrade – let alone upkeep hotels and lodges. Among National Park Service employees in the Park, so many male rangers were drafted that their wives worked their husband's jobs without compensation to keep the park running.

Family members were called away to serve the nation. Huntley Child Jr. registered on October 16, 1940. When called up he was commissioned a 1st Lieutenant in the Army, stationed at the Rock Island Arsenal in Illinois. From September 1942 through the summer of 1944 he was an assistant factory officer in the manufacturing of machine guns. That fall "they were looking for officers overseas." Because of his engineering and production background he was assigned to a Heavy

Maintenance Company in Naples, Italy. With a short stint in a Media Company, he was assigned to organize the 942nd Heavy Maintenance Company in central Florence. He was honorably discharged February 1, 1945.

He returned to the family business after the war, now serving as Manager of the Lodge Division. After three years of spending summers at Mammoth and winters in Helena, he moved to Mammoth year-round in 1949. He was appointed Vice-President of the Yellowstone Park Company in 1950.

Huntley Jr. approached management much like his Grandfather Child had done – he took time to know his hotel staff personally and recognized their unique contributions [126]. He also served as president of the Montana Hotel Association, the Rocky Mountain Hotel Association, and represented the U.S. in trade missions to the Caribbean and Turkey.

John Q. Nichols, Ellen and W.M.'s son, also enlisted. He "served from 1942 until the end of the conflict, attending officers' training school at Miami Beach, receiving a commission as a first lieutenant in army aviation, then being stationed in California, Arizona, and Nevada. The army utilized his experience in Yellowstone by assigning him to operate officers' clubs. He was sent overseas late in 1945 and was among the last [of the family] to return to the park." Johnnie returned to Yellowstone after the war as well, serving as General Manager and President.

In Yellowstone "the increased use of the personal auto reduced the demand for train travel and with it the need for a large bus fleet. There were 240 buses in 1940 and many were sold for ranching, farming and industrial use during the war; 26 were junked outright. When tourists began to return after the war in 1946, only 124 remained in service." The Northern Pacific Railroad ceased passenger service to Gardiner in 1948. Passengers detrained in Livingston so a decision was made to replace the smaller seven- to fifteen-passenger vehicles with larger full-size motor coaches.

As the 1950's dawned, Harry's company had survived for twenty years without his leadership. His heirs were facing the same sort of obstacles that he had battled and conquered in the early 1900s. In the 1930s it was the economic depression that spread across the country. In the 1940s it was WWII and the recovery. The nation's trains were committed to carrying troops and few European tourists found U.S. destinations favorable.

Visitation to national parks across the nation exploded after the war. 1947 brought 900,000 visitors to Yellowstone. By 1948, the one-million mark was reached. The traveling, post-war masses brought changing ideas that required upgraded facilities. To respond to a sudden increase in tourists and faced with neglected guest facilities, the NPS initiated the Mission 66 program.

Starting in 1956, the ten-year goal was to quickly expand accommodations across the national park system. For Yellowstone, that meant a new Canyon Village, a new marina for the Bridge Bay area, and replacing the West Thumb Lodge with a new facility that became Grant Village. All this was to be done to the NPS specifications, but with YPC funds. W.M. had little choice but to comply.

The NPS had come of age and took the reins of the authority they had over the private businesses operating in all the national parks. Mather and Albright had worked a sort of "partnering" plan, whereby they protected and respected the concessionaires' investments in the parks. As administrations in Washington came and went, the new Interior Department Secretaries and NPS Directors were looking at different ways of exercising their oversight of the parks. Now new and unheard of procedures were being presented each season.

In 1951 Conrad Wirth [115] was appointed director of the NPS. He came to Yellowstone to acquaint himself with the current situation and stayed around to become friendly with the YPC people. He seemed interested in working out a good agreement for proceeding with plans for YP improvement. Wirth and W.M. planned to begin with improvements to the Lake area, so W.M. put his crews to work.

Meanwhile the NPS was progressing with plans for the Mission 66 program, whereby all visitor services would be grouped into small areas referred to as villages. The NPS working committee in the Park had submitted its recommendations to the national Mission 66 panel in Washington, D.C., and a tentative program of improvements emerged over the next few months. All three Yellowstone concessioners, Nichols of YPC, Hamilton of the general stores, and Haynes of the photo shops, agreed to participate.

Shortly after Nichols returned from Washington, having hashed out the plan to continue working in the Lake area, Conrad Wirth informed W.M. that he must postpone all other plans, stop the work that he had begun, and concentrate completely on the building of Canyon Village. Nichols and his YPC could do nothing until the NPS did its part – build roads and other infrastructure. The company officers and stockholders recommended that W.M. Nichols invest no more money in a company over which he had so little control. Mr. Nichols and the family members began to search for prospective buyers.

The taxes collected on gasoline sales in the Park were considerable. Yellowstone Park lies mostly in the state of Wyoming, but its outer boundaries spread into Montana and Idaho. The Wyoming governor was the first to express an interest in buying the Yellowstone Park Company, but the other two governors through their congressmen, got that idea blocked.

The scuttlebutt around the park was confusing and unsettling. Workers wondered if they would have a job tomorrow or next week. W.M. Nichols asked Huntley Child Jr. to draft a "prospectus," a statement to be distributed throughout the company explaining to the employees the management view of the current state of the company and future intentions. It did little to quell concerns; however, the vast majority of YPC people remained loyal.

It was not only the workmen who suffered anxiety. Negotiating for concession contracts had taken on increased uncertainty. Harry had operated in the days when he was continually allowed to renew contracts without outside competition. Now bills were floating in Congress requiring the NPS to open bidding to wider competition.

Huntley Child Jr. argued that a concessioner should be able to negotiate a new contract before bids were open to competition – a sort of propriety right. He gathered support from U.S. senators and representatives. He reminded them that the YPC records showed a long history of favors granted to certain elected officials who needed a "payback" for constituents who were heavy donors. Very often this meant summer jobs for sons and daughters who were referred to as "specials," or sometimes entire families were shown a first-class tour of Yellowstone compliments of the YPC – a common practice throughout the national parks.

Huntley Jr.'s was a powerful argument, and he won that round.

———————

In 1956 a YPC Board of Directors was formed. W.M. Nichols was elected chairman of the board of directors, and his son, John Q. Nichols, replaced him as president of the YPC. W.M. signed a new twenty-year contract with the NPS and signed a $3 million line of credit for new construction.

The new Canyon Village was to be the poster child of Mission 66. The architectural firm chosen had a national reputation, but designers failed to consider Yellowstone's unique weather and geology. The ideas of rustic "parkitecture" were abandoned in favor of modern steel and manufactured composite materials. Using the old "lodge" concept, a central building for registration and food service was completed first.

Construction delays hindered the project's completion. By the proposed opening of the New Canyon Village (July 1, 1957) less than one-fourth of the planned 500 cabins were completed. The cabins that did open proved to be undesirable to the tourists. Each night the elegant old Canyon Hotel was filled to capacity while the cabins at the Village were unoccupied.

The stress of the financial commitments and the constant

decisions involved in the development may have taken their toll on W.M. Nichols' health. His death came less than a month before the actual dedication took place. After an illness of ten days, W.M. Nichols died of a heart ailment on August 6, 1957. His widow, Ellen Dean Child Nichols, succeeded him as chairman of the board.

———⟫•⟪———

A short year later it became clear that the Canyon Hotel needed extensive repairs. At the end of the 1958 season it closed. Neither the park engineer, nor the independent engineering firm hired by the hotel company, would sign off on the structural integrity of the building. For four decades the ground under the building, primarily water-laden clay, had been undermining the stability. The hotel was literally sliding down the hillside, twisting sideways as it went. Huntley Child Jr. was present at both of these evaluations. He later said, "The floors were built on top of each other, the only thing keeping them in line was plumbing."

Photographs in the park archives show the massive damage – support beams suspended five feet from their original location; lodgepole logs shoved in to keep them from shifting further. The company's finances were stretched too thinly – the resources for repairs were simply not there. Some thought that the old Canyon Hotel could be remodeled and returned to its former splendor. But the YPC could take on no more debt.

Furnishings from the Canyon Hotel were hauled away by the truckloads and supposedly were being stored at the Gardiner garage. Many of the trucks did not even stop at the garage. In bits and pieces, it all began to show up in the antique shops in the towns around the park.

In 1959, the Carlos Construction Company of Cody, Wyoming assumed ownership of the Canyon Hotel. Their payment was to be whatever materials they could salvage from the structure. And then, one dark, cold night (August 8, 1960), the shell of the hotel burned to the ground. The cause of the fire was never determined.

So many theories have been circulated about the fire.

Yellowstone historian Aubrey Haines paints a picture of conspiracy – that the YPC closed the hotel because it continued to fill, while the new cabins at Canyon remained empty. Another theory was that the Carlos Construction Company started the fire for the insurance. But it was not insured, and they lost much salvage material in the fire and some of their own vehicles that were parked inside. Electrical fire was another theory, but the wiring to the building had already been cut. NPS historian Rod Wheaton called the destruction of the hotel "the greatest architectural loss in Yellowstone's history."

———————

In the 1950s the financial relationship with the railroads was concluded. Not long after, the family had started searching for a buyer for the company. This search would last for another ten years.

But the stress of uncertainty pulled apart the two branches of Harry and Adelaide's offspring. In the spring of 1960, Huntley Jr. sent a letter to his cousin Johnnie suggesting operational changes. He also informed Ellen he could no longer work with Johnnie. But he found that "blood runs thicker than water."

In March 1960 the Board of Directors of YPC informed Huntley Jr. that his services were no longer needed. After twenty-two years of service he was dismissed from the family business. Later that same year, Johnnie Nichols was forced to relinquish his position as general manager, but remained its President and board member.

A promising sale of the company in 1961 was halted when the NPS added high dollar commitments from an incoming concessioner. After the 1965 summer season, only half-way through the twenty-year contract, the National Park Service notified the YPC that they were terminating the contract. "Ellen Dean Child Nichols and her son John – who, together with other family members still controlled 86 percent of company stock – immediately decided to appeal ..." But, having committed so much money and absorbed so much debt to complete Canyon Village, the family was financially drained and could not remain competitive.

"On August 8, 1966, NPS director George Hartzog granted a new thirty-year contract to the Yellowstone Park Company. The family owners immediately sold all their stock in the company to the Goldfield Corporation, whose chairman, [Richard] Pistell, promised to spend $20 million over twenty years on new lodgings and related services. No member of the Child or Nichols family attended the ceremony at Mammoth Hot Springs." After 75 years, no member of the family remained. Huntley Jr., along with many loyal long-time employees went their separate ways. Huntley Jr.'s two sisters, Marion and Betty, made yearly pilgrimages to Yellowstone until the 1990s.

Ellen had to give up her home at Mammoth Hot Springs, the treasured house her mother had carefully planned and tended – a home where she had lived for thirty years since her father's death. She was composed and calm as she closed the door and walked to her waiting limousine. Her chauffeur drove her away from Yellowstone, a place she had visited and called home since she was ten years old.

Just as the stress of the Mission 66-Canyon Village period may have hastened the death of W.M. Nichols, so the heartbreak of the loss of the Yellowstone contract may have contributed to the death of his widow, Ellen Dean Child Nichols. Just months after the sale, "Dean" passed away on October 13, 1966. She was 82 years old.

Huntley Child, son of Adelaide and Harry, lived a life apart from the YPC after being banished from the Park. He had to leave Yellowstone, the home he had built with his wife and three children, his parents, his sister and brother-in-law, memories of his youth and two good friends – Charles Hamilton and Jack Haynes. Many an ex-Yellowstone employee will attest to the fact that after living and working in that wonderful magical place for a few seasons, nothing on the outside can quite measure up.

Huntley Child's term in the military lasted from October 14, 1918 to April 3, 1919. After WWI ended, he remained in Washington D.C.

working for the food administration and living at the Soldier's home.

At some point, Huntley and Emilie divorced. Although family lore believes "he never became involved in any of the three children's lives," Huntley listed Marion, Huntley Jr., and Elizabeth – along with Bessie Ferguson, as members of his household in 1920 after he had moved to New York City – about the time that his aunt Annie and S.B.M. Young returned to Helena.

He seems to have remained in New York for about ten years, at least some of that time working as a salesman. In 1929, he remarried to a Russian immigrant named Marie R. Cruz. Soon after they moved to Seattle, Washington "… where his mother, Adelaide, purchased a pickle factory for him. The *Dean Pickle* did not last long, and they moved to Coronado, California, where Adelaide purchased them a small home and Huntley trained race horses." A granddaughter remembers he retained a fondness for horse-racing – accompanying him to his box at the race track.

"He had no communication with his father after the Yellowstone episode," writes his grandson, Harry W. Child II, "nor with his only sister, Dean. His mother, Adelaide, was always there for him and supported him after 1917."

Harry did not forget his son, however, as the H.W. Child Trust, created from Harry's estate provided for a small monthly income and released Huntley from repaying money he owed to Harry. Huntley retained an attorney to contest the will, but settled with his sister. The action led to another rift within the family between Huntley and his children. It would be years before the family reconciled.

Huntley Child died at the family home in La Jolla, California in 1978, at age ninety-one.

———⊷•⊷———

Many writers have published conflicting opinions about the value of private enterprise providing public services in national parks. In his examination of early concessions policy, Richard A. Bartlett used such phrases as "park nobility," "their fiefdoms," and "aristocratic heiress." "The occupants of those houses [at Mammoth Hot Springs] could have been equally well ensconced," he wrote, "in granite castles protected by moats and portcullises."

Robert Shankland, whose biography of Stephen Mather focuses on the creation of the National Park Service, took time to pay this tribute to national park concessioners who came before:

> In general, the concessioners are due a good deal more praise than censure. Some of them – the railroads – have spent their money more or less lavishly with only feeble expectations of direct profits. Others have plugged along with the parks for many years and, though understandably hopeful of showing a profit, have worked freely for the principle of national-park inviolability and have conducted themselves far more like conservationists than anyone has demanded or expected of them. At the bottom the fact remains that without the concessioners they did have, the national parks would have had no concessioners at all. Congress, in Mather's time, never produced any spare money for investment that way, and if it should do so in the immediate future, it would be well advised to consider first whether somewhere else in the parks the need is not manifestly greater.

Yellowstone Savages Never Say Goodbye: "See You Next Summer!"

This is a story about real people – exceptional people who dove into the tides of progress and assumed leadership roles within those events. Their choices shaped the lives of those around them – and continue to affect us today.

For seventy-four years Harry Child and his descendants held on in Yellowstone. Grandfather Child had no doubt understood early on that the business he and Silas Huntley started would never really belong to him. All Harry's accomplishments in the Park could not remain totally in the family's control. Yet, he never slacked in his efforts to make the hotels, camps, and lodges, and the transportation services, the very best in existence for their time.

It is now over a century since Harry created the face of the accommodations in Yellowstone Park available to the traveling public. Old Faithful Inn, Mammoth Hotel, and Lake Hotel are very much just the way he left them for future generations to see and enjoy – a great legacy.

—➤●◄—

By the 1970s, the Old Faithful Inn's future was in jeopardy. Throughout Mission 66 and then decades of neglect, the idea was circulated that it should be closed to overnight guests, the wings removed, and the original portion, "the Old House," be turned into a visitor center. Those who love the building stood up and cried, "NO."

In 1979 the National Park Service purchased Yellowstone hotels, and since then, concessions partners have been required to commit portions of their revenues to renovation and preservation. In 1987, the Inn was declared a National Historic Landmark – recognizing its role in influencing the spread of rustic national park architecture. After Centennial celebrations in 2004, a multi-year restoration was undertaken including seismic upgrades and structural stabilization.

"Today, the Old Faithful Inn is as much a natural component of the Yellowstone landscape as is Old Faithful Geyser, grizzly bears, and the Lower Falls." wrote Professor Judith Meyer. "Despite the fact that government proposals to remove the hotel's additions and turn the old house (the original 1903 structure) into a museum appear regularly, public outcry is always so great that the proposals are always withdrawn. It is the public's affection for this building and its purpose as an inn–not a museum–that has preserved the inn as part of the Yellowstone experience."

A similar project was performed on Lake Hotel from 2011-2014, culminating in its receiving National Historic Landmark status – touted as a sole Colonial Revival grand hotel remaining in the national park system. "The Grand Lady of the Lake" saw her 125th Anniversary celebration in 2015.

Mammoth Hotel's restoration was completed in August 2019. The public areas of the building have been redesigned and rehabilitated to incorporate the previously-separated ski shop and new conference/event rooms. Historic mahogany woodwork was restored and new matching woodwork was incorporated in the new areas. As an accessioned item in the park's museum collection, Adelaide Child and Robert Reamer's map was restored at the National Park Service Restoration Center in Arizona and returned to the Map Room in all its splendor.

The wing of guest rooms has been reconfigured so all rooms have private baths. Thirteen guest rooms retain the original bathtubs and restored lighting and plumbing fixtures. Structural stabilization, upgrades to the heating systems, and the addition of insulation and new windows bring the hotel to modern energy efficiency. Mammoth Hotel is recognized as one of few remaining Art Moderne-style hotels in the National Park system.

Old Faithful Lodge, Roosevelt Lodge, Lake Lodge, and Canyon Lodge with their adjacent cabins, hearken us back to the history of W.W. Wylie, A.W. Miles, Edward Moorman, and Howard Hays. Other concession companies came earlier to Yellowstone than Harry and Adelaide. Some, like the Haynes family and the Hamilton/Povah dynasty, stayed as long or longer than the Child/Nichols family.

Yellowstone's present hotel and transportation concessionaire, part of the Xanterra Travel Collection, hires 4000 seasonal employees to staff nine hotels, five campgrounds, and to conduct tours on buses, boats, and horses. Human resources staff review 8000-9000 applications every year. Opening and closing procedures are refined and well-practiced – after over one hundred years of trial and error. Knowledge is passed down from one manager to the next. Few seasonal employees, awed with the excitement of the opportunity of a lifetime, realize that they are joining a long legacy of service.

—————

Today's Transportation department celebrates its tradition and its ancestors. From his position as National Park Service Historian in Yellowstone, former driver/tour guide Lee Whittlesey writes:

A fascinating chronology involving Mr. [Gerard] Pesman (1904-2000), can be traced from Yellowstone's stagecoach days to the present in five persons known to have trained concessioner stagecoach drivers, bus drivers, and tour guides. George Wakefield, who established the first in-park stagecoach company in Yellowstone in 1883 and operated it through 1891, no doubt trained his drivers to do the park tour. He trained his son-in-law Dr. S.F. Way, and Way continued in that stead [working for Silas Huntley -rq] through the end of stagecoach travel in 1916 and then for at least ten years into the park's bus era. Gerard Pesman remembers 'Old Doc Way' taking him under his wing in 1926 and teaching him tricks about the park tour, including park facts and storytelling skills. In his late sixties, Pesman returned to the park (1970-1977) as 'Commentary Supervisor' to teach park bus drivers to give park tours. He taught author Lee Whittlesey in 1971-1972 and served as Whittlesey's Yellowstone mentor through 1977. In 1978, Whittlesey took over the teaching reins and trained bus drivers and step-on tour guides to 'commentate the park' through 1982. Whittlesey trained Leslie J. Quinn in 1980, and Quinn assumed the Information Specialist position in 1994 and occupies it today. Thus a direct, pass-it-down connection in the interpretive training of concessioner drivers and tour guides from the stage coach days of 1883 through 2006 [now 2020], a period of 124 [now 137] years, is found in the Wakefield-Way-Pesman-Whittlesey-Quinn lineage. And the training tour is still called a 'frolic' today!

Harry had a great love of cars and buses. His business relationship with Walter White lasted beyond the lives of either man. The *Historic Yellowstone Buses* in use in Yellowstone today were purchased by the YPTC in 1936, 1937, and 1938. Auctioned off in the 1950s, eight of them returned to the park in 2007. Each is now equipped with Ford chassis, engine, and running gear to meet current DOT regulations, so visitors may still experience the park with the "top down" in a White Company motor bus.

George Wakefield and Silas Huntley inaugurated stage travel in the park. Today, one may visit Roosevelt Lodge where replicas of the Tally-ho coaches and cookout wagons require a bevy of wranglers to annually round up and care for the saddle and draft horses.

———◆———

The Great Falls Smokestack did not last as long as Harry predicted. It stood 155 feet high, and had been a loved landmark for over forty years. The smelter "lost money since opening," due to a combination of slow transportation of ore from mines, outside competition, and subsequent mergers.

Old buildings left on the site became a curiosity – then a hazardous liability. "Tottering, decaying remains of the old silver smelter, among the last relics of the boom silver days in the northwest and once a figure in Montana's late '80s and early '90s social whirl …" reported the *Great Falls Tribune* in 1924. After demolition, "their own basements will be their graves."

"When the plant was done away with in 1900 and the buildings removed, the stack stood out by itself, the only structure to mark the one time thriving enterprise. Although it withstood wind and rain for years, small crack appeared at the top …" When the day came to demolish the local landmark an official, a very experienced powder man drilled holes and set charges around the seven-foot diameter base. From 400 feet away he pushed the button that would set off the dynamite. The first charge created only a puff of smoke, but within a few seconds "the remaining 22 shots went off almost at the same moment. The huge stack trembled and then with a cracking sound, it towered to the east and fell a heap of ruins."

The county took over the site in 1936 for non-payment of taxes. A $2.1 million dollar cleanup of the site in the 1970s restored the area. Recovery crews discovered and excavated the base of the blast furnace stack, and it became part of the interpretive story at Giant Springs State Park. High on a hill, overlooking the mighty Missouri River, it remains a silent tribute to the smelter that Harry built.

———————

In 1989 former media executive Ted Turner bought the Flying D Ranch land. "Turner paid $21 million cash and acquired all 107,000 acres, plus the cattle and machinery to operate a legendary ranch. ... A pervasive fear, for some, was that he would turn the ranch into a massive real estate play, dividing it up and selling the pieces."

While that did not happen, Turner's plans were still controversial, ordering his ranch manager "to tear down interior barbwire fences that he and other ranch hands had spent decades erecting and maintaining. Down, too, came power poles and lines, corrals, and outbuildings. Turner put a halt to irrigated hay production on an interior portion of the ranch. That portion of ranch had yielded upwards of 1.5 tons of hay an acre but had pulled water out of the steams. Collectively, this was perceived by some of the traditionalists on the ranch as an order to disavow tradition, to turn their backs on their own sweat equity and the codes of the cowboy way."

By restoring natural processes Turner seeks to demonstrate "– a new model of land management that combines the best land conservation practice with renewable/sustainable commerce that minimizes impact on the land, while generating revenue that can be used to sustain the ranch."

The Flying D is now home to some 5000 native bison, one of the largest known pack of wolves, and other native and endangered species.

On the menu today, at Ted's Montana Grill, in Bozeman, MT (the first of the more that 50 locations of a nationwide restaurant chain), one may order *Karen's Flying D chili*. Although Harry's name is lost when one speaks of the Flying D land, it was his efforts with his partner, Charles Anceney, who assembled this huge tract of land from many smaller holdings.

<hr>

Employees like Beulah Brown and Edward Moorman came for a summer and stayed for decades. Others like Gary Cooper and Gerard Pesman found success and confidence to excel in outside careers. This tradition continues today. We write because, although we worked and lived in different generations of that tradition, we both consider ourselves as belonging to the Yellowstone family of Silas Huntley and Harry and Adelaide Child.

For Nan, their influence started when she arrived in Yellowstone in 1953. Just out of high school, she craved experiences beyond her childhood world. Coworkers with decades of experience in Yellowstone as concession employees mesmerized her with stories. Long after the deaths of the players in our drama, their attitudes, life perspectives, and philosophies of business were spoken through the voices of Lee Martin, Clara and Walley Hendrickson, and Betty Jane and Huntley Child Jr.

For loyal employees who had worked in Yellowstone in their youth and returned every summer for decades, arriving early in the spring was like "old home week." Yellowstone welcomed retired workers who brought life experience and special skills like carpentry and maintenance who continued to contribute and serve upwards of twenty years for YPC. They lingered long after meals in the dining halls or gathered around the old wood-burning barrel stove in the vast open cabin camp lobby. Stories were told and repeated year after year of happy happenings in the past. More serious conversation was about what would be new and different for this summer. Usually with a look of disgust at the new ideas, the response would be something like, "I wonder what 'Old Harry' would say about that," or "Old Harry would turn over in his grave if he knew about that." A young savage, new to the park, could only wonder about "Old Harry" so fondly remembered by this bunch of "Old Timer" employees.

Ruth's experience began in 1990 when she reported as a mid-season replacement – one of the very welcome faces that follow the August exodus of college students. Being in her late 20s, she was drawn to more mature workers – those who had worked more than five summers. They had survived the isolated winters and worked in multiple job categories. Severing ties with home, they built a new Yellowstone family, one to which she was quickly accepted.

We are not government employees. We work for a private for-profit company that contracts with the National Park Service to run hospitality facilities on public lands. Only about 10% are core employees who return year after year, often in management positions. In 2019 Xanterra staff included 107 people with over 20 years' experience each. These employees possessed an accumulated 3239 years of service – averaging around 30 years.

For us in the hospitality business, Harry and Adelaide Child are our revered ancestors. They set the tone of service. They negotiated the contracts, battled governmental changes, and weathered the roller coaster ride of economics. They did so with decorum and professionalism. **We are their legacy.**

Endnotes

Our Purpose

(other historians) Many aspects of this history have been detailed in other publications. We relied most heavily on the following titles:

Albright, Horace M. and Marian Albright Schenck, *Creating the National Park Service: The Missing Years*. Norman, OK: University of Oklahoma Press, 1999.

Barringer, Mark Daniel, *Selling Yellowstone: Capitalism and the Construction of Nature*. Lawrence, KS: The University Press of Kansas, 2002.

Bartlett, Richard A.,*Yellowstone: A Wilderness Besieged*. Tucson, AZ: The University of Arizona Press, 1985.

Forbes, B.C., "Harry W. Child," in *Men Who are Making the West*. New York: B.C. Forbes Publishing Co., 1923, pp. 322-343. A version of this chapter was originally published as B.C. Forbes, "Give Me the West!" *American Magazine*, May 1920, pp. 16, 245-248. There are slight variations in text.

Child II, Harry W., *Montana Pioneers: The Huntley, Child & Dean Families*. privately printed, n.d. (c.2009).

Haines, Aubrey L., *The Yellowstone Story: A History of our First National Park. Vol. II*. Yellowstone National Park, WY: Yellowstone Library and Museum Association, 1977.

Hummel, Don, *Stealing the National Parks: The Destruction of Concessions and Park Access*. Bellevue, WA: The Free Enterprise Press, 1987.

Shankland, Robert, *Steve Mather of the National Parks*. New York: Alfred A. Knopf, Inc., 1951.

Smith, Phyllis, *The Flying D Ranch Lands of Montana: A History*. Bozeman, MT: Gallatin County Historical Society and Pioneer Museum, 2001.

(historic hostelries) Yellowstone National Park Lodges, part of the Xanterra Travel Collection, has operated concessions in Yellowstone under contract from the National Park Service since 1994. Current photos of lodging facilities may be found at their website www.travelyellowstone.com or www.xanterra.com

Prologue

(chapter header) Ruth Quinn photo.

page 1

(old wooden fire watch tower) Our major sources for Helena, Montana history are Ellen Baumler, *Historic Helena Walking Tours*. Helena, MT: Montana Historical Society, 2014; Patricia C. Spencer, *Helena Montana: The Queen City of the Rockies and the Broadwater Hotel*. Chicago: Arcadia Publishing, 2002; Paula Petrik, *No Step Backward: Women and Family on the Rocky Mountain Mining Frontier, Helena, Montana 1865-1900*. Helena, MT: Montana Historical Society Press, 1987, 1990 rev.; and www.helenahistory.org

(W.C. Child) "Death of W.C. Child," *The Anaconda* [MT] *Standard*, (hereafter *AS*) 15Oct1893, p. 1; "The Rueben Bompart Home," in Jean Baucus, *Helena: Her Historic Homes, Vol. II*. Helena, MT: J.G. Publications, 1979, p. 11; "The West," *The Montana Post* [Virginia City, M.T.], (hereafter *MP*) 12Mar1869, p. 4; *William T. McFarland*, in A.W. Bowen & Co., *Progressive Men of the State of Montana*. Chicago: A.W. Bowen & Co., 190?, pp. 293-294; "Personal," *The New North-west* [Deer Lodge, M.T.], (hereafter *NN-w*) 20Jan1871, p. 3; "Library Calico Hall," *The Daily Independent* [Helena, M.T.], (hereafter *DI*) 5Apr1878, p. 3; "Railroad Celebration," *DI*, 9Jun1883, p. 3; Advertisement for Amateur Minstrel Entertainment ...," *DI*, 27Feb1881, p. 1.

page 2

(Lionel R. Nettre) Nettre attended boarding school as a youth and graduated Columbia College in 1869 with a degree in Mining Engineering. In the summer of 1873 he joined the Northern Pacific Railroad Survey as their mineralogist/geologist. The expedition made it up the Yellowstone River as far as Pompey's Pillar, east of present day Billings, Montana, before Indian skirmishes and impending winter turned them back. After a short stint as Superintendent of Chemical Works in Philadelphia, Pennsylvania, Nettre arrived in Helena. Listing for Lionel R. Nettre, *School Catalog, Brooklyn Collegiate and Polytechnic Institute*. New York, 1864, 1865, 1866, www.ancestry.com 16Jan2015; Lionel Robert Nettre, List of Graduates, *School Catalog, Columbia College*, 1870, p. 16, and 1874, p. 61, www.ancestry.com 16Jan2015; "Washington News and Gossip," *Evening Star* [Wash., DC], (hereafter *ES*) 15May1873, p. 1; "Sitting Bull's Band Attack the N.P. Cavalry Escort," *NN-w*, 30Aug1873, p. 2; "Troublesome Indians," *ES*, 28Oct1873, p. 1; D.S. Stanley, *Report on the Yellowstone Expedition of 1873*. Wash., DC: Government Printing Office, 1874, p. 3; M. John Lubetkin, *Jay Cooke's Gamble: The Northern Pacific Railroad, the Sioux, and the Panic of 1873*. Norman, OK: University of Oklahoma Press, 2006, pp. 182, 266; Lionel Robert Nettre, List of Graduates, *School Catalog, Columbia College*, 1875, p. 155, and 1876, p. 113, www.ancestry.com 16Jan2015.

(Silas Huntley) Silas S. Huntley, in Bowen, pp. 922-923; John S. Gray, "The Northern Overland Pony Express," *Montana the Magazine of Western History*, 16(4), Autumn 1966, pp. 61-62.

(Nathaniel Pitt Langford) Haines, Vol. II, pp. 448-449.

page 3

(Fisk's Overland Expedition) Aubrey L. Haines, forward to Nathaniel Pitt Langford, *The Discovery of Yellowstone Park*. Lincoln, NE: University of Nebraska Press, 1972, reprint of 1905 edition, p. viii; Langford, p. xxiv, xxv; George Black, *Empire of Shadows: The Epic Story of Yellowstone*. New York: St. Martin's Press, 2012, p. 102-106.

(lobby for Territorial status) Dorothy M. Johnson, *The Bloody Bozeman: The Perilous Trail to Montana's Gold*. New York and Toronto: McGraw-Hill Book Company, 1971, p. 107; Black, p. 122; Ken Egan Jr., *Montana 1864: Indians, Emigrants, and Gold in the Territorial Year*. Helena, MT: Riverbend Publishing, 2014, pp. 39-43.

(collector of revenues) Dorothy M. Johnson, introduction to Nathaniel Pitt Langford, *Vigilante Days and Ways*. Missoula, MT: The University Press/Montana State University, 1957, p. xxx.

(Samuel T. Hauser) Samuel T. Hauser, in Bowen, pp. 202-203; "The Hauser-Babcock Home," in Jean Baucus and Gayle Shanahan, *Helena: Her Historic Houses, Vol. I*. Helena, MT: J.G. Publications, 1976, not paginated, entry 18; Baumler, *Historic Helena*, p.15; Bill Skidmore, *Treasure State Treasury: Montana Banks, Bankers, & Banking 1864-1984*. Helena, MT: Thurber Printing Co., 1985, pp. 16-17.

(the Yellowstone area) Native Americans used the area's resources for 10,000 years before Euro-American fur trappers and traders such as John Colter, Daniel Potts, Osborne Russell, and Jim Bridger spread word of its wonders. In September 1870 a large expedition left Helena to explore and document the area. Led by Surveyor General of the Montana Territory, Henry D. Washburn, they stopped at Fort Ellis (east of present day Bozeman, MT) to meet their miliary escort led by Lieut. Gustavus C. Doane. Prominent Helenites Nathaniel Langford, Samuel Hauser, and Cornelius Hedges accompanied the party. They followed the Yellowstone River down the east side of the park, members summited the peak now bearing Washburn's name, and traversed the western shore of Yellowstone Lake. They spent less than two days in the Upper Geyser Basin, but are credited with naming such well-known features as Castle Geyser, Giant Geyser, Beehive Geyser, and Old Faithful Geyser. The previous year three men successfully completed a similar adventure, but their reports were dismissed as fanciful. The credibility and reputations of members on the Washburn-Langford-Doane Expedition convinced the U.S. Government to send their own expedition the following year. See Paul Schullery, *Searching for Yellowstone: Ecology and Wonder in the Last Wilderness*. New York: Houghton Mifflin Company, 1997, pp. 51-55; Hiram Martin Chittenden, *The Yellowstone National Park: Historical and Descriptive*. Cincinnati: The Robert Clarke Co., 1895, pp. 75-83; Lee H. Whittlesey, *Yellowstone Place Names*. Gardiner, MT: Wonderland Publishing Co., rev. 2006, pp. 47, 63, 113, 193.

(voice of the expedition) Alfred Runte, *Trains of Discovery: Western Railroads and the National Parks*. Flagstaff, AZ: Northland Press, 1984, pp. 20-24.

(act of Congress) President Ulysses S. Grant signed the bill to create the world's first national park on March 1, 1872.

page 4

(first superintendent) Langford's term as superintendent was 1872-1877. He later published Nathaniel Pitt Langford, *The Discovery of Yellowstone*

Park 1870 (Alternately, *Diary of the Washburn Expedition to the Yellowstone and Firehole Rivers in the Year 1870*). no place: privately published, 1905. He spent much of his later life in St. Paul, Minnesota, and he died there in 1909. Haines, *Vol. II*, p. 449. Langford stayed interested in park matters. As late as 1883, he wrote letters to Congressmen, expressing "his concerns with the park's lease policy..." as related to concessions leases. Karl John Byrand, *The Evolution of the Cultural Landscape in Yellowstone National Park's Upper Geyser Basin and the Changing Visitor Experience, 1872-1990*, Master of Science in Earth Sciences thesis, Montana State University, Bozeman, MT, 1995, p. 59.

Chapter 1: Setting the Scene *(chapter header)* SC 888: Huntley and Clark Records, Montana Historical Society Research Center.
page 5
(gold discoveries of 1864) Baumler, *Historic Helena*, p. 7.
(name was changed to Helena) "In October [1864], residents gathered to properly name the mining camp known as Last Change. After some discussion, they dubbed the new settlement Helena after the Scott County, Minnesota, hometown of one of the men." Baumler, *Historic Helena*, p. 7.
(surface mining) Petrik, p. 146.
(Helena Reduction Works, Lexington Mine) *NN-w*, 16Sept1871, p. 2; "Territorial," *NN-w*, 8Mar1878, p. 2; "The Railroad Silver Welding," *NN-w*, 28May1880, p. 2; Terry Halden, *Ghost Towns and Mining Districts of Montana*. Butte, MT: Old Butte Publishing, 2007, p. 140.
page 6
(Gregory Mine, majority of the wealth) Halden, p. 101. Halden identifies the Gregory as part of the Colorado Mining District, located near "The headwaters of Clancy Creek and the drainage system of Spring Creek."
(Gloster Mine) The Gloster was one of the major mines in the Piegan Mining District, "located on the north slope of Belmont Mountain, Peigan Gulch, a tributary of the Little Prickly Pear." Halden, p. 140; "Gold and Silver Production," *NN-w*, 17Aug1883, p. 2; "Marysville, Montana," *Rocky Mountain Husbandman* [Diamond City, M.T.], (hereafter *RMH*) 30Jun1881, p. 7; "Gloster Clean-Up," *The Benton* [M.T.] *Weekly Record*, (hereafter *BWR*) 29Sept1881, p. 3; "From the North," *NN-w*, 30Dec1881, p. 2.
(sheep ranching) "In Town and Out," *The River Press* [Fort Benton, M.T.], (hereafter *RP*) 22Jun1881, p. 8; "Local News," *RMH*, 15Jun1882, p. 3; "Jottings by our Traveling Man," *RMH*, 10Aug1882, p. 2.
(born in California) Listing for E.F. Child, *1870 US Census Record*, Town of San Francisco, Ward 10, San Francisco County, California, 28Jun1870; Listing for Harry W. Child, 1869, West-Newton English and Classical School, West Newton, Massachusetts, 1895 publication, *High School Student Lists, 1821-1923*, www.ancestry.com 19Jan 2015. The family made the trip via a ship around Cape Horn. "Harry Child, Prominent in Montana, Dies," *The* [Helena] *Montana Record-Herald*, (hereafter *M R-H*) 4Feb1931, p. 1.
(New England roots) Harry's father, E.F. Child, was the son of Sarah Marie Beverly of Providence, Rhode Island, and George Child of Warren, Rhode Island. "George was 12 when his father died. He developed a love for the sea and rose to the command of one of the best of the Long Island Sound Steamers." from Child, Appendix 10: *Harry W. Child - Family Tree*. "The steamer *Lexington* caught fire on Long Island Sound during the night of January 13, 1840. Captain George Child with a crew of forty, tried desperately to head the vessel toward shore. There were 150 passengers on board and a full cargo of cotton bales. This material fed the flames until the fire was out of control. Later the ship sank and there were only four survivors." Paul C. Morris and William P. Quinn, *Shipwrecks In New York Waters*. Orleans, MA: Parnassus Imprints, 1989, p. 2. Listing for Sarah M. Child, *1850 US Census Record*, Town of Providence, Providence County, Rhode Island, 17Aug1850. The names of the six children of Sarah M. Beverley Child and George Child, from www.mckownfamily.com 28Mar2015.
(men's clothing store) "... took a job in a wholesale clothing house in Boston," Forbes, p. 334; "... being a clerk in stationery-house of H.S. Crocker & Co. from 1870-1875," Hubert Howe Bancroft and Frances Fuller Victor, *History of Washington, Idaho, and Montana: 1845-1889*. San Francisco: History Co., 1890, p. 774; "'75-'76, bookkeeper, San Francisco," West-Newton school listing.
("to get up in the world...") Forbes, "Give Me the West," p. 248.
("rather be an asset ...") Forbes, p. 334
page 7
(booked passage on a steamer) Ibid, pp. 334-335.
(San Francisco Stock Exchange) Ibid. Forbes lists Harry as a founder, but no evidence has been found of this. The San Francisco Stock and Exchange Board was formed 11Sept1862. Harry's father E.F. Child joined in 1864 and sold to the Board in 1888. Joseph L. King, *History of the San Francisco Stock and Exchange Board*. New York: Arno Press, 1975, originally published San Francisco: The Stanley-Taylor Company, 1910, pp. 1, 6, 322-323, 336. Forbes' 1920 article in *American Magazine* does refer to the elder Child in reference to the stock exchange, however, that text was edited in the 1923 book.
(Matchless Mine) Halden, p. 101; "Reportorial Notes," *DI*, 16Aug1889, p. 4.
(four year contract, sold their line) Child, Appendix 4: *The Helena-Benton Route*, p. 12; Gray, p. 62. When one delves into the history of transportation between Helena and Fort Benton, it is the names of Thomas C. Power and Samuel T. Hauser that dominate. The short tenure of Huntley & Huntley is largely forgotten. See for instance Baumler, *Historic Helena*, p. 17; Paul F. Sharp, "Merchant Princes of the Plains," *Montana the Magazine of Western History*, 5(1), Winter 1955, pp. 2 -20.
(build a road eastward) Gray, p. 62.
(Pony Express outfit) Ibid, p. 62-63.
(permission from the Assiniboine...) P. 62-64.
page 8
(westward along the Milk, weather conditions ... attacks) Ibid, pp. 64, 67.
page 9
(lazy, worthless dogs, has been discontinued, no excuse, wind up affairs) Gray, p. 71.
(roads connecting the settlements) "He [Silas Huntley] organized the stage lines between Helena and Fort Benton, from Helena to Diamond City, Lincoln, Virginia City and Bannack, also from Helena to Fort Abercrombie, and those between Missoula and Walla Walla, Wash; Virginia City to Bozeman, and from Bozeman and Helena to Tongue river. He and his cousin, Charles C. Huntley, and Bradley Barlow, then president of the Vermont Central Railroad, controlled all stage lines in Montana save that from Helena to Salt Lake City, and held all mail contracts over the great stage lines of the west, the longest being between St. Louis and Walla Walla via Boise, Idaho." Bowen, pp. 922-923.
(health steadily declined) Gray, p. 62; C.C. Huntley death announcement, *ES*, 11Oct1883, p. 3; "Charles C. Huntley's Will," *ES*, 30Oct1883, p. 3. The town of Huntley, Illinois (McHenry Co.) was founded in 1851 by Charles' father, Thomas S. Huntley. Charles C. Huntley died there on 10Oct1883 at age 39. Child, Appendix 1: "The Huntley Family."
page 10
(minimal visitation) Aubrey L. Haines, *The Yellowstone Story: A History of our First National Park. Vol. I*. Yellowstone National Park, WY: Yellowstone Library and Museum Association, 1977, p. 193; Haines, *Vol. II*, p.478.
(last outpost of civilization) Earl of Dunraven, *The Great Divide: Travels in the Upper Yellowstone in the Summer of 1874*. New York: Scribner, Welford, and Armstrong, 1876, p. 207.
(Jay Cooke and Company) Black, pp. 277-278, 338-339.
(appointment was rather ineffective) Haines, *Vol. II*, p. 449.
(Washington social scene) Annie can be found during two seasons (1876 and 1878) in Washington with the Isaiah Hanscom family. In 1876 she and

Silas appear at the same reception. "Society," *National Republican* [Wash., DC], (hereafter *NR*) 8Feb1876, p. 1. The latter year she and her mother acted as hostesses in the Hanscom home. "New Year's Day," *ES*, 31Dec1877, p. 1; "Receiving," *NR*, 1Jan1878, p.1.

(eldest of three sisters) The sisters are Annie, born 1856, Maria, born 1858, and Adelaide, born 1861. A fourth child, a boy named Ervin, was born between Maria and Adelaide, circa 1859. Attempts to locate him after 1870 were unsuccessful. Listing for Simeon Dean, *1860 US Census Record*, Town of Madison, Ward 1, Dane County, Wisconsin, 26Jul1860; Listing for Simeon Dean, *1870 US Census Record*, Town of Prairie du Sac, Sauk County, Wisconsin, 20Jun1870. Child Family tradition lists Annie as the youngest. Emily F. Vucanovich, *The Dean Sisters*, typescript circa 1988, p. 1, vertical file: "Child Family," Montana Historical Society Research Center, Helena, MT (hereafter MHSRC). Annie's age appears to have been hand-altered on one census record, so she seems younger than Adelaide. Listing for Harry W. Child, *1920 US Census Record*, Town of Helena Ward 5, Lewis and Clark County, Montana, 19Jan1920.

(dormitory matron) Listing for Mrs. Simeon Dean, boarder, *Madison, Wisconsin City Directory, 1875*, p. 43, www.ancestry.com 16Jan2015; Listing for Ladies Hall of State University, Ellen Dean, Matron, *1880 US Census Record*, Town of Madison, Dane County, Wisconsin, 11Ju.1880.

(sisters attended classes) Maria appears as a student in 1877, 1878, 1879, and 1880. Adelaide is listed in 1878 (sub-Freshman class), 1879, and 1880 (Freshman Class), Class listings, University of Wisconsin, www.ancestry.com 20Jan2015. Our research shows only Maria graduated from University of Wisconsin. After Maria graduated in 1880 and took up post-graduate studies in Boston, it is likely that mother Ellen and sister Adelaide accompanied her. Adelaide is not listed as a student in 1882 or 1883. Alpha Listings, The *University of Wisconsin Alumni Directory, 1849-1919*, published 1921, p. 80, www.uwdc.library.wisc.edu/collections/uw/AlumniDir 29Jan2015. In her research, Emily Vucanovich, first wife of Huntley Child, Jr., learned that the girls' mother Ellen Dean's "uncle, Dr. John Sterling, had been one of founders of the University [of Wisconsin] and served for a time as its president." Dr. Sterling married Harriet Dean of Raynham, Massachusetts, so he was relative on their father's side of the family. Vucanovich, p. 1; Entry for *John Whelan Sterling*, www.wikipedia.com Jan2015.

(engagement was announced) By-line from the *Washington Herald* in "Personal," *NN-w*, 21Jun1878, p. 3.

(were married) Marriage Record, Dane County, Wisconsin, Vol. 3, p. 0451, located through Wisconsin Vital records online.

(selling routes and equipment) "Local News," *RMH*, 13Jun1878, p. 3.

(filed on a nice piece of land, P.B. Clark) Robert Walker, *Second Annual Report of the Secretary of the Helena Board of Trade for the Year 1879*. Helena, MT: Woolfolk, MacQuaid, and LaCroix, 1880, pp. 54, 56. The version located in the Montana Historical Society Research Center, Helena, MT, chronicles events that happened as late as 1887, although still bearing the 1880 publication date. The two partners corresponded about their plan. "We must control every acre in it [the Crow Creek Valley] possible," wrote Silas, "Prevent others from getting land there – and if possible freeze out stock men living in the valley. ... Do this quietly – and lose no time about it. ..." Silas S. Huntley, to P.B. Clark, 22Nov1877, *Huntley and Clark Records (1877-1883)*, SC 888, MHSRC.

(purchasing trips to the east) "The Territory," *RMH*, 1Aug1878, p. 7; "Territorial," *NN-w*, 20Sept1878, p. 3; "Local News," *RMH*, 1Jul1880, p. 3; "Benton Correspondence," *RMH*, 15Jul1880, p. 2; "Benton Correspondence," *RMH*, 22Jul1880, p. 2.

(sheep fared very well) "Montana Mites," *RP*, 12Jan1881, p. 5; "Local News," *RMH*, 1Jul1880, p. 3.

(but one human habitation) "Local News," *RMH*, 1Jul1880, p. 3.

(Helena) Petrik, pp. 4-5, 14-16; http://en.wikipedia.org/wiki/Northern_Pacific_Railway 19Feb2015; Baumler, *Historic Helena*, pp. 11-12.

(horrific wildfires) Petrik, pp. 6-7; http://www.helenahistory.org/fire_tower.htm 20Feb2015.

(house at 812 Madison) Walker, p. 27; Vucanovich, p. 1, gives credit to Silas for building a house at this address for Annie. In an 1887 publication it is shown as the residence of Harry W. Child, so it may have been a multi-family home for a time. However, no Helena City Directories for this time connect either the Huntleys nor the Childs to this address.

Chapter 2: New Faces in Helena   *(chapter header)* Walker, *Helena Board of Trade*, p. 27.

(they arrived in 1878) "Hotel Arrivals," *NN-w*, 17May1878, p. 3; "Hotel Arrivals," *NN-w*, 12Jul1878, p. 3; "Hotel Arrivals," *NN-w*, 25Oct1878, p. 3.

(job selling cigars) Helena, *Montana City Directory, 1879*, p. 145, www.ancestry.com 14Jan 2015; Listing for Harry W. Child, *1880 US Census Record*, Town of Helena, Lewis and Clark County, Montana,24Jun1880. In this 1880 census Lionel R. Nettre and Harry appear to be roommates.

(agent for a stage company) "... was first associated with the Gilmore and Salisbury stage line." "Harry W. Child Dies at His Home in La Jolla," *The Helena* [MT] *Daily Independent* (hereafter *HDI*), 5Feb1931; Child, p. 29.

(Bach came with him) "Maj. E. W. Bach is Dead at Seattle," *AS*, 21Apr1904; Bancroft and Victor, p. 771.

(dry goods store, North-Western Company) "Personal," *NN-w*, 17May1878, p. 3, "Our Philipsburg Letter," *NN-w*, 4Apr1879, p. 3; Reference to Sheriff's Sale: vs. The North-Western Company ..., *NN-w*, 27Jun1879, p. 2; Entry for quartz mill at Philipsburg, Montana, http://deq.mt.gov/Land/abandonedmines/linkdocs/65tech 12Jul2019.

(champion foot racer) "Our Philipsburg Letter," *NN-w*, 4Jul1879, p. 3; "Pedestrianism," *NN-w*, 8Aug1879, p. 3.

(five feet five inches) Bartlett, *Wilderness*, p. 174.

(Bach, Cory & Company) Bancroft and Victor, pp. 770-771; A. W. Ide, compiler, *Helena City Directory for 1888*. Helena, MT: Journal Publishing Co., 1888, p. 27, includes Wickes Directory for 1888. p. 31; F. Jay Haynes photographs titled "Bach, Cory and Co., LTD, store, Wickes, M.T.R.," 20Dec1886; "The Boston & Montana Gold Mines, Bach, Cory & Co., Gregory, M.T.," Dec1886; "Interior Bach, Cory and Co.'s Store, Gregory, M.T.R.," Dec1886, *Haynes Foundation Collection*, # H-1737; # H-1738; # H-1748, MHSRC Photograph Archives.

(fine brick building) "Montana Melange," *RP*, 8Sept1886, p. 5. The building is called "Broadway Block," in Walker, p. 54. Today, it is known as the Goodkind Building, and it is included in the *Last Chance Gulch, Helena Historic District*, Baumler, *Historic Helena*, p. 17; considered the "oldest standing building north of Broadway," http://www.helenahisotry.org/Goodkind_Building 15Apr2017. In 1890 Bach, Cory & Company conducted over $1 million in business. Bancroft and Victor, p. 771.

(county assessor) "County tickets," *RP*, 6Sept1882, p. 1.

(county delegate) "Democratic Territorial Convention," 25Sept1884," *NN-w*, 26Sept1884, p. 2.

(financial records) "The Legislature," *RP*, 11Mar1885, p. 1; "Local Notes," *RP*, 3Mar1886, p. 6.

(ordinance officer) "Local Notes," *RP*, 18Nov1885, p. 6.

(mining engineer) A.J. Seligman attended Rensselaer Polytechnic Institute. Listing for A.J. Seligman, *Troy, New York City Directory 1877*, www.ancestry.com 15Jan2015.

(Helena in 1881) Carl J. White, "Financial Frustrations in Territorial Montana," *Montana the Magazine of Western History*, 17(2), Spring 1967, pp. 43, 44.

(magnificent home) Listing for The Seligman-Lanstrum Home – 1886, House 16 in Baucus and Shanahan; Walker, p. 27. The Seligman home was designed by architect Cass Gilbert whose notable projects include the Montana Club building in Helena, the Minnesota State Capitol building in St. Paul, five buildings on the campus of Oberlin College, Ohio, Appendix: *Selected Buildings*, in Sharon Irish, *Cass Gilbert, Architect: Modern*

Traditionalist. New York: The Monticelli Press, 1999; Spencer, pp. 25-27; Geoffrey Blodgett and Jane Blodgett, *Oberlin Historic Landmarks.* Oberlin, OH: The Historic Preservation Commission of the City of Oberlin, 1997, p. 12. A.J. also served as delegate to the Montana Territorial Convention in 1884 and 1885. White, p. 43.

(seven brothers) "By 1867 the Seligman firm had branches in New Orleans, San Francisco, London, Paris and Frankfurt." White, p. 35. Branches included J. W. Seligman Company, New York; Anglo-California Bank, Lmtd., San Francisco; Seligman Hellman Company, New Orleans; and Seligman Brothers, London. *The Redemption of New York,* Chapter XXII, www.ancestry.com 18Jan2015. White also lists Seligman, Frerer & Cie in Paris, and Seligman & Stettheimer in Frankfurt.

(Montana Territory, I don't care what.) Joseph Seligman invested in the Bohm and Aub Banking House (S.H. Bohm and Philip Aub). It opened on 25Oct1867 at No. 47 Main Street in Helena. White, p. 36. Our sources for their trials and tribulations are White, pp. 34-45; Skidmore, p. 20.

(Joseph Seligman died in 1880) "[Jesse] Seligman Funeral," *The Evening World* [New York, NY], 2May1894, p. 6.

(correspondence with Lionel Nettre) Lionel Nettre, as superintendent of Gregory Mine, was corresponding with Joseph Seligman's assignees as early as 1876. White, pp. 42, 43.

(1881 A.J. purchased) White, p. 44.

page 18

(Child was manager, development of Gloster and Gregory) "From the North," *NN-w,* 30Dec1881, p. 3; "Territorial News," *RMH,* 17Jun1880, p. 2; Halden, p. 140; "Letter from Wickes," *NN-w,* 24Jun1881, p. 2; "Letter From the Belmont District," *RP,* 29Jun1881, p. 8; "The Swelling Boom," *DI,* 29Jul1883, www.ancestry.com 13Jan2015.

("What's worth doing…") B.C. Forbes, "Give Me the West!" p. 246.

(an investigation) "Capital Topics," *NR,* 24Mar1876, p. 4;"The United States Mail Contractors," *The Abbeville* [SC] *Press and Banner,* 26Apr1876, p. 1.

(equal share of the business) In 1878, the case of *Huntley vs. Huntley* was heard in Equity Court in Wash., DC. In 1880, the case was on the docket of the Supreme Court of the District of Columbia: *Charles C. Huntley Against Silas S. Huntley,* Case No. 6,075. A third suit in Equity Court in 1881 was *Huntley vs. Barlow,* Case No. 8 – "Wants His Share of the Profits," *ES,* 2Feb1878, p. 4; "District Courts," *NR,* 2Feb1878, p. 4; "Wants A Settlement," *ES,* 14Dec1878, p. 8; "The Huntley Case," *NN-w,* 24Dec1880, p. 2; "The Notorious Star Mail Route Service," *ES,* 9Dec1880, p. 1; "Personal Notes," *ES,* 11Dec1880, p. 1; *The Sunday Herald* [Wash., DC] (hereafter *SH*), 12Dec1880, p. 2; "United States Marshal's Sale," *NR,* 26Jan1882, p. 2; "Montana Matters," *RP,* 7Jun1882, p. 1; "Suit for Account. Against Bradley Barlow by C.C. Huntley," *The Evening Critic* [Wash., DC], 18Oct1882, p. 3.

page 19

(grease the wheels) "Mr. S. S. Huntley is defendant…," *SH,* 12Dec1880, p. 2.

(spruce young man) "Personal Notes, Etc.," *ES,* 11Dec1880, p. 1.

(execution of the court) "United States Marshal's Sale," *NR,* 26Jan1882, p. 2; "United States Marshal's Sale," *NR,* 24Feb1882, p. 2; "United States Marshal's Sale," *NR,* 3Oct1882, p. 3; "Real Estate," *NR,* 3Nov1882, p. 3.

(Hershfield's bank) "Territorial Items," *NN-w,* 12May1882, p. 3; Advertisement: "Merchants' National Bank of Helena," *RP,* 16Aug1882, p.5; "Merits Its Good Name, Standing of Montana's Leading Bank in the Financial Centers of the Country," *The Helena* [MT] *Independent* (hereafter *HI*), 10Dec1893, p. 1.

(Silas got contracts) "Mail Contracts," *RMH,* 2Mar1882, p. 2; "Local News," *RMH,* 1Jun1882, p. 3; "Montana Matters," *RP,* 7Jun1882, p. 1; "Local News," *RMH,* 29Jun1882, p. 3; "Local News," *RMH,* 6Jul1882, p. 3.

page 20

(Riverside Stock Farm) "Local News," *RMH,* 4Jan1883, p. 3.

(an early catalogue, treacherous cayuse) "Fine Stock," *RMH,* 15Feb1883, p. 4; "Some New Ads," *RP,* 20Apr1887, p. 5; "Montana Colts at Denver," *HI,* 25Sept1891, p. 8; Child, Appendix 5: *Montana's Great Stud, River Side Stock Farm, Huntley & Clark, Helena and Toston, Montana,* reprint of *1892 Catalogue of Standard and other Choice Bred Trotting Stock.* Lexington, KY: John K. Stringfield of Baxter & Stringfield (hereafter *Huntley & Clark, 1892 Catalogue*).

(demand for road horses, colt named Bishop) Quoted from *Turf, Field and Farm,* in "Live Stock," *RMH,* 11May1882, p. 4.

page 21

(race track) Walker, pp. 54, 59.

(Ben Lomond, fastest trotting horse) Reprinted from *Turf, Field and Farm,* in "Live Stock," *RMH,* 11May1882, p. 4; "The Fair," *RMH,* 5Oct1882, p. 2; "Livestock," *RMH,* 28Dec1882, p. 4; "Local News," *RMH,* 4Jan1883, p. 3; "Kentucky Volunteer," *RMH,* 25Jan1883, p. 4; "Fine Stock," *RMH,* 15Feb1883, p. 4; reprinted from *The Bozeman Chronicle* in "Some Valuable Stock," *RMH,* 3May1883, p. 4. Huntley & Clark began racing horses in 1882 competing in the Territorial Fair in Helena that year. Newspaper reports continue to report the dominant status of their stable at tracks in Butte, Deer Lodge, Anaconda through 1896. But the considerable financial resources of Butte Copper King Marcus Daly who entered the sport in 1887, propelled him the top – overshadowing Huntley & Clark in Montana racing history. See Ellen Baumler, *Lewis and Clark County Fairgrounds Racetrack,* National Register of Historic Places Registration form, National Park Service, 2006; and Catharine Melin-Moser, "In the Winner's Circle: How Montana Thoroughbreds Upset the Nineteenth Century's Racing Establishment," *Montana The Magazine of Western History,* 64(4), Winter 2014, pp. 22-41. The *River Press* noted: "His [Daly's] operations gave the Montana race horses a great name, but Daly never did more for the reputation of horses raised in Montana than did Huntley & Clark, Clark & Larabie and Raymond." "Is a Growing Industry," *RP,* 8Apr1903, p. 4.

(One year later) "Ben Lomond, Jr., Beats the Best," *RMH,* 21Aug1884, p. 2; "Ben Lomond Jr. King of the Montana Turf," *RMH,* 28Aug1884, p. 4.

(throughout the late 1880s, traveled to the fair grounds) Baumler, *Lewis and Clark,* *RMH,* 14Aug1884, p. 4; "West Side Association Races," *NN-w,* 29Jul1887, p. 3; "The Deer Lodge Meeting," *NN-w,* 19Aug1887, p. 3.

(politics governing the growth, first became active, on the Executive Committee) "Officers of the Montana Stock Growers' Association," *RP,* 6Aug1884, p. 8; "Stock Growers' Association," *NN-w,* 24Apr1885, p. 3; "Woolgrowers Association," *Fergus County Argus* [Lewistown, MT] (hereafter *FCA*), 21Nov1895, p. 1; "The Great Northwest," *AS,* 16Jan1891, p. 3; "Local News," *RMH,* 22Mar1883, p. 3.

page 22

(prosperous time) "Fine Stock," *BWR,* 15Feb1883, p. 5; "Sale of Thoroughbred and Trotting Stock," *RMH,* 15Mar1883, p. 4; "Live Stock," *RMH,* 17Apr1884, p. 4; *Daily Yellowstone Journal* [Miles City, M.T.] (hereafter *DYJ*), 22Apr1887, p. 2; "Spray of the Falls," *Great Falls* [M.T.] *Tribune* (hereafter *GFT*), 11Jul1888, p. 4.

(good judges) "Live Stock," *RMH,* 5Jun1884, p. 4; "Live Stock," *RMH,* 19Jun1884, p.4.

(struggles) "Trouble Among the Horses," *NN-w,* 22Feb1884, p. 2; "Territorial," *RMH,* 12Jun1884, p. 2; "More Horses Stolen," *RMH,* 25Sept1884, p. 2.

(Montana Sheep Company) "In Town and Out," *RP,* 22Jun1881, p. 8; "Local News," *RMH,* 15Jun1882, p. 3; "Jottings by our Traveling Man," *RMH,* 10Aug1882, p. 4. W.W. DeLacy, for whom DeLacy Creek in Yellowstone was named, led a group of prospectors through the park in 1863. Whittlesey, *Place Names,* pp. 83-84.

page 23

(D.L. McFarland died) William T. McFarland, in Bowen, pp. 293-294; "Death of 'Linn' [Demas L.] McFarland," *NN-w,* 15Aug1884, p. 2. W.C. Child's wife was a sister to these two men.

(disposed of that ranch) One source says W.C. Child sold the stock, the land, and six bands of sheep to Thomas Cruse for $93,000. Another says W.C. exchanged his sheep ranch with Tommy Cruse for Drum Lummon mining stock. Regardless of how it happened, W.C. no longer worked the ranch, and Harry and E.W. Bach incorporated the Cruse Mountain Consolidated Mining Company, at Marysville, MT on 11Dec1885. "Montana Mention," *DYJ,*

10Jan1886, p. 1; Skidmore, p. 37; Child, pp. 153-154; Listing for Cruse Mountain Consolidated Mining Company, *Helena City Directory, 1886-7*. Helena, MT: Geo. E. Boos, Printer and Binder, 1886, p. 41.

(White Face Farm) "A Flowing Well," *RP,* 7Dec1887, p. 2; Listing for Child Ranch, in Rich Aarstad, Ellie Arguimbau, Ellen Baumler, Charlene Porsild, and Brian Shovers, *Montana Place Names From Alzada to Zortman*. Helena, MT: Montana Historical Society Press, 2009, p. 46; "Better Butter, W.C. Child Establishes a Creamery and Proposes to Show What Montana Can Do," *HI,* 26May1889, p. 8.

(three-story barn, octagonal home) W.C. Child Ranch Barn, in Chere Jiusto, Christine Brown, and Tom Ferris, *Hand Raised: The Barns of Montana*. Helena, MT and Guilford, CT: Montana Historical Society Press, distributed by Globe Pequot Press, 2011, pp. 129-131; John N. DeHaas, Jr., *W.C. Child Ranch,* National Register of Historic Places Inventory – Nomination Form, 14Mar1976. The W.C. Child Barn is also known as The Kleffner Barn, after Paul and Thelma Kleffner bought the property in 1943. Chuck Haney, *Big Sky Barns: Grand and Historic Barns of Montana*. Helena, MT: Riverbend Publishing, 2007, pp. 36-38. In 1977 the W.C. Child Ranch was placed on the National Register of Historic Places. "The barn earned a National Trust for Historic Preservation *Barn Again! Merit Award* in 1988. Today, it is not only a beloved landmark in East Helena Valley but also one of the most desirable destinations in the region for parties, weddings, and family reunions." Jiusto, et al, p. 131.

(gold dust and nuggets) Walker, pp. 56, 58, 60.

(Jefferson County and Elkhorn) Child, Appendix 11: *The History of the Child-Kleffner Ranch*, by Paul Kleffner and Alice Dove; "Many Pleasant Events," *HI,* 3Jul1892, p. 3; "Personal and General," *HI,* 17Jul1892, p. 3; in "Better Butter, …" the reporter writes that "both the Northern Pacific and the Montana Central run very close to it. The N.P. has a spur within a few yards of it."

(completed her studies) Maria Dean graduated UW in 1880. Alphabetical Listings, The *University of Wisconsin Alumni Directory, 1849-1919,* published 1921, p. 80, www.uwdc.library.wisc.edu/collections/uw/AlumniDir 29Jan 2015; "Catalogues of Officers and Graduates," Class of 1880, University of Wisconsin, 1887, p.38, www.ancestry.com 20Jan2015.

page 24

(training abroad) "Neighborhood News," *NN-w,* 23Jan1885, p. 3; "Then she went all alone to Berlin to still further prosecute her studies where she encountered great difficulties gaining admission to a hospital until Prof. Schroeder interested himself in her cause." "Dr. Dean in the East," *HI,* 16Feb1889. "Schroeder was a catalyst in the construction of the new clinic of gynecology and obstetrics at the Berlin-Charité. It first opened in 1881, and was constructed with an emphasis on hygiene and antisepsis. Schroeder specialized in research of gynecological diseases, and is remembered for his surgical work with vaginal and endometrial cancers." Entry for *Karl Ludwig Ernst Friedrich Schroeder (1838-1887)*, www.wikipedia.com Jan2015.

(homeopathic practice) "Montana Mention," *DYJ,* 4Apr1886, p. 1. According to Vucanovich, "When the Berlin Opera House burned, the severest burn cases were her assignment." p. 1. The author's research was unable to locate any more information about this however, there was a fire at the Ring Theater in Vienna on 8Dec1881 which claimed 850 lives. Harry W. Child II writes "Dr. Dean continued her medical studies in Germany and Vienna, again finding she was always given the most harsh cases because of her gender...," Child, p. 12. A fictional depiction of Dr. Dean may be found in the historical novel: Ann Cullen, *Lilly Cullen: Helena, Montana 1894*. Helena, MT: Book Montana, 1999, pp. 153-164.

(diphtheria) Vucanovich, p. 2; "Maria Dean: Woman of Medicine," in Gayle C. Shirley, *More Than Petticoats: Remarkable Montana Women*. Guilford, CT: The Globe Pequot Press, 1995, pp. 62-66, 133; Ellen Baumler, "When Diphtheria Was in Town," in various authors, *More From the Quarries of Last Chance Gulch, Vol. II*. Helena, MT: Helena Independent Record, 1998, pp. 98-102, 105-106; Mari Graña, *Pioneer Doctor: The Story of a Woman's Work*. Helena, MT and Guildford, CT: TwoDot, an imprint of The Globe Pequot Press, 2005, p. 185.

(Adelaide also attended the University of Wisconsin) Vucanovich, pp. 1-2; "Adelaide Dean," Listing for Sub-Freshmen Class, Modern Classical Course, University of Wisconsin, 1878, p. 16; Listing for Sub-Freshman Class, Modern Classical Course, University of Wisconsin, 1879, p. 16; Listing for Freshman Class, Modern Classical Course, University of Wisconsin, 1880, p. 17, www.ancestry.com Jan2015. Adelaide is not listed as a student in 1882 or 1883, which would have been her junior and senior years. Alpha Listings, The *University of Wisconsin Alumni Directory, 1849-1919,* published 1921, p. 80, www.uwdc.library.wisc.edu/collections/uw/AlumniDir 29Jan2015. Adelaide and their mother Ellen Dean may have accompanied Maria to Boston after she graduated in 1880, and perhaps Adelaide completed her studies there.

(Kappa Kappa Gama) Adelaide "furthered her studies at the University of Massachusetts," Child, p. 17; Vucanovich writes that Ellen Dean was "a housemother at the Kappa Kappa Gamma house, at the University of Wisconsin." p. 1. Dr. Dean is listed as member of Kappa Kappa Tau, Listing for Maria Morrison Dean, Class of 1883, School of Medicine, Boston University, 1918, p. 243, www.ancestry.com 20Jan2015.

(NPR tracks) Baumler, *Historic Helena*, pp. 11-12, 59-60; Petrik, p. 14.

(no dearth of young men) Vucanovich, p. 1.

(star of society columns) "Crystal Wedding," *DI,* 21Mar1883, www.ancestry.com 13Jan2015.

page 25

(left for the Gregory mine) "Excursion to the Gregory Mine," *DI,* 6Sept1882. The McFarland reference here is probably to one of W.C. Child's brothers-in-law, Demas L. McFarland or William T. McFarland – both of who were involved in the Montana Sheep Company. Bowen, pp. 293-294.

(strolling Last Chance Gulch) Vucanovich, p. 2.

(mother's family) Harry and Adelaide were married in the home of W.H. Wyman. Wyman was for a time in the insurance business with the girls' father Simeon Dean in Madison, Wisconsin. University of Wisconsin School Catalog, 1858, "Disbursements," p. 33, www.ancestry.com 16Jan2015; University of Wisconsin School Catalog, 1860, "Secretary's Report," no page #, www.ancestry.com Jan2015. W.H. Wyman's wife Isabel, two years younger than her sister Ellen Dean, died in 1880. Listing for Ellen Dean, 1880 US Census Record, Town of Madison, Dane County, Wisconsin, 11Jun1880; Listing for W.H. Wyman, 1880 US Census Record, Town of Cincinnati, Hamilton County, Ohio, 7Jun1880; Listing for Ellen M. Dean, Forestvale Cemetery, Helena, Lewis and Clark County, Montana; Listings for Isabel L. Watson Wyman and William Henry Wyman, Forest Hill Cemetery, Madison, Dane County, Wisconsin, U.S. Find A Grave Index, 1600s - current, https://www.findagrave.com/ 9Jan2015, 19Oct2020.

(extended trip to Cincinnati) Two sources reveal that Harry may have followed Adelaide to Cincinnati, the home of her mother's sister. Listing for R.W. Child (sic), trav. salesman, *Cincinnati City Directory*, 1882, p. 243, www.ancestry.com 21Jan2015; Listing for Harry W. Child: '82 - '83, salesman, Cinn., *West Newton Massachusetts, High School Student Lists, 1821-1923*, www.ancestry.com 19Jan2015. Reprint from the *Cincinnati Commercial-Gazette*, "The Child-Dean Wedding," DI, 31Oct1883, www.ancestry.com 13Jan2015; "Local News," *The Daily Miner* [Butte, M.T.], 2Nov1883, p. 4, www.ancestry.com 13Jan2015; "Territorial Items," NN-w, 2Nov1883, p. 2; H.W. Child to Adelaide Dean, 23Oct1883, Hamilton County Ohio Probate Court, *Marriage Records 1808-1973*, Vol. 89, p. 15, record 30, www.probatect.org/CourtRecordArchive/ 13Jan2015; Listing for W.H. Wyman, Aetna Insurance Company of Hartford, Conn, residence in Walnut Hills, *Cincinnati Ohio City Directory*, 1884, p. 1503, www.ancestry.com 21Jan2015.

page 26

(first born) Child, p. 32.

(concern about adequate facilities) Mary Shivers Culpin, *"For the Benefit and Enjoyment of the People;" A History of Concession Development in Yellowstone National Park, 1872-1966*. Yellowstone National Park, WY: National Park Service Yellowstone Center for Resources, 2003, pp. 6-8; Richard A. Bartlett, "The Concessionaires of Yellowstone National Park: Genesis of a Policy, 1882-1892," *Pacific Northwest Quarterly*, 74, Jan1983, pp. 2-10; Robert V. Goss, *Making Concessions In Yellowstone: A Who's Who of the Explorers, Exploiters, Enthusiasts and Enterprises In Yellowstone National Park*. Gardiner, MT: self-published, 2002.

(he laid out a road system) Karl John Byrand concluded that Philetus W. Norris, by "the laying of the first real road and trail system linking Yellowstone's unique features," "greatly influenced the evolution of the park's interpretive landscape ..." He posits that Norris' five years as

Yellowstone's superintendent were perhaps more influential in creating "an aura of civilization," than the Army's thirty-year tenure. Byrand, p. 11. He quotes Bartlett who wrote, that the "existence [of] the road and trail network encouraged the systematic park tour, helped determine points for hotels and lunch stops, and created an aura of civilization that tourists found comforting amidst the wilderness." Bartlett, *Wilderness*, p. 224.

(Army Corps of Engineers) For history of the Army Corps of Engineers in Yellowstone see Kenneth H. Baldwin, *Enchanted Enclosure: The Army Engineers and Yellowstone National Park. A Documentary History.* Wash., DC: Office of the Chief of Engineers, United States Army, U.S. Government Printing Office, 1976; Mary Shivers Culpin, *The History of the Construction of the Road System in Yellowstone National Park, 1872-1966, Historic Resource Study, Vol. I.* National Park Service, Rocky Mountain Region, 1994.

page 27

(Railroad officials) Culpin, *Concession Development*, pp. 9-12.

(Yellowstone Park Improvement Company) We have chosen to use the simplified YPIC to refer to the company that incorporated in January 1883, under the laws of New Jersey, as the *Yellowstone National Park Improvement Company.* Bartlett, *Wilderness*, p. 129.

(National Hotel) Brit T. Fontenot, "Striking Similarities: Labor Versus Capital in Yellowstone National Park," *Yellowstone Science*, 5(4), Fall 1997, pp. 15-18; Lee H. Whittlesey, "'Oh, Mammoth Structure!' Rufus Hatch, the National Hotel, and the Grand Opening of Yellowstone in 1883," *Annals of Wyoming*, 83(2), Spring 2011, pp. 2-20.

(U.S. Army was sent) H. Duane Hampton, *How the U.S. Cavalry Saved Our National Parks.* Bloomington, IN and London: Indiana University Press, 1971.

(Willows Stock Farm) Walker, p. 60, 63; Child, pp. 155-156; Harriett Meloy, "Harry Child amassed an empire of ranchland," unmarked photocopy, MHSRC; Harriett C. Meloy, "Harry W. Child and Green Meadow Ranch," in multiple authors, *More From the Quarries of Last Chance Gulch, Vol. III.* Helena, MT: Helena Independent Record, 1998, pp. 40-44.

(800 acres of land) "Buying Real Estate," *GFT*, 18May1887, p. 1; "Territorial News," *The Philipsburg* [M.T.] *Mail* (hereafter *PM*), 19May1887, p. 1; "Local Notes," *RP*, 25May1887, p. 6; "A Big Land Sale," *GFT*, 18Jun1887, p. 1; "Real Estate Speculators," *GFT*, 3Aug1887, p. 1; "A Big Transfer," *RP*, 24Aug1887, p. 2.

page 28

(Oro Fino Terrace) Walker, pp. 10, 35; King, pp. 60-61; *Helena City Directory, 1889*, www.ancestry.com 14Jan 2015; "Spray of the Falls," *GFT*, 5Jun1889, p. 3; "Royally Remembered, Judge Bach and Miss Child Receive Wedding Presents," *HI*, 5Jun1889, p. 4; "Orange Blossoms. Judge Bach and Miss Kate Child Married Today," *GFT*, 8Jun1889, p. 4; "Spray of the Falls," *GFT*, 8Jun1889, p. 4; *Thomas C. Bach*, in Bowen, pp. 515-516; *Oro Fino Terrace*, http://helenahistory.org/oro_fino_terrace.htm 20Mar2015; "Personal and General," *HI*, 5Feb1893, p. 3.

(A glance at city directories) MHSRC collection.

(troubles mounted at the Gregory) White, pp. 34-45; Forbes, pp. 335-339; Halden, pp. 101, 103; "Mad Miners Near Helena, Montana, They Capture a Capitalist," *The Daily Herald* [Los Angeles, California] (hereafter *DH*), 29Jan1887, p. 1; "Montana Matters," *RP*, 2Feb1887, p. 6; "A Novel Expedient. How the Gregory Miners Secured Their Pay," *NN-w*, 4Feb1887, p. 3; "In Durance Vile. Four Prominent Helena Gentlemen Held Prisoners by 200 Impecunious Miners at Gregory," *GFT*, 5Feb1887, p. 2; "General Mining News," *PM*, 7Jul1887, p. 3; Skidmore, p. 29. A.J. Seligman later filed suit against the Boston & Montana Mining company in the amount totaling over $83,000. "Sued By Stockholders," *Saint Paul* [Minnesota] *Globe* (hereafter *SPG*), 6Dec1888, p. 2. A few years later he filed a libel suit against the *Anaconda Standard* newspaper, a case which was decided in favor of the defendants. "Eleven to One, Mr. Seligman Can't Heal His Wound With Cash," *AS*, 29Oct1891, p. 1.

page 30

(need to carry a gun) Forbes, pp. 338-339. Lionel Nettre's name does not appear in relation to the Gregory kidnaping incident. In 1881 he was appointed postmaster for the town of Gregory. He was in Vienna, Austria in 1888; by 1891 he was living in London, where he died in 1902. *Appointments of U. S. Postmasters, Vol. 48, 1877- 1884* www.ancestry.com 16Jan 2015; Listing for Lionel Robert Nettre, School Catalog, Columbia College, 1888, p. 250, www.ancestry.com 16Jan2015; Lionel R. Nettre, LifeStory, www.ancestry.com 21May2017.

(Fast Train) "Spray of the Falls," *GFT*, 25Aug1888, p. 4.

Chapter 3: Winds of Change   *(chapter header)* Great Falls Leader Annual 1890, p. 37.

page 31

(Montana Smelting Company's project) "The Great Smelter," *GFT*, 11Jul1888, p. 1; "Ground Broken!" *GFT*, 7Mar1888, p. 1; "The Great Falls Smelting Works," *GFT*, 25Aug1888, p. 2; "The Silver Smelter," *Great Falls and Cascade County: Historic, Scenic, and Biographical.* Great Falls, MT: The Great Falls Tribune, 1899, pp. 14-15.

page 32

(paid one million) Harry W. Child, II to Nan Sigrist, May 2004. Child, an career accountant, has spent much time assimilating the financial records of his great-grandfather. Other statements about Harry's wealth include "Harry Child was a millionaire before he reached the age of fifty." Lee Whittlesey, transcript of speech given at Child Family Reunion, Mammoth Hot Springs, 13Jul1998, vertical file: *History (Whittlesey 6)*, YNPA; and "worth about four million dollars in 1911," Bartlett, *Wilderness*, p. 174.

(dainty hand) "Montana is Growing," *GFT*, 10Oct1888, p. 1; "The Great Smelter ... Mrs. H.W. Child Sets the Machinery in Motion," *GFT*, 6Oct1888, p. 4.

(public relations) [Harry] "... invited the Great Falls guests to dine with him, agreeing to discuss the matter over a cup of coffee or a glass of water from the Giant Spring. Full justice was done the excellent dinner served when the party returned to their homes. ..." "Last Spike Driven, Ceremonies Attending the Completion of the Great Falls & Missouri Railroad," *GFT*, 19May1888, p. 1; "Welcome Visitors, Colonel Broadwater and a Large Excursion Party Come to Town," *GFT*, 14Jul1888, p. 4.

(Press Association) "Notes at Sight," *NN-w*, 6Jul1888, p. 2.

(entertained the eastern financiers) "To Visit the Park," *HI*, 9Jun1888, p. 1; "Spray of the Falls," *GFT*, 12Jun1889, p. 3.

(stopping with her husband, Before many months) "Spray of the Falls," *GFT*, 23May1888, p. 8.

page 33

(French architectural design) "Silver Smelter," source of publication not recorded, reproduced in Child, p. 36; Great Falls Tribune, *Great Falls Memories.* Battle Ground, WA: Pediment Publishing Co., 2008, pp. 94, 95.

(Christmas of 1889) "Spray of the Falls," *GFT*, 25Dec1889, p. 4; "City and County News," *The Great Falls* [MT] *Leader* (hereafter *GFL*), 27Dec1889, p. 4; "Card of Thanks," *GFL*, 27Dec1889, p. 1.

(three sisters) "Spray of the Falls," *GFT*, 28Dec1889, p. 3.

(social and community events) See for instance "Past and Future," *HI*, 24Feb1889, p. 6; "Social Chit Chat," *HI*, 14Jul1889, p. 6; "The Seligman Reception," *HI*, 3Aug1889, p. 8; "Spray of the Falls," *GFT*, 14Aug1889, p. 3.

(long purse) Petrik, p. 72.

(Helena for Capitol) Petrik, pp. 64, 190, n122.

(Helena's Professional Females) *HI*, 12Jan1890, p. 5.

(founding first hospital) http://www.helenahistory.org/st_peters_hospital.htm 20Feb2015; Baumler, *Historic Helena*, pp. 112, 114.

(hunting trips) "General Montana News," *GFT*, 2Nov1887, p. 1; "Personal," *HI*, 29Oct1890, p. 5; "Personal and General," *HI*, 8Nov1891, p. 3; "Movements of Helena People," *AS*, 19Aug1894, p. 10.

(they entertained) "To Welcome Strangers, Informal Receptions to be Given by the Social Society of St. Peters, Tea and Evening Party at the Home of Mr. and Mrs. Child," *HI*, 26Oct1890, p. 2; "An Elegant and Elaborate Reception ...," *HI*, 2Nov1890, p. 2; "Pleasures of the Week." *HI*, 23Nov1890, p. 2.

page 34

(branch in Great Falls) "Visiting our City," *GFT*, 31Dec1887, p. 1; "Spray of the Falls," *GFT*, 28Mar1888, p. 4; "New Enterprises," *GFT*, 11Apr1888, p. 4; Janet Thomson, ed., *Early Settlers of Great Falls: 1884-1920, Vol. I*. Great Falls, MT: Great Falls Genealogy Society, 2012, p. 101. Thomson combed meticulously through early Great Falls City Directories to catalog every name listed. Harry and Adelaide Child were gone before the first one was published for 1887-1888.

(and his wife "Gussie") "Married," *NN-w*, 7Apr1882, p. 3; Edmund W. Bach and Julia A Bach, Marriage Certificate, Gallatin County, *Montana, County Marriages, 1865-1950*, www.ancestry.com 15Jan2015; "Spray of the Falls," *GFT*, 29Aug1888, p. 4.

(frame the constitution) "How to Vote," *GFT*, 8May1889, p. 2.

(choice to amend) "Republican Nominees," *HI*, 2May1889, p. 1; "Republicans in Convention," *GFL*, 2May1889, p.1; "Nominations. Republicans Nominate C.M. Webster and H.W. Child of Helena," *GFT*, 4May1889, p. 1.

(not a good word) "Spray of the Falls," *GFT*, 8May1889, p. 3.

(declined the nomination) "Looking for a Victim, H.W. Child Declines the Republican Delegate Nomination in Cascade," *HI*, 10May1889, p. 1; "Harry W. Child Resigns," *GFL*, 10May1889, p. 1.

(great deal shrewder) "Why Mr. Child Withdrew from the Delegate Contest," *GFT*, 11May1889, p. 3.

(public brawl, There was a knife) "Tripped and Disarmed, An Affair Which Started out as Tragedy and Would up a Comedy. M. A. Meyendorff and Will Bach Have an Encounter at The Helena, There was a Knife and a Good Deal of Talk But Nobody Got Badly Hurt," *HI*, 8Nov1890, p. 5.

page 35

(tragedy struck) "Albert Lionel Bach," http://findagrave.com 19Jan2015; "Died," *GFL*, 23Jul1889, p. 1; "A Sad Death," *HI*, 23Jul1889, p. 4; "A Tribute to the Memory of a Lady Well Known and Esteemed in Helena," *HI*, 28Jul1889, p. 2; "Personal and General," *HI*, 28Jul1889, p. 2.

(after the burial) "Spray of the Falls," *GFT*, 14Aug1889, p. 3; "Personal and General," *HI*, 25Aug1889, p. 6.

(a saner, healthier) Forbes, p. 323.

(you can do more work) Forbes, p. 324.

(Helena Board of Trade) Listing for the Helena Board of Trade members for 1889, *HI*, 2Feb1889, p. 3.

(county election judge) "County Commissioners, Helena Divided Into Three [Voting] Precincts Instead of Two," *HI*, 10Apr1889, p. 4; "Synopsis of Proceedings of Board of County Commissioners in Regular Session, June Term 1889," *HI*, 22Jun1889, p. 3.

(member of the Chamber of Commerce) "A New Era for Helena," *HI*, 8Mar1890, p. 5; "Chamber of Commerce," *HI*, 23May1390, p. 5; "The Election is Over," *HI*, 14Jun1890, p. 5; "The Site Committee," *HI*, 8Jul1890, p. 8; Petrik, p. 18.

(the Athletic Association) "Now For Base Ball," *HI*, 6May1890, p. 5; *HI*, 5Aug1890, p. 5.

(the Commercial Club) "Commercial Club Organized," *HI*, 1Jun1890, p. 4.

(First National Bank) Advertisement for First National Bank, *HI*, 5Apr1893, p. 3. The president was listed as S.T. Hauser; E.W. Bach was listed as a director.

(He disassociated himself) In 1892, Bach was listed as Secretary and Treasurer of Bach, Cory & Company. *R.L. Polk & Co.'s Helena City Directory 1892*. Helena, MT: R.L. Polk & Co., Publ., p. 195, www.ancestry.com 14Jan2015. Three years later, A.J. Seligman was listed as President and Treasurer, and David Cory was listed as Vice President, Secretary and Manager. *R.L. Polk & Co.'s Helena City Directory 1895*. Helena, MT: R.L. Polk & Co., Publ., p. 123. There are allusions to Bach's political trouble around 1893, but the authors have found no specific references to back this up.

(mining broker) Listings for E.W. Bach, *R.L. Polk & Co.'s Helena City Directory 1895*. Helena, MT: R.L. Polk & Co., Publ., p. 123; *R.L. Polk & Co.'s Helena City Directory 1897*. Helena, MT: R.L. Polk & Co., Publ., p. 129; *R.L. Polk & Co.'s Helena City Directory 1898*. Helena, MT: R.L. Polk & Co., Publ., p. 116.

(11,000 acres of land) "Spray of the Falls,"*GFT*, 11Jul1888, p. 4.

(sale of a horse) "Among our Visitors," *HI*, 10Mar1888, p. 4; "Talk of the Turf," *HI*, 19May1889, p. 8.

(sold Ben Lomond) "Neighborhood News," *NN-w*, 13Apr1888, p. 3; "Stock Notes," *RP*, 18Apr1888, p. 4; "Spray of the Falls," *GFT*, 11Jul1888, p. 4.

(hesitated the sale) "Coming Back," *GFT*, 22May1889, p. 1.

(1889 catalogue) "Montana Horses," *HI*, 21Apr1889, p. 6; *Huntley & Clark*, 1892 Catalogue.

page 36

(Helena fair) "The Fair Prizes," *HI*, 1Sept1889, p. 8.

(new Broadwater Hotel) Spencer, p. 45; "The Fair Hop, The New Hotel Broadwater the Scene of a Brilliant Social Gathering," *HI*, 31Aug1889, p. 8; "Personal Mention," *HI*, 1Sept1889, p. 2.

(active in the organizations) "Officers of the Montana Stock Growers' Association," *RP*, 6Aug1884, p. 8; "Montana at St. Louis," *RP*, 26Nov1884, p. 6; "Accomplished. The Heart's Desire of Montana Stock Growers Brought About Yesterday," *DYJ*, 4Apr1885, p. 1; "Stock Growers' Association," *NN-w*, 24Apr1885, p. 3; "Spring Meeting [of the Montana Stock Growers Association]," *DYJ*, 20Apr1887, p. 2.

(large cattle and stock man) "City and County News," *GFL*, 9May1889, p. 4.

(Charles Anceney) "Stock Growers' Association," *NN-w*, 24Apr1885, p. 3; Gen. James S. Brisbin, *The Beef Bonanza; Or, How to Get Rich on the Plains*. Philadelphia: J. B. Lippincott & Co., 1881, pp. 168-170.

(Roosevelt) "Past and Gone, Stock Growers Close their Labors ..." *DYJ*, 19Apr1888, p. 3.

(Chicago and New York) "Montana Horses for Street Cars," *FCA*, 4Apr1889, p. 1; "Montana Horses," *HI*, 21Apr1889, p. 6; "The Great Northwest," *AS*, 16Jan1891, p. 3; "Personal and General," *HI*, 29Nov1891, p. 3.

(horse kings) "Livestock," *RMH*, 28Dec1882, p. 4.

(value of printer's ink) "Local News," *RMH*, 22Mar1883, p. 3.

page 37

(visited the offices) "Spirit of the Turf." reprinted in *DYJ*, 22Apr1887, p. 2; "Chicago Horsemen." reprinted in "The Mecca of Horsemen," *DYJ*, 4Apr1888, p. 3; "Montana Horses," *HI*, 21Apr1889, p. 6.

(While in Chicago, did not thrive any better) "The Great Northwest," *AS*, 16Jan1891, p. 3.

(wrote this letter) "The Montana Horse, 'Si.' Huntley Speaks by the Record ...," *NN-w*, 26Feb1886, p. 3.

(State Board of Stock Commissioners) "The Legislature," *HI*, 6Mar1889, p. 4; "The Legislature," *HI*, 13Mar1889, p. 4; "Northwest News," *AS*, 19Apr1890, p. 3.

(full medical license) Shirley, p. 65; Baumler, *Historic Helena*, p. 106.

page 38

(full of pluck, an excellent shot) "Dr. Dean in the East," *HI*, 16Feb1889, p. 3.

(is a blond, veteran turfman) "Women, God Bless 'Em. Women in Montana Generally and of Helena in Particular Who Work for a Living. The Wealthiest Women in the State – Helena's Professional Females," *HI*, 12Jan1890, p. 5.

(Oro Fino Terrace) Listing for Silas S. Huntley, *R.L. Polk & Co's Helena City Directory, 1898*. St. Paul, MN and Helena, MT: R.L. Polk & Co., Publ., 1898, p. 222; Listing for Silas S. Huntley, *R.L. Polk & Co's Helena City Directory, 1899*. St. Paul, MN and Helena, MT: R.L. Polk & Co., Publ., 1899, p. 222; Listing for Silas Huntley, *1900 US Census Record*, Town of Helena, Ward 5, Lewis and Clark County, Montana, 13-14Jun1900; Listing for

Silas S. Huntley, *R.L. Polk & Co's Helena City Directory, 1901*. Helena, MT: R.L. Polk & Co., of Montana, Publ., 1901, p. 249; "This Week in Helena," *AS*, 18Mar1894, p. 9; Newspaper clipping titled "In the Yellowstone [1896]," *Yellowstone National Park Scrapbook, S12, 1922*, p. 1, Acc. No. 07-812, Yellowstone National Park Archives, Yellowstone Heritage and Research Center, Gardiner, MT (hereafter YNPA).

(tally-ho party) "The World of Society," *HI*, 31Aug1890, p. 2.

(Society in the Solstice) "Society in the Solstice, ..." *HI*, 6Jul1890, p. 2.

page 40

(to act as agents, and independent association, no responsible party) "National Park Management," *GFT*, 5Mar1892, p. 4; "The Hand of the Prince, Two Residents of Helena and a New Lease in the National Park," *HI*, 14Mar1892, p. 5; "The Yellowstone Park," *HI*, 18Mar1892, p. 6; "Bozeman Affairs," *AS*, 24Mar1892, p. 7. In 1883 George Wakefield first received a U.S. mail contract between Livingston, MT and Cooke City, MT via Mammoth Hot Springs. Culpin, *Concessions Development*, p. 31.

(Devil's Stairway) Haines, *Vol. II*, p. 46.

page 41

(Harrison-Huntley relations) Harrison on executive committee with SSH: "The Stock Growers," *HI*, 18Apr1889, p. 1; Involvement in social circles: "Society Getting Lively," *HI*, 16Nov1890, p. 2; criticism: "To Confirm Leases, The Gibson Party Will Introduce a Substitute for the Washburn Bill," *HI*, 14Mar1892, p. 5. In testimony before congress, John Noble confirmed that Russell Harrison, Thomas Carter, and Senator Carey of Wyoming all visited him to vouch for Silas Huntley's suitability. Statement by John W. Noble, 31Mar1892, "Hearing Before the Committee on Territories of the United States Senate in Relation to the Bill (S. 1963) To Incorporate The Yellowstone Park Company," to accompany his testimony before the House Committee on Public Lands, 25Apr1892, published in Thomas C. McRae, "Yellowstone National Park," 52nd Cong., 1st Sess., H.R. No. 1956, 20Jul1892, pp. 48-49.

(received a contract) John W. Noble, Interior Secretary, to Capt. George S. Anderson, Acting Supt. of Yellowstone Park, 14Apr1891, doc 256; George Chandler, First Assistant Secretary of Interior, to Capt. George Anderson, 1Apr1891, doc 356, *First 10,000 Documents*, YNPA.

(Wakefield ... one more summer) F.A. Boutelle, *Annual Report of the Acting Superintendent of Yellowstone National Park*. Wash., DC: Government Printing Office, 1891, p. 7.

(looking over the field) Ibid.

(competitions in Denver and Dallas) "Sports of All Sorts," *AS*, 22Mar1891, p. 9; "Friday's Events," *HI*, 7Aug1891, p. 4; "Jottings About Town," *HI*, 16Sept1891, p. 8; "Winners at Denver," *HI*, 8Oct1891, p. 5; "Mikado Wins at Dallas," *HI*, 29Oct1891, p. 4.

page 42

(disposing of his blooded show horses) "Montana Colts at Denver," *HI*, 25Sept1891, p. 8; "Sold for $10,000. Two Helena Horses Go for Good Figures in Denver," *HI*, 11Mar1892, p. 5; *Huntley & Clark*, 1892 Catalogue.

(heavily into mining) "Anaconda Dates Taken ...," *HI*, 19Jul1891, p. 8; "Court House Cullings," *HI*, 17Jul1890, p. 5; "Court House Cullings," *HI*, 31Jul1890, p. 5; "Castle and Barker News," *HI*, 7Dec1890, p. 8.

(Wakefield ... west side ... Bozeman) "... It is considered to the best interest of the public that a lease be granted George W. Wakefield, of Bozeman, Mont., to draw traffic from the Union Pacific railroad company over the Beaver canyon route, provided if the travel from the Northern Pacific warrants it, the department may find it wiser and to the benefit of the public to extend the lease to Wakefield or to other parties for traffic from that direction also. ..." in "No More Monopolies, The Interior Department Gives Transportation Privileges in Yellowstone Park, Livingston and Bozeman Parties Can Hereafter Look Out for Tourists, Those Who Can Show They Mean Business Will Be Allowed to Put Up Another Hotel," *HI*, 13Jun1893, p. 1; Lon Johnson, *Yellowstone Park Transportation Company Historic District: Determination of Eligibility for Listing in the National Register of Historic Places*. Yellowstone National Park, WY: Branch of Cultural Resources, 21Mar2001, p. 2; Culpin, *Concessions Development*, p. 40.

(hotel in Bozeman) "Spray of the Falls," *The Semi-weekly Tribune* [Great Falls, MT] (hereafter *S-WT*), 28Jan1891, p. 3; Advertisement – "The Bozeman, *AS*, 13Apr1891, p. 8; "Bozeman Hotel is Remodeled," *The Hotel News of the West*, 19(20), May 19, 1923, p. 21.

(Silas' contract) "Lease & Contract Yellowstone Park Transportation Co. #1, 30Mar1891, James W. Noble, Secretary of the Interior & Silas S Huntley, Helena MT: 10 year contract for a stage and transportation line," Item 59, Letter Box: Leases and Contracts for use of Park Lands (expired) 1908-1916, file no. 190 (also called Box no. 28), YNPA.

page 43

(Swearing) Paul Schullery, "A Partnership in Conservation... Roosevelt & Yellowstone," *Montana the Magazine of Western History*, 28(3), Summer 1978, p. 11.

(hiding liquor bottles) Entries for "Whiskey Flats" and "Whiskey Spring," Whittlesey, *Place Names*, p. 262.

(nickname savage) Former NPS Yellowstone Historian, Lee Whittlesey writes, "The name was in use long before this 1891 contract to Silas Huntley, and I've long believed that it somehow came from George Wakefield's stage drivers, but I cannot prove that." Personal correspondence from Lee H. Whittlesey to Ruth Quinn, 5Jun2019. The entry for "Savage Hill," in *Yellowstone Place Names*, Whittlesey, p. 221, quotes Elizabeth Frazer [1May1920, *Saturday Evening Post*, p. 40] "they [the drivers] used to hell-for-leather round those narrow mountain curves in order to hear the doods [sic] and tourist ladies schreeh. So we got to calling them savages because they were such a raw bunch." Another source that ties the name *savage* to stagecoach drivers is Gwen Petersen, *Yellowstone Pioneers: The Story of the Hamilton Stores and Yellowstone National Park*. Santa Barbara, CA: Sequoia Communications, 1985, p. 21.

(old timers) "The Montana Horse," *NN-w*, 26Feb1886, p. 3.

(trotting horse S.S.) Hugh Kirkendall, a prominent area freighter raced a horse named *S.S.* "Spray of the Falls," *GFT*, 11Jul1888, p. 4. Huntley and Clark named one horse *Addie D.* – perhaps for Adelaide Dean Child. "Nomenclature. By Huntley & Clark, Riverside Stock Farm, Montana, 1883," *RMH*, 6Mar1884, p. 4

(staging in Montana) "Montana Stage Coach," *HI*, 27Apr1890, p. 6.

Chapter 4: Tally Ho   *(chapter header)* Bach to Pitcher, 18Jun1902, RG00, series I, box 19, YNPA.

page 45

(ten year contract) "After a Sharp Fight, Helena Men Win the Contest ..." *HI*, 22May1892, p. 8.

(purchased Wakefield's outfit) Child, pp. 38, 46; Statement of Thomas F. Oakes, President of the NPR, before the House (sub)Committee on Public Lands, 13May1892, McRae, pp. 228-229.

(YPTC incorporated) Joining the three principals were Silas Huntley's banking partners L.H. Hershfield and Aaron Hershfield who guaranteed the bond. "County Cullings ... Livingston," *Red Lodge* [MT] *Picket*, 4Jun1892, p. 1. We have chosen to use the abbreviation YPTC, even though the original incorporation was *Yellowstone National Park Transportation Company*. Haines records the company name as *Yellowstone National Park Transportation Company* between 1891 and 1898, and *Yellowstone Park Transportation Company* between 1898 and 1936; while noting that despite these name changes and reorganizations, the names "represent a continuous business operation." Haines, *Vol. II*, pp. 133, 402 n68.

(capital stock of $250,000) Haines, *Vol. II*, p. 406.

(Army Corps of Engineers) Culpin, *Road System*, pp. 25-68; Baldwin, pp. 84-111.

(four hotels) The Yellowstone Park Association operated the four hotels mentioned. George S. Anderson, *Report of the Acting Superintendent of the Yellowstone National Park to the Secretary of the Interior*. Wash., DC: Government Printing Office, 1893, p. 9. Four other hotels were independently operated and are not mentioned in the text. These were McCartney's Hotel at Mammoth Hot Springs, Firehole (Marshall's) Hotel at the Lower Geyser

Basin, Yancey's Hotel at Tower Junction, Cottage Hotel at Mammoth Hot Springs. A YPA hotel at Norris, built in 1886, burned in July of 1887. Personal communication from Lee Whittlesey, to Ruth Quinn, 5Jun2019.

page 46

(had an awful time) Haines, *Vol. II,* pp. 219-220.

(Lieutenant Chittenden ... was sent) Chittenden began his Yellowstone contributions in 1891-1893, and returned 1899-1905. "Chittenden's engineering feats in Yellowstone included at least five masterpieces: The imposing masonry Entrance Gate at Gardiner, the Melan arch bridge over the Yellowstone River above the Upper Falls, the splendid road through Sylvan Pass, the road over the almost impossible summit of Mount Washburn, and the exquisite Golden Gate viaduct, the most difficult piece of work he executed in the park. ... His construction was remarkable, esthetically as well as practically. Whenever possible he provided the tourist with 'a sense of expectancy' by avoiding monotonous straight stretches in favor of roadways that were adapted to the natural terrain and passed by points of interest." Baldwin, pp. 95, 96.

(spare him $500) Ibid; Gordon B. Dodd, *Hiram Martin Chittenden: His Public Career.* Lexington: The University Press of Kentucky, 1973, pp. 14-15.

(up-to-date by telegram) "Jottings About Town," *HI,* 25May1892, p. 4.

(Wakefield house) It is the oldest building (1884) still in use in Yellowstone today. It stands on *Executive House Lane,* next to the Child House. Recognizing its illustrious early residents, historian Lee Whittlesey calls it the *Wakefield/Huntley/Nichols Residence.* Lee H. Whittlesey, *"This Modern Saratoga of the Wilderness:" A History of the Mammoth Hot Springs and the Mammoth Village in Yellowstone National Park,* draft manuscript, 2010, chap. 7, pp. 111-113.

(daintiest little cottage) Annie Jane Pugh, *A Trip to the Yellowstone Park Diary, June 28 - July 28, 1900.* Overbrook, PA: Press of William Mann Co., 1900, p. 34. Original in the Beinecke Rare Book and Manuscript Library, Yale University. Copy courtesy Lee H. Whittlesey.

page 47

(adequate and excellent) George S. Anderson, *Report of the Acting Superintendent of the Yellowstone National Park to the Secretary of the Interior.* Wash., DC: Government Printing Office, 1892, p. 6.

(second phase of his obligation) "Sand Coulee Coal," *GFT,* 18Aug1888, p. 4; "The Great Falls Smelting Works," *GFT,* 25Aug1888, p. 2; "The Great Smelter ... Mrs. H.W. Child Sets the Machinery in Motion," *GFT,* 6Oct1888, p. 4; "Looking for Ore," *HI,* 2Mar1889, p. 3.

(Minneapolis and Manitoba, Montana Central) Skidmore, p. 42.

(Helena, Boulder & Madison) "New Railroads," *GFT,* 30Apr1887, p. 1.

(representative of the Northern Pacific) "Spray of the Falls," *GFT,* 20Mar1889, p. 3. In 1889, Jule M. Hannaford was a Northern Pacific Traffic Manager. He served as president of the road between 1913 and 1920, http://en.wikipedia.org/wiki/Northern_Pacific_Railway 19Feb2015. He and Harry remained friends for the rest of Harry's life. "Prominent Men Express Regret When Informed of Death of Harry W. Child, Pioneer Montana Business Man; Was Known Over Entire Nation," *Livingston* [MT] *Enterprise* (hereafter *LE*), 7Feb1931, p. 2.

(Smelter combined, consolidation of these interests) "Smelting Work United, Two Strong Concerns Join the Great Falls Smelters," *HI,* 6Aug1890, p. 2; "Millions for Montana, A Great Corporation to Control the Helena and Great Falls Smelters," *FCA,* 14Aug1890, p. 1. Although these August notices reported that Harry was to remain as the manager, by October 1890 he was "no longer in charge of the affairs of the Union smelting company." "Spray of the Falls," *S-WT,* 22Oct1890, p. 3. In 1893 Frank Marshall Smith was listed as superintendent. "Silver Smelter," *GFT,* 31Dec1893, pp. 1, 5, courtesy The History Museum, Great Falls, MT, 14Apr2020.

page 48

(closed the Great Falls smelter) Child, p. 36.

(smaller buildings moved away) "Sole Remaining Stack of Old Silver Smelter is Tumbled to Ground," *GFT,* 23Sept1928, p. 7; "Fire to Wipe Out Last Trace of Historic Silver Smelter," *GFT,* 4Apr1924, p. 9, courtesy The History Museum, Great Falls, MT.

(extended vacation to California) "Spray of the Falls," *S-WT,* 22Oct1890, p. 3.

(interesting eastern capitalists) "Good News for Boulder," *S-WT,* 21Nov1891, p. 5.

(incorporating two companies) "Boulder Smelting Co.," *HI,* 6Oct1891, p. 5.

(Ground was broken, surveys for five miles) "Boulder Smelter," *HI,* 14Oct1891, p. 8.

(mines around the town of Basin) "Jefferson County Mines," *HI,* 8Jul1893, p. 8.

page 49

(processed low-grade ores, smelter was well-designed) "The Boulder Smelter ..." *HI,* 2May1892, p. 5; "Post, Politics, Capital, ... " *HI,* 9May1892, p. 1.

(went into operation) The newspapers kept the public apprised of the progress of the smelter's construction. "Jefferson County Mines," *HI,* 20Nov1891, p. 8; "Other Matters," *AS,* 9Dec1891, p. 3; "Jefferson County Mines," *HI,* 2Jan1892, p. 5; "Boulder Notes," *AS,* 31Jan1892, p. 3; "Personal and General Mention of Various Matters of Interest at Boulder," *HI,* 13Mar1892, p. 7; "Boulder," *HI,* 17Apr1892, p. 6; "The Boulder Smelter," *HI,* 13May1892, p. 8; "The Boulder Smelter," *HI,* 25Jun1892, p. 7; "Mining in Jefferson," *HI,* 5Aug1892, p. 8.

(Idle winter) "Boulder Briefs," *AS,* 9Apr1893, p. 6; "In Jefferson County," *AS,* 30Apr1893, p. 8; "Jefferson County Mines," *HI,* 8Jul1893, p. 8; "Mining Notes," *NN-w,* 29Jul1893. Records of the Boulder Smelting Company, incorporated 3Oct1891, extend only until 1894. *Boulder Smelting Company records, 1891-1894,* SC 1036, MHSRC. This enterprise seems to have been short-lived: "the main ore supply which had been depended upon was far too siliceous to be used in quantity, as the ore ran from 65 to 85 percent silica, although the value, chiefly gold, were satisfactory. Purchase ores were very difficult to obtain, so that plant has laid idle most of the time." Edward Dyer Peters, *Modern Copper Smelting.* New York and London: The Scientific Publishing Co., 1899, p. 415. https://books.google.com/ 30May2020.

(There's more to life) Forbes, p. 326.

(interesting foot race) "For a Keg of Beer," *AS,* 10Feb1892, p. 4.

page 50

(accountant at Great Falls) RP, 14Mar1888, p. 2.

(ranch on Belt Creek) "Spray of the Falls," *GFT,* 1Sept1888, p. 4.

(at social events) "Jottings About Town," *HI,* 14May1890, p. 8; "Spray of the Falls," *GFT,* 5Jun1889, p. 3.

(Ben Lomond's death) "Ben Lomond, Jr., Dead," *DI,* 21Aug1892, p. 8.

(Silas had sold Ben Lomond and Maxim) "Neighborhood News," *NN-w,* 13Apr1888, p. 3; "Stock Notes," *RP,* 18Apr1888, p. 4.

(Harry and Val purchased them, standing in stud) "Racing Matters," *DI,* 5May1889, p. 5; "General Turf Notes," *HI,* 14May1889, p. 4; "Whip and Spur," *HI,* 14May1889, p. 4; "Coming Back," *GFT,* 22May1889, p. 1.

(Ben Cole) "Montana's Flyers," *GFT,* 14Nov1888, p. 2; "The Programme for To-day," *HI,* 31Aug1889, p. 8.

(Ida D. and Sweetbrier) "Twentieth Exhibition of the Montana Agricultural, Mineral and Mechanical Association," *HI,* 27Aug1889, p. 8; "The Fair Prizes," *HI,* 1Sept1889, p. 8.

(familiar figure at state fairs) "Harry Child Succumbs," newspaper clipping, vertical file: "Child, Harry W.," MHSRC.

(driven to the ranch of Huntley & Clark) "Park Season Closes," *LE,* 3Oct1896, p. 1.

(served as president) Notice for the annual meeting of the stockholders of the Yellowstone National Park Transportation company, *HI,* 1Nov1893, p. 2; "The Holidays in Bozeman," *AS,* 31Dec1893, p. 9.

(memo, hand-written) Child, pp. 38-39.

page 51

(temporarily at Oro Fino) Listings for Harry W. Child, *R.L. Polk & Co.'s Helena City Directory 1892.* Helena, MT: R.L. Polk & Co., Publ., p. 230; R.L.

Polk & Co.'s Helena City Directory 1893. Helena, MT: R.L. Polk & Co., Publ.; *R.L. Polk & Co.'s Helena City Directory 1894*. Helena, MT: R.L. Polk & Co., Publ., p. 167. In 1893 and 1894 Harry listed his occupation as Vice-President, St. Paul & Helena Land & Improvement Company. The Childs used the Oro Fino address on Benton Avenue through 1909.

(run between the fair grounds) FCA, 30Mar1893, p. 1; "An Old Timer, The Coach Will Be Exhibited at the World's Fair," *HI*, 10Apr1893, p. 1.

(coaches will be run) "Montanans At The Fair," *AS*, 25Apr1893, p. 8.

(Wonderland publications) "Beginning in 1884 with *The Wonderland of the World*, the NPRR published guidebooks illustrated with F. Jay Haynes' photographs. The books, which became known as the Wonderland series, carried information about Yellowstone and about all of the places visitors could see along the railroad's northwestern route. These paperbound books were published from 1884 to 1906." Lee H. Whittlesey, *Yellowstone Place Names*. Helena, MT: Montana Historical Society Press, 1988, p. 136. Byrand discusses how these early guidebooks, distributed through the mail and by local railway agents, provided tourists with "a preconceived notion of the destination." They "literally guide the potential visitor through the park, pointing out what are considered the valuable sights and experiences." Byrand, pp. 227-233; quotes from pp. 228, 236.

(railroad's photographer) Edward W. Nolan, *Northern Pacific Views: The Railroad Photography of F. Jay Haynes, 1876-1905*. Helena, MT: Montana Historical Society Press, 1983, pp. 14, 16; Chris J. Magoc, *Yellowstone: The Creation and Selling of an American Landscape, 1870-1903*. Albuquerque, NM: University of New Mexico Press, 1999, p. 44. See also Jack Davis and Susan Davis, *Haynes Yellowstone Park: The Haynes Family in Yellowstone National Park 1881-1968*. Bozeman, MT: Olde America Antiques, 2013.

(own guidebook) Albert Brewer Guptill, *Practical Guide to Yellowstone National Park*. St Paul, MN: F. Jay Haynes & Bro., 1890. Leslie J. Quinn collection. In 1896, still authored by Guptill, these were published under the title *Haynes Guide to Yellowstone Park*. Beginning in 1910, F. Jay Haynes was listed as author. His son Jack Ellis Haynes was listed as author of *Haynes Official Guide Yellowstone National Park* that were published through 1966. Whittlesey, *Place Names*, [1988 ed.], p. 136.

page 52

(palace car) Nolan, pp. 18-20. Haynes' winter base of operations was St. Paul, Minnesota. A photo of the Haynes Studio at Selby and Virginia Avenue in St. Paul is shown in Richard L. Saunders, *Glimpses of Wonderland: The Haynes and Their Postcards of Yellowstone National Park*. Bozeman, MT: self-published, 1997, p. 31.

(sold as a package) Guptill, pp. 9-10; Anderson, *Report, 1892*, p. 7.

(build his own bunkhouses, kept separate) Telegram from John W. Noble, Interior Secretary, to Capt. George S. Anderson, Yellowstone Superintendent, 17Jun1892, docs 306-310, *First 10,000 Documents*, YNPA;. *Leases in Yellowstone National Park*, S.B.M. Young, *Annual Report of the Acting Superintendent of Yellowstone National Park*. Wash., DC: Government Printing Office, 1897, p. 20.

(Besides the drivers) L.W. "Gay" Randall, *Footprints Along the Yellowstone*. San Antonio, TX: The Naylor Company, 1961, pp. 58- 59. The author's father, James Norris "Dick" Randall, arrived in Yellowstone in 1887 and began working for George Wakefield. He founded the OTO Ranch north of Gardiner, MT and is known as the father of dude ranching in Montana. Ibid, pp. 58, 65, 67-68.

page 53

(the term savage) Petersen, p. 21.

(Savage mess halls) Information from this section, Nan Sigrist, personal knowledge.

(Bozeman schoolteacher) Jane Galloway Demaray, *Yellowstone Summers: Touring with the Wylie Camping Company in America's First National Park*. Pullman, WA: Washington State University, 2015. "… he came to Bozeman, Mont., in September, 1878, where he was superintendent of the public schools for three years, while later he was for four years principal of Bozeman Academy. … He made two tours of the Yellowstone Park in 1880." *William W. Wylie*, Bowen, pp. 974-975.

(three thousand horses) Smith, pp. 30-31. "As of 1900, Wylie Land and Livestock held 600 acres on Middle Creek (Middle Fork of Pole Creek), where Wylie now stored most of his camping company equipment; 7,040 acres (eleven sections) on Cherry Creek, which included several sections of leased state and school land; 1,000 acres on Spanish Creek; and 640 acres (one section) of pasture on Elk Creek, west of Bozeman. Eventually, Wylie purchased 5,120 acres (eight sections) in the Spanish Creek area, south of Bozeman, that once belonged to homesteaders who bought up land in 160-acre parcels in the late 1800s. When many of the settlers proved up and moved away, Wylie bought them out, accumulating more land with each passing year." Demaray, pp. 141-142.

(health concerns of women and children) "Women, God Bless 'Em …" *HI*, 12Jan1890, p. 5; Listing for "Dr. Maria Dean Residence (626 N. Benton Ave)," Baumler, *Historic Helena*, p.106.

(Women's Clinic in Berlin) According to *The Helena Independent* "… she went all alone to Berlin to still further prosecute her studies where she encountered great difficulties in gaining admission to a hospital until Prof. Schroeder interested himself in her cause. "Dr. Dean in the East," *HI*, 16Feb1889, p. 3. Karl Ludwig Ernst Friedrich Schroeder "… was a catalyst in the construction of the new clinic of gynecology and obstetrics at the Berlin-Charité. It first opened in 1881, and was constructed with an emphasis on hygiene and antisepsis. Schroeder specialized in research of gynecological diseases …" https://en.m.wikipedia.org/wiki/Karl_Ludwig_Ernst_Schroeder 17Apr2015.

(first Chinese child) "An Early Morning Arrival," *HI*, 20Jan1893, p. 4.

(Johns Hopkins University) "Personal," *HI*, 23Nov1893, p. 8.

(in-house medical provider) "Women, God Bless 'Em …" *HI*, 12Jan1890, p. 5.

(lecturing around the community) "Woman's Place in Life, Dr. Maria M. Dean Talks About the Matter to the Helena Ladies," *HI*, 15Mar1891, p. 8; "The County Teachers … Dr. Maria Dean to Address the Institute this Evening on Hygiene," *HI*, 19Mar1891, p. 8; "Training the Young, An Able Lecture by Dr. Dean on Forming Habits in Children," *HI*, 16 Aug1891, p. 6; "In Helena," *AS*, 29Apr1894, p. 10; "The Helena Schools," *HI*, 17Jun1894, p. 5.

page 54

(school trustee) "The Helena Election," *AS*, 7Apr1895, p. 7; Listing for "The A.T. Hibbard Home," Baucus, p. 34.

(Associated Charities) "Associated Charities," *HI*, 22Dec1893, p. 5; "They Did Good Work, The Annual Meeting of the Associated Charities …," *HI*, 20Nov1894, p. 1.

(Prevention of Cruelty) "The S.P.C.A.," *HI*, 18May1890, p. 8.

(St. Peter's Episcopal Church) "Personal Mention," *HI*, 10Jan1892, p. 3; "Dr. Dean, Well Known Woman Physician of Capital City Dies," *Great Falls* [MT] *Daily Tribune* (hereafter *GFDT*), 24May1919, p. 13.

(Helena School of Art) "Helena School of Art," *HI*, 25Oct1892, p. 5; Baumler, *Historic Helena*, pp. 91-92.

(balls and parties) "A Silver Anniversary," *HI*, 19Feb1893, p. 3; "The Social Ways of Helena," *AS*, 22Apr1894, p. 9; "An Artists' Evening," *HI*, 25Nov1894, p. 5.

(hunting and camping) "Personal and General," *HI*, 8Nov1891, p. 3; "Personal and General," *HI*, 17Jun1894, p. 7; "Movements of Helena People," *AS*, 19Aug1894, p. 10.

(advancement of society) "Life means growth," she averred, "means progress toward an end and that end is individual perfection. It means working out to the fullest extent the design indicated for the individual. All progress then must coincide with truth, and the first requisite for growth is fidelity to self. Now, if in any stage of the world's growth any individual or class of individual is obligated to live under such circumstance that this cardinal law of growth, viz.; fidelity to self, can not be realized, then that individual or class is living under circumstances unfavorable to complete development. … " "Woman's Place in Life …" *HI*, 15Mar1891, p. 8.

(first annual convention) Graña, p. 213; T.A. Larson, "Montana Women and the Battle for the Ballot," *Montana the Magazine of Western History*, 23(4), Winter 1973, p. 31; Petrik, p. 123; "Ladies on the Silver Question," *AS*, 25Jun1896, p. 8; "Meeting of Women, Second Annual Convention of the

Montana Equal Suffrage Association," *AS*, 18Nov1896, p. 6.

(Ice Cream) "Better Butter ..."; "Busy Week in Society," *HI*, 19Jul1891, p. 3.

(A merry crowd) "At the Child Ranch," *HI*, 28Jun1891, p. 3.

(repaired to the large ball room) "Personal and General," *HI*, 17Jul1892, p. 3.

page 55

(A handsome reception) "Three Large and Pleasant Gatherings Took Place During the Past Week," *HI*, 15Feb1891, p. 3.

(he led the opening dance) "The Merry Dance at the Opening of the Auditorium," *HI*, 5Jun1892, p. 3.

(W.C. mortgaged the ranch) Child, Appendix 11. According to one historian "Although a few silver mines were hanging on, most communities throughout the mining regions – Castle, Park City, Elkhorn, Wickes, Philipsburg, Granite, Glendale, Hecla – were sick, dying, or already dead. ... By the end of the year [1893], Montana's unemployment stood at 20,000 workers, mostly around Butte and Helena. Scores of stores failed, particularly in the mining centers where their prosperity depended on the income of mine and smelter workers." Skidmore, pp. 49-50.

(a falling out) Typescript titled: "H.W. Child," no author listed, vertical file: "Child, Harry W.," p. 8, MHSRC.

(After the Silver Panic) Skidmore, pp. 46-47, 50; Listing for "Child Ranch," in Aarstad, et al, p. 46.

($30,000 in debt) "Death of W.C. Child," *FCA*, 19Oct1893, p. 2; Kleffner and Dove.

(to First National Bank, separate deeds of assignment) "W.C. Child Assigns, He and His Wife Name W. F. Sanders as Assignee," *HI*, 15Sept1893, p. 8.

(found dead, nervous prostration, note was found) "Death of W.C. Child..." *FCA*; "The shocking news ...," *AS*, 15Oct1893, p. 2. Mrs. Mary B. Child died in 1905 in her birth town of Lafayette, Indiana. The couple's two daughters, now married, were living in Helena. "Mrs. M.B. Child Dies in Indiana," *HDI*, 29Nov1905, p. 8, vertical file: "Child, William C.," MHSRC.

(The Society of Montana Pioneers) Kleffner and Dove.

page 56

(A great many ladies) "Columbian Ball To-Night," *HI*, 12Oct1892, p. 1.

(In 1889 ... joined Second National) Advertisement "Second National Bank of Helena," *HI*, 15Nov1889, p. 3. Harry's brother George B. Child was listed as a cashier.

(absorbed into ... First National) Skidmore, p. 51. Advertisement "First National Bank," *HI*, 5Apr1893, p. 3.

(Harry is listed as a Director) Advertisement: "First National Bank, Helena, Mont.," *AS*, 1Jun1896, p. 10.

(E.W. joined Samuel Hauser's) Advertisement "First National Bank," *HI*, 5Apr1893, p. 3.

(Second National Bank failed) "Two Helena Banks Consolidate," *HI*, 28Sept1893, p. 1; Skidmore, pp. 49, 51.

(strongest and best managed) "Helena's Big Buildings, The Pride of the City," *HI*, 1Jan1894, p. 2; "The Merchants National, L.H. Hershfield's bank, had finally failed in 1897 after 32 years in Helena." Skidmore, p. 53. See also pp. 19, 33.

page 57

(Merchant's National Bank of Helena) Advertisement, HI, 28Sept1890, p. 6.

(Anderson seemed satisfied) George S. Anderson, *Report of the Acting Superintendent of Yellowstone National Park to the Secretary of the Interior.* Wash., DC: Government Printing Office, 1894, p. 5.

Chapter 5: In the National Park   *(chapter header)* Farrow to Pitcher, 22Jul1904, RG00, series I, box 19, YNPA.

page 59

(came to the park in 1895) Huntley Child, Interview by author/historian Aubrey L. Haines, 11Sept1961 – audio tape 61-3, side 1, (hereafter: Child-Haines Interview), YNPA.

(back in the park the next year) "In Livingston," *AS*, 5Jul1896, p. 12.

(fond memories ... The harnesses) Child-Haines Interview.

page 60

(big tally-ho) An 1897 inventory shows that Silas operated two six-horse Concord coaches. Young, *Report, 1897*, p. 6.

(Gardiner and Mammoth) Bill and Doris Whithorn, *Photo History From Yellowstone Park.* Livingston, MT: The Park County News, no date, p. 14.

(only one run-away) Child-Haines Interview.

(Champion Fisherman) "In the Yellowstone," newspaper clipping 1896, *Yellowstone National Park Scrapbook No. 3*, Cabinet drawer 1, accession # S71, YNPA.

(weeks spent at Yellowstone Lake) Child-Haines Interview. "Colonel Waters had a fine wife and one son, Amory, and two girls, Edna and Anna." in Edward H. Moorman, "Journal of Years of Work Spent in Yellowstone National Park 1899-1948," pp. 5-6, vertical file: *History-YNP-Journals and Diaries,* "Moorman," YNPA.

(school terms in Helena or California) Child, p. 62; "Spray of the Falls," *S-WT*, 22Oct1890, p. 3; "Personal and General," *HI*, 29Apr1894, p. 7; "Coronado Notes," *The San Diego* [CA] *Union* (hereafter *SDU*), 30Apr1895, p. 8; "Personal," *The San Francisco* [CA] *Call*, 1Oct1895, p. 6; "Coronado Notes," *The San Diego* [CA] *Union and Daily Bee*, 21Nov1895, p. 8; "Coronado, Arrivals at the Big Hotel," *DH*, 4Oct1896, p. 2.

(rights were not being considered) The Bassett Brothers running into the park through the west entrance sought and were denied permission to establish an outpost at Riverside – just inside the west gate. George Chandler, Acting Interior Secretary, to Capt. F.A. Boutelle, Acting Supt., 10Aug1889, doc 218; A.W. Chadbourne, to John W. Noble, Secretary of the Interior, 1Aug1892, doc 235, *First 10,000 Documents*, YNPA.

(One serious issue) An illustration of the conditions before Wakefield and Hoffman (1886) is found in Testimony of Charles Gibson, before the House (sub)Committee on Public Lands, 10May1892, McRae, pp. 187-188; Testimony of George S. Anderson, Acting Superintendent of Yellowstone National Park, before the House (sub)Committee on Public Lands, 12May1892, McRae, pp. 220-221.

(tried not to expand, the only change to be noted) George S. Anderson, *Report of the Acting Superintendent of Yellowstone National Park to the Secretary of the Interior.* Wash., DC: Government Printing Office, 1895, p. 9.

page 61

(last official report, could arrange a stop-over) George S. Anderson, *Report of the Acting Superintendent of Yellowstone National Park to the Secretary of the Interior.* Wash., DC: Government Printing Office, 1896, p. 9. The issue of stop-overs is also discussed by W.G. Pearce, testimony before the House Committee on Public Lands, 2May1892, McRae, pp. 118-119.

(established in 1877) Aarstad, et al, p. 128.

(completed his tour of duty) "Patrolling the Park," *AS*, 27Jun1897, p. 9; Haines, *Vol. II*, p. 455.

(duties until November 15) Haines, *Vol. II*, p. 477.

(extensiveness of Silas' operation) Young, *Report, 1897*, p. 6.

page 62

(Monida & Yellowstone) James B. Erwin, *Report of the Acting Superintendent of the Yellowstone National Park to the Secretary of the Interior.* Wash., DC: Government Printing Office, 1898, p. 4; Randall, p. 48; "Hersey's Letter," *PM*, 4Feb1898, p. 1.

(called the Red Line, guests had their luggage) Child-Haines Interview; Shankland, pp. 66, 118-119.

(By season's end) Erwin, *Report, 1898*, pp. 7, 9, 20; Blueprint: Map showing Monida & Yellowstone sites, 1898 (8 different locations), F. Jay Haynes Papers, Collection 1500, Box 25, Folder 3, Merril G. Burlingame Special Collections, Montana State University–Bozeman Libraries (hereafter BSC-MSU). The Log Cabin Studio at Upper Geyser Basin Faithful was moved from its original location north of Old Faithful Inn in the 1930s. It sits

neglected on the fire road between the Grand Loop Road and the in-bound lanes within Old Faithful Village. Young, *Report, 1897*, pp. 5, 20; Collected pages related to history of buildings, dated 24Feb1955, *Jack Ellis Haynes and Haynes, Inc. Records*, Collection 1504, Box 59, Folder 3, BSC-MSU.

page 63

(praised their operation) Erwin, *Report, 1898*, p. 7.

(identified themselves) "Personal Mention," *DH*, 18Dec1894, p. 12; Listings for Child and Bach, *R.L. Polk & Co.'s Helena City Directory 1895*. Helena, MT: R.L. Polk & Co., Publ.; Listing for E.W. Bach, and Cruse Mountain Consolidated Mining Co., HW Child, pres; EW Bach, sec, *R.L. Polk & Co.'s Helena City Directory 1897*. Helena, MT: R.L. Polk & Co., Publ., pp. 129, 172; Listing for Harry Child, *R.L. Polk & Co.'s Helena City Directory 1900*. Helena, MT: R.L. Polk & Co., Publ., p. 148.

(Boulder Smelting Company) In the 1895 publication of West-Newton English and Classical School, West Newton Massachusetts, *High School Student Lists, 1821-1923*, www.ancestry.com 19Jan2015.

(control of a mine) "Giving Them Pointers. Harry W. Child Tells ... a Few Things. About Montana Mines," *AS*, 9Mar1895, p. 4.

(Seligman now partnered) In 1889, Bach, Cory & Company incorporated, and A.J. Seligman became president of the company. *Helena City Directory, 1889*, Helena, MT: R.L. Polk and Co., pp. 120, 280, www.ancestry.com 14Jan2015. A.J. Seligman was also an investor in the Union Smelting and Refining company that took over the Great Falls Smelter. "Smelting Work United," *HI*, 6Aug1890, p. 2. He served as a director of the Montana Club alongside Harry's brother George B. Child, and brother-in-law, T.C. Bach. *R.L. Polk & Co.'s Helena City Directory 1891*. Helena, MT: R.L. Polk & Co., Publ., p. 127.

(A.J. left Helena) White, pp. 43, 45; Listing for Albert J. Seligman, *New York, New York City Directory, 1911*. www.ancestry.com 15Jan2015. He "... retired from banking in 1927 to devote full-time to mining, rising to the presidency of the Butte Copper and Zinc firm. ... Albert J. Seligman died in New York, April, 1935 at the age of 76." White, p. 43.

(remained active) "Personal and General," *HI*, 5Apr1893, p. 3. In 1893 E.W. married Margaret C. Beattie at Fort Snelling, Minnesota. The couple had a daughter (born 1895) and a son (born 1899). Listing for Edmund W. Bach, *Minnesota Marriages Index, 1849-1950*, on-line data base, Provo, UT; Listing for Margaret Stanislaus Carroll Bach, http://www.findagrave.com/ 19Jan2015. Margaret Bach died in San Francisco in 1936 and is buried in Helena, MT with E.W.

(chief of commissaries) "Maj. E. W. Bach Assigned," *SPG*, 14Jul1898, p. 2; "Will Bring Them Home," *SPG*, 17Sept1898, p. 2; Listing for Major Edmund W. Bach, *R.L. Polk & Co.'s Helena City Directory 1899*. Helena, MT: R.L. Polk & Co., Publ., p. 113; Certificate: Commissary of Volunteers, Rank of Major, 3Jun1898, in vertical file: "Bach, Edmund William," MHSRC.

(Returning to Helena) Ibid, Listing for Edmund W. Bach, *R.L. Polk & Co.'s Helena City Directory 1901*. Helena, MT: R.L. Polk & Co., Publ., p. 125; E.W. Bach, Secretary, YNPTC, to Capt. John Pitcher, 24Sept1901; doc 4766, *First 10,000 Documents*, YNPA; Listing for Edmund W. Bach, *R.L. Polk & Co.'s Helena City Directory 1902*. Helena, MT: R.L. Polk & Co., Publ., p. 149.

page 64

(handling the buggy reins) "Local Layout," *LE*, 11Jul1896, p. 5; Barringer, *Selling Yellowstone*, p. 35.

(other visitors) "Notables to Visit The Park," *DI*, 21Jun1900, p. 8; Daily listings for 22Jun, and 29Jun1900, Bound Volume, Item 143: *Journal of Acting Superintendent Yellowstone National Park 1900-1903*, pp. 59, 62; "Bryan at Mammoth Hot Springs," *AS*, 5Aug1897, p. 1; "In St. Paul Social Circles," *SPG*, 8Jun1900, p. 14; Listings for 4Jul1900, 8Jul1900, 19Aug1900, 13Sept1900, *Journal of Acting Superintendent*, pp. 64, 65, 79, 86; Ruth Quinn, "An Heiress in Wonderland," *Annals of Wyoming*, 87(1&2), Winter/Spring 2015, pp. 17-26.

(escorted them from the Fountain Hotel, see their home at Mammoth, sent his niece Dean) Pugh, pp. 34, 49, 48.

(Jack Haynes was a playmate) Story told by Jack Ellis Haynes, to Aubrey L. Haines, 19Apr1961, Haines, *Vol. II*, p. 182.

page 65

(the hotel company) The Northwest Improvement Company purchased all YPA stock in June 1898. Bartlett, *Wilderness*, p. 172; "Memorandum Re Yellowstone Park Hotel Company & Yellowstone Park Transportation Company," by J.H.P., 12Sept1918, President's Subject file 209 B, folder 9, (137.C.5.7B), Northern Pacific Railway Records, Minnesota History Center, St. Paul, MN, (hereafter NPRR-MHC).

(spoke with him briefly) J.H. Dean, Supt. of YPA hotels, to C.S. Mellen, 26Sept1899, President's Subject file No. 209 A, folder 4; Charles S. Mellen, Pres. of the NPR, was in Yellowstone in July 1899 presumably checking out the hotel situation. C.S. Mellen, Canyon Hotel, to Daniel S. Lamont, New York City, 15Jul1899, President's Subject file 209 A, folder 4, NPRR-MHC.

(regarding Bach and Child) C.S. Mellen, to Daniel S. Lamont, 31Dec1900, President's Subject file 209 A, folder 4, NPRR-MHC; "Local Notes," *The Billings* [MT] *Gazette* (hereafter *BG*), 15Jan1901, p. 5.

(backing behind these men) Bartlett, *Wilderness*, p. 174; Barringer, *Selling Yellowstone*, pp. 36-37; "Memorandum ...," by J.H.P., 12Sept1918, NPRR-MHC.

(the transfer of the YPA stock) "Report on Yellowstone Park Association and Yellowstone National Park Transportation Company and their Successors Yellowstone Park Hotel Company and Yellowstone Park Transportation Company," by E. Askewald, Auditor, Jersey City, NJ, 30Jan1917, President's Subject file 209 B, folder 10, (137.C.5.7B), NPRR-MHC.

(a homemade efficiency) Shankland, pp. 118-119.

page 66

(little had been done) YPA's holdings were outlined in Erwin, *Report, 1898*, p. 6; "Change of Owners, Yellowstone Park Association Sells Out Its Entire Holdings," *BG*, 1Apr1901, p. 7.

(National Hotel at Mammoth) During his 1889 visit, author Rudyard Kipling described the National Hotel as "a huge yellow barn." Paul Schullery, ed., *Old Yellowstone Days*. Boulder, CO: Colorado Associated University Press, 1979, p. 88. The building was originally a terra cotta color, but one photograph shows it with lighter paint – presumably yellow. An 1898 photo on display in the Mammoth Hotel dining room shows light color on the National Hotel. Acting Superintendent Young wrote: "The old, barn-like structure called the 'Mammoth Hot Springs Hotel' should be torn down ..." Young, *Report, 1897*, p. 23.

(facility at Norris) Jonathan Pitcher, *Report of the Acting Superintendent of the Yellowstone National Park to the Secretary of the Interior*, Wash., DC: Government Printing Office, 14Oct1901, p. 9; Lee H. Whittlesey, "'I haven't time to kiss everybody!': Larry Mathews Entertains in Yellowstone, 1887-1904," *Montana the Magazine of Western History*, 57(2), Summer 2007, p. 71.

(fashionable and grand Fountain Hotel) Pitcher, *Report, 1901*, p. 9.

(Upper Geyser Basin Hotel) Anderson, *Report, 1895*, p. 3. Immediately after the fire, there arose talk about moving a portion of the Fountain Hotel to the Upper Geyser Basin. Charles Bihler, Division Engineer, NPR, to E.H. McHenry, Chief Engineer, St. Paul, MN, 20Oct1894, File 375, Box 2, (137.J.18.3B), Branch Lines: Yellowstone Park Association; Statement of J.H. Dean in Record of the adjourned Annual Meeting of the Stock-holders of the Yellowstone Park Association held at the office of the Secretary in St. Paul, MN, 20Dec1897, President's Subject File 209A, folder 5, NPRR-MHC.

(Large tents were divided) Oscar J. Brown, *Report of the Acting Superintendent of the Yellowstone National Park to the Secretary of the Interior*. Wash., DC: Government Printing Office, 1899, p. 50; A. Berle Clemensen, *Historic Structure Report. Old Faithful Inn, Yellowstone National Park Wyoming*. Denver: Denver Service Center, National Park Service, Jan1982, p. 4; "Cottages for the Upper Basin," [Gardiner, MT] *Wonderland* (hereafter *GW*), 20Nov1902, p. 2.

(greatest needs of the Park) Anderson, *Report, 1894*, p. 4.

(an urgent need) Anderson, *Report, 1895*, p. 5.

(frequent demands) Erwin, *Report, 1898*, p. 6.

(what is there in reality) Henry T. Finck, "Yellowstone Park in 1897," *The Nation*, 65(1684), 7Oct1897, p. 276.

(E.C. Waters) Brown, *Report, 1899*, pp. 5-6; Complaints about Waters soliciting passengers and excessive charges (July 1902-Jan 1903) docs 5225 -5258, *First 10,000 Documents*, YNPA. Stephen M. Dale, "Through the Yellowstone On a Coach," *Ladies Home Journal*, 21(9), August 1904, pp. 5-6.

(Lake Hotel) Record of the adjourned Annual Meeting of the Stock-holders of the Yellowstone Park Association held at the office of the Secretary in St. Paul, MN, 20Dec1897, President's Subject file 209A, folder 5, NPRR-MHC; Michelle Trappen, *Grand Lady of the Lake: The Remarkable Legacy of Yellowstone's Lake Hotel*. Helena, MT: Sweetgrass Books, 2016, pp. 2-11, 26-27.

(pre-fab Canyon Hotel) Charles Gibson, YPA, to H.L. Muldrow, First Asst. Secretary of the Interior, 21May1886, doc 199, *First 10,000 Documents*, YNPA.

(permanent structure) Acting Superintendent Boutelle wrote "The hotel at the Cañon is completed; is well and comfortably kept, but is a most unsightly edifice." Boutelle, *Report, 1891*, p. 6.

(Foundation problems) Charles Bihler, Division Engineer, NPR, to E. H. McHenry, Chief Engineer, St. Paul, MN, 20Oct1894, File 375, Box 2, (137.J.18.3B), Branch Lines: Yellowstone Park Association, NPRR-MHS; Anderson, *Report, 1896*, p. 3.

(one very ungainly) "Report of the Association of 1896," from W.G. Johnson, general agent to E.W. Winter, Vice President, 23Apr1897, President's Subject file 210A, folder 14, NPRR-MHC.

(born with a silver spoon) Meloy, "Harry Child amassed..."

Chapter 6: Passing the Reins *(chapter header)* Nichols to Young, 23Jul1908, RG00, series I, box 20, YNPA.

(grief and disruption came) "Died of Heart Disease, S.S. Huntley Passes Away in Yellowstone Park," *BG*, 13Sept1901, p. 3; Listing for Silas Huntley, *U.S. Find A Grave Index*, www.ancestry.com 21Jan2015.

(In his own words) Child-Haines Interview.

(Progressive Men) Bowen, pp. 922, 923.

(one of the picturesque types) The Montana Daily Record of 12Sept1901, as quoted in Bowen, p. 922.

(stood four square) Bowen, p. 922.

(never lost sight of the true interest) Pitcher, *Report, 1901*, p. 8.

(controlled the administration) Hiram Martin Chittenden, *The Yellowstone National Park: Historical and Descriptive*. Cincinnati, OH: The Robert Clarke Company, 4th rev. ed., 1903, p. 116. An attempt was made, after Silas' death, to change the name of Dome Mountain in the Gallatin Range to Mount Huntley. Appearing on maps and guidebooks at the time, the change was not lasting. Ibid, pp. 131, 281; Reau Campbell, *Campbell's New Revised Complete Guide and Descriptive Book of the Yellowstone Park*. Chicago, IL: H.E. Klamer, publisher, 1909, pp. 53-54.

(largest real estate deals) Walter Story of Billings purchased Silas' horses. "Wide Awake In Billings," *BG*, 15Apr1902, p. 8; "Estate of Silas B. Huntley," *The Butte* [MT] *Inter Mountain* (hereafter *BIM*), 31Oct1902, p. 12; "Huntley Ranch Sold," *FCA*, 15Jul1903, p. 1. After Silas' death, Annie continued to take wool to the market in Billings until the ranch was sold. "Large Sales About Over," *BG*, 5Aug1902, p. 7; "Prices are Climbing Up," *BG*, 24Jul1903, p. 8.

(traveled for a few years) "Last rites for Mrs. Young ...," *HDI*, 19Oct1938, p. 5; Vucanovich, p. 4.

(disassociate himself) Haines, *Vol. II*, p. 49. Although E.W. sold his shares of the company, his name continued to appear in the newspaper as a public face of the organization.

(two-thirds shares reverted back) Askewald Report, 30Jan1917, NPRR-MHC. This document also reveals that Thomas Carter owned some percentage of stock as well.

(overcrowding of the hotels) H.W. Child, to Major John Pitcher, 7May1903; H.W. Child, to Sec. of the Interior, 7May1903, H.W. Child, to D.E. Burley, General Passenger and Ticketing Agent, Oregon Short Line Railroad, 6May1903; docs 5533, 5534, 5535 respectively, *First 10,000 Documents*, YNPA.

(land dispute) Lee H. Whittlesey, *Gateway to Yellowstone: The Raucous Town of Cinnabar on the Montana Frontier*. Guilford, CT and Helena, MT: TwoDot, 2015, pp. 10-11, 166, 268-270. Whithorn, *Gardiner*, p. 1. Information about Robert E. Cutler in Bill and Doris Whithorn, *60 Miles of Photo History: Upper Yellowstone Valley*. Livingston, MT: The Park County News, no date, p. 34.

(line to be completed) C.S. Mellen, Pres., NPR, to Capt. H.M. Chittenden, U.S. Engineer Office, Sioux City, IA, 30Apr1902, doc 3673, *First 10,000 Documents*, YNPA; "Road to Gardiner, Northen Pacific will build from Cinnabar to Park Line," *LE*, 10May1902; Report for fiscal year ending June 1904, Item #243: *U. S. Corps of Engineers, Monthly Reports*, 1900-1918, YNPA.

(land in Gardiner) Issac D. McCutcheon, et. ax., to H.W. Child, 5Sept1902, Vol. 30, p. 535; C.B. Scott to H.W. Child, 10Oct1902, Vol. 30, p. 567; J.C. McCartney to H.W. Child, 10Oct10, 1902 , Vol. 30, p. 569; Deed Record Books, Office of the Clerk of the Court, Park County, Livingston, MT. Harry made additional purchases between March and June of 1903. "Copy of Indenture, 10Nov1902, between Harry W. Child and Adelaide Child and the Northern Pacific Railway Company," *Harry W. Child Records*, SC 1667, folder 3, MHSRC.

(sold most of his land) "Our Local Field," *GW*, 5Mar1904, p. 5; "Our Local Field," *GW*, 30Apr1904, p. 5.

(Gardiner Community Church) "Mr. Child has very kindly donated two lots for the building of the new church, and it is to be hoped that the same will be erected at as early a date as possible. Most of the business men have contributed all the way from $25 to $50, and in fact all through the proposition is received with encouragement." "Our Local Field," *GW*, 18Jun1904, p. 5. This notice mentions Bishop Brewer who was also ministering to the communities of Fridley [now Emigrant], Horr, and Aldridge [both extinct]. Episcopal Bishop L.R. Brewer worked with Dr. Maria Dean in the founding of St. Peter's Hospital in Helena and rented, and ultimately purchased, the first home she built in Helena. "The A.T. Hibbard Home," Baucus, p. 34; "Helena's New Buildings," *HI*, 1Sept1889, p. 3; "The Dean-Cooney Home," Baucus, p. 40; "Personal and General," *HI*, 31May1891, p. 3; Dwight Harriman, "Gardiner Community Church celebrates 100-yr. anniversary on Sunday," *LE*, 2Jul2005, pp. 11-12.

(unique window in her memory) The window, in memory of Clara Bicknell Hodgin, was removed in 1933 when the church building was donated to the town of Helena and converted to the town library. Forty years later, an Helena businessman became interested in the window's fate. He was able to locate it, stored in a dark corner of a different building. It was then returned to its original location and reinstalled in what was then the Grandstreet Theatre. Just as early church members such as Ellen Dean saw their building as more than a place of worship, so the Helena community continues to enjoy this gift in which Adelaide Child had a part. Copy of Grandstreet Theatre fund raising brochure, courtesy Harry W. Child, II.

(a western sunset) Child, p. 20.

(rode the trains ... soliciting business) Haines, *Vol. II*, p. 23.

(YPA as winterkeeper) "Martha 'Mattie' Shipley Culver," Elizabeth A. Watry, *Women in Wonderland, Lives, Legends, and Legacies of Yellowstone National Park*. Helena, MT: Riverbend Publishing, 2012, pp. 23-35.

(Firehole Hotel) Also known as Marshall House, after its first operator, it became the Firehole Hotel when it was acquired by the YPA in 1886. It preceded the Fountain Hotel and was located half a mile north of its location, near the present day entrance to Fountain Flat Drive. See Lee H. Whittlesey, "Marshall's Hotel in the National Park," *Montana the Magazine of Western History*, 30(3), Autumn 1980, pp. 42-51.

(brought his wife) Quoted from R.R. Cummings in "Death of Ellis [sic] C. Culver," newspaper clipping in vertical file: *Biography (Culver) – Add-on biography of Ellery Channing Culver – Nan Weber Research*, YNPA.

(tuberculosis) Special kudos to Nan Weber who tackled the original documentation of Mattie's life. She learned that Martha Shipley Gillette Culver was born in Lowell, Massachusetts where her parents were employed in the textile mills. She herself spent her early work life in similar mills of Cohoes, New York. Nan Weber, *Mattie: A Woman's Journey West*. Moose, WY: Homestead Publishing, 1997. Mattie's illness is confirmed in *BG*, 7Mar1889; Weber, p. 111, lists "quick consumption" as cause of death.

(baby girl) Theda Culver was approximately five weeks old when her parents brought her to Yellowstone in the summer of 1887. She was eighteen months old when her mother died 2Mar1889. Weber, p. 103; Watry, p. 28; Whittlesey, *Death in ...*, p. 216. Theda is probably "the baby ... raised on Eagle-Brand milk," Aubrey L. Haines, "The Winterkeeper's Wife," in vertical file: *History (Haines 9)*, Haines, Aubrey L., "Tales from the Yellowstone," YNPA; and the baby "fed on elk's milk," Weber, p. 20.

(body packed in snow) Two versions describe this portion of the tale. From Aubrey Haines: "... the ground was frozen so hard she could not be buried, so the soldiers at the station across Nez Percé Creek helped Culver put his wife's body in two barrels arranged end-to-end and covered with snow until the ground thawed enough for a grave to be dug." Haines, "Winterkeeper's ...." R.R. Cummings, Culver's friend and fellow employee of the YPA, recounted "...we were compelled to remove a partition [of the hotel] in order to secure boards with which to make a coffin. The grave was hewn down into the frozen lava formation, and after two days hard work, she was consigned to rest ..." Culver vertical file, YNPA.

(Adelaide Child) Aubrey Haines wrote "Mrs. H.W. Child, the wife of an early concessioner in the Park, had Mattie Culver's grave neatly fenced, and saw that it was carefully maintained." Haines, *Vol. II*, p. 23. Neither Nan Weber or Elizabeth Watry mention the installation of the gravestone or the construction of the fence.

(woman who died in childbirth) Aubrey Haines heard the story from another ranger in 1939. Author Nan Sigrist heard it told nearly the same way in 1953. Aubrey Haines first published it in *The Yellowstone Story* in 1977. Nan Weber first heard the story in 1984. "Mattie Culver's legendary status in Yellowstone stems more from her untimely death and seemingly misplaced burial site than from her life. ... as with most legends, even Weber's well researched rendering of Mattie's true life, *Mattie: A Woman's Journey West*, published in 1997, has been unable to sway the tenacity of the 'Mattie myths.'" Watry, pp. 23, 24. The authors posit that, with an 18 month old child, it is conceivable – especially in that time period, that Mattie was pregnant with a second child at the time of her death.

page 74

(1900 traveler) Pugh, pp. 31-32.

(superintendent was kinder) Pitcher, *Report, 1901*, p. 9.

(St. Paul architect A.W. Spaulding) E.H. McHenry, to A.W. Spalding, 24Aug1898; E.H. McHenry to J.W. Kendrick,1Oct1898, Chief Engineer Subject Files (134.I.5.5B), file 434: "Hotel in Yellowstone Park at Upper Geyser Basin," NPRR-MHC; Clemensen, p. 5.

(postponed construction) "Letter of Instruction to Bidder" from A.W. Spalding; E.H. McHenry, to A.W. Spalding, 1Oct1898, Chief Engineer Subject Files (134.I.5.5B), file 434: "Hotel in Yellowstone Park at Upper Geyser Basin," NPRR-MHC; A.W. Spalding, "Hotel at Upper Geyser Basin," Sept. and Oct. 1898, *F. Jay Haynes Architectural Drawings Collection*, MC 86, item no. 1, folder 7, MHSRC; A. Walter Spalding, Architect and Superintendent, "Specifications of Hotel for the Northern Pacific R.R. Co.," undated, in *Chief Engineer's Files*, NPRR- MHC.

(erection of five cottages) Daniel S. Lamont, to Charles Mellen, 21Jan1901, File 3.1, Box 3, *Charles S. Mellen Correspondence*, Acc #1938-1, New Hampshire Historical Society, Concord, New Hampshire.

(submitted plans) Blueprint titled "Front Elevation, E.J. Donohue, Architect, St. Paul, Minn." handwritten in ink under the printed words is "Old Faithful Inn, Designed by F.J. Haynes," no date, *F. Jay Haynes Papers*, Collection 1500, Box 25, Folder 6, BSC-MSU; Barringer, *Selling Yellowstone*, p. 50.

(agreed to furnish the money) C.S. Mellen, Pres., NPR, to H.W. Child, 9Nov1902, President's Subject File No. 209 A, Folder 3; The NPR committed $100,000 before construction began. Northern Pacific Railway Company, Executive Committee Report, 26Mar1903, President's Subject File 209A, folder 3, NPRR-MHC.

(cottage idea) "Cottages for the Upper Basin," *GW*, 20Nov1902, p. 2.

(left one hundred head of horses) H.W. Child, to J.M. Hannaford, 8Dec1902, President's Subject file 210A, folder 11, NPRR-MHC; "Local Layout," *LE*, 27Dec1902, p. 5.

(left Montana for San Diego) "H.W. Child, Mrs. Child, Helena Montana" registered at the Hotel del Coronado, Saturday, 17Jan1903 (Room 140). The next guests checked into 140 on Tuesday, 27Jan1903, Series Two: *Registers; Hotel del Coronado*, Special Collections and University Archives, Malcolm A. Love Library, San Diego State University, San Diego, CA (hereafter SCUA-SDSU).

(Babcock ... recommend his architect) E.S. Babcock, Pres. Coronado Beach Co., to R.C. Reamer, 20Jan1903, Book 80 (15Oct1902 to 22Jan1903), p. 972, Series I: *Bound Correspondence Feb 1888-1907*, Hotel del Coronado, SCUA-SDSU. For an expanded covering of the Babcock-Child relationship see Ruth Quinn, *Weaver of Dreams: The Life and Architecture of Robert C. Reamer*. Gardiner, MT: Leslie & Ruth Quinn, Publishers, 2004, pp. 5-8.

page 75

(drafted plans) Blueprint titled: "Old Faithful Tavern," *F. Jay Haynes Architectural Drawings Collection*, MC 86, folder 17, items 1-6; folder 18, item 1, MHSRC. The Department of the Interior approved Reamer's original blueprints on 28May1903. See also Karen Wildung Reinhart and Jeff Henry, *Old Faithful Inn: Crown Jewel of National Park Lodges*. Emigrant, MT: Roche Jaune Pictures, Inc., 2004, pp. 33-39; Karen Wildung Reinhart, "Old Faithful Inn: Centennial of a Beloved Landmark," *Yellowstone Science*, 12(2), Spring 2004, special insert between pp. 22 and 23; Ruth Quinn, "Overcoming Obscurity: The Yellowstone Architecture of Robert C. Reamer," *Yellowstone Science*, 12(2), Spring 2004, p. 34-35.

(still a pile of logs) "Gardiner News," *LE*, 31Jan1903, p. 2; "Larry Link and W. B. Judkins have taken the logging contract for the new hotel at the Upper Basin. More than five thousand logs will be required and it will take some time to deliver them. W. E. Seaman and D. Webb will cut them," *GW*, 7May1903, p. 2; Advertisement for wood choppers, *GW*, 4Jun1903, p. 2. The woodcutters completed their task by August 1903. *GW*, 20Aug1903, p. 2.

(Roosevelt vacationed to Yellowstone) For more about President Roosevelt's 1903 visit to Yellowstone, see Doris Whithorn, *Twice Told on the Upper Yellowstone, Vol. 1*. Livingston, MT: self-published, 1994; Schullery, *Montana*, pp. 2-15; Lee H. Whittlesey and Paul Schullery, "The Roosevelt Arch: A centennial history of an American icon," *Yellowstone Science*, 11(3), Summer 2003, pp. 2-24.

(called upon to transport him) "President After Bear," *RP*, 25Mar1903, p. 4; Notation for 16Apr1903, Bound Volume, Item 143: *Journal of Acting Superintendent Yellowstone National Park 1900-1903*, p. 249, YNPA.

(put his stamp of approval) H.W. Child, to E.A. Hitchcock, Sec. of the Interior, 5May1903, Yellowstone Lake Boat Company (1895-1907), Letters Received by the Office of the Secretary of the Interior, Records of the Office of the Secretary of the Interior Relative to National Parks, 1872-1907, *Records of the National Park Service*, Record Group 29, National Archives at College Park, College Park, Maryland (hereafter NACP). Thanks to Leslie J. Quinn for locating this valuable correspondence.

(Camps of the Adirondacks) David A. Naylor, *Old Faithful Inn and Its Legacy: The Vernacular Transformed*. Cornell University, Master of Arts Thesis, 1990. p. 60; Rodd L. Wheaton, "Architecture of Yellowstone: A Microcosm of American Design," *Yellowstone Science*, 8(4), Fall 2000, p. 15; Ruth Quinn interview with Patricia Lane, Elevation Films, Saratoga Springs, NY, 14Jun2012, at Old Faithful Inn; *Sagamore Lodge, America's Great Camp*, https://www.pbs.org/video/wmht-specials-sagamore-lodge-americas-great-camp/ aired 2Oct2013.

(odd freaks of tree growth) "Merriman Talks of National Park," *Butte* [MT] *Evening News* (hereafter *BEN*), 20Mar1905, p. 5.

(worked out a lot of details) Reference to wood cutting location, Log entry for 8Jun1903, Bound Volume 188: *Permanent Station Records: Upper Basin*, YNPA; Reference to quarry site, Reinhart and Henry, p. 34; Reference to location of water system, "Our local field," *GW*, 3Oct1903, p. 1; Reference to installation of reservoir, "Game is Plentiful," *GW*, 14Nov1903, p. 8; Advertisement for teamsters, "Team Work In Yellowstone Park," *BG*,

29May1903, p. 2. Ad ran for four consecutive weeks.

(enforce wide wheels on freight wagons) "The wide tire regulation went into effect May 1, 1903. It was suspended until May 1, 1904, in favor of the Yellowstone Park Association so far only as the hauling of construction material was concerned – ..." Major H.M. Chittenden, Corps of Engineers, to Major John Pitcher, 19May1904, doc 5526, *First 10,000 Documents*, YNPA.

page 76

(keep running with existing equipment) H.W. Child, President, YPA, to Major John Pitcher, 18Feb1903, doc 5536; The May 29, 1903 advertisement declared "All this hauling can be done on narrow tired wagons." Requesting a 20-day extension, H.W. Child, President, YPA, to Major John Pitcher, 18May1903, doc 5525, *First 10,000 Documents*, YNPA.

(traveled to Washington) Whithorn, *Yellowstone Park*, p. 16. The plans were noted to be on display in Mammoth Hot Springs in March 1903, *GW*, 19Mar1903, p. 1.

(construction commenced) An official date for commencement of construction, 12Jun1903 is listed in "Hotels and Machinery Record," in Box YPC-151, YNPA.

(lived in Haynes' Log Cabin Studio) Page titled "Old Faithful Inn," File 31: *Upper Geyser Basin – Old Faithful Inn*, Box 156, Collection 1504: *Jack Ellis Haynes and Haynes, Inc. Records*, BSC-MSU.

(stranded by an unexpected snowstorm) "Additional Local," *GW*, 5Mar1904. p. 4; "Local Layout," *LE*, 12Mar1904; "Montana Brieflets," *RP*, 16Mar1904, p. 8.

(decorate and furnish the new hotel) Child, p. 18; "Our Local Field," *GW*, 5Mar1904. p. 5. Harry and presumably Adelaide traveled east in the fall of 1903. They often attended furniture shows during this time. "Our Local Field," *GW*, 3Oct1903, p. 1; Returned from an "extended to New York City and other points," "Our Local Field," *GW*, 14Nov1903, p. 5.

(death of Edmund W. Bach) "Local Layout," *LE*, 31Oct1903; "Little Happenings," *The Seattle* [Washington] *Star*, 20Apr1904. p. 5; "Montana News Brieflets," *RP*, 27Apr1904, p. 6.

(He left behind) Daughter Margaret (1895-1971) and son Edmund (1899-1962). Listing for Margaret Stanislaus Carroll Bach (1860-1936), www.findagrave.com/ 19Jan2015. Margaret Bach died in San Francisco in 1936.

(Major Bach was a man) "Maj. E. W. Bach is Dead at Seattle," *AS*, 21Apr1904.

(opened June 1, 1904) Reinhart and Henry, p. 44; Telegram from H.W. Child, to Howard Elliott, 31May1904, President's Subject file 210A, folder 11, NPRR-MHC. The Northern Pacific issued a circular in February 1904 announcing the June 1 date. "Local Layout," *LE*, 13Feb1904. June 1 was still the target date in mid-May. "Additional Local," *GW*, 21May1904, p. 4. Although reportedly open, a visitor who saw the hotel in late June reported that it "is not finished." Entry for 23Jun1904, vertical file: "Diary of S. (Samuel P.) Ewing, Smithfield UT," YNPA. Several newspaper articles agree with the 1Jun1904 opening. "Our Local Field," *GW*, 4Jun1904. p. 5; "Local Layout," *LE*, 4Jun1904, p. 5; "Personal Points," *LE*, 4Jun1904, p. 6.

(castle of logs) "Merriman Talks of National Park," *BEN*, 20Mar1905, p. 5; Mrs. Edward H. [Ruth] Johnson, Fort Dodge, Iowa, *Diary of Trip thru Yellowstone Park, 1905*, Collection 430, Box 2, Item 39, BSC-MSU.

(140 rooms) "How many rooms in the Inn?" unpublished flyer authored by Leslie J. Quinn, Information Specialist, Yellowstone Department of Transportation and Interpretation. At the request of Inn tour guides in the early 1900s, Quinn searched for clues of the exact original room count, using missing room numbers and nail holes in doors to confirm changes over time. Currently 90 revenue rooms remain in the original section of the Inn.

page 77

(Finished in the rough) Yellowstone Park Association Hotels brochure, *Yellowstone Park*. Portland, OR: The James Printing Company, 1905, Quinn collection.

(white linen tablecloths) Sumner Mattson photograph, 1905, Neg. No. 4125, Milwaukee Public Museum.

(silver sterling and Blue Willow) Harry W. Child II to Ruth and Leslie Quinn, Oct2013; Advertising brochure titled "The Willow Ware Pattern Used at the Old Faithful Inn, Yellowstone Park," Chicago: Burley & Co., no date, copy courtesy Harry W. Child II; Elizabeth A.H. Sleeper, "Yellowstone Park. Through Sacramento Valley-Nevada and Utah-Many Canyons-Geysers and ?? in the Park," *Fitchburg* [MA] *Sentinel*, 22Aug1905, pp. 1-2.

(Indian Creek) Robert V. Goss, *Serving the 'Faithful' in Yellowstone: Henry Klamer and the General Store in the Upper Geyser Basin*. Gardiner, MT: self-published, 2003, pp. 14-16.

(Chinamen's Garden) Quinn, *Weaver*, p. 69.

(greenhouse) Reinhart and Henry, p. 95.

(fisherman) Notes by Jack Ellis Haynes, 15Jul1959 from scrapbook of "Dutch" Fred Schultz, Folder 35: *Old Faithful Baseball Team - vs - 14th U.S. Army Infantry 1912*, Box 138, Collection 1504, *Haynes Research Files*, BSC-MSU; Photo captioned "Largest Trout ever caught in the Yellowstone caught by Pete Bergendorff, mounted and hung in Old Faithful Inn," *F.J. Haynes Photograph Collection*, # H-6191, MHSRC Photograph Archives.

(was shipped to St. Louis) "Additional Local," *LE*, 20Aug1904, p. 6.

(one of the largest coaches) "Our Local Field," *GW*, 10Sept1904, p. 5.

(visiting furniture shows) Reference to Harry and Adelaide attending furniture shows, *LE*, 5Oct1910, p. 1; H.W. Child, YPTC, to J.M. Hannaford, Pres., NPR, 22Dec1913; H.W. Child, to Colonel Clough, Chairman of the Board, NPR, 24Feb1914, President's Subject File 209A [?], folder 1, NPRR-MHC.

(Loeb, private secretary) "Last year when President Roosevelt was in the Park he was accompanied by Mr. Loeb. The latter, however, did not get to see much of Wonderland, being required to stay most of the time with the special train at Gardiner so as to be within easy telegraphic reach of Washington. Mr. Loeb saw enough of the Park, to create a desire to see more, so this year he determined to spend his vacation there." "Visits the Park William Loeb, Secretary to President Roosevelt, in Wonderland," *LE*, 11Jun1904; *Livingston* [MT] *Daily Post* (hereafter *LDP*), 2Nov1907, quoted in Whithorn, *Twice Told... Vol. 1*, p. 58; "Local Layout," *LE*, 10Sept1910, p. 5; "Should you wish to communicate with him you can address him care of Mr. William Loeb Jr., Secretary to the President whose guest Mr. Child will be during his stay in Washington." L.S. Wells, Purchasing Agent, YPTC, to Major H.C. Benson, Supt., 1Dec1908, doc 9268, *First 10,000 Documents*, YNPA.

page 78

(Thomas H. Carter) "Elected delegate from Montana to the Fifty-first Congress. [Montana Territory Delegate: March 4, 1889-November 7, 1889]. Elected first representation of the state on its admission to the Union. [State of Montana, Member of U.S. House: November 8, 1889-March 3, 1891]. Commissioner of the general land office from March, 1891, to July, 1892. Elected chairman of the Republican National Committee in 1892. Republican delegate to the national conventions of 1896, 1900, and 1904. ... Elected United States senator for the term beginning March 4, 1895, and ending March 3, 1901 ... Elected to the United States senate for the second time on Jan. 16, 1905..." [until March 3, 1911]. "Senator Carter's Career in Brief," from his obituary, *The Daily Enterprise* [Livingston, MT], (hereafter *LDE*,) 18Sept1911, p. 1. Dates in brackets from biography of "Thomas H. Carter," https://en.wikipedia.org/wiki/Thomas_H._Carter For references to Carter's associations with Child: H.W. Child, to Senator Thomas H. Carter, U.S. Senate, 17Apr1908, doc 9287, *First 10,000 Documents*, YNPA; "Local Layout," *LE*, 6Aug1910, p. 5; "Former Senator Here Sunday," *LE*, 24Jul1911, p. 1. See also Richard B. Roeder, "Thomas H. Carter, Spokesman for Western Development," *Montana the Magazine of Western History*, 39(2), Spring 1989, pp. 23-29.

(on hand to act as his chauffeur) Photo captioned "Theodore Roosevelt's visit to Helena on April 12, 1911. Thomas Carter in back seat," accession #944-647, MHSRCPA. Harry Child is behind the wheel in the right-hand drive automobile. Roeder, p. 26.

(gift to Harry and Adelaide) Harry W. Child II, personal communication with Ruth and Leslie Quinn. After the end of his term in office, Roosevelt spent a year traveling the world, which included big game hunting in Africa. Timothy Egan, *The Big Burn: Teddy Roosevelt and the Fire That Saved*

America. New York: Houghton Mifflin Harcourt Publishing Co., 2009, pp. 11, 89, 134.

  (close friends with four presidents) Child, p. 142.

  (in Yellowstone for one year) Quinn, *Weaver,* pp. 39-55.

  (twenty-five employees) Erwin, *Report,1898,* pp. 7, 9, 20.

page 79

  (toured factories of several auto manufacturers) "No Autos for Park," *BG,* 17Feb1903, p. 6; "Haynes in Butte," *GW,* 1Jan1903, p. 1.

  ("Wylie Way" to A.W. Miles) Mark Barringer, "How Harry Got Taken: The Early Days of the Yellowstone Camps," *Annals of Wyoming,* 69(4), Fall 1997, pp. 4-5.

  (At the age of fifty-seven) Demaray, p. 173.

  (one-third of the company shares) Moorman, pp. 172-173.

  (Wylie Permanent Camping Company, only as a paid employee) Demaray, p. 174. The agreement ended in August 1907. Ibid, p. 177.

  (Spanish Creek properties) Demaray, pp. 177, 178.

page 80

  (Imperial Valley) Smith, p. 31.

  (settled in Pasedena) W.W. Wylie died in Los Angeles in 1930. Demaray, pp. 192, 193.

  (At age 16) "Noyes, A.L. Diary," *Manuscript Collection [NOYES],* YNPA.

  (fastest and most accurate engineer) Child-Haines Interview.

  (building the road from Canyon over Dunraven) "I have the honor to inform you that the road over Mt. Washburn is now completed and open for travel....," E.D. Vincent, Ass't Engineer, U.S. Engineer Office, YNP, to Major John Pitcher, Acting Supt., 17Sept1904, doc 6040, *First 10,000 Documents,* YNPA.

page 81

  (Dunraven pass is in fair condition) H.W. Child, to the Sec. of the Interior, 17Jan1905, doc 5799, *First 10,000 Documents,* YNPA.

  (permit ... of a special character) E.A. Hitchcock, Sec., to H.W. Child, 30Jan1905, doc 5800, *First 10,000 Documents,* YNPA.

page 82

  (assistant to the purchasing agent) Petersen, p. 23. Lansing S. "Daddy" Wells was Purchasing Agent of the Yellowstone Park Association in charge of the Commissary at Mammoth. Withorn, *Gardiner,* p. 14. Wells also has some connections to this story before Yellowstone – having been a manager for Bach, Cory & Company in Great Falls. "Spray of the Falls," *GFT,* 10Jul1889, p. 3. One of the benefactors of Adelaide Child's will was Antoinette S. Wells, which indicates another life-long friendship with the family. "Helena Charitable and Youth Service Organizations Share in Mrs. H.W. Child Will," *HIR,* 23Oct1949, vertical file: "Child Family," MHSRC.

  (Harry Child's secretary) Petersen, p. 29; C.A. Hamilton, secretary to the Superintendent of Hotels, to General S.B.M. Young, 10Oct1907, doc 6470, *First 10,000 Documents,* YNPA.

  (special friends) "Gardiner Notes," *The Livingston* [MT] *Weekly Enterprise,* 30Apr1910, p. 2, "Gardiner Notes," *LE,* 7May1910, p. 2.

  (two photo shops) Young, *Report, 1897,* p. 20.

  (shop just off the Inn lobby) This photo counter in the southwest corner of the Inn lobby operated from about 1923-1927. Chester A. Lindsley, *The Chronology of Yellowstone National Park 1806 to 1939,* typed and bound manuscript, (1939), p. 268, Rare Book Room, YNPA; Clemensen, p. 21.

  (fond of pranks and practical jokes, Charlie took the rap) Child, pp. 74-75; Petersen, p. 29.

  (50-50 ownership) Askewald Report, 30Jan1917, NPRR-MHC; Barringer, *Selling Yellowstone,* pp. 36-37.

Chapter 7: Love In the Rough *(chapter header)* Child to Young, 30Aug1908, RG00, Series I, Box 20, YNPA.

page 83

  (Love In the Rough) The authors have chosen to use this phrase as a chapter title for sentimental reasons – even though Child family tradition attributes it to the *grandchildren* of Harry and Adelaide, not their children as discussed in this chapter. Harry W. Child II wrote, "My Aunt Marion Child Sanger told me that it was my dad Huntley, Jr. and wife Emily were living in the log cabin [the Mail Carrier's Cabin located east of the Mammoth Clinic – rq] in 1938 and she came out to visit, took one look at the cabin, and called it 'love in the rough.' My sister Jane was 3 years old then and I was just 2 months old." Notes from Harry W. Child II to Ruth Quinn, personal correspondence, 20May2019.

  (attended the Baldwin School) S.B.M. Young, to Miss Ellen Dean Child, % Mrs. Baldwin School, Bryn Mawr, PA, 21Nov1903, *Samuel B.M. Young Papers,* Box 7: *Army War College Board and Chief of Staff of the Army 1902-1905, 1916,* n.d., Bound Volume: Letters Sent, p. 397, U.S. Army Archives, Carlisle, Pennsylvania (hereafter Young Papers).

  (accompanied ... to the park) "Personal Points," *LE,* 19Sept1903, p. 6; "Personal Points," *LE,* 18Jun1904, p. 6.

  (1908 class at MIT) Entry for Huntley Child, *U. S. School Year Books, 1880-2012,* Yearbook Title: *Technique, Massachusetts Institute of Technology, Cambridge, 1906,* pp. 90, 166, 347, www.ancestry.com 20Mar2018; Student list, Yearbook Title: *Technique, Massachusetts Institute of Technology, Cambridge, 1907,* p. 346, http://web.mit.edu/tecniques/www/scans/1907_Techique.pdf 20Mar2018.

  (Hunt is the man) "The Naught-Eight Vaudeville Troop," member listed at "Hunt. Childs," Yearbook Title: *Technique, Massachusetts Institute of Technology, Cambridge, 1908,* p. 346, http://web.mit.edu/tecniques/www/scans/1907_Techique.pdf 20Mar2018.

  (Connecticut native, U.S. Military Academy) "Col. Nichols of Yellowstone Park Company Is Stricken," *LE,* 7Aug1957, pp. 1,4. According to family history, he received schooling at St. Matthew's School and Trinity College in Hartford. "History of William Morse Nichols," typescript dated 28Aug1957, vertical files: *History - YNP - Employees, YHC,* "Nichols," YNPA.

  (received an appointment) "San Diego, 75, 50, 25 Years Ago," undated newspaper clipping, *William M. Nichols Papers, 1944-1966,* MC 292, Biographical Materials box 1, folder 1: "Biographical," MHSRC.

  (fencing and football teams) "William Morse Nichols," Vital Statistics Questionnaire, U.S. Military Academy, completed 15Jan1951, by W.M.N., op. cit., *Nichols Papers,* MHSRC.

  (Army-Navy game in 1902) In a photo of the 1902 West Point Military Academy team, one member is labeled as "Nichols." http://tiptop25.com/1902army.png 16Aug2019. Nichols confirmed that he "played in an Army-Navy game at Franklin Field – and the Navy beat us." W.M. Nichols, to Major-General Julian "Baldy" L. Schley, 26Feb1948, op. cit., *Nichols Papers,* MHSRC. Another team member is identified as MacArthur. Douglas MacArthur was "First Captain at the United State Military Academy at West Point, where he graduated top of the class of 1903." http://en.wikipedia.org/wiki/Douglas_MacArthur 15Apr2020.

  (Ellen was present) The game took place at Franklin Field in Philadelphia, Pennsylvania. The outcome was Army Cadets, 40 to Navy, 5. As S.B.M. Young provided three tickets to the game, the authors propose that she either attended with her parents, and met Billie there; or perhaps one of the tickets was for him. It certainly leads to speculation that Ellen and Billie met *before* he was stationed at Yellowstone – not after. It is notable that in Young's collection of clippings related to West Point, he kept a souvenir photo of that game as well. Wikipedia page: *1903 Army Cadets Football Team,* https://en.wikipedia.org/wiki/1903_Army_Cadets_football_team 24Mar2019.; Young, to Ellen Child; photo captioned: *The West Point Foot Ball Players and The Naval Academy Foot Ball Team,* copyright 1903, Box 3, RG 488S: S.B.M. Young Photograph Collection, *Young Papers.*

  (graduated as a second lieutenant, assigned to Fort Yellowstone) William M. Nichols, 2nd Lt. 3rd Cav., Co. D, from 1Dec1903 to 17May1904, Fort Assinibone, MT, Post Commander N.H. Beck, *Returns from U. S. Military Posts: 1900-1916,* National Archives and Records Administration, Washington, D.C. (hereafter NARA-DC), Microfilm Serial: M617, Microfilm Roll: 43, www.ancestry.com 20Mar2018.

page 84

(Harry would have nothing to do with this, Ellen was crushed) Child, p. 65. Family members believe Harry's contact was his friend Theodore Roosevelt.

(Harry's request to transfer) After spending an afternoon with Ellen and W.M., Loeb Jr. wrote, "As I watched them at tea in La Jolla, I felt that my late father must have played a better Cupid than even he knew at the time." William Loeb, III, to Senator W. Stuart Symington, 16Mar1953, *Nichols Papers,* Correspondence box 5, folder 5, MHSRC.

(resigned his commission) Fort Yellowstone, Wyoming, 1898 Jan - 1907 Dec, *Returns from U. S. Military Posts: 1806-1916,* NARA-DC, Microfilm Serial: M617, Microfilm Roll: 1480, www.ancestry.com 20Mar2018.

(Engineering Division) A synopsis of William M. Nichols' life, most probably written by his son Johnnie Nichols, states that W.M. worked as a railroad engineer. "History of William Morse Nichols," YNPA. A biographical note accompanying the William M. Nichols papers at MFSRC more defines this to "he resigned in 1905 to work for the Engineering Division of the Northern Pacific Railway." http://archiveswest.orbiscascade.org/ark/80444/xv79692 20Jul2019. Nichols himself summarizes, "I worked for 'The crookedest railroad in the world,' Mt. Tamalpais, for a few months and thence went to the Western Pacific Railroad at Palermo, California ... From there, to the Northern Pacific Railroad in Montana as resident engineer ..." Nichols to Schley, 26Feb1948.

(Child- Nichols wedding) S.B.M. Young, to William Loeb, Jr., 5Nov1907, *Theodore Roosevelt Papers (1901-1909),* Eli M. Oboler Library, Idaho State University, Pocatello, Idaho (hereafter TR-ISU).

(married in November, private secretary) "History of William Morse Nichols," YNPA.

page 85

(duty in Yosemite) Haines, *Vol. II,* p. 455; Hampton, p. 235, n57; Listing for Samuel Baldwin Marks Young, https://en.wikipedia.org/wiki/Samuel_Baldwin_Marks_Young 3Oct2016.

(five-month tour of duty) Listed as Colonel, Acting Superintendent of YNP, 23Jun1897 to 15Nov1897, Haines, *Vol. II,* p. 465; "Army Officers are Promoted," *The New York* [New York] *Times* (hereafter *NYT*), 4Jan1900, p. 10.

(veteran of the Civil War) Ibid; Young, wikipedia page, op. cit. Yellowstone historian Aubrey Haines suggested he had "one of the most unusual and illustrious careers in the U.S. Army," Haines, *Vol. II,* p. 455.

(Indians in the Southwest) Haines, *Vol. II,* p. 455, Young, wikipedia page, op. cit.

(Spanish-American War) "In Cuba he commanded one of two cavalry brigade that were part of the Cavalry Division commanded by Major General Joseph Wheeler. Young's brigade included Theodore Roosevelt's Rough Riders, the 1st US Volunteer Cavalry Regiment. ... During the Philippine-American War, rank of Brigadier General of Volunteers, commanded brigades in the Northern Luzon District of which he was made military governor." Young, wikipedia page, op. cit. Gifting a copy his book, *Americans and Preparedness Speeches of Theodore Roosevelt, July to November, 1916.* New York: The Mail and Express Job Print, 1917, to Lt. General S.B.M. Young, TR inscribed "from a friend who is proud of having served under him. Theodore Roosevelt, Jan. 29th 1917. I trust that the doctrine herein preached is not entirely unworthy of approval by my old commander ..." Box 5: *Miscellany and Clippings 1881-1932,* Young Papers.

(lieutenant general, chief-of-staff) "Last Rites for Mrs. Young will be Conducted Thursday," *HDI.* 19Oct1938, p. 5.

(second tour of duty) Young retired from the military in 1904. On 1Jun1907, with rank of General, he became full Superintendent of Yellowstone. He held the position until 28Nov1908. Haines, *Vol. II,* pp. 477, 455.

(escapee from Fort Yellowstone) Ibid, p. 153.

(stagecoach hold-ups) A detailed account of a robbery between Old Faithful and the Thumb of Yellowstone Lake is in S.B.M. Young, to Theodore Roosevelt, 7Sept1908, TR-ISU. See also Jack Ellis Haynes, *Yellowstone Stage Holdups.* Bozeman, MT: Haynes Studios, Inc., rev. ed. 1959, pp. 15-20.

(poaching of trophy animals) S.B.M. Young, to Theodore Roosevelt, 14Sept1907, TR-ISU.

(admirable woman) S.B.M. Young, to Theodore Roosevelt, 30Dec1907, TR-ISU.

(dine with us at the White House) Theodore Roosevelt, to S.B.M. Young, 3Jan1908, TR-ISU.

(ceremony will be in Grace Church) S.B.M. Young, to Theodore Roosevelt, undated [marked as received 2Mar1908], TR-ISU; Marriage Announcement, *The National Tribune* [Wash., DC], 26Mar1908, p. 4.

(Heartiest congratulations) Telegram from Theodore and Edith Roosevelt, to S.B.M. Young, 2Mar1908, TR-ISU.

(suggesting improved housing) H.W. Child, to Senator Thomas H. Carter, 17Apr1908, doc 9287, *First 10,000 Documents,* YNPA; "1909 – The new stone buildings at Fort Yellowstone were completed ...," Lindsley, p. 201. Completed in 1909 and known as *Field Officer's Quarters,* it was "the residence of the acting superintendent/post commander." *Fort Yellowstone: Historic District Walking Tour,* pamphlet published by Yellowstone Forever!, May 2018.

page 86

(entered his father's business) Listing for Huntley Child, age 24, occupation: Treasurer, Hotel Company, *U.S. Census Record, 1910,* village of Mammoth Hot Springs, Uinta County, Wyoming [Mammoth Village is now in Park County, Wyoming]; "Additional Local," *The Livingston Weekly Enterprise,* 16Apr1910, p. 8.

(would look at all the women) Child, p. 63.

(married in Memphis) "Huntley Child," LifeStory, www.ancestry.com 18Sept2015.

(house George Wakefield had built) HS-2031: "Nichols' Residence," in "Survey and Evaluation of Historical Buildings in Yellowstone National Park," Historic Structure Survey Form (Draft), prepared by Historical Research Associates, Inc., Missoula, MT, 1999, on file in the Yellowstone Center for Resources, National Park Service, Yellowstone National Park.

(colonial style house) Wheaton, pp. 15-16; Lee H. Whittlesey, et al, *A Yellowstone Album: A Photographic Celebration of the First National Park.* Boulder, CO: Roberts Rinehart, 1997, p. 42; HS-2036: "Mammoth Hot Springs, Nichols Residence," in "Survey and Evaluation of Historical Buildings in Yellowstone National Park," Historic Structure Survey Form (Draft), prepared by Historical Research Associates, Inc., Missoula, MT, 1999, on file in the Yellowstone Center for Resources, National Park Service, Yellowstone National Park. Former Yellowstone historian Lee Whittlesey calls this the *Huntley Child Cottage,* as the Nichols never lived there. Whittlesey, *Mammoth Village* manuscript, chap. 10, pp. 68-70.

page 87

(Their three children) Child, p. 65; Whittlesey, *Mammoth Village* manuscript, chap. 7, p. 113. Additions were constructed by 1902 and a rear addition in 1926. Dan R. Hull, Chief Landscape Engineer, to W.M. Nichols, 8Mar1926, Folder 5: *Landscape Engineer File, F. Y. 1926,* Box D-38: *Landscape Architects & Engineers,* YNPA.

(moved into the Colonial house) Whittlesey, *Mammoth Village* manuscript, chap. 10, p. 68.

(Dr. Maria Dean was once summoned) Child, p. 13.

(Birth dates of the children) Child, p. 64; Child, Appendix 13: *Huntley and Emilie Child's Family.*

(prairie-school style house) Rodd L. Wheaton, Supervisory Historical Architect, NPS, to H.L. Ritchie, TWA Services, Inc., 23Sept1982, Folder H30, Box H-18, YNPA; Wheaton, p. 16; HS-2030: *Mammoth Hot Springs Child Residence,* in *Survey and Evaluation of Historical Buildings in Yellowstone National Park,* Historic Structure Survey Form (Draft), prepared by Historical Research Associates, Inc., Missoula, MT, 1999, on file in the Yellowstone Center for Resources, National Park Service, Yellowstone National Park; Quinn, *Weaver,* pp. 63-67.

(living spaces) Blueprint titled: *Plan of Cottage for Yellowstone Park Transportation Co to be built at Mammoth Hot Springs,* Robert C. Reamer, Architect, 4-1908, approved 1May1908, Map Index, Drawer 9, YNPA. Also on document titled: "site 3, Leases Oct 18, 1907 and May 1908."

(spiral staircase) [H.W. Child], to Senator Thomas H. Carter, 17Apr1908, doc 9287, *First 10,000 Documents*, YNPA; Interior of Child house, photograph YELL 11269, YNPA.

page 88

(similar set of structures in Gardiner) Blueprint titled: "Buildings for Yellowstone Park Transportation Co. to be Built at Gardiner Mont., Robert C. Reamer, Archt. (No date) Approved by E. A. Hitchcock-?, 22Mar1906," includes "Barn, Coach Shed, Bunkhouse, Messhouse," NACP, Record Group 79, Records of the National Park Service, Records of the Secretary of the Interior, Letters Received, Box 86: Yellowstone National Park Transportation Co (1898-1906), Document #250; Quinn, *Weaver*, pp. 61-63.

(to replace the aging) "It is entirely likely that another year will see the commencement of a fine new hotel at Mammoth Hot Springs, the present one being inadequate to the demands upon it." "Local Layout," *LE*, 26Sept1903, p. 5; H.W. Child, President, YPTC, to Howard Elliott, NPR, 2Jan1906, President's Subject file 210A, folder 9, NPRR-MHC.

(in 1906) Reamer produced two separate watercolor renderings with proposals for a new hotel at Mammoth. "Proposed Hotel, Mammoth Springs, Yellowstone Park, Robert C. Reamer, Arch't, July 1, 1906," Architectural Drawings, *Haynes Foundation Collection*, Museum Collection, Accession # 85.63.04, MHSRC; "Proposed Hotel, Mammoth Hot Springs, Yellowstone Park, Robert C. Reamer, Architect, 1906," property of Yellowstone National Park Lodges, displayed in the first floor hallway of the Mammoth Hotel. See Quinn, *Weaver*, pp. 59-60.

(and in 1909) William E. Curtis, "Hotels to be built in Two U. S. Parks," *The Chicago* [Illinois] *Record-Herald*, 23Feb1909, pp. 1, 10; "Proposed Hotel, Mammoth Hot Springs, Robert C. Reamer, August 1909," Black & White Rendering, *F. Jay Haynes Architectural Drawings Collection*, MC 86, folder 2 of 7, MHSRC; "More of the Park," *LE*, 4Sept1909, p. 3; Naylor, pp. 95-96.

(failure to receive government approval) "The Hotel Company is working with the administration during its last hours, for permission to construct a new hotel in front of the old Mammoth Hotel. … I am doing what little I can to block it, but have very little hope of succeeding. Can you do anything with the Chief of Engineers to assist us? The entire symmetry of the Springs would be destroyed if this outrageous proposition receives favorable action. Please do what you can to block it." Major, Fifth Cavalry, to Lieut. Col. H.M. Chittenden, Seattle, WA, 21Feb1909, doc 8564, *First 10,000 Documents*, YNPA; Letters unfavorable about it from Major Benson, 5th Cavalry, to Secretary of Interior, 21Feb1909, Item 45--letter box 45, "Building and Building Sites 1911-1916, box 23-1; File 54, "Yellowstone Park Hotel Co.," YNPA.

(owned a Franklin) "Local Layout," *LE*, 28May1910, p. 7; "Local Layout," *LDE*, 17Sept1912, p. 3.

(handsome garage) "Gardiner Notes", *LE*, 4Jun1910, p. 2; Quinn, *Weaver*, pp. 79, 81; "The Arch House," research file compiled and owned by Beverly Whitman, 1Mar 2001. Data regarding its time as the "Gardiner Store," collected pages related to history of buildings, dated 24Feb1955, folder 3, Box 59, Collection 1504: *Jack Ellis Haynes and Haynes, Inc. Records*, BSC-MSU.

(trip to Helena) "Local Layout," *LE*, 4Apr1911, p. 3; Bill and Doris Whithorn, *Photo History of Gardiner, Jardine, Crevasse*. Livingston, MT: The Park County News, 1972, p. 4.

(special mission) Theodore Roosevelt to S.B.M. Young, 31Jul1907, Young Papers.

page 89

(services … cheerfully given) S.B.M. Young to Theodore Roosevelt, Young Papers.

(National Park Guard) S.B.M. Young, to William Loeb, Jr., Sec. to the Pres., 11Sept1907; addendum titled "Notes for Organization of A Civil Guard for Yellowstone National Park," 11Sept1907; TR-ISU; Demaray, p. 182.

(simply not possible) Theodore Roosevelt, to S.B.M. Young, 11Dec1907, TR-ISU.

(steamboat Zillah) *Northwestern Tourist*, 14Sept1889, p. 2; Boutelle, *Report, 1891*, pp. 7-8.

(consummate businessman) Personal communication, Leslie Quinn, to Ruth Quinn, based on his research of the boat history on Yellowstone Lake.

(annoyance to lunch station staff) Letter dated 15Aug1904, concerns a E.R. Palmer who was ejected from the Lake Hotel; a response is typed on the outside of the document from H.W. Child, 22Aug1904: "The President of the Yellowstone Lake Boat Co. and his employees have been excluded from the hotels of this Association because of their action in making themselves obnoxious to our guests by soliciting business under false statements & misrepresentations." doc 5502; regarding keeping E.C. Waters off YPA property, H.W. Child, to Major John Pitcher, 14Aug1905, doc 6517, *First 10,000 Documents*, YNPA.

(arrangement with W.W. Wylie) Documents concerning Boat Company proposition to carry all passengers of Wylie and the two transportation companies for $1.50 per (April-May 1905), docs 5559-5560, *First 10,000 Documents*, YNPA.

(building a larger vessel) "Our Local Field," *GW*, 16Jul1904, p. 5; "The New Boat Launched," *GW*, 21Sept1905

(set of documents recommending) S.B.M. Young, Supt., to William Loeb, Jr., Sec. to the Pres., 23Aug1907, RG 79: *Records of the National Park Service*, General Records, Central Files, 1907-39, Box 237: "Privileges: …," File: "Privileges - Yellowstone Lake Boat Co. (2 of 7)," NARA-CP.

(cancel Waters' contract) Theodore Roosevelt, to S.B.M. Young, 29Aug1907; S.B.M. Young, to Theodore Roosevelt, 5Sept1907, TR-ISU.

(Soldiers' Home) S.B.M. Young, to Theodore Roosevelt, 12Nov1908, TR-ISU. The mutual affection and admiration between the two men is evident in this letter "The pride of my life is that my whilom pupil (night of June 23 and day of June 24, 1898) became one of the three greatest Presidents our great Republic and still remained my great and good friend." TR replied, "Indeed your whilom pupil is very proud and fond of his teacher!" Theodore Roosevelt, to S.B.M. Young, 17Nov1908, TR-ISU.

page 90

(UPR completed their tracks) Advertising brochure -- "Oregon Short Line R. R. Yellowstone Park, 12Nov1907," doc 7655, *First 10,000 Documents*, YNPA; Lindsley, p. 197; Paul Shea, *Images of America: West Yellowstone*. Charleston, SC, Chicago, IL, Portsmouth, NH, San Francisco CA: Arcadia Publishing, 2009, p. 23.

(to contact Robert Reamer) J. Kruttschnitt, Director of Maintenance and Operation, Union Pacific System, Southern Pacific Company, to Howard Elliott, 11Aug1905; H.W. Child, to E.J. Pearson, St. Paul, 19Aug1905, President's Subject file 210A, folder 10, NPRR-MHC.

(in-house architect) The plans, drawn in 1905, are credited to the Union Pacific Engineering Office in Salt Lake City, not to any architect. Paul Shea, then director of the Museum of the Yellowstone, Walk of Historic District of West Yellowstone, 2000.

(town of Boundary) Regarding the name *Boundary*, Watry, *Women*, p. 73; *Riverside*, Shea, p. 56; *Yellowstone*, Frank Pierce, First Assistant Sec., Department of the Interior, to the Acting Supt., 9May1908, doc 8246, *First 10,000 Documents*, YNPA.

(Museum of the Yellowstone) www.yellowstonehistoriccenter.org/

(stone dining hall) The dining hall was completed in November 1925, and in use the following summer. Shea, pp. 32-33; Joyce Zaitlin, *Gilbert Stanley Underwood: His Rustic, Art Deco, and Federal Architecture*. Malibu, CA: Pangloss Press, 1989, pp. 103, 106-110.

(moved their operations) Lindsley, p. 197; Shea, p. 18.

(Yellowstone-Western) Lindsley, pp. 210, 216.

(1975, the former location of Riverside) The late Joe Mitchell, park bus driver between 1947 and 1996, many times recalled the last event at the Riverside development was a party welcoming the new full-size motor coaches. Leslie Quinn, personal communication, 1Apr2020; Austin, et al, pp. 25-26.

(Monida) Rae Ellen Moore, *Just West of Yellowstone: A Guide to Exploring and Camping*. LaClede, ID: Great Blue Graphics, 1987, p. 96.

(Red Rock Lakes National Wildlife Refuge) "Shambo Stagecoach Station," Interpretive Sign near Upper Red Rock Lake, 30Sept2012; https://www.fws.gov/refuge/Red_Rock_Lakes/about.html 16Apr2020; Moore, pp. 83-85.

(a railroad monopoly) Howard Elliott, to Mr. James N. Hill, Vice Pres, NPR, 1Feb1907, President's Subject file 209A, folder 2, NPRR-MHC.

(dispose of all their hotel stock) Askewald Report, 30Jan1917, NPRR-MHC; Bartlett, *Wilderness*, p. 176.

(now full owner) President of YPA, to Hon. Secretary of the Interior, 24Nov1908, *Yellowstone Park Company Records*, MC 141, box 4: "YPA," folder 4-2: "Annual Reports to Secretary of the Interior," MHSRC; Haines, *Vol. II*, p. 50.

page 91

(The relations between..., satisfactory to the Northern Pacific Company) Howard Elliott, President, to M.P. Martin, Comtroller, 8Mar1907, President's Subject file 209A, folder 1, NPRR-MHC.

(Yellowstone Park Hotel Company) Barringer, *Selling Yellowstone*, pp. 36-37.

(Wylie's four camps) Barringer, *Annals*, p. 5; Demaray, pp. 103-106. These camps were located at Willow Park, Old Faithful, Lake, and Canyon.

(peak year for W.W. Wylie) John Pitcher, *Report of the Acting Superintendent of the Yellowstone National Park to the Secretary of the Interior*. Wash., DC: Government Printing Office, 1902, p. 15.

(company turned a profit) Moorman, p. 8; John Pitcher, *Report of the Acting Superintendent of the Yellowstone National Park to the Secretary of the Interior*. Wash., DC: Government Printing Office, 1905, p. 14.

(larger facility at Swan Lake Flats) Moorman, p. 10; Demaray, p. 179.

(Camp Roosevelt was established) Whittlesey, *A Yellowstone Album*, p. 94.

page 92

(became Miles' assistant) Barringer, *Annals*, pp. 8-9; Jack Ellis Haynes, "Rotarian Howard H. Hays," biographical typescript courtesy Harry W. Child II.

(large Douglas fir tree) Haines, *Vol. II*, p. 233.

("Sleepy Hollow" on the Gibbon River) Lee H. Whittlesey and Elizabeth A. Watry, *Images of America: Yellowstone National Park*. Charleston SC, et al: Arcadia Publishing, 2008, p. 73.

(camp at Riverside) Barringer, *Annals*, p. 5.

(built a bathhouse) "Wylie Company Breaks Camp," *LE*, 24Sept1910, p. 1; "Park Bath House Complete," *LE*, 18Oct1910, p. 3.

(Holm Company on the east side) Aron "Tex" Holm began guiding tourists from Cody in 1901. He organized the Yellowstone Park Camping Company in 1905. W. Hudson Kensel, *Pahaska Tepee: Buffalo Bill's Old Hunting Lodge and Hotel, a History, 1901-1946*. Cody, WY: Buffalo Bill Historical Center, 1987, p. 19. He built Holm Lodge in 1910, eight miles east of Yellowstone's east boundary. It continues to operate as Crossed Sabers Lodge. Kensel, pp. 29; 37-39, 59-60. Mark Spragg, *Where Rivers Change Direction*. New York: Riverhead Books, 1999, p. 1.

(Shaw and Powell) Vivian A. Paladin and S. Rose Shaw, "Yellowstone Park by Camp: Shaw & Powell Camping Company," *Montana the Magazine of Western History*, 22(3), Summer 1972, pp. 94-101; Bound Vol. 140: "Record of Property Purchased & Expended. Office of Supt of YNP, Dept of Interior, 1-935, pp. 28, 120, 128, YNPA; "Local Layout," *LE*, 13Jun1903, p. 5.

(sold half of his share) Barringer, *Annals*, p. 6.

(full owner of the horse operations) Smith, pp. 43-44.

(find a place to winter them) When George Wakefield and Silas Huntley ran the transportation company, they generally wintered horses along the Lower Yellowstone River, east of Livingston, MT. Testimony of George S. Anderson, Acting Superintendent of Yellowstone National Park, before the House (sub)Committee on Public Lands, 12 May 1892, McRae, p. 220. Harry seems to have tried several different locations in the first few years after Silas Huntley's death. Reference to wintering horses near the head of the Stillwater River, "Local Layout" *LE*, 1Nov1902, p. 5. Reference to near Big Timber, *GW*, 11Dec1902, p. 1. Reference to wintering horses near St. Anthony, Idaho, "Local Layout," *LE*, 17Oct1903.

(Charlie Anceney approached him) B.C. Forbes, pp. 181-182. The route used by Anceney was from Mammoth Hot Springs, across Snow Pass, up Panther Creek, through Bighorn Pass, then along the Gallatin River. C.L. Anceney, Chas. Anceney Land and Livestock Co., Salesville, Mont., to General Young, 8Sept1908, doc 8310, *First 10,000 Documents*, YNPA. "The company's herd of 900 horses, which have been wintered 25 miles from Bozeman, will be driven to the park May 25." "Heavy Park Travel," *LE*, 14May1910, p. 5.

("Home Ranch") Smith, p. 15.

(just good grass) "Anceney's theory was that not only was Montana grass more abundant and nutritious, but the northern latitude and higher altitude hastened the growth." Harvey Griffin, "There Was Only One BIG Spread," *BG*, 31Jan1967, vertical file: "Flying D Ranch," MHSRC; "... After the first winter, Child was pleased with the healthy condition of his horses." Smith, pp. 43-44; Demaray, p. 178.

(rumors of loco weed) Child, p. 163.

(Spanish Peaks sparkled, loco weed was forgotten) Smith, p. 44.

page 93

(became his partner, buy all the land within sight) Forbes, p. 182; Child, p. 163.

("One Big Spread") Griffin, *BG*, 31Jan1967.

(bought land in small sections, Cherry Creek area) Smith, pp. 44-45.

(proved up on their land) Child, pp. 164-165.

(The town's namesake) Kensel, pp. 3, 9.

(Tapping the Big Horn Basin's) Ibid, p. 10.

page 94

(road to the park's east border) Kensel, pp. 5, 12; *GW*, 23Jul1903, p. 1; "National Park Improvements," *LE*, 24Oct1903; H.M. Chittenden report in Jonathon Pitcher, *Report of the Acting Superintendent of the Yellowstone National Park to the Secretary of the Interior 1904*. Wash., DC: Government Printing Office, 1904, p. 14.

(Aron "Tex" Holm) Kensel, p. 19; Whittlesley and Watry, p. 75.

(homes at ... Helena, Montana) Harry and Adelaide list their residence at Oro Fino Terrace through 1909. During the same period, Harry's mother occupied a home at 801 Stuart. We might presume that Harry either purchased that home for his widowed mother or inherited it after her death. In the 1910 census, Harry and Adelaide, their two children with spouses and offspring are living at the Stuart Street address. Listing for Harry W. Child, *R.L. Polk & Co.'s Helena City Directory 1909*. Helena, MT: R.L. Polk & Co., Publ.; Listing for Mrs. Sarah Child, *R.L. Polk & Co.'s Helena City Directory 1908*. Helena, MT: R.L. Polk & Co., Publ., p. 138; Listing for Harry Child, 1910 U.S. Census Record, town of Helena, Lewis and Clark County, Montana, 28Apr1910. Harry's father died in 1897; his mother died in 1924. "E.F. Child Dead," *AS*, 29Apr1897, p. 1. Sarah Child's death, Child, p. 33.

(purchasing a home in La Jolla) Listing for Harry W. Child, La Jolla, *San Diego City and County Directory 1920*; Listing for Adelaide D Child (wid Harry W), La Jolla, *San Diego City and County Directory 1931*.

Chapter 8: A Miracle in Hotel Building   *(chapter header)* MSC019, series 7, box 129, file 129.02, YNPA.

page 95

(his "Grand Tour") Haines, *Vol. II*, pp. 100-159, devotes a chapter to a detailed description "On the Grand Tour." Many of his stories date to the 1880 and 1890s, but still give the reader a good taste of the era. The best, most succinct description is found in Dale, pp. 5-6. Dale's visit was probably in the summer of 1903, since he does not mention the Old Faithful Inn that opened in June 1904. See also Lee H. Whittlesey, *Storytelling in Yellowstone: Horse and Buggy Tour Guides*. Albuquerque: University of New Mexico Press, 2007, pp. 167-195; No listed author, [Elizabeth Watry], *The Stagecoach Era*. Yellowstone National Park, WY: Yellowstone Association, 2016.

(precise system) The Hubbards described Harry as "a master" of organization, ... "Mr. Child and his assistants are A students in the subject of economics." Elbert and Alice Hubbard, *A Little Journey to the Yellowstone*. East Aurora, New York: The Roycrofters, 1915, pp. 7-8.

(Robert Reamer designed depot) Quinn, *Weaver,* pp. 39-43.

("tally-ho" stagecoaches) Whithorn, *Gardiner,* p. 4. A nice photo of a six-horse stage underway in the Gardiner River Canyon may be found in the photograph section following p. 80 in Bartlett, *Wilderness.*

(five-mile trip) "Joys of Park Travel. Visitors Should be Prepared for Many Surprises," *GW,* 30Jul1904, p. 1.

(porters then unloaded) "Matt Stewart, who has had charge of the vast amount of baggage going and coming through the Park for many years, returned on Friday with a lot of his help to place things in readiness for the season. It takes a man with a head on his shoulders to handle the car loads of baggage that piles up at the Mammoth, to see that each parcel goes where it belongs, but years of experience has made Mr. Stewart an expert at the business." *GW,* 28May1903, p. 1.

(explore the ... area) Reference to touring the Mammoth Hot Springs Terraces "with a guide," in Diary of Florence E. (Mrs. William S.) Bishop Wallace, Los Angeles, California, trip to through Yellowstone July 13 - 18, 1907, private collection, copy courtesy Shirley Hoffman, San Mateo, CA.

page 96

(orchestra music and dancing) GW, 11Jun1903, p. 1; "Yellowstone Park," *LDE,* 30Jun1913, p. 2.

(luggage was packed, seat assignment for the duration) Dale, p. 6.

(smaller coaches) "When Park Opens, Nation's Playground Begins Summer Season, May 30, E.W. Bach is in Town Today, Preparing to Entertain Tourists – Six-Day Trip This Year – New Hotel at Upper Geyser Basin – Special Rates Made," *BIM,* 6May1902, p. 6.

(Norris Lunch Station) Pitcher, *Report, 1901,* p. 9.

(Fountain Hotel) Lee H. Whittlesey, "'Music, Song, and Laughter,' Yellowstone National Park's Fountain Hotel, 1891-1941," *Montana The Magazine of Western History,* 53(4), Winter 2003, pp. 22-35.

(Three hundred and fifty guests) H.W. Child, Pres., YPA, to Sec. of the Interior, 30Apr1907, *Yellowstone Park Company Records,* MC 141, box 4: "YPA," folder 4-2: "Annual Reports to Secretary of the Interior," MHSRC.

(formation dances) Petersen, p. 33; vertical files: *History-YNP-Journals (Diaries),* "Angelo, Herbert L., Entry for 24Jul[1901], YNPA.

(soldiers stationed) Whittlesey, *A Yellowstone Album,* p. 150.

(practice of feeding bears) Whittlesey and Watry, p. 42; Young, *Report, 1897,* p. 8.

(new Old Faithful Inn) Pitcher, *Report, 1904,* p. 9.

(white linens, silver service) Photo captioned: Old Faithful Inn Dining Room and People, 1917, J.E. Haynes Collection, accession no. 17364, MHSRCPA; M-Y Stage Co., *Yellowstone Park Q and A, 1913.* St. Paul: Pioneer Comapny, 1913, p. 8.

(witnessing eruptions) The importance of a view of geysers can be found in the description of the hotel of cottages planned for Old Faithful: "The cottages will all face 'Old Faithful' geyser. In front of each will be a large covered veranda, from which a fine view may be obtained of the whole formation and from which the eruptions of the 'Giant' 'Giantess' 'Castle' and 'Beehive,' as well as that of 'Old Faithful' can be witnessed." "Cottages for the Upper Basin," *GW,* 20Nov1902, p. 2. One visitor complained, "The stage gives them four or five hours, during which a hurried guide takes them hurriedly across the Basin, and if some of the geysers happen to play while they are being 'done,' the tourists are lucky." Finck, p. 276.

page 97

(Klamer's Curio Shop) Goss, *Serving the 'Faithful,'* p. 19.

(Log Cabin Studio) Young, *Report, 1897,* p. 5.

(West Thumb lunch station) GW, 21May1903, p. 2; Pitcher, *Report, 1903,* p. 7.

(gasoline powered Jean D) "Local Layout," *LE,* 28May1910, p. 7; vertical files: *Diaries,* "The Chapman Party, Yellowstone National Park, July 23 to July 31ˢᵗ, 1914," YNPA; Hubbard and Hubbard, p. 20; James O. Wolfe, *A Yellowstone Savage from Fishing Bridge: Adventures of a Fishing Guide on Yellowstone Lake.* Bloomington, IN: 1stBooks, 2003, p. 108.

(Lake Hotel) Reau Campbell, *Campbell's New Revised Complete Guide and Descriptive Book of the Yellowstone Park.* Chicago: H.E. Klamer, Publisher, 1909, p. 158; Barbara Dittl and Joanne Mallmann, *Plain to Fancy: The Story of the Lake Hotel.* Boulder, CO: Roberts Rinehart, Inc., 1987.

(Canyon Hotel) Tamsen Emerson Hert, "Luxury in the Wilderness: Yellowstone's Grand Canyon Hotel, 1911-1960," *Yellowstone Science,* 13(3), Summer 2005, pp. 21-36; Tamsen E. Hert, "Resort on the Rim: Yellowstone's Grand Canyon Hotel," *The Yellowstone Postcard Exchange,* 3(3), Fall 1998, pp. 10-14.

(ride to the top of Mount Washburn) A.B. Guptill, *Haynes Guide to Yellowstone Park: A Practical Hand Book.* St. Paul: The Pioneer Press, 1905, p. 95.

(Lunch was taken) Whittlesey, *Storytelling,* p. 193-194.

("couponers," cabins with four walls) Bartlett, *Wilderness,* p. 54.

page 98

(cots and mattresses) "Campers' Cabins" or "Housekeeping Cabins" became popular in the automobile era, when travelers enjoyed their convenience and economy. Haines, *Vol. II,* p. 361. Plat plans of the Housekeeping Cabins – as separate from the Lodges – at Mammoth, Canyon, and Old Faithful can be found in *Appraisal Inventory of Yellowstone Park Lodges & Camps Company, Vol. 3.* Milwaukee, WI: The American Appraisal Company, 1929.

("sagebrushers") Bartlett, *Wilderness,* p. 54.

(Cook's Travel Company) Guptill, *Practical Guide,* p. 9.

(Raymond & Whitcomb) Hyde, pp. 212, 249-250; "Opens this Week. Yellowstone Park Season will be commenced Under Especially Favorable Conditions." *DI,* 11Jun1900, p. 2; *GW,* 28May1903, p. 1.

(occupational conventions ...) The columns of local newspapers carried notes about the arrival of these large parties: a party of 125 Shriners from New York and Massachusetts – *LE,* 28Jun1902, p. 5; a party of 44 agriculturalists and scientists from Germany – "Germans Visit Park," *GW,* 11Jun1903, p. 1; "Members of the Montana Press Association numbering 480 – Annual Outing of the Editors," *GW,* 10Sept1903, p. 1; 130 members of the Knights Templar – "Our Local Field," *GW,* 20Aug1904, p. 5.

(handled such "party business" himself) H.W. Child, Pres., YPA, to D.E. Burley, G.P.& T.A., O.S.L.R.R., Salt Lake City, Utah, 6May1903, doc 5535; H.W. Child, Pres., YPA, to Major John Pitcher, Acting Supt., Yellowstone Park, 7May 71903, doc 5533; H.W. Child, Pres., YPA, to Sec. of the Interior, 7May1903, doc 5534, *First 10,000 Documents,* YNPA.

(campaign to divert, "wonders and possibilities ...") Marguerite S. Shaffer, *See America First: Tourism and National Identity, 1880-1940.* Washington and London: Smithsonian Institution Press, 2001, pp. 26-27.

(message across the nation, booster magazine) "From December 1908 until [Fisher] Harris' death in November 1909, the *Western Monthly: A Magazine Devoted to the Art, Literature, Progress, and Development of the Inter-Mountain West* functioned as the 'Official Organ of the See America First Leagues.'" Shaffer, pp. 27, 29, 30.

page 99

(extensive advertising campaign) Shaffer, p. 41.

(promote Glacier National Park) Shaffer, p. 40.

(short-lived magazine, Taft's automobile tour) Shaffer, p. 31.

(Now four railroads) Bruce Austin, Robert Goss, and Gerard Pesman, "Buses In Yellowstone National Park," *Motor Coach Today,* 7(2), April-June 2000, pp. 8, 9; Horace M. Albright, *Annual Report for Yellowstone National Park, 1920.* Wash., DC: Government Printing Office, no date, pp. 31-32. A fifth railroad, the Chicago & Northwestern, arrived for service from Lander, Wyoming to the southeast of the park in 1922. Lindsley, p. 263. Runte, *Trains,* p. 32.

(something of the architecture) H.W. Child, Pres., YPA, to R.A. Ballinger, Seattle, WA, 26Aug1909, folder 6 of 7: *Privileges (Yellowstone) - Yellowstone*

Lake Boat Company, Box No. 237: Privileges: Wylie Permanent Camping Co. – Newsstands to Yellowstone Mining Corporation, Central Files, 1907-39, Yellowstone National Park, General Records, Record Group 79: Records of the National Park Service, National Archives and Record Administration, College Park, Maryland (hereafter NARA-CP).

(leaven Reamer's affinity) Naylor, p. 96.

(set sail October 6) Child letter, 26Aug1909; "Shipping and Mails," *NYT*, 6Oct1909, p. 16.

(returning December 17) "Shipping and Mails," *NYT*, 16Dec1909, p. 16; Passenger Records, Ellis Island Website, www.ellisisland.org

("ugliest building in the world," ugly as the big icehouses) "More of the Park," *LE*, 4Sept1909, p. 3. Reau Campbell observed similarly that the Canyon Hotel "can make no claims to architectural beauty ..." Campbell, p. 158.

page 100

(took up residence at Mammoth) Listing for Robert Reamer, *U.S. Census Record, 1910*, town of Mammoth Hot Springs, Uinta County, Wyoming.

(traveling to Helena, employed a draftsman) "Gardiner Notes," *LE*, 16Apr1910, p. 2; "Gardiner Notes," *LE*, 7May1910, p. 2; "Personal," *LE*, 14May1910, p. 8.

(Blueprints for the structure) Blueprints are filed in the *F. Jay Haynes Architectural Drawings* collection, MC86, folder 1, items 1-7; folder 2, items 1-7; folder 3, items 1-10; folder 4, items 1-8; folder 5, items 1-11; folder 6, items 1-9; MHSRC.

(construction site in January 1911) "The Canyon Hotel – Treasure State Gives New Park Building a Write-Up. – Lauds Child and Reamer – New Building Planned by Same Architect who designed Old Faithful Inn," *LE*, 31Jan1911, p. 3.

(nails by the quart, emulous and undaunted) John H. Raftery, *The Story of the Yellowstone*, Butte, MT: The McKee Printing Company, 1912, pp. 94-103. See also J.H. Raftery, *A Miracle in Hotel Building: The Dramatic Story of the Building of the New Canyon Hotel in Yellowstone Park*, pamphlet published by the Yellowstone Park Hotel Co., c. 1912; and Dan (Alias "Red") W. Gibson, *Souvenir of Construction of the New Canyon Hotel, Yellowstone National Park, 1910-1911*. Tacoma, WA: Acorn Press, 1910.

page 101

(hoping to journey) "Local Layout," *LE*, 29Dec1910, p. 3; "Local Layout," *LE*, 3Jan1911, p. 3.

(Chicago, New York, and Washington) "Local Layout," *LE*, 9Jan1911, p. 3; "Heavy Park Travel," *LE*, 14May1910, p. 5.

(suspended freight charges) Howard Elliott, Pres., NPR, to H.A. Gray, Comtroller, 11Jan1911, President's Subject file 210A, folder 9, NPRR-MHC.

(opened in June) The *Enterprise* reported that Canyon Hotel was "open for guests," but also described it as "partially completed," and "nearing completion." "Local Layout," *LE*, 21Jun1911, p. 3; "Local Layout," *LE*, 3Jul1911, p. 3.

(A grand ball, reception line) "Ball and Reception at Grand Canyon Hotel," *LE*, 3Aug1911, p. 1.

(Hofer ... underwater financially) Howard Elliott, to Warren Delano, New York City, 24Dec1910, President's Subject file 209A, folder 1, NPRR-MHC.

(Waters' ... boats remained) "Park Boats Sold – EC Waters Disposes of Park Property – To Repair Waters Boat – Waters Goes to Miles City to Dispose of Stock – expects to soon leave for East," *LE*, 29Oct1910, p. 1.

page 102

(loan from a wealthy easterner) Haines, *Vol. II*, p. 50.

(let business go to Harry) Barringer, *Selling Yellowstone*, p. 46; Haines, *Vol. II*, p. 52; mimeograph sheet in File #21: Hofer, T. Elwood (Billie), Box 121, Collection 1504: *Haynes Research Files*, BSC-MSU.

(make a nuisance of himself, banned from reentering) Haines, *Vol. II*, p. 77; Bartlett, *Wilderness*, p. 193. Haines contends that Waters' assets were sold to the T.E. Hofer Boat Company. In fact, Hofer purchased his own fleet from the Truscutt Boat Company of St. Joseph, Michigan. It was Harry that ultimately purchased Waters' interest in Yellowstone. Leslie J. Quinn, personal communication.

(buy out his entire outfit) Haines, *Vol. II*, p. 50. Harry paid Waters $50,000 for his assets. "Park Boats Sold ...," 29Oct1910.

(Zillah and E C Waters) The steel-hulled *Zillah* was eventually cut up for scrap. *E C Waters* was moored on the lee side of Stevenson Island. When the ice broke on Yellowstone Lake in 1921, the vessel was shoved up onto the island, destroying its hull. The ribs and portions of the drive train are still visible in and out of the waterline on the north side of Stevenson Island. Report of the Chief Ranger 3Jun1921, p. 14, in Horace M. Albright, *Superintendent's Monthly Report, May 1921*, 10Jun1921; Haines, *Vol. II*, p. 415, n67; p. 316.

(partners had acquired) Smith, p. 45.

(plans for a townsite, hired an architect) Smith, pp. 51, 52.

(fifteen-mile branch line, called Anceney Station) "The line was called the Camp Creek Railway and its terminal was called, of course, 'Anceney Station.' The train was in full operation by 1912 and was successful enough that the Northern Pacific bought it two years later at Harry Child's behest. It continued service, sometimes, sporadically, until 1985." Smith, p. 51. Anceney gave a description of the five hundred mile cattle drive from Montana to Chicago in the pre-railroad days in Forbes, pp. 168-170.

(cattle grazing central) Demaray, p. 179; Barringer, *Selling Yellowstone*, p. 53.

page 103

(contracts for beef, two hundred and sixty) Smith, p. 46.

(variation of an old brand) Smith, p. 49; Child, p. 168. Listings for C.L. Anceney, Child and Anceney, *Livestock Brand Registrations for Montana, 1911-1920*, digital collection, pp. 2442, 5788, https://www.mtmemory.org/

(registered in 1929) Smith, pp. 4, 49, 59-60.

(100 blooded shorthorns) "Big Deal in Land..." *Bozeman Chronicle*, 7Jan1913, p. 8; Smith, p. 15.

(Chilancy) Manager Frank Stone created the name around 1930. Smith, p. 62.

(Chicago Stock Shows) Smith, pp. 55-57.

(Rutledge Hargrove, stayed on with P.B. Clark) Smith, pp. 46-47.

(tenant farmers, unusual arrangement) Smith, p. 47; Forbes, p. 184.

(no inspections and little supervision) Ray Michener and Dorothy M. Vick, "Haying On the Flying D," *In Celebration of Our Past*, [Papers Presented at the Third Annual History Conference], Bozeman, MT: Gallatin County Historical Society, 1991, p. 46.

page 104

(Zachariah Sales, power a sawmill, sleeping children) Smith, p. 18.

(blacksmith, laundry, moved to Salesville, more new businesses appeared) Smith, p. 22.

(water-powered flour mill, "Slabtown, Gallatin Gateway) Smith, p. 18.

(has the same yearning to go camping) Forbes, pp. 330-332.

page 105

(In the fall of 1910) Quoted from "Loeb Got an Elk," *LE*, 8Oct1910 in Doris Whithorn, "The Sec-a-terry to the president [William Loeb, Jr.]," *Twice Told Tales, Vol. 1*, pp. 58, 59.

page 106

(left behind at the railhead) Whithorn, *Twice Told Tales, Vol. 1*, p. 56.

(fall seasons of 1904) "Visits the Park. William Loeb, Secretary to President Roosevelt, in Wonderland," *LE*, 11Jun1904.

(1905) "Loeb did, however return to the Upper Yellowstone Country in 1905." – references to fishing at Slough Creek: *LE*, 22Jul1905; *LDP*, 3Aug1905; *LE*, 19Aug1905; in Whithorn, *Twice Told Tales, Vol. 1*, p. 56.

(1907) Whithorn, *Twice Told Tales, Vol. 1*, p. 57. - *LDP*, 10Oct1907; *LE*, 12Oct1907; *LDP*, 31Oct1907; *LDP*, 12Nov1907.

(a physical wreck) Quoted from "Secretary Gets in the Game," *LDP*, 31Oct1907 in Whithorn, *Twice Told Tales, Vol. 1*, pp. 57-58.

(Madison Valley) "Local Layout," *LE*, 10Sept1910, p. 5.

(handsome promotional pamphlet) Smith, pp. 52-53.

(even with the support) "Supporters of this ambitious operation included the headmasters at Groton and Middlesex prep schools, several railroad presidents, and Samuel Blythe ..." Smith, pp. 53-54.

page 107

(Helena YWCA, independent organization) Ellen Baumler, "Helena YWCA, Independent – A Brief History of the Helena YWCA," presentation given to the Helena Soroptomists, 23Nov 2008, published with permission at www.helenahistory.org/ywca.htm 13Oct2017. "The Helena YWCA chose not to affiliate with the national organization because some of the former's hard-working founders were Jewish." Baumler, *Historic Helena*, p. 38.

(dues from three-hundred members) Ibid, p. 90.

(wrote personally to Howard Elliott) Handwritten letter from Adelaide Child, to Howard Elliott," 1Dec1912, President's Subject file 209A [1], folder 2, NPRR-MHC.

Chapter 9: The Next Generation   *(chapter header)* MSC019 s7 b129 f129.03 YNPA.

page 109

(promoted W.M. Nichols) "History of William Morse Nichols," Typescript, dated 28Aug1957, vertical file: *History - YNP - Employee, YHC.*, "Nichols." W.M. held that position until Harry's death in 1931. "Col. Nichols of Yellowstone Park Company Is Stricken," *LE*, 7Aug1957, pp. 1, 4.

(made General Manager, Treasurer) H.W. Child, YPTC, to J. M. Hannaford, Pres., NPR, 1Mar1914, President's Subject file 209A, folder 1, NPRR-MHC; Listing for Huntley Child, *R.L. Polk & Co.'s Helena City Directory 1915*. Helena, MT: R.L. Polk & Co., Publ.; *R.L. Polk & Co.'s Helena City Directory 1916*. Helena, MT: R.L. Polk & Co., Publ.

(to act as care giver) Child, Appendix 13.

(left there broken-hearted) Personal communication from Harry W. Child II, to Ruth Quinn, 20May2019.

(early 1900s, serving the company, baker for the construction crew, freshly baked apple pies) Reinhart and Henry, p. 81.

(integral part of the families') Listing for Harry Child, *1930 U.S. Census Record*, San Diego County, California, 7Apr1930; Listing for Huntley Child, *1920 U.S. Census Record*, District 0441, Queens Assembly District 6, Queens, New York, www.ancestry.com 20Mar2018.

page 110

(apartments at Oro Fino) Listing for Harry Child, *R.L. Polk & Co.'s Helena City Directory 1908*. Helena, MT: R.L. Polk & Co., Publ., p. 138; and *R.L. Polk & Co.'s Helena City Directory 1909*. Helena, MT: R.L. Polk & Co., Publ.

(home at 801 Stuart St) Listing for Harry Child, *R.L. Polk & Co.'s Helena City Directory 1910*. Helena, MT: R.L. Polk & Co., Publ. The Stuart Street address seems to have first been home to Harry's mother, Mrs. Edwin (Sarah) Child from at least 1905. *R.L. Polk & Co.'s Helena City Directory 1905*. Helena, MT: R.L. Polk & Co., Publ., p. 134.

(Huntley and Ellen) Record for Harry Child, *1910 U.S. Census Record*, town of Helena, Lewis and Clark County, Montana, 28Apr1910.

(Nichols family ... Harrison Avenue) "Personals," *HDI*, 14Oct1914, p. 12; Interpretive street-side sign at 706 Harrison Avenue, *Edward C. Babcock Mansion* [a contributing property to Helena Historic District].

(lived at 706 Monroe) The 1915 city directory lists the address at 706 Monroe, but the 1916 and 1917 list the Huntley Child family at 701 Monroe. Listing for Huntley Child, *R.L. Polk & Co.'s Helena City Directory 1915*. Helena, MT: R.L. Polk & Co., Publ.; *R.L. Polk & Co.'s Helena City Directory 1916*. Helena, MT: R.L. Polk & Co., Publ.; *R.L. Polk & Co's Helena City Directory 1917*. Helena, MT: R.L. Polk & Co., Publ.; Meloy, *More From the Quarries*, lists 706 Monroe as the house affiliated with the family.

(polite and respectful, always addressed) One great-grandchild remembers using the nicknames "Bumpa" and "Muna" for Harry and Adelaide. Child, p. 25.

(Bessie stayed) Listing for Harry Child, *1930 U.S. Census Record*, San Diego County, California, 7Apr1930. A 1936 letter mentions Bessie as a member of the household. Robert C. Reamer, Architect, Stimson Building, to Mrs. Child, 12Oct1936, Box YPC-4, YNPA; Child, Appendix 13.

(New York, New Haven, and Hartford Railroad) Quinn, *Weaver*, pp. 87-93.

(additions to Old Faithful Inn ... and Mammoth Hotel) Quinn, *Weaver*, pp. 93-96; Lindsley, p. 215.

(letter from the acting superintendent) Lieutenant-Colonel, First Cavalry, Acting Supt., to Sec. of the Interior, 1Apr1914, Folder 190: *Yellowstone Park Hotel Company*, Box No. 28, Item 59, Letter Box: *Leases and Contracts for use of Park Lands*, YNPA.

(with an architect on the ground) W.M. Nichols, Sec., YPHC, to Lieut. Col. L.M. Brett, Supt., 18Apr1914, file: *Yellowstone Park Hotel Company*, Item 45: *Buildings and Building Sites*, YNPA.

(Grand Rapid Michigan furniture show) H.W. Child, YPTC, to Jules M. Hannaford, Pres., NPR, 22Dec1913, President's Subject file 209A [1], folder 1, NPRR-MHC.

page 111

(to complete our purchases) H.W. Child, to Colonel Clough, Chairman of the Board, NPR, 24Feb1914, President's Subject file 209A [1], folder 1, NPRR-MHC.

(kept his architect busy) Meloy, *More From the Quarries*, p. 43; David L. Leavengood, "The Green Meadow Ranch," *Perspecta 17: The Yale Architectural Review*. New Haven, CT: 1981, p. 59.

(He re-acquired this land) John DeHaas, *Green Meadow Ranch*, HABS No. MT-35, Historic American Buildings Survey, National Park Service, December 1967, pp. 1, 2.

(one of the interesting points, past thirty years, blooded stock, All varieties of grains) "Green Meadow Farm to Be Finest in the Northwest," *HDI*, 12Jul1914, p. 2.

(Robert Reamer designed) [Architect's Sketch] "Green Meadow Farm; Helena Mont. for H.W. Child [owner]; Robert C. Reamer, Arch't; 5-15-1914," vertical file: *Farms and Ranches*, "Green Meadow Farm, Lewis & Clark Co.," MHSRC; Leavengood, p. 59.

(lost to fire in 1924) DeHaas, *Green Meadow Ranch*, p. 3.

(the barn in 1956) Helena livestock photographer, Edward J. Saxton, captured the blaze. Accession #PAc 89-70, MHSRCPA.

(designed as four separate) Leavengood, p. 59.

page 112

(same heavy timber frame) Meloy, *More From the Quarries...*, p. 43.

(Scandinavian feel) Leavengood, p. 60. The house and bunkhouse are pictured in photo #PAc 89-70, MHSRCPA.

(expended $100,000) "Green Meadow Farm ...," *HDI*, p. 2.

(Strong and sturdy) Mrs. W.J. [Esther] Harrer, "The Green Meadow Barn," typescript in vertical file: "Green Meadow Farm, Helena MT," MHSRC.

(purchasing agent ... land in Gallatin/Madison Valley) Smith, pp. 44-45.

($40.00 an acre) Ibid, p. 46.

(plans ... railroads to build ... into the park) H.W. Child, to Geo. H. Lamar, (YPA attorney in Washington), 21Dec1911, President's Subject file 209A, folder 1; Howard Elliott, to Col. W. P.. Clough, V. P., NPR, 10Nov1912, President's Subject file 209A [1], folder 2, NPRR-MHC.

(coming of the motor cars) Smith, p. 46.

page 113

(Cherry Creek Land Association, twenty-three percent) Smith, pp. 55-56.

(purchased her own home, Mary Wheeler, Georgia Young) "The A.T. Hibbard Home," Baucus, pp. 34-35; Listing for Maria M. Dean, *Helena City Directory, 1911.* Helena, MT: R.L. Polk & Co.'s, pp. 160-161; Listing for *site of St. Peter's Hospital* (Guardian Apartments, 520 Logan St.), in Baumler, *Historic Helena,* pp. 112, 114.

(active in the cause of women's suffrage) Petrik, p. 183; "Meeting of Women, Second Annual Convention of the Montana Equal Suffrage Association," *AS,* 18Nov1896, p. 6; Larson, p. 33.

(assuming presidency) "Woman Suffragists," *AS,* 18Oct1899, p. 2; Graña, pp. 236-237; Larson, p. 34.

(failed to pass amendments) Larson, p. 34; Graña, pp. 250, 251.

(speaking on issues of concern to women) "Without Recommendation, The Bill for Woman Suffrage Given a Hearing in Committee," *AS,* 26Jan1899, p. 1; "Women's Suffrage," *The Kalispell* [MT] *Bee,* 19Aug1902, p. 2; "Know What They Want, All Right, Delegates to Women Suffragist Convention Are Well Informed on Question," *BIM,* 17Sept1902, p. 3; "Woman Suffragists Appoint Committees and Hear Theses on Their Rights to Vote," *BIM,* 18Sept1902, p. 7; "Advocates of Woman Suffrage Have a hearing Before Judiciary Committee," *BIM,* 29Jan1903, p. 2; "Club Lectures," *Montana News* [Lewistown, MT], 14Mar1906, p. 8.

(Montana native Jeanette Rankin) Larson, p. 34.

("old guard of women's rights activists," appeared on the platform) Graña, pp. 258-259, Two photographs in the National Photo Company Collection, Library of Congress, show Dean and Rankin side by side. https://www.loc.gov/pictures/item/2016821746/ and 2016821745.

(1913 a woman suffrage amendment passed) Larson, p. 35.

(focused on the public vote) Larson, p. 36, "Suffragists Plan Big Meeting in July," *The Daily Missoulian* [Missoula, MT], 28Jun1914, p. 8; "Bulletin From the State Equal Suffrage Committee," *Fergus County Democrat* [Lewistown, MT] (hereafter *FCD*), 13Aug1914, p. 5.

(Women's Day at the State Fair) Ibid; "Suffrage Bulletin from The State Headquarters," *FCD,* 20Aug1914, p. 5.

page 114

(marchers from every county, at the front of the pageant) Larson, p. 38; "Suffragists are Busy for Helena Gathering," *FCD,* 17Sept1914, p. 10; Graña, pp. 268-269.

(Young served as hostesses) "Entertainment of visitors," *The Suffrage Daily News* [Helena, MT] (hereafter *SDN*), 26Sept1914, p. 2.

(candidate takes care of the baby) "Eticat Column," *SDN,* 24Sept1914, p. 3.

("Optimism prevailed...") Larson, p. 38.

(handful of states) According to T.A. Larson, "Before another month had passed [after Montana voted for woman's suffrage], the Territory of Alaska and ten of the eleven western states had taken this giant step ..." Larson, p. 25; https://en.wikipedia.org/wiki/Nineteenth_Amendment_to_the_United_States_Constitution 25Aug 2017; Graña, pp. 300-301.

(sent Jeannette Rankin to Congress) Jeannette Rankin (1880-1973) represented Montana with terms in the U.S. House from 1917-1919, and 1941-1943. She is well-remembered for her "no" votes to the United States entry into both World War I and World War II. https://en.wikipedia.org/wiki/Jeannette_Rankin; Jean Hoff Wilson, "'Peace Is a Woman's Job...': Jeannette Rankin and American Foreign Policy: Her lifework as a pacifist," *Montana the Magazine of Western History,* 30(2), Winter 1980, pp. 38-53; Mary Murphy, "When Jeannette said 'No,' Montana Women's Response to World War I," *Montana the Magazine of Western History,* 65(1), Spring 2015, pp. 3-23, n1-n3.

(great enthusiasts) "Local Layout," *LE,* 4Apr1911, p. 3; "Arranging to meet autoists," *LE,* 22Jul1911, p. 1

(right to bring autos into the park) E.A. Hitchcock, Sec. of the Interior, to Colonel John Pitcher, Acting Supt., 12May1902, doc 5018; Petition from citizens of Cody, Wyoming referenced in letter from Frank Pierce, 1st Asst. Secy., 18Jan1908, doc 7985, *First 10,000 Documents,* YNPA.

(moonlight drive through the park) David E. Burley, Gen'l Pass Agt, OSL RR Co., Aug1907, docs 8530 to 8535, *First 10,000 Documents,* YNPA; Richard A. Barlett, "Those Infernal Machines In Yellowstone...," *Montana the Magazine of Western History,* 20(3), Summer 1970, p. 22.

(Other western parks) Bartlett, *Wilderness,* p. 84; Bartlett, *Montana,* p. 23.

page 115

(traveler tried to enter, only under cover of darkness) Chester A. Lindsley, to W.M. Nichols, Sec., YPTC, Helena, MT, 6May1914, YNPA.

(automobilists were exerting such pressure) In 1908, Superintendent S.B.M. Young wrote, "In my judgement it would not only be unwise but wrong to permit automobiles in this great pleasuring ground ..." Bartlett, *Montana,* p. 22. His opinion must be considered in light of his relationship with Harry and Adelaide Child. See also "Will Recommend Autos in the Park," *LDE,* 22Jul1913, p. 3; "Autoists Plan to Meet Secretary of Interior Lane at Gardiner and Bring him Here," *LDE,* 23Jul1913, p. 1.

(ordered to haul ... back to Gardiner) Haines, *Vol. II,* p. 267; unsigned letter to W.M. Nichols, Sec., YPHC, 20Nov1914, YNPA.

(Gallatin River to West Yellowstone) Demaray, pp. 142-143; Fred M. Brown, County Surveyor, to Col. L.M. Brett, Supt., 16Oct1911; "Construction commenced August 8, 1910 and continued until November 10, 1910; was commenced again June 19, 1911 and completed October 10, 1911," – this concerns Taylors Fork & Yellowstone Road, 31.1 miles, Report from Fred M. Brown, Country Surveyor, to Board of Country Commissioners, Gallatin County, MT, 16Oct1911, Item 71, File 345: *Roads Through NW Corner, County Rd [Gallatin Co., Mont.],* YNPA.

(no restrictions against automobile) Lindsley, p. 204; "Local News," *LDE,* 12Apr1913, p. 3; "Autos in the Park," *LDE,* 2Jun1913, p. 3.

(Commercial clubs) "Automobile Road in Wonderland Probable," *LDE,* 5Dec1912, p. 1; "Autoists Plan to Meet Secretary of Interior Lane at Gardiner and Bring him Here," *LDE,* 23Jul1913, p. 1. Travelers mention a Stanley Steamer automobile in use from the park's eastern boundary to Cody, Wyoming in 1914. vertical file: *Diaries,* "The Chapman Party," YNPA.

page 116

(forming The Yellowstone Trail, a yellow circle) "Meeting in Miles City of Twin City - National Park Trail Association," *LDE,* 22Jan1913, p. 1; "Local News," *LDE,* 17Mar1913, p. 3; "A Study in Yellow." *LDE,* 17Mar1913, p. 3; "All Roads Lead to Livingston," *LDE,* 23Apr1913, p. 1; "Preparing to Build Yellowstone Road," *LDE,* 1May1913, p. 1; "Yellowstone Trail Travel Now On," *LDE,* 15Jul1913, p. 1; "First Party to Complete Trip Over the Park Trail Arrives, With Speedometer Registering 999 Miles," *LDE,* 16Jul1913, p. 1.

("A Good Road ...") Doris Whithorn, *Yankee Jim's National Park Toll Road and the Yellowstone Trail.* Livingston, MT: privately published, 1989; Harold A. Meeks, *On the Road to Yellowstone: The Yellowstone Trail and American Highways 1900 – 1930.* Missoula, MT Pictorial Histories Publishing Company, 2000; Alice A. Ridge and John William Ridge, *Introducing the Yellowstone Trail: A Good Road from Plymouth Rock to Puget Sound.* Altoona, WI: Yellowstone Trail Publishers, 2000.

(imposing a franchise or "usage tax," "enlargement of the maintenance fund") Major Benson, to H.W. Child, 4Apr1910, RG00: *Army Era Records,* series II: "Post-1908 Scheduled Files," box 150, file 321: "Rentals, Taxes, etc. – Yellowstone Park Hotel Company;" H.W. Child, Pres., to Major H.C. Benson, Acting Supt., Yellowstone Park, Wyo., 'to Secy Int April 15,' YNPA.

page 121

(twenty-five cents, retroactive to the 1909 season) Major Benson, to W.M. Nichols, 11May1910; Major Benson to Sec. of Interior, 1July1910, RG00, series II, box 150, file 321: YPHC; YNPA.

(subtracted their "dead heads," "do the park some good") W.M. Nichols, to Lt. Col. L.M. Brett, 19Dec1913, RG00, series II, box 150, file 321: "Rentals, Taxes, etc. – Yellowstone Park Transportation Company," YNPA.

(reconciling the payment due date) H.W. Child, to Stephen T. Mather, 27Jul1915; Stephen T. Mather, to Col. L.M. Brett, 30Dec1915, RG00, series II, box 150, file 321: YPHC, YNPA.

(ironed out the final arrangement) Stephen T. Mather, to YPHC, 13Jul1915, RG00, series II, box 150, file 321: YPHC, YNPA.

(astute) "executive ability to an unusual degree, a keen and analytical mind," "Harry Child, Prominent in Montana, Dies, *M R-H*, 4Feb1931, p. 2.

(diagnosis of diabetes) Most sources say it was about 1915-1916 when Harry first became ill. Child, p. 74; Child-Haines Interview. Other references to Harry's ongoing health issues are found in "Harry Child is Here Improved in Health," *GFDT*, 18Jun1920, p. 8; Howard Elliott, Chairman, NPR, to Charles Donnelly, Pres., 5Dec1925, President's Subject file 209B, folder 5, NPRR-MHC. He also refers to consulting doctors at the Mayo Clinic in Minnesota. In his words, "... the Mayo brothers of Rochester told me that if I didn't go back to my out-of-door life in Montana I would very soon go into a box." Forbes, p. 325.

(kept up with political and business trends) "A Builder Passes," *M R-H*, 5Feb1931, p. 4; "Harry Child Will Be Missed," *LE*, 6Feb1931.

(Child had held government contracts) "Harry Child had achieved a balance, managing to earn healthy profits and alter the park to suit both his needs and those of his guests. He operated in a time of consensus, when everyone knew almost instinctively what Yellowstone was supposed to be. His hotels, stagecoaches, camps and buses all fit into the constructed image visitors brought with them to the park. His family business became part of the national experience. ..." Barringer, *Selling Yellowstone*, p. 178.

("The Greatest Tourist Attraction...") Author Nan Sigrist found this quote in her reading. It was in reference to Silas Huntley's stagecoach transportation service in Yellowstone. We have been unable to locate the original source again. RQ

(favored the creation of the National Park Service) Alfred Runte, *National Parks: The American Experience*. Lincoln and London: University of Nebraska Press, 1979, pp. 98-100; Hummel, p. 50. "The agency, particularly under Mather and Albright," observed one historian, " had proven to be philosophically compatible with concessioner promotion, development, and expansion." Barringer, *Selling Yellowstone*, p. 135.

page 118

(ten more parks and twenty-one monuments) Hummel, pp. 49, 50. "In 1910 the Secretary's [Secretary of the Interior Richard A. Ballinger] annual report to the President recommended the creation of 'a bureau of national parks and resorts, under the supervision of a competent commissioner, with a suitable force of superintendents, supervision engineers, and landscape architects, inspectors, park guards, and other employees.'" Hummel, p. 48.

(under the agriculture department) Albright and Schenck, p. 129. Today the National Forest Service, whose roots extend to 1905 with Gifford Pinchot and President Theodore Roosevelt, continues to be administered by the Department of Agriculture. Egan, p. 50; Runte, *Trains*, p. 47, also addresses the multiple overseers in Departments of War, Interior, and National Forest Service.

(known as "orphans") Albright and Schenck, p. 35.

(park superintendents gathered) Demaray, p. 182, Runte, *National Parks*, p. 92.

(At the end of their sessions, recommended the creation) Proceedings of the National Park Conference held at the Yellowstone National Park, September 11 and 12, 1911. Wash., DC: Government Printing Office, 1912; Hummel, pp. 49-50.

(sixty attendees) All are listed in *Proceedings ...1911*, pp. 1-2. Attendees from Yellowstone included Lt. Col. L.M. Brett, Acting Superintendent; R.C. Bryant, Bryant Camping Company; H.W. Child, president, YPHC; F.J. Haynes, president, Monida & Yellowstone Stage Co.; Howard H. Hays, general agent, Wylie Permanent Camping Co.; Walter J. Henderson, concessioner; James R. Hickey, vice president, Monida & Yellowstone Stage Co.; Henry E. Klamer, concessioner; Alexander Lyall, concessioner; A.W. Miles, president, Wylie Permanent Camping Co.; George A. Pryor, concessioner; R.E.L. Smith, Washington, D.C., representing Shaw & Powell Camping Company. In addition to park superintendents and concessionaires, there were representatives from the major western railroads and members of the press.

(no need to sit around camp fires) What the authors have referred to as the "spot of the Washburn pow-wow," is the meadow below the ridge that bears the official place name *National Park Mountain*. During his tenure as Yellowstone's superintendent, Horace Albright promoted this spot, a campsite used by the 1870 Washburn-Langford-Doane expedition, as the birth of the "National Park Idea." Contemporary historians consider the campfire story to be a "creation myth," rather than an actual conversation that took place. See Paul Schullery and Lee H. Whittlesey, *Myth and History in the Creation of Yellowstone National Park*. Lincoln, NE: University of Nebraska Press, 2003.

(Harry Child hosted ... Grand Canyon Hotel) Photo #889: "National Park Conference, Canyon Hotel, 1911," *Haynes Family Photographs*, Collection 1507, series 2: "Yellowstone National Park," sub-series 3: "Collection 1504 Separated Photographs," box 6, folder 39, BSC-MSU, http://lib.montana. edu/digital/objects/coll1507/889.jpg 20Apr2020. Harry Child is standing on the porch, upper left, labeled #26. W.M. Nichols to the Supt. YNP, 27Feb1913, RG00, series II, box 150, file 321: YPTC, YNPA.

(featured speakers) Proceedings ... 1911, pp. III-IV.

("first historic activist mobilization...") Hummel, p. 49. Another conference was held in 1912 in California. Harry also attended this conference. While he did not make an official presentation, he was called upon to comment about hotel conditions in Yellowstone. *Proceedings of the National Park Conference Held at Yosemite National Park October 14, 15, and 16, 1912*. Wash., DC: Government Printing Office, 1913, p. 52.

(chose a graduate ... Franklin K. Lane) Albright and Schenck, pp. 16, 20.

(turned to Berkeley alumni) Adolph C. Miller, Lane's Assistant Secretary of Interior, and Horace Albright, "confidential clerk" to the Interior Secretary, both attended U.C. Berkeley. Albright and Schenck, pp. 16, 18-19.

page 119

(Mather came on board) Runte, *National Parks*, pp. 101-102; Albright and Schenck, p. 35; Runte, *Trains*, p. 50.

(attempt ... bill through Congress) Runte, *Trains*, p. 49.

("public relations man") Albright and Schenck, pp. 39-40.

(his good looks) Albright and Schenck, p. 26; Robert M. Utley, forward to Albright and Schenck, pp. xii-xiii; Shankland, pp. 8, 56-57, 91.

(eight-cylinder, 60 m.p.) Quoting from the *Washington Post*, Shankland, p. 96.

(lobby congressmen and get votes) Albright and Schenck, p. 25.

(not one to sit, entertain lavishly) Albright and Schenck, pp. 43, 63. Mather's way of conducting business as described by Horace Albright, preferring "to conduct business with people he felt were important to his plans over long lunches or at elegant dinners and theater parties. ... Mather of Chicago made himself a known, well-liked, and admired personage in Washington in a very short time," might very well be a carbon copy of the way Silas Huntley found success (and garnered criticism) in his day.

(felt assured of enough votes) Albright and Schenck, pp. 42-44.

(massive dose of favorable propaganda, using his own money) Albright and Schenck, p. 43.

(visit the parks and get to know his personnel) Albright and Schenck, pp. 54, 57.

(his first Superintendent's Conference) 1915 was Mather's first conference. He was not in attendance at the 1911 or 1912 gatherings mentioned earlier. *Proceedings of the National Park Conference Held at Yosemite, California March 11, 12, and 13, 1915*. Wash., DC: Government Printing Office, 1915. A description of the conference is found in Albright and Schenck, pp. 49-57.

(Yard went along) Albright and Schenck, pp. 44, 61.

page 120

(delivered to homes) Albright and Schenck, p. 75, mention the April 1916 issue on the national parks entitled "The Land of the Best," that "greatly influenced the Congress when the time came to vote for the establishment of a National Park Service." Shankland, pp. 196-197, describes how *National Geographic* and *Saturday Evening Post* published articles to promote the Save-The-Redwoods League.

(expositions in San Diego and San Francisco, "On four and a half acres...") Albright and Schenck, pp. 42-43, 45; Demaray, p. 183.

228

(full-size replica) Albright and Schenck, p. 53; Runte, *Trains*, p. 50; "Beyond question, Old Faithful Inn – seating 2000 – is the grand café deluxe of the Exposition." Union Pacific Postcard, Panama-Pacific International Exposition, San Francisco, CA: Cardinell-Vincent Co., circa 1915, Quinn collection; photo by Pacific Photo and Art Co., San Francisco, CA: "1915, Old Faithful Inn (replica)," *Haynes Foundation Collection,* box 158: "YNP-Old Faithful Inn – Exteriors, 1915," MHSRCPA.

(The National Parks Portfolio, "franking") Shankland, pp. 97-99. The General Federation of Women's Clubs lobbied Congressmen in support of the National Park Service bill and "members produced a mailing list of 275,000 names for the *National Parks Portfolio...*" Polly Welts Kaufman, *National Parks and the Woman's Voice: A History.* Albuquerque: University of New Mexico Press, 1996, p. 35; Byrand discusses how, "in trying to prevent resource exploitation," Stephen Mather "intensively promoted the parks and in turn developed them for tourist use." He postulates that "those methods originally designed to preserve the parks from resource development interests almost eighty years ago will ultimately lead to their destruction." Byrand, pp. 18, 24. In ranger-lead interpretive programs today, many in the NPS bring up the two conflicting missions inherent in the bill which created that agency: that of preserving the parks "unimpaired for future generations," while promoting the public to access and benefit from their use.

(group of Reclamation Service people) Albright and Schenck, p. 63; Lindsley, p. 217; Kensel, p. 58.

(first regulations ... published) "The last use of park roads by motor vehicles prior to the official opening occurred on July 4, 1915, when a party of congressmen and officials of the U.S. Reclamation Service were brought to Lake Hotel over the east entrance road. Regulations governing the admission of automobiles in the first season were published on July 8." Haines, *Vol. II,* p. 269.

page 121

(famous "Mountain Party") Albright and Schenck, pp. 64-65. Horace Albright acted as "man Friday, and handler of all details." He provides a list of all invited attendees on pp. 67-68.

(include a visit ... Rocky Mountain) Albright and Schenck, p. 95.

(Mather ... would allow automobiles) Albright and Schenck, p. 63; Stephen T. Mather, Asst. to the Sec. of the Interior, to Colonel Brett, Acting Supt., YNP, 24May1915, referenced Inclosure No. 15445, YNPA.

(Child proposed a test trip, "Mr. Child become a member...," "whip the schedule") Mather to Brett, 24May1915.

(Child's proposition) Mather, Assistant Secretary Interior, Green River, WY, to Col. L.M. Brett, 12May1915, YNPA.

(telegraph wires hummed, trip was planned for June 4th) Brett, Acting Supt., to Sec. of Interior, 31May1915, YNPA; Mather, Asst. to Sec., to L.M. Brett, 1Jun1915, YNPA.

("heavy storms ...") Brett, Acting Supt., to Stephen T. Mather, 5Jun1915, YNPA.

(Huntley Child drove) Whittlesey and Watry, p. 82; Emmett Hood, "A Model D Franklin & Yellowstone," *Air Cooled News,* 53(2), July 2006, pp. 23-25.

(Gardiner resident L.H. VanDyke) VanDyke received a contract to provide meat to park hotels and opened a butcher shop on the northwest corner of Main Street and Second Street in Gardiner. The building is now the K-Bar Pizza business. Description of Van Dyke and Deever Building, designed by A.R. VanDyke of St. Paul & Chicago in *GW,* 18Jun1903, p. 1; Whithorn, *Gardiner,* p. 9; Doris Whithorn, *History of Park County Montana.* Dallas, TX: Taylor Publishing Co., 1984, p. 26.

page 122

("test trip accomplished...") Brett, Acting Supt., to Stephen T. Mather, 8Jun1915, YNPA. Harry Child made an overture to Bozeman tycoon, Nelson Story, inviting him to accompany the test trip. Story contacted Brett proposing "a genuine business proposition and [ask you to] accept these arrangements for a nominal fee." His offer was apparently declined. Nelson Story, Jr., Bozeman, MT, to Col. L.M. Brett, 1Jun1915, YNPA.

("a run" at the park gates) Bartlett, *Montana,* p. 28.

(allowed to permit) Ibid; Hood, p. 25.

(an official White car, promptly at 7:00) "The First Automobile Tour Through Yellowstone Park," *The Albatross,* 4(32), August 1915, p. 5. Although the photographs accompanying this article are not credited, we might presume they (and perhaps the entire article) were submitted by Yard.

(arrived at Old Faithful Inn, good brakes and a substantial) Ibid, p. 7.

(impossible to overheat, night at Grand Canyon) Ibid, p. 8.

(formally signifying) Ibid, p. 5.

(Fifty automobiles) Ibid, Haines, *Vol. II,* p. 271. Karl Byrand argues, that while to some "The automobile had democratized access to the national parks," in his opinion "the process of determining who would visit the parks was still quite selective. This process was based on income and the ability of that income to purchase a certain degree of mobility. To some extent this process is still selective today." Byrand, pp. 14-15. He cites Anne F. Hyde, "From Stagecoach to Packard Twin Six: Yosemite and the Changing Face of Tourism, 1880-1930, *California History,* Summer 1900, p. 162.

("how the mix of car and stagecoach," "pretty good clip," "a terrible time," "fretted and stewed") Albright and Schenck, pp. 98-99. The Park-to-Park Group traveled from Denver in their automobile caravan, after Mather received assurances that the roads were ready for automobile traffic. Mather, Asst. to Secy, to L.M. Brett, Acting Supt., 20May1915; Telegram from Brett, Acting Supt., to Secy of Interior, 21May1915, YNPA. Albright and Mather took the train to Cody and proceeded by stagecoach from there.

page 123

("We stayed in Yellowstone...") Albright and Schenck, p. 99. Harry worried that Mather might force the transportation company to abandon horse-drawn transportation, as he wrote to his friend, Jule Hannaford, now President of the NPR, "... Mather announced yesterday that transportation companies would use horses next year, same as this. The old man won out again. Congratulate me." Harry W. Child, to J.M. Hannaford, 10Sept1915, cited by Bartlett, *Wilderness,* p. 175.

(Huntley heard ... shop ... was for sale) Huntley Child, Jr., Interview by Harry W. Child, II and Lynette Child, 22Aug1992, video courtesy Harry W. Child II. Hereafter, Huntley Child, Jr. Interview.

(Klamer Curio Shop) Henry Klamer died on 13Aug1914 at the Army Post Hospital at Mammoth Hot Springs. He is buried in California. Mary Klamer and Charles Hamilton signed their final agreement on 7Jun1915. Goss, *Serving the 'Faithful,'* pp. 32, 38.

(back home in Minnesota) Petersen, p. 29.

(exactly the kind of business, excitement of merchandising) Petersen, p. 22.

(finance the buy-out, "front man,") Huntley Child, Jr. Interview. This interview is our source for Huntley Child's interest in joining Charles Hamilton in the general store business. Other writers, whose stories come from the Hamilton family, say that "Huntley felt such a small venture was beneath him and didn't feel it was worth his efforts." Goss, *Serving the 'Faithful,'* p. 36; Petersen, p. 29.

("you're staying out of it...") Huntley Child, Jr. Interview.

page 124

(make a deal with, at the Livingston bank early) Petersen, pp. 29-30. The purchase price of the store was $20,000 – Harry's $5,000 loan was the down-payment. The check for the inventory was $512.62. Goss, *Serving the 'Faithful,'* p. 37.

("different from our code out West ...") Forbes, pp. 339, 328.

("Our national parks are ...") Forbes, "Give Me the West!" p. 248.

(over seventy-five years of success, Store could be found at each Park location) Biographies for Eleanor "Ellie" Hamilton Povah and Pat Povah, in Steve Horan and Ruth W. Crocker, *People of Yellowstone.* Old Mystic, CT: Elm Grove Press, 2017, pp. 118-119, 120-121.

(outside businesses in West Yellowstone) Petersen, p. 108. "Miss Ellie" Povah funded the Povah Community/Senior Center in West Yellowstone and

donated her lifetime's collection of Yellowstone memorabilia and American Indian artifacts to the Museum of the Rockies in Bozeman, MT.

(kept an apartment, inviting them up to his office) Petersen, p. 30, Nan Sigrist, personal knowledge.

(walls with canceled checks) Petersen, pp. 30, 111. The Million Dollar Room was restored and conserved in 2012-2013 with a grant from the Yellowstone Park Foundation (now merged into Yellowstone Forever!). During a conservation inventory, it was documented that the canceled checks sum to a total of $1,839,105.60. In the height of the summer, staff at the Old Faithful Lower Store offer one free daily tour to view the room.

(died at his desk) Goss, *Serving the 'Faithful,'* p. 41.

page 125

(Trevor Povah and daughter) Petersen, pp. 108-110.

(contract was not renewed) Horan and Crocker, p. 120.

(from the top down to the most humble) Forbes, p. 326.

(loved time outdoors) B.C. Forbes wrote that Harry was, "so close to Nature, she reveals more of her secrets to him than to others." Forbes, p. 342. Of Mather, Horace Albright observed, "He felt he had to run the parks out in the field. If he could get key men into the parks and they could sit on a rock and talk things out, they could settle problems in a hurry." Albright and Schenck, p. 63.

(frivolous bets) Harry W. Child, La Jolla, CA, to Stephen Mather, 20Mar1920, YNPA. Stephen Mather, to Harry W. Child, 3Apr1922, YNPA.

Chapter 11: "Those Infernal Machines" *(chapter header)* RARE BOOK 12, folder 12, YNPA
page 127

(again become vitally concerned, his wife, chauffeur-driven) Albright and Schenck, pp. 130-131.

(less than favorable) Ibid, p. 132.

(traveled their own, poured over, made copious notes) Ibid, p. 134.

page 128

(the most beautiful in the world) Ibid, pp. 133-134. The quotation, credited to Robert Reamer, was published by J.H. Raftery who visited the construction site in January 1911. "The Canyon Hotel – Treasure State Gives New Park Building a Write-Up. – Lauds Child and Reamer – New Building Planned by Same Architect who designed Old Faithful Inn", *LE*, 31Jan1911, p. 3. The entire quote is "I built it in keeping with the place where it stands. Nobody could improve upon that. To be at discord with the landscape would be almost a crime. To try to improve upon it would be an impertinence." Raftery, *The Story ...*, p. 107.

(Park-to-Park Highway Association, new and grandest hotel, Mather was the featured) Albright and Schenck, p. 136.

(Harry and Adelaide supported) Barringer, *Selling Yellowstone*, p. 66; Forbes, p. 333.

(in the Teton Valley) Albright and Schenck, pp. 138-139; Robert W. Righter, *Crucible for Conservation: The Creation of Grand Teton National Park*. Boulder, CO: Colorado Associated University Press, 1982, p. 27.

(Glacier Mountain Party) Albright and Schenck, p. 149.

(frightening the horses) This issue was being considered as early as 1912. E.A. Hitchcock, Sec. of the Interior, to the Acting Supt., 16Apr1912, doc 5017, *First 10,000 Documents*, YNPA.

(A Motorists Guide) Motorists Guide: Yellowstone National Park, Department of Interior, National Park Service Publication, 1937, Quinn collection; "Regulations governing the Admission of Automobiles ..." and "Schedules and General Instructions," are included in Jack E. Haynes, *Haynes Guide: The Complete Handbook*. St. Paul, MN: The Pioneer Company, 1916, pp. 12-15.

(leave road junctions by certain times) Albright and Schenck, p. 99. Franklin K. Lane, "Automobile Schedules, Yellowstone National Park," published by Department of the Interior, effective 15Jun1916.

https://www.nps.gov/features/yell/slidefile/history/1872_1918/transportation/Images/02825.jpg

page 129

(This 1916 publication) NPS online photograph collection, YELL 02825.

page 130

(a concession was granted) Lloyd M. Brett, *Superintendent's Annual Report for 1916*. Wash., DC: Government Printing Office, 1916, p. 5.

(seven 10-passenger) J.E. Haynes, to Hiram M. Chittenden, 27Ju1916, BSC-MSU, copy courtesy Harry Child, II. Another report says "The company purchased seven eleven-passenger White touring cars and eight seven-passenger M55 Buicks. Wire-enclosed General Motors trucks were used for hauling baggage." Kensel, p. 60. Austin, et al, lists seven Whites and five Buicks, Austin, et al, p. 4.

(directors of this new company) Austin, et al, p. 4; Kensel, pp. 59-60.

(corkscrew bridge) Culpin, *Road System*, pp. 340, 346-347. Today a pullout on the East Entrance Road just east of Sylvan Pass offers an interpretive display and views of the concrete and stone bridge constructed in 1917 to replace the original wooden trestle.

(deal with the railroads, blocking a certain number of rooms) Harry Child, YPA Pres., to Major John Pitcher and Secretary of Interior, 7May1903, docs. 5533-5534, *First 10,000 Documents*; H.W. Child, to Col. L.M. Brett, 22May1915, RG00, series II: "Post-1908 Scheduled Files," box 51, folder 10: 1915-1916, YNPA.

page 131

(just not enough rooms) H.W. Child, to D.E. Burley, Oregon Short Line RR, 6May1903, doc. 5535, *First 10,000 Documents*, YNPA.

("cannot Child aid Haynes") Mather, to Brett, 14Aug1915; Bo Sweeney, Asst Secy, Wash., DC, to Col. Brett, 17-18Aug1915, RG00, series II, box 51, folder 10, YNPA.

(a possible railroad strike) All details in this section are from H.W. Child, to George H. Lamar, Wash., DC, 2Sept1916, RG00, series II, box 51, folder 10, YNPA. The unpopular decision to close the park on 1Sept1916 was made by Robert Marshall in his role as Superintendent of the National Parks. Albright and Schenck, p. 178.

page 132

(wired Col. Brett) Stephen Mather, to L.M. Brett, 2Sept1916, RG00, series II, box 51, folder 10, YNPA.

(most of the credit, made no provision) L.M. Brett, to S.T. Mather, 2Sept1916, RG00, series II, box 51, folder 10, YNPA.

page 133

(passed through Congress) The Senate passed the bill on August 15. The House followed on August 22. President Wilson signed the act into law on 25Aug1916. Albright and Schenck, p. 146.

(Mather was sworn in) Marshall's decision to close the parks under threat of the railroad strike, so angered Stephen Mather that he removed Marshall from position, assuming it himself. Ibid, p. 174.

(plans of developing... Rangers) "During the winter of 1915-16, Mather and Scott [General Hugh Scott, chief of staff of the army] had several meetings to solidify arrangements [for withdrawal of troops]. The transfer from military to civilian control was to become effective on October 1, 1916." Ibid, p. 150.

(agreed to discharge) Hampton, pp. 165, 179. Albright wrote glowingly about these first ranger-recruits, "... I spent a good deal of time talking to each man individually. They were quite a group, tough as nails, but experienced, honest, and excited about their future work. I was very impressed. I always felt they set the standard for our future corps of rangers." Albright and Schenck, p. 150.

(final withdraw of troops) Haines, *Vol. II*, p. 289.

(failed to appropriate, ranger force disbanded) Shankland, p. 106; Albright and Schenck, pp. 150-151.

(recall of the Army) Ibid, p. 224.

(Senator Thomas J. Walsh, Huntley Child had acquired) Ibid, p. 178.

(into a bout of depression) Ibid, pp. 174-175.

(Albright was sent, Chester Lindsley) Albright and Schenck, pp. 150-151.

page 134

(organize the concessioners) Albright credits Mather's idea of "a regulated monopoly" to a speech given by Ford Harvey at the 1915 National Park Conference. Albright and Schenck, p. 55. Hummel, pp. 56-57; Lindsley, p. 232

(not much give and take) Albright and Schenck, pp. 151-152.

(new Yellowstone Park Camping Company) Barringer, *Annals,* p. 8; Demaray, p. 184.

(which camp locations) Lindsley, p. 233; Demaray, p. 189. Three lodges still operate today. Old Faithful Lodge occupies a former Shaw and Powell site; and both Lake Lodge and Roosevelt Lodge occupy former Wylie sites. Moorman, p. 4; Whittlesey, *A Yellowstone Album,* p. 94.

(selection of the YPTC ... out of business) Austin, et al, p. 5; Kensel, p. 63.

(outsting the Haynes family) Barringer, *Annals,* p. 8.

page 135

(at no financial loss) Shankland, p. 124; "... the vehicles and other assets of the Cody-Sylvan Pass Motor Co. were sold to YPTCo. on January 29, 1917, for $25,000." Austin, et al, p. 5.

(retired from the photography) Lindsley, p. 223; Shankland, p. 124.

(fair and honest manner) Demaray, p. 184.

(continued to be depressed) Albright and Schenck, p. 175.

(grooming him to be the director) Ibid, p. 44.

(diligent worker, clumsy administrator) Shankland, p. 106; Albright and Schenck, pp. 142-143.

(did not take it quietly) Albright and Schenck, p. 179; Shankland, p. 107.

page 136

(Wilson's re-election) Albright and Schenck, pp. 182-183; Shankland, pp. 107-108.

Chapter 12: From Wranglers to Gear Jammers   *(chapter header)* MSC019, series 7, box 129, file 129.09, YNFA.

page 137

(sold his stagecoaches) Shankland, p. 124.

(purchase 117 vehicles) Haines, *Vol. II,* p. 273, and Lindsley, p. 229, use 116 as the number of vehicles purchased. Whithorn, *Gardiner,* p. 7, reports 125. We have chosen the number listed in Austin, et al, p. 5, as those authors examined the purchase records directly.

(backing of the railroads) The Chicago, Burlington, and Quincy Railroad and the Union Pacific Railroad each loaned $160,000 to the cause, while the Northern Pacific, through the Northwest Improvement Company, contributed $150,000. "Memorandum ...," by J.H.P., 12Sept1918, NPRR-MHC.

(general manager and treasurer) H.W. Child, YPTC, Helena, MT, to J.M. Hannaford, President, N.P.Ry., 1Mar1914, President's Subject file 209A, folder 1, NPRR-MHC; Listing for Huntley Child, *R.L. Polk & Co.'s Helena City Directory 1917.* Helena, MT: R.L. Polk & Co., Publ.; Listing for Huntley Child, *R.L. Polk & Co.'s Helena City Directory 1918.* Helena, MT: R.L. Polk & Co., Publ., p. 122.

(Nichols ... assistant to the President) "History of William Morse Nichols," typescript dated 28Aug1957, vertical file: *History - YNP - Employees,* "Nichols," YNPA.

page 138

(campaign to recruit) John Terreo, Gerard Pesman Interview, 19Jun1989, Transcript of interview, Oral History 1167, MHSRC. Gerry Pesman worked for Yellowstone transportation from 1926-1941, and 1968-1978 with an aeronautics engineering career at NASA in between.

(try-outs for chauffeurs) "Park Test Car Here," *The Park County News* [Livingston, MT] (hereafter *PCN*), 19May1922, p. 1.

(wanted local people) Austin, et al, p. 12.

("frolickers") Austin, et al, p. 12. The transportation department of Xanterra Travel Collection in Yellowstone holds a twice-annual training tour for new guides. Expanded from two days in Pesman's time, it is now usually 4-6 days. The term *frolic* continues to be used to label this event. Ruth Quinn, personal knowledge.

page 139

("savage programs") In addition to Gerard Pesman's references to the savage shows, another good description may be found in "Memories of Canyon Lodge in the 1940s," vertical file: *History - YNP - Journals & Diaries,* "Janecky, Richard," YNPA.

(had their own mess halls) References to transportation bunkhouses and mess houses are found in Horace A. Albright, *Annual Report for Yellowstone National Park, 1921-1922.* Yellowstone Park, Wyoming, pp. 40-41; Horace M. Albright, *Annual Report, 1923,* p. 46.

(fourth Superintendent's Conference) Albright and Schenck, p. 189.

page 140

(Yard covered for him) Ibid, pp. 190, 192-197.

(sanitarium in Philadelphia, symptoms ... were the same) Ibid, pp. 198-199.

(confinement a secret) Ibid, pp. 200-203.

(uplifting and distracting conversation) Ibid, p. 229.

(reconsidered on the Fountain Hotel, nicely located) Ibid, p. 227.

page 141

(put out an announcement) Ibid, p. 209.

(Selective Service Act) "D.C. Men Drawn For Army," *ES,* 20Jul1917, p. 1; "First Selective Draft makes 1,374,000 Men Liable to Call Into Service of Uncle Sam," *The Washington* [DC] *Herald,* 21Jul1917, p. 1.

(put together some figures) "... the loss of operating revenues during the war period put Mr. Child's businesses in such bad financial condition that he considered disposing of the least profitable part – his hotels." Haines, *Vol. II,* p. 274

(troop trains) Albright and Schenck, p. 303.

(unable to hire adequate staff) Ibid, p. 213.

(answered to the new NPS) "Between 1886, when the U.S. Army assumed responsibility for Yellowstone, and 1916, when the National Park Service took over, the Child, Haynes, and Hamilton executives and employees, as well as park administrators and their families, fraternized, socialized, and even intermarried to such an extent that any divisions became almost meaningless. They all certainly shared a common vision of what the park should be, a basic philosophy that the natural landscape should conform to expectations. ... Within this mix of administrators and entrepreneurs, protectors and profiters, the park superintendent reigned as official chieftain – but those who lived in Yellowstone knew, as did anyone who spent time among them, that Harry Child was the true power behind the throne." Barringer, *Selling Yellowstone,* pp. 56-57.

(traveling in the west) Albright and Schenck, pp. 224-253, 281.

(on Horace Albright's list) Albright and Schenck, pp. 287-288. "The Teton Mountains and the headwaters of the Yellowstone River, with much of the country between, should be added to the park. ..." Horace M. Albright, *Annual Report for Yellowstone National Park 1919.* Wash., DC: Government Printing Office, 1919, p. 97.

page 142

(suggestions to protect) General Philip H. Sheridan, after an 1882 visit, recommended that the boundaries of Yellowstone be expanded to include the area in the Teton valley. Hampton, p. 55; Righter, p. 22.

(Young ... who suggested) Righter, pp. 22-23.

(expedition to ... Mount Moran) "It was their unanimous verdict that Jackson Lake in its towering mountain setting, would soon draw to its shores hundred of recreationists not alone for the romantic interest that attaches to this former rendezvous of the bad men of the West, but for its grandeur, picturesqueness, and the opportunities for mountain climbing, fishing and trail riding." J.E. Haynes, *Haynes New Guide and Motorists' Complete Road Log of Yellowstone National Park*. St Paul: J.E. Haynes, Publisher, 1920, p. 89.

(typical of young men) Huntley Child was born in March 1886; Howard Hays in November 1883; and Jack E. Haynes in 1884. Roe Emery (1875-1953) was 10 years their senior. www.glaciernationalparklodges.com/red-bus-tours/history/ Howard H. Hays, Sr. https://www.findagrave.com/memorial/137083213/howard-h-hays 7Dec2019. Haynes date from Saunders, p. 6.

(Hough published) Albright credits Hough with coining the phrase *Greater Yellowstone*. Albright and Schenck, p. 228; Emerson Hough, "Greater Yellowstone," *Saturday Evening Post*, 190(22), 1Dec1917, pp. 61, 64.

(Idaho senator ... block its passage) Righter, p. 28. President Wilson preserved 600,000 acres with the creation Teton National Preserve in 1918. Albright and Schenck, p. 289. The bill creating Grand Teton National Park was signed by President Coolidge in 1929, but it included the mountain range only – excluding the east-side valley floor. Marian Albright Schenck, "One Day on Timbered Island: How the Rockefellers' Visit to Yellowstone Led to Grand Teton National Park," *Montana the Magazine of Western History*, 57(2), Summer 2007, p. 39; Righter, p. 40.

(now basically a cattle ranch) Demaray, p. 179; Smith, pp. 4, 48.

(went to Mexico each year) "Anceney told the story of a New Mexico friend who generally went to old Mexico with him to buy cattle. There would be no difference between the cattle that went to New Mexico and to the Flying D. But when the steers were marketed as threes, the Flying D cattle would weigh from 150 to 250 pounds more than those run in New Mexico despite Montana's more severe winters. Anceney's theory was that not only was the Montana grass more abundant and nutritious, but the northern latitude and higher altitude hastened the growth." Griffin, *BG*, 31Jan1967.

(with his herd from Salesville, brought the best price) Forbes, p. 183.

page 143

(mill site ... several residences ... Salesville Mercantile, Salesville Bank) Smith, p. 54.

(battling diabetes) Child, p. 74.

(Visitor counts ... 1917 and 1918 summers) Haines, *Vol. II*, p. 479; Lindsley, p. 242.

(only revenue) Haines, *Vol. II*, p. 274; Albright and Schenck, pp. 151-152.

(took a government post) "The State," *Baker* [MT] *Sentinel*, 6Nov1917, p. 6.

(lodging there at Soldier's Home) Listing for Huntley Child, *City Directory, Washington, District of Columbia, 1918*, p. 304, www.ancestry.com 20Mar2018.

(Mather desired ... friendship with Senator Walsh) Shankland, p. 124.

(tried unsuccessfully in 1916) Note attached to letter from Horace Albright, to Mr. and Mrs. John Q. Nichols, 2Jun1978, courtesy Harry W. Child II.

page 144

(back in his Washington D.C. office) Albright wrote, "I'd never seen him look better, so robust, so exhilarated, so charming. He settled right down to his job as though he had never been away." Albright and Schenck, p. 299.

(Huntley being tossed out) Albright says "late in the year" of 1918. Note attached to letter from Albright to Nichols.

(enlisting on October 14) Huntley registered in Montana on 12Sept1918. Registration Card, Draft Card C, Lewis and Clark County, Montana; *U. S., World War I Draft Registration Cards, 1917-1918*, www.ancestry.com 20Mar2018. He was called up in October. Record for Huntley Child, U.S. Department of Veterans Affairs, *BIRLS Death File, 1850-2010*, www.ancestry.com 20Mar2018.

(In his words) Child-Haines Interview.

(calling him a "whipper-snapper") Albright and Schenck, p. 178.

(plans going on between Mather ... Hill) John A. Hill made an inspection of national parks, at the behest of the new National Park Service, in the summer of 1916. John A. Hill, "Report on Inspection of Yellowstone, Rainier, Crater Lake and Yosemite Parks," DOI, 1916, YNP Central Classified file, 1907-1940, Record Group 79.3.1, National Archives & Records Administration, Washington, D.C. The next spring Horace Albright wrote to Hill saying, "Very shortly you will hear officially from the Department with regard to the inspectorship." Horace M. Albright, Assistant Attorney, to J.A. Hill, Stockyard Inn, Chicago, IL, 30Mar1917, YNPA.

(scheme to take over) S.T. Mather, Darien, CT, to John A. Hill, Stockyard Inn, Chicago, IL, 13Oct1918, YNPA; Stephen T. Mather, to John A. Hill, 22Oct1918, YNPA; Stephen Mather, to John A. Hill, 24Oct1918, YNPA.

(did seize the company) Shankland, p. 125; Albright and Schenck, p. 308.

("I've got a wild man...") Shankland, p. 163.

(Albright got to Washington) Albright and Schenck, pp. 308-309.

page 145

(Harry went to Hot Springs ... "I don't care.") Shankland, p. 165, Albright and Schenck, p. 312.

("unfitted to engage...") Note attached to letter from Albright, to Nichols, 2Jun1978.

(relations between father and son) The authors believe, as will be shown in the next chapter, that Huntley Child did have further contact with his father after this event. Although their relationship was strained, it did still exist at a minimal level. Quote from Child-Haines Interview.

(The war was soon over) Child-Haines Interview.

(served in the ambulance/transportation corps) Child, p. 79.

(returned to the Food Administration) MR-H, 25Mar1919.

(discharged) Record for Huntley Child, U.S. Department of Veterans Affairs, *BIRLS Death File, 1850-2010*, www.ancestry.com 20Mar2018.

(moved to New York City) 1920 Federal Census, District 0441; Queens Assembly District 6, Queens, New York, www.ancestry.com 20Mar2018.

(were never reunited) Although Huntley Child and Emilie Child were estranged and living apart, "they didn't divorce for years because Emilie would not give him a divorce for religious reasons. The three children moved to Memphis with Emilie's family." ... "She became deeply involved in the Christian Science religion and moved to Boston to be near the Mother church. On one of her trips to California to visit her daughter Betty, she passed away following a long illness. Emilie was a beautiful southern belle who had a difficult life once she met Huntley. She had a sledding accident in Yellowstone that permanently injured her back and she was in constant pain from then on. She never lost her love for Huntley and also carried this pain forever." Note from Harry W. Child II, to Ruth Quinn, 20May2019; Child, Appendix 13.

(Nichols ... joined the U.S. Army) "History of William Morse Nichols," typescript dated 28Aug1957, vertical file: *History - YNP - Employees*, "Nichols," YNPA.

page 146

(draft deferment) Albright and Schenck, p. 209.

(Universal Military Training) Young addressed the D.A.R. Congress, with a speech entitled: *Universal Military Training*, "Patriotism Rules at D.A.R. Congress," *ES*, 16Apr1917, p. 2.

(he shared the stand) "First Number is Drawn by President," *The Washington Times*, 30Sept1918, p. 1.

(Maria Dean had been asked) Child, pp. 13-14. Miss Jeannette Rankin accepted the challenge and won a seat in Congress in 1916. Larson, p. 41.

(new YWCA building, chairman of the finance committee, financial rescuer, completed February 1919) Baumler, "Helena YWCA," ; Baumler. *Historic Helena.* pp. 107-108.

(Mountain View School) "Saving Girls": Montana State Vocational School for Girls, 26Jun2014, at http://montanawomenshistory.org/saving-girls-montana-state-vocational-school-for girls/ 13Oct2017; Listing for "Dr. Maria Dean Residence (626 N. Benton Ave)," Baumler, *Historic Helena.* pp. 106-107.

page 147

(Dr. Maria was in Washington) Although it is easy to assume that Dr. Dean was in Washington visiting her sister, there was also much activity in the fall of 1918 in Washington as the debate raged for passage of the Nineteenth Amendment. In September 1918, President Wilson addressed the Senate urging its passage "... as vitally essential to the prosecution of the great war of humanity in which we are engaged." He argued," We have made partners of the women in this war; shall we admit them only to a partnership of suffering and sacrifice and toil, not to a partnership of privilege and right? ... The tasks of the women lie at the very heart of the war, and I know how much stronger that heart will beat if you do this just thing and show our women that you trust them as much as you, in fact and of necessity, depend upon them. ..." "President Addresses Congress in Appeal for Woman Suffrage," *The Washington Times,* 30Sept1918, pp. 1, 3.

(President Wilson) Vucanovich, p. 5; Child, p. 14.

(died of cancer) Child, p. 14; "Dr. Dean, Well Known Woman Physician of Capital City Dies," *GFDT,* 24May1919, p. 13. Author Mari Graña points out that Dr. Dean died during the month that the Congress passed the Nineteenth Amendment. "...Maria would miss the reward of final ratification she had worked so hard and so long to achieve ..." Montana was the thirteenth state to ratify the amendment on 2Aug1919. Graña, pp. 300-301; https://en.wikipedia.org/wiki/Nineteenth_Amendment_to_the_United_States_Constitution 25Aug2017.

(Dean Memorial Clock, a friend of the weak) "In Memoriam, Dr. Maria M. Dean," *The Woman Citizen,* 4(2), 14Jun1919, p. 1; http://www.helenahistory.org/Hawthorne_School.htm 20Feb2015. Dr. Maria Dean's tombstone in the Forestvale Cemetery in Helena bears the inscription, "The Beloved Physician." Child, p. 14.

(extensions on his loan) Albright and Schenck, pp. 226-227; "Memorandum ...," by J.H.P., 12Sept1918, NPRR-MHC.

(camps ... did not fare well) Lindsley, p. 233.

(free campgrounds) "During the summer of 1889 and 1890 Boutelle's troops were mainly engaged in fighting and extinguishing fires started by careless campers. In an attempt to prevent this, he established regular campgrounds and limited campers to those places designated. The system of specifically designated campgrounds, subsequently established in all national parks, was thus inaugurated." Hampton, p. 100; Hyde, pp. 297-298; Haines, *Vol. II,* p. 352.

page 148

(soldiers needed overseas) Albright and Schenck, p. 259.

(lack of funds) It was June 1918 before Congressional budgets were approved to fund the National Park Service. Albright and Schenck, pp. 260-261.

(Army left) Albright and Schenck, pp. 260-261; Haines, *Vol. II,* p. 290.

(hotel never opened again) Lindsley, p. 233, Whittlesey, "Music, Song,..." p. 35.

Chapter 13: What's Horace Up To Now?   *(chapter header)* MC 292, MHSRC

page 149

(partners to lead the company) Demaray, p. 184.

(a rough transition) Shankland, p. 125.

(supporting Hays ... Hotel Company) Howard Hays met with Harry Child in California in January 1919 requesting to purchase both the hotel and transportation companies. Harry agreed to sell, but he did not believe in Hays' ability to obtain financing. Barringer, *Anna's,* pp. 9-10.

(recruited a couple of friends ... Glacier and Rocky) Barringer, *Selling Yellowstone,* p. 71.

page 150

(All but one ... stayed loyal) Hays received a negative response from Jule Hannaford, then President of the Northern Pacific Railroad. But Hannaford's connections with Harry went back to 1889 when Harry was developing the Great Falls smelter and he was a NPR traffic manager – only beginning to work his way up through the ranks. Barringer, *Annals,* p. 10; "Spray of the Falls," *GFT,* 20Mar1889, p. 3.

(White ... did put up some money) Barringer found that "White concealed his stake in the company by having his stock issued in Hays' name and keeping it, along with a deed of trust for his wife, in a Cleveland safe deposit box. In this way, whenever Child came East to purchase more busses for this transportation business, White could deny holding stock in the camping company ..." A third financial partner was Roe Emery, but "Emery was least involved, as his interest in the camps was purely financial and the transportation franchise in Rocky Mountain National Park occupying most of his attention." Barringer, *Annals,* pp. 10-11.

(April 1919) Lindsley, p. 252; Shankland, p. 125.

(Harry's brother sent him a clipping) E.O. Child, San Francisco, to Harry Child, 25Jun1919, YNPA. The fact that Mather made this announcement again confirms his desire to oust Harry from Yellowstone hotel operations.

page 151

(fired off a letter) Harry W. Child, to Stephen Mather, 1Jul1919, YNPA.

(keep his job as Director) Robert M. Utley, forward to Albright and Schenck, p. xiii.

page 152

(Albright would come to Yellowstone, house and an official car) Albright and Schenck, pp. 333-334, 336. Horace Albright served as superintendent from 28Jun1919 to 12Jan1929. Haines, *Vol. II,* pp. 458-459.

(overseeing all the field operations) Albright and Schenck, p. 281.

(personal gift) Ibid, p. 334.

(NPS creed) Horace Albright was assigned the task of penning the NPS creed, with input from his wife and Robert Sterling Yard. It was published in Franklin Lane's *Annual Report of the National Park Service* in 1918 as *Statement of National Park Policy, 13May1918, from Franklin K. Lane to Mr. Stephen Mather.* Albright and Schenck, pp. 274-275.

(public auto camps) Haines, *Vol. II,* p. 359.

(museums where educational programs) Whittlesey, *A Yellowstone Album,* p. 163. Zillah Pocock White served as a nature guide for the Yellowstone Park Camps Company at Old Faithful Geyser in 1921. In her study of women's roles in national parks, Polly Welts Kaufman applauds Horace Albright's policy of employing women as nature guides and lecturers. She points to a subsequent policy which excluded them until the 1960s. Kaufman, p. 253, n14. Beulah Brown began a similar role in 1915. Elizabeth A. Watry, *Women in Wonderland: Lives, Legends, and Legacies of Yellowstone National Park.* Helena, MT: Riverbend Publishing, 2012, p. 114. In 1920, Albright hired Isabell Bassett (Wasson) as the second naturalist. Whittlesey and Watry, p. 104. "It was at Yellowstone, under Superintendent Horace Albright, that the Park Service hired the most women naturalists. There the visibility of women attracted the attention of Washington officials, with servicewide repercussions that eventually discouraged all but the most secure superintendents from hiring women–even as seasonal ranger-naturalists–until the 1960s. Beginning with Isabel Wasson in 1920, Yellowstone hired ten women as rangers or ranger-naturalists. After Herma Albertson Baggley resigned in 1933, the park hired only men as ranger-naturalists. The chief exception was a brief period during World War II when Yellowstone paid rangers' wives to perform essential services." Kaufman, p. 77. For the NPS policy which

excluded women see Kaufman, pp. 79-80.

(spoke with admiration) Albright and Schenck, pp. 226-227.

page 153

(a little full of himself) Albright wrote of Harry, "I had hoped that I would be able to get along with Child, but no superintendent can get along with him unless he wants his individuality completely subordinated, his judgements formed for him, his initiative completely eliminated, and his operations in the park guided by Child, as a teacher would guide the faltering hand of a child learning to write." postscript enclosed with letter from Horace M. Albright, to Stephen T. Mather, 21Oct1920, YNPA.

(trying to dig up now, let you run the outfit) Notes found attached to letters referenced here, YNPA.

(poison pen letter, let him do as he pleases, keep it in your confidential) Horace M. Albright, to Stephen T. Mather, 21Oct1920, YNPA.

(his son is now serving his country, acres to growing wheat, use automobile trucks) "Turn Great Cattle Ranch To Wheat Farm To Help Feed U.S. Army and Allies: Child & Anceney Will This Year Sow to Cereal 12,000 Acres Heretofore Used to Raise Hay for Fattening Stock," *MR-H*, 25Mar1919.

page 154

(use their success, France can raise) Huntley Child, to Harry Child, 3Mar1919, quoted in "Turn Great Cattle ...,"

(Harry visited his son, turned up in my office, sore as a boil) Horace Albright, to Howard Hays, 11Dec1919, as sent to John Q. Nichols with letter dated 2Jun1978, and forwarded to from Jock Nichols, to Harry W. Child II, 25Mar 2018, courtesy Harry W. Child II.

page 155

(told him I was sorry) Child-Haines Interview.

(Galusha Financial Firm) Barringer, *Selling Yellowstone*, p. 86.

(a loop of Yellowstone approach roads, Yellowstone Car Party) "Yellow Car Party Making Some Time," *GFDT*, 1May1919, p. 5.

(mission ... was two-fold) "Yellow Car Party Boosting National Parks, Two Big Cars Filled With Prominent Persons Reach Klamath Falls on Swing Around the Circle of America's Scenic Spots," *The Evening Herald* [Klamath Falls, OR] (hereafter *EH-KF*), 10Oct1919, p. 4; "Good Roads Advocates of State to Meet in Helena May 23," *GFDT*, 17May1919, p. 5; "Plan Big Meeting of Western States in Good Road Work, Will Call Highway Advocates from Various State to Meet in Yellowstone," *GFDT*, 24May1919, p. 5.

page 156

(road records ... were smashed) "Yellow Car Party ..."

(invited representatives, support and help of Secretary) "Plan Big Meeting of Western States..."

(Geysers to Glaciers Trail) Spencer, p. 107.

(operated passenger cars on scheduled time) "Auto Touring Party Boosting..."

(purchasing Broadwater Hotel) Harry W. Child, to Stephen T. Mather, 29Apr1920, YNPA.

(meeting was held in Glacier) "Montana and Canada Will Combine Parks," *GFDT*, 4Aug1919, p. 2.

page 157

(motor tour from Montana to California) "Child and Hill Plan Park-to-Park Crusade," *GFDT*, 28Aug1919, p. 2; "Plans Made for Tour," *EH-KF*, 17Sept1919, p. 7.

(arrived in Hood River) "National Park Party Visits Here," *The Hood River Glacier* [Hood River, OR] (hereafter *HRG*), 9Oct1919, p. 2.

(newspaper reporters were busy) "West Will Prepare for Coming Tourists," *Grant's Pass* [OR] *Daily Courier* (hereafter *GPDC*), 23Oct1919, p. 1; "Kingman Will Be On Park To Park Road," *Mohave County Miner and Our Mineral Wealth* [Kingman, AZ] (hereafter *MCM*), 25Oct1919, p. 1; "30 Are Coming From Billings To State Road Meeting," *GFDT*, 5Nov1919, p. 9.

(a featured speaker) "Auto Touring Party Boosting National Parks," *EH-KF*, 10Oct1919, p. 4; "Hood River to be on Park Highway," *HRG*, 16Oct1919, p. 8; "Park-To-Park Loops Boosted by Road Meet," *GFDT*, 17Nov1919, p. 2.

(stop in Grand Canyon) "Kingman Will Be On Park To Park Road," *MCM*, 25Oct1919, p. 1. Grand Canyon area was federally protected as a Forest Reserve in 1893. It became Grand Canyon National Monument in 1908, but did not achieve full National Park status until 1919. Albright and Schenck, p. 119, Runte, *National Parks*, p. 112. In September 1920, the American Automobile Association and the National Park Service sponsored a 76-day, 5,000 mile dedication tour for the Park-to-Park Highway. Stephen Mather and his heightened publicity of this trip largely overshadowed Harry's efforts in the historical record. The Park-to-Park group entered the east gate of Yellowstone on 3Sept1920. Supt. Horace Albright posed with them at the Roosevelt Arch on September 7, after they left the Mammoth Hotel. Brandon Wade, dir., *Paving the Way: The National Park to Park Highway.* Depth of Field Productions, 2009. Forbes writes "Not so long ago Mr. Child drove his own car on a 6,000 mile tour from National Park to National Park stirring up interest in a movement to construct good roads to link up the nation's pleasure grounds so that automobile tourists can 'See America First' in comfort." Forbes, p. 333. Harry Child's name is never mentioned in relation to this 1920 trip, so the authors are uncertain if he hosted the group in Yellowstone. We believe Forbes' is a reference to Harry's trip in the fall of 1919 – a full year before Mather's trip.

(When your road is marked) "Plans Made to Mark Highway to Tap all Important Trails," *GFDT*, 14Mar1920, p. 12.

(Forty thousand tourist) "West Will Prepare for Coming Tourists," *GPDC*, 23Oct1919, p. 1.

Chapter 14: Harry Spreads His Wings   *(chapter header)* MSC019, series 7, box 139, file 139.12, YNPA.

page 159

(year 1920 would) "Auto Touring Party Boosting National Parks, Two Big Cars Filled With Prominent Persons Reach Klamath Falls on Swing Around the Circle of America's Scenic Spots," *EH-KF*, 10Oct1919, p. 4.

(controlled 120,000 acres) Smith, p. 46.

(cattle empire) Meloy, "Harry Child Amassed ..."

(ranch-style house) Architect's drawing, unsigned, "Flying D Ranch, Harry W. Child's Ranch, Spanish Creek, Mont.," circa 1921, *Haynes Foundation Collection*, box 27, folder: "Flying D. Ranch - Montana," (H-21248), MHSRCPA. The house still stands and is visible from highway US 191, just south of the crossing of Spanish Creek.

(elegant residence, delightfully rustic) Smith, p. 57.

page 160

(golf course, polo ponies) Michener and Vick, p. 46.

(favorite residences) Smith, p. 46; "When Harry Child retired and moved to La Jolla, California, he came to Spanish Creek less often; he was not in good health the last years of his life. When his son-in-law Billie Nichols moved his family to the La Jolla residence, they continued to spend at least part of their summers at Spanish Creek Ranch, entertaining friends for weeks on end." Ibid, p. 57. Huntley Child Jr. reminisced about summers when the six cousins (three children of Ellen and Billie Nichols and three children of Emilie and Huntley Child) spent weeks at the ranch,"playing and riding horses." The children and Bessie Ferguson where driven in a big yellow bus by chauffeur to the ranch from Yellowstone. Harry and Adelaide would occasionally visit from Mammoth. Huntley Child, Jr. Interview.

(required a ready supply of gas) "The first automobilists were enjoined to carry tires, oil, and gasoline with them ..." Haines, *Vol. II*, p. 357.

(stores at Canyon and Mammoth) George Whittaker sold his stores at Canyon and Mammoth to Anna Pryor and Elizabeth Trishman in 1932. Charles Hamilton acquired both locations in 1953. Lindsley, p. 300; Petersen, p. 103; Watry, pp. 56, 59. See also Robert V. Goss, *Yellowstone's George Whittaker: Soldier, Scout and Storekeeper.* Gardiner, MT: self-published, 2002.

(three joined forces) Albright, *Report, 1920*, p. 36; Lindsley, pp. 256, 261-262; Barringer, *Selling Yellowstone*, p. 78.

(attractive gas stations) Chas. P. Purchard, Jr., Landscape Engineer, to Horace M. Albright, Supt., 21Jul1920, folder 1: *1919-1920 – Correspondence and Memoranda*, box D-38: *Landscape Architects & Engineers*, YNPA. Three buildings of historic note are the Mammoth station that was designed by Bozeman architect Fred Willson, the Old Faithful upper station, and Fishing Bridge station designed by National Park Service Landscape Architect Kenneth C. McCarter. Ann Butterfield to Ruth Quinn, 28Jul2000; "Proposed Plans for Old Faithful Tourist Camp Service Station," NP-YEL-5555, unsigned, submitted by C.A. Hamilton, 1Sept1929, copied from the files of the Technical Information Center, National Park Service, Denver, CO, copies courtesy Yellowstone Business Management Office to Ruth Quinn; "Report of Kenneth C. McCarter, Junior Landscape Architect, Week of August 5-11, 1929," folder 8: *Landscape Division Matters, F. Y. 1930*, box D-38: *Landscape Architects & Engineers*, YNPA; Roger W. Toll, Supt., to C.A. Hamilton, 4Sept1930, file: *Building Construction, C. A. Hamilton, F. Y. 7/1/34 to 6/30/35*, box C-28: *Correspondence regarding building projects by Hamilton Stores, 1928-1953 plans of Hamilton's buildings, 1941-1947*, YNPA.

(Yellowstone-specific changes, twenty-four new vehicles) Austin, et al, pp. 9, 10.

(each of the next two years, sixty in 1924) Ibid, p. 10.

(forty-nine 7-passenger) Ibid, p. 11.

(hiring cars from outside) Albright, *Report, 1920*, p. 32; Albright, *Report, 1923*, pp. 2-3.

page 161

(three cars were driven cross-country) Austin, et al, p. 9. Other cars were driven from Denver. "Local News," *PCN*, 16Jun1922, p. 6; "New Motor Cars on Way to Yellowstone," *LE*, 10Jun1922, p. 6.

(Harding Presidential party) "Whites in the Wake of the News," *The Albatross*, IX(62), [1923?], no page #. The Hardings spent one night in the park at Old Faithful Inn on 30Jul1923. Bartlett, *Wilderness*, p. 97.

(host 600 teachers) Austin, et al, p. 10; "Harry W. Child and White Motor Company touring buses," Scrapbook Collection (Child), YNPA.

(began construction, disastrous blow) Johnson, p. 8.

(Seventy-five vehicles were saved, ninety cars in fifty-nine days) Austin, et al, p. 11; Whittlesey, *Yellowstone Album*, p. 173.

(White Motor Company responded) Austin, et al, p. 11.

(new Gardiner complex, YPTC logo) The concrete structures remain standing along the park's northern border at Gardiner, MT. Those two, and a third sitting behind and between them built as a driver's dormitory (now known as the Gardiner Bunkhouse), were designed by Helena, MT architects J.G. Link and C.S. Haire. Johnson, pp. 1, 4; Horace M. Albright, *Monthly Report for June, 1924*, 8Jul1924, p. 22; Wheaton, p. 18. The westernmost building houses the Xanterra Travel Collection's vehicle service center and the human resources offices. New hotel concessions employees are welcomed here by the hundreds every spring and summer. One new recruit later wrote, "By its appearance, the grey stone building looked more like a forgotten warehouse than administrative offices for Yellowstone Park Company. ... I had driven 1100 miles to get here [1973] and this building was almost a disappointment." Joyce B. Lohse, *A Yellowstone Savage: Life in Nature's Wonderland*. Colorado Springs, CO: J.D. Charles Publishing, 1988. The easternmost building houses the company's recycling hub, parkwide laundry, and support services operations.

(two new homes, for the district ranger) Quinn, Weaver, pp. 161-164. These houses, along with the concrete structures, today line the northern boundary of the Park, and are visible across the open meadow slightly east of the Roosevelt Arch. In 2012 the NPS appropriately named this interior park roadway *Robert Reamer Avenue*. "Gardiner YPT Address," map produced by the Spacial Analysis Center, National Park Service in Yellowstone National Park, 1May2012. Ruth A. Quinn, "New Street Names Honor Park Architects," *Commentary Newsletter*, 28(3), Jun2013, pp. 7-9, inhouse publication of the Department of Transportation & Interpretation, Xanterra Parks & Resorts, Inc., Yellowstone National Park, WY.

(chalk board, same signal the park over) Pesman interview.

page 162

(carefully prepared schedules) Albright, *Report, 1920*, p. 32.

(1923, Gary Cooper) Whittlesey and Watry, pp. 99-100; Amanda Ricker, "A Star Among Us. Bozeman's Hollywood Star: Gary Cooper," *Bozeman Daily Chronicle*, 27Mar2011, pp. E1, E7. The Ellen Theater on Main Street in Bozeman placed a star for Gary Cooper in their sidewalk. Cooper graduated from Gallatin Valley High School in 1922. A home the family occupied while he was attending high school in Bozeman lies between downtown and the university campus. Thanks to Nic Sinnott for sharing information about this historic site.

(Bachelor of Philosophy) Personal knowledge, Nan Sigrist. Her late husband Bruce Sigrist's mother was a college roommate of Beulah Brown at Wooster College, Ohio. She recruited his sister Margaret into employment with National Park Concessions in Big Bend National Park. Bruce later worked with his sister for that organization in Olympic National Park. Other family members worked at Mammoth Cave and Blue Ridge Mountains. See also Watry, *Women*, pp. 113, 137.

(minister father) Watry, *Women*, p. 112.

page 163

(well-modulated voice) Nan Sigrist, personal communication.

(starting in 1915, total of eleven seasons) Watry, *Women*, pp. 111, 131.

(guide for ... Camps Company) Ibid, p. 114. While Beulah Brown Sandborn spent her career in hospitality management, Polly Welts Kaufman found other women who started as concessions tour guides in Yellowstone and found subsequent careers as National Park Service Interpreters. Kaufman, pp. 69, 253, n14.

(recruited fellow "savages") Whittlesey, *A Yellowstone Album*, pp. 121, 166; Watry, *Women*, p. 115. "The 'savages have always produced good programs nightly for the guest and savage entertainment. ... Please bring your music, musical instruments, costumes, and ideas for new entertainment." Letter from YPC to prospective employees, Ralph Bush, "Scrapbook from summers of 1953-1956," vertical file: *Employees – Bush*, YNPA.

(wrote and directed a series of skits) Watry, *Women*, pp. 116-117, 284 n19; "Memories of Canyon Lodge in the 1940s," vertical file: *History - YNP - Journals & Diaries*, "Janecky, Richard," YNPA.

(singing of campfire songs) This had been a major component of an evening's entertainment in the Wylie Camps. Whittlesey, *A Yellowstone Album*, p. 121.

(sung to familiar tunes) For example, "Camping with the Y.P.C," sung to the tune "Jingle Bells;" and "Eat Song," sung to "Turkey in the Straw." Beulah Brown, *Songs of the Yellowstone Park Camps*, c1924, pp. 2, 35. Quinn collection.

("Rotten-logging ...") Petersen, p. 100.

(singing out the dudes) Mary Dawe Lowry and Denise Mackesy, "Working in Yellowstone: Then and Now," from *Montana Outdoors*, July/August 1985, 16(4), pp. 27-30, clipping in vertical file: *History – YNP – Journals & Diaries*, "Lowry, Mary Dawe and Denise Mackesy," YNPA.

(booklet titled Songs) Watry, *Women*, pp. 129-130, 285 n7.

(doing the winter keeper chores) Mr. and Mrs. Morris Musser, who employed Miss Brown, spent winters in the park as early as 1910-1911. "Local Layout," *LE*, 28Dec1910, p. 2.

(tutor the three children) The Musser's three boys were seven, nine, and eleven years old during the winter of 1922-1923. Watry, *Women*, p. 119.

(greenhouse, comfort of steam heat, My Winter in Geyserland) Beulah Brown, *My Winter in Geyserland*. self-published, 1924, pp. 6-8. copy in the Rare Book room, YNPA.

page 164

(sold it next summer, travel through Europe) Personal knowledge, Nan Sigrist. Betsy Watry found documentation of this trip from December 1924 to March 1925. Beulah visited Hawaii, Japan, China, the Philippines, Sumatra, Ceylon, Egypt, Italy, France, and England. Watry, *Women*, p. 128.

(Canyon, Mammoth, and Old Faithful) Watry, *Women*, pp. 127, 129, 131.

(began managing the new Furnace Creek Inn) Hummel, p. 88; Christine Barnes, *Great Lodges of the National Parks, Volume Two*. Portland, OR: Graphic Arts™ Books, 2008, p. 58.

(followed her in the winters) G. Nelson, "The History of Furnace Creek," typescript of undocumented source, vertical file: *Biography*, "Brown, Beulah," YNPA; Watry, *Women*, p. 131.

(officer in the National Park Concessions, Inc., in smaller areas) Hummel, pp. 117-118, 121; Watry, *Women*, p. 137.

(until they retired) Miss Brown did not return to Yellowstone after 1929. She married Henry S. Sanborn in 1928. They managed Lake Arrowhead's Village Inn for five years, the Arlington Lodge at Lake Arrowhead, and Mammoth Cave Hotel. They retired in 1958. Beulah died in Sedona, Arizona in 1976 at the age of 87 ... "A thoroughly modern woman for her time, Beulah fashioned her own success as a vibrant guide, an amusing entertainer, a congenial hostess, and an accomplished hotel manager in a hospitality career that spanned three states and more than forty years of her active life, a career that she had unassumingly begun in Yellowstone." Watry, *Women*, pp. 133-138.

(Lander-Yellowstone Transportation) Lindsley, p. 263; Barringer, *Selling Yellowstone*, pp. 66-67.

(elegant Gallatin Gateway Inn) Austin, et al, pp. 8, 9; Lindsley, p. 286. It was added to the National Register of Historic Places in 1980. Information from "A Brief History" distributed by the Gallatin Gateway Inn, circa 2010. Descriptive pages and photographic views may be found in Thornton Waite, *Yellowstone By Train: A History of Rail Travel to America's First National Park*. Missoula, MT: Pictorial Histories Publishing Co., Inc., pp. 120-123. At the time of this writing, the Inn is used as employee housing for staff commuting to jobs at the Yellowstone Club in the Big Sky, MT environs.

(YPTC pick-up point) "New Entrance to Park is Success," *The Hotel News of the West*, 22(38), 18Sept1926, p. 10.

(changed its name) Smith, p. 18.

(Burlington Inn in 1924) Thornton Waite writes that the Burlington Cody Inn existed in some form since 1903, but that building was expanded in 1924. Waite, pp. 90-92.

(five railheads) *Circular of General Information Regarding Yellowstone National Park Wyoming*. Washington, DC: Government Printing Office, 1929, p. 12.

page 165

(landscape architecture division) Harvey Kaiser, *Landmarks in the Landscape: Historic Architecture in the National Parks of the West*. San Francisco: Chronicle Books, 1997, pp. 22-23; Horace Albright, "The National Park Policy," *The Western Architect*, 39(6), June 1930, pp. 93-96.

(Reamer added one hundred rooms) Quinn, *Weaver*, pp. 149-152.

(expanding the dining ... Presidential Suite) Trappen, pp. 56, 60.

(granddaughters recalled) This story was told by Marion Sanger and Betty Pomeroy (daughters of Huntley Child) during a visit to Yellowstone to Steve Blakeley, bell porter of Lake Hotel in the early 1990s. Steve has shared it with concession tour guides for two decades.

(Coolidge ... did occupy the suite) "Memorandum for drivers relative to stops on Presidential Party Trip," Aug1927, p. 5, in vertical file: "Coolidge Visit to YNP," YNPA.

(informed him ... a decision) Horace Albright, forward to Dittl and Mallman, p. 5; Whittlesey, *Yellowstone Album*, p. 132. President Coolidge engaged in an activity still available to visitors to Yellowstone in modern times. A rainbow trout he himself caught became part of his own dinner the next day. "Coolidges Visit Grand Canyon, Marvel at Scenery as They Stand at an Altitude of 7740 Feet, Start Tonight for Black Hills," newspaper clipping dated 28Aug1927, from Park Scrapbook S41, "Presidential Parties," accession no. 08-327, p. 8, YNPA.

(melody of an old-time waltz) "Mrs. Coolidge, Led to Dance by Waltz, Finally Two-Steps," newspaper clipping dated 27Aug1927, Ibid, p. 8A, YNPA.

(a joint loan) joint mortgage – dated 26Jul1928, Yellowstone Park Hotel Company, Yellowstone Park Transportation Company, Yellowstone Park Camps Company, with Northwestern Improvement Company [Northern Pacific], Union Pacific Railroad Company, Chicago, Burlington & Quincy Railroad Company, and Chicago, Milwaukee, St. Paul and Pacific Railroad Company. President's Subject file 209B, folder 4, NPRR-MHC.

page 166

(they demanded he continue) Horace Albright, to Stephen Mather, 1Jun1927; Thomas C. Vint, Associate Landscape Engineer, to Stephen Mather, 8Jun1927; H.W. Child, to R.C. Reamer, 24Jun1927; box C-14, YNPA.

(I was not shot) Robert C. Reamer, to Harry W. Child, 25Jun1927, box C14, YNPA.

(won the argument) Quinn, *Weaver*, pp. 151-155.

(received ninety-six new rooms) Lindsley, p. 295; Roger W. Toll, *Superintendent's Monthly Report, May 1930*, Wash., DC: Government Printing Office,5Jun1930, p. 6.

(new dorm at Old Faithful Inn) Windows, doors, and staircases of Laurel Dormitory at Old Faithful were constructed with re-claimed materials from the Fountain Hotel. Lee Whittlesey interview with John Egger, 17Jan1981, cited in Reinhart and Henry, pp. 82, p. 141 chap. 13 n21. An former employee of the Yellowstone Park Service Stations who worked at the lower YPSS station at Old Faithful in the 1950s recalled a newspaper article taped to the wall claiming *that* building had been constructed from wood from the Fountain Hotel. Homer Rudolf to Ruth Quinn, Jul2002; Albright, *Report, 1921-22*, p. 39.

(Mather visited Yellowstone in 1925) Harry Child, to Howard Hays, 5Sept1925, file: *1925-26 correspondence*, box 3, *Howard H. Hays Collection*, American Heritage Center, Laramie, WY cited in Barringer, *Selling Yellowstone*, endnote 15, pp. 193-194; Shankland, p. 209.

(Fountain Hotel was razed) Lindsley, p. 287.

(built "recreation halls") Albright, *Report, 1920*, pp, 30, 31; Albright, *Report, 1921-1922*, pp. 39-40; Albright, *Report, 1923*, pp. 2-3; Lindsley, p. 285.

(Sylvan Pass Lodge) A Wylie camp was established just inside the east entrance in 1913. Lindsley, p. 210. Sylvan Pass Lodge, which was probably on the same site, was demolished in 1940. Kensel, p. 85; telegram from Horace Albright, to Director, NPS, 11Aug1923, folder 4: *D.R. Hull, General Correspondence, F.Y. 1924*, box D-38: *Landscape Architects & Engineers*, YNPA; Whittlesey, *A Yellowstone Album*, p. 84. This is distinguished from a lodge at Sylvan Lake, nine miles west of the east gate, originally built by Aron "Tex" Holm in 1911. It was later absorbed into the camps' operation and removed in 1928. Kensel, pp. 37-39; M.F. Daum, Acting Superintendent, *Superintendent's Monthly Reports, November 1928*. Wash., DC: Government Printing Office, 5Dec1928, p. 4.

(called the Thumb Lodge) The Hotel Company abandoned the lunch station at Thumb in 1917. Lindsley, p. 233. Charles Hamilton occupied the building, operating a store there in 1920. Albright, *Report, 1920*, p. 37. He completed his own building at Thumb in 1924. Lindsley, p. 277. By 1990, all that remained of the concession buildings in and around what is now the West Thumb Geyser Basin parking lot, was the former Haynes photo shop – then used as a convenience store and coffee shop. It was gone the following spring. Leslie Quinn, personal communication. The ranger station remains. Merilyn Peterson Grosshans, *West Thumb Remembered, 1958, 1959, 1960*. Las Vegas: self-produced DVD, 2014.

(they were followed) For instance a map of the West Thumb developed area includes Ranger Station, Cafeteria, Gas, Hamilton Store, Haynes Picture Shop, Cabins, Campground and amphitheater. Jack Ellis Haynes, *Haynes New Guide: the Complete Handbook of Yellowstone National Park*. St. Paul: Haynes, Inc. 1936, p. 76.

(delicatessen tents) Howard H. Hays, to H.W. Child, 8Feb1921, box YPC-85, YNPA; Albright, *Report, 1923*, pp. 45-46; Paul Schullery, *Nature and Culture at Fishing Bridge: A History of the Fishing Bridge Development In Yellowstone National Park*. Yellowstone National Park, WY: National Park Service, Yellowstone Center for Resources, YCR-2010-02, 2010, p. 30.

(very popular) Albright, *Report, 1923*, pp. 2-3.

page 167

(free NPS auto camps) Lindsley, p. 265; Haines, *Vol. II*, p. 359.

(housekeeping cabins) "Report of Kenneth C. McCarter, Junior Landscape Architect, Week of July 7-14, 1929," folder 8: *Landscape Division Matters, F.*

236

Y. 1930, box D-38: *Landscape Architects & Engineers*, YNPA; Lindsley, p. 295. A 1929 inventory shows "housekeeping cabins" as distinct from lodges at Mammoth, Old Faithful, West Thumb, Canyon, and Roosevelt. When author Ruth Quinn worked at Lake Hotel front desk in 1990 and 1991, "rustic shelters" were still rented at Roosevelt. With furniture and wood burning stoves, guests were expected to provide their own linen. The remaining housekeeping cabins at Old Faithful had been relegated to employee residence use, and they were removed during the 1997-1999 construction of the current Old Faithful Snow Lodge.

(a new partner, Vernon Goodwin) Barringer, *Selling Yellowstone*, p. 74.

(prestige and expertise) "Yellowstone Parks Company Purchased," *The Hotel News of the West*, 20(22), 7Jun1924, p. 3.

(made Manager ... Nichols was President) Demaray, p. 189.

(more pies than fingers) Petersen, p. 42.

(From this point forward, he controlled) "So, as of 1925, Harry Child finally secured what he had coveted for years, a practical monopoly of all Yellowstone Concessions ..." Barringer, *Selling Yellowstone*, pp. 74-75.

(a cow camp is) Smith, pp. 48-49.

(Cow Camp consisted) Ibid, p. 49.

(when she wasn't milking, pies and cakes, for twenty-one years) Ibid, p. 59.

page 168

(haying time ... thirty-five) Ibid, p. 48.

(referred to as "the company") Michener and Vick, p. 46.

(Flying D Ranges, Inc.) Smith, pp. 59-60.

(agriculture empire) Forbes, p. 182.

(real ranchman) Ibid, p. 167.

(is as modest) Ibid, p. 184.

(registered their brand) Smith, pp. 49, 61.

(retired to Helena, 705 Harrison) "Last rites for Mrs. Young will be conducted Thursday," *HDI*, 19Oct1938, p. 5. The address for this home is now 529 Floweree St. It is known as the *Tatum-Young Residence*, and is a contributing home of Helena Historic District, NRHP; "Tatum-Young House," House 14, Baucus and Shanahan; Listing for Annie D. Young, *Helena Montana City Directory, 1927*, R.L. Polk & Co., p. 317, www.ancestry.com 21Jan2015..

(again became active) "Last rites..."

page 169

(General Young died) Haines, *Vol. II*, p. 455. He was honored with a state funeral and is buried in Arlington National Cemetery. Young, wikipedia page, op. cit.

(winters in La Jolla) Listing for Annie D. Young, *San Diego California City Directory, 1921*, p. 1016, www.ancestry.com 21Jan2015; "Last rites ..."

(purchased a home on Stuart Street) Listing for Harry W. Child, *R.L. Polk & Co's Helena City Directory 1910*. Helena, MT: R.L. Polk & Co., Publ.; Listing for Adelaide D. Child, *R.L. Polk & Co.'s Helena City Directory 1931*. Helena, MT: R.L. Polk & Co., Publ.

(held on to Oro Fino Terrace) Oro Fino Terrace, http://helenahistory.org/oro_fino_terrace.htm 20Mar2015.

(active in the Unitarian, died in February, most beloved) "Mrs. Ellen Dean Dies," *HDI*, Sunday, 24Feb1924, p. 5. The Grandstreet Theatre, Helena, MT, began as the First Unitarian Church. The society donated the building to the city in 1933, at which time it became the town's library and the Tiffany widow was removed. In the 1970s the window was re-discovered, restored, and returned to the building.

(five night visit to Yellowstone) Horace M. Albright, *Monthly Report of the Superintendent for August 1927*, 7Sept1927, p. 1.

(whisked off ... Roosevelt area, gear was transferred) "Coolidges Begin Vacation in Park," newspaper clipping dated 22Aug1927, from Park Scrapbook S41: *Presidential Parties*, accession no. 08-327, p. 4A, YNPA.

page 170

(Secret Service staff, planned execution date) Paul Mallon, "Coolidge Sees Park Wonders. Through Fantastic Geyser Region, President Follows Tin Can Trail," newspaper clipping from Park Scrapbook S41, p. 6, YNPA; Horace M. Albright and Robert Cahn, *The Birth of the National Park Service: The Founding Years, 1913-33*. Howe Brothers: Salt Lake City, 1985, pp. 210-211; Donald C. Swain, *Wilderness Defender: Horace M. Albright and Conservation*. Chicago and London: University of Chicago Press, 1970, p. 174. "In 1977, on the fiftieth anniversary of the executions, Governor Michael Dukakis of Massachusetts after a review of the case vindicated the pair in a proclamation that recognized the faults of the trial and declared that 'any stigma and disgrace should be forever removed from their names.'" "Sacco-Vanzetti Case," in Ted Yanak and Pam Cornelison, *American History Fact-Finder*. Boston & New York: Houghton Mifflin Company, 1993, p. 342.

(spent a quiet, happy evening) Thank you note from Grace Coolidge, to Adelaide Child, found tucked in the pages of Adelaide's guest book, courtesy Harry W. Child II.

(1928, he suffered a stoke, named Horace Albright) Shankland, p. 284.

(continued to see improvement) Shankland, p. 286.

(died unexpectedly) Shankland, p. 287. Each national park displays a bronze plaque dedicated to the memory of Stephen Mather. Yellowstone's is located at the confluence of the Gibbon and Firehole Rivers, just down the hill from the Madison Information Station. Lindsley, p. 298. The inscription concludes, "There will never come an end to the good he has done." Shankland, pp. 289-291. Named in his memory are *Mount Mather* in Denali National Park, *Mather Point* overlook at the Grand Canyon, *Mather Gorge* on the Potomac River, and *Mather Forest* near Lake George, New York. Dayton Duncan and Ken Burns, *The National Parks: America's Best Idea*. New York: Alfred A. Knopf, 2009, p. 241.

(first superintendent under the NPS) After leaving YNP, he became the second director of the National Park Service until 1933, "When he at last withdrew from active direction of the federal park system ... it was well organized and secure under the management of a service with an outstanding sense of mission." Haines, *Vol. II*, p. 459. He returned to the private sector, finishing his career as president, general manager, and director of the U.S. Potash Company. Righter, p. 80. Horace Albright died in 1987 at the age of ninety-seven. Named in his honor are *Albright Grove* in Great Smoky Mountains National Park, the *Albright Training Center* at Grand Canyon National Park, the *Albright Visitor Education Center* and *Albright Avenue* in Yellowstone, and *Albright Peak* and the *Albright View Overlook* in Grand Teton National Park.

Chapter 15: Riding into the Sunset   *(chapter header)* MC292, MHSRC

page 171

(Child entered the Park) Roger W. Toll, *Superintendent's Monthly Report, August 1930*, 5Sept1930, p. 16.

(died at his home) "Harry W. Child Dies in La Jolla," *SDU*, 5Feb1931, p. 10; *California Death Index, 1905-1939*, www.ancestry.com 14Jan2015.

(liked owning champions) Vertical file: "Child Family," MHSRC.

page 172

(passion for running water) Robert Davis, as quoted in Forbes, p. 332.

(an efficient and successful business man) Horace Albright as quoted in "Harry W. Child was One of the Most Colorful and Interesting of Montana's Early-Day Builders," *MR-H*, 5Feb1931, p. 6; and "Prominent Men Express Regret ..." *LE*, 7Feb1931, p. 2.

(promoting an intimate knowledge) "Harry Child Will be Missed," *LE*, 6Feb1931. A similar thought was expressed by J. M. Hannaford, who called Harry "one of my first Montana friends of 50 years ago." See note for page 49 for reference to Jule Hannaford dining with Harry in Great Falls in 1889.

(tourist tide was turned) "Harry Child, Head of Park Firms, Dies," *GFT*, 5Feb1931; Forbes, p. 341.

(unaustentatious in his benefactions) "Death Comes As Climax to Long and Useful Life Devoted Always to Best Interests Northwest Area," Livingston, MT, 5Feb1931, newspaper clipping, vertical file: *Biography*, "Child, Harry," YNPA.

page 173

(the noblest host) quoted in Forbes, p. 332.

(names in his guest book) "Harry Child Will be Missed," *LE*, 6Feb1931.

(Sweden's Crown Prince) "Royal Heads of Sweden Headed Toward Montana," *Big Timber* [MT] *Pioneer*, 17Jun1926; "Prominent Citizens From All Over To Greet Crown Prince," *Big Timber Pioneer*, 1Jul1926, p. 1. This visit is thought to be the origin of the naming of *King Geyser* in the West Thumb Basin. Whittlesey, *Yellowstone Album*, p. 128. Cross of the Royal Order of Vasa of Sweden, July 14, bestowed on H.W. Child, in possession of Harry W. Child II.

(associated with pioneer history) "Death Comes As Climax ..."

(A more humorous characterization) Lee Whittlesey, transcript of speech given at Child Family Reunion, Mammoth Hot Springs, 13Jul1998, vertical file: *History (Whittlesey 6)*, YNPA.

(early in 1931) Barringer, *Selling Yellowstone*, pp. 82-83.

page 174

(Charles Anceney died, Stone ... took over as manager) Smith, p. 61; "Charles Anceney Dies at Bozeman," *Judith Basin County Press* [Stanford, MT], 2Mar1936, vertical file: *Flying D Ranch*, MHSRC.

(not a cattle man) Smith, p. 57.

(used proceeds ... to finance their hobby) Smith, p. 59, Child, pp. 166-167.

(could not financially support, decided the shorthorns, Best is none to good, sale ... was most successful) Smith, p. 62; "Famed 'CA' Brand Will Be Revised," *FCA*, 31Aug1937, vertical file: *Flying D Ranch*, MHSRC.

page 175

(a new Secretary of Interior) Harold L. Ickes was appointed Secretary of the Interior in January of 1933. He openly promoted what "would mean the end of the private sector in the national parks." He advocated for the United States "to nationalize all concession companies in the parks and operate them itself." Hummel, p. 103. Barringer, *Selling Yellowstone*, pp. 94-95. One might speculate that W.M. Nichols, sensing a threat to his continued Yellowstone business, chose to "circle his wagons," consolidating his businesses as a form of defense.

(Yellowstone Park Company formed, listing of officers) Lindsley, pp. 313-314; Charles Donnelly, Pres., NPR, to Mr. D. F. Lyons, General Counsel, 22Jul1936, President's Subject file No. 209 B, folder 2; "Consolidation Agreement," dated 10Apr1936, President's Subject file 209B, folder 2, NPRR-MHC.

(Galusha firm) Barringer, *Selling Yellowstone*, p. 86.

(aspect of the operations, Division heads) Personal knowledge, Nan Sigrist. "He [Nichols] ran the companies almost by committee, by allowing managers much leeway in their daily operations. Fortunately, Child had left him capable individuals in these positions." Barringer, *Selling Yellowstone*, p. 86.

(20-year contract) Bartlett, *Wilderness*, p. 367.

(graduated from MIT) Listing for Phi Beta Epsilon, Massachusetts Institute of Technology, Year 1932 & Year 1933, *U.S., School Yearbooks, 1880-2012*, www.ancestry.com 28Jun2019.

(mechanical and electrical engineering) Huntley Child, Jr. Interview.

(Murray Corporation, designing machinery, plant layout) Huntley Child, Jr. Interview; Child, Appendix 13.

(wrote W.M. and Adelaide) Huntley Child, Jr. Interview.

(fall of 1938) Huntley Jr. mentions living at 706 Harrison, the house purchased by Ellen and Billie Nichols in the nineteen-teens. Huntley Child, Jr. Interview; Child, p. 141.

(to Murray Hotel, assistant in the Lodges) Huntley Child, Jr. Interview; *1940 U.S. Census Record*, Livingston, Montana; Roll: m-t0627-02226, Page 81B, Enumeration District: 34-7, www.ancestry.com 28Jun2019.

page 176

(mail carrier's cabin, electricity, wood stove) Huntley Child, Jr. Interview.

(love in the rough) Personal correspondence from Harry W. Child II to Ruth Quinn, 20May2019. Lee H. Whittlesey, interview with Marian Child Sanger, at Robert Reamer Executive House, Mammoth Hot Springs, 12Jul1997, cited in Whittlesey, *Mammoth Village* manuscript, chap.10, p. 32.

(three bedroom house, Helena during the winters) Huntley Child, Jr. Interview. Huntley says that "the winterkeeper's house behind the Mammoth pool" was being fixed up for their use. This is shown on the Plat Plan for the Lodge Section of the Mammoth Hot Springs Group, *Inventory of Yellowstone Park Lodge and Camps Company*. Milwaukee, Wisconsin: The American Appraisal Co., 1929, Rare Book room, YNPA. The plat plan also shows "Moorman Residence," and "Goodwin Residence," both located northeast of the Mammoth Lodge proper.

(transportation managers and representatives, met to evaluate chassis) Austin, et al, p. 19.

(Its designer) Leslie J. Quinn, "Count Sakhnoffsky, Czar Nicholas II, and Yellowstone," *Commentary Newsletter*, in-house publication of the Department of Transportation and Interpretation, Yellowstone National Park Lodges, 32(1), May 2019, pp. 3-5.

page 177

(a rock star) Jay Kissell comment to a park visitor, overheard by Ruth Quinn at Old Faithful Inn, Aug2019.

(driver between 1947 and 1996) Joe Mitchell, *My Thirty-five Years Driving Bus in Yellowstone National Park*. Billings, MT: Aspen View Retirement Center/Frenchy LaJesse, [self-published], 2006. Mitchell's celebrity passengers included John Wayne, Gen. James Doolittle, Astronaut Wally Shirra, then-governor Ronald Reagan, and First Lady "Lady Bird" Johnson, p. 41.

(remembers Mrs. Nichols) Joe Mitchell to Ruth and Leslie Quinn.

(Wizardy? Shucks!) Forbes, p. 343.

Chapter 16: Grandmother Child, Anchor of the Family   *(chapter header)* NPS photo, YELL 133540

page 179

(Caption for family photograph) Back row, left to right: Johnnie Nichols, Jackie Nichols Casserly, W.M. Nichols, Dean Nichols, Huntley Child Jr., Marion Child, Betty Child. Middle row: Marianna Casserly, Ellen Dean Nichols, Harry W. Child II, Adelaide Child, James Child, Jane Child, Bonnie Child. Front row: Jock Nichols, Joan Casserly.

(using a guest book) The first entries are from July and August 1932. This book is in the possession of one of Adelaide and Harry's great grandson's Harry Child, II. The authors thank him for sharing it with us.

(recently widowed himself) Quinn, *Weaver*, p. 169.

page 180

(found a new brat) Adelaide Child guest book entry, 20Aug1934.

(My first visit to La Jolla) Adelaide Child guest book entry, 3Jan1937.

(sent his first sketches) W.M. Nichols, to Robert C. Reamer, 24Sept1934, folder: *Old Faithful 1935-1938*, box YPC-141: *Yellowstone Park Company Maintenance*; Robert C. Reamer, Architect, to W.M. Nichols, Pres., YPHC, 18Oct1934, box YPC-33, YNPA.

(They replaced the remains, into the new vision) Quinn, *Weaver*, pp. 156-159; "$200,000 Hotel to Replace Razed Mammoth," *The Hotel News of the*

West, 34(2), 15Jan1937, p. 14.

(making the business decisions) In one letter, Nichols wrote, "I would like to go over the matter with Mrs. Child before making any final answer ..." W.M. Nichols, Pres., to R.C. Reamer, 3Dec1936, box YPC-4, YNPA.

("work her magic," to prevent the cabin people) James R. McDonald, *Mammoth Hot Springs Hotel: Historic Structures Report.* Missoula, MT: Historical Research Associates, November 1995, pp. 15-16.

(worked together ... a large map) Robert C. Reamer, to Mrs. Child, 12Oct1936; correspondence related to the cost of the map – W.M. Nichols, Pres., to R.C. Reamer, 16Oct1936; Robert C. Reamer, to W.M. Nichols, 27Oct1936, box YPC-4, YNPA.

(The finished full-size map) R.C. Reamer, to W.M. Nichols, 27May1937, YPC-142, YNPA.

(sent by rail ... in six panels) W.H. Fey, "How Map of United States, in Mammoth Springs Hotel Lounge, Was Made," 3Aug1939, box YPC -4, YNPA. Reamer mentions the sections of the map being crated for shipping and acknowledges that W.H. Fey made the map in R.C. Reamer, to W.M. Nichols, 27May1937, YPC-142, YNPA.

(highlighted ... highways ... railroads) Robert C. Reamer, to W. M. Nichols, 23Nov1936; W. M. Nichols, Pres., to R.C. Reamer 9Dec1936, box YPC-4, YNPA.

(Inlaid wood) "Interesting Facts Concerning the Large Inlaid Map of the United States," publication by Yellowstone Park Co , and available map-side in the Mammoth Hotel.

(small scale sample) Robert C. Reamer, to Mrs. Child, 12Oct1936, box YPC-4, YNPA.

page 181

(locations related to the family) Reamer originally suggested, "You might as well give the map a personal family touch and if it would be of interest to show where they live, were born, married or an incident of unusual interest occurred, let's put it on. The Public will never even wonder why. ..." Robert C. Reamer, to W.M. Nichols, 23Nov1936, box YPC-4, YNPA.

(W.M. requested be included) "In Montana I think we will want Gallatin Gateway and Anceney, besides Helena and Butte, . . Of course La Jolla and San Mateo and Burlingame should be in California, ... Darned if I know where you were born, but I think that wherever it was, you should put it on the map. Seattle, of course, will go on anyway. ..." W. M. Nichols, Pres., to R. C. Reamer, 9Dec1936, box YPC-4, YNPA.

(Reamer died) Quinn, *Weaver*, p. 170.

(partners in his office) W.H. Fey, to W.M. Nichols, 18Jan1938, box YPC-142; B.O. Hallin, to W. M. Nichols, 11Feb1938, folder *Construction -- Gardiner 1936-1938*, box YPC-141: *Yellowstone Park Company Maintenance*, YNPA.

(prohibition had ended) Lindsley, pp. 302, 306. 309.

(garbage dumps, bring life ... inside the hotel) Alice Wondrak Biel, *Do (Not) Feed the Bears: The Fitful History of Wildlife and Tourists in Yellowstone.* Lawrence, KS: University Press of Kansas, 2006, pp. 17-21; Paul Schullery, *The Bears of Yellowstone.* Worland, WY: High Plains Publishing Co., 1992, pp. 102-108. Robert C. Reamer, to W.M. Nichols, 26Mar1935, W.M. Nichols, to Robert C. Reamer, 3Apr1935, file: *Old Faithful, 1935-1938*, box YPC-141, YNPA.

(W.M contacted ... Oehrle) Walter Oehrle, to W.M. Nichols, 7May1935; W.M. Nichols, to Walter Oehrle, 14May1935; Walter Oehrle, to W.M. Nichols, 20May1935, file: *Old Faithful 1935-1938*, box YPC-141, YNPA.

(cover art for the Union Pacific Railroad) Thornton Waite, *The Yellowstone Bears of the Union Pacific Railroad.* Columbia, Missouri and Idaho Falls, ID: Brueggenjohann/Reese, Inc. & Thornton Waite, 2000. In addition to this portfolio collection, Mr. Waite also reproduced twelve cover images as postcard sets. "Yellowstone Bears of the Union Pacific, Series I: 1936-1957," and "Series II: 1930-1934. Waite Publications, Idaho Falls, Idaho. In 1998 Paul Shea, former Director of the Yellowstone Gateway Museum, Livingston, MT, and Lee Whittlesey, retired Yellowstone Park NPS historian, traveled to the Union Pacific Archives, then located in Omaha, Nebraska to view the original brochures. According to Shea, besides being entertaining, the bears can be viewed because of the social commentary they offered about society. Many images reflected national events and feelings of the time. Paul Shea, slide presentation: "Union Pacific Bears of Yellowstone," presented for Heritage Days, 28Aug2004, at Old Faithful Warming Hut, Yellowstone National Park, Wyoming. The UP Archives moved across the river to Council Bluffs, Iowa in 2003. http://www.uprrmuseum.org/

(imagining ... and imposing ... "animalize humans") Excerpt from U.P. publication, "Evolution of Union Pacific's Famous Yellowstone Cubs," *William A. McKenzie files 1875-1966*, box 4 (135.I.19.5B), file: "Yellowstone Animals, Advertising Files," NPRR-MHC.

page 182

(bears strolled, danced, cut into stencils) "The Beguiling Bear Pit Cocktail Lounge," undated brochure printed by the YPC, MSC 019: *Yellowstone Park Company Records*, Series IX: "Brochures and Publications," Folder B: "1911-1939," YNPA. Each of the twelve panels was photographed by Wheale in September 1936, *J.E. Haynes Collection*, images 36418-36420, box 159: "YNP- O.F. Inn – Interiors 1936," and images 36421-36429 in box 158: "YNP - O.F. Inn – Interiors, 1936," MHSRCPA.

(visit of President ... Roosevelt) Whittlesey, *Yellowstone Album*, p. 135. Photographs of the President and First Lady touring the park and stopping at Old Faithful Geyser were published in Carl Schreier, ed., *Yellowstone: Selected Photographs 1870-1960.* Moose, WY: Homestead Publishing, 1989, pp. 90, 91. Several details of their visit to the Fishing Bridge and Yellowstone Lake area are in Schullery, *Fishing Bridge*, pp. 45-46, 64.

(extended their hospitality) Lindsley, p. 318. Richard Bartlett concluded this proved "that Harry Child's son-in-law was carrying on a family tradition of always catering to whomever occupied the White House, regardless of political party." *Wilderness*, p. 101.

(impressed by the plan) Vucanovich, p. 4. Huntley Child, Jr. believed that FDR copied the plans at his Georgia resort. Huntley Child, Jr. Interview.

(Adelaide lost her sister, kindly woman) "Last rites for Mrs. Young ..."

(returned to the Wakefield-Huntley house) "Following Mr. Child's death, his widow found the house too large so my father remodeled a small house next door for her and the Nichols took the big house, where they lived henceforth." Correspondence from Jane R. White, to Richard A. Bartlett, 21Sept1970, copy in Ruth Quinn collection, courtesy Richard A. Bartlett. After his death Dr. Bartlett's papers went to Florida State University, of which he was then Professor Emeritus.

(throughout the 1940s) Harry W. Child II to Ruth Quinn, 7Jan2021.

(after November 1948) Miss Adeline Moulton began working for the Yellowstone Park Company in 1946. She remembers 1947 as the last summer Adelaide Child spent in the park. Adeline Moulton to Ruth Quinn and Nan Sigrist, Aug2019. Miss Moulton retired from the YPC in 1990 after decades of service as secretary to Huntley Child Jr., then Tom Hallin. She worked about four years for Mrs. Isabel Haynes, before returning to the YPC, working for Art Bazata and several of his successors. She died in Gardiner, MT, 15Jan2020 at the age of 95.

(vice president) Child, p. 19.

page 183

(new dimension to their life) quote from Emily Child Vucanovich, in Child, p. 24.

(all livestock, poultry) Child, Appendix 21: *Harry W. Child, Last Will and Testament, H.W. Child Trust.*

(the one entity) Child, pp. 158-159. Multiple files show he was very involved in the Green Meadow Farm. *William M. Nichols papers, 1914-1966*, MC 292, Financial Records box 15, folders 2-7: "Green Meadow Farm," MHSRC.

(unsuccessful attempts, sold in 1947, 2741 acres) Child, p. 159; DeHaas, *Green Meadow Ranch*, p. 3.

(Green Meadow Country Club; St. Peter's Hospital) Child, p. 21.

(wading pools) Child, p. 23.

(gift of 17 acres, continue to support the camp) Child, pp. 22-23.

(land for a new school) Child, p. 23; Whithorn, *Park County*, p. 24; Whithorn, *Gardiner*, p. 22.

(*1952 school annual*) Child, p. 23.

(*final lots in Gardiner*) Child, p. 171.

(*Adelaide died in October*) "Huntley Child," LifeStory, www.ancestry.com 18Sept2015; Adelaide Dean Child, Death Date: 20Oct1949, Forestvale Cemetery, Helena, MT, *Find A Grave Index*, http://www.findagrave.com 20 Jan 2015; "Pioneer in Yellowstone Park Development Taken by Death," *GFT*, 19Oct1949, p. 4.

(*Bessie stayed with her*) Listing for Harry W. Child, *1930 U.S. Census Record*, San Diego County, California, 7Apr1930.

page 184

(*last entries were addressed to Bessie*) Entries addressed to Bessie begin in 1951. The last entry is 25Sept1959. On14Feb1954 Huntley Child, Jr.'s second wife, Betty Jane, wrote, "Dearest Bessie ... both of us love you – and *you* are Huntley's mother!..." Adelaide Child guest book, courtesy Harry W. Child, II.

(*family bought Bessie a house in La Jolla*) Ellen Dean Child Nichols retained ownership of the house, and maintained the taxes and insurance. W.M. Nichols, to T.B. Weir, First National Bank, Helena, 1Feb1950; Deeds of sale, 22Jun1960. *Nichols Papers*, Financial Records box 13, folder 8: "Bessie Ferguson House," MHSRC.

(*death in 1960*) Child, Appendix 13.

(*anchor of the family*) Elizabeth "Betty" Child Pomeroy, quoted in Child, p. 25.

(*crossword puzzles, fried chicken dinners*) Huntley Child, Jr. quoted in Child, pp. 25, 26. He also mentions jigsaw puzzles. Huntley Child, Jr. Interview.

(*friend to everyone*) Child, p. 17.

(*drafted over forty projects*) Quinn, *Yellowstone Science*, p. 47.

("*ability would be recognized*") Elisa T. Babcock, to Robert C. Reamer, 20Jan1903, Book 80 (15Oct1902 to 22Jan1903), p. 972, *Series I: Bound Correspondence Feb 1888-1907*, Records of Hotel del Coronado, SCUA-SDSU.

(*most cherished and beloved man-made spaces*) For a list of Robert C. Reamer's extant buildings by state see Quinn, *Weaver*, p. 181. For some comments summarizing his architectural style and his legacy see Ibid, pp. 172-176.

Chapter 17: The Last Roundup   (*chapter header*) Quinn collection

page 185

(*Flying D Ranch was sold*) Smith, pp. 73, 74.

(*continued to winter horses*) Nan Sigirist and her family attended the last roundup in 1964. For many recent decades, Livingston area rancher Tom Venable wintered company horses, and leased his own horses to the park concessioner to operate corral operations at Canyon, Mammoth, and Roosevelt. Beginning in 2019, horses are leased from an outfitter in the Jackson, Wyoming area. Lori Todd, ed., "Staff Spotlight: Bailee Morrison-Fogle, Roosevelt Wrangler," *Insider's Guide to Yellowstone*, in-house publication, department of Employee Communications, Yellowstone National Park Lodges, Xanterra Travel Collection, 2019, p. 13.

(*retained fifteen sections, tenant farmers stayed on, hired Archie Martin II*) Smith, p. 74. Harry W. Child II writes, "From 1952-1957, I spent my summers working on the Spanish Creek Ranch (Flying D off-spring) which Archie was the foreman. My second Dad." Email from Harry W. Child II, to Ruth Quinn, 9Aug 2019. Archie Martin (1906 - 1987) "A.L. Martin," Madison County History Association, *Pioneer Trails and Trials: Madison County 1863-1920*. Sheridan, MT: Madison County History Association, 1976, p. 257, courtesy Harry W. Child, II; https://findagrave.com/memorial/181826871/archie-martin 5Apr2020.

page 186

(*worked in the Park, family homestead between Pony and Harrison*) "It's my understanding that Archie ran the horses in the Park in the 1930s." Email from Harry W. Child II, to Ruth Quinn, 2Dec2019. Personal knowledge Nan Sigrist who knew Lee Martin (1912-1981) and his wife Hazel. Lee's obituary states he came to work in Yellowstone in 1933, working first as a wrangler, before being promoted to manager of the saddle horse division – a post he held for 33 years. https://findagrave.com/memorial/38584826/lee-r-martin 5Apr2020.

(*last roundup in 1964*) Nan and Bruce Sigrist attended this event at the invitation of Lee Martin. This section is written by her based on her memories of that day. This was during the time the company was leasing Flying D land. After this year, she remembers the company leasing land farther to the west in the Madison Range area.

page 187

(*sold the Spanish Creek Ranch*) Smith, p. 80.

(*visitation reached an all-time high, dropped below 100,000*) Haines, *Vol. II*, pp. 479.

(*Lake Hotel did not open*) Trappen, pp. 78,81.

(*Old Faithful Inn stayed closed*) Reinhart and Henry, p. 76.

(*Mammoth Hotel was shuttered, as was Canyon Hotel*) Child, p. 102. An employee from 1942 remembers Canyon Hotel being closed during the war. "Memories of Canyon Lodge in the 1940s, vertical file: *History - YNP - Journals & Diaries*, "Janecky, Richard," YNPA.

(*little spare money to upgrade*) "In August 1942, Nichols began drastically scaling back operations. He cut executive salaries 25 percent, asked department heads Kammermeyer and Brown, who were too old to serve in the military, to find outside employment, and offered another three hundred vehicles for sale to reduce expenses." Barringer, *Selling Yellowstone*, p. 98.

(*wives worked their husband's jobs*) Kaufman, pp. 92-93.

(*registered on October 16*) WWII Draft Registration Cards for Montana 10/16/1940-3/31/1947, Record Group: Records of the Selective Service System 147, box 8, National Archives in St. Louis, www.ancestry.com 28Jun2019.

(*Rock Island Arsenal, looking for officers overseas, Heavy Equipment, discharged*) Huntley Child, Jr. Interview. He mentions that W.M. was also stationed at the Rock Island Arsenal.

page 188

(*Manager of Lodge Division, year-round in 1949*) When moving to Mammoth year round, Huntley Jr. began living in the Wakefield-Nichols house. Huntley Child, Jr. Interview. "Yellowstone Park Company Employment Contract," Richard M. Janecky, Racine, WI, 1Apr1947 - 15Sept1947, vertical file: *History - YNP - Journals & Diaries*, "Janecky, Richard," YNPA.

(*appointed Vice President*) Child, p. 141.

(*took time to know his hotel staff*) Personal knowledge, Nan Sigrist.

(*Montana Hotel Association, trade missions*) Child, Appendix 13. Huntley Jr. became involved with the Montana Hotel Association in the late 1940s, and he became its president in 1953. He became president of the Rocky Mountain Hotel Association in 1955. He was contacted by the Department of Commerce in Cheyenne, Wyoming and agreed to participate in a six- week trade mission to the West Indies, British Guyana, South America, and Puerto Rico in 1961, promoting tourism and development. In 1967 he was contacted again, and he served a four-week trade mission to Turkey. Huntley Child Jr. Interview.

(*served from 1942*) Barringer, *Selling Yellowstone*, p. 100.

(*General Manager and President*) Bartlett, *Wilderness*, p. 367; "Col. Nichols of Yellowstone Park Company Is Stricken," *LE*, 7Aug1957, pp. 1, 4; Barringer, *Selling Yellowstone*, p. 109.

(*increased use of the personal auto*) Austin, et al, p. 20.

(*ceased passenger service to Gardiner*) Haines, *Vol. II*, p. 372; Fred T. Johnston, Acting Superintendent, "Concessioners," *Superintendent's Monthly*

Report, September 1948, 6Oct1948, p. 5. "Yellowstone Specials," carrying park employees continued service to Gardiner for four more years, but "the last passenger train of any sort to arrive was a special trip in 1952 carrying a group of farmers from Michigan and Indiana." Timothy R. Manns, Park Historian to Mr. Donald N. Hammarstrom, Aurora, CO, 15Sept1982, box H-18, YNPA.

(replace the smaller, full-size motor coaches) Austin, et al, pp. 24-26. Although the White open-top buses are generally thought to be the longest standing veterans of the park roadways, another style of bus has earned that distinction. A total of 25 Motor Coach Industries parlor coaches model MC-5B were purchased between 1975 and 1976. Austin, et al, pp. 26-27. Leslie Quinn, a tour guide and Interpretive Specialist for Xanterra Travel Collection, drove the lower loop tour (now called the Circle of Fire Tour) from Old Faithful Inn on Saturday, 9Oct2019. It was the final day of revenue service for these venerable coaches, retiring after 45 years of service. As of this writing only 1 remains in Yellowstone. It is used for employee trips and as a backup vehicle.

page 189

(the economic depression) "The only component ... that had successfully weathered the difficult years of 1932 and 1933 was the Yellowstone Park Lodges and Camps Company. ... It had virtually carried the hotel and transportation divisions through the rough years." Barringer, *Selling Yellowstone*, p. 89.

(WWII and the recovery) Huntley Child Jr. said about 1946 "all facilities were open, but help was so hard to come by. We closed Roosevelt Lodge a week after it opened. It was touch and go all summer." Huntley Child, Jr. Interview.

(900,000, one-million mark) Haines, *Vol. II,* p. 479.

(brought changing ideas) Barringer, *Selling Yellowstone*, pp. 101-103.

(initiated the Mission 66) "Mission 66 was without question the largest, best-organized, and most slickly packaged initiative ever undertaken by the NPS, as well as the most ambitious attempt to redesign national parks. ... The plan called for a ten-year appropriation in excess of $785 million, with more than $48 million of that total to be spent in 1956 alone." Barringer. *Selling Yellowstone,* p. 120.

(new Canyon Village ... Grant Village) Barringer, *Selling Yellowstone*, p. 131. "Although Mission 66 was the well-intentioned fiftieth anniversary program designed to improve visitor services, it resulted in some regrettable architectural legacies for the national parks." Kaiser, p. 41. The authority on Mission 66 is Ethan Carr, *Mission 66: Modernism and The National Park Dilemma.* Amherst, MA: University of Massachusetts, 2007.

(took the reins of the authority) "In 1946 newly appointed Secretary of the Interior Julius Klug ... attempted to alter the traditional NPS-concessioner 'partnership' approach to park management, launching a crusade to reassert authority over both the NPS and concession operations. ... Operators had always been assured of preferential treatment in the renewal process; in fact, most contract expirations were never announced or opened for competitive bids. Krug wanted to encourage competition for the lucrative operations. He also wanted to shorten the twenty-year standard contract and raise franchise fees from 3 percent of net income to 5 percent." Barringer, *Selling Yellowstone,* pp. 104-105.

("partnering" plan) Barringer. *Selling Yellowstone*, pp. 103-104.

(Wirth was appointed, acquaint himself with the current situation) Barringer, *Selling Yellowstone,* pp. 116-117.

(improvements to the Lake area) W.M. Nichols was in Washington, DC in November 1953 to hash out the plans with the government. Ibid.

page 190

(small areas referred to as villages) Wirth was trained as a landscape architect. Ibid, p. 117.

(NPS working committee) Hummel, pp. 182-185; Barringer, *Selling Yellowstone,* pp. 120-121.

(All three ... agreed to participate) Photograph caption, "Breaking ground for Canyon Village, 1956," Barringer, *Selling Yellowstone,* photo section between pages 108 and 109. Also attending the groundbreaking were Anna Pryor and Elizabeth "Belle" Trishman who had sold their general store concession to Charles Hamilton three years earlier. *Yellowstone's Weekly News,* 10(26), 28Jun1956, p.1; Watry, *Women,* p. 59.

(must postpone all other plans) Barringer, *Selling Yellowstone*, p. 117.

(build roads and other infrastructure) Ibid, p. 118.

(invest no more money) Ibid, pp. 112-113.

(search for prospective buyers) The search began in 1952 when stockholders "quietly offered the YP Company for sale through a New York investment banker." Barringer, *Selling Yellowstone,* p. 118. Barringer notes that "by 1950 he [W.M. Nichols] seemed to be losing interest in the YP Company ... In 1951 his son John and nephew Huntley Child Jr., both executives in the company, expressed a desire to sell the family holdings." Ibid, p. 107.

(Wyoming governor ... express an interest) Barringer, *Selling Yellowstone,* p. 119.

(confusing and unsettling, did little to quell) Nan Sigrist, personal knowledge.

(draft a "prospectus") Barringer, *Selling Yellowstone,* pp. 118-119.

(allowed to renew contracts) Back in Silas Huntley's reign as transportation overseer, Secretary of Interior John W. Noble argued "if you want to preserve the park to the people of the United States at anything like reasonable prices, you have to have competition come in, and in order to do that you must get the hotels and the transportation and the boats and as many of these different things as arise as separate as you can, ..." Statement by Hon. John W. Noble, Secretary of the Interior, 31Mar1892, "Hearing Before the Committee on Territories of the United States Senate in Relation to the Bill (S. 1963) To Incorporate The Yellowstone Park Company," to accompany his testimony before the House Committee on Public Lands, 25Apr1892, McRae, p. 66. One early park superintendent maintained, "So as long as the regular company maintains its very high standard of excellence, it is right and proper that it should be protected in this manner." Anderson, *Report, 1895,* p. 9.

page 191

(open bidding to wider competition) Barringer, *Selling Yellowstone,* pp. 104-105, 112.

(Huntley Child, Jr. argued, propriety right) Ibid, p. 112.

(gathered support from U.S. senators, summer jobs ... "specials") In Huntley Jr.'s words, "I made it a point to know all the Senators, to hire the kids they recommended. Probably one third of our staff were those kids. I made sure they knew how the kids did." Huntley Child, Jr. Interview. Barringer, *Selling Yellowstone,* pp. 112-113. The term "specials" was in use in the mid-1950s when Nan Sigrist arrived as a YPC employee.

(YPC Board of Directors) Barringer, *Selling Yellowstone,* pp. 138-139.

(twenty-year contract) Bartlett, *Wilderness,* pp. 370-371. Part of Huntley Jr.'s argument was that in order to find a bank willing to finance new construction, they would have to go to Congress to extend the lease to thirty years. Huntley Child, Jr. Interview.

($3 million line of credit) Barringer, *Selling Yellowstone,* pp. 126-127.

(poster child of Mission 66) Lesley M. Gilmore, *Canyon Village in Yellowstone: The Model For Mission 66.* Charleston, SC: The History Press, 2017, pp. 11-12. "Canyon Village was the single most important project of the entire ten-year scheme to rebuild and expand national Park facilities." Barringer, *Selling Yellowstone,* p. 133.

(architectural firm chosen) Johnnie Nichols and Huntley Child, Jr. went to Los Angeles to hire the architectural firm of Welton Becket & Associates (WB&A) and the McNeil Construction Company. McNeil had just finished building Disneyland, Huntley said, so it was thought they would fit well for their idea of a centralized community/registration/dining building and cabins for guest accommodations. "We thought we could prefab [the cabins] in Gardiner in the winter." He said the 1957 winter was "too cold - we couldn't work." Huntley Child, Jr. Interview. Gilmore, pp. 72-75, 91-95. WB&A specialized in department store design, large shopping centers, and the theory of total design. Gilmore, pp. 39-41, 76.

(failed to consider) The last of the 1950s cabins were removed from the Canyon area in 2017. One of the mock-up cabins still stands in Gardiner, MT, used as employee housing by Yellowstone Park Service Stations. Designed for use in warmer climates, its flat roof design proved problematic when facing winters at nearly 8000 feet in elevation. "Canyon Village was WB&A's first foray ... into design in the national parks, yet its prior experience ...

demonstrated its ability to design large complexes and respond to a variety of climates. However, ... it had not designed in heavy snow country like Yellowstone." Gilmore, p. 76.

(modern steel and manufactured composite materials) Kaiser, p. 38; Gilmore, pp. 82-89.

(hindered the project's completion, less than one-fourth) A formal dedication ceremony was held at Canyon Village on 31Aug1957, but most of the cabins were not completed until October. Barringer, *Selling Yellowstone*, p. 140. Bruce Sigrist was the Manager of Canyon Lodge in 1958, its first full season of operation. Nan Sigrist recalls "mud everywhere," "roads not built." See also Gilmore, pp. 102-105.

(undesirable to the tourists, cabins ... were unoccupied) "Those units that were serviceable rarely filled with guests even during the busiest months. ... Underground pipes were so poorly sealed that workers flushed rocks, rubbish, and welding beads out by the bucketful, and miniature 'geysers' began appearing between cabins. Plumbers had also left gaps between fixtures and the floors, allowing ground squirrels unimpeded access to bathrooms, while frost heave occurring during the winter loosened waste pipes so that toilets flushed directly onto the ground. Equally disconcerting, the bare plywood walls between cabins were devoid of soundproofing materials ..." Barringer, *Selling Yellowstone*, p. 140. Gilmore, p. 94, also addresses cabin deficiencies.

(Canyon Hotel was filled) Ibid, p. 141.

page 192

(toll on W.M. Nichols' health) Mark Barringer points out that by the time of the Mission 66 plans, W.M. had already reached his seventies. Barringer, *Selling Yellowstone*, p. 117.

(illness of ten days) History of William Morse Nichols, 28Aug1957, vertical file: *History - YN - Employee, YHC*, "Nichols," YNPA; "Col. Nichols of Yellowstone Park Company Is Stricken," *LE*, 7Aug1957, pp. 1, 4.

(succeeded him as chairman) Barringer, *Selling Yellowstone*, p. 150.

(needed extensive repairs) "...the existing foundations [of the lounge] have been badly broken by frost action. The front of the porch has raised approximately 1 foot, and the north wall has been displaced inward approximately 10 inches. As a result of this pressure, the main structure of the lounge has been put under severe strain and a number of the supporting columns and trusses have been distorted. This condition has been observed for several years, but it has now reached a point where repairs are absolutely necessary. ..." Thomas J. Hallin, Manager of Construction Dept., YPC, to Lemuel A. Garrison, Supt., 12Sept1957, vertical file: *History – Structures*, "Canyon Hotel Demolition," YNPA.

(structural integrity) "Inspection of Canyon Hotel, September 13, 1958; ... we evidently have many secondary structural members now taking direct primary loads as a result of the inability of primary members to sustain actual loads. ... It is true that in any large city or municipality covered by zoning codes there is little doubt that the owner of such a structure would have been ordered a number of years ago to either correct the structural condition of this building or close it down. ... The Company hired an architectural firm to make a structural analysis of the building to determine the relative merits of continuing to operate this unit ... It has been determined by the architectural firm of Orr Pickering and Associates that as a result of their study of the structure, they were of the opinion that it was not economically feasible to rehabilitate the building and that it should be abandoned. They also expressed an opinion that the present structural condition of the older portions of the hotel are definitely unsafe for occupancy. ..." Gerald A. Rowe, Park Engineer, to Supt., 16Jan1959, vertical file: *History – Structures*, "Canyon Hotel Demolition," YNPA.

(undermining the stability) Gerald Rowe wrote that due to a combination of snow loading, heavy winds, and frost action "the resultant effect of these indeterminate stresses has obviously changed basic loadings on the various structural members of this building and we evidently have many secondary structural members now taking direct primary loads as a result of the inability of primary members to sustain actual loads. ... " Ibid.

(park engineer) "... it was determined that the Canyon Hotel is structurally unsound and is unsafe for further occupancy and it will not be open this summer. Inspection of the building was made this fall by Engineer Miller of the Washington Office, our own engineers and representatives of the concessioner and we are all agreed that we can no loonger permit guests to use the building." Lemuel A. Garrison, Supt., to Region Two [NPS], 16Jan1959, vertical file: *History – Structures*, "Canyon Hotel Demolition," YNPA.

(only thing keeping them in line) Huntley Child, Jr. Interview.

(Photographs in the park archives) Vertical file: *History – Structures*, "Canyon Hotel Demolition," YNPA.

(resources ... simply not there) "... By the spring of 1957, with reserves all but depleted, the company was basically broke, and interest payments on the $5 million note further exhausted available funds. To exacerbate the situation, payments on the loan principal – $500,000 per year beginning in 1958 – promised to prevent any possible recovery." Barringer, *Selling Yellowstone*, p. 139. Huntley Jr. mentioned that Canyon Village had a planned budget of $3 million, but it ended up closer to $5 million. Huntley Child, Jr. Interview.

(could be remodeled) This was the opinion of Thomas Hallin, Director, Construction and Engineering for the Yellowstone Park Company, personal knowledge, Nan Sigrist.

(Furnishings ... towns around the park) Personal knowledge, Nan Sigrist. Some Canyon Hotel furniture is still in use today in the lobby of Old Faithful Inn.

(Carlos Construction Company) "World-Famed Grand Canyon Hotel to be Razed," Press release [inviting bids], 15Jul1959, Public Relations Office, Yellowstone Park Co.; and Contract between the Yellowstone Park Company and Carlos Construction Company, William W. (Bill) Henry of Cody, WY, 9Sept1959. Vertical file: *History - Structures*, "Canyon Hotel Demolition," YNPA. Huntley Jr. said they were receiving quotes in the $100,000 to $200,000 range to demolish the building. Then "a guy from Cody told us he'd do it for nothing, or just do it for the materials." Huntley Child, Jr. Interview.

(one cold dark night) According to one researcher the fire started 8Aug1960. The fire was reported to have started on upper floor in back of the building's shell at 11 p.m. The cause of fire on official report was listed as "unknown." The fire burned until August 23, burning a total of 5.6 acres, with many spot fires. Personal communication during walk around Canyon developed area with then NPS Interpretive Ranger, David Rothenburger, 3Jul1996. Someone, living in a government bunkhouse at Canyon, remembers the night the Canyon Hotel burned, charred shingles were found 3-4 miles away. He said that when they looked into the foundation pits, that radiators were twisted and bath tubs had all the enamel burned off, and "they opened up like flower petals from the heat." Personal communication Lee Osmansky, to Ruth Quinn, 26Sept2012. Some of the structure remained until 1962. Thomas J. Hallin, First V.P., YPC, to L.A. Garrison, Supt., 12 Aug1961, vertical file: *History – Structures*, "Canyon Hotel Demolition," YNPA.

page 193

(So many theories) One recent publication claims that the hotel was a victim of the 1959 Hebgen Lake Earthquake, but clearly the damage was noted before that time. Jill Bullock, *Yellowstone National Park*. Postcard History Series, Charleston, SC: Arcadia Publishing, 2011, p. 99. "I guess he'd [reference to Bill Henry of Cody] gotten everything out of he wanted so it burned down. That's my guess." Huntley Child, Jr. Interview.

(picture of conspiracy) Haines, *Vol. II*, p. 377.

(for the insurance, lost much salvage material) Jack E. Haynes quoted in Hert, "Luxury ... ," p. 35.

(wiring ... had already been cut) Henry's contract required him to provide his own electricity. Contract between the Yellowstone Park Company and Carlos Construction Company, William W. (Bill) Henry of Cody, Wyoming, 9Sept1959, vertical file: *History - Structures*, "Canyon Hotel Demolition," YNPA.

(greatest architectural loss) Wheaton, p. 16.

(relationship with the railroads) Austin, et al, p. 21.

(sent a letter to his cousin, "blood runs thicker ...", services were no longer needed) Child, p. 122.

(dismissed from the family business) Although Mark Barringer used the word *resigned*, Huntley Jr. describes being enroute to Hawaii to attend the American Hotel Association meeting in the spring of 1960, when he was informed he had until the end of May to be out of the park. Friends had

called to "let us know something was coming." Barringer, *Selling Yellowstone*, p. 150; Huntley Child, Jr. Interview. In 1957, Huntley Child Jr. was a charter member of the Treasure State Life Insurance Company in Butte, MT, serving as Senior Vice-President. After leaving Yellowstone, he moved to Butte, spent a short time in Red Lodge, and finally settled in Billings, MT. There, in 1962, he also co-founded the Kampgrounds of America [KOA] – having noticed the high number of travelers coming through the area on their way to the Spokane World's Fair that summer. He served as Executive Director of the Montana Action Program, advocating for sales tax in Montana. Huntley Jr. died in 1993 after a long battle with cancer. Child, Appendix 13; http://www.michelottisawyers.com/betty-jane-oslund-child/ 28Jun 2019; "'Happy Kampers' at the Montana Historical Society," *Society Star*, Spring/Summer 2018, p. 4; Huntley Child, Jr. Interview; advertisement advocating sales tax in Montana, *The Dillon* [MT] *Daily Tribune-Examiner*, 21Oct1968; Listing for Huntley Child, Jr., *Find-A-Grave Index*, 28Jun2019.

(Johnnie Nichols ... relinquish his position) Child, p. 124. Barringer reports on the extreme drama that took place between 1960 and 1965 when three different General Managers, LeMarr Bittinger, George Beall, and Art Bazata, tried unsuccessfully to set the company back on track. Barringer, *Selling Yellowstone*, pp. 154-155; 166-169.

(promising sale) Barringer, *Selling Yellowstone*, pp. 155, 156.

(terminating the contract, decided to appeal) Ibid, p. 169.

page 194

(new thirty-year contract) Ibid, p. 171.

(yearly pilgrimages) The sisters graciously shared family stories with long time hotel company employees during their visits. They attended the Child Family Reunion, Mammoth Hot Springs, Jul1998. Marion passed away in 2009, and Betty died in 2010. Lee Whittlesey interview Marion Child Sanger at Mammoth Hot Springs in 1997. Notes from Lee Whittlesey to Ruth Quinn, 5Jul2019.

(She was composed and calm) On her way out of the park, Mrs. Nichols made a stop at the Wakefield House where Bruce and Nan Sigrist were living.

("Dean" passed away) "Huntley Child," LifeStory, www.ancestry.com 18Sept2015.

page 195

(term in the military) Record for Huntley Child, U.S. Department of Veterans Affairs, *BIRLS Death File, 1850-2010,* www.ancestry.com 20Mar2018.

(remained in Washington) MR-H, 25Mar1919; Listing for Huntley Child shows his residence in Washington, D.C., *R.L. Polk & Co.'s Helena City Directory 1920.* Helena, MT: R.L. Polk & Co., Publ., .p. 93.

(Huntley and Emilie divorced) "When Huntley left the Park to join the Army it was the last time he lived with Emilie. they didn't divorce for years because Emilie would not give him a divorce for religious reasons." Personal communication from Harry W. Child II, to Ruth Quinn, 20May2019.

(never became involved) Child, Appendix 13.

(moved to New York City) Marion was 10 years old, Huntley Jr. was 8, and Elizabeth "Betty" was 6. *1920 U.S. Federal Census,* District 0441, Queens Assembly District 6, Queens, New York, www.ancestry.com 20Mar2018.

(for about ten years) Listing for Huntley Child, *1930 Federal Census Record,* Manhattan, New York County, New York, 14May1930.

(he remarried) "Huntley Child," LifeStory, www.ancestry.com 18Sept2015; Listing for Huntley Child, *1930 Federal Census Record,* Manhattan, New York County, New York, 14May1930.

(purchased a pickle factory) Child, Appendix 13; Listing for Huntley Child, Manager, Dean Pickle Co., *City Directory, Seattle, Washington, 1934,* p. 355, www.ancestry.com 20Mar2018.

(fondness for horse-racing) Personal communication, Bonnie Stern, to Ruth Quinn, 19Jun2015.

(had no communication) Child, Appendix 13.

(released Huntley from repaying) Child, Appendix 21.

(died at the family home) "Huntley Child," LifeStory, www.ancestry.com 18Sept2015.

page 196

(used such phrases as) Bartlett, *Pacific Northwest Quarterly,* p. 2.

(more praise than censure) Shankland, pp. 142-143.

Yellowstone Savages Never Say Goodbye: "See You Next Summer"

page 197

(future was in jeopardy) Bartlett, *Wilderness,* pp. 372-373.

(closed to overnight guests) Byrand, pp. 202-203; Huntley Child Jr. takes credit for initiating this idea. Huntley Child, Jr. Interview. William S. Ellis, "Yellowstone at 100: The Pitfalls of Success," *National Geographic,* 141(5), May 1972, p. 631.

(stood up and cried) A. Clark Stratton, Chairman, Department of the Interior, NPS to George Beall, President, YPC, June 1, 1964; Beall to Stratton, July 14, 1964; Box YPC-150, YNPA

(purchased Yellowstone hotels, portions of their revenues) Bartlett, *Wilderness,* p. 377; John A. Townsley, *1981 Annual Report of the Superintendent,* Yellowstone National Park, 2Mar1982; Robert D. Barbee, *1982 Annual Report of the Superintendent,* Yellowstone National Park, 4Mar1983; Robert D. Barbee, *1987 Annual Report of the Superintendent,* Yellowstone National Park, 3Apr1988, YNPA; Lecture given by Andy Beck, NPS Architect, 17Jan2001, Mammoth Hot Springs, WY; Reinhart and Henry, pp. 124-125.

(National Historic Landmark) Laura Soulliere Harrison, *Architecture in the Parks: National Historic Landmark Theme Study.* Washington, D.C.: National Park Service/Department of the Interior, Nov1986, pp. 61-76.

(multi-year restoration) Thomas Beaudette and Janna Moser, "Faithful Preservation – Another 100 Years," *Structure Magazine,* Sept2009, pp. 18-20, www.STRUCTUREmag.org/; Kim Briggeman, "Architect gets 'once-in-a-lifetime' Yellowstone Project," *BG,* 15Jan2012, p. C7; Jason Bacaj, "Historic Preservation: Restoration to shore up Old Faithful Inn's structural integrity," *Bozeman* [MT] *Chronicle,* 10Jun2012, pp. A1, A8.

page 198

(as much a natural component) Judith L. Meyer, *The Spirit of Yellowstone: The Cultural Evolution of a National Park.* Lanham, MD: Rowman & Littlefield Publishers, Inc., 1996, p. 79.

(Lake Hotel from 2011-2014) R. Laurie Simmons and Thomas H. Simmons, National Historic Landmark Nomination Form, 16Apr 2015.

(Landmark status) – "Lake Yellowstone Hotel Designated National Historic Landmark," NPS press release, 15-020, 16Apr2015.

(Mammoth Hotel's restoration, redesigned and rehabilitated) Personal communication Peter Galindo, National Park Service Architect and Project Engineer, to Leslie and Ruth Quinn, 30Aug2019.

(Reamer's map was restored) NPS interpretive sign in Mammoth Map Room, summer 2019.

(wing of guest rooms, Art Moderne style hotels) Personal communication Peter Galindo, NPS Architect and Project Engineer, to Leslie and Ruth Quinn, 30Aug2019.

page 199

(hires 4000 seasonal employees) Ruth Quinn has been a seasonal member of Human Resources staff since 2004.

(joining a long legacy) Correspondence of the YPA, file J, July1891, NPRR-MHC; Clara Green, "Comments on Working in Yellowstone National Park 1891 & 1892," vertical files: *History-YNP-Journals (Diaries),* YNPA; "Local Layout," *LE,* 4Jun1904, p. 5; Richard Janecky, "Memories of Canyon Lodge in the 1940s," typescript, vertical file: *History-YNP-Journals & Diaries,* YNPA; Mary Dawe Lowry and Denise Mackesy, "Working in Yellowstone: Then and Now," from *Montana Outdoors,* July/August 1985, pp. 27-30, in vertical file: *History-YNP-Journals & Diaries.* YNPA; James Perry, *Squatters in Paradise: A Yellowstone Memoir.* Bloomington, IN: iUniverse, 2009, p. 138.

(a fascinating chronology) Whittlesey, *Storytelling*, p. 348.

(in use in Yellowstone today) Austin, et al, pp. 28-29; "Yellow Buses Return to Yellowstone to Join Park's Historic Vehicle Collection," *Yellowstone Discovery*, 17(2), Summer2002, p. 8; "Return of the Old Yellow Bus: A History of Transportation in Yellowstone National Park," marketing brochure, Yellowstone National Park Lodges, 2007.

(lost money since opening) Christopher C. Dantic, "The Montana Smelting Company," *River Edge*, June 2006, p. 9; *Montana Smelter Reclamation, Cascade County Montana: A Cultural Resource Inventory and Evaluation*. Butte, MT: Renewable Technologies Incorporated, 2003, pp. 43-52, courtesy the History Museum, Great Falls, MT.

(tottering, decaying remains) "Fire to Wipe Out Last Trace of Historic Silver Smelter," *GFT*, 4Apr1924, p. 9, courtesy The History Museum, Great Falls, MT.

(stack stood out by itself, remaining 22 shots) "Sole Remaining Stack of Old Silver Smelter is Tumbled to Ground," *GFT*, 23Sept1928, p. 17.

page 200

(county took over, cleanup of the site) Dantic, p. 10. The Silver Smelter at Great Falls was operation for only twelve years. Nearby, on the opposite side of the river, upstream, is the site of the Boston & Montana Mining Company facility that opened in 1893. Later known as Anaconda Copper Company, it was primarily engaged in refining copper and later zinc. That facility closed in 1980 and its great stack was demolished in 1982. Craig Wirth and Jim Meinert, producers, *Under the Big Stack: The Great Falls Smelter Remembered*. Great Falls, MT: The History Museum Film Production, 2013.

(Turner bought the Flying D) Smith, pp. 85-86.

(paid $21 million) Todd Wilkinson, *Last Stand: Ted Turner's Quest to Save a Troubled Planet*. Guilford, CT: Lyons Press, 2013, pp. 24-25.

(ordering his ranch manager, to disavow tradition) Ibid, pp. 25-26.

(new model of land management) Ibid, p. 342.

(5000 native bison) Ibid, p. 7.

(pack of wolves) Ibid, pp. 292-293.

page 201

(nationwide restaurant chain) Ibid, p. 322.

(107 employees) Email from Lori Todd, Employee Engagement & Communications Manager, Yellowstone National Park Lodges to Ruth Quinn, 17Jul 2019. Lori notes that five will receive 40 year pins in 2019, bringing that current total to eight, including the employee with the longest record of service at 47 years. Seven new employees reached the 20 year milestone.

Citations for photograph pages

[5] (piercing eyes and a drooping moustache) William Loeb, III, to W. Stuart Symington, Wash., DC, 16Mar1953, *William M. Nichols Papers, 1944-1966*, MC 292, Correspondence box 5, folder 5: "William Loeb," MHSRC. Signature of HW Child from HWC to SBM Young, 16Sept1908, RG00, s1, b20, YNPA.

[6] (our handsome Harry) "Local News," *The Daily Miner* [Butte, MT], 2Nov1883, p. 4, www.ancestry.com 13Jan2015

[8] (beautiful eyes and a lovely expression always on her face) Child, p. 24.

[20] (water cress near Giant Spring) Child, p. 37.

[36] (150 men, a full moon ...) Hiram M. Chittenden, *Yellowstone National Park: Historical & Descriptive*. Stanford University Press, 4th ed. rev. Eleanor Chittenden Cress and Isabelle F. Story, 1933, pp. 248-249.

[49] Back cover, *The Broadwater Hotel, camp and natatorium, Helena, Montana. A day's drive to geysers or glaciers*. Ephemera collection: Broadwater Hotel and Natatorium, MHSRC Library.

[69] Schullery, *Old Yellowstone Days*, p. 82.

[72] (It is a craftsman's dream realized) Mrs. Edward H. [Ruth] Johnson, Fort Dodge, IA, *Diary of Trip thru Yellowstone Park, 1905*, Collection 430, Box 2, Item 39, BSC-MSU.

[86] (the greatest architectural loss in Yellowstone history) Wheaton, p. 16.

[97] (Harry can handle a Rainbow ...) Forbes, p. 332.

[102] Brands recreated from *Livestock Brand Registrations for Montana, 1911-1920*, digital collection, pp. 2442, 5788, https://www.mtmemory.org/

Newspaper and archives abbreviations used

	The Abbeville [South Carolina] *Press and Banner*
AS	*The Anaconda* [Montana] *Standard*
	Baker [Montana] *Sentinel*
BWR	*The Benton* [Montana Territory] *Weekly Record*
	Big Timber [Montana] *Pioneer*
BG	*The Billings* [Montana] *Gazette*
	Bozeman [Montana] *Chronicle*
BEN	*Butte* [Montana] *Evening News*
BIM	*The Butte* [Montana] *Inter Mountain*
	The Chicago [Illinois] *Record-Herald*
LDE	*The Daily Enterprise* [Livingston, Montana]
DH	*The Daily Herald* [Los Angeles, California]
DI	*The Daily Independent* [Helena, Montana Territory and state]
	The Daily Miner [Butte, Montana Territory]
	The Daily Missoulian [Missoula, MT]
DYJ	*Daily Yellowstone Journal* [Miles City, Montana Territory]
	The Evening Critic [Washington, D.C.]
EH-KF	*The Evening Herald* [Klamath Falls, Oregon]
ES	*Evening Star* [Washington, D.C.]
	The Evening World [New York, New York]
FCA	*Fergus County Argus* [Lewistown, Montana]
	Fergus County Democrat [Lewistown, MT]
	Fitchburg [Massachusetts] *Sentinel*
GPDC	*Grant's Pass* [Oregon] *Daily Courier*
GFDT	*Great Falls* [Montana] *Daily Tribune*
GFL	*Great Falls* [Montana] *Leader*
GFT	*Great Falls* [Montana Territory and state] *Tribune*
HI	*The Helena* [Montana] *Independent*
HDI	*The Helena* [Montana] *Daily Independent*

HRG	*The Hood River Glacier* [Hood River, Oregon]
	Judith Basin County Press [Stanford, Montana]
	The Kalispell [Montana] *Bee*
LDP	*Livingston* [Montana] *Daily Post*
LE	*Livingston* [Montana] *Enterprise*
MCM	*Mohave County Miner and Our Mineral Wealth* [Kingman, Arizona]
	Montana News [Lewistown, Montana]
MP	*The Montana Post* [Virginia City, Montana Territory]
MR-H	*The* [Helena] *Montana Record-Herald*
NR	*National Republican* [Washington, D.C.]
	The National Tribune [Washington, D.C.]
NN-w	*The New North-west* [Deer Lodge, Montana Territory]
NYT	*The New York* [New York] *Times*
PCN	*The Park County News* [Livingston, Montana]
PM	*The Philipsburg* [Montana Territory and state] *Mail*
	Red Lodge [MT] *Picket*
RP	*The River Press* [Fort Benton, Montana Territory and state]
RMH	*Rocky Mountain Husbandman* [Diamond City, Montana Territory]
SDU	*The San Diego* [California] *Union*
	The San Diego [California] *Union and Daily Bee*
	The San Francisco [California] *Call*
SPG	*The Saint Paul* [Minnesota] *Globe*
	The Seattle [Washington] *Star*
S-WT	*The Semi-Weekly Tribune* [Great Falls, Montana]
SDN	*The Suffrage Daily News* [Helena, Montana]
SH	*The Sunday Herald* [Washington, D.C.]
	The Washington [D.C.] *Herald*
GW	[Gardiner, Montana] *Wonderland*

BSC-MSU	Merrill G. Burlingame Special Collections, Renee Library, Montana State University Libraries, Bozeman, Montana
MHSRC	Montana Historical Society Research Center, Helena, Montana
NACP	National Archives at College Park, College Park, Maryland
	New Hampshire Historical Society, Concord, New Hampshire
NPRR-MHC	Northern Pacific Railway Records, Minnesota History Center, St. Paul, Minnesota
SCUA-SDSU	Special Collections and University Archives, Malcolm A. Love Library, San Diego State University, California
Young Papers	Samuel B.M. Young Papers, U.S. Army Archives, Carlisle, Pennsylvania
TR-ISU	Theodore Roosevelt Papers (1901-1909), Eli M. Oboler Library, Idaho State University, Pocatello, Idaho
YNPA	Yellowstone National Park Archives, Yellowstone Heritage and Research Center, Gardiner, Montana

Special Note: Documents in the YNPA have been reclassified and reordered since some of this research was originally done. For instance, those previously known as First 10,000 Documents may now be found in RG 00, Series I, Boxes 009-021. My apologies to researchers following in my footsteps and to the library staff who have already helped others locate these important documents. RQ

Abbreviations used in photograph citations and special thank yous

Our photograph pages were assembled during the COVID-19 pandemic in the spring and summer of 2020. We are grateful to the many staff in libraries and archives who assisted us in obtaining images and permissions, while working remotely and under conditions of reduced staffing. We honor your commitment!

BSC-MSU	Merrill G. Burlingame Special Collections, Montana State University Library, Bozeman, Montana. Thanks to Gary Barnhart.
GHM	Gallatin History Museum, Gallatin Historical Society, Bozeman, Montana. Thanks to Rachel Phillips.
HM, GF	The History Museum, Great Falls, Cascade County Historical Society, Montana. Thanks to Megan Sanford.
LC	Library of Congress Photograph Collection
MHSRC	Montana Historical Society Research Center, Helena, Montana. Thanks to Zoe Stoltz and Jodie Foley.
MHS	Montana Historical Society Photograph Archives. Thanks to Kellyn Younggren and Jeff Malcomson.
	Those bearing a number beginning with H- are part of the Haynes Foundation Collection.
MoR	Museum of the Rockies, Bozeman, Montana. Thanks to Steve Jackson.
YELL	Yellowstone National Park Photograph Archives, Gardiner, Montana. Thanks to Anne Foster, Sarah Marino, Melanie Cutietta, Kimberlee Roberts, and Jackie Jerla.
YGM	Courtesy of the Yellowstone Gateway Museum of Park County, Montana. Thanks to Rob Park, Park Photo, Livingston, Montana.

We owe a debt of gratitude to our early readers whose suggestions have made this better. All errors are our own. Thanks to Joni Sigrist, Linda McDonald, Mary Jane and Winston Hoskins, Gillian Hennessey, Leslie Quinn, Joanne Kearney, Lee Whittlesey, and Sabra and Harry W. Child II.

Timeline of Selected Dates

1841	May 2, birth of Silas Stilwell Huntley
1856	May 8, birth of Annie Dean Huntley Young
1856	birth of Harry W. Child
1858	birth of Dr. Maria Dean
1861	October 2, birth of Adelaide Dean Child
1867	arrival of Silas Huntley to Montana Territory
1870	Washburn Expedition to Yellowstone from Helena
1872	March 1, signing of bill to create Yellowstone National Park
1877	initiation of road building in Yellowstone
1878	arrival of Harry W. Child and E.W. Bach to Helena
1878	Silas and P.B. file on Tosten land
1879	February 11, marriage of Annie Dean to Silas S. Huntley
1882	management of Gloster and Gregory assumed by HWC
1883	arrival of Northern Pacific Railroad to Livingston Montana
1883-1885	construction of National Hotel by YPIC
1883	October 23, marriage of Adelaide Dean and Harry Child
1884	August 12, birth of daughter Ellen Dean Child Nichols
1886	March 5, birth of son Huntley Child
1887	kidnaping at the Gregory Mine
1886-1891	construction Fountain, Canyon, Lake Hotels by YPA
1888-1890	construction of Great Falls smelter
1889	statehood for Montana, Dr. Dean receives medical license
1892	May 20, SSH, EWB, HWC incorporate YPTC and begin in YNP
1893	October 15, death of W.C. Child

1901	April 4, transfer of hotel ownership to SSH, EWB, HWC
1901	September 11, death of Silas S. Huntley
1902	arrival of Northern Pacific Railroad to Gardiner Montana
1904	June 1, opening of Old Faithful Inn
1907	formation of ranch partnership between HWC and Anceney
1907	November 6, marriage of Ellen Dean Child and W.M. Nichols
1908	March, marriage of Annie Dean Huntley and S.B.M. Young
1908	October 12, marriage of Huntley Child and Emilie James
1911	formal establishment of Flying D Ranch
1911	June, opening of Grand Canyon Hotel
1911	September, National Park Conference, Canyon Hotel
1914	purchase of Green Meadow Farm, Helena
1915	January 1, appointment of Mather as Asst to Secy of Interior
1915	August 1, admittance of automobiles into YNP
1916	August 25, signing of bill creating National Park Service
1916	December 10, forced merger of Yellowstone concessioners
1919	May 23, death of Dr. Maria Dean
1924	February 23, death of mother Ellen Watson Dean
1924	September 1, death of S.B.M. Young
1931	February 4, death of Harry W. Child
1936	merging of all YP companies by W.M. Nichols
1949	October 20, death of Adelaide Child
1960	August 8, Canyon Hotel lost to fire
1966	sale of YPC outside the family
1979	purchase of YNP hotel structures by NPS

Our Creative Team

Nan and Bruce Sigrist

Nan Sigrist grew up in Missouri, but after discovering Yellowstone, chose to make it her home. She worked for the Yellowstone Park Company in the Old Faithful Cafeteria (demolished), Old Faithful Camper's Cabins (demolished), and the Old Faithful Lodge Dining Room (now the cafeteria). She met her husband Bruce at Old Faithful and raised three children through summers at Old Faithful Lodge and Canyon Village where Bruce was manager. He became General Operations Manager under the Nichols family ownership and through the sale and transition. She returned after retirement to work in the Computer Center for TW Recreational Services, Inc. She lives in Emigrant, Montana.

Leslie and Ruth Quinn

Also a native Midwesterner, Ruth Quinn hails from Kansas. She has called Yellowstone home since her first summer in 1990, meeting her husband Leslie at Lake Hotel. She authored Weaver of Dreams: The Life and Architecture of Robert C. Reamer. She spends summers at Old Faithful, Wyoming, conducting tours of Old Faithful Inn. She lives in Gardiner, Montana and works winters as part of the hotel concessionaire's Onboarding and Talent Teams.

Jim and Donna Reed

James Reed painted the cover for the book and his wife Donna did the graphic layout for the cover. Native Wyomingites, Jim and his wife Donna met on a blind date in 1987. In the summer of 2003 Jim was awarded the honor of being the "Artist in Residence" at the Old Faithful Inn in Yellowstone National Park. Each year since, they have spent the 5 summer months in the Park and the other 7 months in Casper, Wyoming. Donna continues to be the driving force behind Jim's professional art career.

Harry and Sabra Child

Harry & Sabra Child live in California. "When someone writes a complete history of your family it truly fills your heart. Nan and Ruth have done a beautiful and exceptional job of researching and writing this story. Yes, they are part of Harry's legacy, and that makes me so happy. Harry was my great grandfather and I also was raised in Yellowstone Park, my true home." Harry W. Child II.

Carl and Becky Sheehan

Becky met Carl Sheehan at college in Michigan, then she transferred to Montana State University in Bozeman in 1975. Carl soon followed and they married. Graduating in 1977 Carl taught art for two years, while potting evenings. He connected with the buyer for TWA Services, who contracted him to be Potter in Resident at Old Faithful starting in 1980, which he continued to enjoy for the next 27 summers. Becky and their three children joined him there, making many lifelong family friends. Becky eventually finished her degree at MSU in graphic design, working in Bozeman, retiring in 2020. She was excited to design the cover for Ruth Quinn's book, Weaver of Dreams. And she has enjoyed the task of designing the interior of this book. Carl continues to produce his pottery at their home in Bozeman, Montana.